REFERENCE BOOK
Use in Reference
Dept. Only

D1260996

BRITISH
LITERARY
MAGAZINES

HISTORICAL GUIDES TO THE WORLD'S PERIODICALS AND NEWSPAPERS

This series provides historically focused narrative and analytical profiles of periodicals and newspapers with accompanying bibliographical data.

Black Journals of the United States
Walter C. Daniel

Mystery, Detective, and Espionage Magazines
Michael L. Cook

American Indian and Alaska Native Newspapers and Periodicals, 1826–1924
Daniel F. Littlefield, Jr., and James W. Parins

British Literary Magazines: The Augustan Age and the Age of Johnson, 1698–1788
Alvin Sullivan, editor

British Literary Magazines: The Romantic Age, 1789–1836
Alvin Sullivan, editor

British Literary Magazines: The Victorian and Edwardian Age, 1837–1913
Alvin Sullivan, editor

Children's Periodicals of the United States
R. Gordon Kelly, editor

International Film, Radio, and Television Journals
Anthony Slide, editor

Science Fiction, Fantasy, and Weird Fiction Magazines
Marshall B. Tymn and Mike Ashley, editors

American Indian and Alaska Native Newspapers and Periodicals, 1925–1970
Daniel F. Littlefield, Jr., and James W. Parins

Magazines of the American South
Sam G. Riley

Religious Periodicals of the United States: Academic and Scholarly Journals
Charles H. Lippy, editor

BRITISH LITERARY MAGAZINES

The Modern Age, 1914–1984

Edited by

Alvin Sullivan

Historical Guides to the World's Periodicals and Newspapers

Greenwood Press
New York • Westport, Connecticut • London

Library of Congress Cataloging-in-Publication Data
(Revised for vol. 4)
Main entry under title:

British literary magazines.

   (Historical guides to the world's periodicals and
newspapers, ISSN 0742–5538)
   Includes bibliographies and indexes.
   Contents: [1] The Augustan age and the age of
Johnson, 1698–1788 — [2] The romantic age, 1789–
1836 — [etc.] — [4] The modern age.
   1. English periodicals—History.   2. Literature—
Periodicals—History.   3. English literature—
Periodicals—History.   I. Sullivan, Alvin.   II. Series.
PN5124.L6B74   1983   820'.8   82–21136
ISBN 0–313–22871–X (v. 1 : lib. bdg.)
ISBN 0–313–24336–0 (v. 4 : lib. bdg.)

Copyright © 1986 by Alvin Sullivan

All rights reserved. No portion of this book may be
reproduced, by any process or technique, without the
express written consent of the publisher.

Library of Congress Catalog Card Number: 82–21136
ISBN: 0–313–22871–X (vol. 1)
ISBN: 0–313–22872–8 (vol. 2)
ISBN: 0–313–24335–2 (vol. 3)
ISBN: 0–313–24336–0 (vol. 4)
ISSN: 0742–5538

First published in 1986

Greenwood Press, Inc.
88 Post Road West
Westport, Connecticut 06881

Printed in the United States of America

The paper used in this book complies with the
Permanent Paper Standard issued by the National
Information Standards Organization (Z39.48–1984).

10   9   8   7   6   5   4   3   2   1

Contents

Preface   vii

Acknowledgments   xiii

Introduction by Muriel Mellown   xv

Profiles of British Literary Magazines, 1914–1984   1

Appendix A: Titles Included in *The Augustan Age and the Age of
            Johnson, 1698–1788*   513

Appendix B: Titles Included in *The Romantic Age, 1789–1836*   517

Appendix C: Titles Included in *The Victorian and Edwardian Age,
            1837–1913*   521

Appendix D: Titles Included in *The Modern Age, 1914–1984*   525

Appendix E: A Chronology of Social and Literary Events and British
            Literary Magazines, 1914–1984   529

Appendix F: Scottish Literary Periodicals: A Selected List   555

Appendix G: Magazines with Short Runs   559

Index   573

Contributors   625

Carrie Rich Memorial Library
Campbell University
Buies Creek, NC 27506

186216

Preface

British Literary Magazines: The Modern Age, 1914–1984, concludes a four-part reference guide. Previous volumes include *The Augustan Age and the Age of Johnson, 1698–1788 (AAAJ)*, *The Romantic Age, 1789–1836 (RA)* (both published in 1983), and *The Victorian and Edwardian Age, 1837–1913 (VEA)* (1984). In total, all four parts profile 369 magazines and treat over 400 others in appendixes, making *British Literary Magazines* the most comprehensive reference work on its subjects.

The Modern Age profiles 108 titles. To those titles, hundreds of others might easily have been added, for literary magazines proliferate so today as to require monthly bibliographic journals just to keep track of their appearance and demise. In choosing among the plethora of titles, several principles of selection, not mutually exclusive, have been applied: the literary importance of editors and contributors; the influence of the magazine on its time; the subjects and issues it defended, attacked, or promulgated; and, to suggest the character of the publishing enterprise in any age, the notably eccentric behavior or policies of some editors and contributors. Some purely "literary" magazines have been excluded because they produced work of little value; while others, for whom literary affairs were merely ancillary interests, attracted some of the most important literary figures of the time. A. R. Orage's *New English Weekly*, for example, was founded essentially to promote the Social Credit scheme of C. H. Douglas; but it is remembered today as the first publisher of Dylan Thomas's poetry and of T. S. Eliot's *Four Quartets*.

The marriage of politics, literature, and economics in the magazines of the period is hardly surprising. The beginning of "modernism" in English literature was, in part, a reaction to the social and economic realities brought about by the first world war, and the term persisted at least to the second war, to denote a period of general strikes, revolutions in Russia and Spain, economic depression, and the war itself. The avoidance of politics became in itself a political act, and no magazine was able quietly to ignore the surge of events. Old-line magazines, like the *Adelphi*, became organs for such Marxist groups as the Independent Socialist Party. Editors transformed themselves into activists. The *Adelphi*'s Richard Rees went off to fight in Spain in 1938, while former editor John Middleton Murry founded *Peace News*. Edgell Rickword abandoned the *Calendar of Modern Letters* for the overtly political *Left Review* and progressed to the doctrinaire Communist *Our Time*. Cyril Connolly attempted to keep *Horizon* apolitical at its beginning in 1945, but soon began to advocate international socialism as a means to defeat the Germans' nationalist brand. George Gooch tried in 1945 to transform the *Contemporary Review* into the leading British journal in foreign affairs and freely supported the Labour government.

As larger, older literary journals and reviews inevitably became political, new ones began from the premise that art and politics were inseparable. Some, like *Gangrel*, believed that their literary reviews could halt the rush to totalitarianism. Edwin Muir and Janko Lavrin thought that by exposing the 1930s German Nazi regime—as reflected by *European Quarterly* contributors—they could promote international peace. Stephen Spender and Irving Kristol founded *Encounter* in 1953—with the backing of the Congress for Cultural Freedom, and later, to their chagrin, of the American CIA—to break down barriers between politics and art. More doctrinaire literary magazines, like the pro-Soviet *Left Review* and the Communist *Arena*, simply announced that art was propaganda. Some, like *Now*, eschewed all political parties and favored anarchism: socially relevant literature, such as W. H. Auden's poetry, was merely an attempt to escape the self.

Amid the dazzling array of Guild socialists, internationalists, Communists, activists, pacificists, and moderates, other more idiosyncratic voices added to the wilderness of literary journals. Count Potocki established *Right Review* to prove that the only viable political system rested in the divine right of kings. In the *Enemy* Wyndham Lewis classed D. H. Lawrence as a political writer and therefore a bad writer; the critical mind should weed out politics. Lewis was himself free from that censure, however; he was not a critic, but instead conducted "investigations into contemporary states of mind."

One important by-product of the magazines' political emphases has been the frequent publication of non-British writers. Some magazines, such as the *European Quarterly* and *Horizon*, set out deliberately to include Continental figures; one is not surprised to find in their pages work by Franz Kafka, Hermann Broch, Otokar Brezina, M. O. Gershenzon, and Ivan Vazov alongside that by familiar British figures. Other magazines—even the Scottish regional *Northern Review*— turned to American as well as Continental figures. Its editor, Hugh MacDiarmid, believed that as the British Empire shrank, English literature would lose its ascendancy. Many British magazines began to feature Commonwealth literature, notably *Nimbus*; one such magazine, whose title indicates its focus, *Poetry Commonwealth*, survived for eight issues in the late 1940s. Even nationally focused titles, such as *London Magazine*, have eschewed parochialism and published issues on Malaysian and Vietnamese as well as Commonwealth literatures.

In many ways the struggle of modernism is itself a rebellion against English traditions, especially in poetry, in favor of Continental movements. Many of the titles profiled in *The Modern Age* trace the reaction against Georgianism in the 1910s and 1920s in favor of imagism. Orage's *New Age* (see *VEA*) provided T. E. Hulme and Ezra Pound space to explain the movement, and the *Egoist* served as advocate for the movement. The profile of *Arts and Letters* traces the transition of English verse from 1917 to 1920, while that of the *Decachord* records the staunch defense of classicism. One magazine, the *London Mercury*, became the epitome of a dead, Georgian tradition that virtually every "new" magazine set out to pull down: the *Enemy, Coterie, Experiment,* and especially the *London Aphrodite*. A decade later the Continental surrealist movement provided the spark for new magazines, like *Contemporary Poetry and Prose*, and all of the other magazines in the 1930s appropriated surrealism as a movement to be defined, excoriated, or transformed by English hands. Concomitantly in that decade, psychoanalytic themes were grafted onto geographical and industrial images; strict observation created a poetry that becomes a catalogue of images; and *New Verse* came to stand for modernist, "objectionist" verse, with Auden the prototypical figure. By the 1940s a tainted surrealism, fused with Georgian subjects and war imagery, produced the Apocalyptic poets; *Poetry (London)* became, unwillingly at first, their "official" voice, followed by *Kingdom Come*. In the 1950s all of the Romantic excesses of the Apocalyptics were thrown over for a lean austerity reminiscent of the thirties, and Movement poets found eager editors at *London Magazine* and a dozen other magazines.

Any doubts that art was a function of social, political, and economic variables were challenged during the 1930s and 1940s. Proletariat literature acquired greater viability when magazines like the *Bermondsey Book* printed work by laborers alongside that by intellectuals. Phenomena such as Mass Observation—where teams of "reporters" were asked to record their impressions of national events, such as the coronation of Edward VIII—were given space in *New Verse, Twentieth Century Verse,* and other 1930s magazines. In the 1940s *Our Time* solicited reports from laborers about their jobs. And by 1945, with Labour Party victories, the great British working class must have seemed, at last, the national voice.

With such revolutionary change came a revival of drama in London theaters, with the working class and their "liberated" morality as subjects. Not since Shaw had drama been a popular and artistic success in Britain. As John Osborne was followed by Arnold Wesker, Harold Pinter, and Tom Stoppard, the movement for a national theater, modeled on the Berliner Ensemble of Bertolt Brecht, found eager voices in new theater journals: *Encore*, which was the first to applaud the Angry Young Men playwrights, *Drama, Plays and Players,* and *Gambit*. *Plays and Players* for a dozen years published the complete texts of plays; *Gambit* arranged for licensing and staging of productions that had never been mounted in England.

British Literary Magazines: The Modern Age includes the titles that allow one to trace British literary history since 1914: the growing political preoccupations, the critical revaluations of literature, the succession of movements in poetry, the involvement of a growing middle class and working class in national life, the emergence of a new British drama. Additionally, the volume treats the growth of specialized, academic magazines that supplanted the reviews of earlier centuries: *Scrutiny*, the *Criterion*, the *Critical Quarterly*, and *A Review of English Literature*. It permits one to see how British magazines, severely hampered by World War II, attempted to "fill in" the missing years: *Horizon*'s publication of *La littérature anglaise pendant la guerre*, and the *British Museum Quarterly*'s special retrospective in 1951 of the war years. Regional interests are indicated by the profiles of Scots magazines—*Akros, Gangrel, Lines Review*, the *Northern Review, Poor. Old. Tired. Horse.*—and Welsh magazines—the *Anglo-Welsh Review, Poetry Wales, Wales*. Lastly, *The Modern Age* includes some of the "fringe" magazines that suggest the vitality of British publishing—*Enquiry*, with its interests in parapsychology; *New Writers*, which has staged festivals to promote poetry "happenings"—and irregular minor magazines that have become central to contemporary literature, such as Michael Horovitz's *New Departures*. Even as *The Modern Age* goes to press, some magazine, probably provincial, is beginning to print the literature we shall read ten or even a hundred years hence. Such is the function of literary magazines that histories like *The Modern Age* cannot fully capture, but only suggest, and send readers in search of the real thing.

Each profile in this book concludes with sections in which data on Information Sources and Publication History are provided in tabular form. The section on Information Sources gives bibliographic information, index sources, reprint sources, and location sources. The section on Publication History lists title changes and alternative titles, volume and issue data, publisher and place of publication, and editors.

The Information Sources have been supplied by the authors of essays and verified in the *National Union Catalog* and the *British Museum Catalogue of Printed Books* (vols. 184–86), the catalogues of microform reprints by University Microfilms International, the *British Union Catalogue of Periodicals*, and the *Union List of Serials*. The last two are frequently unreliable, and where additional information (from other works or authors' sources) is given, we have relied on that. If, for example, authors advise that only a partial run may be found at "Xy" though the *ULS* lists a complete run there, we have indicated a partial run. In most cases, however, for locations we have had to rely on the *BUCOP, ULS* and *NUC* listings. We have also relied extensively on the *BUCOP* to list reprint editions. For reprint microforms, we have also searched the 1982 *Guide to Reprints* and the *Guide to Microforms in Print*, and the catalogues of houses such as University Microfilms International and Brookhaven Press. We have tried to list all the index sources and reprints available, but given the vagaries of publishing history, others undoubtedly remain to be discovered.

Indexes are listed only if the magazine is completely indexed by author, title, and/or subject, either internally or in a separate publication. Items from some magazines have been included in general indexes, such as the *British Humanities Index*, which are not listed. Two specialized indexes have included titles in *The Modern Age*, and they are listed when a magazine is indexed: *The Comprehensive Index to English Language Little Magazines 1890–1970*, ed. Marion Sader (Millwood, N.Y., 1975), and *An Author Index to Selected British Literary Magazines 1930–1939*, ed. B. C. Bloomfield (London, 1976). Some editions may be facsimiles, but not described as such.

Location sources are listed by complete and partial runs and by reprints, when that information is available. If a title is held by ten or more libraries, we report it as "widely available," and users should consult the *Union List of Serials* and the *National Union Catalog* for American holdings, and the *British Union Catalogue of Periodicals* for holdings in the United Kingdom.

The following information is also helpful for users of this work:

When the magazine being discussed is cited, the citation is given in the text in parentheses by volume and page or by number and page, unless a note specifies another system of citation. When another source is cited, the citation is given in a numbered note at the end of the profile.

When magazines spanned two or more eras, they are assigned to parts of *British Literary Magazines* according to the year in which they began publication:

1698–1788   *The Augustan Age and the Age of Johnson (AAAJ)*
1789–1836   *The Romantic Age (RA)*
1837–1913   *The Victorian and Edwardian Age (VEA)*
1914–1984   *The Modern Age (MA)*

There is only one entry for magazines spanning two or more ages, with the exception of five titles. The longevity of these five and their literary importance call for entries in both the age in which they began publication and *The Modern Age: Blackwood's Edinburgh Magazine (RA, MA), Contemporary Review (VEA, MA), Cornhill Magazine (VEA, MA), Fortnightly Review (VEA, MA)*, and *Quarterly Review (RA, MA)*. Appendixes A through D—which list the titles included, respectively, in *The Augustan Age and the Age of Johnson, The Romantic Age, The Victorian and Edwardian Age*, and *The Modern Age*—will help those who are not certain when a magazine began publication to locate specific profiles.

The inclusion of cross-references within the text provides further access to the profiles. An asterisk following a periodical title mentioned in the text indicates that the periodical has been profiled in *British Literary Magazines*. In some cases a *see* reference to another part of *British Literary Magazines* appears after the asterisk, for example, "*Cornhill Magazine** (see *VEA*)." An asterisk not followed by a *see* reference indicates that the profile appears in this part of *British Literary Magazines*. When a magazine began publication close to the end of an age or is more in spirit with the preceding or the following age, thus making it likely that a reader might look under the wrong age for a profile, there is an entry providing a cross-reference to the proper part of *British Literary Magazines*; for example:

SATURDAY REVIEW, THE. See VEA

Finally, when a magazine underwent title changes, cross-references are provided to the title under which the magazine is discussed.

Errata

On page 93 of *British Literary Magazines: The Augustan Age and the Age of Johnson* dates for publishers of the new series of the *Edinburgh Magazine, or Literary Miscellany* are listed 100 years later than the actual dates of tenure.

On Page 258 of *British Literary Magazines: The Romantic Age* two items should be added to the bibliography for the *Literary Journal*: Fenn, Robert A. "James Mill's Political Thought," Thesis, University of London, 1971; and Lazenby, A. L. "James Mill: The Biography of a Scottish Emigré Writer," Thesis, University of Sussex, 1972. Both list contributors to the *Literary Journal*.

The editor welcomes additions and corrections.

Alvin Sullivan

Acknowledgments

In memory of Nicholas Joost and Richard P. Adams, and to Ralph Cohen: a personal acknowledgment of the power of their teaching. And to Southern Illinois University at Edwardsville (School of Humanities, The Graduate School) for its support of this project over the past six years.

Introduction

In 1963, looking back on the first ten years of *Encounter*,* Melvin Lasky declared: "A review is a way of looking at the world, a record of glimpses and perspectives, concerned with the colour of things and not only with their meaning, with the visible surface of life as well as its hidden patterns."[1] An examination of the literary magazines produced in England since 1914 bears out the accuracy of his statement. These magazines present the outward events that transpired in the course of the century and interpret for us the inner significance of those events. Since the beginning of World War I, England has passed through more, and more radical, changes than at any other period of its history. Those tumultuous years saw its transformation from an imperialist world power to a small nation serving as an adjunct to the two superpowers; from a country whose economy was based on a thriving capitalist system to one in which the principles of the welfare state are firmly entrenched; from a rigidly stratified and homogeneous society to one that is flexible and multiracial. The record of these upheavals is written in the literature and literary magazines of the era as fully, if not as specifically, as in the newspapers and news reports. To read the literary magazines of the twentieth century, therefore, is to read not only the literary but also the cultural, social, and political history of England in three periods: 1914 to 1939, 1940 to 1959, and 1960 to 1984.

Before turning to the historical development of these three periods, however, we should consider some of the distinctive features which set the journalism of the twentieth century apart from that of the nineteenth. Of these features two are preeminent: the growth of the reading public and the influence of advertising. In combination these two led to the nearly complete destruction of periodical literature as it had been practiced in the nineteenth century—the *Edinburgh Review** (see *RA*); the *Quarterly Review*,* *Blackwood's Edinburgh Magazine** (for both, see *RA, MA*); and, later in the century, the *Saturday Review*,* the *Cornhill Magazine*,* the *Pall Mall Gazette*,* and the *Fortnightly Review** (for all, see *VEA*; for the *Cornhill* and *Fortnightly*, see also *MA*)—appealed to a middle-class, educated public, well able to afford a relatively high price for the entertainment and information which the journals provided. The reviews exercised immense influence, and few self-respecting households were without access to at least one, and more likely several, of them. Moreover, they paid their writers well and published a multitude of important figures—Thomas Carlyle, Matthew Arnold, John Ruskin, Thomas Hardy, and George Gissing, to name only a few of the notable writers. But by the end of the nineteenth century what Denys Thompson in his historical survey of periodical literature calls "the disintegration of the reading public" had already begun. Thompson takes the year 1914 as marking the end of the old style of review, and comments, "The War destroyed the last vestiges of the nineteenth century tradition of journalism by increasing the demands for cheap stimuli, and supplying improved machines to meet it."[2]

This whole process was pessimistically explained by an anonymous correspondent to the *Times Literary Supplement* who in August 1938 contributed a series of three articles entitled "Present Discontents." There he pointed out that the cultivated audience of the previous century had now, with the spread of general education, been replaced by a massive, quasi-literate public, able to read and seeking entertainment, but lacking culture, intellectualism, and the capacity for serious literary appreciation. The technological advances which made possible cheaper printing and the new pressures of advertising meant that, in order to survive, periodicals must satisfy the demands of the new readership. In consequence, the correspondent argued, the editor's task was no longer to educate and stimulate his readers or to provide an organ for the dissemination of higher culture, but simply to keep up the circulation. His first responsibility, then, was to give the public what it wanted. The result was that England, "once the home, and now the grave, of the great review," had experienced the decline of what had been for 200 years a major outlet for its literature.[3] Further testimony to the collapse of the literary review was provided by John Middleton Murry. In response to the *Times* series, Murry wrote to support the general conclusions and to cite in particular the disappearance of substantial reviewing as a major loss to the literary scene.[4]

There is no denying the truth of these charges. The changes in circulation and audience undoubtedly brought about changed standards and new directions for the periodicals themselves. Nonetheless, the literary magazines of the present century have not proved themselves in all respects inferior to their great predecessors. They are characterized by a rich diversity in format, contributions, and contributors; and they have attracted as editors and as writers some of the keenest intelligences and most creative imaginations of the age. They include established quarterlies such as the *Criterion** and *Scrutiny,** directed at a small, intellectual, and often academically oriented public; a variety of monthlies ranging from the solidly traditional *Contemporary Review** (see *VEA, MA*) to the more innovative and lively *London Magazine** and *Encounter*; weeklies such as *Time and Tide** and *New Statesman** (see *VEA*), usually primarily concerned with politics and designed for a wider readership, educated and liberal in outlook; and many little magazines, often published erratically and catering to all kinds of special interests—regional, social, artistic, or political. Some magazines have been devoted entirely to creative work; a growing number have combined poetry and short stories with criticism; others, whose chief focus has been politics, have yet maintained a distinguished tradition of reviews and essays by eminent writers. The contributors are as varied as the publications. Throughout the century the literary magazines have been enriched by the works of professional journalists, established and emerging poets and novelists, working-class writers such as coal miners and factory workers, and academics who provided critical articles and in some instances creative work. The periodicals, moreover, have to a far greater extent than in the past transcended national boundaries, and their editors have proved receptive to new work by writers from all over the world. The story, then, of periodical literature since 1914 is not simply one of loss and deterioration but also one of compensations and even gains or improvements.

The first period, from 1914 to 1939, the period of modernism, is the most complex and most significant of the three. In the years between the wars, artists and writers, from T. S. Eliot and the Bloomsbury group to the Auden generation, struggled to find new patterns of meaning and new value systems to replace the traditional modes of life and thought which had been wiped out in World War I in the carnage on the Western front. These interim years, punctuated at the beginning by the Russian Revolution and toward the end by the Spanish Civil War, saw the growth of socialism; the establishment in 1924 of the first Labour government, headed by Ramsay MacDonald; the formation and failure of the League of Nations; the spread of both communism and pacifism; and, heralding the end of the era, the dark rise of fascism on the Continent. Confronting these experiences, writers espoused new ideals and took up new causes, many of which they were eventually compelled to modify as the period ground to its end with Hitler's invasions, first of Czechoslovakia and then of Poland. Out of the conflicting elements of the time, the mixture of anxiety and idealism, despair and optimism, emerged the full flowering of modernism. This development is inextricably connected with the creative and critical work of the literary magazines of the period.

In the years during and just after the war came the establishment of a number of magazines which advanced the work of the first moderns and revealed some of the tensions between them and the outmoded Georgians. The *Egoist*,* of which Richard Aldington was assistant editor until 1917, was at first primarily concerned with the imagists of the prewar years, but in 1917, when T. S. Eliot became an assistant editor, it began to include a new group of contributors, notably Eliot, Herbert Read, and Aldous Huxley. Other magazines publishing the new young poets were *Coterie*,* edited by Chaman Lall from Jesus College, Oxford; *Wheels*,* edited by Edith Sitwell; and *Art and Letters*,* for which Osbert Sitwell was poetry editor. These magazines were consciously avant-garde advocates of experimental poetry and defenders of the radical left in literature. Other journals, however, assumed more moderate positions or less controversial stances: *Nation and Athenaeum** (see *RA*), the *Owl,** and *To-Day** (see *VEA*). They avoided the extreme fringe of modernism but by no means restricted themselves to the Georgians, instead offering a wide selection of writers old and new. The *Owl*, for example, printed Thomas Hardy, John Masefield, W. H. Davies, Robert Graves, Siegfried Sassoon, and Edmund Blunden. The champion of the extreme right was J. C. Squire, editor of the powerful *London Mercury.** A Georgian poet himself, Squire was vehemently antipathetic to modernism. "With him," writes Robert H. Ross, "as with most of the post war Right Wing, incomprehensibility was the poetic sin of sins."[5] On these grounds he vigorously criticized the leftist journals and their authors, reserving his sharpest attacks for *Coterie* and Edith Sitwell's group. A much less strident defense of conventional poetic style is found in the *Decachord,** which was established in 1924 to combat modernism and preserve the conservative approach to literature embodied in the Georgian manner.

But it was soon apparent that, despite the bitterness of the literary warfare, Squire was fighting a rear-guard action, and by the mid–1920s the moderns, including Eliot, Huxley, E. M. Forster, and Virginia Woolf, had become the accepted literary establishment. The quick rise of modernism was due in large part to the publication in 1922 of three significant works: T. S. Eliot's *The Waste Land*, James Joyce's *Ulysses*, and Virginia Woolf's *Jacob's Room*. These works had a tremendous impact and opened the way for other modernist works. With the recognition of modernism as the literary mode of the age came the creation of new magazines to promote the work of the new writers. In fact, the moderns of the twenties and thirties published more of their work in periodicals and anthologies than did any of their predecessors except for the nineteenth-century writers of serial fiction. Eliot's *The Waste Land* and *Four Quartets*, for example, Ezra Pound's Cantos 38 and 41, many of W. H. Auden's poems, parts of Christopher Isherwood's *Goodbye to Berlin*, and the work of many thirties poets, including Stephen Spender, C. Day Lewis, Louis MacNeice, and Dylan Thomas, all achieved their first publication in literary magazines.[6]

During the twenties the moderns appeared in a wide range of periodicals, among which several are outstanding. First, from both a chronological and a literary standpoint, is Eliot's own *Criterion*. Founded in 1922, the *Criterion* was planned as an intellectual review for a highly cultivated audience. In it Eliot adopted the classicist position; his purpose was to maintain literary traditions and preserve the continuity of Western culture. This emphasis on authority and tradition eventually manifested itself in a theological and political rather than a literary theory, and the review became the expression of Eliot's conservatism and high Anglicanism. Even on the literary side, the magazine was not without defects. Julian Symons remarks that the prose published was thin compared with the poetry, and that the critical articles appear to a later generation of readers "dismally old fashioned and uninteresting."[7] Nonetheless, the position of the

Criterion is secure. Its first issue included *The Waste Land*; in its early years it printed Huxley, Forster, Woolf, D. H. Lawrence, James Joyce, and W. B. Yeats; through its pages Eliot introduced Marcel Proust, Paul Valéry, and Jean Cocteau to English readers; in the next decade its contributors included Auden, Spender, MacNeice, and Dylan Thomas.

Two other noteworthy magazines of the twenties were the *Calendar of Modern Letters** and *Life and Letters.** In the two years of its existence, the *Calendar*, edited by Edgell Rickword, published a wide selection of modernist writers and critics. Symons maintained that "in the creative work it printed [it] was surely the best literary magazine of the last fifty years,"[8] while Malcolm Bradbury ranked it with the *Criterion* and the *Adelphi** as one of the three great reviews of the twenties and attributed to it responsibility for "the growth of modern criticism."[9] *Life and Letters* is important chiefly for its publication of the Bloomsbury group, including Huxley, Woolf, Forster, Lytton Strachey, and Clive Bell, but its editor, Desmond MacCarthy, also welcomed fresh talent. Writing in 1951, John Lehmann recalled nostalgically "the excitement with which, nearly twenty-five years ago, I devoured the first number."[10]

But modernism, of course, was not single or uniform, any more than Romanticism or Victorianism had been, and the conflicts of the various factions are likewise revealed in the magazines. The *Adelphi*, founded by John Middleton Murry in 1923 to promulgate his own philosophies and those of his friend D.H. Lawrence, represented a deliberate turning away from the experimental work of Joyce and Woolf in favor of ideas appealing to the general reader. In addition, the *Adelphi* reflects something of the division between Eliot's new classicism and Murry's own brand of antitraditional Romanticism. A somewhat different kind of conflict is revealed in the *Transatlantic Review.** This short-lived journal was established in 1924 by Ford Madox Ford with the help of his Paris-American friends Ezra Pound, Ernest Hemingway, and William Carlos Williams. The ensuing struggle between Ford and Hemingway for control of the magazine dramatizes the struggle between literary conservatism and modernism. A final example of the literary feuds of the decade may be seen in the opposition of two Cambridge magazines, *Experiment** and *Venture*, both established in 1928. The latter is described by Lehmann, who was one of its contributors, as "a magazine of the 'centre' in what was already being called a Cambridge poetic renaissance."[11] Its rival, *Experiment*, on the other hand, was much further to the left, as was evidenced by its reproductions of abstract and surrealist paintings and its inclusion of surrealist and imagist poems.

By the 1930s the temper of the times had changed, and modernism assumed a new shape as a fresh generation of writers appeared on the literary scene. This was the decade of the slump, unemployment, the dole, the Jarrow hunger march, worker protests, and the rise of Nazism. Stephen Spender, as spokesman for the thirties generation, has described how these events precipitated a crisis of conscience among the middle-class writers, who suddenly "felt themselves divided by the thinnest of walls from destructive forces which seemed absolute, from terrible suffering, and pure evil.''[12] The result was the well-documented shift among the younger generation toward socialist, often Marxist politics. Yeats, Eliot, Pound, and Wyndham Lewis had all valued traditionalism and remained politically conservative. Members of the Bloomsbury group, while generally liberal or leftist in their sympathies, were for the most part indifferent to politics and politicians, whom they tended to regard as philistines. But the writers of the thirties could no longer separate literature from action. As they turned to revolutionary causes, they began to chart a fresh, markedly different course for modernism, a shift reflected in the sudden burgeoning of new literary journals.

The decade of the thirties produced arguably the most valuable magazines of the century, all of them betokening in some way the drift to the political left. *Left Review*,* edited by Edgell Rickword of the *Calendar*, was founded in 1934, four years after the *Daily Worker*. From its origin it was committed to strict socialist doctrine, and it became "the nearest thing to an official organ that the intellectuals of the Left had."[13] Another politically oriented journal was the *Adelphi*, which in the 1930s proclaimed the socialist and pacifist philosophies of Murry and succeeding editors. Other magazines, while ostensibly declaring their political independence, obviously supported leftist tendencies: *New Verse** and *New Writing*,* for example. In the opening manifesto of the latter, John Lehmann declared that the journal would be apolitical, placing literature above politics. In practice, however, it was too antifascist and left-wing. In fact, politics played a part in it from the very beginning, and Symons theorizes that its foundation had been prompted by a "realization of the change in British intellectual life, a change that was pushing the Audience slowly towards sympathy with all Left-wing ideas and movements."[14] Looking back later, Lehmann himself acknowledged the political bias, writing that his object had been to demonstrate among contemporary writers "an awakened conscience and interest that impelled them to look for their material in new fields, and produce . . . 'a literature arising from the violent conflicts of human life in our time.' "[15] Symons's *Twentieth Century Verse** was one of the few leading magazines to stand outside the general pattern and avoid direct political involvement.

Although left-wing politics provided the main foundation for the literature of the thirties, another element was, at least for a short time, that of surrealism. Surrealism in art and literature originated on the Continent in the twenties, and it had no lasting effect on British painters and writers. But for a brief period in the thirties it enjoyed a considerable vogue. Amid much fanfare the International Surrealist Exhibition opened in London in June 1936, and under its impetus two magazines were founded, *Contemporary Poetry and Prose** in 1936 and *London Bulletin** in 1938. The former started a month before the exhibition, devoted its June issue to the surrealists, and through its year's history emphasized their work. The latter was designed specifically to explain and defend surrealism theory and published essays and poems by surrealists both in English and in French. A number of surrealist poems also appeared in *New Verse*, as did a series of essays outlining the development of the movement. Even this channel of literature, however, retained political connections, for the surrealists were closely aligned with socialism, although doctrinaire Marxists denounced them as reactionary and irresponsible and dismissed their work as the product of bourgeois decadence.

One of the most striking characteristics of the literary magazines of the early period—and one which remained constant through the century—was the international outlook. In 1865, in "The Function of Criticism," Matthew Arnold had condemned insularity and stressed the need for an international community of culture, but it was not until the twentieth century that the kind of internationalism he advocated became a significant reality. Of key importance in this development were Eliot and the *Criterion*. As firm an internationalist as Arnold, Eliot saw his review as belonging to the European republic of letters and assumed the task of acquainting his readers with Continental literatures. European authors were also published extensively in the *Calendar of Modern Letters*, the *Transatlantic Review*, and *Experiment*. In addition, these periodicals included works by many American writers—Ernest Hemingway, Ezra Pound, Gertrude Stein, E. E. Cummings, Djuna Barnes, Hart Crane, John Crowe Ransom, Allen Tate, Conrad Aiken—thus beginning that English-American interaction of culture which has been so marked in this century.

In the thirties the international orientation was further intensified by political events. From Hitler's accession to power in 1933 English writers were involved in international movements and found themselves drawn to their compeers on the Continent not just by the community of letters but by the united effort to combat fascism. Thus Edwin Muir and Janko Lavrin set up the *European Quarterly** to apprise readers of events in Europe and alert them to the intellectual movements taking place abroad. *New Writing* prominently included the writings of André Gide, Jean-Paul Sartre, and Ignazio Silone; and when the Spanish Civil War broke out, Lehmann made an eager search for Spanish materials. Other periodicals, such as the *Contemporary Review*, promoted internationalism by opening their pages to newly arrived refugees from Hitler's Germany.

Another feature of this first period was the interest in and demand for proletarian literature. As early as 1923 the *Bermondsey Book** printed, along with the work of established authors, the poems, stories, and essays of the inhabitants of London's East End. In the socialist thirties the emphasis on proletarian literature deepened, and magazines such as *New Writing* and *Left Review* actively sought contributions by working-class authors. In these years a sudden flourishing of intellectual activity occurred among the working classes, and for the first time working-class writers of genuine significance—Walter Greenwood and Ralph Bates, for example—began to emerge. But such writers were still comparatively few, and it soon became clear that proletarian art on a wide scale was not yet a viable option. Stephen Spender struck at the root of the problem in his essay "Poetry and Revolution," when he asserted that working-class writers and readers had in fact moved into the bourgeois cultural tradition by their very concern for writing and reading.[16] The consequence was that social realism came to be sought in other ways—especially in the documentary and in the experiments of Mass Observation. The first theory of the documentary as a literary form was propounded in 1937 by Storm Jameson in *Fact*, the socialist magazine designed to spread information.[17] Mass Observation was an attempt to record the realities of contemporary life by teams of observers. Since one of its leaders was Charles Madge, a frequent contributor to *New Verse*, that periodical became connected with the movement.

One last phenomenon of the first period was the advance of literary criticism. Scholarly interest in the theory and practice of criticism began with the *Criterion*, the *Calendar of Modern Letters*, and the distinguished reviews in the *Athenaeum*. These prepared the way for the most famous critical journal of the time, *Scrutiny*, which took its name from a series of "Scrutinies" published in the *Calendar*. Edited and produced at Cambridge, *Scrutiny* marks the beginning of modern academic criticism. F. R. Leavis, the most celebrated critic of the day, was its editor and principal contributor throughout its twenty-one-year history. Under his direction the journal formed a new method of literary criticism based on textual analysis, undertook revaluations of the entire body of English literature, and exercised immense influence not only on its own but on subsequent generations of writers, scholars, and readers.

These developments came to an abrupt halt in 1939, when the rising tensions of the decade reached the culmination toward which they had been inexorably moving. On the literary as well as the political scene, 1939 was a time of endings and of the gathering of resources for the challenges that lay ahead. The year saw the closing of some of the most important magazines of the period: in the first six months the *Criterion*, the *London Mercury*, *New Verse*, and *Twentieth Century Verse* all ceased publication.

The second period, from 1940 to 1959, spans the war, the postwar reconstruction, and the gradual move to affluence in the late 1950s. It was a period marked by unexpected reversals and readjustments. After the unrest and civil disturbances of the thirties, the war actually created a regeneration of the national spirit. Under the pressure of Dunkirk, the Battle of Britain, and the Blitz, there developed—to use the words of Spender—a "strange aura which was also that of the last flicker of the England which began with the reign of Queen Elizabeth and which ended with the war and the diminution of England to our Welfare State."[18] During the war itself, however, the prospect of the welfare state seemed not a diminution but an ennoblement of the old order, and innumerable writers testified to the widespread hope that after the war a new England would arise in which social and economic justice would at last prevail. By contrast, the postwar years following the great Labour Party victory of 1945 were filled with bitterness and disillusion as the nation struggled with fuel shortages, stringent rationing, and the immense cost of setting up the first socialist programs. Only in the last years of the period did the austerity relax and a new prosperity make itself felt.

These same pendulum swings are mirrored in the art and magazines of the time. In wartime England culture was by no means dormant. In fact, London experienced something of a renaissance: concerts were given; Shakespearean plays starred actors like John Gielgud and Peggy Ashcroft; art flourished among such practitioners as Henry Moore, Graham Sutherland, and John Piper; and literary production was vigorous, with new work by Eliot, Edith Sitwell, Dylan Thomas, and Roy Fuller appearing.[19] This revitalization clearly owed something to a general feeling that the arts represented the civilized values for which England was fighting. It was the same sense that produced an upsurge in new periodicals.

Despite paper rationing and the 1940 ban on new magazines, a number of journals began to appear during the war. Chief among these was the monthly *Horizon*,* edited by Cyril Connolly with the assistance of Spender, which put out its first number in January 1940. In that first issue, Connolly insisted that the magazine would concern itself only with aesthetic principles and eschew politics, but he rapidly diverged from that ideal and became caught up in political questions. A brilliant, if idiosyncratic and inconsistent editor, he started by asking well-known authors for contributions, but also proved receptive to new talent and ultimately published whatever appealed to his own somewhat wayward but never dull taste. Largely because of the imprint of his vital, temperamental style, *Horizon*, along with *Folios of New Writing* and *Penguin New Writing*,* came to dominate the literary scene during the war.

Also important were the magazines associated with the Apocalypse movement, which began with an anthology of prose and verse edited in 1940 by J. F. Hendry and Henry Treece entitled *The New Apocalypse*. It was followed by two other anthologies, *The White Horseman* (1941) and *The Crown and the Sickle* (1944). The Apocalyptics, whose chief figures, in addition to Treece and Hendry, were G. S. Fraser and Norman MacCaig, were a divergent group, united mainly by their hostility to Auden. Often labeled the new romantics, they attempted to explore themes of death and chaos by use of symbol and myth and to convey descriptions and psychological conditions through series of images. Their work appeared in the *Adelphi, Life and Letters Today*, and several new magazines such as *New Road** and *Now*.* When Treece became editor of the Oxford-based *Kingdom Come** in 1941, he used that magazine to propagate Apocalyptic poems and theory. Another popularizer of the Apocalyptics was J. M. Tambimuttu, editor of *Poetry (London)*,* and one of the most flamboyant figures of the war years. As the Apocalyptics reacted against Auden, so Tambimuttu reacted against Auden's supporter Geoffrey Grigson and adopted a romantic critical theory directly opposed to the objectivity demanded by *New Verse*. He was, however, catholic in his tastes and refused to ally himself exclusively with any one literary movement. Thus he came to publish a wide range of eminent authors, maintaining a consistently high standard of poetry and criticism in his lively, if irregularly issued, magazine.

The sudden burst of vitality diminished in the postwar era. In this time of disappointment and disillusion, the old causes—socialism, Marxism, and pacifism—could not longer kindle enthusiasm or arouse the imagination. Although left-wing political theory had provided much of the impulse underlying the literature of the thirties, the retreat from communism had already begun toward the end of that decade. With the onset of the Cold War there was a switch to the right. Former radicals retracted or modified their views, and liberal editors such as Lady Rhondda of *Time and Tide* began to express opinions veering toward conservatism. Even the ostensibly communist *Arena,** founded in 1949, adopted a position very different from the official party line, thus arousing the disapproval of the orthodox *Daily Worker*.

Literary movements, like the national spirit, seemed in abeyance, awaiting a fresh impetus. Admittedly, a few new magazines such as the *Mint** and *New Poetry** offered work by major authors. But these ventures were short-lived, and as a whole the postwar years were more notable for endings than for beginnings. The last issue of *New Writing and Daylight* was published in 1946. *Now* ceased publication in 1947, *New Road* and *Horizon* in 1949. *Poetry (London)* continued until 1951, but under new editorship after Tambimuttu left for America in 1949. In 1950 Penguin Books decided to cancel *Penguin New Writing*, and that series too came to an end. *Penguin New Writing*, although not strictly a magazine, had become one of the best serial publications of the time. It was primarily devoted to literature and printed an impressive array of poetry and prose by young writers from both England and America: its last number included contributions from Lionel Trilling, Eudora Welty, Tennessee Williams, and Saul Bellow. At the same time it covered the other arts, with articles on theater, ballet, music, cinema, and radio. It had acquired the support of an enthusiastic band of followers, and its passing marked the nadir of literary magazines.

The limbo of these years was eventually dispelled in the fifties by the Movement poets: Kingsley Amis, Philip Larkin, John Wain, Donald Davie, John Holloway, Elizabeth Jennings, Robert Conquest, D. J. Enright, and Thom Gunn. These poets, who for only a very short time cohered as a group, spurned the romantic lavishness of the Apocalypse poets and rejected posture and idiosyncrasy in poetry in order to develop new techniques. They aimed at clarity and exactitude of statement rather than at profusion of image and metaphor, and their work is characterized by a dry, carefully controlled intensity. Several of the Movement poets were equally important as novelists, striking new ground in fiction as well as poetry. Their novels, of which Amis's *Lucky Jim* (1954), one of the first, is also one of the most representative, depict a new social realism, an exact, yet satiric, portrayal of the newly educated lower middle classes. Not so exclusively connected as the Auden group had been with the upper middle class and the public school, Oxbridge tradition, these writers voice the attitudes of the new generation of the grammar school, the redbrick universities, and the welfare state.

Simultaneously with the Movement writers came a new crop of magazines which usually proved sympathetic to their work. In 1953 Lehmann started *London Magazine*, a monthly which printed both creative work and criticism and drew on established and new talent. Lehmann had already introduced several of the

Movement poets on his 1951–1952 radio series *Soundings*, and he now included them in *London Magazine*. Another vehicle for the Movement writers, as well as for older, established figures, was *Encounter*, also founded in 1953. Edited by Spender, *Encounter* was a stylish monthly dealing with current affairs, literature, and the arts, one of its goals being to demonstrate that politics and the humanities may be rendered compatible with each other. Since it was a joint English-American production, it drew on well-known writers from both sides of the Atlantic, printing the works of such authors as the British Robert Graves, Evelyn Waugh, C. P. Snow, Philip Larkin, Elizabeth Jennings, and Ted Hughes, alongside those of Americans Theodore Roethke, Robert Lowell, and Katherine Anne Porter. Not all magazines were as receptive to the latest generation of poets as *London Magazine* and *Encounter*. *Nimbus*,* for example, which first appeared in 1951, published writers from England, Europe, and America, but remained largely hostile to the Movement poets.

The most significant progress in the fifties, however, took place in the drama. The first indication of change came in 1954 with the English production of Samuel Beckett's *Waiting for Godot*, in which Beckett dispensed with regular plot and characterization and used bizarre happenings and cryptic dialogue to portray his sense of the isolation and despair of human existence. This was followed by the 1956 presentation of John Osborne's highly influential *Look Back in Anger*, with its explosive depiction of the bitterness and frustrations prevailing among the younger generation. In the next few years these two works together initiated a new kind of theater characterized by the shocking realism inherited from Osborne and by the experimental techniques and bleak philosophy derived from Beckett. Whereas the developments in poetry and fiction in the fifties had been largely based upon English traditions, remaining aloof from European influence, this new drama built upon the work of European dramatists, particularly Bertolt Brecht, Eugene Ionesco, and Friedrich Dürrenmatt. One of its leading champions was Kenneth Tynan, theater critic for the Sunday *Observer*. Among literary magazines it was *Encore** that most fervently supported the new style. Following Tynan, *Encore* deliberately set out to reshape popular taste. It attacked insipid drawing room comedies and expressed warm admiration for new dramatists Arnold Wesker, Harold Pinter, and John Arden. Its role in fostering an understanding and appreciation of their work makes it one of the most valuable periodicals of the age.

Although the magazines of the second period were in form and content different from those of the period before, they retained some of the distinctive features of the earlier time. The international approach, propounded by Eliot and evident in almost all of the major periodicals, expanded to include more contributions by foreign writers. *New Road* contained sections on South American as well as European writing; *Poetry Commonwealth** and *Nimbus* both featured Commonwealth literature. When Lasky summed up the achievements of the first ten years of *Encounter*, he singled out this kind of broad internationalism as one of the journal's strengths. Like the *Criterion*, he declared, *Encounter* was based upon an awareness of the international community of artists, but "with the new and additional range which is characteristic of our time: not merely international but intercontinental; not merely European but with a vital sense of the world-wide unities which embrace Europe, Africa, Asia and America."[20]

In the same way, the trend toward academic criticism, begun in the first period, was extended in the second. When *Scrutiny* came to an end in 1953, its place was taken by *Essays in Criticism*, whose purpose was to continue the tradition established by the earlier journal. Thus, in an editorial of July 1954, *Essays in Criticism* followed the Leavis line as it defended academic reviews and the unique role of the universities in elevating public taste and promoting the serious study of literature. The year 1959 saw the founding of another important critical periodical, the *Critical Quarterly*.* The *Quarterly* attempted to avoid Leavis's dogmatism and aimed at readable, unpedantic criticism. Its particular concentration was modern literature, and it printed both critical articles and many poems by the Movement poets and others. Despite their differences of approach, the founding of these two important journals in the fifties confirmed the shift of literary criticism away from professional writers to the academicians which had been increasing throughout the century.

The third period, from 1960 to the 1980s, is the most nebulous and difficult to define, not merely because time has not yet set events in perspective and made the broad outlines clear, but also because in these two decades the process of change speeded up at a bewildering rate. The sixties were an interval of boom after the long, drawn-out austerity of the postwar years. Harold Macmillan's campaign slogan, "You've never had it so good," testified to the new affluence that set the tone of the age. These were the years typified by the image of swinging London, Beatlemania, pop art, and the discarding of old modes and mores. But prosperity ended with the rise of new problems in the seventies. In the last fifteen years England has confronted the emotional and economic strains of the Common Market, widespread unemployment among young people, crippling national strikes, the decline of the pound, and increased troubles in Ireland. In the period as a whole the country has adjusted to changes great and small. It has seen the end of the Empire, the formation of a European economic community, the building up of a multiracial society through Commonwealth immigration, even the extinction of its old currency and of the ancient county lines.

Not surprisingly, this has also been a period of renewed experiment with a wide diversity of poetry that defies rigid categorization. This innovative poetry appeared in a variety of little magazines, most of them short-lived, irregularly produced, and aimed at a restricted audience. *New Departures** represents the radical "underground" writing and includes avant-garde poetry, music, and artwork. *Poor. Old. Tired. Horse.** publicized the concrete poetry of the sixties, while it also demonstrated the contemporary interest in graphics as an adjunct to poetry. An undergraduate magazine from Cambridge, *Solstice,** assumed an antiestablishment stance, endorsing political radicalism and, like *New Departures*, printing experimental and concrete poetry. *Samphire** provided another outlet for the concretists and for the jazz poetry designed for performance at large gatherings. *New Writers** included experimental fiction and issued volumes dealing with the "happenings" in vogue during the sixties. All these magazines demonstrated the international spirit and an interest in the Third World. *Poor. Old. Tired. Horse.* had the closest connections with foreign literature since it derived much of its inspiration from the international concrete movement, but all of these journals published translations of writers from many different countries, including the Soviet Union and China.

Other magazines of the period dealt with more recognized authors and had a broader appeal. Chief among these were *Encounter* and *London Magazine*, which both continued relatively unchanged, although *London Magazine*, when Alan Ross became editor in 1961, widened its focus to become a magazine of the arts as well as literature. Another continuation from the fifties was *Lines Review.** When it first began in 1952, this periodical had been devoted strictly to the publication of Scottish poetry, and throughout its history it retained its national emphasis, printing some of the best-known Scottish poets—Hugh MacDiarmid, Norman MacCaig, Iain Crichton Smith—as well as relatively obscure figures. In the late 1960s and 1970s, however, it also began to include important English, European, and American authors. *Agenda,** founded in 1959 under the influence of Ezra Pound, took as its mission the advancement of English poetry and criticism by a study of American verse, and published issues featuring a wide range of authors from England and America. Another noteworthy journal is *Gambit,** founded in 1963, which has established itself as the foremost magazine in international drama.

Despite these varied achievements, however, it is impossible to avoid the conclusion that these last years saw a diminution in the publishing of literary periodicals. The new magazines, for the most part, had only a small circulation, while some of the most notable older journals ceased publication. *Time and Tide*, which dated back to 1920, and *Blackwood's*, the *Cornhill Magazine*, and the *Quarterly Review*, which had originated in the nineteenth century, all closed their doors. Moreover, many of the surviving periodicals, such as the *Listener*, *New Statesman*, and *Contemporary Review*, are political rather than literary in their orientation. As early as 1959 Malcolm Bradbury was deploring the demise of periodical literature, remarking that it was now left to the *Sunday Times* and the *Observer* to fulfill some of the functions of the earlier reviews.[21] The vacuum which he noted twenty-five years ago has not yet been filled.

Many factors account for this decline. Chief, of course, is commercial pressure. In recent years even national newspapers have fallen victim to mergers and takeovers by the monolithic publishing empires. It is hardly surprising, then, that periodicals which reckoned their circulation in thousands, at most, rather than in millions, were unable to continue. Other, broader, causes are also involved. In the past few years it appears that the audience for serious literature has split into a number of different groups which lack common standards and even a recognized critical language. The result has been a plethora of little magazines and the disintegration of a general readership. Even more telling is the oft-touted decline of the act of reading itself in the face of television and the demand for easy entertainment. The serious book reviews which were still produced in the first part of the century have now largely been replaced by the best-seller list and the mini-ratings column.

The loss is not one to be passed over lightly. The first-class literary magazines of the early period were a vital, not a peripheral, force in literature. Matthew Arnold, in "The Function of Criticism," justified criticism as an act which supports creativity. And Eliot, in his best-known pronouncement about the importance of good literary reviews, declared: "A review should be an organ of documentation. That is to say, the bound volumes of a decade should represent the development of the keenest sensibility and the clearest thought of ten years."[22] Periodicals of the kind Eliot had in mind serve a threefold function, for the public, for the general intellectual atmosphere, and for the writers themselves. They serve to educate the public by encouraging the serious study of literature and by deepening literary appreciation. They help to create an intellectual climate since they provide a forum for critical discussion and establish critical standards. And they mirror the spirit of the age as they build up and preserve tradition.

When one considers the history of the magazines in the entire century, one is struck not so much by the poverty of the last few years as by the rich achievements of the period as a whole. The literary magazines of the twentieth century have been directed by distinguished editors possessed of both critical acumen and imaginative flair. Eliot, Murry, Grigson, Lehmann, Connolly, and Spender are just the foremost among many notables. By their contributions to modernism the periodicals have helped to change the mood and direction of literature. Moreover, they have published major works, provided serious reviews, charted the erratic course of literary trends and conflicts, and fostered new developments in academic criticism. And if they have not always lived up to Eliot's demand for disinterestedness, as voiced in the first number of the *Criterion*, they have assuredly satisfied his requirement that they "exhibit the relations of literature—not to 'life,' as something contrasted to literature, but to all other activities, which together with literature, are the components of life."[23]

Notes

1. Melvin J. Lasky, Preface to *Encounters: An Anthology from the First Ten Years of Encounter Magazine*, ed. Stephen Spender, Irving Kristol, and Melvin J. Lasky (New York, 1963), p. xiii.

2. Denys Thompson, "A Hundred Years of the Higher Journalism," *Scrutiny* 4 (June 1935):31, 32.

3. "Present Discontents: I. The Author; II. Editor, Publisher and Public; III. Signs for the Future," *Times Literary Supplement*, 6 August 1938, p. 518; 13 August 1938, p. 530; 20 August 1938, p. 542.

4. John Middleton Murry, "Thoughts on Reviewing," *Times Literary Supplement*, 17 September 1938, pp. 597–98.

5. Robert H. Ross, *The Georgian Revolt 1910–1922: Rise and Fall of a Poetic Ideal* (Carbondale, Ill., 1965), p. 188.

6. For *The Waste Land*, see entry on the *Criterion*; for *Four Quartets* and Cantos 38 and 41, that on *New English Weekly*; for *Goodbye to Berlin*, that on *New Writing*.

7. Julian Symons, "The Cri," *London Magazine*, 7 (November 1967):22.

8. Ibid., p. 19.

9. Malcolm Bradbury, "*The Calendar of Modern Letters*," *London Magazine*, 1, no. 7 (October 1961):37.

10. John Lehmann, "The Case for the Literary Magazine," *Listener*, 15 February 1951, p. 263.

11. John Lehmann, *In My Own Time* (Boston, 1969), p. 96.

12. Stephen Spender, *The Thirties and After: Poetry, Politics, People 1933–1970* (New York, 1978), p. 12.

13. Samuel Hynes, *The Auden Generation: Literature and Politics in England in the 1930s* (London, 1976), p. 12.

14. Julian Symons, *The Thirties: A Dream Revolved* (London, 1960), p. 59.

15. Lehmann, *In My Own Time*, p. 155.

16. Spender, pp. 34–35.

17. See Hynes, pp. 268–73.

18. Spender, p. 69.

19. Ibid., p. 68.

20. Lasky, p. xiii.

21. Malcolm Bradbury, "Will There Always Be an English Periodical?" *Saturday Review*, 18 July 1959, p. 12.

22. T. S. Eliot, "The Idea of a Literary Review," *Criterion* 4 (January 1926):1–6.

23. T. S. Eliot, "The Function of a Literary Review," *Criterion* 1 (July 1923):421.

Bibliography

Bradbury, Malcolm. "*The Calendar of Modern Letters*: A Review in Retrospect." *London Magazine*, n.s. 1, no.7 (October 1961):37–47.

———. "The *Criterion*." *London Magazine* 5, no. 2 (February 1958):41–54.

———. "Will There Always Be an English Periodical?" *Saturday Review*, 18 July 1959, pp. 11–12, 40.

Cox, R. G. "The Critical Review Today." *Scrutiny* 14 (1947):256–68.

Eliot, T. S. "The Function of a Literary Review." *Criterion* 1 (July 1923):421.

———. "The Idea of a Literary Review." *Criterion* 4 (January 1926):1–6.

Hamilton, Ian. *The Little Magazines: A Study of Six Editors*. London, 1976.

Hewison, Robert. *Under Siege: Literary Life in London 1939–1945*. London, 1977.

Hoffman, Frederick J., Charles Allen, and Carolyn F. Ulrich. *The Little Magazine: A History and a Bibliography*. 2d ed. Princeton, 1947.

Hynes, Samuel. *The Auden Generation: Literature and Politics in England in the 1930s*. London, 1976.

Lehmann, John. "The Case for the Literary Magazine." *Listener*, 15 February 1951, pp. 262–64.

———. *In My Own Time*. Boston, 1969.

Murry, John Middleton. "Thoughts on Reviewing." *Times Literary Supplement*, 17 September 1938, pp. 597–98.

"Present Discontents. I. The Author. II. Editor, Publisher and Public. III. Signs for the

Future." *Times Literary Supplement*, 6 August 1938, p. 518; 13 August 1938, p. 530; 20 August 1938, p. 542.

Ross, Robert H. *The Georgian Revolt 1910–1922: Rise and Fall of a Poetic Ideal.* Carbondale, Ill., 1965.

"Running a Literary Review." *Times Literary Supplement*, 29 August 1952, p. xlvii.

Spender, Stephen. *The Thirties and After: Poetry, Politics, People 1933–1970.* New York, 1978.

———. *World within World.* 1951. Reprint. Berkeley, 1966.

Spender, Stephen, Irving Kristol, and Melvin J. Lasky, eds. *Encounters: An Anthology from the First Ten Years of Encounter Magazine.* New York, 1963.

Stanford, Derek. *Inside the Forties.* London, 1977.

Symons, Julian. "The Cri." *London Magazine*, n.s. 7 (November 1967):19–23.

———. *The Thirties: A Dream Revolved.* London, 1960.

Thompson, Denys. "A Hundred Years of the Higher Journalism." *Scrutiny* 4 (June 1935):25–34.

Muriel Mellown

PROFILES OF BRITISH LITERARY MAGAZINES, 1914–1984

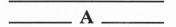

A

ABINGER CHRONICLE, THE

The outbreak of World War II caused the serendipitous convergence of several aging, prominent English writers and artistic figures just south of London in and around Abinger, near Dorking, Surrey. E. M. Forster, whose principal residence, when he was not traveling, had been the family home at Abinger Hammer since 1902, was forced by the war to stay at home. The career of Ralph Vaughan Williams had always been closely tied to this area because of his family home at Leith Hill Place. Max Beerbohm, whose limited finances had exiled him to Rapallo, Italy, left the Continent to take up residence with his friends Sydney and Violet Schiff at their country house at Abinger. They were brought together by R. C. Trevelyan, a man of their generation (the 1870s), and a young woman, Sylvia Sprigge, in a literary enterprise that in 1939 became the *Abinger Chronicle*, perhaps recalling Forster's 1936 collection of essays *Abinger Harvest*, but certainly devoted to their mutual love of the countryside and writing.

Sprigge, the second wife of Cecil Jackson Squire Sprigge—Reuter's chief correspondent in Italy during the war and a writer on Marx, modern Italy, and Benedetto Croce—provided the direction and energy for the project. She introduced Beerbohm to Forster and persuaded the former to read *Howard's End*. She organized the *Chronicle* with Robert Trevelyan, a poet, playwright, and translator of classical verse, whose wife Elizabeth had worked with Ralph Vaughan Williams to organize and conduct the Leith Hill Festivals since 1904. Her home address—Cherry Cottage, Abinger Common—became the editorial address. Yet, perhaps because she was unsure of herself in such company or maybe because she wanted the magazine to project a communal image, she was never identified as the editor, nor did she sign her many poems and articles in any way but "S.S." Although the *Chronicle* seems to want its readers to believe that it is the jointly managed venture of a group of local writers, it has about it a kind of single-minded sense that one is not likely to find in the output of a committee. In fact, it reads like the project of one person who is continually pushing for its publication.

The first issue of the *Abinger Chronicle* was published in October 1939 and dated Christmas 1939. Its square border of repeated holly leaves and berries with the title and table of contents in script became the standard title page format. Its contents consisted of a modest four articles, including "Local Musicians" by Vaughan Williams, articles by Beerbohm and Oliver W. F. Lodge, and poems by S. S. On the last page appeared a message that ran with variations through most issues of the magazine: "The Abinger Chronicle appears monthly. The chief contributors are Max Beerbohm, E. M. Forster, Ralph Vaughan Williams, Desmond MacCarthy, Oliver W. F. Lodge, Robert Trevelyan and others. The annual subscription is 6/- post free, 3/- for six months post free."

Two articles written by Forster for volume 1 express the tone and range of the magazine: "*The Abinger Chronicle* is not one of those magazines which give you a bang for your sixpence. . . . Left to itself, there is not a safer place in England than Abinger, and it would be unfitting if it produced a volcanic chronicle." In "Luncheon at Pretoria" he recounts comically a series of events that occurred to him while traveling in Africa that ruined his blue serge suit. The *Chronicle* is resolutely local, provincial in the best sense, communicating a strong awareness of time and place, a part of the English countryside that has stood still for a long time and is one of the few havens from the raging violence outside. But it is also aware of the larger world, especially the war, and takes positions that exhibit a sophistication and world view that one would not expect of such a publication.

The *Abinger Chronicle* published, for example, many childhood stories and reminiscences, including a series by Sarah Shore Gill. Sometimes the contributors wrote about or to each other, and from time to time, of course, Beerbohm drew them. A slightly fictionalized prose piece by Sprigge that criticized the insensitive treatment of refugees by the Home Office led to a published exchange of letters between her and Beerbohm, the latter threatening to separate himself from the magazine if it continued to publish such political material. The history and geography of the Abinger environs were regularly featured. The magazine does not, however, fall into easy sentimentality or simple pastoralism. In contrast to these everyday village concerns, the reader finds essays on the artistic history of England, poems and articles published in or translated from other languages, and constant reminders of the war.

Often printed, for instance, were poetry and prose sketches about English literary figures—Robert Browning, Jane Austen, David Garrick, Virginia Woolf, and even a poem on Milton in German. The *Abinger Chronicle* makes its strongest statements, however, when it implies or directly writes about the contrasts between the haven of Surrey and the death and destruction elsewhere. Two essays entitled "In London Now" (1, no. 2) remind the reader of that contrast. Poems such as Douglas Gibson's "To a Skylark over an Aerodrome" discuss aerial warfare. By the end of the first year, we are told, thirty writers, including sixteen locals, had contributed to the *Chronicle*. "About a third had never published before, including men and women now serving with the Forces."

The *Abinger Chronicle* carried through to 1944. But, finally, the people who began it found their lives turning away from Abinger. In August 1944 a flying bomb demolished the cottage in which Beerbohm lived; he and his wife left the community. By the following year, Forster had been forced by the owner to vacate his longtime home at West Hackhurst, and took up residence at Cambridge. Sprigge had by this time gone to Italy where, as a writer and journalist, she followed her husband's interests, writing, for example, *The Lagoon of Venice*. Perhaps inspired by R. C. Trevelyan's poem "To Bernard Berenson" (1, no. 2), she eventually published *Berenson, a Biography*.

In a farewell to the readers on the first page of the final issue, Sprigge wrote of the *Chronicle*:

> It was a small and happy venture in grim and unhappy times. It was wayward and irregular . . . and it will not appear again. . . . One day, when men will wrongly envy the times we live in, . . . they will find at least one wisp of paper which enjoyed the old lights, grieved over the present darkness, and felt a little doubt about the new twilight, lest there be insufficient vigor to turn it into daylight. [5, no. 1]

There was to be one more farewell—a 1945 supplement—sold for two shillings and sent free to former subscribers. The *Abinger Garland* was a collection of poems by Nicolai Gumilev translated from the Russian by Yakov Hronstein, a Dorking resident who had published a translation of a Gumilev poem in the final issue of the *Chronicle*.

Information Sources

BIBLIOGRAPHY
Furbank, P. N. *E. M. Forster, a Life*. New York, 1978.
McElderry, Bruce R. *Max Beerbohm*. New York, 1972.
Vaughan Williams, Ursula. *R.V.W.: A Biography of Ralph Vaughan Williams*. London, 1964.
INDEXES
Volume 1, number 1 in *An Author Index to Selected British Little Magazines*, ed. B. C. Bloomfield (London, 1976).
REPRINT EDITIONS
None.
LOCATION SOURCES
American
Complete runs: Harvard University Library; New York Public Library; University of Minnesota Library; Yale University Library.
Partial runs: Newberry Library; University of Illinois Library; University of Texas, Austin, Library.

British
   Complete runs: Bodleian Library; British Museum.

Publication History

MAGAZINE TITLE AND TITLE CHANGES
   The Abinger Chronicle.
VOLUME AND ISSUE DATA
   Volume 1, numbers 1–12, 1939–1940; volume 2, numbers 1–8, 1941; volume 3,
   numbers 1–5, 1942 (number 5 is numbered 5/6); volume 4, numbers 1–4, 1943
   (not 5, as listed in the final number); volume 5, number 1, 1944.
FREQUENCY OF PUBLICATION
   Irregular. See above.
PUBLISHERS
   Sylvia Sprigge and R. C. Trevelyan.
EDITOR
   Sylvia Sprigge.

Frank Edmund Smith

ACADEMY, THE. See VEA

ADAM INTERNATIONAL REVIEW

The first English issue of *Adam*, number 152 in its run, appeared in September
1941. In its new homeland *Adam* "endeavoured to gather round it almost all
the foreign writers, members of the various P.E.N. centres now assembled in
England" (no. 152:1). *Adam* is an acronym for arts, drama, architecture, and
music. An international review published in English and French, *Adam* extends
over the entire range of the arts: poetry, short stories, sculpture, painting, music.
It reflects the cosmopolitan tastes of its creator and sole editor, Miron Grindea,
who came to Britain on 1 September 1939, two days before World War II was
declared. In prewar Bucharest and Paris, Grindea and his wife, the distinguished
pianist and musicologist Carola Grindea, had been members of avant-garde
musical and literary circles. They numbered among their closest friends Eugene
Ionesco and Jean Cocteau. Between 1940 and 1946 Miron Grindea was music
critic for the French daily *France* and wrote feature articles for the Ministry of
Information and the British Broadcasting Corporation. In 1943, in the midst of
the German blitz on London, the Grindeas, along with Henry Moore, Stephen
Spender, and others, founded the International Arts Guild, which promoted
concerts, recitals, and exhibitions in the besieged capital.

The magazine is noted for the number of its distinguished contributors, especially T. S. Eliot. Eliot contributed "Reflections on the Unity of European
Culture" (nos. 158–161) and "The Aims of Poetic Drama" (no. 200:10–16),

which subsequently appeared, after much revision, as *Poetry and Drama*. His
personal message for *Adam*'s twenty-first birthday celebration appeared in the
issue for January 1953. The first English appearance of Charles Moncheur's
French translations of Eliot's "Rhapsody on a Windy Night," "The Hollow
Men," "A Song for Simeon," and "Marina" appeared in May 1948 (no. 182:6–
8), as did an English-French parallel text of Georges Cattaui's translation of
"The Hollow Men" (pp. 8–10). Issue 186 for September 1948 was a sixtieth
birthday tribute to Eliot, with poems by Hugh MacDiarmid, G. S. Fraser, and
J. M. Tambimuttu. From the beginning, Grindea attracted the most prominent
midcentury artists. The first English issue of *Adam* contained a contribution from
H. G. Wells, a note from Storm Jameson, president of the London P.E.N., and
articles by Thomas Mann, Georges Duhamel, and Stefan Zweig. C. Day Lewis
contributed a powerful short poem, "The Watching Post." Subsequently, con-
tributors to *Adam* have included Edith Sitwell, Walter De la Mare, Joyce Cary,
E. M. Forster, Jean Cocteau, André Gide, François Mauriac, Paul Claudel, Jean-
Paul Sartre, Augustus John, Pablo Picasso, Ronald Searle, Nicholas Bentley,
Herbert Read, John Lehmann, Stephen Spender, W. H. Auden, Tristan Tzara,
Marc Chagall, Joan Miró, and Georges Simenon.

In his editorial in the 200th issue of *Adam* for November 1949, Grindea cites
T. S. Eliot's *Criterion** commentary for July 1938: "So far as culture depends
upon periodicals, it depends upon periodicals which exist as a means of communication between cultivated people, and not as a commercial enterprise: it
depends upon periodicals which do not make a profit" (p. 5). In the magnificent
wrapper illustration to the 200th issue, by Ronald Searle, Grindea is seen naked.
A large apple, shaped rather like a time-bomb, with "200" written on it, serves
as a fig leaf protecting the editor's delicate parts. A taller T. S. Eliot looms
behind Grindea, his angelic wings protecting the editor from three demonic
figures with swords raised, ready to plunge them into Grindea's private parts.
All are flanked by the tree of knowledge from which Grindea has removed an
apple. Searle's vision echoes Grindea's opening editorial in the first English
issue: "Adam was driven out last year from the Eden of its readers," and its
rebirth is compared to the process of starting to eat again from "the tree of the
knowledge of good and evil" (no. 152:2).

Adam's longevity has frequently been commented upon; perhaps its sheer
diversity of materials partially explains why it has survived. A 1969 issue devoted
to Baudelaire and Berlioz contained, among other attractions, sixty-one letters
by Berlioz, some in the original French, others in English translation. Several
of the French originals are reproduced in facsimile, and there are also copies of
scribbled bits of musical scores. In 1971, the Dickens centenary and the Beethoven bicentenary year, *Adam* ranged in content from eight unpublished Dickens
letters, written in French to his friend Alfred d'Orsay, to an article on Proust's
love of Beethoven, to a one-page tribute by J. B. Priestley on Beethoven, to
Raymond Mortimer on "The Fascination of Mauriac," to a poem by Miltonic
scholar E. H. Visiak. One of *Adam*'s strengths has been its awareness of an-

niversaries of one kind or another, and it has made a practice of devoting whole
numbers to a single topic or writer of special interest. Nevertheless, frequent
pleas for subscribers and funds punctuate *Adam*'s history. In his editorial to the
200th issue Grindea revealed that the journal had fewer than 1,000 regular
subscribers. *Horizon*,* which had just ceased publication, claimed, by comparison, "eight thousand readers, half of whom were subscribers" (p. 4).

The 400th number was a special tribute to the London Library. Grindea's
usual lengthy editorial pays fulsome tribute to the library, to which he and so
many others were indebted: "Hardly a single issue would have been possible
without having had the privilege of foraging among the stacks, quarrying through
endless volumes" (no. 400:3). In addition to a black-and-white Nicolas Bentley
cover design and drawings by Edward Ardizzone and Michael Lasserson, there
are short paeans of praise to the London Library by thirty different hands in the
ninety-page issue. Black-and-white photographs are complemented by manuscript reproductions from Virginia Woolf's childhood efforts at journalism. Letters to the London Library from Edmund Gosse, Henry James, T. E. Shaw
(T. E. Lawrence), and J. M. Barrie are reprinted.

Issues devoted to individuals range from numbers on Proust, Chopin, H. G.
Wells, L. P. Hartley, and Dylan Thomas to an eightieth birthday tribute to
Graham Greene. *Adam* special issues are indispensable for study of their subjects,
critically, biographically, and bibliographically. Usually they contain hitherto
unpublished childhood memoirs and reflections, poems, articles or short stories,
drafts, and bibliographically forgotten contributions. For example, in 1961 an
L. P. Hartley issue included an editorial tribute in French to its subject, followed
by articles in English and French on Hartley, memoirs from Oxford of the early
1920s, two hitherto unpublished short stories, "The Fact" and "A Very Present
Help," and P. Bien's "A Hartley Bibliography," the first to be published. The
Graham Greene tribute in 1984 (nos. 446–448), published to coincide with
Greene's eightieth birthday and the 1984 Brighton Festival, at which all Greene's
major films were shown, packs twenty contributions into fifty-five pages. (The
Grindeas live on the ground-floor flat of a tall house in a Regency square alongside
the seafront of this well-known English resort.) The issue includes rare photographs of Greene's mother punting, of Greene at a fancy dress party when very
young, and of a much older Greene, sitting with his brother and sister in the
garden in the summer of 1983. In addition to Grindea's witty, learned, and
informative editorial introduction, "A la Recherche de Graham Greene," there
are articles by his brother, Hugh Greene, on "Childhood with Graham"; observations by Father Leopoldo Duran, Greene's close friend; views and reviews;
and the publication of Greene's speeches on receiving literary prizes in Hamburg
and Jerusalem.

In addition to serving the famous, *Adam* has given the unknown artist, writer,
poet, or dramatist a chance to break into print, and has supplied welcome payment
to contributors in need. It has thus published some notable "firsts." Within its
pages may be found the text of Bernard Kops's brilliant drama depicting the

anguish, guilt, and despair of Ezra Pound during his post–1945 imprisonment and release (nos. 431–433). The front cover of the issue contains a photograph of Pound in bed at Olga Rudge's bungalow at Sant 'Ambrogio overlooking Rapallo. The same issue publishes a speech cut out of Tom Stoppard's *Travesties*; the first contribution to *Adam* by Arthur Calder-Marshall, an autobiographical memoir set in 1916; four posthumous poems by John Mander; twelve by Yves de Boyser, translated by David Gascoyne; and a poem by Jeremy Reed, ''The Ides of March.''

Such a survey hardly does justice to the rich and complex diversity of Grindea's *Adam International Review*. Eclectic cosmopolitanism with a bias toward literature, music, and the pictorial has long been characteristic of this bilingual journal. It is a tribute to its importance that the *Adam* archive has gone to the library of King's College, London University, where it can be studied by future scholars of European culture. The words of Cyril Connolly, writing on ''Fifty Years of Little Magazines'' in *Art and Literature* (April 1964), seem appropriate to sum up *Adam*: ''I know of only three magazines which survive unaltered from the 'thirties: *Partisan Review, The Wine and Food Quarterly* and Miron Grindea's indestructible *Adam*.''[1]

Notes

1. Quoted in *Adam*, no. 300 (1965): cover 1.
Miron Grindea has been most helpful in providing information about his journal, and I am grateful for his assistance.

Information Sources

BIBLIOGRAPHY

Grindea, Miron. ''Cultivating One's Garden—The Story of *Adam*,'' The Adam Lecture, 1985. Given in the Great Hall, King's College, London University, 20 February 1985.

Marder, Irving. ''*Adam*—A Literary Cliffhanger.'' *International Herald Tribune*, 29 February 1972.

INDEXES

Numbers 152–200, 1941–1949, by genre.

REPRINT EDITIONS

None.

LOCATION SOURCES

American

Partial runs: Widely available.

British

Complete runs: Bodleian Library; British Museum; Cambridge University Library; National Library of Scotland, Edinburgh; Trinity College Library; University of London Library.

Partial runs: Widely available.

Publication History

MAGAZINE TITLE AND TITLE CHANGES
 Adam. International Review.
VOLUME AND ISSUE DATA
 Number 152, September 1941. Numeration continues that of the periodical of the
 same title formerly published in Bucharest.
FREQUENCY OF PUBLICATION
 Irregular, but announced as monthly, numbers 152–300, 1941–1965; quarterly,
 number 301–, 1966–. Frequently issued as joint or triple numbers.
PUBLISHERS
 St. Clements Press, 66 Woodlands, London NW 11, numbers 152, 153. Adam
 International Review, 28 Emperor's Gate, London SW7, number 154–. (In as-
 sociation also with University of Rochester, New York, numbers 325–360.)
EDITOR
 Miron Grindea.

William Baker

ADELPHI, THE

The *Adelphi* was published from 1923 to 1955 under three sequences of volume
numbers, and these three divisions mark the changes and even the significance
of the journal. The first four volumes (1923–1927) consist of forty-seven monthly
issues and present the work of Katherine Mansfield, D. H. Lawrence, and John
Middleton Murry, as well as that of other writers sympathetic to their philosophies
and ideas. The second sequence of three volumes, entitled the *New Adelphi*
(1927–1930) and issued quarterly for a total of twelve numbers, still reflects the
Laurentian philosophies, but there is a broader literary concern, while in format
the quarterly is more like the other journals of the time. In the final sequence
of thirty-one volumes (1930–1955), the first twenty-five reflect certain social
and political issues, and the last six present a general review of the arts, including
opera, ballet, and the theater. The central figure to 1948 is the founder of the
journal, John Middleton Murry. The *Adelphi* was published to express and
promote his ideas and beliefs, as well as those of his friend Lawrence; and it
stands as a record of the literary world to which Murry belonged and of the
social and literary history of a certain segment of English life.

Like many other literary figures of this period, Murry rose in the world by
his innate intellectual abilities and his literary efforts; while improving his situation in life, he influenced his age by his literary activities. Scholarships took
him through Christ's Hospital and Brasenose College, Oxford; his keen sensitivity to art gained him entrance into the artistic circles of Paris and London;
his ability to express his appreciation for art and literature enabled him to support
himself by writing for London and European newspapers. From 1911 to 1913
he edited the periodical *Rhythm** (see *VEA*), and from 1919 to 1921, the *Ath-*

enaeum* (see *RA*). In 1911 he met Katherine Mansfield, who was the most lasting influence on his work, and in the following year he met D. H. and Frieda Lawrence. The relationship between these two couples is of the greatest significance to students of Lawrence, not only because of the personal attachments and animosities that developed, but also because of the models they provided for Lawrence in *Women in Love* and various short stories. When Katherine Mansfield died in 1923, Murry despaired until he experienced a psychic "affirmation of life" and an exalted realization that he continued to live. Lawrence's *Fantasia of the Unconscious* had recently been published in the United States. Murry immediately accepted Lawrence's ideas and decided to "launch an independent journal—a mouthpiece for Lawrence and himself."[1]

Between March and June 1923, when the first issue appeared, Murry located a financial backer, Vivian Locke-Ellis, asked S. S. Koteliansky to be business manager, wrote and distributed a prospectus, and contacted the writers who would contribute in the first year. In addition, he wrote the first of the editorial essays which were to be a regular feature of the journal. Entitled "The Cause of It All," its wide-eyed, ingenuous tone characteristically projected the image that Murry fostered (which Aldous Huxley so accurately satirized in the figure of Burlap in his 1928 novel, *Point Counter Point*).[2] Beginning with personal anecdotes which disarm the hostile reader, Murry simply states his point of view:

> We know we are not isolated. That is enough. But we can say more. We believe in life. Just that. And to reach that belief, to hold it firm and unshakable, has been no easy matter for some of us. We have paid for it. ... [We] know it is a precious thing. We have to fight for it. We know it is worth fighting for, the only thing worth fighting for. We fight in our way with our pens. [1, no. 1:5, 6]

Simple as this manifesto may be, it brought forward a response from a reading public confused by the current difficult and seemingly life-denying modernist literature: the first issue of the *Adelphi* was sold out shortly after publication and was twice reprinted within the first month.[3] Of course, Murry's facile optimism was not the sole influence upon readers. Throughout each issue there was an emphasis on ideas that were new, provocative, yet easily grasped, and a deliberate turning away from the experimental, difficult work of such writers as James Joyce and Virginia Woolf. Murry consciously addressed his magazine to the general reader who wanted moral and practical ideas that had relevancy to his own life and were immediately accessible to him.

The first issue set the format used in the first four volumes. Each issue began with a long introductory essay by Murry, followed most frequently by writings by Mansfield and Lawrence, essays and stories by other writers (H. M. Tomlinson and J.W.N. Sullivan appeared regularly in the first volume), and translations from Russian (often by S. S. Koteliansky). There would be a personal essay by "The Journeyman" (often Murry, although other writers also used this pseudonym); short unsigned paragraphs entitled "Multum in Parvo"; and a column entitled "Contributors Club." The latter consisted of signed paragraphs of comment, or reviews, or indeed whatever the contributor chose to write about. Some of the best-known writers of this period—Arnold Bennett, H. G. Wells, Harold Laski, R. Ellis-Roberts—as well as younger authors—Mark Gertler, Frank Swinnerton, Catherine Carswell—contributed to the "Club," testifying to Murry's central position in the London literary world.

But the main purpose of these monthly issues, bound in bright yellow paper covers, was to gain a wider circulation for the ideas of Lawrence and to insure that the work of Mansfield unpublished at the time of her death would be printed. Murry was ultimately to publish every fragment of his wife's work, no matter how unfinished it was. This practice did not help the circulation of the new journal, since few readers shared the editor's interest in Mansfield, while those who did inevitably thought that Murry was exploiting his wife's work rather than establishing her literary reputation.

While Murry was his wife's literary executor and could do as he wished, he faced a different situation with Lawrence. Their friendship, pondered and argued by all of their biographers, was always an uneasy relationship: Murry's devotion to Lawrence was never precisely what Lawrence wanted, while Lawrence in person was usually a very different creature from the Lawrence whom Murry found in the philosophical and critical essays. But in the first forty-seven issues Murry printed at least nineteen separate items by Lawrence: chapters of *Fantasia of the Unconscious* (printed without prefatory material or other explanation of the whole from which they were taken); translations of Giovanni Verga's stories; essays such as the two-part "Hopi Snake Dance" and "Indians and an Englishman"; the poem "Creative Evolution"; and even a book review of Baron Corvo's *Hadrian the Seventh*. Meanwhile, Murry was receiving Lawrence's letters. The novelist had at first responded to Murry's requests for material with his typical enthusiasm for such new enterprises; but when he saw the first issue he was "badly disappointed" and wrote to S. S. Koteliansky that it "seemed . . . so weak, apologetic, knock-kneed, with really nothing to justify its existence. A sort of beggar's whine through it all." Some weeks later he was more temperate in writing directly to Murry, referring merely to his disappointment "with the apologetic kind of appeal in the Adelphi" but continuing to promise to contribute. Later he encouraged the editor to be more forceful in his satire and to be less "vague," to "put a bit of gunpowder in your stuff, and fire a shot or two" instead of being "soft and . . . stirring your own finger in your own vitals." But the letter of 17 November 1924 makes clear Lawrence's feelings that Murry would not alter, and anticipates the counsel offered in 4 January 1926: "In short, shut up. Throw the Adelphi to the devil, throw your own say after it." The offering of the disciple to the master ultimately proved unsatisfactory—and may even have harmed Lawrence's immediate reputation, for the pieces which Murry chose to print without context or explanation must have been quite unintelligible to many readers. Lawrence never had any misconceptions about the *Adelphi*: on 3 June 1924 he remarked to Frederick Carter that it "does one no good."[4]

While Mansfield and Lawrence were the mainstays for the *Adelphi*, other writers appeared almost as frequently. The changing fortunes of the *Adelphi*, as well as Murry's own shifting allegiances, are reflected in the fact that while the first two volumes present the work of well-known authors of the period, the next two contain the writing of an entirely different group, most of them obscure in the extreme. In the first two there appeared J. D. Beresford, Walter De la Mare, Dorothy Richardson, Robert Graves, Sarah Gertrude Millin, Edmund Blunden, Edwin Muir, and Geoffrey Wells. Many of the contributors to the last two volumes are virtually unknown sixty years later. One exception can be found in the last number of volume 4: fifteen pages are given over to W. B. Yeats's verse-drama "The Resurrection." Other less expected contributions include Charles Chaplin's biographical essay, "Does the Public Know What It Wants?"; an essay by Edwin Muir on Friedrich Hölderlin; and Dorothy Richardson's "About Punctuation."

While the *Adelphi* served primarily as a platform for its editor and his interests, it also played a part in the emergence of T. S. Eliot as a public figure. Eliot and Murry became friends when Murry published at least thirty-five pieces by Eliot in the *Athenaeum* in 1919–1920. Indeed, the founding of the *Adelphi* may have been a reaction not only to Mansfield's death, but also to Eliot's new quarterly *Criterion*,* which appeared in the autumn of 1922. In it were two works that represented the type of literature to which Murry was opposed: *The Waste Land* and the subject of an essay by Valery Larbaud, Joyce's *Ulysses*. Murry's "pro-life" stand in his first editorial, whether he was aware of it or not, was probably shaped by his belief that these two works were antireligious and life-denying. In retrospect one sees that the struggle was between the new classicism of the modernist writers and the unabashed romanticism of Murry. Their conflict became apparent to readers of both the *Adelphi* and the *Criterion*, as first Murry and then Eliot put forth their opposing points of view. In a debate largely carried on in the *Criterion*, although there are many passing references to it in the *Adelphi*, Eliot developed his "interest in theological matters: what had begun as a dispute over classicism and romanticism became one over medievalism and modernism."[5]

The immediate justification for the *Adelphi* was to serve as a voice for Murry's ideas and philosophies, expressed in editorials and essays, most of which reappeared in his later books and collections. Through the years, *Adelphi* readers were given parts or all of *The Life of Jesus* (London, 1926), *The Unknown God* (London, 1924), *Things to Come* (London, 1928), and *Son of Woman: The Story of D. H. Lawrence* (London, 1931), as well as other collections of essays and studies. Between 1923 and 1930 there is no distinction between the *Adelphi* and the man and his writings. Precarious as its existence was—hardly an issue came forth without an appeal for subscribers or for financial assistance—it reached a considerable body of readers and was an important influence. Murry was the chosen teacher for many serious, well-meaning, and sensible persons to whom the *Adelphi* was more than a monthly journal of entertainment. The social and cultural changes that have taken place since World War II make it difficult to appreciate the attitudes toward ''self-improvement'' that prevailed in the early years of the century in both England and America. While there was a strong sense of the social hierarchies, there was also an awareness that one could—and should—improve oneself through the acquisition of the cultural awareness that belonged to the higher classes. The literary knowledge that belonged to this cultural awareness was not to be acquired solely in formal academic training, but in independent reading of the great writers, especially contemporaries. Thus Lawrence was read as a provocative thinker who spoke directly to the individual reader, no matter what his station or place in life, and who demanded an immediate, direct, and personal response. The change of attitude that has come about in later decades—the feeling that one must ''study'' Lawrence (or Woolf, or Joyce, or Eliot) in an academic setting—is in some ways foreshadowed by the differences between the *Criterion* and the *Adelphi*. Eliot promoted those creative writers whose work demanded study before it could be fully appreciated and who rarely appealed to the general reader, while Murry addressed the *Adelphi* to an audience which was more interested in developing its own ideas and understanding than in the appreciation of works of literary art.

The second phase of the *Adelphi* began in September 1927, with a title change to the *New Adelphi*, quarterly publication, and a format more like that of other literary reviews. The ''Contributors Club'' continued to be a regular feature, although the authors were not quite unknown figures, and Murry began each issue with his own ''Notes and Comments.'' Nothing by Lawrence appeared until the last issue of the new series, although all of his books were reviewed as they were published. Issues normally contained short stories and poems, conventional in form, for the *New Adelphi* did not welcome experimental or avant-garde writers. Short story writers included H. E. Bates, Frances Gregg, Mary Arden (the pseudonym of Violet le Maistre, Murry's second wife), and Malachi Whitaker; poets included Edwin Muir, Stella Gibbons, Romer Wilson, George Rostrevor Hamilton, Michael Roberts, Theodore Morrison, Frances Cornford, William Jeffrey, and Robert Hillyer. Many were represented by more than one contribution. The main concern of the new quarterly was to present essays dealing with religious issues, social concerns, and most frequently, literary matters. Murry contributed essays on Keats, Shakespeare, Hardy, and Anne, Countess of Winchilsea (all reprinted in later books). T. S. Eliot continued his controversies with Murry over religious matters, while Lawrence Hyde wrote on Aldous Huxley as a ''Life-Worshipper''; Max Plowman discussed Blake; John Shand, Ibsen; and Orlo Williams, Hardy. Other essayists included Hugh I'Anson Fausset, Jules de Baultier, C. G. Jung, Waldo Frank, William Plomer, and Geoffrey Sainsbury. The quarterly offered its readers serious studies that made no concessions to popular taste.

The major change was the inclusion of signed book reviews. Robert Hillyer was a frequent reviewer of new books of poetry; Richard Murry, the editor's young brother, noticed art books and related studies; and the editor himself reviewed many types of books, including those by Lawrence. Other reviewers were Herbert Read, H. P. Collins, Dorothy Richardson, M. Robinson, James Young, and Geoffrey West.

The end of this second phase came with the last issue of volume 3 in June–August 1930. On the first page was the announcement that henceforth the journal would be issued monthly. And while Murry would "remain as intimate as before . . . [in] his connection with the magazine . . . and his contributions [would] be more regular," the editor would be Max Plowman, "assisted by Sir Richard Rees" (3, no. 4:241). This last issue edited by Murry was a memorial to Lawrence, who had died in March. It included photographs of him and of one of his manuscripts, his essay "Nottingham and the Mining Countryside," nine letters by him to Katherine Mansfield, and extracts from several of his nonfiction works. The main obituary was entitled "Elegy" and was written by Rebecca West (later reprinted as a separate pamphlet). The issue also included the first installment of Murry's *Reminiscences*, subsequent parts of which were published in later issues of the *Adelphi*. This publication marked the beginning of Murry's controversial handling of Lawrence's life that culminated in *Son of Woman* (1931) and *Reminiscences of D. H. Lawrence* (1933). The *Adelphi* began with a death, and, after a period of alienation between Murry and Lawrence, its second phase concluded with another death. When the journal reappeared in September, again entitled the *Adelphi*, Katherine Mansfield's work had already been published and Lawrence's writings were controlled by his literary executors, and the original justification for its publication had disappeared. It still continued to be closely associated with Murry, however, and until 1948 his changing political and religious outlooks shaped its interests.

The third phase of the *Adelphi* has two parts: the first twenty-five volumes (1930–1948) reflect the philosophies and ideas of Murry and his followers—who were not always in agreement with one another or with Murry—while the last six volumes (1948–1955) have no connection with Murry and present a general review of the performing arts and of literature, with no particular philosophy or creed underlying the journal. As Murry had announced, Max Plowman took over as editor in 1930, but he had political views as strong as Murry's, and within the year he resigned. Sir Richard Rees, who also subsidized the journal, assumed the editorial duties. Murry and Rees soon found that their socialism had led them to the Independent Labour Party: in October 1932 Rees announced that the *Adelphi* would henceforth express the views of the I.L.P., and reflect a Marxist attitude. In September 1934 Murry announced his resignation from the I.L.P., and by November he was reporting on the Convention of the Independent Socialist Party. Meanwhile, influenced by Max Plowman, he was turning toward pacifism. In late 1936 his pacifist views proved to be too much for Rees—the specific point of disagreement was the Spanish Civil War—

and Rees withdrew his support from the *Adelphi* and went to Spain to fight. The immediate result was a reduction in the size of the journal and the announcement that it was available by subscription only.

In May 1938 Plowman resumed editorial chores and continued to make the *Adelphi* into an organ of the pacifist movement. Meanwhile, Murry had taken over editing of *Peace News*, the official voice of the Peace Pledge Union. Various assistant editors helped during these years, one being F. A. Lea, later Murry's biographer. These new influences helped to give the journal a better balance of content, for although wartime restrictions forced the monthly to become a quarterly in 1942, and to print double-columned pages, the physically unimpressive magazine was actually considerably more interesting to the general reader than earlier issues had been. Max Plowman died in June 1941, and once more Murry took over the editor's job and provided the financial support which kept the *Adelphi* going. In the summer of 1948 he "gave the *Adelphi* away," and its final phase began.[6]

While there are exceptions, the writers published in the *Adelphi* between 1930 and 1948 are those who can be identified with the cause for which the magazine stood at that time. Thus, during the 1930s and 1940s a frequent contributor of poems, personal essays, and reviews was George Orwell. Readers of the *Adelphi* were presented with his current sociological studies, as well as stories reflecting his experiences in Burma ("A Hanging") and poems. After Murry and Rees joined the I.L.P. they printed extracts from the writings of Marx, Lenin, and Rosa Luxemburg. They were also receptive to the writings of various Americans associated with leftist politics. Edmund Wilson was a not infrequent contributor; in October 1933 he wrote the lead article, "Art, the Proletariat, and Marx." Essays by Waldo Frank were featured in various issues, and several pieces by Sherwood Anderson appeared in the early 1930s, including the prolabor, anti–big business "Loom Dance" in the issue for July 1931. In a lighter vein, personal humorous essays by Will Cuppy and E. B. White were reprinted from the *New Yorker*. Another writer associated with the *New Yorker*, James Thurber, published several of his stories in the *Adelphi* in 1933, including the often anthologized "The Night the Bed Fell."

Such material was the exception rather than the rule, however, for the larger part of the magazine was given over to serious essays, generally with a political or sociological slant. G.D.H. Cole's "Communism for Englishmen" (April 1932) or J. T. Murphy's writings on problems of the unions in 1933 were typical offerings; but there were frequent essays, at least in the first part of the 1930s, on literary topics. Hugh de Selincourt wrote on Goethe; Robert Graves examined a new edition of John Skelton; Catherine Carswell wrote her reminiscences of D. H. Lawrence; Hugh I'Anson Fausset studied Wordsworth; and Rayner Heppenstall discussed Edward Carpenter. But as the decade progressed, political concerns became paramount, to the extent that in July 1934 one reader complained that "literature is being swamped . . . by all this Socialistic propaganda. . . . *Must* the *Adelphi* pursue this dull path much longer?"

There were grounds for the complaint, for up to 1934 the *Adelphi* had published many short stories and poems which, rarely being experimental or difficult, appealed to a conservative, middle- to highbrow reader. The stories tended to reflect "realistic" situations and themes and usually had a proletarian or rural setting. Some of the fiction writers at this time included Malachi Whitaker, T. O. Beachcroft, Jack Common, Rhys Davies, Roger Dataller, and, in December 1934, the twenty-year-old Dylan Thomas. The *Adelphi* was one of the first London journals to publish Thomas's work, and many of the emerging poets of the decade were published early in their careers in the *Adelphi*: W. H. Auden, Stephen Spender, C. Day Lewis, Bryan Guinness, A.S.J. Tessimond, Michael Roberts, William Plomer, Allen Tate, Edouard Roditi, Theodore Roethke, George Barker, Rayner Heppenstall, Jesse Stuart, and Boris Pasternak. The literary inclinations of the *Adelphi* editors were certainly shaped by political consider-ations, but for the most part the editors had discerning taste that enabled them to appreciate new poets. The books chosen to be reviewed, similarly, were ones which interested the editors, and hence they tended to be the work of political or religious thinkers, or the writings of new poets. An unexpected feature of these issues is the attention given to the dance. Both Rees and Rayner Heppenstall were interested in ballet and wrote reviews of books on the dance and of per-formances by the ballet companies of the period.

When Max Plowman resumed the *Adelphi* editorship in October 1938, he directed the journal toward a pacifist policy and the endorsement of Canon Dick Sheppard's Peace Pledge Union, but he continued to publish in each issue stories, usually very short, and poems. Typical essays of the time were his own essay in October 1940, "Stop Bombing!," an attack on the saturation bombing by the British military of German cities, and an anonymous "Tribunal Statement," evidently offered as a model for men who wanted to claim conscientious objector status. In the same issue also appeared poems by William Soutar, Alexander Comfort, and J. F. Hendry. The book reviews at this time were noteworthy, for Plowman was able to find critics who had special interest in the books he wanted reviewed. Thus Maud Bodkin, author of *Archetypal Patterns in Poetry*, reviewed T. S. Eliot's *The Family Reunion* in 1939, later developing her essay into a book-length study, *The Quest for Salvation in an Ancient and a Modern Play* (1941). A younger reviewer was Iris Murdoch, who, unknown as a novelist, wrote notices of books in her area of academic expertise, philosophy.

Throughout the war years the *Adelphi* appeared regularly, edited from the Adelphi Centre in Norfolk. With all journals of the period required to conform to publication restrictions, its double-column pages were not unusual, and while it was of course subject to censorship, the measure of civil liberties which the English continued to enjoy during wartime can be judged by the open discussion and criticism of political and even military matters. Murry continued to publish promising young poets: in the July-September 1943 issue, for example, there are two poems by Denton Welch and three by James Kirkup. When one notes that the journals with which the *Adelphi* could be compared in the 1920s and

1930s—specifically the *Criterion*—had ceased publication in 1939, one sees the importance of the *Adelphi* as a voice for criticism and as an outlet for new literature. Murry shared the pages of his journal with those who were once his opponents, and in the postwar years he published several essays by Eliot, including "The Social Function of Poetry" in 1945 and "Culture and Politics" in 1947.

After Plowman's death in 1941 Murry continued to edit the *Adelphi* and to provide the financial subsidy that was required to keep it going. Finally, in 1948, in its twenty-fifth year, he decided to bring it to a close; but various friends and readers refused to let the magazine die. Primary among them was Henry Williamson; and in the July–September 1948 issue, Murry wrote that he had "gladly made [the *Adelphi*] over to" him (24, no. 4:193). Williamson edited only three issues; beginning with the issue for July–September 1949, George Godwin conducted the next five issues. In 1950 Ronald Staples bought the periodical, and B. Ifor Evans became the editor and continued in that position until 1955, when the magazine finally ceased publication.

In this last phase, the *Adelphi* became a journal of the arts directed to the general, educated public, eschewing any political or philosophical point of view. Indeed, in the first issue that Williamson edited he rejected Murry's pacifism by writing on and publishing writings by James Farrar, an English airman who had been killed in battle in 1944. Some of the other writers published by Williamson included Herbert Read (who had been a longtime contributor), Charles Causley, Richard Aldington, Donald Davie, Vernon Scannell, and Rolf Gardiner. When Godwin took over the journal, he promoted his special interest in gardening and ecology. B. Ifor Evans, in his first editorial, gave a clear statement of the directions the journal would take in the future. It was to be "a quarterly of the arts. Though literature and the theater will occupy a major place, attention will be given to opera, ballet, music, painting, sculpture and architecture" (27, no. 1:7). In addition to this survey of the contemporary scene, the editor proposed to publish poems and short stories, meanwhile avoiding political essays and reviews of political books.

In its last years the *Adelphi* became in almost all ways the opposite of the journal that Murry originally founded. Instead of one, idiosyncratic point of view, it aimed for a general, wide-ranging understanding; instead of a political attitude, it turned its back on politics; and instead of examining the religious and philosophical bases of contemporary culture, it looked at the artistic manifestations of culture and particularly at the forms these manifestations took in London. Opera, ballet, and theater—which readers of the *Adelphi* in the 1920s would have considered the frivolous interests of Bloomsbury—were now the main items in the journal. Arnold Haskell wrote on the need for training ballet dancers, while various ballerinas contributed their memoirs and autobiographical sketches; critics commented on the opera and theater, and such writers as John Whiting discussed the emerging neo-Elizabethan theater. At the same time, every issue gave lengthy literary essays. In 1951, R. A. Scott-James wrote on E. M.

Forster, and Neville Braybrooke on Graham Greene as a critic; in the following year Lionel Trilling considered the work of William Dean Howells. Later there was Alida Monro's memoir of the once popular Charlotte Mew. The death of Dylan Thomas in late 1953 occasioned various eulogies and memoirs in the February 1954 issue—although no writer realized that the *Adelphi* had been one of the first journals to publish Thomas. Finally, the earliest interest of Murry's *Adelphi* was celebrated when Graham Hough, near the end of the magazine's run, in 1954, published its last essay on D. H. Lawrence.

Notes

1. F. A. Lea, *The Life of John Middleton Murry* (London, 1959), p. 105.
2. While Huxley's is the best-known satire, there are others, including D. H. Lawrence's "Jimmy and the Desperate Woman," published by Eliot in the *Criterion* 3 (October 1924) :15–42.
3. John Carswell, *Lives and Letters* (London, 1978), p. 199, reports that 15,240 copies of the first number were printed; there were 12,000 copies for the second; and later numbers averaged between five and six thousand: "During its first year of life the *Adelphi* circulated more than 100,000 copies."
4. *The Collected Letters of D. H. Lawrence*, ed. Harry T. Moore (New York, 1962), 2:747, 749, 753, 821, 875, 792.
5. John D. Margolis, *T. S. Eliot's Intellectual Development, 1922–1939* (Chicago, 1972), pp. 67–68.
6. Lea, *Life*, p. 320.

Information Sources

BIBLIOGRAPHY
Alpers, Anthony. *The Life of Katherine Mansfield*. New York, 1980.
Carswell, John. *Lives and Letters*. London, 1978.
Lea, F. A. *The Life of John Middleton Murry*. London, 1959.
INDEXES
    Each volume indexed.
REPRINT EDITIONS
    None.
LOCATION SOURCES
  American
    Widely available.
  British
    Widely available.

Publication History

MAGAZINE TITLE AND TITLE CHANGES
    The Adelphi, volumes 1–4. *The New Adelphi*, new series volumes 1–3. *The Adelphi*, new series volumes 1–31.

VOLUME AND ISSUE DATA

Volumes 1–4, June 1923–June 1927. New series volumes 1–3, September 1927–August 1930. New series volume 1–volume 18, number 3, October 1930–December 1941. New series volume 18, number 4–volume 31, January 1942–September 1955.

FREQUENCY OF PUBLICATION

Monthly, June 1923–June 1927, October 1930–December 1941. Quarterly, September 1927–August 1930, January 1942–September 1955.

PUBLISHERS

June 1923–September 1930: British Periodicals Ltd., Cursitor Street, Chancery Lane, London, E.C. 4. October 1930–August 1934: The Proprietors, Bloomsbury Street, London, W.C. 1. September 1934–March 1937: The Proprietors, Russell Street, Downing Street, Manchester. April 1937–August 1937: The Proprietors, Adelphi Centre, Langham, nr. Colchester. September 1937–September 1938: The Proprietors, The Old Rectory, Larling, nr. Norwich. October 1938–June 1941: The Proprietors, 12 Woodside, Erskine Hill, London, N.W. 11 (temporary address, October 1940–June 1941, as below). July 1941–September 1942: The Proprietors, Adelphi Centre, Langham, nr. Colchester. October 1942–September 1948: The Proprietors, Lodge Farm, Thelnetham, via Diss, Norfolk. October 1948–June 1949: The Proprietors, Upper Welland, Malvern, Worcestershire. July 1949–June 1950: George Godwin, Old Buildings, Lincoln's Inn, London, W.C. 2. July 1950–September 1955: Staples Press Ltd., London, W. 1.

EDITORS

John Middleton Murry, volumes 1–4, new series volumes 1–3 (1923–1932). Max Plowman, new series volumes 1–2 (1930–1932); assisted by Sir Richard Rees. In late 1930 Rees began serving as editor, but Plowman still wrote for the *Adelphi* and had many connections with the journal. Murry, too, was always present on the editorial scene between 1930 and 1941, and it is often difficult to determine which of the three men (or their changing assistants) was the actual editor for a given issue between 1930 and 1941. Sir Richard Rees, new series volumes 3–8 (1932–1937).

Elgin Mellown

AGENDA

The first, four-page issue of *Agenda* in 1959 was enigmatic and cryptic; it billed itself merely as a "continuation" of a little program, *Four Pages*. Yet the editorial voice sounded suspiciously familiar: appalled by the small number of vital ideas among all that was published, it called for

communication between isolated outposts. Some of these are no doubt frivolous, some eccentric—outposts cannot be central. London at this moment has no map of European thought. We are all too ignorant of most Continental groups—a few it is difficult not to regard with suspicion. [No. 1:1]

Twenty-one years later, in an issue commemorating Ezra Pound, William Cookson, editor for all of *Agenda*'s twenty-five years to date, reproduced Pound's correspondence to him, begun when Cookson was only sixteen, up through the beginning of *Agenda* (17, nos. 3, 4; 18, no. 1:5–48). This correspondence shows that *Agenda*'s inaugural editorial derived from a letter of Pound's to Cookson. In his usual tireless way, Pound also tailored reading lists, suggested contacts in America, England, and Europe, and urged as model periodicals *Strike* and *Four Pages*. *Agenda* committed itself in 1959 to resuscitate poetry and criticism in England by the model of Pound's cultural warfare and the example of American verse: "If our poetry is to be revitalized it will be by a study of modern American poetry" (2, no. 1:cover 2). *Agenda* has remained attentive to Pound by special issues commemorating him (4, no. 2; 8, nos. 3–4; 17, nos. 3–4/18, no. 1), through innumerable articles on his work, and by publishing Pound himself (3, nos. 3, 5; 9, nos. 2–3; 17, nos. 3–4/18, no.1). More generally, Pound's interests set the agenda: economics and language study in the earliest issues, and translation throughout (6, nos. 3–4, a translation issue; 7, no. 1, modern Greek poetry; 12, no. 3, Rumanian poetry; 15, no. 4, French poetry; 20, nos. 3–4, Chinese poetry).

The featuring of other poets, in addition to Pound, has produced some of *Agenda*'s most attractive work. Special issues have been devoted to David Jones (5, nos. 1–3; 11, no. 4/12, no. 1), Geoffrey Hill (17, no. 1), William Carlos Williams (3, no. 2) Theodore Roethke (3, no. 4), Louis Zukovsky (3, no. 6), Basil Bunting (4, nos. 5–6), Hugh MacDiarmid (5, no. 4/6, no. 1), Wyndham Lewis (7, no. 3/8, no. 1), Giuseppi Ungaretti (8, no. 2), W. B. Yeats (9, no. 4/10, no. 1), Thomas Hardy (10, nos. 2–3), and Robert Lowell (18, no. 3). Issues are forthcoming on T. S. Eliot and Ford Madox Ford.

Notably, *Agenda* has featured poets who have used their own study of American verse—Jones's study of Eliot, Hill's of "the Fugitives," Tomlinson of Williams, Moore, and Zukovsky, Bunting of Pound himself—to create an intensely "local" British poetry. But while the selection of poets may appear partisan, the editors try for balance in their treatment.

The editorial introduction to the second issue on Bunting (16, no.1) confesses a lack of disagreement in previous special issues, and identifies a contribution by Peter Dale to that issue as "advocatus diaboli" (16, no. 1:3). This transformation from a journal that simply enforces Pound's ideas to a forum that, however faithful to its master, sets its own agenda, was won by timely, exemplary acts of self-criticism. After only six issues, *Agenda* estimated its own effect:

We have not yet become sufficiently a forum for intelligent discussion among those thinking actively at the present time. There has been too much general statement along lines which either our readers are too familiar with for anything to be achieved, or the opposite, which has meant a failure of communication. [No. 6:1]

Self-criticism gives point to the criticism of others. The ambitious issues devoted to English rhythm (10, no. 4/11, no. 1) and the "Supplement on Rhythm: From America" (11, nos. 2–3) print the lively replies of, among others, Auden, Bunting, Thom Gunn, Michael Hamburger, George MacBeth, Tomlinson, Richard Eberhart, Lowell, William Stafford, and Zukovsky to a questionnaire about poetic practice. The issue is prefaced by an acerbic contrast between *Agenda*'s self-criticism and the *Review*'s* self-regard: "It had certainly never occurred to us to celebrate a decade with a rigmarole of timid literary chat and cautious qualified praise from penpushers we most pushed" (10, no. 4/11, no. 1:3).

Agenda has sponsored criticism of Pound as well. *Ezra Pound Talking*, the transcripts of Pound's notorious radio broadcasts from Italy during World War II, was responsibly reviewed in the twenty-first anniversary issue devoted to Pound. The most stringent, telling criticism of Pound's "case" is Geoffrey Hill's "Our Word Is Our Bond" (21, no. 1:13–49), which scrupulously attends to the poet's responsibility for social forms, latent and expressed, in the language.

Pound's paideuma comes to the care of verse in this language by way of all that surrounds it. In a recent *Agenda* essay, "The Egotistical Banal, or Against Larkitudinising," Christopher Miller marks the limits of the parochial movement of much recent English poetry. If Philip Larkin and Ted Hughes constitute the " 'fully inherited imaginative and linguistic wealth of English poetry,' then English poetry is a paltry thing indeed, made up of the addition of mechanized, strip-cartoon violence and jeering and unremarkable boredom" (21, no. 3:102). In 1984 *Agenda* was continuing the argument of Pound against inbred English verse.

Information Sources

INDEXES
> Volumes 1–8, number 3/4 in *Comprehensive Index to English Language Little Magazines 1890–1970*, series 1, ed. Marion Sader (Millwood, N.Y., 1976).

REPRINT EDITIONS
> Kraus Reprint, Nendeln, Liechenstein (vols. 1–5 only).
> Microform: University Microfilms International (1959, apply UM/1; 1971, apply UM/5,6; 1975, apply UM/9).

LOCATION SOURCES
American
> Complete runs: Cornell University Library; Harvard University Library; Indiana University Library; Johns Hopkins University Library; New York Public Library; Northwestern University Library; Rice University Library; University of Illinois Library; University of Iowa Library.
> Partial runs: Widely available.

British
> Complete runs: British Museum; National Library of Scotland, Edinburgh; University of London College Library.
> Partial runs: Widely available.

Publication History

MAGAZINE TITLE AND TITLE CHANGES
>   *Agenda.*

VOLUME AND ISSUE DATA
>   Volume 1, numbers 1–12, January 1959–July 1960. Volume 2, numbers 1–12, September 1960–March/April 1963. Volume 3, numbers 1–6, August/September 1963–December 1964. Volume 4, numbers 1–6, April/May 1965–Autumn 1966. Volume 5, numbers 1–4, Spring/Summer 1967 (nos. 1–3)-volume 5, number 4/ volume 6, number 1, Autumn/Winter 1967/1968. Volume 6, numbers 1–4 (5, no. 4)/6, number 1, Autumn/Winter 1967/1968–volume 6, number 4, Autumn/ Winter 1968. Volume 7, number 1–, 1969–.

FREQUENCY OF PUBLICATION
>   Irregular. Issues are frequently combined (see above). After volume 4: quarterly.

PUBLISHER
>   William Cookson, "The Agenda and Editions Charitable Trust," 5 Cranbourne Court, Albert Bridge Road, London SW11 4PE, England.

EDITORS
>   William Cookson, 1959–. Peter Dale (coeditor), 1981–.

W. A. Johnsen

AKROS

In 1965, when Duncan Glen founded *Akros*, the only regularly appearing Scottish literary magazine was the Gaelic *Gairm*. The lack of native publishing outlets and the resultant self-alienation of Scottish poets forced to meet standards set in London or New York were, in Glen's view, a threat to Scottish cultural integrity: "It's as if critics of Baudelaire scrievit aye in Spanish" (17, no. 50:76). This concern, expressed polemically as a continuation of Hugh MacDiarmid's struggle "against the betrayers and Philistines who would return Scottish literature to being a sub-literature to English literature," animated *Akros* from its inception to its final issue in October 1983 (17, no. 51:118). Glen's interest in promoting poetry in Scots is the review's most immediately striking feature. Not only did he provide space for poets writing in that language, but he wrote essays on the vitality of Scots as a spoken language that continues to develop "new urban words [that] are genuine Scots words and not part of Scottish-English" (17, no. 50:120) and argued for increasing its prominence in Scottish universities. Nonetheless, *Akros* was always open to poetry in English, especially Scottish English, on the view that what really matters is that poets use their own "true-to-themselves" language (17, no. 50:122). Less often, it included poetry in Gaelic, a language Glen himself does not read.

To an unusual degree *Akros* always reflected the temperament and interests of its editor. In the early years, Glen, a teacher of graphic design, not only edited the magazine but undertook most of the physical labor of producing it. Although

from its sixth issue on *Akros* had the support of the Scottish Arts Council, the
first five volumes were hand-set and hand-printed by the editor, and the first
fourteen were "gathered and hand-sewn" by himself and his wife (7, no. 21:75).
Glen also designed many covers for the review, to which he contributed numerous
editorial essays, self-interviews, and poems—some published in his own name,
and others pseudonymously. In addition, the magazine carried numerous reviews
of Glen's own works and advertisements for the productions of his publishing
company, Akros Publications. Number 21, for example, carried largely admiring
review essays on the journal itself by John Herdman and J. K. Annand (both
regular contributors); the last, number 51, contained twenty critiques of "famous" modern Scottish poems, including a favorable if not adulatory review
by Michael K. Glenday of Glen's "My Faither." "I believe that Duncan Glen
is one of the most important poets writing in Scots today," says Donald Campbell
(7, no. 21:29).

Glen's attitude toward two Scots poets is revealed in the editorial choices in
Akros. The editor's deep admiration for Hugh MacDiarmid is a consistent theme.
Glen selected his "The Burning Passion" as the first poem in the first number,
staged a poetry competition for his eightieth birthday (no. 19), and devoted two
double issues (nos. 13/14; 34/35) to MacDiarmid's previously unpublished poems
and critical essays about him. Edwin Muir, at least as famous abroad, borders
on being an object of suspicion: "It may be that some anglicised individuals
such as Muir . . . have, indeed, been 'educated' out of their childhood Scottishness and have ended up as cultural refugees in the no man's land between the
Scottish and English tradition."[1] It is a fairly safe generalization that *Akros* has
over the years published far more poems showing MacDiarmid's influence than
it has poems exhibiting what Glen regards as the deracinated manner of Edwin
Muir.

Yet if every issue of *Akros* had the unmistakable accent of its editor, it is
equally true that the review was unusually varied in its format and contents. As
J. K. Annand remarked, by 1972 there had already been four changes in format
that "must be very frustrating to librarians and others who have to deal with the
problems of binding and storing" (7, no. 21:27). The changes in physical appearance were accompanied by more significant experiments with content. While
journals typically ration the number of pages devoted to poems, articles, and
book reviews, *Akros* was never wedded to any editorial formula. Even Edwin
Muir finally got his special issue (no. 47), devoted exclusively to critical essays.
Among the most imaginative issues have been number 18, a "visual" issue
featuring concrete poetry and photography; number 9, a translation issue, featuring translation into Scots of not only English and Gaelic, but Russian, Italian,
Latin, and Afrikaans poems. Number 49 was a special issue on criticism of
recent American poetry. The special situation of Sicily and its language vis-a-
vis Italy, as well as the excellence of its little-known poetry, attracted Glen's
sympathy in number 27. The amount of space devoted to Sicilian poetry testifies
to the sincerity of his expressed desire to encourage not only Scots poets, but

others in danger "of being condemned to conformity with the large culturally powerful nations in the name of universality" (17, no. 50:119).

Over the years the quality of the poetry in *Akros* varied as much as its format. The magazine's most distinctive feature—the number and variety of its poems and translations in Scots—could convince any skeptic that that language is a vital contemporary idiom suited to more than quaint imitations of the more popular poems of Robert Burns. The magazine had regular contributions from the best-known Scottish poets and critics—among them Alexander Scott, Alastair Mackie, Donald Campbell, Edwin Morgan, John Herdman, Robert Garioch, J.K. Annand, Eric Gold, Ruth McQuillan, and Andrew Greig. At its best an *Akros* poem is the astonishing experience of, say, Raymond Vettese's "By Words Alone," in which the poet refuses to be consoled for his lover's loss by the putative immortality of his verse: "I'm left wi words, sleekit as liars / malevolent craws on raucous wire / skriechin reminder: you arena here" (5, no. 15:81). That *Akros* produced its share of forgettable verse in both Scots and English was no scandal to its editor or contributors, since the magazine's role was always defined as encouraging the young and unconfident: "I will continue to print poems which show the marks of a poet still learning, even if some superior critics attack me for printing lesser—or bad poems" (17, no. 50:134).

In 1982 Glen announced his intention of making *Akros*, which had been appearing three times a year, an annual publication. The magazine appeared as planned in October 1983, but carried an editorial notice that this issue would be the last. "I have had enough of being a magazine editor," Glen remarked with characteristic candor, "especially as I am now having to turn away poets to whom I would have been able to give the encouragement of publication when *Akros* appeared three times a year" (17, no. 51:3). At the time of its last issue, *Akros* left the Scottish publishing scene considerably improved, with such journals as *Chapman, Lines Review*,* and the *Scottish Literary Journal* (see Appendix F) regularly appearing. Glen's own Akros Publications continues to prosper, and some of the changes in the curriculum of Scottish universities for which he argued have become a reality. Glen has, in Trevor Royle's words, been "a driving force behind the promotion of Scottish poetry."[2] Without arguing for direct cause and effect, the view that *Akros* succeeded in fulfilling its editor's objectives carries conviction.

Notes

1. Duncan Glen, *The Individual and the Twentieth-Century Scottish Literary Tradition* (Preston, Eng., 1971), p. 13.
2. Trevor Royle, *A Companion to Scottish Literature* (Detroit, 1983), p. 121.

Information Sources

INDEXES
"Check-List" of numbers 1–20 in number 21 (April 1973).

REPRINT EDITIONS
 Numbers 1–22, Kraus Reprint, Nendeln, Liechtenstein.
LOCATION SOURCES
 American
  Widely available.
 British
  Complete runs: British Museum; Cambridge University Library; University of
  Glasgow Library.

Publication History

MAGAZINE TITLE AND TITLE CHANGES
 Akros.
VOLUME AND ISSUE DATA
 Volumes 1–17, numbers 1–50, August/November 1965–October 1982; volume
 17, number 51, October 1983.
FREQUENCY OF PUBLICATION
 Three times a year (irregular), 1965–1982. One annual issue appeared in 1983,
 when the magazine ceased publication.
PUBLISHER
 Akros Publications, 25 Johns Road, Radcliffe-on-Trent, Nottingham, N612 15W.
EDITOR
 Duncan Glen.

Margaret Scanlan

ANGLO-WELSH REVIEW, THE

On the title page of each issue of the *Anglo-Welsh Review* from 1958, just
before the list of contents appears the note, "Published by Five Arches Press
and issued from 1949 to 1957 under the title *Dock Leaves*." Eight volumes (or
twenty-two numbers) appeared under a title many readers thought ambiguous
because they did not know whether it referred to a weed or to Pembroke Dock,
the magazine's place of origin. Whichever it referred to, the magazine flourished,
much to the surprise of the small literary group whose idea it was. They had
planned to publish just a single collection of their work. But the original subscription list (which included mostly family members and relations of the group)
grew from 89 for number 3 to 96 for number 5, 202 for number 7, and then (by
no. 22, the last as *Dock Leaves*) to seven closely printed pages of names.

When this group decided to publish some of their own work—critical papers,
stories, and poems they had read to one another at their regular meetings during
the first half of 1949—Roland Mathias, then headmaster of Pembroke Dock
Grammar School and founder of the group, suggested that they persuade his
English master, Raymond Garlick, to put the collection together. They had been
listening for six months to one another's papers on such famous writers as Goethe
and T. S. Eliot and to their own creative efforts, first at Mathias's house, 10

Argyle Street, and then at each member's house as the group grew. Probably it was Mathias who thought it a good idea to publish their work, though his innate modesty has never let him say so. The group also thought it a good idea as "a one time thing," and they read with astonishment in the first number that *Dock Leaves* would be published three times a year.

Except for four poems by C. C. Reed, all the contributions to the first issue came from members of this group. There were four poems each by Olwyn Rees, Roland Mathias, Nora E. Davies, and Raymond Garlick; stories by Mathias, Morwyth Rees, and Garlick; and an article, "The World of T. S. Eliot," by Alun Page. Unhappily, the issue was rather carelessly printed and assembled, so that one wonders if the editor really did not intend to publish further issues. Fortunately, Garlick saw beyond such petty details.

The remaining twenty-one numbers of *Dock Leaves* ran about fifty or sixty pages and included reviews as a prominent section. Writers from outside the group as well as other members of the group were added to the list of contributors. Some names of previous contributors may seem new to readers unfamiliar with the group and only indifferently acquainted with the characteristics of Welsh names. Olwyn Rees in the first number, for example, is Olwen in the second, where he reviews Saunders Lewis's play *Blodeuwedd, The Lady Made of Flowers*. Among the expanding list of contributors were Henry Treece, Neville Braybrooke, Paul Ferris, and R. S. Thomas; and the expanding list of subscribers included addresses in France, South Africa, and Buffalo, New York. In the third number Mathias commented on "some recent poems by Vernon Watkins" and was treated to a reply by Watkins in a few lines of doggerel in the fourth. As the audience grew and the writers became more eclectic, Garlick added a subtitle (no. 5), "A National Review in English of Welsh Arts and Letters," and reprinted an article from the *British Weekly* by A. G. Prys-Jones on the history of Anglo-Welsh poetry. In his seventh number he gloated a little, pointed to the failure of *Horizon*,* *Wales*,* and the *Welsh Review*, and attributed the success of his magazine to "faith and good works, partially subsidized by sales, subscriptions and good will offerings" and by voluntary workers and writers who accepted complimentary copies as fees.

In the spring of 1954 appeared "A Dylan Thomas Special Number" (no. 13), copies of which, seven years later, the magazine wanted to buy back because the editors had kept none. Included in this issue are poems in tribute (Anthony Conran's had been selected by Louis MacNeice to receive the Dylan Thomas Award), an editorial by Garlick asserting that Thomas's greatness is in his poems, the text of a broadcast in English and Welsh by Saunders Lewis, and articles of assessment. Aneirin Talfan Davies assesses Thomas's reading aloud; Henry Treece remembers, evaluates, and ranks; Glyn Jones finds no influence of Welsh poetry on Thomas but the capacity to have been good at it; A. G. Prys-Jones describes the genius and influence of Thomas; and Roland Mathias analyzes poems. Then follow reviews of *Under Milk Wood* and of Treece's "dog among the fairies" book.

186216

With number 23, *Dock Leaves* became the *Anglo-Welsh Review*. Garlick explained that the title change gave readers a clearer idea of what to expect and outlined the history of "Anglo-Welsh." Now that Professor Gwyn Jones has delivered a lecture on the subject at the University College of Swansea, he says, this literature may be accepted. From this number on, contents and editorials became strongly Anglo-Welsh and Welsh, though occasional articles had nothing to do with Wales but only with literature. The magazine at this point announced that it would be issued twice a year and nearly doubled the number of pages. The dating of the issues became complicated, however, because some years have three issues and other years seem to have but one. Nor did the editors help present-day bibliographers by omitting the date from the cover and pages of the magazine; restoring it later adds to the difficulty of dating the numbers accurately because of the irregular frequency of issues.

On the tenth anniversary of *Dock Leaves* (no. 25) Garlick elaborated his explanation and defense of Anglo-Welsh as a literature. His editorial cited poets Dylan Thomas, Vernon Watkins, David Jones, and R. S. Thomas; novelists Gwyn Jones, Jack Jones, Glyn Jones, Emyr Humphreys, Dannie Abse, and Alexander Cordell; collections of short fiction in the World's Classics and Faber anthologies; satire by Gwyn Thomas; and criticism by David Jones, Roland Mathias, Pennar Davies, and R. George Thomas. As further evidence Garlick surveyed various activities: a research degree granted by the University of Wales for a thesis on Idris Davies; the formation of several Anglo-Welsh societies; a summer school on Anglo-Welsh at Coleg Harlech; the resumption of the publication of *Wales*; and last, "the Third Programme put out an elusive symposium on the Anglo-Welsh."

In 1960 Roland Mathias replaced Raymond Garlick as editor, having assumed his duties after the Winter 1959 issue when Garlick resigned to take a post at the International School, Eerde Castle, Holland. Mathias's editorial expressed appreciation for Garlick's services and sketched his biography. The following year, Mathias became disheartened by the dwindling amounts of money granted by the Arts Council and the growing costs of producing each issue. Since subscriptions covered only about half the costs, he gloomily announced in number 29 the probable demise of the magazine. But the next issue duly appeared in July, and Mathias, through exuberance or perhaps modesty, neglected to explain how he had managed it. Not until summer 1969 (no. 41) did he satisfy his readers' curiosity in an editorial reviewing the twenty years of the magazine's existence. Apparently the Welsh Committee of the Arts Council had followed the lead of the English Arts Council, which decided to increase its grants to literature that year, and granted money to the *Anglo-Welsh Review*, reversing its previous position. Later, in 1965, as insurance for future issues, Mathias applied to have the magazine included on the Central Register of Charities and received approval in May 1966. These two sources of financial support, along with aid from Welsh Church Funds Committees, brought a reasonable degree of health.

Roland Mathias remained sole editor until Gillian Clarke, whose poems had appeared in the magazine from time to time and in *Poetry Wales*,* joined him as editor with number 50. When Mathias retired in autumn 1976, Clarke became editor and asked John Davies to help her as review editor. Davies, as head of the English department in Prestalyn High School, however, found the work of both positions too burdensome within a few years and left after the Spring 1979 issue. Clarke replaced him with Tony Bianchi, who served until 1981 (no. 68), when Greg Hill joined the staff as review editor.

After Roland Mathias, the editorial tone of the *Anglo-Welsh Review* took a more nationalistic slant, though not in any strident way. Gillian Clarke has understandably concerned herself with the immediate political conditions and events around her, in contrast to Mathias, who concentrated on artistic and linguistic conditions. Today these matters seem closely allied, as in, for example, the decisions of the Arts Council on the relative size of grants for any given year. And, of course, the cultural climate of Wales is directly affected by what happens in London. Thus Clarke's editorials talk about television, women writers, devolution, and, among other topics, the penuriousness of the Arts Council.

The present-day editorial policy is very clearly represented by Gillian Clarke's assertion in number 66: "Literature does not live in a void. Wales needs all the good writing it is offered, good journalism as well as literature."

Information Sources

INDEXES
  None.
REPRINT EDITIONS
  None.
LOCATION SOURCES
  American
    Complete runs: Harvard University Library; New York Public Library; University of California Library, Los Angles; University of Colorado Library; University of Michigan Library; University of Pennsylvania Library.
    Partial runs: Widely available.
  British
    Complete runs: British Museum; Cambridge University Library; National Library of Scotland, Edinburgh; Swansea Public Library; University College of South Wales Library, Cardiff; University College of Swansea Library.
    Partial runs: Bodleian Library; London University Library; University College of Wales Library, Aberystwyth.

Publication History

MAGAZINE TITLE AND TITLE CHANGES
  Dock Leaves, 1949–1957. *The Anglo-Welsh Review*, 1958–.
VOLUME AND ISSUE DATA
  Volumes 1–27, numbers 1–60, Christmas 1949–Spring 1978. Number 61—, Summer 1978–.

FREQUENCY OF PUBLICATION
    Biannually until 1956, then irregular.
PUBLISHERS
    1949–1977: The Dock Leaves Press, Pembroke Dock, Pembrokeshire.
    1978–: H. G. Walters, Ltd., Five Arches Press, Knowling Mead, Tenby, Dyfed.
EDITORS
    Raymond Garlick, 1949–1959. Roland Mathias, 1960–1976. Gillian Clarke, 1976–.

Martin E. Gingerich

ARENA

In 1949 Fore Publications, founded by Randall Swingler and run chiefly by
Jack Lindsay, became Arena Publications; an earlier magazine, *Our Time*,* was
supplanted by *Arena*, edited by Jack Lindsay with the assistance of Swingler
and John Davenport. Large-format populism had given way to a more defensive
stance:

> *Arena* is a literary magazine interested in Values. . . . The work in which
> *Arena* is interested is the sorting-out of . . . confused and often vital trends
> of resistance—the clarification of the valuably formative from the false
> and the merely fashionable (a feeble conformity trying to exploit what was
> for a moment a genuine adventure). [No. 1:1]

But continuous with Edgell Rickword's *Our Time* is the desire of the new *Arena*
to "draw on European sources—or still further afield—as well as on English"
(no. 1:2–3). Indeed, the spirit of the wartime Resistance was to inform the
postwar (Cold War) cultural struggle.

In order to revitalize culture it would be necessary to re-evaluate the English
tradition as it might be experienced in the present. The "Editor's Note" for the
second issue explained: "Tradition and culture: the words ring like a cracked
bell; and indeed the dreary ritual reminds one of a middle-class funeral, even
down to the sherry. The loved one died of sleeping sickness—*encephalitis leth-
argica*, caused by the T.S.E.-T.S.E. fly" (no. 2:3). England would have to look
to contemporary Europe "or further afield" for inspiration and, in that light,
discover those vital native elements which were being overshadowed by writers
such as T. S. Eliot.

The first issue carried not only poetry by Paul Eluard, an essay by Tristan
Tzara, and an excerpt from *The Plague* by Albert Camus, but also poems by
Hugh MacDiarmid and Edith Sitwell, and essays by Lindsay and Alick West.
Subsequent issues featured works by Eugenio Montale, Pablo Neruda, Leonid
Leonov, Aragon, and Jan Kott, as well as essays by Britishers Arnold Kettle,
E. P. Thompson, and, of course, Lindsay. " 'European, with no iron curtain'—

we have been called. Which describes our intention aptly enough,'' the editor admitted (no. 3:3).

However, the inclusiveness which the magazine managed within its declared limits—''A Literary Magazine''—and its constant reference of British cultural problems to Europe and beyond did not impress the Communist Party, of which the editors were members. The *Daily Worker* was particularly hostile to the first issue and ignored it thereafter. Apparently the *Arena* was insufficiently pro-Soviet: the decadence of British literature should have been referred to Russia specifically, where lay the answer to all problems, economic or cultural.

There is also another explanation for the Communists' displeasure. Lindsay was already unpopular with many of his comrades because of his constant critique of their mechanical interpretation and application of dialectical materialism. In this respect he was carrying on where his *London Aphrodite*,* which had attacked bourgeois philosophy, left off. In becoming a Marxist himself in the early 1930s, Lindsay did not thereby forgo the hard-won benefits of his theoretical work of the 1920s. Informing the *Aphrodite* was an ideal of human development and synthesis which brought Lindsay very close to English Romanticism; by the time of *Arena* he had decided that the Romantics were not only compatible with Marx but were, indeed, his precursors. One can imagine how bizarre it would have seemed to orthodox Stalinists for an explicitly (if not officially) communist magazine to carry two long articles on the significance of Coleridge. But Lindsay, author of the articles, knew what he was about. In the ''Foreword'' to issue 6, by which time he was sole editor, he explained:

> Coleridge has been chosen as the one English thinker who, working from bases in our own tradition, came close to a form of dialectical thought (akin to that of Hegel). His strengths and weaknesses are thus of basic significance if we are to understand both what is our own vital tradition to be revived, and what it was that went wrong with our culture after Shelley and Keats. [No. 6:2]

Lindsay's prefatory note indicates that *Arena*'s exploration of the creative mind of the late eighteenth and early nineteenth centuries bears little relation to the fashionable neo-Romanticism of the 1940s. The magazine has its own Marxist impetus. The four sections which comprise the two articles on Coleridge represent original and serious speculation—on Coleridge's thought, as it relates to the dialectic of Hegel (no. 6:36–43); his use of light-imagery, as suggestive of a possible transformation of man and society in a new relation to nature (no. 6:43–49); and his concept of ''Hope,'' seen as persistent despite disillusionment with personal circumstances and political events (no. 7:29–33).

The discussion of Coleridge, in such depth, puts Lindsay's enterprise outside the ranks of both communist dogma and the new Apocalypse. Similarly, his references to Blake carry their own distinctive weight. He had written his first full-length study of that poet as early as 1927, and in *Arena* undertook a revaluation in the light of his own political development. In the *Arena* essays he discovers a continuity between the work of Blake and that of Dickens (one to be discovered, in a different political mood, rather later by F. R. Leavis): both "grew up out of ferment of popular forms and forces"; both center on "the notion of transformation"; both resist the "bourgeois distortion" of life which is to culminate in naturalism (no. 4:44–45).

In its generous internationalism and its seriously selective traditionalism, *Arena* represents a triumph over Cold War consciousness. The Marxism of which it was a medium was always alert to the forces threatening "humanism," to use Lindsay's recurrent word. *Arena* opposed the extensive submission by the dominant intellectuals to *angst*: the way that "the Cocktail Party in the Wasteland" was considered the sole literary event of merit, or that *1984*, with its identification of fascism with "the mass movements which alone can prevent the emergence of such a state," was taken as "the last word about contemporary politics and the human condition itself" (no. 5:54,56). But at the same time it refused to mouth the "mechanist" platitudes of contemporary Marxist aesthetics, such as "the representation of the problem of the working-class." What was needed was to recognize and encourage any signs in "Western culture" of "the liberating comprehension of the true pattern of human evolutionary process"—without forgetting that "the problem of *man*" could only finally be solved by the working class alone (no. 5:62).

A systematic study of *Arena* is facilitated by the logical form of its own brief existence. Volume 1 (nos. 1 to 4) seeks to register the vitality of contemporary European literature. Volume 2 (nos. 5 to 7) keeps the European connections open but seeks also to remind readers of the vitality of the British tradition, specifically of the Romantics and those who followed them: John Ruskin, William Morris, Charles Dickens, George Meredith. In its last year, 1952, *Arena* takes the form of two pamphlets, arising from conferences conducted by Lindsay, the first of which concludes the argument for Britain ("Britain's Cultural Heritage") and the second of which glances prophetically across the Atlantic, stressing the extent of the struggle which *Arena* has only initiated ("The American Threat to British Culture").

Information Sources

BIBLIOGRAPHY
Coupe, Laurence. "From the *Aphrodite* to *Arena*." In *Jack Lindsay: The Thirties and Forties*. London, 1984.
Lindsay, Jack. *After the Thirties*. London, 1956.
———. *Life Rarely Tells*. Harmondsworth, Eng., 1982.
INDEXES
      Volume 1, numbers 1–4 in *An Author Index to Selected British Little Magazines*, ed. B. C. Bloomfield (London, 1976).
REPRINT EDITIONS
      Kraus Reprint, Nendeln, Liechtenstein. Scholars' Facsimilies and Reprints, Delmar, N.Y.

LOCATION SOURCES

American

Boston Public Library; Harvard University Library; New York Public Library; University of Arkansas Library; University of Pennsylvania Library; Wellesley College Library.

British

British Museum; National Library of Scotland, Edinburgh; University of London Library.

Publication History

MAGAZINE TITLE AND TITLE CHANGES

Arena: A Literary Magazine.

VOLUME AND ISSUE DATA

Volumes 1–2, numbers 1–9, Autumn 1949–(?) 1952. The last two issues took the form of undated pamphlets published by "Arena Publications."

FREQUENCY OF PUBLICATION

Monthly, volume 1, numbers 1–4, then bimonthly, volume 2, numbers 5–7. Irregular, numbers 8, 9.

PUBLISHER

Arena Publications, 28/29 Southampton St., London WC2.

EDITORS

Jack Lindsay, John Davenport, and Randall Swingler, volume 1; Jack Lindsay, volume 2.

Laurence Coupe

ART AND LETTERS

The moment of *Art and Letters* (1917–1920) is one of transition to an English modernism. Its particular interest lies in the opposing tendencies manifest in its pages between the Georgians and the imagists, and the uneasy urge—essentially true to both yet tactically closer to the latter—toward something more comprehensive. *Art and Letters* had originally been planned in the spring of 1914, but, as the opening editorial of July 1917 explained, the impact of the war had delayed it. On one hand, the scarcity of paper had made the editors—Frank Rutter, Charles Ginner, and H. Gilman—think carefully about their responsibilities; but on the other, they were acutely conscious of the mass of periodicals being blithely produced in England already: periodicals which gave "vulgar and illiterate expression to the most vile and debasing sentiments" (1, no. 1:1). Moreover, it was the very continuance of the war which had caused the initiative of *Art and Letters* to be fulfilled, since the editors felt that they had a responsibility for the civilization which the ordinary soldiers were fighting to defend. "Engaged, as their duty bids, on harrowing work of destruction they exhort their elders at home never to lose sight of the supreme importance of creative art" (1, no. 1:2). Indeed, *Art and Letters* was dedicated to upholding "the highest standards in all the arts, paying no respect to popular sentiment and ephemeral opportunities'' (1, no. 1:2).

In their justification of art by reference to the sufferings of the ordinary fighting man, the editors displayed an antagonism to the "imperialist" school of poetry— the bluff didacticism of Henry Newbolt and William Watson, and to an extent of Rudyard Kipling—which might suggest an affinity with the early Georgian poets. But editorial proclamation of "the highest standards" and the refusal of any claims made by "popular sentiment and ephemeral opportunities" reveals also an affinity with the imagists. A sense of concern for the conscience of an existing audience and direct duty to a given civilization is balanced by a show of detachment, aestheticism, even arrogance.

Between 1917 and 1920 the Georgian movement became the neo-Georgian movement, which one may, for convenience, identify with the *London Mercury*.* The *Mercury* coterie of J. C. Squire, John Freeman, Edward Shanks, and others (the "Squirearchy," as Osbert Sitwell dubbed them) was guided only by some of the incidental mannerisms of their predecessors; it had lost that fidelity to lived experience which had informed the early movement. Augustine Rivers's review of *Georgian Poetry 1918–19* in *Art and Letters* traces that falling off. Squire's poetry, he noted, was only superficially "matter-of-fact," his content limited to "Birds and Trees," his subjects chosen "from Latin gender rhymes. . . . Mr. Squire is an exhaustive exponent of Nature." Few other poets in the volume are spared this irony. Positive praise is reserved only for Robert Nichols and Siegfried Sassoon: "These two are the new lighthouses against whom other people's birds will smash their heads" (3, no. 1:51). The best Georgian poems were those which could comprehend the particular horrors of war, not those which led to genteel delectation in a neutralized and generalized "Nature."

Art and Letters published the poetry of Sassoon, Wilfred Owen, and Isaac Rosenberg. Resisting the temptation of technical innovation (other than the recurrent use of assonance), Owen effectively realized as a war poet the initial Georgian impulse toward emotional precision and integrity in traditional form.

The first issue contained Sassoon's "Wraith"; the Spring 1920 issue featured Owen's "Greater Love," "Arms and the Boy," and "The Next War." Nearly half of the Spring 1919 issue was dedicated to the life and work of Rosenberg: a memoir by Anne Rosenberg; poems—"In Piccadilly," "If You Are Fire," and "Heart's First Word"—and a pencil study by Isaac. The war poets represent that side of *Art and Letters* which, linking with imagism, anticipates the formal aspect of 1920s modernism.

Art and Letters demonstrates a tendency—inevitable anyway in such unpromising, hostile circumstances as the jingoism of the war and the immediate peace— to controversy and outrage. The Sitwells' verse, aggressively free, is there in issue 1 (Sacheverell's "Bird-Actors," Edith's "The Lady with the Sewing Machine") and thereafter, thus suggesting a proximity to the conspiratorial and notorious *Wheels** (1916–1921). A provocative formalism also characterizes some of the central critical pronouncements of *Art and Letters*. In the winter of

1918–1919 Frank Rutter offered "Nine Propositions" on art that add up to a case for cultural elitism as the appropriate context for artistic innovation: "Vital art-work is controversial and displeasing to the majority. . . . A minority is not always right, but right opinion can only be held by a minority. . . . Ignorance triumphs at a general election" (1, no. 1:52). In the previous issue Herbert Read offered a "Definition towards a Modern Theory of Poetry." Axioms are offered as "necessary dogmas" for any new aesthetic of value which will emerge: "*i* Form is determined by the emotion which requires expression. . . . *ii* The poem is an artistic whole demanding strict unity. . . . *iii* The criterion of the poem is the quality of the vision expressed, granted that the expression is adequate" (1, no. 3:73).

Art and Letters also anticipates a more mature modernism, such as one associates with the 1920s and such magazines as the *Criterion** and the *Calendar of Modern Letters.** Richard Aldington, for example, was a contributor from the first issue ("Postlude," "Concert"); and some of Herbert Read's poems ("Winter Grief," "Promenade Solennelle") suggest retrospectively an affinity with T. E. Hulme and the early Pound. One may recall Ezra Pound's reflection on the postwar years and the necessity to move beyond imagism, to consolidate the more important earlier gains with a new rigor and discipline. "Rhyme and regular strophes" is his phrase for the prescription.[1] He is thinking of his own *Hugh Selwyn Mauberley*, of course, but also of the tight quatrains to be found in Eliot's *Poems 1920*. Two of the most striking of those pieces—"Burbank with a Baedeker" and "Sweeney Erect"—appeared in *Art and Letters* for Spring 1919, in the same issue that celebrated Rosenberg. Eliot's essays on drama also appeared in the magazine, most notably his "Notes on the Blank Verse of Christopher Marlowe" (2, no. 4:194–99) and "Euripides and Gilbert Murray" (3, no. 1:36–41). Illustrations by Lucien Pissarro and Wyndham Lewis complemented the modernist fiction by Katherine Mansfield and Lewis, and the criticism of I. A. Richards.

It is fascinating also to read *Art and Letters* simply as a student of Herbert Read's career. The key to Read's total contribution is the understanding of modernism as a further working-out of the Romantic movement in poetry, philosophy, and politics. The attention of the imagists to the pure, value-free image was tactically effective, he argued, but any valid aesthetic must rest on some deeper notion, such as Coleridge's "organic form," and a wider view of poetry which recognizes the pervasive importance of the rhythm—understood as expressive of the poet's relation to nature and history—which carries and synthesizes the imagery.[2] There is, for example, his "Neglected Aspect of Edgar Allan Poe," an essay in which Poe's own poetic theory, continuous as it is with Romanticism, is gleaned for insights appropriate to emergent modernism (3, no. 3:137–41). Read's review of Joyce's *A Portrait of the Artist as a Young Man*, though clumsy in its attempt to view form and content as complementary, offers an insight which anticipates his own later aesthetic: praising "a style of clarity and even of radiance, an economy and exactness of description, and a purity of phrasing which makes us wonder at the possibilities,'' he yet regrets Joyce's neglect of ''the intenser spirituality of life'' (1, no. 1:26, 30). In exploring that intense spirituality, and in restoring modernism to the context of Romanticism, Read was to move beyond his formulations in *Art and Letters*. But the magazine remains indispensable for students, not just of his work, but for everyone interested in how modernism itself came into being in England.

Notes

1. Ezra Pound, ''Harold Monro,'' *Criterion* 11 (July 1932):590.
2. Herbert Read, *The True Voice of Feeling: Studies in English Romantic Poetry* (London, 1953).

Information Sources

BIBLIOGRAPHY

Hoffman, Frederick J., Charles Allen, and Carolyn F. Ulrich. *The Little Magazine: A History and a Bibliography*. 2nd ed. Princeton, 1947.

Press, John. *A Map of Modern English Verse*. London, 1969.

Read, Herbert. *The Innocent Eye*. London, 1930.

INDEXES

None.

REPRINT EDITIONS

Frank Cass & Co., London, 1971.

LOCATION SOURCES

American

Complete runs: Harvard University Library; U.S. Library of Congress; University of Minnesota Library; Yale University Library.

Partial runs: California State Library; Cleveland Public Library; Gardner A. Sage Library; Princeton University Library; University of California Library; University of Chicago Library.

British

Complete runs: Bodleian Library; British Museum; Cambridge University Library; Glasgow University Library; National Library of Scotland, Edinburgh.

Partial runs: Manchester Public Library; Victoria and Albert Museum Library; Westminster Public Library.

Publication History

MAGAZINE TITLE AND TITLE CHANGES

Art and Letters: An Illustrated Quarterly.

VOLUME AND ISSUE DATA

Volume 1, number 1–volume 3, number 1, July 1917–Winter 1920.

FREQUENCY OF PUBLICATION

Quarterly.

PUBLISHER

Arts and Letters, 148 Lower Richmond Street, London SW15 (1917–1919); 9 Duke Street, London WC2 (1919–1920).

EDITORS
    Frank Rutter, Charles Ginner, and H. Gilman.
FREQUENCY OF PUBLICATION
    Quarterly.

Laurence Coupe

ATHENAEUM, 1921–1931. See NATION AND
ATHENAEUM, THE

AYLESFORD REVIEW, THE

The Aylesford Review appeared in 1955 as a devotional publication of the English Carmelite Fathers. Intended primarily for their tertiaries (the Carmelite Third Order) and other friends, the first issues included only essays on religious topics, such as "Carmelite Spirituality," religious book notes, and a few nineteenth-century style poems. When the prospective audience displayed little interest in the new review, the editor, Father Brocard Sewell, began to extend its coverage. The editorial comment in the Autumn 1956 issue recalls that the church has traditionally been a patron of the arts and announces that the magazine "will not be confined to specifically Carmelite or . . . religious subjects." An article on wood engraving appears in the same issue, almost as a token of good faith. Although the journal continued to discuss religion, especially mystical theology, and to survey Carmelite scholarship in particular, it gradually evolved into a literary quarterly. Father Sewell, sole editor from beginning to end, mapped its course.

Throughout the 1960s the *Review* became increasingly sophisticated and comprehensive. An insert in the Winter 1959–1960 issue looks to the future: the editor regards the journal not as just another "house organ" but as a "serious review of spirituality, literature, and the arts," concerned also with "current questions of the day," albeit "from a friar's cell." The insert adds that "after four years of experimentation the *Review* has developed a character of its own, and it seems to fill a want that is not quite supplied by any other Catholic periodical. It admits to its columns a certain proportion of non-Catholic writers in the belief that it is good, and even necessary, for Catholics to know something of the best current non-Catholic thought, and that it is good also for non-Catholic writers to make contact with Catholic writers and thinkers." The Winter 1960–1961 issue states more clearly that the *Review* is "intended to serve as a forum where Catholics and non-Catholics can discuss topics of common interest" (4:1). Although those topics did, in fact, come to include the arts in general as well as religious, political, and social concerns, the *Review* is primarily important for its contribution to literary history.

The *Review*'s approach to literature is illustrated in Rachel Attwater's early essay "Piers Plowman," in which she presents Langland as "our very English Dante" (1:168–70). Attwater's article, like others that followed, is an introduction and an appreciation. The "critical" approach of the journal is typically biographical and historical. Unreadable esoteric criticism is, in fact, refreshingly absent. One of the most significant contributions of the *Review* was the special numbers devoted to minor writers who are generally neglected but who reflect the intellectual and artistic currents of their times. The first such issue (1, no. 7 [1957]) was a tribute to Elizabeth Myers, who wrote novels—*A Well Full of Leaves, The Basilisk of St. James's, Mrs. Christopher*—and other stories, but who may have been most talented as a letter writer. The issue is largely biographical and explores Myers's connection with the Powys family, another literary interest of the *Review*.

The Carmelites' St. Albert's Press, which printed the early issues of the *Aylesford Review*, also published a memoir of Elizabeth Myers. Since the *Review* received no subsidy from any source, it was kept afloat partly from the sale of books published by the Press. These publications reflect the interests of the *Review*, and several were in fact edited by Brocard Sewell.

The Winter 1957–1958 number (2, no. 2), the second special issue, introduces Henry Williamson, a writer who gained fame as an author of such nature books as *Tarka the Otter*, and then went on to write chronicles of country life (*The Story of a Norfolk Farm*) and two series of novels, one detailing the life of Willie Maddison in the quartet *The Flax of Dreams*, and a second recounting the adventures of his cousin Phillip Maddison in "the London Novels," sometimes called *A Chronicle of Ancient Sunlight*. Although most critics since the 1940s have dismissed Williamson as an artist, the *Review* presents him as "a great living writer." W. Gore Allen emphasizes the contemplative, theological character of Williamson's work. Malcolm Elwin calls him "an English Proust," and John Middleton Murry, who compares him to D. H. Lawrence, writes that "it is high time we awoke to the splendour and scope of his achievement in *A Chronicle of Ancient Sunlight*" (2:55). Williamson himself contributes an autobiographical note on his work. Several years later, Colin Wilson, pointing out that Williamson's life and work are curiously mixed, discusses his confusing fame as novelist, writer of animal books, and follower of Sir Oswald Mosley, the British fascist leader. Wilson's conclusion, however, is that Williamson's art, viewed in proper perspective, reveals "the presence of an extraordinary creative spirit" (4:121–43). Williamson also appeared as a frequent and valued contributor, and any students of him rely on the *Review* as a primary source.

Arthur Machen, author of *The Hill of Dreams, Far Off Things*, and many tales of the supernatural, is the subject of a largely biographical special issue (2, no. 8), which includes Henry Williamson's recollections of his friend. Brocard Sewell also examines Machen as "a consistent upholder of Catholic doctrinal and moral teaching in the Anglican Communion" (2:302–8). The issue on Machen was reprinted by St. Albert's Press as a miscellany.

Other special issues continued over the years. "The John Gray Commemorative Number" in the spring of 1961 (4, no. 2) presents rare insight into the *fin de siècle* poet and elegant man about town who is perhaps best known for *Silverpoints* (1893). Gray, later Canon Gray, was the friend of Oscar Wilde, the Rhymers' Club poets, Aubrey Beardsley, and, most especially, of Andre Raf-falovich, who maintained a literary salon in Edinburgh. In addition to the biographical essays of this issue, Ian Fletcher ("The Poetry of John Gray," 4:60–72) provides an introductory critique of Gray, whom he sees as outsider in the 1890s. Like Lionel Johnson, he considers Gray's poetry "a beautiful oddity." The Winter 1965–Spring 1966 issue includes articles on Gray's novel *Park* (1932), an unusual work of science fiction. Bernard Bergonzi, writing an introduction for a new edition, considers Gray as a stylist and sees him echoing the fantasy fiction of the 1880s and 1890s (7:206–15).

The Summer 1962 issue (4, no. 7) devoted to Joseph Delteil is unusual, in part, because it includes two notes (one in French) by Henry Miller, who did not usually contribute to religious publications. Delteil himself also assisted with the symposium, and two of his essays, including one on Henry Miller, appear along with his own abridged introduction to his *Oeuvres Completes*. The editorial states that this issue is offered as an "*introduction* to Delteil: nothing more." It is, in fact, a panegyric. The issue nonetheless has value and was reprinted in hardcover by St. Albert's Press.

The *Review*'s continuing interest in the 1890s is demonstrated in the Autumn 1966 number (8, no. 2) featuring Aubrey Beardsley. The illustrated issue examines Beardsley's contribution to the "decadent" magazine the *Savoy** (see *VEA*) and includes notes on a Beardsley exhibition.

The Summer 1967 special issue (8, no. 4) was "Homage to E. H. Visiak," poet, critic, and novelist. Along with commentaries by Kenneth Hopkins and Colin Wilson, the editor includes two essays by Visiak: "In Life's Morning Hour" (8:245–52), poetic memories of his early childhood; and "The Adolescent Age" (8:237–44), a study of Romantic novelists of the 1890s—Max Pemberton, Jules Verne, Robert Louis Stevenson, H. Rider Haggard, Stanley John Weyman, Gilbert Parker, and others. Colin Wilson, who praises Visiak's unpublished autobiography, speaks of him as "a writer of considerable complexity," potentially of the stature of Proust or Joyce (8:221–36).

Although not a "special issue," the *Review* devoted most of the Spring 1965 number (7, no. 1) to Hilary Pepler, a sometime writer best known as the founder of the St. Dominic's Press and cofounder with Eric Gill (who also figures in the pages of the *Review*) of a community of craftsmen on Ditchling Common, once described as a "fascinating sort of communal early Christianity." Sewell was once a member of the community.

Following its policy of introducing minor writers, the *Review* paid a centenary tribute to the novelist M. P. Shiel, a writer whom H. G. Wells found "colossal . . . brilliant." The issue (7, no. 3) for the first time prints a speech and a short autobiographical note by the eccentric writer, whose eccentric father had him

crowned king—a bishop apparently officiated—of the West Indian island of
Redonda on his fifteenth birthday. Shiel later held "court" in London and
bestowed titles on his friends: Arthur Machen was an archduke.

Another noteworthy interest of the *Review* was Frederick Rolfe, who used the
pen name Baron Corvo. Alexandra Zaina writes about his curious novel *Hadrian
the Seventh* (3:61–64) and about "The Corvo Revival," dated from 1950. *Don
Renato*, which appeared posthumously in 1964, was reviewed by Archibald
Colquhoun (4:78–81). Colin Wilson, one of the most important contributors to
the *Review*, reviewed a volume of *Centenary Essays on Frederick William Rolfe*,
commenting that the chief justification for the book is that it raises the question
of Corvo's literary value at a time when he might have been on the edge of
oblivion.

Although the same observation might be made about a number of authors
discussed by the *Aylesford Review*, it also included articles on such famous
writers as T. S. Eliot, Ernest Hemingway, Aldous Huxley, Marcel Proust, and
William Shakespeare. The president of the durable Bacon Society, for example,
presents his case for Bacon's authorship of the Shakespeare canon (6:168–76).

Along with its interests in religion, literature, and the arts, the *Review* was,
to some extent, concerned with social and political philosophy. In 1960, the
tercentenary of the Restoration, the *Review* gave special attention to *Sovereignty*
by Bertrand de Jouvenel, and presented a strong defense of the theory of monarchy (3, no. 2). After 1962 it also spoke out clearly on topical political matters
whenever it saw fundamental justice involved. The editorial in the Spring 1962
issue condemns the conduct of an "Official Secrets" trial in which the judge
disallowed evidence important for the defense. The editorial notes, moreover,
a "momentous happening"—the willingness of Catholics in Britain to resort to
nonviolent resistance (4:205–7). The *Review* also condemned apparent police
connivance in attacks on the life of Sir Oswald Mosley. "We publish these
facts," Father Sewell writes, "because we believe that one of the functions of
a small independent magazine should be to publish (at least for the record)
matters of public importance which the national press 'plays down' or ignores"
(4:282). In the Winter 1963–1964 issue, Father Sewell excoriates the Denning
Report (which relates to the Profumo affair and its sequel in the trial of Dr.
Stephen Ward) and speaks of the "immoral doctrine" that fails to restrict police
power (6:3–8).

However sincere its social commentary, the *Review* was more important as a
magazine for poets, known and unknown. The early years saw the publication
of generally prosaic traditional verse, such as that by Lady Margaret Sackville,
but its poetry became increasingly contemporary in style. In 1963, in a special
number on poetry (5, no. 3), the editor noted the kinship of mystic and poet,
and remarked on the "special fittingness" of devoting a number of the *Aylesford
Review*, published under Carmelite auspices, to poetry and essays on poetry.
Gregory Corso, writing in striking contrast to the usual conservative tone of the
Review, contributes a more stylistically outrageous piece entitled "Beat and

Afterbeat—Poetry and Theology." A second issue on poetry in Winter 1964–
1965 (6, no. 4) included critical studies on poetic technique—meter, rhyme, and
other musical effects. In 1966 the *Review* reprinted Francis Thompson's long
poem, "The Mistress of Vision," along with the 1918 commentary of Father
John O'Connor, the original of Chesterton's Father Brown (8:4–23).

Over the years, the *Review*, along with some literary oddities, included an
impressive sampling of modern poetry. Among the poets it published were
Thomas Merton, Carol Bergé, Stevie Smith, Alan Neame, Cressida Lindsay,
John Gawsworthy, Anselm Hollo, Michael Horovitz, Elizabeth Jennings, Robert
Nye, and Ian Hamilton Finlay. The *Review* was also open to young poets:
Penelope Shuttle, Francis Horovitz, Angela Carter, and Peter Redgrove.

In 1965 the *Aylesford Review* rightly described itself as "rather different from
the usual run of periodicals published under religious auspices." With *Carmelus*,
published by the Carmelite Institute in Rome, it helped to maintain the order's
reputation for learning and demonstrated "that an ancient religious order can be
genuinely 'involved' in the thought and aspirations of the contemporary world"
(7:92). But the *Review* always existed precariously from number to number.
While a number of American university libraries eventually subscribed to it, its
circulation never exceeded 500. Always handsomely printed, it began with twelve
pages, quickly expanded to sixteen, and ended with sixty to seventy pages. The
price registered similar increases. The last issue appeared in the summer of 1968.

Note

In writing this history, I am indebted to Father Brocard Sewell, who shared his perspective on the magazine he created in a letter to me, dated 30 May 1984.

Information Sources

INDEXES
    None.
REPRINT EDITIONS
    None.
LOCATION SOURCES
    American
        Complete runs: Indiana University Library; Johns Hopkins University Library;
        University of Colorado Library.
        Partial runs: Harvard University Library; New York Public Library; Tulane Uni-
        versity Library; U.S. Library of Congress; University of West Florida Library.
    British
        Complete run: British Museum.

Publication History

MAGAZINE TITLE AND TITLE CHANGES
    The Aylesford Review.

VOLUME AND ISSUE DATA
> Volumes 1–9, Autumn 1955–Autumn 1967. New Series, volume 1, number 1, Summer 1968.

FREQUENCY OF PUBLICATION
> Quarterly.

PUBLISHER
> The English Carmelites.

EDITOR
> Brocard Sewell, O. Carm.

Lawrence H. Maddock

B

BELL, THE

In 1940, the year after the death of W. B. Yeats and the one before the death of James Joyce, Ireland was a country stumbling into a new political identity, a neutral nation on the edge of a war-divided Europe and a land with increasingly faint memories of its own literary revival. In October of that year a forty-year-old short story writer from Cork named Sean O'Faolain (born John Francis Whelan, taking the Gaelic form of his name at age eighteen) launched his magazine, the *Bell*, as much because of these circumstances as despite them. Such attempts at an Irish literary journal were not altogether new. George Russell ("A.E."), mystic, poet, and friend to Yeats, had made a similar attempt with the *Irish Statesman* (1923–1930). Russell had published not only O'Faolain's early stories but work by Padraic Colum, Frank O'Connor, Seamus O'Sullivan (who went on to edit the *Dublin Magazine**), and James Stephens. Like Russell, O'Faolain disliked naturalistic literature and sought instead an Irish art with preferences for "intuition over rationalism" while still displaying a "developed social conscience."[1]

Subtitled variously throughout its existence (1940–1954) "A Survey of Irish Life," "A Magazine of Creative Fiction," and "A Magazine of Ireland Today," the *Bell* always combined dissemination of new fiction, poetry, plays, reminiscences, and reviews with an interpretation of what it meant to be Irish. In his initial issue, O'Faolain explicitly linked his country's artist and citizen: "You who read this know intimately some corner of life that nobody else can know. You and Life have co-operated to make a precious thing which is your secret" (1, no. 1:6). In the second and third numbers of the *Bell*, O'Faolain repeated expectations for an Ireland capable of taking its place among its international neighbors. Idealistically fighting against narrow brands of nationalism, O'Faolain opposed the Gaelic revivalists, insisting that it was possible for Irish "life to speak for itself'' (2, no. 6:5) to "project a picture of popular life" (2, no. 6:7). His vision, he said, was "Nationalist, Democratic, and Catholic" (2, no. 6:10), combining what he saw as the five strains of Irish culture: Gaelic, classical, Norman, Anglo-Irish, and English. He had in mind for his new magazine an Irish equivalent of *Horizon** or the *New Statesman and Nation** (see *VEA*) in England and the *Partisan Review* or *New Republic* in America (Vivian Mercier, "The Fourth Estate: Verdict on *The Bell*," 10, no. 2:159).

The *Bell* took a moralistic view both of its country and of itself. Each issue began with a free-ranging, self-assured editorial, with O'Faolain acting as a latter-day Joseph Addison or Richard Steele (see *The Spectator and The Tatler*, in AAAJ). Censorship, the Church's heavy hand, and reactionary views on politics and the arts were all frequent targets of O'Faolain's polite wrath. The literary works which followed each editorial were meant to set out suitable alternatives. Editing responsibilities of the ninety-six-page monthly were very much O'Faolain's alone, and he was not above launching his own campaigns within the *Bell*'s pages—an activity that won and lost readers for the new periodical. Its first issue sold out its printing of 500 copies within days; the number printed per issue increased tenfold within the first year. Paper shortages and related difficulties of wartime release plagued the magazine's first years. Appeals for British and, later, American audiences met with limited success.

Throughout its life the *Bell* fulfilled its aim of presenting "the best work of Irish writers" (12, no. 1:5). W. B. Yeats's novel *The Speckled Bird* appeared there. Countless stories by O'Faolain and Frank O'Connor (who served briefly as poetry editor of the *Bell*, as well) found their first readers in the *Bell*, as did scores of poems and several works of fiction by Patrick Kavanagh, Brendan Behan's *Borstal Boy*, and Michael MacLiammoir's memoirs. Elizabeth Bowen, Mary Lavin, Flann O'Brien, Austin Clarke, Lord Dunsany, Oliver St. John Gogarty, C. Day Lewis, Louis MacNeice, Sean O'Casey, Liam O'Flaherty, Denis Johnston, Lennox Robinson, W. R. Rodgers, and Jack Yeats all contributed frequently. Among younger writers, Benedict Kiely, Thomas Kinsella, James Plunkett, and John Montague all received early publication in the *Bell*. Sir Arnold Bax wrote several pieces of music criticism, some under the pen name "Bellamy." Evelyn Waugh's famous statement on whether he was a snob appeared in a letter he wrote to the *Bell* (14, no. 4:77) in response to a review of *Brideshead Revisited*. George Bernard Shaw and Sean O'Casey each wrote articles on censorship for the February 1945 issue (9, no. 5). William Saroyan, Osbert Sitwell, and Erskine Childers also were among the distinguished list of the *Bell*'s contributors.

In addition to a steady diet of new fiction and poetry, the *Bell* usually included pieces devoted to ordinary aspects of Irish life: Irish crafts, pubs, prisons, postage stamps, architecture, days in the life of a mechanic or a school teacher. Occasional volumes were devoted exclusively to Ulster or international writers. Regular columns reviewed the Irish theater and the film scene in Ireland; a general look-round appeared under the by-line "Gulliver" (Michael Farrell wrote most of these).

Beginning with the January 1944 issue, O'Faolain wrote an editorial series entitled "One World"—in part to counter an official wartime suppression of most international news, in part to combat isolationist attitudes held by many of his countrymen. The United Nations (and Ireland's eventual membership in it), other smaller European countries with situations parallel to Ireland, hopes for a new era of British-Irish relations—these were subjects that the editor chose to discuss which had "a valuable historical impact on the Irish scene. Some intelligent and influential Irish writer had of necessity at that period to enunciate what to the majority of the people in Ireland were startlingly advanced ideas."[2]

After six years of combining his editorship of the *Bell* with his other creative work, O'Faolain decided to "stop being didactic" (11, no. 2:649) and turned over his role as editor to Peadar O'Donnell, who had been responsible for the production of the *Bell* since its inception. Because he continued to write essays and stories for the magazine after his resignation as editor, O'Faolain's hand was never really absent. He served officially as book review editor after O'Donnell's elevation, and his last contribution was a story, "Childybawn," for the penultimate November 1954 issue. O'Donnell, a socialist whose interest in political and social issues was at least as strong as O'Faolain's, avoided any major changes in the *Bell*, reserving the editorials for his own points of view. From 1947 onward, however, economic difficulties increased, with publication suspended from the April 1948 issue for two and a half years. In O'Donnell's announcement of suspension is an admission that the *Bell's* useful life might be coming near its end:

> From an editorial point of view a temporary shutdown should be very useful. I have been of the opinion that the original impulse in *The Bell* has exhausted itself, and that if we are to serve any real purpose we must move closer to the problems of the moment—domestic and international. [16, no. 1:4]

O'Donnell's vision of a more socially committed publication was not to be. When the *Bell* reappeared in November 1950, it was with a different design format and a shorter (seventy-two page) length, but without fundamental alteration. From April 1951, the *Bell* was available only on direct order from the publisher and ceased publication altogether three years later.

Under O'Faolain the *Bell* became one of modern Ireland's most important intellectual journals. His own contributions, fiction and nonfiction, helped it to achieve its high literary reputation. Although some of his editorials were either long-winded or discursive or both, his skill as an advocate of native Irish talent was his strongest contribution. John Kelleher finds that O'Faolain "produce[d] piecemeal in his articles and editorials the fullest analytic description of contemporary Ireland, and of its strengths, faults, and derivations, ever given."[3] The forum that it offered Ireland's most talented writers, during an era in which those same writers often did not receive adequate presentation abroad, served to "build up real standards worthy of . . . dreams about a great, modern Ireland" (2, no. 3:11). It is an appropriate, if slightly ironic, tribute to O'Faolain's internationalistic outlook that the final issue of the magazine was a completely non-Irish one with, among its contributions, Jean-Paul Sartre's 1954 antinuclear speech to the World Peace Council in Berlin, Alberto Cavalcanti's essay on film and the novel, a Vietnamese folktale, and pieces on Henri Matisse and Anton Dvorak. Urging Ireland to look beyond its boundaries—and, in turn, allowing Irish writers to speak to a universal audience—was the *Bell*'s ever-prominent purpose.

Notes

1. Maurice Harmon, *Sean O'Faolain: A Critical Introduction* (Notre Dame, Ind., 1966), p. 55.
2. Paul A. Doyle, *Sean O'Faolain* (New York, 1968), p. 103.
3. John V. Kelleher, "Sean O'Faolain," *Atlantic* 199 (May 1957):68.

Information Sources

BIBLIOGRAPHY

Doyle, Paul A. *Sean O'Faolain*. New York, 1968.
———. "Sean O'Faolain and *The Bell*." *Eire-Ireland* 1 (Fall 1966):58–62.
Harmon, Maurice, *Sean O'Faolain: A Critical Introduction*. Notre Dame, Ind., 1966.
Holzapfel, Rudi. *An Index to Contributors to "The Bell."* Blackrock, Ireland, 1970.
Kelleher, John V. "Sean O'Faolain." *Atlantic* 199 (May 1957):67–69.
MacMahon, Sean, ed. *The Best from "The Bell": Great Irish Writing*. Dublin, 1978.
INDEXES

Rudi Holzapfel, *An Index to Contributors to "The Bell"* (Blackrock, Ireland, 1970).

REPRINT EDITIONS

None.

LOCATION SOURCES

American

Partial runs: Harvard University Library; Lehigh University Library; Newberry Library (Chicago); New York Public Library; U.S. Library of Congress; University of Kansas Library; Yale University Library.

British and Irish

Complete runs: National Library of Scotland; University College, Cork, Library; University College, Galway, Library.
Partial runs: Bodleian Library; British Museum; Cambridge University Library.

Publication History

MAGAZINE TITLE AND TITLE CHANGES

The Bell. Subtitle varies: *A Survey of Irish Life*, *A Magazine of Creative Fiction*, and *A Magazine of Ireland Today*.

VOLUME AND ISSUE DATA

Volume 1, number 1–volume 19, number 11, October 1940–December 1954.
Publication suspended, April 1948–November 1950.

FREQUENCY OF PUBLICATION

Monthly.

PUBLISHERS

1940–1948: Cahill & Company Ltd., Parkgate Printing Works, Dublin/43 Parkgate, Dublin (1940–1945)/2 Lower O'Connell Street, Dublin (1946–1948). 1950–
1954: Martin O'Donnell Ltd., Dublin/Fleet Printing Co. Ltd., 6–7 Eccles Place,
Dublin (1950–1951)/Cahill & Company Ltd. (as agents for Martin O'Donnell),
14 Lower O'Connell Street, Dublin (1952–1954).

EDITORS

Sean O'Faolain, October 1940–March 1946. Peadar O'Donnell, April 1946–December 1954. Poetry editors: Frank O'Connor, 1941; Geoffrey Taylor, 1941–
1945; Louis MacNeice, 1945–1947. Associate editor: Anthony Cronin, 1951–
1954. Music editor: John Beckette, 1951–1952. Book and theater editor: Val
Mulkerns, 1954.

Ronald L. Dotterer

BERMONDSEY BOOK, THE

Taking its name from the London working-class district that both inspired and
supported its publication, the *Bermondsey Book*, first published in 1923, advertised itself as "The Review with *Life* in It" (2, no. 3:100) and aimed at opening
the minds of the tanners, shipyard laborers, and factory workers of South London
to a new world of ideas. It hoped also to bring the lives and concerns of such
men and women to the attention of the privileged classes and, more generally,
"to increase the love and knowledge of the written word" (1, no. 1:3). As the
magazine's assiduously anonymous editor put it, "Life without Literature and
the ideals which flower from its reading, is barbarism, and a nation in which
the humblest and poorest cannot have free access to the thought and beauty
which are its heritage, EXISTS, but does not LIVE" (1, no. 1:3).

The *Bermondsey Book* was founded in December 1923 by Ethel Gutman, an
intensely humanitarian crusader who just three years earlier—convinced of the
spiritual and intellectual hunger of London's poorest working-class citizens—
had gone into their depressed neighborhood in Southwark Borough and there
had opened the Bermondsey Bookshop at 89 Bermondsey Street. In the early
1920s, Bermondsey was not materially better off than it had been almost a
century earlier when Charles Dickens used its gray and sordid dockside slum as
the background for young Oliver Twist's life of crime. Given the wretched living
conditions in Bermondsey, the bookshop's success seems very nearly miraculous;
for very soon after opening, it was to become widely (if ephemerally) recognized
as a cultural center. Every issue of the magazine begins with a report, several
pages long, listing the rich array of speakers and debaters—businessmen, poets,

novelists, musicians, and intellectuals, British and foreign—who participated in the events sponsored by the bookshop and held on its premises. Clearly, the Bermondsey Bookshop, today virtually unheard of, vied for fame in its own day with that other celebrated bookselling establishment, Harold Monro's Poetry Bookshop (1912–1935). Just as clearly, the Bermondsey Bookshop owed its own brand of broad appeal to the open-mindedness of its founder and her successors.

The magazine was, likewise, broad-minded—bearing equally the mark of Gutman's considerable influence. When she died in March 1925, the *Bermondsey Book* praised Ethel Gutman for having become

> a need; a part of many lives, someone very sure and safe who always gave to friends or strangers freely and without thought of the giving, just what they lacked. . . . she took the troubles of others and made them her own to ease. She smoothed lives that lay in rough places, and gave them purpose and meaning. [2, no. 3:3]

Like her contemporaries and friends Dr. Alfred Salter and his wife, Bermondsey's mayor Ada Salter—two similarly inspired social reformers with a zeal for bettering the living conditions of Bermondsey's citizenry[1]—Ethel Gutman was an activist, an intellectual devoted to cultivating local interest in government and politics, education, and the arts. Happily, the times were ripe to reward their efforts, for 1924 was the year in which Ramsay MacDonald at last succeeded in forming the first British Labour government. The pages of the *Bermondsey Book* convey something of the spirit of the times, the enthusiasm and optimism of people struggling to improve their lives and their minds. One gets glimpses of the lives of many who, like D. H. Lawrence, moved from poverty and obscurity to some measure of fame and good fortune, by sheer force of character.

In keeping with the vision expressed in its "Dedication," the magazine featured pieces by dozens of the most highly esteemed authors of Europe—alongside poems, stories, and articles written by Bermondsey's humbler, local sons and daughters. Among the established men and women of letters who contributed to the *Bermondsey Book* were Bertrand Russell, George Bernard Shaw, Emile Cammaerts, Julian Huxley, Virginia Woolf, Sir Hugh Seymour Walpole, Israel Zangwill, Edna St. Vincent Millay, William Archer, Thomas Hardy, John Drinkwater, Laurence Binyon, John Galsworthy, Luigi Pirandello, André Maurois, Alberto Panzini, Aldous Huxley, Siegfried Sassoon, J. B. Priestley, A. A. Milne, Harold Laski, Ernst Toller, Vita Sackville-West, Wilfred Gibson, Conrad Aiken, Sylvia Townsend Warner, Humbert Wolfe, Herbert Read, and Walter De la Mare, to name a few. But the magazine also published, in serial form, the quietly sensational, anonymous *Autobiography of a Bermondsey Boy* and numerous essays by young, then unknown members of the bookshop. For instance, it featured essays by Jack Uglow, a working-class youth, on John Ruskin's criticism (1, no. 1:41–42) and Cardinal Newman's "Idea of a University" (2, no. 2:90–

93); and it launched the successful writing career of James H. Wellard, later a scholar of classical literature and a prolific novelist (2, no. 2:6–7). Frank Bellamy, a Yorkshire miner, contributed a number of eye-opening pieces—some factual, some fictional (1, no. 1:51; 4, no. 4:61–63; 5, no. 4:90–93). Most of the short stories written by working-class authors are equally candid. Brief synopses suggest both their lower-class settings and their universal themes. Ashley Smith's "The Atlas Café," for instance, tells the rough and tumble love story of a hard-working barmaid named Anna and her proud, proletarian swain, Jim (6, no. 2:50–60). A. E. Coppard contributed "Fine Feathers," a story about a clerk in a brewery whose driving passion is ambition (5, no. 1:22–43). "Colour" by Mabel Dean is the story of a tragic mulatto (6, no. 3:110–14), and Liam O'Flaherty's "The Strange Disease" is about a sex-obsessed country youth who drives a priest into a frenzy of punitive violence (5, no. 2:32–37). Because the contributions were so well written, the fame of the magazine spread, and soon it was publishing autobiographical pieces like "The French Working Man" by René Massé (1, no. 2:44–47), "From a Russian Workman" by P. A. Romanoff (1, no. 3:65–66), "The Workers in Spain" (1, no. 4:61–63), "Italian Workmen and Fascism" by Yoi Mariani (2, no. 2:86–89), "A Belgian Miner's Life" by Emile Erculisse (2, no. 3:81–83), and "An Indian Workman's Life" by "Mazdura" (3, no. 3:94–96). Articles by journalists for the *Times* were balanced by others written by the music and drama critics on the staff of the *Daily News*. The general idea was to build bridges of concern across the boundaries separating the nations and classes of the world—to kindle a small flame of enthusiasm to warm the human spirit and banish the postwar blues.

One of the hallmarks of the *Bermondsey Book*'s style is succinctness. Here, eminent writers frequently treated their large subjects in no more than three pages. Only a few subjects received fuller treatment. In an article entitled "Nationality and Research," J.B.S. Haldane, for example, authoritatively explains how the conditions under which scientific investigation must take place around the world appear to affect the development of knowledge in various fields; and he says what he has to say in fewer than six pages. André Maurois assesses "English Novelists of To-Day" in a little less than five pages (3, no. 2).

Most of the articles aim to engage as broad an audience as possible. In an eight-page essay, long by *Bermondsey Book* standards, Bertrand Russell examines the relationship between psychology and politics. Without political or psychological jargon, it makes its points straightforwardly, to wit: "In politics, especially, sex is chiefly important when thwarted. In the war, elderly spinsters developed a ferocity partly attributable to their indignation with young men for having neglected them"; or again:

> It would be easy, with our present knowledge to make instinctive happiness almost universal if we were not thwarted by the malevolent passions of those who have missed happiness and do not want anyone else to get it. And if happiness were common it would preserve itself, because appeals

to hatred and fear, which now constitute almost the whole of politics, would fall flat. But if psychological knowledge is wielded by an aristocracy, it will prolong and intensify all the old evils. [3, no. 2:13, 15]

Russell's observations are provocative, of potential interest to all thinking people, regardless of their class or political affinities. And, while his ideas are in no way typical of the ordinary Englishman's, the tenor of his discourse is in accord with the magazine's editorial policy of offering views that transcend the narrower preoccupations of particular groups.

Julian Huxley's essay "The Courtship of Animals" recommends itself to the attention of a similar range of readers. "Remembering our incorrigible passion ... for anthropomorphism," Huxley wonders "whether much of human behaviour had better not be interpreted from the animal side rather than the animals's from ours, and asks us to consider how much we are walled in by our biological heritage." His essay, rich in scientific detail but in no way pedantic, aims "to throw a little light upon this subject and to give a few of the facts which may enable us to gain a true perspective" (3, no. 3:58).

The articles written by members of the working classes are similarly universal in their appeal, primarily due to their literate tone and intelligent grasp of realities, qualities not generally associated with nor expected of the common laborer. One may, for example, be struck by the sophistication of the essay by "F." entitled "The Miner and His Hours." "We look and feel like the denizens of a Dantesque world," writes the coal miner. "Although we look upon perils lightheartedly, the presence of danger weighs heavily on our sub-conscious minds" (3, no. 3:55). The point of the essay is not, however, to show off his erudition—his acquaintance with *La Divina Commedia* and the terms coined by Sigmund Freud—but to commend certain reforms in the labor laws, especially those reducing the number of hours laborers must work for a day's pay. He argues that conditions are nowhere near perfect, by any means; there is much yet to strive for, decent housing and minimal welfare programs, for example. "Meanwhile," he explains, "our dearest possession is the seven-hour day. It is the stepping-stone from the industrial dark ages to the millennium. It has added more to our status than any other reform, for with it we have lived a fuller life, and have broadened our minds and developed a little our personalities" (3, no. 3:57). The *Bermondsey Book*, founded to further the same ends, was no doubt proud of the opportunity to publish this and similar testaments to the validity of its general aims.

Several regular features of the magazine combine the functions of journalism and criticism. Beginning with the first issue of volume 3, the *Bermondsey Book* ran a series of essays entitled "A Critic in the Gallery" by A. Paget, drama critic for the *Daily News*. Paget's reviews, because they are punctuated by observations on the nature of drama and on the social value of theatrical productions in general, evince more than a topical interest in the plays being staged on the London boards. In accounting for the appeal of comedy, for instance, he argues that comedy and tragedy are more closely allied than many would suspect:

"Pay a visit to a musical comedy that has been running for months and months,"
he urges. "Here you will find the tragedies of life, not in small numbers, but
in battalions" (3, no. 3:42). Beginning with volume 4, number 3, James Wellard
contributed a comparably thoughtful series of pieces entitled "At the Cinema."
Fairly regularly, the magazine ran a section called "Letters from Abroad," a
showcase for correspondence from foreign readers of the magazine. Many of
the letters are, in fact, essays on political and cultural developments in such
places as Rome, Berlin, Paris, Jerusalem, New York, and the Gold Coast.

Perhaps the single most important serial feature of the *Bermondsey Book* is
its large collection of book reviews, most of which are excellent. The majority
of these, signed "F.H.," are informative, intelligent, and inviting. But their
primary function seems to be to call attention to the most important books being
published; and this they do with impressive regularity. One issue's fairly typical
assortment included Walter De la Mare's *Stories from the Bible*, H. G. Wells's
The Common Sense of World Peace, Erich Maria Remarque's *All Quiet on the
Western Front*, Theodore Dreiser's *Dreiser Looks at Russia*, and Mrs. Le-
Mesurier's *The Socialist Woman's Guide to Intelligence*, a spirited rebuttal of
George Bernard Shaw's *The Intelligent Woman's Guide to Socialism and Capitalism* (6, no. 3:119–26). The reviews, modestly set in much smaller type than
the featured pieces, constitute a significant proportion of the *Bermondsey Book*'s
intellectual substance.

In November 1926, the Bermondsey Bookshop and the editorial offices of the
Bermondsey Book moved to 171 Bermondsey Street, formerly the site of a public
house. The original house "had proved too small for the growth in membership"
(4, no. 1:3). Both the shop and the magazine were thriving financially. Whoever
was in charge following the death of Ethel Gutman apparently possessed good
business sense. But we can only surmise his identity. All but one of the magazine's "Editorial Notes" are unsigned. The second page of each issue bears a
notice that begins, "The Editor will be very pleased to consider contributions,
which need not be typewritten." The one editorial that is "signed" is only
initialed "F.H." It is not unreasonable to hypothesize that "F.H." is Frederick
Heath, who contributed a number of essays, book reviews, and poems to the
publication. Whether he was indeed solely responsible for continuing Gutman's
mission or not we cannot be absolutely sure. That "F.H." contributed massively
to the enterprise is, on the other hand, obvious.

In the spring of 1930 the *Bermondsey Book* abruptly ceased publication. The
reason is not readily apparent. The "Editorial Notes" for that issue offer no
clues. "*The Bermondsey Book* is now in its seventh year of publication," writes
the editor. "It has met with all the usual difficulties that beset any independent
literary review. Some of these difficulties have still to be faced, but most of
them have now been overcome" (3, no. 2:3). The problem was not a lack of
subscribers or a lack of contributions; for, the editor reports:

We are able to record a very significant increase in the number of subscribers. Contributions submitted from all parts of the world have more

than trebled in number during the past year, and we are now receiving them almost at the rate at which they are submitted to a monthly magazine.

All the same, the issue was the last of the bright blue and yellow *Bermondsey Book* and the end of a noble and successful venture.

Note

1. Mary Boast, *The Story of Bermondsey* (London, 1978), p. 23.

Information Sources

BIBLIOGRAPHY

Boast, Mary. *The Story of Bermondsey*. London, 1978.
Dimoldenberg, Paul. *The Evolving Role of the State and Its Impact on the Development of Bermondsey, 1850–1975*. Oxford, 1977.
Grant, Joy. *Harold Monro and the Poetry Bookshop*. London, 1967.

INDEXES

Volume 7, number 2 in *An Author Index to Selected British Little Magazines*, ed. B. C. Bloomfield (London, 1976).

REPRINT EDITIONS

None.

LOCATION SOURCES

American

Complete runs: New York Public Library; Northwestern University Library; U.S. Library of Congress; Yale University Library.
Partial run: Minnesota University Law Library.

British

Complete runs: Bermondsey Public Library; Bodleian Library; British Museum; Cambridge University Library; National Library of Scotland, Edinburgh.
Partial runs: British Library of Political Science; Leeds Public Library.

Publication History

MAGAZINE TITLE AND TITLE CHANGES

The Bermondsey Book: A Quarterly Review of Life and Literature.

VOLUME AND ISSUE DATA

Volume 1, number 1–volume 7, number 2, December 1923–March/April/May 1930.

FREQUENCY OF PUBLICATION

Quarterly.

PUBLISHERS

December 1923–March 1925: Cecil Palmer, 49, Chandos, Charing Cross, London.
June 1925–March/April/May 1930: William Heinemann, Ltd., London.

EDITORS
> Anonymous (Ethel Gutman?), December 1923–March 1925. Anonymous (Frederick Heath?), September 1925–March/April/May 1930.

R. Victoria Arana

BLACK ART, THE

The *Black Art* was not, as one might assume initially from its title, an overdue forum for one of Great Britain's racial minorities. The "black art" referred to therein is the art of printer's ink; this distinctive periodical published between 1962 and 1965 was devoted exclusively to an underrepresented minority of the modern publishing world—the private press. Elegantly set with quality typefaces and at high production standards, the *Black Art* offered to its readers articles, illustrations, and even advertisements (usually for either small press publications, antiquarian bookshops, print designers, or other compatible journals) with a legitimate measure of style. Many of the articles in the twelve issues that appeared focus directly upon technical or historical aspects of book printing: logotypes and ligatures, the invention of the roll-press or the relief press, the printing and proofreading of Shakespeare's First Folio, Irish scribal influence on modern type design, for example. But the greater bulk of the *Black Art*'s articles dealt with the literary uses for which a handpress had been pulled. More than such contemporary journals as *Printing Technology, Printers' Register*, or *Graphic Technology*, the *Black Art* concerned itself directly with artistic aspects of the printing trade.

James Charles Moran, the *Black Art*'s editor and driving force throughout its short life, had been editor of *Book Design and Production* (1958–1964), subsequently incorporated into *Print Design and Production*. In the decade following the *Black Art*, he was to become, at least in Britain, "the acknowledged authority on printing history" and author of several books on the subject including a 1973 Faber and Faber volume that became the standard in the field.[1] After the *Black Art* ceased publication, he contributed to its revamped successor, the *Journal of the Printing Historical Society*, before his death on 24 February 1978. As editor of the *Black Art*, Moran took William Caxton and William Morris as models of the type of printer whose work would receive attention in this special periodical: printers who were authors themselves, combining knowledge of the other arts with their own literary inventiveness. (see 1, no. 2; 3, no. 1). Sensing "a growing interest in the historical and antiquarian side of printing, and the practice of the old craft by private presses" (1, no. 4:119), Moran sought to praise the virtues of these forebears by practicing as he preached.

In addition to its obvious value as a chronicle of the technological history of book publication and its interest as a record of British (and, less comprehensively, Continental and American) trade craftsmanship, the *Black Art*'s claim as a critical journal of literary merit falls into two categories: first, the articles it devoted to early book publishing, primarily in Britain but also in the rest of Europe; and, secondly, articles discussing the expansion, since Morris's Kelmscott Press, of an important part of literature written in English—small press publications. John Mountford of London's Merrythought Press praised the *Black Art* as a needed vehicle in which small presses might "discuss their problems, their hopes and perhaps, how they can help each other" (1, no. 1:31). As a narrow-interest periodical with an admittedly short (although adequately circulated) run, the *Black Art* left its recognizable, if limited, mark. While it did not achieve the universal discourse Mountford predicted, it served during its existence as a collective house organ for a diverse group of small presses. For the general reader with literary interests, it helped to place the small-press movement in an appropriate context while giving solid information about the actual works printed by Morris at Kelmscott, and by Laura Riding and Robert Graves's Seizin Press (2, no. 2), and through its review sections highlighted the issues of such contemporary presses in Britain, Ireland, and America as Swallow, Adagio, Signet, and Three Candles. Among others reviewed, Thomas Merton's volumes for the Saint's Press deserve mention for their detail and insight.

Beginning in March 1965, publication of a new magazine entitled the *Journal of the Printing Historical Society* dictated that, as Moran announced in the *Black Art*, this new journal would undoubtedly "cover much the same ground" as the *Black Art*—not a completely accurate statement, since the *Journal of the Printing Historical Society* chose to be more exclusively historical than its predecessor.[2] (Moran, in turn, served as first chairman, from May 1964, of the London-based Printing Historical Society.) The initial editor of this second journal was James Mosley, librarian of the St. Bride's Institute; its printer was the University Printer at Oxford. Annual subscriptions (four issues) to the *Black Art* cost forty-two shillings ($6.00 for the first volume, $7.00 thereafter) for the 6 1/4 by 9 1/4 inch publication.

Melvin G. Williams's reassessment of the role of Caxton as printer typifies the distinctive approach of the *Black Art* (1, no. 4). Discussing Caxton's conflicting personae as imaginative artist and profit-seeking businessman, Williams defines the pattern of printer as "editor/publisher" overtaking that of a journeyman-artisan following the established patterns of his trade. Articles on Wynkyn de Worde, Caxton's assistant, and on the von Stern Press of Lüneberg in Germany complement one by John C. Tarr (1, no. 3) on John Day, printer of the *Chronicles of King Alfred*, the *Queen Elizabeth Prayer Book*, Roger Ascham's *The Scholemaster*, and the English edition of Euclid's *Elements of Geometrie*. Moran himself wrote a descriptive account of the volumes issued by Riding and Graves's Seizin Press (2, no. 2). As supplements to feature articles such as these, short reviews of recently issued literary works produced by small presses were included in most issues of the *Black Art*—for example, Thomas Merton's *Hagia Sophia*, John Ruskin's *The Contemptible Horse*, and Charles Dickens's *Public Dinners*.

Booklovers, antiquarians, and professionals in the printing world all found items of value in the *Black Art*, and its refusal to separate publishing technique from literary artistry is noteworthy. Throughout its run, the *Black Art* depended upon outside contributions as well as those from its editor, but the books which Moran later wrote had their germination in these pages. By reminding its readers of the artistic standards possible in book printing, the *Black Art* used its backward glances to set out clear glimpses of the best current practice.

Notes

1. Anonymous tribute to the late author, *"Fit to Be Styled a Typographer"*: *A History of the Society of Typographic Designers, 1928–78* (London, 1978), p. vi.
2. *Journal of the Printing Historical Society* 3 (1965):66.

Information Sources

INDEXES
Each volume indexed.
REPRINT EDITIONS
None.
LOCATION SOURCES
American
Widely available.
British
Widely available.

Publication History

MAGAZINE TITLE AND TITLE CHANGES
The Black Art.
VOLUME AND ISSUE DATA
Volume 1, number 1–volume 3, number 4, Spring 1962–1964/65.
FREQUENCY OF PUBLICATION
Quarterly for volumes 1 and 2, semiannually for volume 3.
PUBLISHERS
Volume 1–volume 2, number 2: The Furnival Press, 31 Furnival Street, London EC4. Volume 2, numbers 3/4: Taurus Press Ltd., London EC4. Volume 3: Thomas Rae Ltd., Greenock, Scotland.
EDITOR
James Charles Moran.

Ronald L. Dotterer

BLACKFRIARS

Blackfriars: A Monthly Review Edited by the English Dominicans was begun in 1920 as a continuation of the defunct *Catholic Review* and a student Dominican publication, the *Hawkesyard Review*. Into the chaos of the 1920s the Dominicans thrust their magazine, determined to wrestle with the issues of the day in a realistic manner. It was apparent that the working classes were lost—if indeed the Church had ever had them. But something could be saved—and the struggle for God was on. This would be nothing less than an attempt to save the Faith, now rapidly eroding under the attacks of secularism, hedonism, and materialism. The founder, Father Bede Jarrett, had his own ideas as to how to combat the age:

> We have a popular gospel to preach to the disinherited; yet are losing in the poorer quarters thousands whom the communists gain. . . . We are afraid to tackle the single, central fabric on which all rests. We put ointment on the sores; we leave the social body's inner ailments timidly alone.[1]

Blackfriars remarkably appeased and combined at least two of the disparate factions in the English Catholic Church. There was, first, an ancient and very small group of aristocrats who never lost or gave up the faith. Another group consisted of the Irish, fleeing poverty, famine, and the never-ending sorrows of their homeland. An enormous part of the Church in England was Irish, clustered with their priests in Liverpool, London, and the other great cities. A third group came in during the "Second Spring" as converts of the Oxford Movement, not a homogeneous community. Still others came from diverse backgrounds—pagans, Quakers, Nonconformists. When they entered the Church, they brought with them the tattered clothing of their former secular beliefs. Submitting to the Church, they wore their political and economic opinions like banners, refusing to shed them: Eric Gill (who designed the cover of *Blackfriars*), with his concept of an ideal community, or Stanley Morison, self-declared communist and a member of the editorial board from the magazine's inception.

The nexus for agreement among the second and fourth factions was a strange, determined man, Father Vincent McNabb, a member of the ancient religious Order of Preachers, founded by St. Dominic. Banished in Penal Times to exile in Brussels, Tangier, and Rome, they returned in the late nineteenth century to England. Under Father Bede, they built their new priory at Oxford: the House of Studies for the English Province of the Order. Born in Ireland, one of a large family of devout Catholics, McNabb was an eminent theologian, a vigorous controversialist, and a man of great charity. To many of his coreligionists, he was a saint; to others, he was also a socialist, a designation he refused with determined vigor.

One cannot escape the implications of the fact that the periodical was founded in 1920. The war to end all war was succeeded by revolutions upon revolutions, some nationalistic (in Ireland, Finland, Poland), some ideological (in Russia, Germany, Hungary). The old order had at last shown its total bankruptcy: the Hapsburgs, Romanovs, Hohenzollerns, Wittelsbachs were scattered in exile. Terrible suffering was the lot of vast numbers of the new and old poor of Germany, Austria, and England. Inflation and the destructive effects of war industry had produced economic chaos in England, France, and other European nations. Reparations and punishment would pave the way for such socialist experimentation as National Socialism in Germany under Hitler.

Distributism, as developed by Hilaire Belloc, was to be the banner under which *Blackfriars* would fight. In its pages Belloc argued for a synthesis of private property and cooperation, with wealth distributed and safeguards established against the rebuilding of the enormous capitalistic structures of modern times. To Belloc and his allies, there was little difference between the capitalists and the communists or socialists. The socialist state would exist wherein the means of production—land, machines—would be owned or controlled by the politicians. The socialists, however much they might war with the capitalists, were at one with them in this: they both wanted to take over and concentrate wealth. Belloc and his allies wanted to divide it.[2]

Many of the ideas the periodical supported in its early day are now dead. McNabb fought feminism with the same vigor that he fought sin and heresy. The breakup of the family, with working wives, the disappearance of the family wage, contraception, the extension of state control over children, mass unemployment with the dole becoming a way of life—all these he consistently attacked. The *New York Times* obituary noted that he was a critic of the feminist movement, and that the entire English nation followed his clashes with Arnold Bennett in 1920 over this issue.[3] The feminists today go from victory to victory. The back-to-the-land movement supported by McNabb never caught on either in any formidable way. For McNabb, with his anti-industrial attitudes, the city was a cemetery for the Faith; religion simply could not survive there. One can only conjecture out of what Romantic notions this idea was born. However, despite his best efforts, the people never returned to the land. Even when transferred to the United States, the Catholic Rural Life Movement was never a success, with more and more farms going under, and more and more people moving to the cities. The idea that the machine age was evil, that industrialism would bring with it only sorrow, was also a Romantic notion; a drive against the machine was a lost cause indeed.

Among all the lost causes, however, there was one triumph: ecumenism. Early on, McNabb supported an earnest dialogue with other Christian churches, long before it was popular in the Catholic Church to do so. He and others of the Order of Preachers supported the famous Malines Conversations of 1921–1925 when talks were held between the Established Church of England and the representatives of the Catholic faith.

Blackfriars did well. The first number sold out completely, largely because of an article on the Anglican Lambeth Conference, an article which gave the periodical considerable favorable publicity. The editor always insisted that the Established Church should be treated with courtesy and consideration.

Over the years all of the eminent scholars and writers of Catholic England have written for *Blackfriars*. Not all contributors have been Catholic, though

186216

the majority have been; nor have they all been English. The authors range from David Mathew to Howard Root, Thomas Merton to Robert Charles Zaehner.

Despite the sympathies of the founders with the Chesterbellocian view of economic reality, it must not be assumed that *Blackfriars* pushed a strident campaign for the adoption of this panacea. Indeed, most of the articles dealt with a virile defense of Catholicism, not distributism. *Blackfriars* strongly supported the papal condemnation of communism. Rather, it put before its readers a balanced viewpoint—indeed, a decidedly vigorous Catholic viewpoint of the questions of the day. The issue for June 1931, for example, featured an article by Alexander Parker on the Spanish Republic, two notes on papal infallibility, and an article by Thomas Gilby, "The Obsolescent Parrot," on catechetical instruction. In March 1934, at the Great Depression's height, the contents included McNabb with a report on sterilization, H. Somerville on Karl Marx and capitalism, and Hilary Pepler on "Church, Stage and Soviet," among other features. All through the 1930s *Blackfriars* published articles on the ethics of war under modern conditions, the Catholic viewpoint on international relations, and the utility of modern peace policies. During World War II the editors believed that a periodical more explicitly devoted to things spiritual, without the admixture of worldly concerns, should be started, and began the *Life of the Spirit*. It was at first published as a supplement to *Blackfriars* from February 1944 through June 1946, at which time it became a separate publication. Less concerned with worldly matters, it featured, for example, articles on the reconversion of Scotland (Peter Anson), a sermon for Corpus Christi (St. Thomas Aquinas), the beautiful names of God (E. E. Evans-Pritchard), and the spiritual traditions of East and West (Bernard Kelly). As always, the Dominicans held out "the pursuit of truth with the tradition and present authority of the Catholic Church as norm and guide" (6, no. 58:9).

In October 1964, after some twenty years of independent existence, the *Life of the Spirit* was amalgamated with the *New Blackfriars*. The *Life* was concerned with prayer and contemplation, and after Vatican II it was thought best that spiritual insights with theological application should be presented side by side with the practical examination of the moral and material dilemmas of the world and the involvement of the Church. Since that day, the *New Blackfriars* has continued on its serene, vigorous, and highbrow way. Edited from Oxford, *New Blackfriars* concerns itself still with ecumenical thought as well as other diverse issues—the celibacy of the clergy, the poetry and life of Sylvia Plath, apartheid in South Africa—all from the viewpoint of the Christian Catholic theologian.

Notes

1. Kenneth Wykham-George and Gervase Mathew, *Bede Jarrett of the Order of Preachers* (Westminster, Md., 1952), p. 144.

2. Hilaire Belloc, *Hilaire Belloc's Prefaces Written for Fellow Authors*, ed. G. A. De Chantigny (Chicago, 1971), pp. 319–20. See also Robert Spaight, *The Life of Hilaire Belloc* (New York, 1957).

3. *New York Times*, 18 June 1943, p. 21.

Information Sources

BIBLIOGRAPHY

Barker, Dudley. *G. K. Chesterton: A Biography*. New York, 1973.

Belloc, Hilaire. *Hilaire Belloc's Prefaces Written for Fellow Authors*. Edited by G. A. De Chantigny. Chicago, 1971.

McCarthy, John P. *Hilaire Belloc: Edwardian Radical*. Indianapolis, 1978.

Spaight, Robert. *The Life of Hilaire Belloc*. New York, 1957.

Valentine, Ferdinand. *Father Vincent McNabb, O.P.: The Portrait of a Great Dominican*. Westminster, Md., 1955.

Ward, Maisie. *Gilbert Keith Chesterton*. New York, 1943.

Wykham-George, Kenneth, and Gervase Mathew. *Bede Jarrett of the Order of Preachers*. Westminster, Md., 1952.

INDEXES

Each volume indexed. *Catholic Periodicals Index*.

REPRINT EDITIONS

Microform: UMI (*New Blackfriars* only).

LOCATION SOURCES

American

Widely available.

British

Widely available.

Publication History

MAGAZINE TITLE AND TITLE CHANGES

Blackfriars: A Monthly Review, April 1920–1950. *Blackfriars: A Monthly Review Edited by the English Dominicans*, 1951–1964. *New Blackfriars (Incorporating Blackfriars and The Life of the Spirit)*, new series, October 1964–.

VOLUME AND ISSUE DATA

Blackfriars: volumes 1–45, numbers 1–531, April 1920–September 1964. [*Life of the Spirit*: volumes 1–3, numbers 1–28, February 1944–June 1946. *Life of the Spirit: A Blackfriars Review*, volumes 1–19, numbers 1–215, July 1946–August/September 1964.] *New Blackfriars*, volume 1, number 1, October 1964–.

FREQUENCY OF PUBLICATION

Monthly.

PUBLISHERS

April 1920–June 1934: Basil Blackwell, 49 Broad Street, Oxford. July 1934–December 1938: The Rolls House Publication Company Ltd., 2 Breams Buildings, London. January 1939–December 1950(?): Basil Blackwell, 49 Broad Street, Oxford. January 1951–1952: Blackfriars, St. Giles, Oxford. 1953–1970: Blackfriars Publications, London. 1971: Blackfriars, St. Giles, Oxford.

EDITORS

Blackfriars: Bernard Delany, 1920–1924. Edwyn Essex, 1924–1925. Bernard Delany, 1925–1932. Bede Jarrett, 1932–1934. Hilary Carpenter, 1934–1940. Conrad Pepler, 1940–1950. Illtud Evans, 1950–1958. Ronald Torbet, 1958–1959. Illtud Evans, 1959–1964.

Life of the Spirit: Conrad Pepler, 1946–1955. Henry St. John, 1955–1958. Edmund

Hill, 1958–1960. Lawrence Bright, 1960–1964.
New Blackfriars: Illtud Evans, 1964–1966. Herbert McCabe, 1966–1967. Pascal
(now Marcus) Lefébvre, 1967–1970. Herbert McCabe, 1970–1979. Alban Weston, 1979–1982. Fergus Kerr, 1982–1983. John Orme Mills, 1984–.

William Clarkin

BLACKWOOD'S EDINBURGH MAGAZINE

Blackwood's ceased publication in 1980, putting an end to a venerable Scottish
institution. Founded in 1817 as a leaner and tougher Tory review than the
*Quarterly Review** (see *RA, MA*) had proven to be, it made literary history in
its early years, and it continued to exert some force throughout the nineteenth
century, attracting some of Britain's best writers to its pages. At the turn of the
century, for example, it was serializing Joseph Conrad's *Lord Jim*. But from
1914 on *Blackwood's* was a far less vital force, and one reads through its run
in our century with the sense that the once fiery "Maga" had simply grown old
and tired and had placed itself *hors de combat*. One finds here no engagement,
either progressive or reactionary, with any of the major literary issues and personalities of the twentieth century.

Maga enjoyed some continuity with the nineteenth-century tradition, in the
person of Charles Whibley, who wrote for nearly every issue from the 1890s to
his death in 1930. His column, "Musings without Method," ran at the end of
each issue, being in flavor, if not in actuality, a continuing editorial. He was
not in fact an editor; except for a short period toward the end, one of the
Blackwoods was always at the helm of the magazine. Whibley's column was
unsigned, though, and the anonymity and regularity together created the editorial
effect.

His columns were intentionally diffuse and rambling, liable to settle on any
topic at any time. They attack literary experimenters, like E.F.T. Marinetti and
the futurist group, and then, a paragraph or two later, praise the organic sentence
style of Henry James. During the war years, Whibley wrote patriotic attacks on
Germany and on pacifists, especially Bertrand Russell. He presented Charles
Péguy, soldier-poet, by contrast, as a sound example for moderns. Whibley's
subjects were more often political and social than literary: he decried the rise of
the Labour Party, trade unions, and psychoanalysis; in the phenomenon of the
suffragettes he saw a symptom of a decadent society.

While this summary may suggest that Whibley (and with him *Blackwood's*)
stood squarely against every important movement of our time, one must qualify
that somewhat by noting that T. S. Eliot—virtually a symbol and rallying point
in the 1920s for literary progressivism—admired Whibley greatly and eulogized
him in essays, seeing him as the last great man of letters. And indeed, while
today one sees much in Whibley that is simply obstinate and overconservative,

the "Musings" nevertheless often reveal a forceful and fascinating mind—not greatly unlike what one feels in reading *The Sacred Wood*.

Apart from Whibley, and certainly after him, the magazine had no single distinctive intellectual character, but turned to promoting a species of refined amateurism in its fiction, essays, and poetry. The closest to a major author or title published in the twentieth-century *Blackwood's* is a serialization of John Buchan's *The Thirty-nine Steps*, later adapted into the Hitchcock film. *Blackwood's* fiction otherwise has very often an imperialist air. It is usually set in an outpost of the empire—most often India and Burma—and balances a thin line between fiction and memoir concerning the military or administrative life. One seems always to be hearing Rudyard Kipling just in the background—and, in fact, many of these amateur tales are quite as readable and entertaining as Kipling's, which is no doubt a tribute to the magazine's editors. The authors write under names like "Zeres," "Odysseus," "A Royal Field Leech," "Officier de Liaison," or "Ironside"; when a real name is used, it is most often prefaced by a "Major" or "Colonel."

Some fictional items deserve a closer look—for example, a serialized science fiction novel by Hamish Blair, printed in 1930 and titled *1957*, set in a future strife-torn British India. In the 1950s and 1960s, the subject matter of the fiction becomes somewhat less military, but still emphasizes the personal narrative with an exotic setting. Frequent contributors in the latter decades were Leslie Gardiner, Lawrence G. Green, and J. K. Stanford.

Blackwood's printed little poetry, averaging perhaps two poems or so per year, more in the 1960s and 1970s. Moira O'Neill, Neil Munro, and Alfred Noyes contributed poems, some of them in semi-dialect. There is little discussion of poetry or poetic principles aside from the "Musings" of Whibley.

Most issues published nonfiction in addition to memoirs, usually of a light historical character. There is an article on Sir Walter Scott's service as a quartermaster on the home front in the 1790s and a number of articles on eighteenth-century figures, such as Dr. Johnson and Thomas Gray. The discovery of the Boswell papers at Auchinleck led to several articles on Boswell.

Compton Mackenzie, writing in the 150th anniversary issue for April 1967, praised the House of Blackwood as a great bulwark of conservatism, saying that "what has enabled 'Maga' to live for a hundred and fifty years are the countless articles by writing amateurs . . . bringing to life in its pages the far-off unfamiliar corners of this green world of ours. Those amateurs who write every month . . . are an antidote to the Cockney School of Criticism bleating in unison like sheep, as destructive as goats and almost as lecherous" (301:294). Mackenzie's praise amounts to a eulogy, however, for the publishing world and the reading public were ceasing to have much room for the amateurs anymore; and the green corners of the world were delivered more vividly on television.

In 1976 there was an attempt to halt the erosion of the magazine's public. An article called "Two Hundred Years On" (319:449–52) is a mine of information about editorial changes and issues over the preceding couple of decades, and it announces David Fletcher's appointment as editor—the first non-Blackwood to take the helm. The article promises that the magazine will not change just for the sake of change, but Fletcher did indeed make a real effort to attract well-known contributors, abandoning the amateurs-only policy. Lawrence Durrell published a short story in 1978, and A. L. Rowse contributed a host of articles on topics ranging from Hilaire Belloc to John Betjeman. An editorial column began each issue, taking stands on topics from defense spending to slang words.

Fletcher was replaced in 1980 by Michael Blackwood, who inaugurated a new format; the magazine looked slicker and more modern, and Blackwood openly announced that he did not want the magazine to stagnate and die like many other venerable old titles had—the *Cornhill Magazine** (see *VEA, MA*), the *Strand Magazine** (see *VEA*), and *Chambers's Journal** (see *RA*). But in October, he announced that the magazine had only two choices: to die out altogether, or to go to a biannual. He made a plea for subscriptions to float the biannual; 3,000 would be needed in advance. In November he wrote to reassure the readers that "the material [planned for the new biannual] will be of a kind which has been well received by the majority of *Blackwood's* readers over many years. I can categorically state that we will not venture into controversial and educative areas. Our intention is to provide a collection of entertaining and gently informative articles and short stories" (327:323).

In December only 200 subscriptions had come in for the biannual, and Blackwood wrote that Maga "has provided a medium through which the ordinary person with a story to tell, an experience to relate, or an opinion to air, has been given a hearing. That this opportunity will no longer be is the greatest shame" (327). He went on to speculate that the world has changed into a place without time for leisurely reading or writing. That diagnosis is surely not all wrong. But had the modern Maga been allowed to have some of the bite of its nineteenth-century ancestor, it might have survived. [See also the article on *Blackwood's Edinburgh Magazine* in *RA*.]

Information Sources

INDEXES
> Each volume indexed.

REPRINT EDITIONS
> Microform: UMI.

LOCATION SOURCES
> *American*
>> Widely available.
> *British*
>> Widely available.

Publication History

MAGAZINE TITLE AND TITLE CHANGES
> *Blackwood's Edinburgh Magazine.*

VOLUME AND ISSUE DATA
1817–1913: See entry in *RA*. Volumes 195–328, issues 1179–1982, January 1914–December 1980.

FREQUENCY OF PUBLICATION
Quarterly.

PUBLISHER
William Blackwood and Sons, 32 Thistle Street, Edinburgh EH2 1HA.

EDITORS
1817–1911: See entry in *RA*. George William Blackwood, 1912–1942. James H. Blackwood, 1942–1948. George Douglas Blackwood, 1948–1976. David Fletcher, 1976–1979. Michael Blackwood, 1980.

Raymond N. MacKenzie

BLAST

Blast: The Review of the Great English Vortex sprang upon London in the summer of 1914 with the five letters of its title flung in huge black letters across an outsize, blazing-pink cover. Inside, the reader found over 150 pages of daringly modern art, prose, and poetry, of manifestoes and challenges, in typography as dramatic as the content. The magazine announced itself as a quarterly, but it is doubtful that under the best of circumstances the energy and quality, or even the quantity, of that first issue could have been sustained. With World War I breaking out only a few weeks after publication, the magazine was doomed. The second issue, a year later, was still exciting—it contains the first English publication of T. S. Eliot's poetry—but it was the last. *Blast*, however, has an importance out of all proportion to its short life. It captures the energy and daring of an exciting group of young artists out to revolutionize the world of English art, and marks the point of greatest confidence and optimism of its two major creators, Wyndham Lewis and Ezra Pound.

Of the two, Lewis is by far the most important in *Blast*'s history. He not only began the magazine and borrowed the money for it, but found the contributors, designed its dramatic layout, and wrote most of its manifestoes and its most daring fiction. For a few months in 1913 and 1914, Lewis was the dynamic center of a circle of young artists determined to lead the London art world, and *Blast* was to be the organ of their movement.

Percy Wyndham Lewis began his art study at the Slade in London, but spent seven years in France, and came back to England in December of 1908 as fully aware of the challenges posed by postimpressionism and cubism as anyone in England. He exhibited with forward-looking art groups, the Camden Town Group and the Allied Artists Association, and finally, in 1913, joined the Omega Workshop of the champion of postimpressionism, Roger Fry. After only a few weeks, Lewis and three fellow artists left the Omega: the immediate cause was an argument over a commission, but the deeper cause was division over artistic aims. In an angry letter sent to the press, Lewis grumbled that the aim of the Omega was "Prettiness, . . . its skin is 'greenery-yallery', despite the Post-What-Not fashionableness of its draperies."[1] With financial backing from fellow artist Kate Lechmere, Lewis founded the rival Rebel Art Centre in Great Ormond Street, promising an ambitious program of lectures, lessons, musical perform-ances, exhibitions, and a magazine. A prospectus was printed, the rooms were decorated, and a few programs were held, but Lewis showed no evidence of the mundane talents that would keep a fragile artistic venture financially sound. The centre lasted only until Lechmere withdrew her subsidy in June 1914.

But if Lewis had no talent for running a formal organization, he had at this period a talent for finding and bringing together daring young artists. Like the centre, *Blast* was a cheerfully communal affair. The three artists who had joined Lewis in leaving Omega and signing the round robin letter—Frederick Etchells, Cuthbert Hamilton, and Edward Wadsworth—contributed to the magazine. Wadsworth was especially helpful: he provided a place to meet, helped write a manifesto, helped to develop mailing lists, and arranged for pictures to be taken of the artwork. The name was contributed by C.R.W. (Christopher) Nevinson, Lewis's closest collaborator in the early stages. Kate Lechmere provided a 100 pound loan, after Lewis gave her some of his paintings as collateral; Lewis's mother also lent money. And on the literary side, Lewis had the enthusiastic participation of the American poet Ezra Pound.

It would seem that in late 1913 Pound could hardly have had the time or the need to contribute to another magazine. Since 1912 he had served as foreign editor of Harriet Monroe's Chicago-based *Poetry* and was sending a steady stream of poetry, criticism, and advice. At the request of Rebecca West, who, like Lewis and Pound, was a member of the circle around Ford Madox Hueffer, he had taken on the post of literary editor of a struggling magazine, the *New Freewoman*—renamed in January 1914 the *Egoist*.* In addition, he was con-tributing poems, reviews, or articles to A. R. Orage's *New Age*,* to *Smart Set, Poetry and Drama* (earlier the *Chapbook** [see *VEA*]), the *Quarterly Review*,* the *Fortnightly Review** (for both, see *VEA, MA*), the *Modern Review* of Calcutta, and *T. P.'s Weekly* (formerly *To-Day** [see *VEA*]). In 1912 he had founded a new movement in modern poetry, imagism, and made certain it would catch on by providing it with publicity, a body of principles, and an anthology (*Des Imagistes*, published as an issue of still another magazine, the *Glebe*, in February 1914). But by the end of 1913, Pound was dissatisfied with the limitations of his own movement, developing a concept both wider and more dynamic, which he named vorticism. He was also impatient with his editors, especially with the too-eclectic policies of Harriet Monroe. He was enthusiastically working with the Chinese materials of Ernest Fenollosa, and was more and more interested in painting and sculpture. At an art exhibit he met Henri Gaudier-Brzeska, a young French sculptor newly arrived in London, and immediately took to him. He wrote to his college friend William Carlos Williams about Gaudier-Brzeska and another new friend, John Cournos, "We are getting our little gang after five years of waiting.''[2] At this period of rapid change, Pound was ready for a new magazine with artistic aims purer and more daring than those of any existing magazine. He had known Lewis since 1908 and had lectured at the Rebel Art Centre; when *Blast* was planned he was ready to help with publicity and with searching out material. In April he wrote to James Joyce suggesting he submit something to Lewis's "Futurist, Cubist, Imagiste Quarterly."[3]

The "Futurist, Cubist, Imagiste Quarterly" did not become the "Review of the Great English Vortex" until very shortly before it was published, even though Pound had spoken on vorticism in February at the Rebel Art Centre. Originally, Lewis was not deeply concerned with labels. But suddenly, in June, he found it necessary to keep his own little gang distinct from the Italian import, futurism. Futurism had been well known in England since the first visit of its leader, E.F.T. Marinetti, in 1909; the man in the street tended to call all semi-abstract or modern-looking art "futurist." The movement had much in common with Lewis and the artists around him—a willingness to not only reject but insult the nineteenth-century tradition, a fascination with the modern world's violence and speed, a pull toward abstraction, and an honest appreciation of the necessity of publicity. But similarity is not identity, and the arch-publicist Marinetti and his English supporter Nevinson went too far when they signed the names of the Rebel Art Centre group to one of their own manifestoes, without permission. Lewis took action. In fact, he first took physical action, as he describes with relish in his autobiography, *Blasting and Bombardiering*, bringing together a group of "anti-Futurists" including Wadsworth, Gaudier-Brzeska, T. E. Hulme, and Jacob Epstein to break up a Marinetti lecture with catcalls and heckling.[4] On 14 June he published his own antifuturist manifesto in the *Observer*, signed by himself, six other artists Marinetti had claimed and, for good measure, Gaudier-Brzeska, Pound, and Richard Aldington.[5] When *Blast* appeared two weeks later, it was complete with vorticist manifestoes and symbols, and attacks on futurism.

Vorticism was too short-lived and the vorticists were too individualistic for the movement to develop its own firm definition. Historians and critics have not agreed on whether it should be restricted to the *Blast* group or expanded to like-minded artists, whether it is exemplified in many works or in just a few, whether it is to be seen as a technique or a spirit of the age. Lewis himself thought (at one point, at least) that the term could only be usefully applied to the visual arts, while Pound saw it as cutting across all the arts. A few elements, even in the confusion, are central, however. First, vorticism was English: though its participants could be French or American, it was a movement tied to England, not an island version of something from Europe, and of course specifically not futurism. Second, it was new; without rejecting all of the past in a Marinetti way, it still was breaking new ground, especially by turning to pure abstraction. Futurism was still tied to natural forms: "Futurism, as preached by Marinetti, is largely Impressionism up-to-date. To this is added his Automobilism and Nietzsche stunt" (no. 1:143). Third, and most important, the symbol of the vortex held in tension the ideas of energy and stillness, of the still point in the midst of surging force.

Blast was originally announced for April, but publication was delayed even past the cover date of 20 June.[6] It was already printed when its publisher, John Lane, found three lines of Pound's poem "Fratres Minores" offensive; distribution was delayed while young ladies blacked out "With minds still hovering above their testicles" and "That the twitching of three abdominal nerves / Is incapable of producing a lasting Nirvana."[7]

Even without Pound's lines, the reader of 1914 found *Blast* the most daring, the most arrogant of any of the English or American little magazines, and it has brought to generations of readers since the same delighted shock. First, it is simply big—157 pages, 12 1/2 by 9 1/2 inches, printed on coarse, thick paper. Second, the cover shouts for attention, with its three-inch letters in darkest black against a color somewhere between pink and purple that Lewis called puce (Lewis called the magazine "the puce monster," but it is probably best described in Pound's phrase, "steam-calliope pink").[8] Within, the pages of manifestoes are laid out in lines and blocks of print ranging from large to very large, with generous use of boxes and rules, exclamation points, capital letters, and underlining. Almost every sentence in these pages is its own paragraph, surrounded with white space. This kind of typography, echoing posters and tabloids, had been used in futurist publications, but no futurist publication and certainly no previous English publication had used it in such variety and abundance.

This dramatic typography is not decorative; as in concrete poetry, the written word and the physical form interact to form a work different from both. The statements are not arranged to make connected argument: they explode out of the white space like firecrackers. The words are not simply read, they are heard. "Long live the great art vortex sprung up in the centre of this town!" shouts Lewis in the first two pages.

> We believe in no perfectibility except our own. Intrinsic beauty is in the Interpreter and Seer, not in the object or content. . . . Blast sets out to be an avenue for all those vivid and violent ideas that could reach the public in no other way. . . . We will convert the king if possible.
> "A VORTICIST KING! WHY NOT!
> "DO YOU THINK LLOYD GEORGE HAS THE VORTEX IN HIM?"
> [No. 1:7–8]

This "Great Preliminary Vortex" is followed by what have become the most famous pages of the magazine, the eighteen pages of "blasts" and "blesses." Although cooperatively compiled at a meeting at Lewis's studio, credit for their full effect goes mostly to their arranger and designer.[9] The lists themselves are partly attacks on the traditional and established, partly serious art criticism, partly a chance to pay off personal scores, and partly pure high spirits. "BLAST First (for politeness) ENGLAND" (no. 1:11), especially her weather and her newly

appointed poet laureate: "CURSE *the flabby sky that can manufacture no snow,* but can only drop the sea on us in a drizzle like a poem by Mr. Robert Bridges" (no. 1:12). Blast France for, among many other things, "Bad change" and "Imperturbable, endless prettiness" (no. 1:13). "CURSE . . . THE BRITANNIC AESTHETE . . . SNEAK AND SWOT OF THE SCHOOLROOM" (no. 1:15) and "BLAST years 1837 to 1900" (no. 1:18). Page 21 explodes with a solid mass of fifty-two items to be blasted, including whole groups, such as "Bishop of London and all his posterity" and "Beecham (Pills, Opera, Thomas)."

Immediately the magazine turns about just as confidently to "BLESS ENG-LAND!" (no. 1:22), especially her ships and her ports, and to

> BLESS   cold
> magnanimous
> delicate
> gauche
> fanciful
> stupid
> ENGLISHMAN.   [No. 1:24]

Hairdressers are blessed, English humor (blasted a few pages before) is blessed, and so is France. The page of seventy-six people and things to be blessed that ends the section includes Kate Lechmere, Charlotte Corday, and Castor Oil (no. 1:28).

The manifesto continues for ten more pages, each page holding only a few boldly numbered sentences. "We are Primitive Mercenaries in the Modern World" (no. 1:30), it states. A new independent art will rise in the north, in England, not only in spite of but because of her lack of any artistic history: "but with this LIFE-EFFORT, she has been the last to become conscious of the Art that is an organism of this new Order and Will of Man." The manifesto was signed by eleven poets and artists: Richard Aldington, Malcolm Arbuthnot, Lawrence Atkinson, Henri Gaudier-Brzeska, Jessica Dismorr, Cuthbert Hamilton, Ezra Pound, William Roberts, Helen Saunders (misspelled Sanders), Edward Wadsworth, and Wyndham Lewis. Within this group there were widely differing degrees of interest and involvement in vorticism and in *Blast*.[10] Pound, who considered himself the founder of vorticism, and Gaudier-Brzeska contributed "Vortices" that appeared with "Vortex and Notes" by Lewis at the back of the book, boldly presented but without the typographical pyrotechnics of the opening pages.

The daring of the manifestoes was well supported by the reproductions of paintings and sculpture, and by the photograph of Gaudier-Brzeska's sculpture "Stags." Never before had so much radical and abstract English art been presented in one magazine. The literary material, however, was far less consistent in its style. The longest, and finest, literary work in the magazine was a section of Ford Madox Ford's novel *The Good Soldier*, titled in *Blast* "The Saddest

Story." While its dissection of the sham and suffering within polite English society was damning, its success comes from effects as subtle as *Blast* is strident. Rebecca West's short story, "Indissoluble Matrimony," was daring enough to be rejected by the *English Review** (see *VEA*), but the daring is in its feminist theme more than in its style. A man attempts to murder his wife because she is, simply, too much woman for him. Although a vortex appears in the story, the mocking, grim, understated style has no connection with the new movement.

And although Ezra Pound created the movement, his poetry in this first *Blast* does not provide convincing examples. In his "Vortex" statement he provides distinctions between vorticism and imagism—"The vortex is the point of maximum energy," it is "man DIRECTING . . . CONCEIVING instead of merely observing and reflecting" (no. 1:153), but the example he presents, H.D.'s "Oread" ("Whirl up, sea / whirl your pointed pines"), was one of the poems he had presented to *Poetry* as the first examples of imagism two years before. His twelve poems in *Blast* do not provide any indications of new ground. He begins with a series of polemics against those "who objected to newness"; the invective is distinctive only for its brutality: "You slut-bellied obstructionist . . . You fungus, you continuous gangrene . . . Here is the taste of my Boot, / Caress it, lick off the Blacking" (no. 1:45). The other poems are slight, although interesting in terms of his development: all are in the stripped language, free of poeticisms, that he had been developing since 1912, and two show the influence of the Chinese material of Ernest Fenollosa that was affecting not only his practice but his theory of poetry.

It is not Pound, however, but Lewis who creates a radically new language. The events of "Enemy of the Stars," a play "VERY WELL ACTED BY YOU AND ME," have the simplicity of a fable: Arghol, the "enemy of the stars," rejects his companion Hanp; Hanp kills Arghol and then commits suicide. Arghol is the artist-hero, regularly beaten by a "boot, and heavy shadow above it" (no. 1:63), who rejects Hanp because "I wanted to make a naif yapping Poodle-parasite of you. . . . You are the world, brother, with its family objections to me" (no. 1:73). The world fears the artist most when the artist has become free and individual, so the cowardly Hanp waits for Arghol to sleep, and slits his throat: "There was only flesh there, and all our flesh is the same. Something distant, terrible and eccentric, bathing in that milky snore, had been struck and banished from matter" (no. 1:84). The events take place in a half-lit urban wasteland, contrasted with the violent energy of the stars. The prose is fragmented, jagged as bolts of lightning. Violent images, red and black, are juxtaposed without connections or explanations. He is pushing his prose almost as far as it can go toward the energy-filled abstract patterns of his art of this period.[11]

When *Blast* was finally published, it created enough sensation to satisfy even Wyndham Lewis, and he became a lion on the social circuits of Mayfair. For a few months in "the snobbish social sunset of 1914" everyone "wanted to look at this new oddity, thrown up by that amusing spook, the Zeitgeist."[12] But this social popularity was not accompanied by much serious interest in the art, graphic

and literary, of *Blast*. Lewis was invited to dinner, but the inviters were not interested in buying his pictures. The magazine was widely reviewed, but except in places like the *Egoist*, not with sympathy. At least one editor was actively hostile. G. W. Prothero of the *Quarterly Review* closed the magazine to Pound (and thus cut him off from an important part of his small income) because of his association with *Blast*. Most editors and reviewers, however, were not so much hostile as sarcastic or condescending. They were not interested in vorticism as a movement, and its daring was simply put down to the influence of Marinetti. "The Press simply treated it as the latest in a long series of cranky Bohemian publicity stunts."[13] As for the public at large, or as much of it as was aware of *Blast*, the general reaction was a kind of delighted shock. Lewis wrote years later: " 'Kill John Bull with Art!' I shouted. And John and Mrs. Bull leapt for joy, in a cynical convulsion. For they felt safe as houses. So did I."[14]

Given time, the vorticists might have capitalized on the sensation they had caused to educate the public and convince the critics, and to further develop their own movement. That they would be denied that chance by World War I was not clear in the first months after the August outbreak. The second issue of *Blast* was considerably delayed—*Blast* had announced itself as a quarterly, but the second issue came out a year after the first—but the delay was not entirely caused by the war. Lewis, under the best of circumstances not an ideally efficient editor, was busy with other projects and ill for most of the year.[15] There were money problems; the first issue did not make a profit or even pay for itself.

The second *Blast* appeared in July 1915. Although smaller than the first it was still over 100 pages. A much larger portion of it was written by Lewis himself, but the contents still provide impressive variety and feature new contributors—Helen Saunders, Jessie Dismorr, Jacob Kramer, Pound's wife Dorothy Shakespear, and a young poet whom Pound was pushing, T. S. Eliot. "The Saddest Story" was not available because the novel had been published, but Ford contributed a poem. Pound provided one of his most experimental and vorticist poems, "Dogmatic Statement on the Game and Play of Chess" ("Whirl, centripetal, mate, King down in the vortex: / Clash, leaping of bands, straight strips of hard colour" [no. 2:19]), as well as one of his most successful parodies, "Ancient Music" ("Winter is icumen in, / Lhude sing 'Goddamm' " [no. 2:20]). *Blast* 2 confidently looks to the future ("The Review of the London Vortex may not always appear to date, but two further numbers will probably come out before next January") and starts off with the same confident tone: "We have subscribers in the Khyber Pass, and subscribers in Sante Fe. The first stone in the structure of the world-wide reformation of taste has been securely laid" (no. 2:7).

But at other points in the magazine the confidence rings hollow. Gaudier-Brzeska, who had volunteered almost as soon as the war began, sent a "Vortex (written from the trenches)." It describes how he studied the shape of a Mauser rifle butt taken from a German soldier, until "I broke the butt off and with my knife I carved into it a design, through which I tried to express a gentler order of feeling, which I preferred" (no. 2:34). But this assertion of art over brutality is immediately followed by the black-bordered announcement of Gaudier-Brzes-ka's death in battle. Pound contributed a poem mocking a well-known young poet who, after an amorous interlude with a Tahitian maiden, came home and wrote a hundred Petrarchan sonnets. Between the time the poem was written and the time it was published, the poet, Rupert Brooke, had died on the way to Gallipoli, turning the joke nasty.

Most of the contents reflect the new and grimmer world. Half of the prints and the cover print (Lewis's *Before Antwerp*) have the war as subject. Lewis's fiction in this issue is "The Crown Master," a vivid description, in perfectly conventional style, of the English crowd reacting to the opening of the war.

The poems by T. S. Eliot fit this soberer mood. He had first offered Lewis two poems titled "Bullshit" and "The Ballad for Big Louise"; Lewis wrote to Pound, "I am trying to print them in *Blast*, but stick to my naif determination to have no "words ending in -Uck, -Unt, and -Ugger."[16] The poems finally accepted, four "Preludes" and "Rhapsody on a Windy Night," are more typically the Eliot of "The Love Song of J. Alfred Prufrock" (published the month before in *Poetry*) and *The Waste Land*.

Even though this issue contained more quality material than the reader would find in any other single magazine of the period, number 2 was the last issue. Its editor did not expect it to end so quickly. As late as 1919 he was planning *Blast* 3, as he described in a letter to John Quinn: "one half, the matter of my pamphlet: these theories illustrated by fifteen or twenty designs by Roberts, Etchells, Wads-worth, Turnbull, Dismorr and myself; the other half consisting of less specific matter: a story by myself, a long, new poem by Eliot, and some other things."[17] But by then Pound was in France, the vorticists were dispersed, and Lewis himself was involved in many projects. Most important, the world, and with it the artistic world, had changed. The war had effectively sunk Lewis's "puce cockleshell."

However, in the decades since, one young artist after another has discovered the magazine with the same surprised delight. Derek Stanford writes of the 1940s, when he put in the slip for *Blast* at the Victoria and Albert Museum and was brought the magazine "of 'bright puce colour . . . a page area of 12 inches by 9 1/2 . . . in general appearance not unlike a telephone book' . . . its contents struck me like a torpedo. One talked much then about art and revolution and revolutionary art (not necessarily the same thing). *Blast* was certainly the second with a vengeance."[18] No magazine of that exciting period has kept its freshness and energy as well as Wyndham Lewis's *Blast*.

Notes

1. *The Letters of Wyndham Lewis*, ed. W. K. Rose (Norfolk, Conn., 1963), p. 49. He also called Omega "Mr. Fry's curtain and pincushion factory."

2. *The Letters of Ezra Pound, 1907–1942*, ed. D. D. Paige (New York, 1951), p. 27.

3. *Pound/Joyce: The Letters of Ezra Pound to James Joyce, with Pound's Essays on Joyce*, ed. Forrest Read (New York, 1967), p. 26.

4. Wyndham Lewis, *Blasting and Bombardiering* (London, 1967), p. 33.

5. Marinetti's manifesto specifically mentioned Lawrence Atkinson, David Bomberg, Jacob Epstein, Frederick Etchells, Cuthburt Hamilton, C.R.W. Nevinson, William Roberts, Edward Wadsworth, and Wyndham Lewis. The repudiation was signed by all except the turncoat Nevinson and the fiercely independent Epstein.

6. Lewis himself says that the magazines appeared 20 June (*Blasting and Bombardiering*, p. 46), but records of the John Lane's Bodley Head set the official publication date at 2 July (William C. Wees, *Vorticism and the English Avant-Garde* [Toronto, 1972], p. 242, n. 21.) Review copies were distributed before that date.

7. Not all copies were censored. See Omar S. Pound and Philip Grover, *Wyndham Lewis: A Descriptive Bibliography* (Hamden, Conn., 1978), p. 80. The Kraus reprint of *Blast* has only blank space where the lines were.

8. Walter Michel declares that the cover color is officially violet-red, as determined by the *Methuen Handbook of Colour. Wyndham Lewis:Paintings and Drawings* (Berkeley, Calif., 1971), p. 151, n. 62. Wees calls it "pinkish purple" but quotes sources who suggest "violent pink," "purple," "magenta," "bright cerise . . . that makes one feel as if the outer cuticle had been removed" (*Poetry*, 1914) and "the color of an acute sick-headache" (*The Little Review*, 1914). Wees, pp. 165, 242, n. 1. It has also been called "rosy," "pucey-pink," "shocking pink," "violet-red," and "raspberry."

9. Douglas Goldring, quoted in Wees, p. 160. Identification of most of the people and things blasted and blessed is in Wees, pp. 217–27. Like the typography, the "blasts and blesses" had futurist predecessors—a few months before, Guillaume Apollinaire had published two lists headed "rose a" and "merde a" in *Lacerba*.

10. Wadsworth, who had worked with Lewis on the first issue, reviewed Vasily Kandinsky's *On the Spiritual in Art* in *Blast* 1 and contributed art to both issues. Roberts, who said his name was signed without his permission, appears in both issues. Hamilton has art in the first issue only; Arbuthnot (better known as a photographer) and Saunders in the second issue only. Dismorr has art, poems, and a "vortex" in the second issue. Atkinson exhibited with the vorticists, but has no work in *Blast*. Richard Aldington, one of Pound's original imagists, was not interested in either the movement or in contributing to the magazine.

11. Lewis revised "Enemy of the Stars" for republication in 1932 into a much more conventional style. See Wendy Stallard Flory, "Enemy of the Stars," in *Wyndham Lewis: A Revaluation*, ed. Jeffrey Meyers (Montreal, 1980), pp. 92–106.

12. Lewis, *Blasting and Bombardiering*, pp. 46–47.

13. Richard Cork, *Vorticism and Abstract Art in the First Machine Age* (Berkeley, Calif., 1976), 1:264.

14. Lewis, *Blasting and Bombardiering*, p. 36. Lewis published an article with the title "Kill John Bull with Art" in the *Outlook* in July 1914.

15. Some examples of his lack of attention to detail: *Blast* 1 was filled with misprints and errors, and the only errata list he provided was corrections to his own "Enemy of the Stars"; the subscription price on the cover page is higher than four issues bought individually; soon after *Blast* 1 was published he lost part of the subscription list.

16. Lewis, *Letters*, pp. 66–67. The letter was probably written in January 1915; on 2 February Eliot writes to Pound, "I fear that King Bolo and his Big Black Kween will never burst into print" ("A Bundle of Letters," in *Ezra Pound: Perspectives*, ed. Noel Stock [Chicago, 1965], p. 111).

17. Lewis, *Letters*, p. 111.

18. Derek Stanford, *Inside the Forties: Literary Memoirs 1937–1957* (London, 1977), p. 21.

Information Sources

BIBLIOGRAPHY

Cork, Richard. *Vorticism and Abstract Art in the First Machine Age*. Volume 1: *Origins and Development*. Volume 2: *Synthesis and Decline*. Berkeley, Calif., 1976.

Kenner, Hugh, *The Pound Era*. Berkeley, Calif., 1971.

Lewis, Wyndham. *Blasting and Bombardiering*. London, 1967.

————. *The Letters of Wyndham Lewis*. Edited by W. K. Rose. Norfolk, Conn., 1963.

————. *Rude Assignment*. London, 1950.

Materer, Timothy. *Vortex: Pound, Eliot, and Lewis*. Ithaca, N.Y., 1979.

Meyers, Jeffrey. *The Enemy: A Biography of Wyndham Lewis*. London, 1980.

Meyers, Jeffrey, ed. *Wyndham Lewis: A Revaluation*. Montreal, 1980.

Michel, Walter. *Wyndham Lewis: Paintings and Drawings*. Berkeley, Calif., 1971.

Pound, Ezra. *Gaudier-Brzeska: A Memoir*. New York, 1970.

————. *The Letters of Ezra Pound, 1907–1942*. Edited by D. D. Paige. New York, 1951.

INDEXES

Comprehensive Index to English Language Little Magazines 1890–1970, ed. Marion Sader (Millwood, N. Y., 1976). List of contents in William C. Wees, *Vorticism and the English Avant-Garde* (Toronto, 1972), pp. 213–15.

REPRINT EDITIONS

Kraus Reprint, Millwood, N.Y.

Microform: Kraus Microform, Millwood, N.Y.

LOCATION SOURCES

American

Complete runs: Widely available.

Partial runs: Columbia University Library; Free Library of Salt Lake City; Louisiana State University Library; Oberlin College Library; Philadelphia Museum of Art; University of Minnesota Library.

British

Complete runs: Birmingham University Library; Bodleian Library; British Museum; Cambridge University Library; National Library of Scotland, Edinburgh; Victoria and Albert Museum Library.

Partial runs: Durham University Library; London University Library; Warburg Institute Library.

Publication History

MAGAZINE TITLE AND TITLE CHANGES

Blast: The Review of the Great English Vortex.

VOLUME AND ISSUE DATA

Two issues only, July 1914 (dated on cover page 20 June) and July 1915.

FREQUENCY OF PUBLICATION

Irregular.

PUBLISHER
    John Lane, The Bodley Head.
EDITOR
    Wyndham Lewis.

Susan J. Hanna

BOOKMAN, THE. See VEA

BRITISH MUSEUM QUARTERLY

Although many periodicals have had odd beginnings, none has been of more prosaic origin than *British Museum Quarterly*, which was the progeny of bureaucratic procedure. It was born in 1926 as an alternative to a long-standing requirement by the British government that the museum trustees render to the House of Commons an "account of Income and Expenditure of the British Museum for the year ending the 31st day of March." In addition to such tabulations, a statement of the progress made in the arrangement and description of the collections was submitted, together with remarks prepared by the various heads of the museum departments giving an account of the objects added to the collections during the year.

The museum's "Return" to Parliament, as the report was called, averaged between 160 and 240 pages prior to World War I, and although it contained a complete list of the museum's newest holdings and acquisitions, it was not expansive. The Return "did not err on the side of exuberance," according to Sir Frederick Kenyon, the director of the British Museum in 1926 and the founder of *British Museum Quarterly*. In fact, as Sir Francis comments in the foreword to the first number of *British Museum Quarterly*, "the official volume had all the austerity of an unillustrated Blue Book," and, he adds, "the Return was a valuable record, but it was not calculated to stir emotions" (1:4). While not exactly a journal created to stir emotions, the *Quarterly* was conceived with the idea of enhancing the information provided Parliament annually. Thus, a quarterly magazine was decided upon by the trustees of the museum as the means of letting the public as well as the politicians know what was being done by the nation's greatest museum. An inexpensive journal containing descriptions and illustrations of important additions to collections was issued in April 1926 with the accurate but unadorned title of *British Museum Quarterly*.

British Museum Quarterly was immediately welcomed by the public and professionals alike. Museum visitors could consult the *Quarterly* to gain insights into the objects they had seen, and those in remote parts who could not visit the displays were kept abreast of the museum's latest acquisitions. Since the magazine was a quarterly (each volume being issued in four parts), it was possible for readers to keep very current through *British Museum Quarterly*; each number dealt with the major acquisitions of the previous quarter. The descriptions of the additions were written by the staffs of the various departments, which included printed books and manuscripts, Greek and Roman antiquities, Egyptian and Assyrian antiquities, coins and medals, ethnography, and the library. The editorial and publication process naturally fell most heavily on the library department, and the head librarian in fact acted as editor, selecting and assigning the articles that would go into each number of the magazine.

The accounts of the objects obtained by the museum were, in matters of style and substance, something of a compromise, not too technical, and yet not without interest and use for the expert, who could keep abreast of the latest finds in archaeology or the most recent acquisition of manuscripts. Although the *Quarterly* was by no means purely concerned with literary matters, devoting most of its space for archaeological news, it was nevertheless a journal that those with a scholarly interest in literature would have found useful and interesting. Typical are two articles by T. C. Skeat in 1951. The first, pertaining to a series of letters between Charles and Mary Lamb to S. T. Coleridge, shows that the Lambs provided Coleridge an element of emotional stability before he passed into the hands of Doctor Gillman. Coleridge's need for assistance and assurance during the years 1811–1816 was acute. As a revealing remark in a letter to Charles (published in volume 26) indicates, his self-esteem was at its nadir; he writes, "My face is not a manly face . . . it is an exceedingly weak and strengthless face. My face was ever painful to me."

A more important manuscript concerning Coleridge is discussed in a second article, relating to the composition of "Kubla Khan." Acquired by the museum from the Marchioness of Crewe, this document is the only autograph copy of the poem known to exist. Its significance, as Skeat points out, is that it throws doubt on Coleridge's famous account of the composition of the poem that he printed in a preface in 1816. Here, for instance, there is no mention of the interruption by a businessman, no reference to a specific number of words composed automatically, as in the 1816 version; nor is there any allusion to purchase or the poet's ill-health. Most significantly, Coleridge admits to the exact dosage of opium he took on this occasion: two grains, a substantial amount of drugs for one ingestion, which explains the phantasmagoric quality of "Kubla Khan."

One could find numerous items of literary interest in any issue of *British Museum Quarterly*, but some of the accessions stand out over others. For example, in 1967 the British Museum acquired autograph drafts of Lytton Strachey's *Eminent Victorians* which reveal that his original intention was much larger in scope and that he aimed to include Charles Darwin, John Stuart Mill, and Benjamin Jowett among others in his book. Some of the portraits were to be favorable, but as the length of his biographical sketches of Florence Nightingale, Cardinal Manning, Dr. Thomas Arnold, and General "Chinese" Gordon increased he was forced to stop with these four, all of whom were treated negatively. Thus, Strachey acquired a reputation as an iconoclast, which it was not his intention to be.

In addition to fully developed articles that explained the significance of literary objects, there were also numerous shorter items in a typical issue of *British Museum Quarterly*. These notes of paragraph length called attention to the reception of such items as a draft of Jane Austen's *Persuasion*, a copy of Dryden's poem "Annus Mirabilis" with cancelled lines, first editions of works by Daniel Defoe, Jonathan Swift, the diaries of Lord Byron's friend John Cam Hobhouse, and Sir Walter Raleigh's commonplace book. The format for articles in *British Museum Quarterly*, signed only by the initials of the contributors until volume 6, was, with small variations, standardized. The item was identified and enough exposition given to explain the historical and cultural importance of the object, whether it be a coin, vase, sword, or manuscript; and donors were thanked for their gifts. In fact, an original function of *British Museum Quarterly* by which the trustees set considerable store was to provide a place for expressions of gratitude to benefactors of the museum, and thus "to let the public know the variety and generosity of those whose gifts have been received."[1]

Other functions of the *Quarterly* were to call attention to museum exhibitions, report the results of excavations, and announce additions to the publications list of the British Museum. In addition, the journal carried notices of staff appointments, promotions, retirements, and deaths.

The magazine's size remained constant from 1926 to 1973, averaging twenty-four pages per number, with usually at least eight to ten plates of color and black-and-white illustrations. In outward appearance *British Museum Quarterly* was austere, appearing in plain blue-gray covers. This style prevailed until 1953, when a cover design appeared on volume 18. The design was usually a woodcut of some important or interesting item in the British Museum, and the blue-gray covers gave way to soft yellow, pink, and cream tones. Overall, the *Quarterly* was a journal that reflected the substantial institution that published it. The paper was of sturdy stock, the illustrations were handsome, and there were no obtrusive advertisements other than those calling attention to British Museum publications.

Shortly after the advent of World War II, in 1940, publication was suspended with volume 14. After a hiatus of over a decade, the *Quarterly* was resumed in January 1951 with volume 16; no reference was made to the break in publication, nor was any reason given for the missing volume 15. It was as if there was nothing to be said about the war years, during which the museum had been closed, and the following five years, during which the *Quarterly* was defunct. Actually, the trustees were reserving the whole of the volume 15 for a special retrospective issue on the years from 1941 to 1950. This volume, dedicated to Sir John Forsdyke for his part in safeguarding the building and collections from German bombs during the war, makes interesting reading. Numerous photographs depict the ravages of modern war upon culture. The King's Library with its priceless manuscripts is shown in shambles, the great rotunda of the Reading Room punctured by bomb fragments. After these close calls, all the collections of art, manuscripts, and archaeology were moved underground, going into the deepest London subway tunnels and down mine shafts out in the Midlands. As well as giving the reader an understanding of how the museum survived the war, this special volume reflected on the ten years' total of additions to the museum collections.

Publication of the *Quarterly* was uninterrupted from 1951 to its demise in 1973. Like its inception, its end was due to bureaucratic policy within the museum, rather than public response or reader reaction to the magazine. In 1973 the Library Department of the British Museum became the Reference Division of the British Library, an internal restructuring that caused the trustees to reconsider the basis for *British Museum Quarterly*. The Library Department from the outset of the *Quarterly*'s life had contributed most extensively, and with the severance of this unit from the museum, it was evident that the magazine was also cut adrift.

In the forty-seven years of *British Museum Quarterly*'s existence, the original terms of reference were modified considerably. It went beyond the short notes on recent acquisitions that it was created to promulgate, and more and more featured longer, more substantial articles. Furthermore, the *Quarterly* evolved into a journal of a dual character, publishing articles by outside contributors as well as staff.[2] It was decided that *British Museum Quarterly* was due replacement. In 1976 a new magazine entitled *British Museum Yearbook* began publication as its successor. Though the two journals had a common parent, the *Yearbook* differed from the *Quarterly* in quite a few ways: the frequency of issue; longer essays that averaged thirty-forty pages; articles grounded not on single items in the museum, but on retrospective research on entire collections; and issues organized around a single theme. All four feature essays in volume 1 of *British Museum Yearbook* dealt with the "Classical Heritage," which was the subtitle of that volume. An article by Jessup Price shows how much ancient coins can tell us about the architecture of antiquity. Another essay by Ralph Pinder-Wilson discusses links between Islamic and Greek astronomy. Robert Carson contributed an article that reveals the decline of Roman administration through the discovery of hoards of coins and medals in Britain. And in a richly illustrated essay Andrew Wilton looks at William Blake's response to the art of the classical world. In only one respect was the *Yearbook* similar to the *Quarterly*; a series of notes or articles on major museum acquisitions were contributed by the keepers of the various departments, but these items were much reduced in number, each department only noting one item.

Subsequent volumes of *British Museum Yearbook* took themes that would appeal to laymen and scholars alike. In this respect, too, the new magazine was like its predecessor; it was scholarly but not pedantic and addressed the museum visitor rather than the specialist as its audience. In summing up the significance of the *British Museum Quarterly*, one can do no better than to apply Sir Frederic Kenyon's original estimation of the "Record" to the *Quarterly*: "It was a valuable record, but it was not calculated to stir emotions." However, *British*

Museum Quarterly lived up to the expectations of the trustees when the magazine was founded because, if nothing else, it met their modest hope that "over a term of years it would be a not unimportant addition to the library of art and architecture" (1:5).

Notes

1. Initially the museum's director, who was also head librarian, was primarily concerned with the editorship, until about 1950, when, under the directorship of Thomas Kendrick, the editing of the *Quarterly* tended to be placed in the hands of the assistant to the museum secretary. This arrangement lasted until 1961, when a full-time publications officer was appointed and took on the job of editing the *Quarterly*. In 1969 the trustees decided that as a result of other changes the museum secretary should take over the editorship of the *Quarterly*. This meant that he was responsible for the content of the *Quarterly*, including the assembling of material and editorial selection of contributions offered by the departments: the publications officer continued to be responsible for the form of the publication, including layout, typography, and the normal executive work of seeing it published. Letter (*Times Literary Supplement*) received from Ben Bayliss, librarian, secretariat, British Museum, 22 May 1984.
2. John Pope-Hennessy, "Foreword," *British Museum Yearbook* 1 (1976):3–4.

Information Sources

BIBLIOGRAPHY
Crook, Joseph M. *The British Museum*. London, 1972.
Miller, Edward. *That Noble Cabinet: A History of the British Museum*. Athens, Ohio, 1974.
INDEXES
Volumes 1–5 in volume 5, 6–10 in volume 10, 11–19 in volume 20, 21–30 in volumes 30–31.
REPRINT EDITIONS
Volumes 1–31, 1926–1971, Swets and Zeitlinger, Lisse, the Netherlands.
LOCATION SOURCES
American
Widely available.
British
Widely available.

Publication History

MAGAZINE TITLE AND TITLE CHANGES
British Museum Quarterly, 1926–1973. (Replaced by *British Museum Yearbook*, 1976–.)
VOLUME AND ISSUE DATA
Volumes 1–14, numbers 1–56, April 1926–December 1940. Volume 15, special issue for the years 1941–1950. Volumes 16–37, numbers 57–110, January 1951–1973.
FREQUENCY OF PUBLICATION
Quarterly.

PUBLISHER
British Museum Publication Ltd., Great Russell Street, London, 3C1B.
EDITORS
Sir Frederic Kenyon, 1926–1931. Dr. George F. Hill, 1931–1936. Edgar J. Fors-
dyke, 1936–1950. Thomas D. Kendrick, 1950–1959. Frank C. Francis, 1960–
1967. Sir John F. Wolfenden, 1968–1973.

Hallman Bell Bryant

BRITISH MUSEUM YEARBOOK. See BRITISH MUSEUM
QUARTERLY

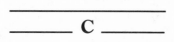

C

CALENDAR, THE. See CALENDAR OF MODERN LETTERS, THE

CALENDAR OF MODERN LETTERS, THE

In 1925 Edgell Rickword and Bertram Higgins came down from Oxford, Douglas Garman down from Cambridge to London to found a new monthly, the *Calendar of Modern Letters*.[1] In its two-year existence the *Calendar* succeeded in publishing a remarkable range of contemporary poetry, fiction, and essays, as well as a number of reviews of the literary productions of several nations. The memoirs of Fyodor Dostoevsky's wife, translated by S. S. Koteliansky, a play by Anton Chekhov, the meditations of Vasili Rosanov; and stories by Isaac Babel, Leonid Leonov, and Aleksey Remizov and Alexander Nievierov developed the English interest in contemporary Russian literature. Italy was represented by Luigi Pirandello, and Robert Nichols wrote from California on Petrarch and Gabriele D'Annunzio. From France came translations from Charles Baudelaire and sympathetic discussions by Samuel Hoare of Marcel Proust, Arthur Rimbaud, and Paul Valéry. Ireland was represented by Liam O'Flaherty, but unfortunately not by James Joyce, whose contribution ran afoul of the prudery of the printers.[2] The United States furnished poetry by Hart Crane, Robert Frost, John Crowe Ransom, and Allen Tate, criticism by Iris Barry, and an essay on Kenneth Burke by Gorham Munson.

At home, contributors of poetry included Edmund Blunden, Roy Campbell, Richard Church, Robert Graves, D. H. Lawrence, Laura Riding, Edwin Muir, Peter Quennell, and Siegfried Sassoon; of fiction, A. E. Coppard, William Gerhardi, D. H. Lawrence, Llewelyn Powys, William Plomer, and Edward Sackville-West; of critical prose, E. M. Forster, Robert Graves, H. C. Harwood,

J. F. Holms, L. P. Hartley, Aldous Huxley, D. H. Lawrence, Wyndham Lewis, Desmond MacCarthy, and Bertrand Russell.

The creative liveliness and catholicity of taste suggested by this list of contributions were reinforced by the development and quiet assertion of firm critical positions. Indeed, the critical attitudes are of more interest than the miscellaneous creative writings themselves, however representative these may be. The critical attitudes may be traced back to S. T. Coleridge with their insistence on the combination of emotion and intellect in literature. Though E. M. Forster writes of the mystery of literature (2:153), the general position of the *Calendar* critics is a much more clear-headed one, sympathetic toward the rational critical attempts of I. A. Richards (1:162).[3] In this post-Romantic phase of the late 1920s, special emphasis is placed on the objective and the intellectual component, including the satiric. For example, John Skelton, Alexander Pope, Jonathan Swift, and Charles Churchill are praised. However, the attempt to revive satire was less than successful, judging by the examples provided in the *Calendar* itself, from Wyndham Lewis downwards. The critics of the *Calendar* stressed the integration and integrity of the work of literature. At the same time that they placed some emphasis on the technique of poetry, this concern was not much evidenced in the practical criticism in the journal itself. More broadly, as H. C. Harwood argued, the critics felt the importance of their own function as mediating between the artist and the inchoate mass of the public of the day at a time of a "crisis of taste" (1:407).

For the *Calendar* critics, literature continues, in increasingly difficult circumstances, the heroic Arnoldian process of turning philistinism in the direction of civilization. Indeed, Douglas Garman put forward a bold case for going beyond Arnold. A "bloodless revolution" was offered by Arnold's Hellenism. But the audience was as important as the poet if "a regeneration of intelligent sensibility" were to come "after a devastating and bloody revolt against the sickly, bourgeois, animal consciousness of our age" (2:49). Edwin Muir is less revolutionary and more philosophical when he writes, also after Arnold: "We live in an interregnum. . . . if civilised societies change they also tend perpetually to integrate themselves; at its moment the stable order of life and thought, better or worse than its preceding type, returns" (2:329). The role of poetry is expressed most succinctly by "E.R.": it must "find its audience and assert true values" (1:483).

In concrete terms the valiant attempt of the *Calendar* failed. Faced with the growing economic and political crisis of the 1930s, its leading contributors, Rickword and Garman, turned leftward in a more politically active and popular direction.[4] Rickword went on to assist in the editorship of *Left Review** (1934– 1938) and to edit *Our Time** (1944–1947).[5]

The more covertly political and strictly literary-critical battle was taken up most successfully by F. R. Leavis, an admirer of the *Calendar*. He praised it as "uniquely intelligent . . . the critical consciousness of the younger adult generation."[6] Rickword published *Scrutinies*, based on the series of examinations in the *Calendar* of popular authors of the day—J. M. Barrie, Arnold Bennett,

Walter De la Mare, John Masefield, G. B. Shaw, H. G. Wells—in 1928 and 1933. Leavis published *Towards Standards of Criticism, A Selection from The Calendar*, in 1933. He intended this as a text exemplary of a healthy creative-critical response to contemporary social disintegration. He edited his own deeply influential *Scrutiny** from 1932 to 1953. However, what Leavis gained massively in influence, he lost in breadth and geniality of approach. These are the qualities for which in looking back one most admires the *Calendar of Modern Letters*.

Notes

1. Malcolm Bradbury, "A Review in Retrospect: *The Calendar of Modern Letters*" (New York, 1966). Reprinted from *London Magazine*, n.s. 1 (October 1961):xi.
2. James Joyce, *The Letters of James Joyce*, ed. Richard Ellmann (New York, 1966), 3:121–27.
3. Arnold Rattenbury, "Total Attainder and the Helots," in *The 1930s: A Challenge to Orthodoxy*, ed. James Lucas (Sussex, Eng., 1978).
4. Francis Mulhern, *The Moment of "Scrutiny"* (London, 1979).
5. Alan Young and Michael Schmidt, "A Conversation with Edgell Rickword," *Poetry Nation* no. 1 (1973):73–89.
6. F. R. Leavis, *New Bearings in English Poetry* (London, 1932), p. 1.

Information Sources

BIBLIOGRAPHY

Bradbury, Malcolm. "A Review in Retrospect." *The Calendar of Modern Letters*. Edited by Malcolm Bradbury. New York, 1966.
"A Conversation with Edgell Rickword." *Review*, no. 11/12 (1964):17–20.
Hayman, Ronald. "The Calendar of Modern Letters." *New Review* 1 (1975):14–19.
Leavis, F. R. "A Retrospect." *Scrutiny* 20 (1963).
Lucas, John. "An Interview with Edgell Rickword." In *The 1930s: A Challenge to Orthodoxy*. Edited by John Lucas. Sussex, Eng., 1978.
Mulhern, Francis. *The Moment of "Scrutiny."* London, 1979.
Pritchard, William H. *Seeing through Everything*. London, 1977.
Rattenbury, Arnold. "Total Attainder and the Helots." In *The 1930s: A Challenge to Orthodoxy*. Edited by John Lucas. Sussex, Eng., 1978.
Rickword, Edgell. *Essays and Opinions 1921–31*. Edited by Alan Young. Cheadle, Eng., 1974.
Towards Standards of Criticism: Selections from "The Calendar." Edited by F. R. Leavis. London, 1933.
Young, Alan, and Michael Schmidt. "A Conversation with Edgell Rickword." *Poetry Nation* 1 (1973):73–89.

INDEXES

Comprehensive Index to English Language Little Magazines 1890–1970, series 1, ed. Marion Sader (Millwood, N.Y., 1976).

REPRINT EDITIONS

Barnes and Noble, New York, 1966.

LOCATION SOURCES

American

Complete runs: Widely available.
Partial runs: New York Public Library; Rutgers University Library.

British
> Complete runs: Bodleian Library; British Museum; Cambridge University Library.
> Partial runs: Leeds Public Library; London University Library.

Publication History

MAGAZINE TITLE AND TITLE CHANGES
> *The Calendar of Modern Letters*, March 1925–March 1926. *The Calendar*, April
> 1926–July 1927.

VOLUME AND ISSUE DATA
> Volume 1, number 1–volume 4, number 2, March 1925–July 1927.

FREQUENCY OF PUBLICATION
> *The Calendar of Modern Letters*: monthly. *The Calendar*: quarterly.

PUBLISHER
> Wishart, London.

EDITORS
> Edgell Rickword, Douglas Garman, and Bertram Higgins. (These are the names
> given by Bradbury, p. xi, on the authority of Rickword.)

Peter Morgan

CAMBRIDGE JOURNAL, THE

From 1947 to 1954, the *Cambridge Journal*, mainly under the editorship of the conservative political philosopher Michael Oakeshott, served as a vehicle for learned articles on historical, political, philosophical, literary, and artistic topics, some of contemporary relevance, others of scholarly interest. The *Journal* aimed at being "culturally conservative" (7:707). It set itself up as an organ of culture, a voice for the permanent in an age given over to the transient and fragmentary, an agent for the promotion of civilized values and the advocacy of intellectual pursuits at a time when these were devalued, even ignored. It aimed at the disinterested study of "the best that is known and thought" in a style that had high seriousness, but not pedantry. The *Journal* was a general intellectual review, not a specialist organ. It shared, however, one important feature with the specialist reviews that sprang up on university campuses in the postwar years: it drew its contributors mainly from academia. The majority of *Cambridge Journal* contributors held university posts of one kind or another. While this may reflect broader changes in the world of "higher journalism," it is also a clue to the defining impulse of the *Journal*.

The *Cambridge Journal* originated as a response to postwar "anarchy." The editorial board shared with many other Britons a sense that theirs was an age of crisis. In the twentieth century, as the first general editor, T.F.D. Williams, observed, "the retreat from the optimism of the golden days of Victoria and Edward VII, has been obvious, and we have entered—as far as psychological analysis goes—an age of neuroses, crisis, and tension" (1:78). But the *Journal* was not given to crisis-talk; in fact, it was critical of the practice. Such talk was the jargon of the day, inappropriate for the complex problems facing modern, industrial societies. What the age needed was not unreflecting journalistic chatter, but a broader perspective based on the "higher interests of any civilized society" (7:707).

The problem was, who was to provide the civilizing commentary? One group who might be expected to take a part were university intellectuals, yet they— in particular, the conservatives—found themselves at the center of a controversy over the nature and goals of higher education and their place in the university. The higher education controversy—the "University Question"—arose out of increased public attention occasioned by the commitment of Clement Attlee's Labour government to invest large sums of money in university development and expansion, especially in science and technology. From a conservative point of view, the government's assistance was not entirely a blessing. In a *Cambridge Journal* editorial, Denis Brogan, an original member of the editorial board, expressed the conservative fears: "At first sight, the universities are in an especially favoured position. His Majesty's Government is pouring out money for higher academic purposes on an unprecedented scale . . . [but] the government is more and more the payer of the piper and will be tempted to call the tune" (1:143). In an era that saw Parliament enact a number of bills nationalizing health services and the electrical and gas industries as well as iron and steel, Brogan feared that the signs of the times pointed to a curtailment of what remained of university financial independence as well as to a decline in the status of the humanities, especially in the face of numerous government reports arguing for educational reform in the areas of science and technology.[1]

What the editors of the *Cambridge Journal* feared was the force behind the government reports: the urgent sense that British schools needed to produce more scientists and technicians to meet industrial and commercial demands for trained administrators, managers, engineers, physicians, nurses, teachers, and architects. Their aim was to promote the study of the pure and applied sciences as well as the social sciences in universities. As such, they posed a threat to the humanistic traditions of the universities. Humanities and sciences competed for the same government pound, and the reports backed the sciences. Nor could the humanities compete in public appeals: they could not point to modern gadgetry for improving the "quality" of life, as could the sciences. Finally, the basic tenets of a humanistic education were threatened by a view of education as job training.

For the *Cambridge Journal*, the universities were on the defensive. They faced a public that little understood, or cared for, the university's intellectual traditions and values—objectivity, leisure for study and thought, tolerance of intellectual eccentricity, even idleness and incompetency.[2] The real strengths of the university, argued T.F.D. Williams, lay in its being behind the times, in not being avant-garde, and in its being an institution independent of public whim and caprice. Instead of being given to faddish toing-and-froing in response to public demands, the university provided a center for perspective, a place removed from the jargon and crisis-talk of the daily newspapers, a place for the disinterested reflection upon modern problems and the best of culture's achievement. This last phrase might well describe the fare the *Cambridge Journal* editorial board intended to serve its readers.

In a series of editorials in the opening three numbers of the *Journal*, members of the editorial board addressed themselves to the issues raised by the expansion of university education, especially the place of science and technology in education. The question found its way into articles as well. In "Progress in the Twentieth Century" R.W.K. Hilton, a Fellow of Peterhouse College, Cambridge, divided modern attitudes toward progress along lines defined by the university debate. On the one side were the practical-minded, those who were in favor of science and technology. They formed the party of progress. On the other side were the intellectuals, the learned, the scholars, who made up the antiprogress party. R. F. Harrold's "What Is the Correct Number of Nurses?" is a pointed critique of the Minority Report of the Working Party on the Recruitment and Training of Nurses. He argued against the social engineering that lay behind the so-called scientific study aimed at determining the extent of reform in nursing education. A similar antitechnological bias is evident in an eccentric article, "An Apology for Scholarship," based on a sermon delivered by the Canon of Westminster, Charles Smyth. He defended scholarship as a means not simply to better one's life, personal fortune, or even mind, but as a means to glorify God and attain a heavenly reward.

It was Michael Oakeshott, however, who provided the most sustained and thoughtful reaction to the issues raised by the University Question. In a series of essays and reviews, beginning with the two-part "Rationalism in Politics" in the second and third numbers of the *Journal*, he dealt with the false philosophical foundations of the various reports.[3] His term for this type of thought is rationalism, that is, a way of thinking that recognizes only the authority of reason and is opposed to thinking based on tradition, custom, or habit. In politics, the rationalist wants to start fresh, discarding all that has gone before, and his aim is to produce perfection in detail and uniformity in state and society. In education, the rationalist aims at "training in technical knowledge" because the only proper knowledge is technical knowledge. He finds no use for or value in what Oakeshott sees as the aim of traditional humanistic education: "an initiation into the moral and intellectual habits and achievements of his society, an entry into the partnership between past and present, a sharing of concrete knowledge" (2:523). The result of a rationalist education, for Oakeshott, would be only half-training, half-knowledge.

For that reason, Oakeshott opposes contemporary trends in university expansion. "My own view," he writes, "is that the contemporary world offers no desirable model for a university, and that the current activity of approximation is lacking not in speed, but in discrimination." Oakeshott is not opposed, he goes on to explain, to change, but to what he sees as indiscriminate change.

Universities cannot be islands, isolated from the world in which they exist, as he readily admits. For him, the real issue is how they meet change:

> A war, a Royal Commission, a Barlow Committee, a specific benefaction, a government grant, each involves the approximation of a university to something in the world outside; pressure is continuous and no pressure is neutral, no gift is without strings, and the politician loves the unseen string. But merely to be in the fashion and to accept what comes is no very exalted ideal, and a university which has power to refuse a benefaction thought to be eccentric to its character must, when it exercises that power, have some sense of its own character and identity. This character may change, it certainly has changed, but what is to be avoided is change of such a kind that the university loses its sense of identity. [2:523]

The University Question formed the background against which the *Cambridge Journal* first appeared, but the journal was not devoted to the issue. Instead, it made itself a forum for those academic virtues it saw threatened, and set itself the task, as its opening editorial announces, of restoring the balance between the humanities and the sciences by showing the quality of work the humanistic values could produce (1:4).

During its seven-year run, the *Cambridge Journal* published some of the most distinguished scholars of the day. Rereading its numbers amounts to a who's who of some of the most prominent philosophers, historians, and literary critics of the last twenty-five years. The *Journal* published in philosophy Stephen Toulmin's "World-Stuff and Nonsense" and Ernest Gellner's "Use and Meaning." Michael Polanyi contributed "On the Introduction of Science into Moral Subjects." But the majority of the philosophical papers, reflecting the editor's interest, dealt with aspects of political theory. Richard Wollheim wrote on the political philosophy of existentialism; Eugen Weber on political language and political realities; C. B. MacPherson on the deceptive task of political theory; Frederick Hertz on nationalism; G. L. Arnold on realpolitik; and G.R.G. Mure on international socialism.

Among historians, the *Journal* published articles by Herbert Butterfield, Norman Sykes, Alfred Cobban, Asa Briggs, R. R. Bolgar, Duncan Forbes, E. J. Hobsbawm, R. J. White, G. S. Kirk, Shirley Letwin, and H. M. Pelling. The papers were as distinguished as the roll of names. Asa Briggs first published several of his best-known essays in the pages of the *Cambridge Journal*— "*Middlemarch* and the Doctors," "Ebenezer Elliott, the Corn Law Rhymer," "Samuel Smiles and the Gospel of Work," and "Trollope, Bagehot, and the English Constitution"—the last two of which became chapters in his well-known *Victorian People*. Duncan Forbes, whose essay on the Liberal Anglican idea of history appeared in 1952, published essays on *Historimus* in England, James Mill and India, the rationalism of Walter Scott, and the scientific whiggism of Adam Smith and John Millar. The labor historian H. M. Pelling published a paper on H. H. Champion, and Shirley Letwin presented an article on utilitarianism and tolerance. But the *Cambridge Journal* did not treat only English history. Alfred Cobban published studies on the historical significance of Marcel Proust and on Laval and the Third Republic; R. R. Bolgar wrote papers on Victor Cousin and on Ernest Renan. E. J. Hobsbawm wrote two articles on the political theory of Auschwitz and of the Mafia.

The *Cambridge Journal* also published a significant amount of literary criticism. Each issue of the review contained, on the average, four articles, of which at least one, but very often two, were devoted to literary subjects. If one criterion for judging quality articles is the fame they acquire when presented in book form, then the *Cambridge Journal* during its relatively short run published a remarkable group of midcentury literary studies.

One most distinguished set of literary essays began to appear in the *Journal*'s opening number. Graham Hough published a paper entitled "Ruskin and Fry: Two Aesthetic Theories." The following April, his essay "Marius the Latitudinarian" appeared. The set was completed by a two-part article in the February and March 1949 numbers called simply "A Study of Yeats." Together, these essays formed important chapters in his highly regarded study, *The Last Romantics*, a volume that continues to be a standard commentary on aesthetics and literary culture in England in the second half of the nineteenth century. Although not given to advocating poetic causes as did the "little magazines," the poet and critic Donald Davie, one of the chief voices of the Movement, found space in the *Journal*'s pages for his admittedly conservative critique of literary modernism.[4] He published papers on Cowper and Dryden, and on the style of Berkeley's *Siris*. His essay "Hopkins as a Decadent Critic" first appeared in the *Cambridge Journal* and later became a chapter in *Purity of Diction in English Verse*, the first of two studies (the second being *Articulate Energy*) that advocated syntax over imagery and the native English tradition over modernist poetics. John F. Danby, at the time lecturer in education at the University of Sheffield, published articles that eventually formed part of his two studies: *Poets on Fortune's Hill* and *The Simple Wordsworth*. His friend Frank Bradbrook also published articles that became part of his *Jane Austen and Her Predecessors*. In Continental literature, the *Cambridge Journal* published papers by the distinguished German scholar Erich Heller. Between 1948 and 1951 appeared his "World of Kafka," "Ambiguity of Faust," "Goethe and the Idea of Scientific Truth," and "Nietzsche and Goethe"—all of which became part of his classic study of German modernism, *The Disinherited*. Perhaps it was only fitting, then, that the *Journal* ended as it had begun, by publishing Dorothea Krook's articles on Henry James's *The Wings of the Dove* and *The Golden Bowl*, which also became chapters in her *The Ordeal of Consciousness in Henry James*. Of course, not all important articles became parts of later publications. The *Journal* published essays by Kenneth Muir on the uncomic pun, Frank Kermode on Richardson and Fielding, Maurice Evans on Elizabethan spoken English, John

Holloway on the odes of Keats, Bernard Blakestone on Blake and Keats, D. J. Enright on Goethe, and L. D. Lerner on Bunyan and Puritan culture.

The final number of the *Cambridge Journal* appeared in September, 1954, when it fell victim to financial difficulties, as did other publications at the time: *Scrutiny*,* the *Adelphi*,* *Horizon*,* and the *Fortnightly Review** (incorporated in the *Contemporary Review** [for both, see *VEA, RA*] in 1954). A second cause was the development of specialized academic publications. With the growth of English studies at the university level, more and more literary criticism found its way into academically oriented journals. Joining the established *Review of English Studies* in 1951 was F. W. Bateson's *Essays in Criticism*. Eight years later, C. B. Cox and A. E. Dyson began editing the *Critical Quarterly*.* Critics such as Graham Hough, Donald Davie, Frank Kermode, and John Holloway began to appear in their pages. The *Cambridge Journal* was unable to sustain its efforts to promote a general intellectual review. It failed to carve out a niche for itself as a comparable U.S. publication, *American Scholar*, had done. But the *Journal* was far from being unsuccessful, as in its pages appeared some of the best critics of midcentury.

Notes

1. Numerous government reports on higher education appeared in the years immediately after World War II. In May 1946 the report of the Scientific Man-Power Committee, known as the Barlow report after the committee's chairman, Sir Alan Barlow, became the focus of public debate by calling for the expansion of university facilities to produce as soon as possible twice the number of trained scientists at British universities. The previous year, the report of the Percy Committee touched off a decade of debate. Appointed by the Minister of Education, the Percy Committee outlined a plan for universities and technical colleges to coordinate their programs in the training of engineers. Other reports—the Goodenough, McNair, and Clapham reports—also called for changes in professional training in medical education, teacher training, and the study of the social sciences, respectively. For a summary of the changes, see H. C. Dent, *Universities in Transition* (London, 1961). The story can also be followed in the pages of the *Times Education Supplement*. In particular, see Sir Ernest Simon, "University Reform," *Times Education Supplement*, 3 August 1946, p. 367.

2. The academic virtues are those of Brogan; see "Editorial Note," *Cambridge Journal* 1 (December 1947):144.

3. Oakeshott's other contributions touching on the University Question are "Scientific Politics," 1 (1948):347–58; "Science and Society," 1 (1948):689–97; and "The Universities," 2 (1949):515–42. In addition, he published "The Tower of Babel," 2 (1949):67–83, and "The Political Economy of Freedom," 2 (1949):212–29. Together with the two-part "Rationalism in Politics," these essays provided the opening for his collection entitled *Rationalism in Politics* (1962).

4. Donald Davie, *Articulate Energy* (New York, 1955), p. 161.

Information Sources

INDEXES

Public Affairs Information Service (P.A.I.S.).

186216

REPRINT EDITIONS
>   Kraus Reprint, Nendeln, Liechtenstein. Scholars' Facsimiles and Reprints, Delmar, N.Y.
>   Microform: UMI.

LOCATION SOURCES
>   *American*
>   Widely available.
>   *British*
>   Widely available.

Publication History

MAGAZINE TITLE AND TITLE CHANGES
>   *The Cambridge Journal.*

VOLUME AND ISSUE DATA
>   Volumes 1–7, October 1947–September 1954.

FREQUENCY OF PUBLICATION
>   Monthly.

PUBLISHER
>   Bowes & Bowes, Cambridge, England.

EDITORS
>   T.F.D. Williams, October 1947–January 1948. Michael Oakeshott, February 1948–September 1954.

Mark A. Reger

CATHOLIC REVIEW, THE. See BLACKFRIARS

CHAMBER'S JOURNAL. See RA

CHAPBOOK, THE. See VEA

CONTEMPORARY POETRY AND PROSE

Although *Contemporary Poetry and Prose* lasted only ten issues beginning in May 1936, Roger Roughton's magazine provides one of the most fascinating cases of the uneasy alliance between left-wing politics and avant-garde art in the mid–1930s. The magazine has frequently been seen as a "semi-official" organ of the surrealist movement in England, and there is some justification for the label.[1] The second issue was a "Double Surrealist Number" including work by Paul Eluard, André Breton, Alfred Jarry, Luis Bunuel, and Salvador Dali. English surrealists such as David Gascoyne and Humphrey Jennings were among the most frequent contributors, particularly in the early issues. But by the final issue of Autumn 1937, political satire, frequently directed against the insufficiency of art, dominates the contents, and only a single surrealist piece appears. A major shift of sensibility had occurred since, only a year earlier, Roughton wrote what might serve as a credo for leftist surrealism: "Surrealist work, while not calling directly for revolutionary intervention, can be classed as revolutionary in so far as it can break down irrational bourgeois-taught prejudices, thus preparing the mental ground for positive revolutionary thought and action" (no. 4/ 5:74). The reasons for the ensuing disillusionment can be traced partially to a worsening international situation—the Spanish Civil War broke out as the third issue went to press—and partially to Roughton's failure to generate a coherent aesthetic to clarify the meaning of his credo.

When the nineteen-year-old editor, who published *Contemporary Poetry and Prose* at his own expense, opened shop at 1 Parton Street, which also served as the headquarters of Contemporary Poetry and Prose Editions and the Arts Cafe, literary surrealism had just begun to attract widespread attention in England.[2] Gascoyne had published *A Short Survey of Surrealism* in 1935, and Herbert Read's *Surrealism* was to appear in 1936. *Contemporary Poetry and Prose* published work by most of the prominent English surrealists—Francis Scarfe, Gascoyne, Jennings, Hugh Sykes Davies, Valentine Penrose, and Roughton—many of whom were slightly younger than Auden, Spender, and the rest of the *New Signatures* group (see *New Verse**). To some degree, the magazine challenged what by 1936 had come to be seen as a new poetic establishment. But Roughton insisted that *Contemporary Poetry and Prose* was not the official magazine of any clique. Noting that even in volume 1 (nos. 1–8) only about 40 percent of the contributors could be called surrealists, Roughton wrote:

Although the editor is at the moment a member of the loosely-constituted English Surrealist group, *Contemporary Poetry and Prose* is in no way an official Surrealist magazine. . . . Thus, the Surrealist group is not responsible for the political or other opinions expressed in the paper. [No. 8:143]

The contents of *Contemporary Poetry and Prose* largely justify Roughton's insistence that no party line existed for editorial decisions. Early issues of the magazine included poems by E. E. Cummings (nos. 1, 3, 4/5) and Wallace Stevens (no. 3), and poems and stories by Dylan Thomas (nos. 1, 3, 4/5, 9) which bear only tangential relationship to either surrealism or communism. Poems by Auden, Spender, Marianne Moore, and C. Day Lewis were announced for forthcoming issues, but the magazine folded before they appeared. Next to these "independent" contributors, the work of the English surrealists appears both philosophically tame and technically conservative. This is somewhat surprising when juxtaposed with parodic rejections of established poets such as Roughton's own "The Foot of the Stairs," which satirizes T. S. Eliot (no. 10:29). Similarly iconoclastic is William Empson's "Just a Smack at Auden" (no. 10:24–25). Both of these appear to demand new poetic modes. Yet most of the English surrealists, at least within the pages of *Contemporary Poetry and Prose*, gravitate strongly toward traditional iambic forms. Philosophically, they share a vague belief in "discovered images." As A. T. Tolley summarizes the theory, "The poet was not to invent images, because poetry had to do with historical and collective reality."[3] Many shared Roughton's fascination with folk forms, and the magazine frequently printed old English ballads, Afro-American spirituals, and folk songs from throughout Europe. Gavin Ewart (no. 1), Edgar Foxall (nos. 4/5, 9), and others imitated these forms in their own poetry. But this loose identification of imagination with the folk seems more the heritage of "Preface to Lyrical Ballads" than of Pablo Picasso or Tristan Tzara. The iconoclastic confidence, in retrospect, appears almost entirely unsupported by poetic achievement.

Still, *Contemporary Poetry and Prose* played an important role in translating and publishing standard texts of the Continental tradition such as *Les Chants de Maldoror* by Isadore Ducasse, Comte de Lautréamont (nos. 6, 9), and poems by Tristan Tzara (no. 10). The translated materials clearly reveal the importance of the visual arts in works such as Paul Eluard's poems on Max Ernst and Paul Klee (no. 2) and in six prose poems by Picasso accompanied by a Salvador Dali essay on Picasso (no. 4/5). Curiously, the English surrealists, despite their participation in the International Surrealist Exhibition of June 1936, reveal little direct concern with the aesthetic issues raised by modern painting. Gascoyne, whose "The Very Image, to René Magritte" (no. 2) is a salient exception, translated a statement by Eluard which concluded with a sentence that seems to imply a clear surrealist aesthetic: "THE POET IS HE WHO INSPIRES FAR MORE THAN HE WHO IS INSPIRED" (no. 2:18). But *Contemporary Poetry and Prose* never grappled with the philosophical or aesthetic issues raised by such statements, and most of the penetrating criticism of surrealism as an artistic movement appeared in *New Verse* and, later, the *London Bulletin** and *Arson, an Ardent Review*.

It did, however, directly confront some of the political implications of surrealism, most notably in an exchange between Roughton and Ezra Pound (no. 7:136–38). Pound, identified in a footnote as "admirer of Mussolini . . . no enemy of surrealism at its start, but no friend of some surrealists," blasts Roughton and the younger surrealists for ignorance of history and sloppy use of language: "The mere flight from and evasion of defined words and historic fact is NOT *sur* but SUB-realism; it is no more revolutionary than the dim ditherings of the aesthetes in 1888." Roughton responds that surrealism is in fact deeply rooted in history and that only the surrounding discourse has changed: "Surrealism as an unconscious element has existed since prehistory, and the only novelty of the twentieth century is that Freud's discoveries have made it possible for the first time to analyse, define and hence exploit this element." In response to Pound's assertion that "the simple practice of using WORDS with clear and unequivocal meaning will blast all the London Schools of economics; history or other bourgeois dribble; without any -isms being needed as hyperdermic," Roughton makes a statement which marks a significant retreat from his earlier political-aesthetic confidence:

> If it were true, no-one would be more delighted than myself. The Communist Manifesto is a brilliant pamphlet using WORDS with clear and unequivocal meaning, containing nothing but true statements based on a rational and correct analysis of capitalism; no doubt Mr. Pound has read it . . . he remains an admirer of Italian fascism.

By the end of his response, Roughton advances a much more modest claim for surrealism than he had only a few months previously:

> Too much is often made of the directly revolutionary significance of present-day surrealism: the part it has to play in helping to bring over a small section of that small section of the bourgeoisie which in times of capitalist crisis joins the class-conscious militant workers, that part in comparison with the direct impact of economic circumstances is very very minute; but the role exists and the revolutionary sincerity of its players is usually genuine.

Several external factors may have contributed to this defensive posture. Federico García Lorca had been murdered just prior to this exchange, and an unsigned article, most likely written by Roughton, declared: "There is no longer a fence for intellectuals to sit on: they must choose between fascism and anti-fascism; and magazines of modern poetry can no longer pretend they are Something Apart" (no. 6:106). In assessing the contents of *Contemporary Poetry and Prose*, Roughton must have perceived that much remained on the fence. Jennings's "The Boyhood of Byron" and Gascoyne's "The Light of the Lion's Mane" (no. 8:160–62) typify the vaguely political stance of many contributions. Gascoyne's long prose poem encourages the reader "to consider the cause of the disturbance that is taking place at the far end of this corridor" and notes that "the final explosion has been timed to coincide with the demolition of the plaster-of-paris monument that has been set up in the middle of the park to commemorate the victims of a savage watchdog who wrought great ravages in these parts towards the end of the 19th century." The political allegory is murky—why is the monument to the *victims* of tyranny being destroyed if this is a Marxist vision?—and the poet remains distanced from the disturbance. The poem's conclusion, while probably intended as a leftist statement, merely presents a simplistic vision of art undermining oppression: "Clusters of sharp little shells are growing beneath my eyelids, ants' eggs to throw to the fishes, chrysalises lying quietly in the dust beneath the feet of the marching tyrants, who will all fall down with fatigue in the end, and bury their arrogant faces in the mire."

Roughton appears to have grown increasingly impatient with this stance, an impatience no doubt fueled by hostile reviews in the leftist press.[4] He began devoting more space to proletarian poetry, such as Horace Gregory's "Dempsey, Dempsey" (no. 7), a plea for an end to American isolationism. In addition, practical problems beset the magazine. Number 8 included an announcement of the change from monthly to quarterly publication and a price increase from six pence to one shilling six pence. The same issue included two blank pages because an Isaac Babel story was censored. Roughton had faced censorship before in relation to an unidentified Cummings poem and the "Contemporary Poetry and Prose Edition" of Benjamin Péret's *Remove Your Hat*. Roughton's editorial comment on the censorship is bitter. *Contemporary Poetry and Prose* number 10 begins with a terse statement announcing the suspension of publication because "the Editor is going abroad."

Roughton won the Harriet Monroe Lyric Prize from *Poetry* (Chicago) in 1937, but he would never again play an active role in British literary journalism. He committed suicide in Dublin in 1941. Francis Scarfe, a frequent contributor to *Contemporary Poetry and Prose*, later came to view surrealism as a sign of "psychological illness in society." Nevertheless, he dedicated his study of 1930s poetry to Roughton and provided a fitting epitaph for his intriguing magazine: "His review, whatever its faults, was perhaps the most international review produced in the thirties with the exception of 'Transition.'"[5]

Notes

1. See William York Tindall, *Forces in Modern British Literature 1885–1946* (New York, 1947), p. 351, and Paul C. Ray, *The Surrealist Movement in England* (Ithaca, N.Y., 1971), p. 183.
2. George Barker, "Coming to London," *London Magazine* 3 (January 1956):49–54.
3. A. T. Tolley, *The Poetry of the Thirties* (New York, 1975), p. 230.
4. Derek Kahn, "They See Where the Menace Lies," *Daily Worker*, 14 October 1936, p. 7.
5. Francis Scarfe, *Auden and After: The Liberation of Poetry 1930–1941* (London, 1942), p. 149.

Information Sources

BIBLIOGRAPHY

Hynes, Samuel. *The Auden Generation: Literature and Politics in England in the 1930s.* New York, 1976.
Matthews, J. H. "Surrealism and England." *Comparative Literature Studies* 1 (1964):55–72.
Ray, Paul C. *The Surrealist Movement in England.* Ithaca, N.Y., 1971.
Scarfe, Francis. *Auden and After: The Liberation of Poetry 1930–1941.* London, 1942.
Tolley, A. T. *The Poetry of the Thirties.* New York, 1975.

INDEXES

An Author Index to Selected British Little Magazines, 1930–1939, ed. B. C. Bloomfield (London, 1976). *Comprehensive Index to English Language Little Magazines 1890–1970*, series 1, ed. Marion Sader (Millwood, N.Y., 1976).

REPRINT EDITIONS

Kraus Reprint, Nendeln, Liechtenstein. Scholars' Facsimiles and Reprints, Delmar, N.Y.

LOCATION SOURCES

American

Complete runs: Harvard University Library; Newberry Library, Chicago; Ohio State University Library; University of Alabama Library; University of Michigan Library; Yale University Library.

Partial runs: Brown University Library; New York Public Library; University of Buffalo Library.

British

Complete runs: Bodleian Library; British Museum; National Library of Scotland, Edinburgh.

Partial run: Cambridge University Library.

Publication History

MAGAZINE TITLE AND TITLE CHANGES

Contemporary Poetry and Prose.

VOLUME AND ISSUE DATA

Numbers 1–10, May 1936–Autumn 1937.

FREQUENCY OF PUBLICATION

Number 4/5 is a double issue. Numbers 1–8 are monthly. Numbers 9–10 are quarterly.

PUBLISHER

Roger Roughton, 1 Parton Street, London W.C. 1.

EDITOR

Roger Roughton.

Craig Werner

CONTEMPORARY REVIEW

The *Contemporary Review*, founded in 1866 and still issued today, is one of the longest-lived of the great British reviews. It is also one of the most consistent in its editorial policies and contents, showing little radical or abrupt change in over 100 years. Certainly it has undergone modification, but essentially it retains the format and standards established at its beginning. This consistency has been made possible in part by the fact that the journal has remained an independent publication, privately owned and managed, and free of formal connections with any political party. It is also due to the continued direction of two distinguished editors, Sir Percy Bunting in the nineteenth century and George Peabody Gooch in the twentieth.

The *Contemporary* was designed to provide entertainment and information for the educated upper classes, for those "to whom 2/6d. represented not a week's supply of bread for a large family, but rather two or three pleasant

evenings' reading'' (208:2). It assumed that its audience was cultivated, interested in politics, foreign affairs, and history, and familiar with literature both
modern and classical. Its aim was to provide such an audience with substantial
articles and reviews in all these areas. In time it began to direct itself to a more
strictly academic readership while still not excluding articles of a more general
nature which would appeal to a wider audience. Throughout its history the journal
has represented the liberal tradition, standing, as Gooch remarked, ''just a little
to the left of the centre, abhorring extremes on either side of the line'' (208:4).
On social and cultural as well as political issues, the journal has supported liberal
values, welcoming change consonant with those values but deploring radical
overthrow of the old standards and ideals. In short, it has embodied the views
of the cultured, intellectual establishment. The tradition of substantial content,
discriminating readership, and moderate liberalism can be traced in an unbroken
line through the three distinct periods of the journal's history: the period from
1866 to 1911, when Bunting died; the period from 1911 to 1970, dominated by
the influence of Gooch; and the final period from 1970 to the present.[1]

One of the most striking features of the *Contemporary* at the turn of the century
was its involvement with social conditions and with the women's movement.
Many articles dealt with the poor, the conditions in prisons and workhouses,
and political issues such as the miners' strike of 1893, unemployment, and old
age pensions. In addition, the *Contemporary* not only supported the women's
movement but also published many articles by women. Bunting was an ardent
follower of Josephine Butler in her campaign against the Contagious Diseases
Act, and for many years he served as chairman of the National Vigilance Association. These connections led him to open the journal to such women writers
as Emily Davies, Josephine Butler, and Bessie Raynor Belloc. Julia Wedgwood
was a regular writer, and for some time was in charge of fiction reviews. Millicent
Garrett Fawcett wrote on such matters as women's suffrage (June 1892), degrees
for women at Oxford (March 1896), and the imprisonment of the suffragettes
(December 1906). Another important writer was Teresa Billington-Grieg, who,
in ''The Rebellion of Women'' (July 1908), identified the women's movement
as the main fact of the age, and who in the next few years contributed many
articles on feminism and politics. Other typical articles are Elizabeth Sloan
Chesser's ''The Treatment of Women Prisoners'' (October 1908), Lady Bunting's ''Mistress and Maid'' (May 1910), Elizabeth Robins's ''Sermons in
Stones''—a defense of suffragette violence—(April 1912), and Bertrand Russell's ''Liberalism and Women's Suffrage'' (July 1908).

On the literary side, as in its other departments, the *Contemporary* published
the most celebrated authors of the day. Writers close to the twentieth century
include Rudyard Kipling, who contributed short stories in the 1890s; H. G.
Wells, who in August 1897 offered a critical appraisal of George Gissing's
novels, and W. B. Yeats, whose ''Ireland Bewitched'' appeared in September
1899. Other established authors were Walter Pater, Robert Louis Stevenson,
James M. Barrie, Edmund Gosse, and a number of the writers associated with

the nineties, such as Arthur Symons, John Addington Symonds, and "Fiona McLeod" (William Sharp). Foreign authors were represented by Leo Tolstoy, who contributed "Religion and Morality" in March 1894, and Henrik Ibsen, whose "The Saga and the Ballad" appeared in September 1906.

The journal issued essays on major authors past and present and usually provided balanced appraisals. In May 1900, for example, William Larminie wrote an essay on Thomas Carlyle and Percy Bysshe Shelley in which he traced the influence on English political thought of Carlyle's twin hostilities to materialistic values and to abstract theorizing on revolution. Likewise, G. K. Chesterton in July 1909 formulated a provocative estimate of George Meredith, contending that Meredith combines a pagan acceptance of the mystery of the universe with the materialism of the true mystic. George Barlow's review in August 1905 of Algernon Charles Swinburne's six-volume *Poems* stresses the poet's spiritual side as his most characteristic and least understood quality.

During the first period the *Contemporary* also published articles on special, often controversial, literary topics. One such topic was that of the Romantic novel as opposed to the realistic. In February 1897 Rider Haggard defended his own type of Romantic fiction, a position which immediately won support from Andrew Lang in "Realism and Romance" (November 1887) and from Harry Quilter in "A Living Story-Teller, Mr. Wilkie Collins" (April 1888). More far-reaching was the subject of realism in the novel and in drama, a controversy which centered around Ibsen and on which the *Contemporary* published essays representing a wide range of critical opinion. At one end of the spectrum stand Norman Hapgood and A. Maynard Butler. Hapgood in November 1898, while acknowledging Ibsen's greatness as a craftsman, deplored the "harsh and joyless criticism of life, which is now condemned in the pulpit [and which] must be banished from the stage" (74:723). Butler wrote in a milder tone but found Ibsen lacking in sympathy and common humanity (May 1902). In contrast to such evaluations may be placed Edward Dowden's essay of November 1906, which gives detailed analyses of the plays and points out the deeply personal philosophy underlying them. Henry Rose in June 1908 stressed the religious side of Ibsen, and in April 1913 Edwin Björkman explained how Ibsen fought through despair to a philosophy of faith and hope. Other special groups of literary essays at the turn of the century are those by "Vernon Lee" (Violet Paget) on aesthetics and literary psychology and those on Irish poetry and the Celtic revival. Into the last category fall Havelock Ellis's "The Celtic Spirit in Literature" (February 1906) and Yeats's "Literature and the Living Voice" (October 1906). Ellis describes the remoteness and supernatural interest of Celtic literature, contrasting these qualities with the emotional intensity and realism of Nordic literature. Yeats, on the other hand, endorses the work of the Gaelic movement as a means of maintaining the old imaginative life.

One other noteworthy type of essay belongs to the first period: the personal recollections of famous authors by family, friends, and acquaintances. As a periodical of high reputation, the *Contemporary* was the recipient of many such reminiscences. William G. Kingsland, for example, reported on "Some Browning Memories" in August 1912. Agnes Grace Weld, Tennyson's niece, contributed articles in March 1893 and November 1897 containing personal anecdotes of the poet. Similarly, Mrs. Disney Leith in April 1910 recounted her early memories of her cousin, Swinburne. Other personal recollections include those by John Masefield of John Millington Synge (April 1911), by Percy Fitzgerald of Carlyle (June 1913), and by John Drinkwater of Rupert Brooke (December 1915).

In addition to long literary essays, the *Contemporary* also published regular reviews, and in October 1907 there appeared the first "Literary Supplement," a feature which has continued without interruption up to the present day. At its inception the supplement included a leading article on some general literary subject, reviews of books in a variety of fields, and a section of shorter reviews, notices, and literary notes. It was started by the jurist J.E.G. De Montmorency, who remained in charge of it until his death in 1934. Augustine Birrell wrote the first lead article, "The Critical Faculty"; thereafter both the lead articles and the main reviews were largely the work of Montmorency.

The second period of the *Contemporary*, from 1911 to 1970, covers the half century of Dr. G. P. Gooch's editorship. When Gooch was elected to Parliament as a Liberal in 1906, he was invited by Bunting to join the *Contemporary* as one of its directors. Five years later, on Bunting's death, he succeeded to the editorial chair, with Lady Bunting's nephew, the Nonconformist spokesman Dr. J. Scott Lidgett, as coeditor. Gooch dealt mainly with political issues, and the more conservative Lidgett supervised philosophical and theological matters and problems of London government.[2] The partnership continued for almost three decades, but it was Gooch who was the more active partner and who provided the shaping force in the review.

For the first three years of Gooch's editorship the *Contemporary* continued along the lines established by Bunting. When change did come, it came not as a result of policies or procedures but because of the war and new political situations. Between 1914 and 1918 the journal was inevitably dominated by articles about the war, the course of the war in foreign nations, and the involvement of the United States. In the last two years Irish affairs also occupied much space, as did the Russian Revolution, which the *Contemporary*, like most liberal journals, at first welcomed enthusiastically as the beginning of a new and better age.

The articles of the war years which dealt with broader issues often did so by connecting those issues with war and politics. Thus these years were marked by a spate of articles on women in relation to war, women's work in wartime, and conscription for women. The same trend is reflected in the literary essays. October 1914 saw the publication of Montmorency's article "Shakespeare and War," followed a month later by one on Cervantes and Shakespeare. Similarly, in November 1918 Zabelle C. Boyajian contributed "War and Peace in Shakespeare," pointing out that while Shakespeare apparently extolled the glories of war he also understood and recognized the philosophy of pacifism. Ernest A. Baker's essay "The Muscular Novel" (November 1917) analyzes the depiction of the Crimean War by Charles Kingsley, Thomas Hughes, and Tennyson, and discusses the literature which embodies the ideal of physical courage and prowess. A more strained connection of literature and politics is seen in E. Lyttelton's essay "Henry Vaughan and Optimism" (April 1916), in which the author uses Vaughan's poetry as a springboard to present his views on the need for national penitence and a far-reaching peace of conciliation.

After the war Gooch was free to fulfill the aim which had been his from the first, to make the *Contemporary* "the leading monthly in the field of foreign affairs" (200:503). Politics and world affairs were, therefore, the central concern for the next four decades.[3] During Bunting's editorship the leading contributor on foreign affairs had been Dr. E. J. Dillon, the Eastern European correspondent for the *Daily Telegraph*. In August 1902 Dillon instituted a separate Foreign Affairs Section which continued until August 1914, and for the next eight years he remained a frequent contributor. In 1922 Leonard Woolf resumed the Foreign Affairs Section, but dropped it after a year. George Glasgow took over the section in 1923 and managed it until 1954. Other important writers on foreign affairs were Sir Edwin Pears, H. N. Brailsford, and Gooch's friend Noel Buxton.

Along with this emphasis on the international scene, the *Contemporary* also published articles on social conditions, history, education, travel, and the arts. Each issue usually contained one article on nature and country life and at least one on literature. Major contributors in these various areas included Francis Hirst, later editor of the *Economist*; the historians H.A.L. Fisher and Arnold Toynbee; the Labour politician Arthur Greenwood, who contributed several articles in the 1920s; Gilbert Murray, the classical scholar and pacifist, who wrote regularly up to the end of the 1940s; and Julian Huxley, who contributed articles on scientific humanism in July 1931 and on Charles Darwin in October 1932.

In the years between the wars and during World War II, the literary department, even though not the principal focus of the journal, attracted notable writers, provided a wide variety of literary studies, and made a significant contribution to literary journalism and criticism. The number and quality of its articles on foreign literature were outstanding, largely because of the editor's own interests and principles. Gooch was deeply concerned with European culture, and from 1921 onwards he began to increase the number of articles on French, German, Italian, and Russian literature. These essays ranged from scholarly studies of established classical figures such as Dante and Goethe to perceptive appraisals of the moderns. Bernard Causton, for instance, in August 1925 gave a detailed analysis of Luigi Pirandello's plays, identifying in them the themes of alienation and introspection and discussing in particular *The Man with A Flower in His Mouth* as an expression of the utter loneliness of the human soul.

The essays on European literature multiplied in the 1930s. Gooch had strong personal and intellectual ties with Germany, and for him the rise of Nazism came to assume something of the nature of a personal tragedy. Thus after Hitler's accession to power in 1933 he became an active supporter of Jewish and political refugees from the Continent, and he welcomed the contributions of their writers and sympathizers to the *Contemporary*. One of the authors to receive extensive critical attention at this time was Thomas Mann, whose philosophy, politics, and denunciation of the Nazi movement were analyzed at length, most particularly by the scholar Dr. J. Lesser. Typical of the political articles is one by Fritz Gross, who in "The Literature of Exiles" (March 1944) wrote on Heinrich Mann, Bertolt Brecht, and Max Herrmann-Neise, and their struggles against ignorance, lies, brutality, and madness. A similar political slant is reflected in "Literature in Fascist Italy" by Dr. Paolo Treves (January 1940). Treves's thesis was that fascism had not succeeded in producing a body of literature or even history and that the books about fascism, although numerous, were unread. Such political analyses were not restricted to European literature. In the same issue as Treves's article, for example, D. L. Hobman gave a survey of the depiction of the Jew in Gentile fiction, drawing on works ranging from Marlowe to Joyce and Lawrence.

The most significant aspect of the literary articles in this period was the increasingly scholarly and academic approach. Contributors included such distinguished figures as Augustine Birrell, John Shawcross, and C. H. Herford, while Professors Frederick Boas and B. Ifor Evans were regular writers. Many of the articles, moreover, rose above the level of transitory literary journalism to criticism of permanent value. Gilbert Thomas, for example, when writing on the Everyman edition of Daniel Defoe's *A Tour through England and Wales*, provided an illuminating estimate of Defoe's place in history. Similarly penetrating is Thomas's November 1931 article on Cowper, an essay which anticipated his own book *William Cowper and the Eighteenth Century* (1936). Not all essays, of course, were of the same quality or detail. The frequent articles on centenaries and other anniversaries often offered only general surveys and appreciations. And some writers were limited by the preconceptions of their time. C. K. Allen, to cite one example, in January 1924 praised Joseph Conrad's skill in depicting character and setting but considered his devious method of narration in *Lord Jim* to be a blemish on the work, a "trick of construction which some writers seem to regard as a mark of superior intelligence" (125:59).

Ironically, the "Literary Supplement" had the least to offer in the way of substantial literary criticism. After the 1920s the lead articles gradually became fewer, although Montmorency continued to produce a story or sketch each year. The signed reviews were mainly the work of Montmorency and Salvador De Madariaga. Together they regularly reviewed works of literature and literary criticism, as well as history, politics, education, and theology. The reviews, however, were unusually short, consisting of only one or two pages, and not highly analytic of either texts or authors. When Montmorency died, a larger team of reviewers took over, including, among others, Gooch, Robert Murry, George Glasgow, and in the 1940s Deryck Abel and Theodora Roscoe. At this time the reviews concerned with literature declined slightly in number, while the coverage of history increased. In 1941, when wartime restrictions caused the periodical to be reduced in size, the "Literary Supplement" suffered further curtailment, providing fewer reviews in all areas.

The last year of Gooch's editorship, the postwar period from 1945 to 1960, saw some new developments, most importantly the absorption of the *Fortnightly Review** (see *VEA, MA*). The *Fortnightly*, founded in 1865 by Anthony Trollope and edited by George Henry Lewes, ceased publication in 1954 and was merged with the *Contemporary*, which thereafter included the words "Incorporating the Fortnightly Review" as part of its title. Another development was that, toward the end of the 1950s, the review began for the first time in many years to publish poems in almost every issue. In these years appeared the work of such authors as Lord Gorell, Phoebe Hesketh, and Alfred Noyes. Such changes as these, however, were external; in both politics and literature the general tenor of the journal remained unchanged.

The political orientation was consistently left-wing. Gooch explained the position in the postwar years as follows:

> We approved the larger part of Labour policy and particularly the two most important achievements of the Labour Government of 1945–50 under the wise leadership of Clement Attlee. The first was the completion of what is called the Welfare State, which went far to bridge the gulf between the haves and the have-nots. The second was the transformation of the British Empire into the British Commonwealth in which no state became or remained a member except by its own will. [208:7]

Among the important new contributors in the area of politics and economics were Frederick Pethick-Lawrence, elder statesman of the Labour Party and chief architect of Indian independence, and Joseph Grimond, leader of the Liberal Party from 1956 to 1967. Grimond was one of a group of liberals who in 1956 issued in the *Contemporary* a series of special supplements entitled "Contemporary Commentary," in which they expounded Liberal policy and encouraged the reviving interest in the Liberal Party as an alternative to the Conservative and Labour parties.

In the field of literature the *Contemporary* continued to publish personal and academic essays, though new names came to be added to the list of writers. W. H. Graham wrote frequent articles on the eighteenth and nineteenth centuries. Joan Harding wrote on twentieth-century figures ranging from Arnold Bennett to T. S. Eliot, Charles Morgan, and Dylan Thomas. Derek Stanford was the author of many reviews and articles on the moderns. In August 1957 he discussed Dorothy Richardson's novels and her use of the interior monologue and stream of consciousness technique. The following year (June 1958) he defended Graham Greene's *The Potting Shed*, responding to rationalist critics like Kenneth Tynan who had objected to the miraculous element in the play. Four months later he reviewed Eliot's *The Elder Statesman*, a play which he found to be both religious and deeply humane. In this play, he felt, "the world of 'the hollow men,' terminating with a whimper, now regenerates itself with a kiss" (194:201).

Articles such as these indicate an increasing concentration on modern literature. In the 1950s articles on the major twentieth-century authors abound, and writers as diverse as Joseph Conrad, E. M. Forster, W. Somerset Maugham, George Orwell, T. S. Eliot, Edith Sitwell, and Jean Anouilh were the subjects of critical analysis. But interest in the established moderns did not mean that the *Contemporary* was always highly receptive of the new poets of the 1950s or that the magazine supported radically new departures in literature, as is clearly seen from Carl Bode's review of Alfred Alvarez's *The Shaping Spirit* in July 1958.

Gooch retired from the editorship of the *Contemporary* in 1960, and the following decade was marked by several major upheavals in organization and management. Gooch's immediate successor was the political economist Deryck Abel. In 1965, just before his untimely death, Abel handed over the editorship to Dominic Le Foe, under whose leadership the journal weathered financial difficulties and celebrated its centenary with special issues throughout the year. In June 1968 Gordon Godfrey succeeded Le Foe. He accepted the post of editor on a temporary basis, serving only until July 1970.

Despite these administrative changes, the journal retained the format set up half a century earlier. The various editors were united in maintaining the general character and Liberal tradition. Moreover, Gooch himself continued to act as a guiding spirit for several years after his retirement, for he still served as consulting editor and, until shortly before his death in 1968, contributed articles and reviews. Continuity was also ensured by Arnold De Montmorency, who remained as editor of the "Literary Supplement," and by the assistance of Professor Herbert Butterfield and Sir Denis Brogan, both of whom agreed in 1965 to become editorial advisors.

In the 1960s the literary department continued as it had in the last years of Gooch's editorship. Chief reviewer for the "Literary Supplement" at this time was William Kean Seymour, who provided balanced, though often brief, reviews of poetry and literary criticism. Other regular reviewers were Richard Whittington-Egan, Francis Grierson, and Molly Tibbs in literature, David Thomson in history, and George Catlin in politics. Full-length essays continued the scholarly approach of earlier years. Between 1967 and 1970, for example, Stanford issued a number of articles on the short story of the 1890s in which he outlined the themes, characteristics, and sources of the then emerging literary genre. Many articles dealt with modern literature. Howard Sergeant contributed "Siegfried Sassoon—Poet of War" in July 1962 and in February 1963 surveyed the archetypal imagery of Edwin Muir, Dylan Thomas, and Elizabeth Jennings. A notable article on contemporary literature is John Ferguson's "A Christian Laureate" (November 1969), an introduction to Gwendolyn Brooks (215:268).

The retirement of Gordon Godfrey in 1970 brought to an end the long period of Gooch's influence, and when the novelist Rosalind Wade became editor in July, the *Contemporary* entered the third phase of its history. While she made no sudden changes, Wade gradually widened the scope of the journal, trying to broaden its appeal while at the same time retaining its high quality and standards. Politics, world affairs, and economics were still the chief focus, but more articles on education, the arts, literature, and the women's movement began to appear. Wade's first innovation was the "Quarterly Fiction Review"; she took charge of this special feature herself, with the first issue appearing in July 1970. Since then the "Fiction Review" has been a regular feature, each one providing reviews of about a dozen significant new novels. It was followed by a "Quarterly Record Review" begun in May 1976 by David Fingleton, and by a "Quarterly Film Review" begun in September 1976 by James Morton.

Another development under Wade's direction was the inclusion of creative writing. The poems which Gooch had introduced in the last years of his editorship had disappeared in the 1960s, but now poems and stories for the first time were regularly included. Among the short story writers published were L. P. Hartley, James Hanley, Edwin Samuel, and John Elsom. Numbered among the poets were such figures as William Kean Seymour, A. L. Rowse, and Robert Gittings. The change in tone which accrued from this imaginative writing was further increased by a new emphasis on the familiar essay. Many issues were enlivened by at least one essay of this kind, in which the author expressed personal ideas and recollections, usually in a style both intimate and urbane. A. L. Rowse's "Oxford—Then and Now" (November 1983) is an example of this type of essay. So too is Tom Lannon's "The Spirit of Stirling Bridge" (October 1983), in which he describes how, when he studied history as an adult, he finally came to understand the significance of the Wallace Monument under which he had played as a child. More politically oriented is George Beattie's championship of the miners in "The Story of the Miners" (November 1979), which recounts the author's experiences growing up as the son of a small shopkeeper in a Scottish mining village.

While these developments brought about a change in the character of the journal, many features were unaltered. The "Literary Supplement" retained the same team of reviewers and continued to review works on literary criticism, history, psychology, politics, and foreign affairs. Distinguished scholars and academics still contributed articles on literature past and present. The 150th anniversary of Keats's death was the occasion for Robert Gittings's essay on "Keats and Medicine" (September 1971), in which he demonstrated Keats's serious interest in medicine and refuted the popular notion of his unhappiness at Guy's Hospital. Mary Moorman, author of the standard biography of William Wordsworth, wrote a biographical study of Dorothy Wordsworth in December 1971. G. Wilson Knight contributed several articles on John Cowper Powys, the most ambitious being a two-part essay entitled "Powys and the Kundalini

Serpent'' (July and August 1978), in which he traced references to the Yoga Kundalini Serpent in several twentieth-century authors.

While articles such as these by eminent scholars ensured that the journal retained its academic appeal, literary essays of a different character were also published. These are more informal essays which present the author's own experiences or casual reflections on literature. An example is A. L. Rowse's ''Holywell Cemetery: Victorian Oxford'' (August 1971), where Rowse offers his musings on some of the headstones, including those of Kenneth Grahame, A. C. Bradley, Walter Pater, and Charles Williams. In the same category is E. A. Markham's ''Visiting a 'Fellow's' Flat'' (November 1979), in which the author gives a sketch of his year as a creative writing fellow at Hull University. Another interesting personal essay is that by John Elsom entitled ''Samuel Beckett, Max Wall and Me,'' which appeared in May 1983. The previous month Elsom had directed Wall in readings from *Malone Dies* at the National Portrait Gallery, and in the essay he recounts his childhood delight in the radio comedian Max Wall, his later fascination with Beckett, and the chain of events by which he was able to bring these seemingly diverse enthusiasms together.

These years also saw an increased attention to the theater, reflected not only in reviews of productions but in the discussion of current issues and problems in the theater. Academic articles include Edmund Miner's ''The Theme of Disillusionment in the Drama of Arthur Pinero'' (April 1975) and Holly Hill's ''Rattigan's Renaissance'' (January 1982). Both of these articles apply the methods of scholarly analysis to these popular dramatists. More frequent are essays dealing with experimental drama and with the developments in British drama since the war: David Morgan's ''And Now the Void: Twentieth Century Man's Place in Modern Tragedy'' (June 1979), and Glynne Wickham's ''British Theatre: 1949–79'' (February 1980), an essay-review of John Elsom's *Postwar British Theatre*. Other articles took up practical matters, in particular the importance of fringe theater and the need for continued support from the Arts Council. Writers on these topics include Robert Rubens, Clare Colvin, theatre critic for the *Tatler* and the *Evening News*, and David Cregan, novelist, teacher, and dramatist. In addition, the contributions of at least two celebrated directors enhanced the theater offerings of the *Contemporary*. E. Martin Browne, founder of Pilgrim Players and director of the 1951 revival of the York Mystery Plays, wrote on ''The Medieval Play Revival'' in September 1971. The essay, written to mark the 1900th anniversary of the city of York, describes the circumstances of the 1951 production, the first since 1562, and its influence on subsequent revivals of other cycle plays. At the other pole of dramatic experience is Charles Marowitz, American-born artistic director of the experimental Open Space Theatre, well known for such productions as the 1972 *An Othello*, his own rewriting of Shakespeare featuring a black Iago. Marowitz contributed several articles, such as ''Ibsen, Strindberg and the Sex War'' (March 1980) and ''Playing to the House'' (July 1980).

In the last decades of the twentieth century, the *Contemporary* has thus acquired a broader range and assumed a different tone, becoming less formal both in subject and style. Usually its writers present themselves in a more relaxed mood, and are perhaps readier than their predecessors to accept experiment and innovation in literature and the arts. Such changes were inevitable in a changing society. Writing in 1966 on the *Contemporary*'s centenary, Gooch remarked: "So to today. The Contemporary faces a different world. The churches empty, the bingo halls fill up. The television companies coin millions and the ballet companies go bankrupt. Our national theatre has been secured by destroying two excellent individual companies, our national press and periodicals contract" (208:2). Yet Gooch saw such changes not as a threat but as a challenge. It is a challenge which the *Contemporary* seems to have met.

The changes in the journal, though real and significant, have not been fundamental ones. It was never the role of the *Contemporary* to appeal to the semi-literate Victorian reader of pulp fiction or to the modern patron of the bingo halls. It is directed now, as it was in its beginnings, at educated, informed readers concerned about the arts and about events in the world around them. Its mission has been to provide reliable information, thorough scholarship, and penetrating criticism. At the same time it has welcomed a variety of opinions and has encouraged that free play of the mind on the object which is the essence of the liberal attitude. Its articles are well—even elegantly—written and reveal good judgment and perceptive evaluations. Its contributors have been famous writers, distinguished scholars, and recognized authorities in all the branches of human learning. Its editors have all maintained the tradition of English liberalism, with its emphasis on truth, tolerance, and reason. Throughout its long history the *Contemporary* has been characterized by high standards, both intellectual and moral, seriousness of purpose, and commitment to the pursuit of knowledge and the dissemination of truth. If Bunting were to see it now, he might be surprised—Gooch a little less so. Neither would be disappointed. [See also the article on the *Contemporary Review* in *VEA*.]

Notes

The article on the *Contemporary Review* was originally assigned to Professor Mark Reger. Shortly after he had started work on the project illness forced him to resign, and he generously agreed to share his materials with me. I should like to thank Professor Reger for permitting me to see and use his working bibliography, his list of editors, and some information regarding writers on politics and foreign affairs. (See also the article on the *Contemporary Review* in *VEA*.)

1. For a discussion of the magazine before 1900, see the entry in *VEA*.
2. G. P. Gooch, *Under Six Reigns* (London, 1958), pp. 162–63.
3. Ibid., p. 200.

Information Sources

BIBLIOGRAPHY

"About Ourselves." *Contemporary Review* 198 (July 1960):1.

Butterfield, Sir Herbert. "George Peabody Gooch." *Contemporary Review* 200 (October 1961):501–5.

———. "George Peabody Gooch, O.M., C.H." *Contemporary Review* 213 (November 1968):226–28.

Dictionary of National Biography. S. v. "Alford, Henry"; "Bunting, Sir Percy"; "Gooch, George Peabody"; "Knowles, Sir James"; "Lidgett, John Scott."

Eyck, Frank. *G. P. Gooch: A Study in History and Politics.* London, 1982.

Godfrey, Gordon. "G. P. Gooch, O.M., C.H., F.B.A., D. Litt." *Contemporary Review* 213 (November 1968):225.

Gooch, G. P. "About the Review." *Contemporary Review* 208 (January 1966):1–3.

———. "The Centenary of the *Contemporary Review.*" *Contemporary Review* 208 (January 1966):4–7.

———. "Deryck Abel: A Tribute." *Contemporary Review* 207 (September 1965):153.

———. *Under Six Reigns.* London, 1958.

Henkel, Dorothy. "George Peabody Gooch." *Contemporary Review* 214 (February 1969):103–4.

Hirsch, Felix E. "Published Works of George Peabody Gooch, 1898–1960." In *Studies in Diplomatic History and Historiography in Honour of G. P. Gooch, C.H.* Edited by A. O. Sarkissian. London, 1961.

Lidgett, J. Scott, and William T. Stead. "Sir Percy Bunting." *Contemporary Review* 100 (September 1911):301–8.

Rossman, Alexandre. "Dr. Gooch: A Friend." *Contemporary Review* 213 (November 1968):229–30.

Wedgwood, C. V. "G. P. Gooch." *Contemporary Review* 198 (August 1960):405–8.

INDEXES

Each volume indexed. 1866–1880 in *Poole's Index.*

REPRINT EDITIONS

Microform: UMI.

LOCATION SOURCES

American

Widely available.

British

Widely available.

Publication History

MAGAZINE TITLE AND TITLE CHANGES

Contemporary Review, 1866–1955. *Contemporary Review, incorporating The Fortnightly*, 1955–.

VOLUME AND ISSUE DATA

Volumes 1–243 + , numbers 1–1410 + , February 1866–present.

Volumes 1–18: four issues per volume; volumes 19–30, six issues per volume; volumes 31–36, four issues per volume; volumes 36–, six issues per volume.

FREQUENCY OF PUBLICATION

Monthly.

PUBLISHERS

1866–June 1912: See entry in *VEA*. Volumes 102–118, July 1912–December 1920: The Contemporary Review Company, Ltd., 10 Adelphi Terrace, London W.C. Volumes 119–121, January 1921–June 1922: The Contemporary Review Company, Ltd., 170 Fleet Street, London E.C. 4. Volumes 122–128, July 1922–December 1925: The Contemporary Review Company, Ltd., 12 Cursitor Street, London E.C. 4. Volumes 129–158, January 1926–December 1940: The Contemporary Review Company, Ltd., 19–19a Cursitor Street, London E.C. 4. Volumes 159–163, January 1941–May 1943: The Contemporary Review Company, Ltd., Breams Buildings, 11–13 Chancery Lane, London E.C. 4. Volumes 163–198, June 1943–July 1960: The Contemporary Review Company, Ltd., 46–47 Chancery Lane, London W.C. 2. Volumes 198–199, August 1960–January 1961: The Contemporary Review Company, Ltd., Fulwood House, Fulwood Place, High Holborn, London W.C. 1. Volumes 199–205, February 1961–June 1964: The Contemporary Review Company, Ltd., 42 Broadway, Westminster, London S.W. 1. Volumes 205–213, July 1964–December 1968: The Contemporary Review Company, Ltd., 36 Broadway, Westminster, London S.W. 1. Volumes 214–218, January 1969–June 1971: The Contemporary Review Company, Ltd., 38 Farringdon Street, London E.C. 4. Volumes 219–229, July 1971–September 1976: The Contemporary Review Company, Ltd., 37 Union Street, London S.E. 1. Volumes 229–October 1976–: The Contemporary Review Company, Ltd., 61 Carey Street, London WC2A 2JG.

EDITORS

1866–1910: See entry in *VEA*. George P. Gooch, 1911–1960. Deryck Abel, 1960–1965. Dominic Le Foe, 1965–1968. Gordon Godfrey, 1968–1970. Rosalind Wade, 1970–.

Muriel J. Mellown

CORNHILL MAGAZINE, THE

The *Cornhill Magazine*, which began so successfully in 1860 under Anthony Trollope and William Thackeray as editors, retained its reputation for quality through the years of Leslie Stephen's editorship (1871–1882), and then floundered in the 1880s, a period of decline for miscellanies, when it changed editors and attempted to become a popular magazine with lighter material and more short fiction. By the mid-1890s the *Cornhill* sought to regain some of its original flavor with a vigorous new editor, John St. Loe Strachey, who appealed more directly to readers' taste; but it had little success in the face of new competitors. In 1898, the year before he gained sole control of Smith, Elder, the *Cornhill*'s publishing company, Reginald John Smith began the style of editing which he continued until his death in 1916.

Smith emphasized patriotism, sought interesting, skillfully written articles and fiction by famous authors, and attempted to recreate the quality and prestige of the earliest years of the magazine. He reprinted original works by major writers from earlier issues. The first editor, Thackeray, was the most frequently reprinted, with fourteen items, six of them appearing in 1911 to celebrate the centennial of his birth. Six works by Charlotte Brontë reappeared. And although Dickens was not associated with the magazine, two of his works were reprinted in honor of his centennial. Mrs. Gaskell's centennial was also honored with reprints, and one work each of Trollope and Robert Louis Stevenson appeared.

Like his father-in-law, George Murray Smith, Reginald John Smith sought to win the confidence of authors and their public by becoming an agent between them. He conscientiously read everything that was published by his firm.[1] Aware of the advantages of keeping a coterie of authors and experts loyal to his magazine, Smith frequently wrote charming letters, and "correspondence with old and trusted friends of the *Cornhill* often brought words of praise for new writers appearing on its pages."[2] Appreciative notices from the papers were passed on, with a note in his own hand, to encourage young writers:

> A contributor said that to have known him was "a liberal education in human kindliness, in thoughtful courtesy and in love of letters." Many of his authors dedicated their books to him. One called him an "inexhaustible fount of kindness." Mrs. Humphry Ward said he had been "shelter and comfort, advice and help, through many years."[3]

He was able to attract major writers, including Thomas Hardy, who published several poems and prose pieces in the magazine after a long silence following the rejection of *The Return of the Native* in the 1870s.

The new century provided an opportunity to look back with pride at the forty-year history of the magazine, especially since so many of its rivals and imitators were defunct. And, unlike the less successful houses, Smith, Elder had retained key members of the staff. John Aitchison remained for forty-five years as a sagacious and prudent business manager for the firm from before the advent of the magazine until 1915. Similarly, William Partledge served for forty years as principal accountant for author and publication accounts.[4] With this strong continuity it was not difficult for an energetic man with good business instincts, who also seemed to be a spiritual son of his father-in-law, to recapture some of the spirit and force of the brilliant early years, despite a decreasing interest in serious literary work in popular magazines. George Murray Smith, who had founded the *Cornhill Magazine* with Thackeray as his editor and Trollope as his chief novelist, cooperated in the celebration of continuity by writing his memoirs, the best chapters of which appeared in the *Cornhill*. Anne Thackeray Ritchie, who had been associated with the magazine from its first decade, wrote a reminiscent article and began a series of twelve essays, like her father's *Roundabout Papers*, called *The Blackstick Papers*. The quality of her writing was uneven, because she was verbose and uncritical of her own work. Editing her pieces was a chore which not every editor would attempt, but Smith continued to publish her work—including a piece coauthored with her daughter Hester—because he saw the marketability of her name and the charm of her writing.

As publisher, Reginald Smith brought out major posthumous editions of the best Smith, Elder writers—the Brownings, the Haworth edition of the Brontës, the biographical edition of Thackeray, and the Knutsford edition of Mrs. Gaskell. Because he appreciated the value of nostalgia and of celebrating anniversaries, he printed special articles during 1900 and 1901. The Jubilee issue of January 1910 had 32 pages more than the usual 144, featured nine special contributors, and bore an orange design on a white cover.

Some highlights of the magazine during Smith's tenure included miniature biographies of men of letters. Arthur C. Benson contributed a series of impressions of notable men who had influenced his life, called "Leaves of the Tree." There were historic mysteries by Andrew Lang; scientific articles by W. A. Shenstone; serial fiction by Henry Seton Merriman, Anthony Hope, A.E.W. Mason, Stanley Weyman, and Mrs. Humphry Ward; poetry by Alfred Noyes, Robert Bridges, and George Meredith, as well as Hardy; and essays by Arthur Quiller-Couch, Julian Huxley, and A. I. Shand. W. B. Yeats contributed "What Is 'Popular Poetry'?" and Sarah Bernhardt "The Moral Influence of the Theatre," and practical advice was made available in such pieces as "Family Budgets" on 1,800 and 10,000 pounds a year (n.s. 10:446, 656, 790); "Prospects in the Professions," an extensive series covering such fields as the military, law, farming, acting, engineering, and medicine (n.s. 13:317, 471, 635, 764); and "Household Budgets Abroad," covering six countries in as many articles (n.s. 17:87, 181, 336, 467, 631, 806). Exotic adventure was offered in "Elephant Hunting in Siam" (n.s. 9:350) and "Tiger Shooting in Central India" (n.s. 27:318). For the ladies, Frances Hodgson Burnett wrote "The Making of a Marchioness" (n.s. 10:730; n.s. 11:3, 146) and A. W. Ward "The Girlhood of Queen Louisa" (n.s. 9:509). Essays appeared on "French Housekeeping" (n.s. 16:367), "Georgian Gossips" (n.s. 8:814), and "French Wit in the Eighteenth Century" (n.s. 9:688). During a year when Thackeray's daughter's work did not appear, Virginia Woolf contributed a series of six pieces, "The Book on the Table" (n.s. 24:190, 469, 765; n.s. 25:217, 523, 794). Other notable authors included W. D. Howells, Edmund Gosse, Max Beerbohm, Sidney Webb, E. V. Lucas, Ford Madox Hueffer, Austin Dobson, Churlton Collins, Katherine Tynan, G. M. Trevelyan, and Henry James.

During the Great War, the cost of labor for printing rose by 300 percent. To offset the rising costs, the *Cornhill* reduced its length, first to 128, and then to 112 pages, and the price was increased from 1 shilling ordinary to 1 shilling net.[5] Yet circulation had finally risen, Leonard Huxley believed, because the magazine provided solace and satisfaction that was appreciated both at home and by the soldiers at the front. There was a succession of war stories in the magazine, beginning with Boyd Cable's "Pride of Service" in the issue for July 1914 (n.s. 37:91). Numerous articles on military matters appeared by Hesketh Prichard, A. Conan Doyle, C. H. Firth, Rev. W. H. Fitchett, and Frank Bullen. There were even articles on "French Refugees to England 1871–72" (n.s. 18:607),

"Women's Suffrage: In Time of War" (n.s. 9:210), and "War and Diplomacy in Shakespeare" (n.s. 41:400).

Leonard Huxley, the reader for the firm, assumed the editorship upon the sudden death of Reginald Smith in 1916. The magazine moved to John Murray Publishers, who purchased Smith, Elder in 1917. There were no members of the Smith family in the business at that time. Reginald Smith had been so forceful and energetic in his management that no line of succession had been foreseen as necessary. Huxley sought to please the new owners, who desired that the magazine retain its character. Continuity was suggested visually to the public by keeping the same design and format. The publisher maintained an active interest in the magazine, offering suggestions but leaving the final decisions to the editor, especially during the first years under the new proprietorship. As time passed, the publisher exerted more influence, as his working relationship with the editor became more collegial. For example, Murray cautioned Huxley in 1921: "What some people seem to crave for are short stories and adventures. Whatever happens we must try and avoid a reputation for dullness however undeserved."[6]

While the war lasted, the magazine was able to retain its vigor through preoccupation with military events. Although patriotic articles continued to appear, a somber tone predominated with such titles as "How to Be a Patient" (n.s. 44:303), "A Prisoner of War in Germany" (n.s. 44:511), "Home from a German Prison Camp" (n.s. 45:235), and "At a Y.M.C.A. Hut Somewhere in France" (n.s. 42:20). The deaths of such frequent contributors as Anne Thackeray Ritchie and Stanley Weyman were noted in memorial articles, as were those of Reginald John Smith and Thomas Hardy. Hardy, like Anne Thackeray Ritchie and Edmund Gosse, came in for critical inspection posthumously. The centenary of former editor James Payn's birth was noted by an article, as was the fiftieth anniversary of the publication of *Far from the Madding Crowd*. While researching a history of the publisher, George Paston wrote a series of three articles about Albemarle Street in the 1940s and 1950s. Similarly, while writing *The House of Smith, Elder*, Huxley printed "Chronicles of *Cornhill*" in the magazine in an attempt to keep the illustrious history of the journal alive in the memory of the readers. Because of Huxley's own interests in Elizabeth Barrett Browning's and Jane Welsh Carlyle's letters, he wrote about both; and articles appeared about them and their spouses with greater frequency than about Shakespeare, the perennial favorite. Huxley contributed more regularly than had any editor of the *Cornhill* since Leslie Stephen.

After the war the Victorian era seemed more remote, but, like earlier periods, worthy of study; and in an attempt to return to normality, literary history, biography, and criticism flourished. Dr. Johnson, Jane Austen, Charlotte Brontë, Charles Dickens, and Oscar Wilde were discussed, separately, in at least five articles. Special notice was taken of such nineteenth-century giants as Thackeray, John Henry Newman, John Ruskin, and Sir Walter Scott, while Matthew Arnold, Lord Byron, Lewis Carroll, Charles Darwin, Gilbert and Sullivan, George Bernard Shaw, Robert Louis Stevenson, and George Meredith were each discussed in at least two articles. Joseph Addison, James Boswell, Chaucer, Benjamin Disraeli, John Keats, Charles Lamb, Karl Marx, Christina Rossetti, Leslie Stephen, Jonathan Swift, Tennyson, and Trollope each received one. Series of remembrances of the past were written by Mrs. Humphry Ward about Frederick Locker-Lampson.

Succeeding Huxley as editor after his death in 1933 was Lord Gorell, a novelist, poet, and partner in John Murray Company. He retained the post until 1939, when the beginning of World War II forced Murray to discontinue the magazine. During Gorell's relatively brief editorship, there was little to distinguish the *Cornhill*; his conservative attitude did not allow for innovations.

After the war, when the paper allowance was no longer a problem, John Murray VI persuaded his uncle that the *Cornhill* was worth reviving.[7] Peter Quennell, who had done research for his Byron volumes at Murray's and thereby become acquainted with members of the firm, became editor, with John Murray VI as assistant editor. The magazine appeared three times each year in 1944–1946; beginning in 1947 it became a quarterly. The length of the issues varied from fewer than sixty to more than ninety. Payment to contributors varied accordingly: from slightly under 100 pounds per issue to under 150, except for the centennial issue, which paid nearly 300. The magazine did not make money, but it provided an outlet for Murray Company authors to appear before the public more frequently, as well as being a source for advertisements for John Murray titles. A half-crown quarterly with a modernized cover design, the *Cornhill* included fiction, verse, belles lettres, and criticism of a high literary standard. Installments of novels no longer appeared, with longer pieces reserved for special issues.

Postwar articles included several on Franklin Roosevelt, Winston Churchill, and relations between France and England. Balancing a consciousness of tradition with an intense awareness of modern times, writers supplied criticism, poetry, philosophy, travel, fiction, and history. Contributors included Max Beerbohm, Clive Bell, John Betjeman, Elizabeth Bowen, Maurice Bowra, Truman Capote, Kenneth Clark, Patrick Leigh Fermor, André Gide, Harley Granville-Barker, Margaret Lane, Rose Macaulay, Somerset Maugham, Harold Nicolson, William Sansom, Osbert Sitwell, Freya Stark, Hugh Trevor-Roper, Evelyn Waugh, and H. G. Wells.

Quennell reminisced with pride, "I was able to put on record an interesting piece of social history—a letter from Jane Austen's best-loved niece, Fanny . . . in which she informed her sister that Aunt Jane's immediate domestic circle was not everything that they themselves esteemed." He treasured this find because it clearly displayed "the spirit of an age and the effect of the time-spirit upon individual human beings."[8] Quennell enjoyed working on the magazine in the little room at the top of the building, where he was independent of the firm and could do his own work, yet be helped by members of the staff with technical details. Sir John, "a formidable traditionalist, though, being at heart a just and generous man . . . [undoubtedly did not wholly approve] of some of the stories and essays," but he did not interfere any more than he had with earlier editors. Quennell remembered running into difficulty only over his smoking a cigar which was tracked down by Sir John, who himself despised cigars.[9]

Late in 1950 Osyth Leeston and John Murray VI became the first anonymous editors of the *Cornhill Magazine* in this century in order to keep the identity of the magazine separate from the publishing company. Having served as assistant editor under Huxley from 1931, the year after he joined the firm controlled by his uncle, John Murray VI extended the family continuity. Under his direction the magazine continued as a quarterly, publishing occasional supplements containing work as long as 35,000 words. Special issues commemorated the centenary of the magazine in a six-shilling edition, and 200 years of publishing by John Murray were celebrated in a 206–page double issue for Autumn/Winter 1968/1969. In the "Foreword to the Centenary Number" Quennell, although no longer editor, emphasized that the consistent aim of the magazine had been to publish writing that appealed to educated readers and reflected civilized taste.

The press picked up, whenever possible, the unusual in each issue of the *Cornhill*. During John Murray VI's tenure, most celebrated was the correspondence between George Bernard Shaw and the Benedictine Abbess of Stanbrook, which appeared in the *Cornhill* for Summer 1956. According to the *Sunday Times* of 18 July 1954, the *Cornhill* had

> strong individuality without eccentricity; in its pages sensibility, good taste, a feeling for tradition and a zest for adventure peacefully co-exist. Not in the least political, not much concerned with literary experiment, it reflects and caters for the diversions of civilized minds, and deserves hearty congratulations upon its achievement.

Among the contributors during the last two decades were John Betjeman, Elizabeth Taylor, Sean O'Faolain, Iris Origo, May Sarton, X. J. Kennedy, Kenneth Clark, Betty Miller, Frank O'Connor, Eva Le Gallienne, Alfred Kazin, Sylvia Townsend Warner, Elizabeth Berridge, Joyce Cary, Philip Larkin, Robert Graves, C. Day Lewis, Arnold Toynbee, Nadine Gordimer, James Pope-Hennessy, H. E. Bates, Isaiah Berlin, Laurens van der Post, John Fowles, Clive Bell, Margaret Lane, and Laurie Lee. Henry James and Mrs. Humphry Ward received retrospective articles in honor of the centenary of their births.

In 1954, according to the *Advertiser's Weekly*, the circulation of the *Cornhill* increased to 20,000, primarily intelligent and literary readers with an income of at least 400 pounds. But by 1955 a circulation of 10,000 was reported, too low to meet rising costs. The habits of the reading public were changing; mass circulation newspapers were becoming more like magazines, and radio and television were increasingly encroaching upon the quiet hours. These trends brought about the demise of many monthly and quarterly magazines. The last few years of the magazine showed increasing subscription prices with fewer items per issue, and faithful subscribers were implored to find other subscribers or to make gifts to keep the *Cornhill* alive. In the "Publisher's Note" that prefaced the final issue of the *Cornhill*, Leeston expressed gratitude and good wishes to its contributors and regular subscribers and hoped for an early reunion. John Murray VI, who had become senior director of the publishing house in 1968, received his C.B.E. two years before the demise of the *Cornhill* with the Spring/Summer issue of 1975. [See also the article on the *Cornhill Magazine* in *VEA*.]

Notes

1. Leonard Huxley, *The House of Smith, Elder* (London, 1923), pp. 225, 227.
2. Ibid., p. 229.
3. W. Robertson Scott, *The Story of the "Pall Mall Gazette"* (London, 1950), p. 98.
4. Huxley, *House of Smith, Elder*, p. 245.
5. Ibid., p. 136.
6. John Murray to Leonard Huxley, 27 May 1921, John Murray Archive.
7. Conversation with Sir Peter Quennell, 22 August 1984.
8. Peter Quennell, *The Wanton Chase* (London, 1980), pp. 64–66.
9. Ibid., p. 63.

Information Sources

BIBLIOGRAPHY
Huxley, Leonard. *The House of Smith, Elder*. London, 1923.
John Murray Archive.
Quennell, Peter. *The Wanton Chase*. London, 1980.
Scott, J. W. Robertson. *The Story of the "Pall Mall Gazette."* London, 1950.
INDEXES
Indexed semiannually until 1944; at eighteen-month intervals thereafter (with exceptions).
REPRINT EDITIONS
Microform: UMI.
LOCATION SOURCES/
American
Widely available.
British
Widely available.

Publication History

MAGAZINE TITLE AND TITLE CHANGES
Cornhill Magazine, The.
VOLUME AND ISSUE DATA
January 1860–June 1896: see entry in *VEA*.
New series (3), volume 1, number 1, July 1896–volume 181, number 1084, Spring/Summer 1975.
FREQUENCY OF PUBLICATION
Monthly until 1939; quarterly, with exceptions, 1944–1975.

PUBLISHERS
  1860–1917: Smith, Elder. 1917–1975: John Murray.
EDITORS
  1860–1898: see entry in *VEA*.
  Reginald John Smith, 1898–1916. Leonard Huxley, 1917–1933. Lord Gorell,
  1933–1939. Peter Quennell, 1944–1950. [John Murray and Osyth Leeston], 1950–
  1975. See also the entry in *VEA*.

Barbara Quinn Schmidt

COTERIE

Without even so much as an opening editorial, *Coterie, A Quarterly: Art,
Prose, and Literature* was published by Hendersons, a highbrow London book-
store, on May Day 1919. Chaman Lall, the editor and then a student in Jesus
College, Oxford, apparently was about to leave the university, for the September
issue directed correspondents to write him at the fashionable bookseller's address—66 Charing Cross Road. Each of the seven numbers (6/7 was a double
issue) of *Coterie* (1919–1921) and the six of its successor, *New Coterie* (1925–
1927), included eight to fifteen poems, occasional short stories or plays, translations of European writers (especially in *New Coterie*), and four to six drawings.
Avant-garde imagist poetry was its leading characteristic, although newspaper
critics regularly commented on the drawings by such artists as Nina Hammett,
René Durey, Ossip Zadkine, and Modigliani. On the mastheads of numbers 2–
5 were the names of two American editors, Conrad Aiken (of South Yarmouth,
Massachusetts, although between 1916 and 1927 he lived in England for parts
of each year) and Stanley I. Rypins (of the University of Minnesota). Also, at
one time or another the editorial committee included T. S. Eliot, T. W. Earp,
Aldous Huxley, Nina Hamnett, and Russell Green. Lall continued as editor until
Green assumed the post beginning with the Winter 1920–1921 number (6/7).
Because the *New Coterie* continued *Coterie*'s practice after number 5 of not
having a masthead, it can not be established with certainty who was the editor
of the succeeding journal. However, the format and design, the same general
stable of contributors, the same type of bookseller-publisher, and especially the
regular appearance of Green's poetry in *New Coterie* support the view that he
continued as editor. Until he assumed the editorship, Aiken appeared to be the
agent between the journal and its sizeable number of regular American contributors. After the change, dropping the masthead, *Coterie* and *New Coterie* took
on a decidedly British-Continental rather than British-American flavor.

The initial number had a mixed reception in the 22 May 1919 issue of the
Times Literary Supplement. The reviewer thought that with Eliot and Huxley as
its nucleus, *Coterie* "has every opportunity of producing really interesting experiments." On the other hand, the magazine's "lack of spiritedness, its timid-
ity" were found to be "disappointing." This critic was joined by many who

immediately located *Coterie* in the vast and shifting literary sands of the late Edwardians; like a dozen or so British and American journals, its "young writers were not interested in the political issues that had been so important to the preceding generation; hence they submitted their works to *Art and Letters*[*], *Wheels*[*], *Coterie*, or *Voices*[*] rather than to *The New Age*[*]'' (see *VEA*).[1]

Coterie did not publicly respond to criticisms of the journal until Green (presumably) wrote its first editorial (nos. 6/7, winter 1920–1921) to hotly refute comments in the *Daily Herald* of 24 November 1920, the *London Mercury** of November 1920, the *Manchester Guardian* of 9 October 1920, and the *Times Literary Supplement* for 28 October 1920. It opens with the observation that *Coterie*'s "vitality and sincere originality" have been well received by "all readers whose critical flair is not warped by malice or rusted with ineptitude." In keeping with the sharpness of Edwardian journalism, the writer then attacks the "puerility" of the *Daily Herald*'s attempt to make something out of the title. But even a cursory look at the issues shows that thirty–forty like-minded writers and artists, a coterie, used the journal to advance their views. Having dispensed with the ineptitude of one organ, the writer blazes away at the malice of the *Mercury*. The first charge is about its neglect: the *Mercury* was silent about the existence of *Coterie* until the appearance of its fifth number. Then, calling the writers for the *Mercury* "renegades from the fraternity of letters [because they] betray the solidarity of culture," the writer proudly asserts that his journal has stayed within the mainstream of literature yet "is not . . . perpetuating the barrel organs of Georgian poetry . . . [and] the accumulated rubble of sombre academicism."

Although belatedly, this editorial articulated how those associated with *Coterie* saw it as an important outlet for British and American creativity. Conrad Aiken, the enthusiastic promoter of American letters in Britain, fictionalized these years in *Ushant*:

> And the wonderful decade or more was to unravel itself as predestined— in the Arnault bookshops, at Soho restaurants, in the Bloomsbury tea-shops, Lyons or ABC's, and at Inglesee and Saltinge [Winchelsea, where Aiken lived between the spring of 1922 and the winter of 1923, when he moved to Rye, leaving there for a teaching post at Harvard in 1927]. A time of blooming, of profusion, of hard work and endless debate; of good food, good drinks, and good living. But a time of competitive stress also, of unceasing literary *sauve-qui-peut*. . . . Which of them would survive? which of them wouldn't? The various cliques formed or fell apart, new coteries rose and fell; but central among them, and in the end omnipotent, was the group that erratically and fluctuatingly arranged itself, or rearranged itself, round the Tsetse's quarterly [*Criterion**], and the luncheons and dinners that intermittently celebrated its appearances.[2]

Coterie is an important little magazine for several reasons. It is a fine example of the closeness of British and American letters in the decade surrounding World

War I, for in its pages appeared many of the leading younger poets, playwrights, and short story writers eager to go beyond the Age of Tennyson: Eliot, Huxley, Aiken, Richard Aldington, Herbert Read, H. J. Massingham, John Gould Fletcher, the three Sitwells, E. C. Blunden, Wilfred Owen, H[ilda] D[oolittle], Frank Harris, Amy Lowell, and Harold Monro, among others. While there is no evidence in *Coterie* on payment to contributors, it might be concluded from the second issue of *New Coterie* that there was no payment; contributors gave to a cause, expecting nothing in return. Many pieces in the maiden issue of May 1919 expressed the artists' revulsion with the carnage of war; having made that statement, the remaining issues of both *Coterie* and *New Coterie* ignored the international economic and political turmoil. In fact, *New Coterie* seemed to go out of its way to praise Continental artists—including the recent German enemies—perhaps attempting to reconcile the Western world's creative people.

No circulation figures are available, but *New Coterie* printed 1,000 numbered copies of one issue. By extension, its predecessor may have had similarly large runs for a little magazine. The several pages of advertising, chiefly by publishers of fiction such as Chapman and Hall or by exclusive London book dealers such as Hendersons, kept down the costs, but the magazine still was fairly expensive: in England, two shillings, eight pence per issue or ten, eight per year; at Brentano's, in New York, seventy-five cents per issue or three dollars per year. The rates remained unchanged for both journals.

Until its end in 1921, *Coterie* narrowly focused on a well-to-do, literate audience which wanted to be *au courant* in arts and letters; and further steps in that direction were taken in *New Coterie*, which succeeded it four years later. Both journals died after six quarterly issues (*Coterie* had a final double number). In addition to the many notable writers and artists who continued to contribute to what was essentially the same journal, major new artists donated their work: Liam O'Flaherty, Augustus John, William Rothenstein, Faith Compton Mackenzie, and D. H. Lawrence.

The key difference between the two titles is the sharp decline of contributions by Americans and the increase in Continental writers in *New Coterie*. John Gould Fletcher was the only notable American poet who published in the new journal; Paul Selver regularly included a section entitled "European Anthology"—translations of contemporary writers. Although E. Archer succeeded Hendersons as the publisher, both booksellers, concentrating on trading quality literature, seemed to exercise little control over the editorial policies of the journals. Particularly in the late numbers, *New Coterie* took on the sassy tone of *New Yorker*: regular editorials addressed pressing literary issues, and a chatty, unsigned insider's column picked up the artsy gossip of London. All in all, the special qualities of *Coterie* were, if anything, a bit more sparkling in *New Coterie*.

Notes

1. Wallace Martin, *The "New Age" under Orage: Chapters in English Cultural History* (New York, 1967), p. 275.

2. As quoted in *The Selected Letters of Conrad Aiken*, ed. Joseph Killorin (New Haven, 1978), p. 61. A fuller picture of the history of *Coterie* probably lies buried in the 3,000 letters written by Aiken from which Killorin selected less than 10 percent. See his preface for details on the holdings. Furthermore, an interesting book could be written about Aiken's promotion of various little magazines between 1916 and World War II.

Information Sources

BIBLIOGRAPHY

"*Coterie.*" *Times Literary Supplement*, 22 May 1919, p. 274.

Hoffman, Frederick J., Charles Allen, and Carolyn F. Ulrich. *The Little Magazine: A History and a Bibliography*. 2nd ed. Princeton, 1947.

Killorin, Joseph, ed. *The Selected Letters of Conrad Aiken*. New Haven, 1978.

Martin, Wallace. *The "New Age" under Orage: Chapters in English Cultural History*. New York, 1967.

INDEXES

Comprehensive Index to English Language Little Magazines 1890–1970, series 1, ed. Marion Sader (Millwood, N.Y., 1976).

REPRINT EDITIONS

Kraus Reprint, Millwood, N.Y., 1967.

LOCATION SOURCES

American

Widely available.

British

Widely available.

Publication History

MAGAZINE TITLE AND TITLE CHANGES

Coterie, A Quarterly: Art, Prose, and Literature, May 1919–1921. *New Coterie*, 1925–1927.

VOLUME AND ISSUE DATA

Coterie: numbers 1–7, May 1919–Winter 1920–1921. *New Coterie*: numbers 1–6, November 1925–Summer/Autumn 1927.

FREQUENCY OF PUBLICATION

Quarterly.

PUBLISHERS

Coterie: Hendersons, 66 Charing Cross Road, London. *New Coterie*: E. Archer, 68, Red Lion Street, Holborn, London.

EDITORS

Coterie: Chaman Lall, 1919–1921; Russell Green, number 6/7, Winter 1920–1921. *New Coterie*: Russell Green, 1925–1927.

Vincent L. Tollers

CRITERION, THE

When T. S. Eliot published *The Waste Land* in the first number of the *Criterion* in October 1922, he thereby assured the magazine's literary immortality. Often overlooked, however, is the magazine's additional seventeen-year run, containing some of the most interesting and significant critical and creative work produced between the wars. The *Criterion* not only helped to shape European culture during a difficult period, but it also became a vehicle through which Eliot pursued his own self-definition. Eliot's interest in editing a critical review surfaced immediately following World War I. Living more or less permanently in England, Eliot felt that to be the editor of a critically important magazine would greatly enhance his own literary reputation and hasten his acceptance in British intellectual circles. He had been approached by A. R. Orage, editor of the *New Age** (see *VEA*), to assume editorial responsibilities for that journal, but the arrangements came to nothing. There was also some talk of his being involved in the newly constituted *Dial*, edited by a former classmate at Harvard, Scofield Thayer, and to which he had been contributing a "London Letter," but that too collapsed. In 1921, through his acquaintance with Richard Cobden-Sanderson, Eliot was introduced to Lady Rothermere, the wife of the newspaper magnate Viscount Rothermere, owner of the *Daily Mail*, the *Sunday Dispatch*, and the *Evening News*, and a supporter of artistic projects, one of which was a particular desire to fund a literary quarterly.[1] Eliot seized the opportunity to edit a magazine financed by her and published by Cobden-Sanderson, himself an independent publisher of fine books.

The initial agreement was made for three years and worked well until the end of that period, when Eliot's patroness decided that she no longer wished to carry the entire financial burden of the journal by herself. There is some conjecture whether or not Lady Rothermere wanted a magazine that was less intellectual and a bit more "arty," and there was additional speculation about a rift in the relationship between the editor and her ladyship. Whatever the reasons, Eliot confessed his problem to Bruce Richmond of the *Times Literary Supplement*, one of whose protégés, Frank Morley, had just begun work for the publishing firm of Faber and Gwyer, later Faber and Faber. Through Morley's intercession Faber agreed to split the economic subsidy with Lady Rothermere while retaining Cobden-Sanderson as the publisher. Eventually, after a couple of years, Faber assumed complete control of the *Criterion* when Lady Rothermere moved permanently to France and gave up her good works. By then the firm of Faber realized that the journal was not only good publicity for its own publications but also served as a feeder for its collection of authors.

Part of the initial arrangement between Faber and Eliot included a position for the editor within the publishing house. Eliot, relieved of his job at Lloyd's, which had become increasingly frustrating, and exhausted by his editorial efforts, perhaps could not have continued the *Criterion* without such a change. The move to Faber and Gwyer did not relieve Eliot of all of his duties or of his financial responsibilities, but it did provide him with a more congenial workplace and reduced somewhat the demands on his already divided life. Vivienne, Eliot's first wife and, incidentally, the one who gave the *Criterion* its name, was ill and demanded much of Eliot's time and energy.[2] The gradual collapse of his marriage and the deterioration of Vivienne's mind plagued Eliot during the entire run of the magazine. As Eliot's energies underwent one of their periodic collapses, and at the onset of the new war, the *Criterion* published its last issue in 1939.

The first issue of the *Criterion* was announced in the *Times Literary Supplement* in mid-August 1922 in a short notice that stated that the new journal would have more in common with the critical quarterlies of a hundred years ago than with the currently fashionable literary miscellanies, and that it would help to fashion European opinion by providing a method of exchange among thinkers while maintaining what the article described as "international standards."[3] At the end of October, following the first number, the *Times* again ran an item which began: "If we are to judge by its first number, *The Criterion* is not only that rare thing amongst English periodicals, a purely literary review, but it is of a quality not inferior to that of any review published either here or abroad." The notice concluded on a note that surely pleased Eliot immensely: "What literary school, then, does this new quarterly represent? . . . There is no such school, obviously. It becomes apparent that the only school represented is the school of those who are genuinely interested in good literature."[4] Eliot had achieved the right tone from the beginning and would maintain it throughout the run of the journal.

The history of the *Criterion* might be generally characterized in the following way: in the 1920s, especially through the middle of 1925 (when the journal once failed to meet its quarterly publication schedule), the *Criterion* contained substantially more literary material than was included later. Eliot himself wrote more literary works for the magazine as well, later restricting his contributions largely to his "Commentaries." In the later 1920s and early 1930s the pages of the *Cri*, as it was often affectionately known, contained an increasing number of book reviews and essays of political character, especially of rightist *Action Française* and Marxist leanings, and the journal maintained its international flavor by publishing translations and even some work in the original languages; in the late 1930s Eliot turned more and more to topics of religious significance, as his own interests shifted in that direction; and when he was not concerned with religious questions, the magazine concentrated on political ones, in keeping with the temper of the times. As he remarked later, the international content began to diminish as the attention of European intellectuals turned increasingly inward to the pressing events within their own countries; first the Italians, then the Germans and Spaniards, and finally the French ceased to appear in the *Criterion*. To Eliot's credit, the magazine did continue to survey the contents of foreign periodicals right up to the end in an attempt to keep current with Continental European thought and literature.

The *Criterion*'s initial issues contained a potpourri of essays and creative work, most of it vaguely modernist in flavor. In the first volume, for example, Eliot published not only his own work and that of Ezra Pound, but also pieces by Hermann Hesse, Fyodor Dostoevsky, Roger Fry, Luigi Pirandello, Julien Benda, Virginia Woolf, Herbert Read, Paul Valéry, William Butler Yeats, E.

M. Forster, and Richard Aldington. In addition, the first four issues contained essays on James Joyce's *Ulysses*, Gustav Flaubert, Stéphane Mallarmé, Honoré de Balzac, contemporary Spanish literature, and Sigmund Freud. In the third number there appeared for the first time the feature "Foreign Reviews," which would continue to grace the pages of the *Criterion* to the end. In a series of short notices about foreign periodicals, the readers of the *Criterion* were kept abreast of what was being published on the Continent and in America. This feature was in keeping with Eliot's intention to use the pages of his journal to attempt to present the best of international thought. The "Foreign Reviews" complemented the internationalist list of contributors and the fair number of translations which appeared throughout the run of the journal.

In addition to reviewing Dutch, German, French, American, Italian, Spanish, and Danish periodicals on a regular basis, by the eighth number Eliot had introduced a book review feature, "Books of the Quarter," which by the beginning of the third volume grew large enough to comprise one of the main features of the journal. The books Eliot chose to review reflected, once again, his interest in a wide range of intellectual and artistic topics, and included volumes on contemporary affairs, politics, and economics. The first of Eliot's "Commentaries" appeared in the seventh issue; this feature would appear in almost every number and would allow Eliot free range over a variety of topics. Collectively they form a sort of intellectual diary, and through them one can plot Eliot's developing political, religious, and aesthetic ideas.

In the New Year issue of January 1926 (4, no. 1), Eliot contributed "The Idea of a Literary Review," in which he outlined the editorial practices, already in force, which would shape the journal to the end. Eliot felt rather strongly that a literary review should be more than a miscellany but less than a polemic, that such journals should walk the fine line between having no editorial policy and having one which was too rigid and constricting. The adjustment between editors, collaborators, and occasional contributors must result in a "tendency" rather than a dogmatic program. Eliot's "tendency," the one which guided his editorial policy, was to make the *Criterion* an "organ of documentation"—"that is to say, the bound volumes of a decade should represent the development of the keenest sensibility and the clearest thought of ten years." Even the single numbers, he felt, should attempt to illustrate, within their limits, the "time and the tendencies of the time."

In spite of Eliot's later "tendency" for his journal, the early issues of the *Criterion* do read like a miscellany, drawing together a body of work from a disparate, if not uninteresting, group of modern writers of varying national backgrounds. There appears to be no "tendency" here unless one calls the publication of good writing a tendency. Nevertheless, the collection of early contributors to the pages of the *Criterion* was truly impressive: May Sinclair, Ford Madox Ford, Hugo von Hofmannsthal, Wyndham Lewis, Gerhart Hauptmann, Hugh Walpole, Sacheverell Sitwell, Marcel Proust, C. P. Cavafy, Osbert Sitwell, Gilbert Seldes, Benedetto Croce, T. E. Hulme, James Joyce, and I. A.

Richards. The experience of reading the early issues is a heady one. Many ideas flowered in the period immediately following the war, and the pages of Eliot's journal captured all of their diversity and excitement. Perhaps the reason readers have found the later issues of the magazine less interesting has less to do with a shift in Eliot's perception than with the gradual winding down of the postwar euphoria. Not only did writers of the 1930s turn their attention to other matters— ones of social and political import—but they lost some of the vigor of the decade before, rendering their writing in many cases less dynamic, less appealing.

The January 1926 issue contained roughly 190 pages of articles and creative work and 27 pages of reviews; a year later the January issue contained 108 pages of articles and poetry and almost 75 pages of reviews. Although the magazine still published work of literary interest by such writers as John Gould Fletcher, Aldous Huxley, Gertrude Stein, Jean Cocteau, Ada Leverson, Ivan Bunin, Archibald MacLeish, F. S. Flint, and Harold Monro, more and more space was given over to critical writing and reviews. It was as though once Eliot officially set a policy, albeit a loose one, for the *Criterion*, he felt obliged to make it more serious, more critical, and less artistic. In May 1927 the journal also began publishing as a monthly, a move which would continue for only a year, but which would have a lasting effect on the subsequent numbers. In order to keep up with the schedule Eliot was obliged to let out more reviews and to accept more essays in place of creative material. Since his own interests were turning more toward critical writing, such a move was undoubtedly congenial. After the appearance of his "Fragment of an Agon" in the January 1927 issue, a poem, "Salutation," a year later, and "Five-Finger Exercises" in July 1933, he published no more creative work in the *Criterion*, confining himself almost exclusively to writing his "Commentaries" and reviewing.

The year 1928 opened for the *Criterion* with a significant article, Charles Murras's "Prologue to an Essay on Criticism," translated by Eliot, which involved the editor in a rather long and often rather uneasy association with right-wing politics. It was a connection from which Eliot was able to extricate himself, but it reflected the sort of political fascination that threw Eliot's friend and contributor to the *Criterion*, Wyndham Lewis, into the arms of Hitler and was to have a similar effect on Ezra Pound and his fascination with Italian fascism.[5] The pages of the *Criterion* of the late 1920s are peppered with essays and letters debating various political systems. A. L. Rowse wrote about communist literature and Eliot the literature of fascism, J. S. Barnes and Rowse exchanged letters, and Eliot's "Commentaries" increasingly dealt with political subjects. In the October 1921 issue Eliot devoted a long editorial to a comparative review of books on politics by Harold Laski and Lord Lymington. This piece highlights Eliot's own apparent confusion about warring political factions, but its approach reflects his attitude in dealing with political issues in the pages of the *Criterion*. Not only did the magazine deal with political issues before other "literary" journals would do so, but the emphasis was always on balance and interaction of opposing points of view. Eliot did strive to keep an open forum in his magazine even when he himself had rather strong views on the matters at hand.[6]

The early thirties saw a new generation of writers appear in the *Criterion*: Stephen Spender, Louis Zukovsky, W. H. Auden, Conrad Aiken, Hugh MacDiarmid, Peter Quennell, Gordon Bottomley, Kay Boyle, Louis MacNeice, Caroline Gordon, John Cournos, T. F. Powys, Marianne Moore, André Malraux, and Francis Birrell. In addition, the *Criterion* had been running a series of "chronicles" on music, art, verse, fiction, Italy, Spain, and even for a brief time on broadcasting, which was designed to keep the readers current on these subjects.

The final years of the *Criterion* were characterized by essentially the same format and editorial policy. The issues published new writers, not perhaps as dynamic as when the journal first began, but interesting nevertheless. The last volume, which consisted of only two issues, contained work by John Betjeman, Dylan Thomas, Hugh MacDiarmid, and Henry Miller. The articles over the last four or five years tended to be a little less internationalist in content, although the October 1938 issue carried an article on Franz Kafka and the January 1939 issue published Friedrich Gundolf's "Bismarck's Reflections and Reminiscences as a Literary Monument." Eliot's "Commentaries" dealt with political issues, the British press, and the Nuffield Endowments At Oxford University. There was little indication in the journal that it was winding down.

In the final editorial, "Last Words," Eliot remarked that the coming war and his own exhaustion were the two main reasons for the journal's immediate cessation. There is a nostalgic tone to "Last Words," a recognition that the "European mind" which the *Criterion* wished to reflect was no longer a viable entity; it had evaporated, because, in Eliot's opinion, few writers of one country appeared to have anything to say to the intellectual public of another. As the divisions of political theory became increasingly important, the *Criterion* dealt less with an international audience than with an ever-narrowing insular one. The last vestiges of the original scope resided in the "Foreign Chronicles" and the "Reviews of Foreign Periodicals," which concluded each number of the magazine. With his audience largely gone and his own energies flagging, Eliot prepared to give up the journal he had begun and sustained with so much intellectual vigor. His view for the future of literary quarterlies was guarded but not pessimistic: "It will not be the large organs of opinion, or the old periodicals; it must be the small and obscure papers and reviews, those which hardly are read by anyone but their own contributors, that will keep critical thought alive, and encourage authors of original talent" (18:274). One need not add that the *Criterion* was a periodical that fit all of these particulars. Eliot's own lack of "enthusiasm," as he described it, did not permit him to continue to edit his journal in the manner he wanted it edited. So, amid the increasing violence of 1939, with World War II imminent and the European mind shattered, Eliot stopped the *Criterion*.

Eliot himself has provided the best short assessment of the impact of the magazine. In 1967, almost thirty years after the cessation of the *Criterion*, Faber and Faber issued a collected edition of the full run of the magazine, complete with author and subject indexes. Eliot wrote a preface to this edition, in which he provided a brief history and what was to become his final assessment of the importance of his enterprise. It is a more balanced view than the one he supplied in "Last Words" or in "The Unity of European Culture." In this preface he noted that he had wanted to present the work of both old and new writers, was proud to have introduced English-speaking readers to Marcel Proust, published Lawrence, Wyndham Lewis, James Joyce, and Ezra Pound, and included the work of such young poets as Auden, Spender, and MacNeice. He also mentioned the contributions of both George Saintsbury and G. K. Chesterton. The two aims he always had in mind were to introduce to English readers the work of important new foreign writers and to provide space for longer and more deliberate reviews than was otherwise generally available in magazines. "I think that both my aims were realized," he summed up, "and that the eighteen volumes of *The Criterion* constitute a valuable record of the thought of that period between two wars."

Notes

1. There seems to be some disagreement about the first meeting between Eliot and Lady Rothermere and just exactly who introduced them. See Frank Morley's "A Few Recollections of Eliot," *Sewanee Review* 74 (January-March 1966):110–33, and Robert Sencourt's *T. S. Eliot: A Memoir*, ed. Donald Adamson (New York, 1971).

2. Vivienne (or Vivien) Eliot also contributed several items to the *Criterion* during a brief period from early 1924 until mid-summer 1925.

3. *Times Literary Supplement*, 26 October 1922, p. 525.

4. "Periodicals: *The Criterion*," *Times Literary Supplement*, 26 October 1922, p. 690.

5. Stephen Spender, among others, has noted that Eliot's turn to religion saved him from the kind of political excess engaged in by Pound and Lewis. See *T. S. Eliot/ Stephen Spender* (New York, 1976), p. 51.

6. For more lengthy discussions of Eliot's social and political thought, see Russell Kirk, *Eliot and His Age: T. S. Eliot's Moral Imagination in the Twentieth Century* (New York, 1971); Roger Kojecky, *T. S. Eliot's Social Criticism* (London, 1971); and William M. Chace, *The Political Identities of Ezra Pound and T. S. Eliot* (Stanford, 1973).

Information Sources

BIBLIOGRAPHY

Bergonzi, Bernard. *T. S. Eliot*. New York, 1972.

Boardman, Gwenn R. "T. S. Eliot and the Mystery of Fanny Marlow." *Modern Fiction Studies* 7 (1961):99–105.

Bradbury, Malcolm. "*The Criterion*: A Literary Review in Retrospect." *London Magazine* 5 (February 1958):41–54.

Cox, C. B. "Eliot's *Criterion*." *Spectator*, 25 August 1967, pp. 216–17.

Cox, C. B., and Arnold P. Hinchliffe, eds. *T. S. Eliot, The Waste Land: A Casebook*. London, 1968.

Dobrée, Bonamy. "T. S. Eliot: A Personal Reminiscence." *Sewanee Review* 74 (January-March 1966):85–108.

Donoghue, Denis. "Eliot and the *Criterion*." In *The Literary Criticism of T. S. Eliot*. Collected and edited by David Newton-De Molina. London, 1977.

Freed, Lewis. *T. S. Eliot: The Critic as Philosopher*. West Lafayette, Ind., 1979.

Gordon, Lynall. *Eliot's Early Years*. Oxford, 1977.

Howarth, Herbert. "T. S. Eliot's *Criterion*: The Editor and His Contributors." *Comparative Literature* 2 (Spring 1959):97–110.

Kenner, Hugh. *The Invisible Poet: T. S. Eliot*. New York, 1959.

Kirk, Russell. *Eliot and His Age; T. S. Eliot's Moral Imagination in the Twentieth Century*. New York, 1971.

Kojecky, Roger. *T. S. Eliot's Social Criticism*. London, 1971.

Leavis, F. R. "T. S. Eliot as Critic." In *Anna Karenina and Other Essays*. New York, 1968.

Margolis, John D. *T. S. Eliot's Intellectual Development, 1922–1939*. Chicago, 1972.

Matthews, T. S. *Great Tom: Notes towards the Definition of T. S. Eliot*. New York, 1974.

Morely, Frank. "A Few Recollections of Eliot." *Sewanee Review* 74 (January-March 1966):110–33.

Oras, Ants. *The Critical Ideas of T. S. Eliot*. 1932. Reprint. Folcroft, Pa., 1969.

Peter, John. "Eliot and *The Criterion*." In *Eliot in Perspective: A Symposium*. Edited by Graham Martin. New York, 1970.

Read, Herbert. *The Innocent Eye*. New York, 1947.

Schwartz, Delmore. "*The Criterion*, 1922–1939." *Kenyon Review* 1 (Autumn 1939):437–49.

Scott-James, R. A. "Mr. T. S. Eliot and 'The Criterion.' " *London Mercury* 39 (February 1939):280–81.

Sencourt, Robert. *T. S. Eliot: A Memoir*. Edited by Donald Adamson. New York, 1971.

Spender, Stephen. *T. S. Eliot/Stephen Spender*. New York, 1976.

Symons, Julian, "The Cri." *London Magazine*, n.s. 7 (November 1967):19–23.

T. S. Eliot: Symposium. Compiled by Richard March and J. M. Tambimuttu. Chicago, 1949.

Tate, Allen. *T. S. Eliot, The Man and His Work: A Critical Evaluation by Twenty-six Distinguished Writers*. New York, 1966.

INDEXES

Each volume indexed. Author and subject index by E. Alan Barker in *The Criterion, 1922–1939*, 18 vols., ed. T. S. Eliot (London, 1967).

REPRINT EDITIONS

The Criterion, 1922–1939, 18 vols., ed. T. S. Eliot (London, 1967).

Microform: New York Public Library.

LOCATION SOURCES

American

Widely available.

British

Widely available.

Publication History

MAGAZINE TITLE AND TITLE CHANGES

> *Criterion; a Quarterly Review*, October 1922–July 1925. *The New Criterion; a Quarterly Review*, January 1926–January 1927. *The Monthly Criterion; a Literary Review*, May 1927–March 1928. *The Criterion; a Literary Review*, June 1928–January 1939.

VOLUME AND ISSUE DATA

> Volumes 1–18, numbers 1–71, October 1922–January 1939.

FREQUENCY OF PUBLICATION

> Quarterly, except from May 1927 to March 1928, when *The Criterion* appeared monthly. No issue appeared for October 1925.

PUBLISHERS

> 1922–1925: Cobden Sanderson Ltd. 1926–1929: Faber and Gwyer Ltd. 1929–1939: Faber and Faber Ltd.

EDITOR

> T. S. Eliot.

Charles L.P. Silet

CRITICAL QUARTERLY, THE

During the 1950s, the need for a replacement for F. R. Leavis's *Scrutiny*,* which ceased publication in 1953, became "a common university topic of conversation."[1] In the summer of 1958, C. B. Cox and A. E. Dyson, both young lecturers in English literature at provincial universities, determined to start a new literary journal which would reflect the values of their creative contemporaries and would be addressed to a large audience. In these intentions, as well as in others, the negative example of *Scrutiny* loomed large. Indeed, the nature and character of the *Critical Quarterly* in its early years—it began publication in the spring of 1959—can best be understood as a reaction to Leavisite values and stances. As Cox observed in 1961: "The figure of Dr. Leavis overshadows our literary appreciation for good and ill. Being heirs to *Scrutiny* is a complex fate" (3:292).

While the third issue of the *Critical Quarterly* contained a symposium entitled "Our Debt to Dr. Leavis," there could be no doubt to whom the editors referred in the foreword to their first issue and in subsequent editorials: "Too much can be written, too solemnly, about the critic's 'responsibilities'; . . . he is not really a priest, a prophet, a hero, a saviour or a sage, and he confuses everyone, including himself, if he pretends too hard that he is" (1:3); "A critic or teacher of literature should not spend overmuch time in denunciation" (1:274); "Literature is, after all, one of the civilised pleasures of life, and to turn it into a battlefield for the puritanical and disgruntled is no service"; "his inability to do justice to anything but the very best is [Leavis's] major flaw as a critic" (2:3,

5); "what is dangerous is the assumption that final conclusions can be reached. The desire for certainty, for authority, for definitive judgments, leads both to excessive dogmatism and to the turgidity of thesis-dominated criticism. Literary taste must always vary" (6:7)

In contrast to Leavis's journal, the *Critical Quarterly* aspired to be undoctrinaire, catholic in taste, constructive, "lively and responsible, intelligent and readable" (1:3). The aim was "to make literature accessible to any student with goodwill."[2] The journal's particular interest was in twentieth-century literature, British, American, and European, "for contemporary writers inevitably set us the greatest critical challenge. . . . they throw us back inescapably on our own experience, our own sense of what is true and valuable" (1:3). While *Scrutiny*, started in 1932, "by and large reflected the literary values established by Eliot and the moderns, so our journal," Cox wrote, "was influenced by the assumptions of Philip Larkin, Donald Davie and the Movement poetry of the 1950s."[3] In the late 1950s, Cox was lecturing at the University of Hull, where Larkin had become university librarian in 1955. Larkin contributed poems and reviews to the *Critical* during its early years, and since its inception the journal has followed his poetic development closely and admiringly. Davie also became a contributor, the editors having been influenced by his early critical books, *Purity of Diction in English Verse* (1952) and *Articulate Energy* (1957). In them the poet "is no longer seen as the guardian of T.S. Eliot's 'unified sensibility,' uttering fine sentiments to a small elite of initiates. He is a man speaking to men. And the critic no longer claims special insights beyond the comprehension of the common reader."[4]

Other poets of emerging distinction also contributed verse: Ted Hughes, Charles Tomlinson, Thom Gunn, D. J. Enright, Sylvia Plath, R. S. Thomas, Louis Simpson. Articles and reviews were contributed by critics of emerging distinction: Raymond Williams, G. K. Hunter, Bernard Bergonzi, John Wain, and Malcolm Bradbury. These and other contributors made the early issues eclectic, lively, and fresh. In addition to new poems and articles on both modern literature and major works of the past, there were assessments of postwar authors (Larkin, Hughes, R. S. Thomas, John Osborne, William Golding, Angus Wilson, Thom Gunn, Iris Murdoch); symposia on the teaching of literature, the influence of Leavis, Dickens, "the living theatre," the idea of a literary elite, and pornography and obscenity; analyses of poems; surveys of recent criticism on major authors or works; reviews of new books; and a correspondence section.

The editors' assumption that a journal which aimed "to bring lucidity and intelligence to bear on the whole realm of literature" could attract a large audience and even pay for itself was soon proved correct (2:197). Two thousand copies of the first issue were printed, and a reprint of 1,000 was soon necessary. Circulation rose steadily to around 5,000, where it was to remain for a dozen years, before dipping to 4,000 in the 1970s. Much of the positive response had come from school teachers, and it was not long before the journal and its enterprising editors were to develop ancillary functions with more explicitly educational aims. Since the purpose of the *Critical Quarterly* was "to help people understand and enjoy literature," and since new poetry seemed comparatively neglected, the editors decided to produce an annual poetry supplement, priced at one shilling (1:179). The first of these, *Poetry 1960*, had three parts: a selection of poems of the 1950s; new poems by established poets; and three prize poems by new writers. The second supplement, *American Poetry Now*, "a selection of the best poems by modern American writers," was edited by Sylvia Plath. These and their annual successors sold between 10,000 and 12,000 copies each. Other shoots from the parental stem were the organization of conferences designed to foster among teachers and students a more informed understanding and enjoyment of literature; and the *Critical Survey*, a semiannual publication that addressed itself to the educational needs of the schools and that served during the late 1960s as the vehicle of publication for three substantial "Black Papers" on education, in which the egalitarian excesses of the Labour government were vigorously opposed by a variety of contributors.

The *Critical Quarterly* celebrated its tenth anniversary with a special double issue, *Word in the Desert*, published in hardcover by Oxford University Press. During its first decade the journal had remained true to its original aims (though some numbers had few or no articles on twentieth-century literature). In their introduction to *Word in the Desert*, Cox and Dyson reaffirmed their constructive, undogmatic principles. They recognized in George Steiner's influential *Language and Silence* a post-Holocaust restatement of Leavis's "cultural pessimism" and "myth of decline," and restated their belief that "we are living through a great period of art, that it is worth devoting one's life to presenting, teaching and celebrating this art, and that academic literary criticism can be enormously beneficial to the new reading public."[5]

During its second decade there were some changes of emphasis. In the last number of the eleventh volume, Cox struck a Leavisite note in condemning "the current phenomenon of Pop and Op art, concrete poetry, etc. . . . We detest the neo-modernists' lack of moral purpose, their contempt for traditional wisdom and civilized order" (11:291–92). This opposition to the new avant-garde was continued in editorials during the early 1970s. As the years passed, articles tended to get longer and therefore fewer in number, a process which the editors tried to reverse in 1976 by soliciting shorter review articles. The commitment to modern and contemporary literature weakened and had to be renewed in the late 1970s; this was visually underlined by the adoption of a new, more *au fait* format. Younger critics, who could not usefully be described as the heirs of Leavis, were attracted to the journal; their contributions naturally tended to reflect the methodologies and concerns of the 1970s. This heterogeneity and openness to change did not lead to a loss of identity; it rather bespoke the journal's commitment to undogmatic, pluralistic, constructive criticism and to what in 1976 one of its contributors called "the great ordinary work of literary criticism: the mediation between writer and reader through the provision of relevant context, the witness of disinterested care and catholic sensibility, and the saying of fresh, intelligent and interesting things about literary works" (19:72).

Notes

1. C. B. Cox, "The Editing of *Critical Quarterly*," in *From Parnassus: Essays in Honor of Jacques Barzun*, ed. Dora B. Weiner and William R. Keylor (New York, 1976), p. 135.
2. Ibid., p. 139.
3. Ibid., p. 136.
4. Ibid., p. 140.
5. C. B. Cox and A. E. Dyson, "Word in the Desert," in *Word in the Desert: The Critical Quarterly Tenth Anniversary Number*, ed. C. B. Cox and A. E. Dyson (London, 1968), pp. 2, 5–6.

Information Sources

BIBLIOGRAPHY
Cox, C. B. "The Editing of *Critical Quarterly*." In *From Parnassus: Essays in Honor of Jacques Barzun*. Edited by Dora B. Weiner and William R. Keylor. New York, 1976, pp. 135–46.
INDEXES
None.
REPRINT EDITIONS
Kraus Reprint, Millwood, N.Y.
LOCATION SOURCES
American
Widely available.
British
Widely available.

Publication History

MAGAZINE TITLE AND TITLE CHANGES
The Critical Quarterly.
VOLUME AND ISSUE DATA
Volume 1, number 1, Spring 1959–. (Volume 10, number 1/2 was a double issue.)
FREQUENCY OF PUBLICATION
Quarterly.
PUBLISHERS
Volume 1, "edited at Bangor and Hull," The University, Hull. Volume 2, number 1, Spring 1960–volume 14, number 4, Winter 1973: Oxford University Press, Amen House, Warwick Square, London, EC4. Volume 15, number 1, Spring 1973–: Manchester University Press, Oxford Road, Manchester MlE 9PL.
EDITORS
C. B. Cox and A. E. Dyson. D. J. Palmer was acting editor for volume 6, number 4 and volume 7, numbers 1 and 2. Since 1978 the journal has been edited by a

board composed of J. R. Banks, C. B. Cox, A. E. Dyson, W. Hutchings, and D. J. Palmer.

Kerry McSweeney

D

DECACHORD, THE

Founded in 1924—a year in which modernism burst vigorously upon the literary consciousness of even the most conservative men and women of letters—the *Decachord* was committed to a very traditional, some might say reactionary, critical posture. The traditional attitude of Georgian poets toward versification was being attacked critically on both sides of the Atlantic; and astute literary commentators were beginning to think that the modernist experiments in the arts would alter permanently the ways future writers would look at the world. Against this belief, the *Decachord* stubbornly set its sights on fostering a sense of continuity with the past, looking back as far as classical antiquity for poetic models. Its founding editor, Charles John Arnell, undertook an explanation of the magazine's policy in the first editorial essay, "What Poetry Is" (no. 1:2). Poetic "wit," he argued, is the "sophistication" that permits a poet to select, from the vast resources of poetry produced in the past, those tried and true strategies best suited to the poet's own temperament and times. While weakly conceding that "each generation of poets must find a new mode of expression," Arnell contended that to relish discontinuity for the sake of discontinuity is always simply and outrageously bad mannered. The *Decachord*'s mission would be to encourage poets to produce "song" on the old, familiar themes (the wonders of nature, the virtues of optimism, and so on), composed, of course, in traditional verse forms.

A native of Wessex, Arnell eventually succeeded in gathering around him a quite sizeable coterie of regional poets. Prior to the *Decachord*, he had founded (in 1917) another serial publication, *Poetry: A Magazine of Verse, Comment, and Criticism*, which later "under the name of *Poetry and the Play* became the organ of the Poetry League" (no. 31:2). Besides devoting himself to the production of these literary periodicals, Arnell authored two volumes of verse, compiled at least four regional poetry anthologies, and published a students' handbook on prosody. When he began the *Decachord*, Arnell was at retirement age, and his physical frailty may account for the magazine's faltering publication schedule in its early days. Arnell bore "the entire burden, both editorial and managerial, as well as [the] pecuniary sacrifice" necessary to keep the venture afloat (no. 29: Editor's Note). And when the *Decachord* changed editorial hands in mid–1931, it was not for lack of subscribers but because Arnell was too infirm to manage the labors involved.

Given Arnell's devotion to his native soil, it is no surprise that the *Decachord* served initially as a showcase for "the best work" being done by the poets of England's "West Country"—the regions of Cornwall, Somerset, Devon, and the Isle of Wight. As he put it,

The scenery of the West has a peculiarity not found to the same extent in any other part of England, that of exhibiting side by side an excessive luxuriance and fertility with austere moorlands and all the bleak majesty of the Unsown. The charm of Devon lies as much in Dartmoor as in its leafy woodlands and its high embowered lanes.[1]

Arnell generally felt, too, "that the beautiful West Country [had] inspired even in those commercial and materialistic days, much work that the world should not willingly let die." He believed in his "stalwarts," the contributors to the *Decachord*, and elsewhere wrote that "the poetic accomplishment of some of them excels, in beauty and charm, a great deal that has become familiar under the authorship of certain famous names."[2] In a sense, his was a true conservationist's project. If the magazine's title suggests a deliberate effort to recall ancient songs, like the psalms David composed on a pastoral lyre, it also hints at the bucolic nature of its newer contents.

Arnell's emphasis on the richly historic English countryside and English experience (the Arthurian legends and "the spacious days of Elizabeth"),[3] on the traditional mode of versification, and on a selection of lyrical poems in a somewhat discursive, and not infrequently didactic, mode creates the impression that this magazine is dedicated to the formation and education of "taste" conceived of in an old-fashioned, Addisonian sense. That impression is reinforced by certain features of the magazine: its regular sponsorship of poetry contests, for which the editor set the prosodic and thematic constraints; frequent essays explaining in fairly general terms the value of poetry; and a regular section featuring the editor's brief responses to the technical and tonal problems of poems submitted to him for criticism.

Obviously, Arnell never meant for his periodical to cater to the tastes of the avant-garde or the intelligentsia. In her essay "The Modern Spirit in Poetry," Eleanor Hebblethwaite expresses the magazine's basic premise:

According to the orthodox poets and critics, poetry is ageless and timeless. Therefore *modern* poetry cannot exist. Contemporary poetry there must always be, but as soon as verse of any age makes a claim to be modern it ceases to be poetry, for poetry deals with that part of human experience which does not change with time or fashion. [No. 2:142]

Another of the magazine's "stalwarts" objects to modernist motives: "The primal urge of this poetry is usually revolt, conscious or unconscious." The same contributor writes: "To sum up, we don't understand it [modernism] and we don't want to" (no. 1:144).

Except for an occasional piece by such popularly esteemed writers as Eden Phillpotts, Ernest Rhys (founder of the Everyman Library), Siegfried Sassoon, Graham Greene, Robert Graves, T. Sturge Moore, and Sir Arthur Quiller-Couch, the *Decachord* mostly featured the writing of a slowly evolving clique. From 1924 to 1932, S. Matthewman and Edwin Faulkner contributed heavily to its pages—poems and essays as well as editorial assistance. The fairly tight circle of regular contributors included William Rowland Childe, Eric Chilman, Leonard Galletley, C. Elissa Sharpley, and Alberta Vickridge—writers who, except for high visibility in Arnell's magazines and anthologies, have not emerged in literary histories of the period. By the early 1930s, a few more regular contributors were added: Stanley Stokes, Herbert Tremaine, Ursula Lock, E.H.W. Meyerstein, Thomas Thornely, and Marjorie Mackesy—likewise only locally recognized. Under the direction after 1931 of Phillipa Hole, the *Decachord* gradually and subtly shifted its interests, so that by the mid–1930s it featured a much greater proportion of works by women writers. Brenda F. Skene, Helen Stone, and Margaret Stanley Wrench contributed many poems; Clara Candlin supplied a stream of translations from the Chinese; and the works of a few foreigners were welcomed—principally the poems of the Yugoslavian Sibe Milicic, the Russian Anna Ahmatova (translated by Princess Sophy Dolgoronsky), and the grande dame of Wichita (Kansas) letters, Kunigunde Duncan. In her editorial essays, Phillipa Hole repeatedly invited her readers to observe the fine qualities shared by poets dedicated to writing within traditional prosodic constraints.

Not surprisingly, the political enthusiasms of "the Pink Decade" had only the most minimal effect on the magazine's poetic offerings. Phillipa Hole discussed Benito Mussolini at length with E.F.T. Marinetti and discovered that Mussolini and Marinetti were "devoted" friends. She attended the left-leaning 1933 P.E.N. Congress in Yugoslavia and witnessed "the confused and agitated scenes which accompanied the withdrawal of the Hitlerite delegates." But her magazine remained staunchly West Country in its attitude. The references to international events to be found in the pages of the *Decachord* were mostly accompanied by asseverations on the universality of the English countryside experience. In January 1933 Hole wrote: "As a magazine born with good West Country ink in our veins and bred near Exeter, we recall our origin with pride and hail the news that a Devonshire man has been awarded the Nobel Prize" (no. 37:1); the man was John Galsworthy. Clearly, Arnell's provincial zeal was not lessened in his successor.

In 1939 Phillipa Hole composed an editorial piece entitled "Poetry and Politics." Without mentioning W. H. Auden, Stephen Spender, Christopher Isherwood, and C. Day Lewis by name, she writes:

> Recently, for several years, the young experimental poets of our decade have been interesting themselves in political ideas: though abandoning traditional models, they perforce meditate long and anxiously, cudgeling their brains to explain to themselves, and to others, how and why politics provide themes meet for poets.

But it is in keeping with the *Decachord*'s philosophy that she adds: "All people to-day are interested in politics, even poets, and the truth is that politics have provided a stimulus for poets ever since civilization began." Her discussion then centers on what is political in the greatest poetry of Dante, Chaucer, William Langland, Spenser, Milton, Wordsworth, Shelley, and Whitman. The editorial position of the *Decachord* is that the "young experimental poets" of the 1930s were definitely out on a limb—both politically and artistically. West Country common sense governs the critical insight:

> The poetic expression of a mood being the most brilliant and legitimate quality of the experimentalists, their allegiance would hardly seem likely at present to recommend itself to any experienced party. Either intellectual balance is still to seek, or they show great singlemindedness in having to a man re-inforced the party which, owing to extreme paucity of numbers, can offer the minimum circulation for their books—stimulating and provocative as these are to the poetic connoisseur. [No. 77:73]

That sort of thinking may have been the editor's basis for having ignored the poetry of the political left. Whatever the case, more urgent preoccupations arose with the declaration of war against Hitler. And the *Decachord* addressed them with renewed determination, if in the old ways.

In the 1940s editorial interest focused once again upon the home shires, the strong bonds of culture and language, and the sustenance a nation derives in wartime from its songs. Editorial rhetoric swelled: "Already poets, freed from uncertainty by a certainty however cataclysmic, should have something to feel, and something to sing"; "A common language, a common literary tradition, is one of the strongest bonds of race, and sometimes it has proved to be a factor in the moral history of the world" (no. 78:92–93). Although editorial rhetoric swelled, in the poems themselves diction and imagery, reference and allusion contracted to understatement. Nevertheless, it is possible to reconstruct a history of prevalent wartime emotions by reading attentively what the magazine published during the war—such poems, for instance, as Ernest Rhys's "To the All-

But 'Impossible She' " (no. 84:92); Mary Mair's "1941" (no. 88:60); M. E. Allen's "Night in War-Time" (no. 88:63); M. C. Sidgwich's "Vision" (no. 93:46).

The *Decachord*'s roots in the English countryside and folkways may account for its longevity; it survived when the *London Mercury*,* T. S. Eliot's *Criterion*, *Isis*, and the *Cornhill** (see *VEA, MA*) went under. The *Decachord* offered the middlebrow English reading public a homegrown collection of simple, little songs when it most needed them. It is difficult not to agree with Denis Turner's assessment of the magazine's manner of helping its subscribers to survive the horrors of war; for survival is effected, as he put it, "by our own occupations and interests, our art, and our crafts, the whole pathetic little box of toys that each of us carries about" (no. 79:5–6).

One regular feature of the *Decachord* after 1932 was the "Notice-Board," an annotated calendar of literary events, most taking place in or near London. Here, in the margins, really, of the *Decachord* appear the names of writers we tend to think of as the center of British literary life at that time: Harold Monro, Alida Klemantaski, Lascelles Abercrombie, Laurence Binyon, Gordon Bottomley, Edmund Blunden, T. S. Eliot, Stephen Spender, Louis MacNeice, C. Day Lewis, George Barker, David Gascoyne, and so on. Occasionally, a brief report may amuse. In 1945, for example, when T. S. Eliot and C. Day Lewis read their translations of Paul Valéry's erudite poems to an audience gathered at the International Arts Guild (to commemorate Valéry's death), the "Notice-Board" succinctly commented: "This proved something of a test for the listening capacity of the audience" (no. 114:67).

From first to last, the *Decachord* bravely dedicated itself, in a sense, to sustaining popular interest in the poetic ideals of the Georgian poets—long after the initial and universal enthusiasm for their poetry had waned. What Ezra Pound deprecatingly called the "Abercrombie element" of Georgian verse (a discursive as opposed to an imagistic mode) decidedly pervades the magazine. Its poetic selections often recall Abercrombie's trendy 1912 review of Edward Marsh's anthology *Georgian Poetry*, in which Abercrombie heartily approved both the Georgians' break from Victorianism and their "determination to undertake new duties in the old style."[4] After World War II, it would have taken an optimist more cockeyed than the West Country was likely to produce to cry, as the *Decachord* had done nearly a quarter of a century earlier, in defense of its old-fashioned taste. The war over, and nearly a year after the Allied forces leveled Nagasaki and Hiroshima and demonstrated "the old earth's" awful vulnerability, the *Decachord*, unstrung at last, ceased publication without so much as a "Brief Notice."

Notes

1. *A West Country New Anthology of Contemporary Poets*, ed. Charles J. Arnell (London [after 1928, before 1931]), p. 7.

2. *An English Lute: A New Anthology of English Verse*, ed. Charles J. Arnell (London, 193[?]), unpaginated "Preface."

3. *A West Country New Anthology*, p. 7.

4. *Dictionary of Literary Biography*, s.v. "Lascelles, Abercrombie."

Information Sources

BIBLIOGRAPHY

Arnell, Charles John. *Random Rhymes of a Vectensian*. Newport (Isle of Wight), 1914.

Phillpotts, Eden. *From the Angle of 88*. London, 1952.

Rhys, Ernest P. *Everyman Remembers*. London, 1931.

Ross, Robert H. *The Georgian Revolt, 1910–1922: Rise and Fall of a Poetic Ideal*. Carbondale, Ill., 1965.

Simon, Myron. *The Georgian Poetic*. Berkeley, Calif., 1975.

Spender, Stephen. *The Struggle of the Modern*. Berkeley, 1963.

INDEXES

Volume 7, number 26–volume 11, number 48 in *An Author Index to Selected British Little Magazines*, ed. B. C. Bloomfield (London, 1976).

REPRINT EDITIONS

None.

LOCATION SOURCES

American

Complete runs: Harvard University Library; New York Public Library; Yale University Library.

Partial run: U.S. Library of Congress.

British

Partial runs: Bodleian Library; British Museum; Cambridge University Library; London University Library.

Publication History

MAGAZINE TITLE AND TITLE CHANGES

The Decachord: A Magazine for Poets and Students of Poetry (cover); subtitle on title page: *A Magazine for Students and Lovers of Poetry*, numbers 1–15. *The Decachord: A Magazine of New Verse, Critical Essays, Reviews, etc.*, numbers 16–30. *The Decachord: A Magazine of Verse*, number 31. *The Decachord: A Magazine for Poetry-Lovers*, numbers 32–119; subtitle on title page, *A Magazine of Verse*, numbers 32, 91–119.

VOLUME AND ISSUE DATA

Volumes 1–23, numbers 1–119, March/April 1924–September/October, 1946.

FREQUENCY OF PUBLICATION

Bimonthly, except 1927–1931: volume 3 contains only one issue (no. 13), volume 4 only four (nos. 14–17), volume 5 only five (nos. 18–21), volume 7 only two (nos. 26–27), volume 8 only three (nos. 28–30).

PUBLISHERS

1924–January/February 1931: Poetry Publishing Company, 64, Fleet Street, Torquay, & 173, Fleet Street, London. July/August 1931–Christmas Issue [No. 30] 1931: The Poetry Publishing Company, Inc., Haven Road, Exeter. 1932–1946:

Phillipa Hole and The Women's Printing Society, Ltd., 31, Brick Street, Picca-
dilly, W. 1, London.
EDITORS
Charles John Arnell, 1924–1931. Phillipa Hole, 1931–1946.

R. Victoria Arana

DOCK LEAVES. See ANGLO-WELSH REVIEW, THE

DRAMA

Drama appeared in July 1919, one month after the first public meeting of the
British Drama League. The ties between the magazine and the league were strong
from the outset and remained strong for the next thirty years, largely because
Geoffrey Whitworth, founder of the league, also founded *Drama* and served as
its editor until 1948. Chatto and Windus, which employed Whitworth as an art
editor, published the magazine every other month during its first year. Since
November 1920 *Drama* has been published by the British Drama League (or the
British Theatre Association, as it has been known since 1972). In the first number
Whitworth identified the magazine "as the official organ of the British Drama
League." Yet he also expressed the desire that *Drama* might become "a high-
class theatrical magazine of interest to the general public." "We hope that *Drama*
may be the means of putting every member of the League in touch with the best
thought about things pertaining to the theatre. And to this end it is essential that
the magazine should be conducted in a free spirit, not as a mouthpiece of a
particular organization" (1:31).

Under Whitworth's editorship *Drama* was first published as a thirty-two page
bimonthly, then became a monthly that grew from eight to twenty pages between
1920 and 1939: it survived the war years as an "occasional bulletin" and in the
summer of 1946 assumed its present shape as a quarterly. Throughout Whitworth's tenure the role of *Drama* as official organ of the league took precedence
over its offerings to the general public. As a monthly, the magazine's coverage
expanded to keep pace with the growth in the league's membership (5,000 strong
by 1925) and in the scope of its theatrical activities. In addition to publishing
regularly a column of news from and about league members and affiliated societies, *Drama* also printed the league's membership lists, its annual reports,
and the minutes of its annual meetings. Each year after 1927, when the league
inaugurated its National Festival of Community Drama, *Drama* devoted one
monthly number (seventeen of twenty pages) to a listing of the festival's plays
and players. During the 1920s and 1930s league subcommittees were actively
engaged in other projects that were discussed frequently in reports and notes in
the magazine: the league's theatrical library, schools of acting and production,
annual theater conferences, drama in education, and community theater. All in

all, *Drama* provided a full account of league affairs and of developments in the amateur theater in England between World War I and World War II.

During this interwar period the pages of *Drama* were not given over exclusively to the burgeoning community theater movement. The magazine provided a forum for the discussion of issues of importance to amateurs and professionals alike. The question of the dramatist's right to fees for amateur productions generated lively debate, in which A. A. Milne and Bernard Shaw participated (n.s. 7:26–27; n.s. 12:34–37; n.s. 16:55). Shaw also registered his opposition to Sunday theater openings (n.s. 9:139), another issue discussed in the magazine. Yet no issue received more attention than the establishment of the national theater, one of Whitworth's primary objectives in founding the league. *Drama* not only recorded the vicissitudes of the crusade but actively supported the cause until the passage of the National Theatre Bill in 1951. The most intense campaigning took place between July 1929 and December 1930 in articles and testimonials by Harley Granville-Barker, Shaw, Whitworth, and many others. In December 1929 *Drama* published a "Special National Theatre Number" which was intended, as Whitworth put it, "to register our support of . . . the foundation of a National Theatre" (n.s. 8:33).

While the contents of *Drama* between 1919 and 1939 frequently followed the agenda of the British Drama League, the magazine did publish notes on plays and playwrights "of interest to the general public," and particularly to students of dramatic literature. There were many review-articles as well as pieces reprinted from other publications or transcribed from speeches. Regardless of source or format, they are more accurately described as notes, since they are rarely longer than two pages. Notes appear on the form and theory of drama, including Gordon Bottomley, "A Note on Dramatic Poetry" (n.s. 6:146–48); Malcolm Muggeridge, "The Impossibility of a Romantic Revival in Drama" (n.s. 10:114–16); Angus Wilson, "The Three Unities" (n.s. 13:87); and T. S. Eliot, "The Future of Poetic Drama" (n.s. 17:3–5). Drama in other media also received attention: "Radio Drama and Its Critics" (n.s. 10:122–24); "Shakespeare on the Wireless" (n.s. 12:69–70); "Radio Drama" (n.s. 13:61–62); "Cinema v. Theatre" (n.s. 12:115–16); and "Television and Drama" (n.s. 16:119–20). There was more discussion of modern dramatists than old masters: G. B. Shaw (n.s. 2, no. 13:2–3); Luigi Pirandello (n.s. 4:41–42; n.s. 5:90); Eugene O'Neill (n.s. 5:34–35); Henrik Ibsen (n.s. 6:98–101); John Galsworthy (n.s. 8:76); Arnold Bennett (n.s. 9:117–18); J. M. Barrie (n.s. 14:97–98; n.s. 17:87–89). Edward Gordon Craig wrote "Tolstoy and Shakespeare" (n.s. 10:18–20), and Montague Summers contributed "The Censorship of Restoration Plays" (n.s. 2, no. 8:57–59). Yet the most engaging commentary on old drama appeared between May 1925 and April 1926 in "The Theatre of the Past," a series of "research notes" by Allardyce Nicoll on the history of drama and theater (n.s. 3:22). *Drama* showed more interest in the German theater than in any other foreign drama and even printed translations of essays by two German playwrights—Hermann Sudermann's "Drama of Yesterday and To-Day" (n.s. 7:50–51) and Ernst Toller's "As Others See Us" (n.s. 13:50–52).

During World War II *Drama* was reduced to eight pages and published as *War-Time Drama*, "an Occasional Bulletin from the British Drama League." Between October 1939 and February 1946 the contents of the magazine reflected the contributions of theater people to the war effort as well as the deprivations they and the theater suffered. As a sampling of the titles of notes and news items suggests, *War-Time Drama* stressed the importance of producing and reading plays to bolster the morale of the troops and the folks at home: "British Equity and the War," "Drama in the Reception Centers," "Entertaining the Troops," "Festivals in Wartime," "Drama de Profundis," "The British Theatre Carries on in America," "Bolshoy Theatre Defies the Siege," "Play-Readings for the Black-Out," "Soldier Amateurs," "Munition Hostel Drama," "The Theatre in Liberated Belgium," "—And in a Prison Camp." Two problems, aggravated by war conditions, were discussed at some length: the competition between amateur and professional actors during a period of drastically reduced theatrical activity and the need to maintain standards in choosing plays for production. In its thirty-nine numbers *War-Time Drama* carried out the mission "For Victory" that Whitworth accepted for the magazine in 1939: "It will be our privilege to open its columns to news or helpful criticism of every kind of stage activity, whether professional or amateur, which has for its prime object the heartening of our people for their great task, the maintenance of their good humour, their courage, and their will to victory" (no. 1:1).

Interim Drama, the last of *Drama*'s bulletins, was published in February 1946 and carried Whitworth's prospectus for a "completely new version of the magazine." He claimed once again that *Drama* would "entertain and instruct" the "general public . . . who form the theatre audience"—while continuing to "publish news of our affiliated societies" and a "good proportion of articles directly helpful to amateur producers and the like" (no. 39:1). Whitworth also promised that the "new version" would "provide what has been lacking in dramatic journalism, a worthy review of the theatrical scene at home, with constant allusion to the theatre abroad" (no. 39:1). *Drama* kept Whitworth's promise and became a "worthy review of the theatrical scene," but only with the direction and innovations provided by the three editors who succeeded him—E. Martin Browne (1948–1957), Ivor Brown (1957–1967), and Walter Lucas (1968–1980). Under these men the magazine spoke less for or about the league and more about the literature of the theater, plays, and playwrights.

The most significant change in *Drama* during E. M. Browne's term as editor was the rise in the quality and prominence of its book reviews. A column devoted to theatrical publications and variously titled the "Month's Book List," the "Month's Books," and "Recent Books" was written between 1925 and 1932 by Norman Marshall and between 1932 and 1945 by F. Sladen-Smith. Only one or two pages long, the column provided brief notices—not reviews—of new books. After the war the column reappeared with a new title, "Theatre Bookshelf," and enlisted more writers, but there was little improvement in its contents until 1948, when Browne became editor and set an example with his own reviews. By the end of the 1950s substantial review essays offering critical judgments and commentary had become more common in the "Theatre Bookshelf." The new importance attached to book reviews was signaled in the number for Spring 1950 (n.s. no. 16) which for the first time printed the titles of reviews and the names of reviewers in the table of contents. In addition to E. M. Browne and Ivor Brown, who also became a regular reviewer, the better known writers for "Theatre Bookshelf" in the 1950s and 1960s included more scholars than journalists: Anne Ridler, W. M. Merchant, Frederick S. Boas, J. C. Trewin, Hugh Hunt, C. B. Purdom, Janet Leeper, Allardyce Nicoll, E. F. Watling, and W. Bridges-Adams. J. C. Trewin continued to write book reviews in the 1970s and 1980s, and he was joined by many of the leading dramatic critics of the modern age: John Russelll Taylor, John Russell Brown, John Peter, Ronald Hayman, Martin Esslin, Clive Barker, J. W. Lambert, Katharine Worth, James Roose-Evans, David Thompson, John Lahr, and Richard Findlater. Since 1965 *Drama*'s reviews have been cited in the *Book Review Index*.

In an editorial in 1982 Giles Gordon could state as a matter of fact that *Drama* was, "to a considerable extent, a journal of theatrical record" (n.s. no. 145:1). Gordon was referring to the magazine's extensive coverage of "exciting work being staged throughout the country—as well as abroad" (n.s. no. 145:1). During its first thirty years, however, *Drama*'s play reviews were no better than its book reviews. In 1919 the magazine touted its "review" column as a "causerie on the London State . . . giving an opportunity for eminent dramatic critics of various schools of thought to express their unrestrained opinions" (1:54). Yet until the late 1940s and early 1950s *Drama* provided only skimpy notices of London productions, squeezed together on a page or a page and a half that left little space for "unrestrained opinions." William Archer, highly esteemed as a veteran critic, wrote the notices for the magazine's first number (1:25). Thereafter, occasionally until 1925 and then regularly throughout the 1930s, a group of London journalists, including several "eminent dramatic critics," took turns as guest reviewers: E. A. Baughan, S. R. Littlewood, Percy Allen, G. W. Bishop, Hubert Griffith, J. T. Grein, Ivor Brown, C. B. Purdom, Stephen Williams, and A. E. Wilson. A freer expression of judgments is discernible in reviews written by Clifford Bax, Peter Forster, and several others at the end of the 1940s.

But it was J. W. Lambert, a literary editor and drama critic for the *Sunday Times*, who from 1951 developed "Plays in Performance" into a first-rate column of criticism. He reviewed London productions for the quarterly for twenty-five years and managed to increase the review section to ten pages by 1964—evidently with the blessing of Ivor Brown, the editor at the time. Shortly after Walter Lucas became editor, the format for reviews was revised, and two new critics joined Lambert in writing "Plays in Performance": Eric Shorter, who began covering productions in the "Regions" in 1969, and Randall Craig, who started filing reports on the experimental or "fringe" theater in 1970. "Plays in Performance" expanded again in 1977 to make room for "Hobson's Choice" by Harold Hobson, who came to *Drama* after thirty years as drama critic for the *Sunday Times*. By 1981 "Plays in Performance" had grown to twenty-six pages and featured "Hobson's Choice," separate reviews of radio and television drama, commentary on the London stage by John Russell Taylor, and reviews of productions in the "Regions" and on the "Fringe." In the 1970s *Drama* was transformed into a "journal of theatrical record" without rival.

The impressive advances in the reviewing of books and plays were indicative of a more fundamental change in *Drama* following the war. The magazine's attention shifted gradually but surely from the amateur to the professional stage, and the reviews, notes, and articles published between 1950 and 1983 confirm that, increasingly, the play and the playwright became the magazine's primary topics. However, with few exceptions, the drama and dramatists of earlier ages were ignored in postwar *Drama* just as they had been ignored in Whitworth's time. There were two notes by John Klein—"Was Mercutio Christopher Marlowe?" (n.s. no. 60:36–39) and "Byron's Neglected Plays" (n.s. no. 63:34–36)—and three articles by Hovhanness Pilikian—"Comedy in Greek Tragedy" (n.s. no. 98:46–51), "The Swollen-Footed Tyrant" (n.s. no. 113:31–36), and "Ancient Echoes in *King Lear*" (n.s. no. 127:25–31). In addition, Neville Coghill speculated about Hamlet's father (n.s. no. 15:10–12), Ivor Brown contributed "Dickens as a Dramatist" (n.s. no. 98:43–46), and J. W. Lambert wrote "Shakespeare and the Russian Soul" (n.s. no. 126:12–19).

A preponderance of *Drama*'s notes and articles between 1946 and 1984 treated the modern dramatist. A memorial, "Tribute to George Bernard Shaw, 1856–1950," was published in the Spring 1951 issue (n.s. no. 20:7–34) and included, among others, essays by Gilbert Murray, Lewis Casson, F. S. Boas, Geoffrey Whitworth, Barry Jackson, and J. C. Trewin. In his brief series entitled "Contemporary British Dramatists," Clifford Bax assessed the careers of James Bridie (n.s. no. 26:10–13), J. B. Priestley (n.s. no. 27:21–23), Noel Coward (n.s. no. 29:25–27), and Terence Rattigan (n.s. no. 30:22–24). There were also notes or articles on works by Gerhardt Hauptmann (n.s. no. 4:18–19), Christopher Fry (n.s. no. 13:6–10), Jean Anouilh (n.s. no. 25:14–18; n.s. no. 60:27–30), Eugene O'Neill (n.s. no. 32:24–29), Luigi Pirandello (n.s. no. 35:21–26; n.s. no. 46:35), Georg Kaiser (n.s. no. 37:18–21), James Barrie (n.s. no. 38:28–30; n.s. no. 56:30–32), Henrik Ibsen (n.s. no. 39:26–29), Eugene Ionesco (n.s. no. 58:35–39), T. S. Eliot (n.s. no. 60:27–30; n.s. no. 76:41–43), Friedrich Dürrenmatt (n.s. no. 60:30–33), Bertolt Brecht (n.s. no. 63:29–31; n.s. no. 72:40–42), Arthur Miller (n.s. no. 74:39–40), J. M. Synge (n.s. no. 90:35–38), August Strindberg (n.s. no. 92:30–35), Peter Weiss (n.s. no. 101:57–63), Edward Bond (n.s. no. 118:28–32), Philip Barry (n.s. no. 121:14–16), Sean O'Casey (n.s. no. 136:22–25), Anton Chekhov (n.s. no. 145:14–15), David Hare (n.s. no. 149:26–28), and Christopher Hampton (n.s. no. 150:21–23). Of special interest are essays and letters written by playwrights as well as transcriptions of interviews and discussions in which playwrights took part: J. B. Priestley, "Some Aspects of the Soviet Theatre" (n.s. no. 1:16–19); Bernard Shaw, "Granville-Barker: Some Particulars by Shaw" (n.s. no. 3:7–14) and "Six Letters from G.B.S. to Dr. Gilbert Murray" (n.s. no. 42:24–28); T. S. Eliot, "Gordon Craig's Socratic Dialogues" (n.s. no. 36:16–21); "A Lecture (1921) by William Archer on Galsworthy, Barrie, and Shaw" (n.s. no. 42:29–37); Harold Pinter, "A Letter to Peter Wood" (n.s. no. 142:4–5); E. M. Browne, "Translation or Adaptation: A Discussion between Elizabeth Sprigge, Ronald Duncan, and Christopher Fry" (n.s. no. 45:53–55); and Ronald Hayman, "Conversation with David Storey" (n.s. no. 99:47–53).

In recent years the editors of *Drama* have taken justifiable pride in the quality and longevity of their magazine. On *Drama*'s sixtieth anniversary Walter Lucas boasted that the magazine had the "most distinguished record and the longest continuing history of any publication devoted to the theatre in this country at the present time" (n.s. no. 134:11), Lucas's claim was substantiated more fully in the early 1980s after *Drama*'s two strongest rivals, *Plays and Players** and *Theatre Quarterly*, ceased publication.[1] By 1982 *Drama*'s circulation had climbed to 15,500.[2]

Notes

1. In 1981 *Drama* added a new feature, "Drama Awards of the Year," a legacy from the lapsed *Plays and Players*, and at the same time adopted the larger page size and glossier finish of the defunct magazine (n.s. no. 139:3).

2. *Ulrich's International Periodicals Directory*, 22nd ed. (New York, 1983), 2:1390.

Information Sources

BIBLIOGRAPHY

Boas, F. S. "The British Drama League and Its Founder." *Drama*, n.s. no. 23 (Winter 1951): 14–16.

Briggs, Frances. "Early Days of the British Drama League." *Drama*, n.s. no. 148 (2nd quarter 1983):26–27.

Dictionary of National Biography. S.v. "Whitworth, Geoffrey Arundel."

Norgate, Matthew. "Now 62 Years Back." *Drama*, n.s. no. 140 (2nd quarter 1981):19–20.

Whitworth, Robin. "The First Fifty Years." *Drama*, n.s. no. 95 (Winter 1969):37–40.

INDEXES

Annual subject index, 1955–1983.

REPRINT EDITIONS

Microform: UMI.

LOCATION SOURCES

American

Partial runs: Widely available.

British

Complete runs: Bodleian Library; Cambridge University Library; Leeds Public Library; National Library of Scotland, Edinburgh; Victoria and Albert Museum Library.

Partial runs: Widely available.

Publication History

Magazine Title and Title Changes
> *Drama*, 1919–1939. *War-Time Drama*, numbers 1–34, October 1939–March 1945.
> *VE-Time Drama*, numbers 35–36, May–July 1945. *VJ-Time Drama*, number 37,
> October 1945. *Interim Drama*, numbers 38–39, November 1945–February 1946.
> *Drama*, 1946–.

VOLUME AND ISSUE DATA
> Volume 1, July 1919–July 1920. New series, volumes 2–17, November 1920–
> July 1939. Numbers 1–39, October 1939–February 1946. New series, numbers
> 1–, Summer 1946–.

FREQUENCY OF PUBLICATION
> Volume 1: bimonthly. New series volumes 2–17: monthly (ten monthly numbers
> each year, October through July). Numbers 1–39: irregularly (an average of six
> numbers each year). New series numbers 1–: quarterly.

PUBLISHERS
> 1919–1920: Chatto & Windus, 97, 99, St. Martin's Lane, London, W.C. 1920–:
> British Drama League (British Theatre Association since 1972): Dudley House,
> Southampton Street, Strand, London (1920–1921)/10 King Street, Covent Garden,
> London, W.C. (1921–1925)/8 Adelphi Terrace, London, W.C. (1925–1935)/9
> Fitzroy Square, London, W.1 (1935–).

EDITORS
> Geoffrey Whitworth, 1919–1948. E. Martin Browne, 1948–1957. Ivor Brown,
> 1957–1967. Walter Lucas, 1968–1980. Ion Trewin, 1980–1982. Giles Cooper,
> 1982–1984. Christopher Edwards, 1984–.

Ted R. Ellis III

DUBLIN MAGAZINE, THE

James Sullivan Starkey began his *Dublin Magazine* in 1923, when the two-year-old Irish Free State was just beginning its struggle against Partition. Officers of the new government had been made to take an oath to the British Crown, a fealty the Irish Republican Army was loath to make. The Republicans viewed those who accepted the Free State as traitors. Civil war resulted with Irishman against Irishman: killings and torturings and imprisonings. A gentle, rather fey poet and essayist and an earnest disciple of George Russell, Starkey eschewed violent partisanship, whether religious, political, or ideological, when he founded his periodical. Russell called him "the literary successor of those old Gaelic poets who were fastidious in their verse, who loved little in this world but some chance light in it which reminded them of fairy land."[1] Unlike another famous Irish magazine, the *Bell*,* the *Dublin Magazine* was in no way political.

The journal was to be literary and international: all literary culture was welcome. The first issue featured the Irish voices of Padraic Colum, F. Newland Smith, Donn Byrne, Seumas O'Kelly, and James Stephens, the French of Gerard de Nerval, a translation into Gaelic of Catullus by Padraic de Brun, and a poem (in English) by Mona Price. There were reviews of Italian, Portuguese, and English books. A review of the literary scene was a feature of "Notes of the Month." One item which caught the eye—and held it—was a short story by Liam O'Flaherty: "Going into Exile."

Seldom would some of the most notable names in modern Irish literature be included. Liam O'Flaherty was usually left out because of his leftist sympathies, Peadar O'Donnell because he was the leader of the Irish Communist Party, Sean O'Faolain for his strident liberalism. Sean O'Casey and Lennox Robinson were two others who seldom made the pages of the *Dublin Magazine*. The *Dublin Magazine* did not want to pillory Ireland and the Irish with self-hate. Ireland's faults—poverty, puritanism, silly Romanticism, showy emotionalism—were so evident that no more journals were needed to hold up an Irish mirror to the world. As the *Bell* noted, there were only two independent, nonaffiliated periodicals in the entire country: the *Bell* itself and "the exclusively literary *Dublin Magazine*."[2] Being nonaffiliated, Starkey could select what he wanted to publish without any pressure from other sources.

Even on the issue of censorship, the editorials cautioned with gentle understatement. The liberals, of course, fought vigorously against censorship; W. B. Yeats and G. B. Shaw, according to Grattan Freyer, founded the Irish Academy of Letters to fight the monster, and both Peadar O'Donnell, editor of the *Bell*, and James Starkey—each at opposite ends of the ideological pole—were founding members.[3] The censorship law of 1928 had nothing to do with politics, theology, or ideology; it forbade only material which was pornographic. The *Dublin Magazine* was satisfied to warn that good and bad were netted alike by the Censorship Board. For since no first-rate writer would agree to judge his peers, judgments would be made by second- or third-rate minds. This would doom creative literature.

The editorial argument was nothing if not perspicacious. In the *Bell* for April 1941, Sean O'Faolain listed the writers who had been banned by the censorship law: George Moore, James Joyce, Sean O'Casey, Con O'Leary, Rearden Connor, Austin Clarke, F. R. Higgins, Francis Stuart, Liam O'Flaherty, Frank O'Connor, Louis Lynch, Elizabeth Connor, Kate O'Brien, Nora Hoult.[4] It is apparent where Starkey's sympathies lay in this matter, but never in his life, apparently, did he join the liberal pack. "One periodical, at least, of a purely non-sectarian and non-political character would seem to be a necessity to a modern country which hopes to voice its artistic and literary life" (n.s. 1, no. 1:1). The *Dublin Magazine* went its serene way, little noting the enormous cataclysms which convulsed the world: the Great Depression of the thirties, the rule of Eamon De Valera, the start and the fighting of World War II, the neutrality of Ireland, even the continuance of Partition. No strident Celticism found its way into its pages. It had no concern with political internationalism, it did not call for Ireland to jump into the world war any more than it upheld any Gaelic Twilight claptrap, nor did it have any shamrocks, harps, or wee folk in Hollywoodish Glockamorra. Withal, it did not eschew the Irish nation, but rather propounded the Irish point of view in art and literature. Nor did it support a parochial or provincial view of its nationality. It also insisted that the material it published should be of the highest quality. Starkey maintained that it would govern itself "entirely in conformity with spiritual principles." It hoped to be hospitable "on the edge of the future for gathering together of . . . poets, story tellers . . . essays . . . economics, craft, science" (n.s. 1, no. 1:3).

Thus the less strident L. A. G. Strong, Michael Scot, Frank O'Connor, R. L. Megroz, F. R. Higgins, Michael McLaverty, George Fitzmaurice, Monk Gibbon, and Rhoda Coghill found a warm reception in the *Dublin*'s hospitable precincts. Many other Irish writers found their first outlet, and continued publishing, in Starkey's magazine, which, by the time it ceased publication in 1958, was sold not only in Ireland, but all over the world.

Notes

1. George Russell, *Imaginations and Reviews by A.E.*, 2nd ed. (Dublin, 1921), p. 55.
2. Sean O'Faolain, "1916–1941: Tradition and Caution," *Bell* 2, no. 1 (1941):6.
3. Grattan Freyer, *Peadar O'Donnell*, Irish Writers Series (Lewisburg, Pa., 1973), pp. 105–6.
4. O'Faolain, "1916–1941," pp. 8–9.

Information Sources

BIBLIOGRAPHY

Bennett, Arnold. *Arnold Bennett: The Evening Standard Years: "Books and Persons" 1926–1931*. Edited with Andrew Mylett. London, 1974.

Doyle, Paul. *Liam O'Flaherty*. New York, 1971.

Freyer, Grattan, *Peadar O'Donnell*. Irish Writers Series. Lewisburg, Pa., 1973.

Russell, George. *Letters from AE*. Edited by Alan Denson. New York, 1961.

Zneimer, John. *The Literary Vision of Liam O'Flaherty*. Syracuse, N.Y., 1970.

INDEXES

Original series: each volume indexed. *Comprehensive Index to English Language Little Magazines 1890–1970*, series 1, ed. Marion Sader, (Millwood, N.Y., 1976).

REPRINT EDITION

Kraus Reprint, Millwood, N.Y., 1967.

LOCATION SOURCES

American

Complete runs: Amherst College Library; Dartmouth College Library; Miami University Library; New York Public Library; Ohio State University Library; University of Cincinnati Library; Yale University Library.

Partial runs: Widely available.

British and Irish

Complete runs: Bodleian Library; British Museum.

Partial runs: Cambridge University Library; Manchester Public Library; National Library of Scotland, Edinburgh; Queens University of Belfast Library; University College Library, Cork; University College Library, Galway; University College Library, London; University College Library, Swansea.

Publication History

MAGAZINE TITLE AND TITLE CHANGES

The Dublin Magazine, 1923–1925. *The Dublin Magazine, A quarterly review of literature, science and art*, 1926–1958.

VOLUME AND ISSUE DATA

Volume 1, number 1–volume 3, number 1, August 1923–August 1925. New series, volume 1, number 1–volume 33, number 2, January 1926–June 1958.

FREQUENCY OF PUBLICATION

Original series, monthly; new series, quarterly.

PUBLISHER

New Square Publications, Ltd., Elstow, Knapton Road, Dun Laoghaire, Dublin, Ireland.

EDITOR

James Sullivan Starkey [Seamus O'Sullivan].

William Clarkin

E

EGOIST, THE

The appearance of the first issue of the *Egoist*, in January 1914, attracted attention to the formation of a dynamic, if unstable, intellectual coalition. Dora Marsden, the periodical's first editor, had founded a feminist journal, the *Freewoman*, in 1911. Approached by American expatriates John Gould Fletcher and Ezra Pound, she had agreed in June 1913 to change the name of the publication and broaden its scope. For six months, through thirteen issues, the *New Freewoman* sustained the concern of the earlier publication with challenges facing the "new woman." Under the literary direction of Pound, however, the publication began to show increasing interest as well in philosophical issues and in new poetry and fiction. The flag of the periodical now bore the subtitle "An Individualist Review."

When the shareholders of the *New Freewoman* voted on 23 December 1913 to change the publication's name to the *Egoist*, they confirmed the result of a brief, dramatic evolutionary process. While still concerned with the rights and obligations of women, the *Egoist*, bearing the subtitle of its predecessor, would develop under Pound's insistent influence into a medium for the publication and discussion of "advanced" art and ideas.

First as editor, then, after six months, as contributing editor, Dora Marsden worked assiduously to define the character and the audience of the journal. Her lengthy leading articles on "all the debatable and insoluble problems in philosophy" challenged the preconceptions of her loyal readers and tested their patience. While "stating afresh the ambitions" of the periodical, in a leader titled "I Am," Marsden acknowledges that her writing may often have resulted in "the bewilderment of our readers" (2 [1 January 1915]:2). Spirited responses from readers, published in a correspondence column, testify to the stimulation her essays provided for some.

But a reader of the *Egoist* diagnosed early the publication's problematical split focus when he complained about the division of the paper between two interests, "certain movements in belles-lettres and art" and "the Marsdenian treatment of ethics." "The connection is not so close as to establish any very strong presumption that one who is especially interested in the one will be especially interested in the other," he wrote to the editor [2 (1 February 1915]:31). Pound prevailed. "Damn the man in the street, once and for all, damn the man in the street who is only in the street because he hasn't intelligence to be let in to anywhere else," Pound wrote (1 [15 June 1914]:233). Expressing his contempt for popular reaction to Wyndham Lewis's "Timon," a portfolio of designs and illustrations, Pound voiced the assumption of cultural and intellectual superiority which was to become characteristic of the editorial posture of the *Egoist* throughout its brief but influential run. Assistant editor Richard Aldington would make an engaging attempt to see both sides of aesthetic arguments: "I do not see why new fashions in artistic creeds should compel us to say that simple and happy and healthy works of art are entirely bad" (1 [15 January 1914]:35). But Pound would insist, repeatedly, that the "war" between the artist and the world must end in "slaughter" (1 [16 February 1914]:68).

Assuming a natural antipathy between art and public taste, Pound addressed readers presumed to have enlisted on the right side of the struggle. So, instead of mounting defenses for the fiction of James Joyce or the poems of T. S. Eliot, Pound supported their publication, then developed carefully measured, paradoxically subdued appreciations of their distinctive strengths.

It was as a source of imagist poetry, of unconventional fiction, and of solid critical statements that the *Egoist* attracted and held the attention of most of its subscribers. During its six-year life, the journal printed poems by such poets as H.D., D. H. Lawrence, Amy Lowell, William Carlos Williams, and Marianne Moore. French poems, as well as translations from French, German, and Italian, also appeared. Most striking were the serial appearances of Joyce's *A Portrait of the Artist as a Young Man* and of parts of *Ulysses*. Attempts by Pound and others to define, describe, and defend imagism provided a useful balance in the periodical's early issues to reviews of particular imagist works.

When T. S. Eliot became literary editor of the *Egoist* in 1917, following Richard Aldington's departure for the war, readers were able to observe, issue by issue, the development of a brilliant young critic's principles and priorities. In brief reviews of new works, most of which he did not admire, Eliot began to articulate his prerequisites for successful writing and his priorities as a critic. For instance, while giving some attention to *Strange Meetings*, a new book of poems by Harold Monro, Eliot manages to criticize the provinciality of English poetry in general, to define the difference between the emotional yield of objects in Donne's poetry and those in Wordsworth's, to admit a condescending tolerance for Georgian poetry (a "bypath of poetry"), and to reach a memorable conclusion: "The vague is a more dangerous path for poetry than the arid" (4[September 1917]:118).

"Tradition and the Individual Talent," published in the final issue of the *Egoist*, remains Eliot's best-known and most influential statement of the need for broad cultural awareness in contemporary literature. The preceding issues of the *Egoist*, to a considerable extent, show how the ideas which Eliot would continue to argue first took shape.

By the end of 1919, when the *Egoist* suspended publication, its subscription list had declined as dramatically as its costs of publication had risen. But its influence had been felt. Through Marsden's opaque essays, Pound's generous (and not so generous) reviews, the publication of important avant-garde literary works, and the maturing critical competence of Eliot, the *Egoist* through its short life justified fully its subtitle: "An Individualist Review."

Information Sources

BIBLIOGRAPHY

Bergonzi, Bernard. *T. S. Eliot*. New York, 1972.
Gallup, Donald. *T. S. Eliot and Ezra Pound: Collaborators in Letters*. New Haven, Conn., 1970.
Gates, Norman T. "Richard Aldington and Marianne Moore." *Marianne Moore Newsletter* 1, no. 1 (1977):16–19.
Kenner, Hugh. *The Invisible Poet: T. S. Eliot*. New York, 1959.
———. *The Pound Era*. Berkeley and Los Angeles, 1971.
MacKendrick, Louis K. "T. S. Eliot and the *Egoist*: The Critical Preparation." *Dalhousie Review* 55 (Spring 1975):140–54.
Paige, D. D., ed. *The Letters of Ezra Pound 1907–1941*. New York, 1950.
Read, Forrest, ed. *Pound/Joyce: The Letters of Ezra Pound to James Joyce*. London, 1968.

INDEXES
> (*New Freewoman*) numbers 1–13; (*Egoist*) volumes 1–6, number 5, in *Comprehensive Index to English Language Little Magazines 1890–1970*, series 1, ed. Marion Sader (Millwood, N.Y., 1976).

REPRINT EDITIONS
> Kraus Reprint, Millwood, N.Y., 1967.
> Microform: Datamics, Inc., New York, N.Y.

LOCATION SOURCES
American
> Complete runs: Harvard University Library; New York Public Library; U.S. Library of Congress; Yale University Library.
> Partial runs: Brown University Library; Ohio State University Library; Princeton University Library; Stanford College Libraries; University of Buffalo Library; University of Chicago Library; University of Minnesota Library; University of Washington Library.

British
> Complete runs: Bodleian Library; British Museum; Edinburgh Public Library.
> Partial run: Women's Service Library.

Publication History

MAGAZINE TITLE AND TITLE CHANGES
The Egoist: An Individualist Review.
VOLUME AND ISSUE DATA
Volume 1, numbers 1–24, 1 January 1914–15 December 1914.
Volume 2, number 1–volume 6, number 5, January 1915–December 1919.
FREQUENCY OF PUBLICATION
Volume 1, numbers 1–24, 1 January 1914–15 December 1914: biweekly. Volume 2, number 1–volume 5, number 9, January 1915–October 1918: monthly. Volume 5, number 10–volume 6, number 2, November/December 1918–March/April 1919: bimonthly. Volume 6, numbers 3–5, July, September, December 1919: irregular.
PUBLISHERS
1 January 1914: The Egoist, Ltd., Oakley House, Bloomsbury St., London, W.C. 15 January 1914–December 1916: The New Freewoman, Ltd., Oakley House, Bloomsbury St., London, W.C. January 1917–January 1918: The Egoist, Ltd., Oakley House, Bloomsbury St., London, W.C. February 1918–December 1919: The Egoist, Ltd., 23 Adelphi Terrace House, Robert St., Adelphi, London, W.C. 2.
EDITORS
Dora Marsden, editor; Richard Aldington and Leonard A. Compton-Rickett, assistant editors, 1 January 1914–15 June 1914. Harriet Shaw Weaver, editor, 1 July 1914–December 1919. Richard Aldington, assistant editor; Dora Marsden, contributing editor, 1 July 1914–1 May 1916. Richard Aldington and H[ilda] D[oolittle], assistant editors; Dora Marsden, contributing editor, 1 June 1916–May 1917. T. S. Eliot, assistant editor, Dora Marsden, contributing editor, June 1917–December 1919.

Paul L. Gaston

ENCORE

Proclaiming itself "The Voice of Vital Theatre" in each bimonthly issue, *Encore* magazine, first published in 1954, vigorously defended Britain's most original and controversial playwrights throughout the decade after Jimmy Porter's harangues first startled the audiences of *Look Back in Anger* at the Royal Court Theatre in 1956. With evangelical fervor, acerbic wit, and an iconoclastic intensity seldom equalled among British literary magazines since the heyday of Wyndham Lewis's *Blast,** *Encore* set out not only to reshape the form and content of the modern stage but also to reform popular tastes in theater as well. However much the works of such new young authors as Harold Pinter, Arnold Wesker, and John Arden might be deplored and denounced by reviewers in the popular press or scorned by the public at large, *Encore* regularly championed the revolution of which these playwrights were in the forefront. Though sometimes exhortative in its enthusiasm, it provided the foremost outlet of its time for sustained, thoughtful, and detailed criticism of experimental and innovative contemporary drama.

Founded in 1954 as a student publication at the Central School of Speech Training and Dramatic Art, *Encore* was originally underwritten by the school's Students' Association and was described in an editorial in the Winter 1954 issue as a "purely parochial effort" (p. 2). Editorial responsibilities were shared among a number of students, including Robert Pinker (described in the same editorial as "the original volition for this magazine"), Clive Goodwin, Vanessa Redgrave, Antony Ferry, Judy Wright, and Diana Harker. Struggling to build a subscription list of 500 during the first two years, *Encore* gained increasing attention with such articles as Sean O'Casey's assessment of *Waiting for Godot* and Eli Wallach's discussion of the then controversial Actors' Studio in New York and its experimentation with Stanislavskian "method." Attention given the magazine by Kenneth Tynan in the *Observer* widened public awareness of its offerings, and it soon gained autonomy (and a bimonthly rate of publication) under its business manager and patron, Owen Hale. Expenses for issue 7—featuring reportage on an *Encore*-sponsored symposium on the need for a national theater, with participants including Tynan, Tyrone Guthrie, and Peter Hall—were underwritten by Carolyn Green, whose play *Janus* was a popular success of the day. Such popular successes were hardly the primary interest of *Encore*, however; its fervor and sometimes strident idealism remained undiminished from the days of its inception as a student publication, as it sought to provide a corrective not only for the stage itself but for the audiences and critics as well.

Nowhere was the scorn of *Encore*'s writers more relentlessly and unstintingly targeted than on the stolid revivals and bland popular fare that were regularly offered in the theaters along Shaftesbury Avenue during the mid-1950s and early 1960s. The principal problem, as Julian More contended in early 1958, was theater's tendency toward "living in the past. Shakespeare-worship is paralleled by Novello-worship and a terrible nostalgia for secret hearts, roses and flowers, and a plethora of phony aristocrats" (no. 12:38). Several months earlier, David Watt had complained of currently popular plays that were "as remote [from contemporary life] . . . as an evening's recitation in ancient Rome and not quite as convulsing," while numerous others "appear[ed] to have been written by the inhabitant of one penthouse in Knightsbridge for the amusement of the girl in the flat below" (no. 10: [35]). Without radical change, the English theater would soon receive "an hygienic, expensive, and exceedingly tasteful burial" at a suitably fashionable crematorium, Watt suggested (no. 10: [35]). Even six years later, Charles Marowitz (then one of *Encore*'s editors) complained that the central problem was "not only the crusty old playwrights, the Rattigans, Christies, and Duncans, but the entire diction of that theatre . . . which begs to be annihilated" (no. 45:6). Inveighing against such authors' "insidious influence," he concluded that the essential problem of contemporary theater was "the language they have hardened, the patterns they cause to be repeated, [and] the creaking stagecraft they have dignified and entrenched" (no. 45:6).

To some of *Encore*'s writers, even the theaters themselves seemed hopelessly outmoded relics of the Victorian and Edwardian periods, physical embodiments of values (architectural, social, dramatic, literary, and moral) to which self-consciously contemporary young playwrights were deliberately and defiantly unattuned. Thus, as Alfred Emmet complained in 1957, authors who were "tired of Great Grandmother's theatre" needed a more contemporary stage for which to write (no. 11: [44])—though no such thing existed at the time. Though *Encore* consistently opposed the destruction of numerous theaters by commercial property developers (primarily because such demolition meant the loss of yet another outlet for the creative artists involved in theater productions of *any* kind), the need for additional, more functionally designed stages that could accommodate innovative, more challengingly conceived plays remained a recurrent concern.

Predictably, the audiences that filled such theaters and supported such plays also came under frequent attack in the pages of *Encore*—as did the critics (often cited by name) who praised such offerings. Scorning alike the charabanc crowds of tourists and the undemanding theater-goers seeking only a "good night out," *Encore*'s writers shared Lindsay Anderson's detestation of "passive" audiences—those who seek merely facile diversion, vicarious emotional gratification, or cultural reassurance. In their place, Anderson and others sought "audiences who come, not with the passive expectation of 'entertainment,' not just with mouths wide open for another slab of minority culture, but themselves prepared to give something, to work, with minds open and alert, themselves creative" (no. 11: [13]). Yet, as Anderson conceded, such an audience did not then exist in London, and even the English Stage Company at the Royal Court (where Britain's most innovative plays were regularly offered) could build no core audience on which it could consistently rely.

There was, therefore, an urgent need to develop a new audience, attracting it away from the television and movie screens by offering a form of theater that would address contemporary realities in bold and meaningful new ways; yet the plays that attempted to do just this met all too frequently a hostile reception from reviewers in the popular press, whom *Encore* termed "the *critici infallibombasts*" (no. 10: [41]). Accordingly, the author of an unsigned editorial in 1964 lamented the lack of worthwhile drama criticism in London's daily, weekly, and monthly press and complained that its reviewers were "about as penetrating as an Indian-rubber knife, and as stimulating as three-day-old, caffeine-free, sugarless coffee re-heated over a wet wick" (no. 45:4). *Encore*, of course, provided the much-needed alternative.

Notwithstanding its famous excoriations, *Encore* was equally vigorous in defending the "new" drama and in articulating its goals: a theater of "commitment" and "engagement," concerned with—and commenting seriously on —contemporary social issues through not only a new (and politically leftist) perspective based in the working class but a new poetry as well. The paradigm for such a theater was the Berliner Ensemble under Bertolt Brecht, for whom the writers for *Encore* held an almost adulatory esteem. Alongside Kenneth

Tynan, who, more than any other critic, fostered an appreciation of Brecht's work in Great Britain, *Encore* found in his work an embodiment of the social commitment, the strong artistic conception, the innovative dramatic techniques, and the type of new demands on the audience that would, they hoped, characterize England's own "theatre of commitment" as well. "Vital Theatre," John Arden argued, "consists of plays which must be organic events—[which must] get hold of their audiences by laughter, by pain, by music, dancing, poetry, visual excitement, rhythm: and occupy not merely the minds of the people . . . but their stomachs and loins as well" (no. 20:42). It would be, Lindsay Anderson suggested, "a theatre which relates to life rather than to culture" (no. 11: [13]); its audience would "come to the theatre to work—not just to sit, and be 'absorbed,' made to laugh or cry by an expert machine, being 'entertained.' . . . Not school of Vilar, you see, but school of Brecht" (no. 11: [12])—no matter how discomforting such presentations might be to audiences that were accustomed to more conventional theatrical fare and less than receptive to full and frank presentations of contemporary life replete with its problems and anxieties, its sporadic violence and myriad frustrations, and the countless injustices against which the Angry Young Men and "kitchen-sink dramatists" tirelessly railed.

With such broadly defined and ambitious goals for the theater and such receptiveness toward the variety of theatrical means by which they could be achieved, *Encore* was remarkably consistent in responding to the widely diverse output of the emerging playwrights of the day. With very few exceptions (most notably Samuel Beckett and Joe Orton), the authors who would later be recognized as the foremost dramatists of their time were first acclaimed in the pages of *Encore*— even when its writers stood alone, as in the magazine's defense of Harold Pinter, whose first play, *The Birthday Party*, was almost unanimously denounced by other critics when it opened in 1958 (and closed after only sixteen performances). Similarly, the works of John Osborne, John Arden, Arnold Wesker, Ann Jellicoe, David Rudkin, Alun Owen, Joan Littlewood's Theatre Workshop, Doris Lessing, Jean Genet, Jean-Paul Sartre, and even Lenny Bruce (who was banned from entering the country) were discussed and defended at length in its pages. In several instances, the magazine's commitment went even further: *Encore* published the first editions of Pinter's *The Birthday Party* and *The Caretaker* in book form, as well as the first editions of Alun Owen's *The Rough and Ready Lot* and Ann Jellicoe's *The Knack*. Even with its constrained budget and its limited staff (which included among its prominent reviewers Penelope Gilliatt, Richard Findlater, Charles Marowitz, and John Russell Taylor), *Encore* quickly established itself not only as the foremost platform for many of the liveliest writers about contemporary theater but as a promulgator of the plays they championed as well. Beginning in 1961, a series of probing interviews also provided significant insights into the works of John Whiting (no. 29), Robert Bolt (no. 30), John Arden (no. 32), Peter Hall (no. 35), Arnold Wesker (no. 37), William Gaskill (no. 38), David Rudkin (no. 50), and Peter Weiss (no. 56).

In addition to its championing of the works of individual playwrights and directors, *Encore* wholeheartedly supported the two major theatrical crusades of its decade: the campaign for a national theater and the movement to abolish the censoring authority of the Lord Chamberlain's Office, without whose approval no play could be publicly produced (though unauthorized plays could be presented in ostensibly private "club" showings which were accessible to anyone willing to pay the nominal "membership" fee at the door in addition to buying a ticket). The national theater campaign, which *Encore* dubbed "The Hundred and Ten Years War" (no. 12:2), had begun in 1848 with a proposal for such a theater by Effingham Wilson, a publisher whose idea gained the support of Charles Dickens and others; it was won at last in 1963 with the opening production of *Hamlet* directed by Laurence Olivier at the Old Vic (a production which, perhaps predictably, received a negative review in *Encore* as yet another stolid instance of Shakespeare-worship). As envisioned by the writers for *Encore*, at least, the National Theatre would not merely preserve the classics of the past in the manner of the Comédie Française but would actively encourage—and produce—new works from the foremost playwrights of the day, while developing the talents of those who were yet unknown. The abolition of censorship, a prerequisite to such development, was the goal of an even lengthier struggle which *Encore* traced back to 1843 (no. 15:5); the reform was finally accomplished in 1968, three years after the demise of *Encore* as a separate publication.

Although the magazine tirelessly campaigned for new and innovative approaches to the theater and acclaimed Brecht's works even before the Berliner Ensemble arrived in Great Britain,[1] its hostility toward the works of Samuel Beckett was extraordinarily adamant and long-sustained. Far from representing the sort of "vital theatre" which *Encore*'s writers advocated, Beckett's works offered a landscape (moral as well as geographical) with no barricades for the engagés to assail. *Waiting for Godot* was reviewed in 1955 by Sean O'Casey as "a rotting and remarkable play" offering nothing more than "lust for despair" (no. 6:7), and it was denounced in an editorial (signed "Osric") as a "snot-ridden lament . . . [being] given wider coinage by emasculated dilettantes" (no. 6:4). Five years later, *Endgame* was decried as "the fantasy of a sick mind" (no. 23:28), and in fact no work of Beckett's received a positive review in *Encore* until Peter Brook's assessment of the New York production of *Happy Days* appeared early in 1962 (no. 23:34–38).

During its later years, *Encore* devoted increasing attention to Brecht's life and works. An entire issue (no. 55) was devoted to reprinting his notes for *Mother Courage and Her Children*; another (no. 51) featured articles on "The Artist on Trial," reprinting a lengthy selection from Brecht's testimony before the House Un-American Activities Committee ten years before—alongside an account of charges brought in New York against Julian Beck, Judith Malina, and the Living Theatre over nonpayment of back federal taxes. However interesting and relevant such matters may have been, they also seemed remote from the concern with specifically British theater which had, from the outset, provided the magazine with its animus (in both senses of the word) since its founding as a quarterly in 1954.

In 1965 *Encore* was absorbed by *Plays and Players*,* the popular monthly which often prominently featured cover stories, photographs, and lengthy reviews of the sort of revivals, musicals, and "star vehicles" that *Encore* had long deplored. Although a number of *Encore*'s writers and several of its features (including the editorial series "A View from the Gods") were incorporated into *Plays and Players*, the iconoclastic fervor for which *Encore* was renowned did not—and perhaps could not—accommodate itself entirely to the more popular, less abradantly partisan magazine. The inimitable "Voice of Vital Theatre" had been muted if not entirely stilled, and its idealistic, ardently sought transformations of the theater itself remain unachieved—as the record-breaking runs of *The Mousetrap, Oh! Calcutta, No Sex Please, We're British*, and other anodyne fare make abundantly clear. Yet even though such plays continue to thrive, and even though the magazine's incipient vision of an audience (and thus a society) that would be transformed through theatrical events may now seem as hopelessly quaint and impractically utopian as the ideals of the Fabian Society at its founding a century ago, *Encore*'s achievements are nonetheless remarkable for all that. Often standing alone against the prevailing critical opinions of its day as well as against the indifference and derision of the philistines, *Encore* was not only "present at the creation" of the revolution in contemporary British drama in 1956; it actively assisted in the birth of the movement through its extraordinary commitment to the new authors, and it continued to nurture their development throughout the early years of their careers. Few magazines have achieved so much in a single decade of existence.

Note

1. According to the prefatory editorial "Presenting Brecht" in the combined issue of *Adam International Review*, no. 254, and *Encore*, no. 8, Eric Bentley came to England

> in the hope of inciting a general "Brecht-consciousness" and to stimulate, if possible, the publication of an authoritative booklet which would collate as much information as was available in English prior to the arrival of the Berliner Ensemble. *Encore* was entrusted with this altruistic mission. ... [and] he and Brecht provided basic articles for a special issue and many of Brecht's colleagues in this country, notably Joseph Losey, Ella Winter, Sam Wanamaker, George Devine, and Donald Stewart, provided much of the background research which was necessary. The project gathered momentum and soon loomed so large that it became evident that a work of this kind would impose an impossible production problem for a small magazine, unless another adventurous publication were ready to join in.

The combined issue of *Adam International Review* and *Encore* was the result of this undertaking, and the issue contains five contributions by Brecht himself ("On Shakespeare's Play 'Hamlet' "; "Practice Scenes for Actors"; "On Watering the Garden"; "The Fourth Wall of China"; "Prologue to 'Puntila' ").

Information Sources

BIBLIOGRAPHY

The Encore Reader: A Chronicle of the New Drama. Edited by Charles Marowitz, Tom
Milne, and Owen Hale, with a foreword by Richard Findlater. London, 1965.

Marowitz, Charles. *Confessions of a Counterfeit Critic: A London Theatre Notebook,
1958–1971.* London, 1973.

————. "What Happened to *Encore.*" *Plays and Players* 13, no. 3 (December 1965):13.

*New Theatre Voices of the Fifties and Sixties: Selections from Encore Magazine, 1956–
1963.* Edited by Charles Marowitz, Tom Milne, and Owen Hale, with an introduction by Michael Billington. London, 1981. [Reprint of *The Encore Reader*
with a new introduction.]

INDEXES

None.

REPRINT EDITIONS

None; selected articles are reprinted in the collections listed above.

LOCATION SOURCES

American

Partial runs: widely available. Among sources having the most complete runs
(from vol. 3) are: Carleton University Library; Columbia University Library;
Harvard University Library; New York Public Library; University of California
at Berkeley Library; University of Chicago Library; University of Colorado Library; University of Florida Library; University of Kentucky Library; University
of Pennsylvania Library. Copies of some individual issues published in 1954 and
1955 are privately owned and were made available in preparation of this account.
Entries in *New Serial Titles* listing complete runs at Carleton University and at
the University of California at Berkeley are erroneous.

British

Partial runs: British Library; London Museum; Cambridge University Library;
National Library of Scotland, Edinburgh; Reference Library, Manchester Public
Libraries; University Library, University of Cambridge; University Library, Uni-
versity of London.

Publication History

MAGAZINE TITLE AND TITLE CHANGES

*Encore: The Magazine of the Central School of Speech Training and Dramatic
Art*, 1954. *Encore: The Magazine of the Students' Association, Central School
of Speech Training and Dramatic Art*, 1954–1955. *Encore: The Magazine of the
Central School*, 1955–1956. *Encore: A Quarterly Review for Students of the
Theatre*, 1956. *Encore: The Quarterly Review of World Theatre*, 1956. *Encore:
The Voice of Vital Theatre*, 1957–1965.

FREQUENCY OF PUBLICATION

Quarterly, 1954–1956, though the (presumably annual) subscriptions offered in
early issues promised three such issues for 3s.6d. Bimonthly, 1957–1965.

PUBLISHERS

1954–1956: The Students' Association, The Central School of Speech and Drama,
Royal Albert Hall, London S.W.7; 52 Hyde Park Gate, London S.W.7. 1956:

Adam International Review, 28 Emperor's Gate, London S.W.7 (no. 8 only; published with *Adam International Review* no. 254 [1956]). 1957–1965: Encore Publishing Co. Ltd., 25 Howland St., London W.1. Encore Publishing Co. Ltd., 41 Great Russell St., London W.C.1.

EDITORS

Robert Pinker and Clive Goodwin, 1954. Clive Goodwin, 1954 (listed as one of a number of associate editors in subsequent issues). Vanessa Redgrave, Judy Wright, Diana Harker, 1956 (also listed as associate and/or assistant editors in other issues). Antony Ferry, 1956. Gordon Rogoff, 1957. Gordon Rogoff and Clive Goodwin, 1957–1959. Clive Goodwin (general editor), Tom Milne (editor), and Gordon Rogoff, 1959–1962. Clive Goodwin, Tom Milne, and Charles Marowitz, 1962–1964. Clive Goodwin, Tom Milne, Charles Marowitz, and Michael Kustow, 1964–1965.

William Hutchings

ENCOUNTER

Encounter, a magazine of literature, the arts, and politics, appeared in October 1953 as one of the family of journals sponsored by the Paris-based Congress for Cultural Freedom (CCF); this distinguished family included at one time or another *Der Monat*, *Preuves*, and *Tempo Presente*. The founding editors of *Encounter* were Stephen Spender, formerly (1939–1940) coeditor of Cyril Connolly's *Horizon*,* and Irving Kristol, who had edited the American periodical *Commentary* from 1947 through 1952.

With the demise of *Horizon*, *Life and Letters*,* and *Penguin New Writing** in 1950, as C.L.R. James wrote in his early comparative review of *Encounter* and *London Magazine*,* "These last years English literature has felt terribly the need of literary periodicals."[1] There was also a political reason for founding *Encounter*, and the catalyst was the initial meeting of the CCF in Berlin during 1950: "The reluctance of the British delegates to join a rhetorical crusade against communism seems to have suggested to the officers of the Congress for Cultural Freedom that British intellectuals needed to be approached more energetically than before. . . . The founding of *Encounter* magazine . . . was the official answer to the 'anti-Americanism,' as it was now called, which disfigured the English cultural scene."[2] Independently, Spender had suggested to John Lehmann, on the termination of *Penguin New Writing*, "Wouldn't it be possible now to start a magazine of all the talents? Couldn't we, say, try to draw up a list of those who are simply the best writers in England and try to get the collaboration of all of these, old as well as new?"[3] *Encounter* was planned as a bi-national magazine, to be produced in London from a British viewpoint, and to have one editor from England, one from the United States. It was to encourage contributors from all nations and have worldwide distribution. On the cover of the first issue "LITERATURE ARTS POLITICS" appeared as a subtitle, although by volume 4 the last word had given way to "CURRENT AFFAIRS." While this avowed political intention occasioned some alarm in British literary circles, Spender and Kristol maintained that they wished to break down the "departmentalization" of literature and politics, and promised to print opinions which dissented from their own and those of invited contributors.

In his "Postscript" to the 100th number of the magazine, Spender presented a further justification for the linking of politics with the creative arts in a journal: "In *Encounter* we have always been concerned with the conditions which affect the kind of culture we live in. . . . Politics is, of course, the most intrusive of the sets of circumstances conditioning sensibility today" (18, no. 1:124). He then addressed the parameters which the editors had established:

> Politically our idea in *Encounter* has been to provide a platform for the greatest possible amount of disagreement within a broad area of agreement. We are agreed that in the present state of the world, democracy provides the basis for individual freedom that is denied under Communist and other dictatorships; and that therefore this freedom should be exercised, maintained, and defended. . . . this means that we have a debate rather than an *Encounter* line. [18, no. 1:124]

The political bias of the magazine was not surprising, given the "devotedly anti-Communist" stance of the underwriting CCF.[4]

The editors themselves represented divergent political views, both through their past associations and their positions in 1953. Spender had joined the Communist Party while working as a propagandist for the Loyalists during the Spanish Civil War, because he "saw the communists as the defenders of freedom against the fascists";[5] subsequently, he had become disillusioned with the left, although he remained liberal in politics. Kristol has described himself as a "Trotskyist" while he attended the City College of New York during the late 1930s, but he had later become a self-styled "Neoconservative." How successful they were in maintaining a balanced editorial position is an open debate; certainly right, center, and left have been heard in *Encounter*, although not in equal proportions.

From the outset, Spender established what was to be the characteristic literary image of *Encounter*, an emphasis on recognized authors over little-known and highly experimental writers. "The political articles," wrote Spender, "were the domain of the American editors."[6] The "Editorial" in the first issue, written by Kristol but approved by Spender, emphasized the political stand of the magazine, and in his article in the same number, "Men of Science—and Conscience," a report on a CCF-sponsored conference of July 1953 at Hamburg, Kristol proclaimed:

> Above all, what this conference made clear was the impossibility of solving the major practical issues plaguing modern science . . . while the world of politics remained half-slave, half-free. It is all well and good for conscientious scientists to worry about the possible misuse of the power they

have conjured up. But as long as one of the world's great empires is obviously intent upon misusing it, there is nothing left to do but conjure up more power, and still more, in the hope of frustrating this intention— but also in the knowledge that this "more" would soon be the common property of friend and enemy, and that they would have to renew their efforts without cease. [1, no. 1:59]

This pragmatic statement by the American editor was both a call to Cold War confrontation with the ultimate aim of overcoming the other "great empire," and a justification for the interim necessity of the arms race. Criticism of *Encounter* over the years has centered on the extent to which the magazine has served as a mouthpiece for American political and military objectives.

If there was cause for unease on political grounds in the first number of *Encounter*, there was also ample demonstration of what was fine in the early issues. Included were a hitherto unpublished excerpt from Virginia Woolf's diary; two short stories by Dazai Osamu; poetry by C. Day Lewis and Edith Sitwell; essays by Albert Camus, Leslie A. Fiedler, Christopher Isherwood, and Denis de Rougemont (president of the Executive Committee of the CCF); book reviews by John Kenneth Galbraith and Spender. In future issues, nonfiction in the form of essays and reportage on political and social topics would take up, typically, 59 percent of the 80–124 pages (96 is the median page count); book reviews and critical articles on literature, theater, film, and other arts would run to about 30 percent; creative fiction, verse, and correspondence a mere 4 percent each. Advertising accounts for approximately six pages in most numbers. The balance varies, naturally enough; for instance, the issue for January 1960 contains "The Trial Begins," a thirty-four page story by a young Soviet writer with the nom de plume "Abram Tertz"; the January 1965 *Encounter* includes fifty-five pages of essays; the July 1980 number has a thirty-five page "Special Book Section." The early numbers have only a few topic headings, varying from issue to issue: "Comment," "Books," "Communications." In July 1954 a special feature, "Letter from Finland," initiated a series of reports of several pages each from various places, including Paris, Holland, Mexico, Vienna, Saigon, America, and Rangoon. Over the years other divisions have included "Men and Ideas," "Table Talk," "TV and Films," "Theatre," and "From the Other Shore." Many early numbers contain a few black-and-white plates, a feature rare after volume 7.

Among the most frequent contributors to *Encounter* have been its editors. Spender not only published poems and essays in the magazine, but personal memoirs running in many numbers under the heading "Notes from a Diary"; these last he considers his best work to appear. Kristol continued to write on political subjects for *Encounter* after his resignation as editor in 1958; Melvin J. Lasky, who succeeded him, wrote for the magazine beginning with the first volume; the four men who followed Spender in the British editor's chair, Frank Kermode, Nigel Dennis, D. J. Enright, and Anthony Thwaite, were all contrib-

186216

utors well before their names appeared on the masthead. Naturally enough, the editors brought into *Encounter* their friends and close colleagues in the craft: prominent in the first fourteen years of the magazine are W. H. Auden, Day Lewis, Louis MacNeice, Edith Sitwell, and various other poets whom Spender had published as editor of *Horizon* or who had appeared in *New Verse,* Penguin New Writing*, and other magazines of the 1930s and 1940s. Kristol had known Nathan Glazer and Lasky at the City College of New York, Saul Bellow and Fiedler at the University of Chicago; *Encounter* also published various writers he had admired in the pages of the *Partisan Review* (sponsored since 1959 by the American branch of the CCF), among them Sidney Hook, Mary McCarthy, Harold Rosenberg, and Lionel Trilling. Lasky, who joined *Encounter* after ten years as the founding editor of *Der Monat*, knew most of the notable European anticommunist writers. Besides Hook and Lasky, a number of the other participants in the 1950 meeting of the CCF also became important contributors, including Franz Borkenau, James Burnham, James T. Farrell, Arthur Koestler, and Arthur Schlesinger, Jr.

Among the frequent contributors on social and political topics have been Raymond Aron, Daniel Bell, Max Beloff, D. W. Brogan, Alastair Buchan, Colin Clark, Herbert Luethy, Dwight Macdonald, Michael Polanyi, Hugh Seton-Watson, Edward Shils, and Ignazio Silone. The economists C.A.R. Crosland, Andrew Schonfield, and, recently, Milton Friedman have appeared often, as have historians George F. Kennan, Schlesinger, and Hugh Trevor-Roper. Few contemporary issues of major significance have escaped discussion in *Encounter*: the Suez crisis, Cuba, Vietnam; Allende in Chile; race relations in America and the repression of minorities in the Soviet Union; the European Common Market; and, time after time, the relations between the two superpowers. Criticism of literature and the arts by Walter Allen, Cyril Connolly, David Daiches, Martin Esslin, K. W. Gransden, Frank Kermode, Malcolm Muggeridge, Herbert Read, Philip Toynbee, and Lionel Trilling, to name just a few of the many distinguished critics, has been consistently provocative in *Encounter*. Book reviewers for the magazine have included Kingsley Amis, W. H. Auden, Hilary Corke, Geoffrey Grigson, Steven Runciman, Bertrand Russell, Karl Shapiro, and Rebecca West. Although the largest number of pages has always been devoted to nonfiction, the list of creative writers whose work has appeared in the magazine makes up a virtual honor roll of contemporary world literature: Bertolt Brecht, Heinrich Böll, and Gunter Grass; Albert Camus, Blaise Cendrars, and Jean-Paul Sartre; Jorge Luis Borges, Pablo Neruda, and Octavio Paz; Doris Lessing, Nadine Gordimer, and William Plomer; Harold Pinter, Alan Sillitoe, and Arnold Wesker; Paul Bowles, Lawrence Durrell, and George Seferis; Boris Pasternak, Wole Soyinka, and Henry Miller; Samuel Beckett, Eugene Ionesco, and Vladimir Nabokov; Saul Bellow, William Faulkner, and Robert Penn Warren.

Special issues of *Encounter* have appeared occasionally. Koestler edited the number for July 1963 (21, no. 1), published later the same year, slightly revised, as a book, *Suicide of a Nation? An Enquiry into the State of Britain Today.*

Other special numbers treated Germany (22, no. 4), Latin America (25, no. 3), and "The New Asia" (27, no. 6). Some of *Encounter*'s best featured subjects ran through several numbers: C. P. Snow's "Two Cultures" essay was published in volume 12, number 6 and volume 13, number 1, and the two following issues contain related discussion by Walter Allen, Michael Polanyi, Bertrand Russell, and others. Excerpts from Koestler's *The Sleepwalkers* appear in three consecutive numbers (11, no. 6; 12, nos. 1, 2), and a pair of issues with sections headed "The Life and Death of Arthur Koestler" (61, nos. 1, 2) repaid the magazine's substantial debt to its leading anticommunist light. Special sections comprising up to two-thirds of an issue began in October 1959 with "Turismo—Inquest on a Holiday Season" (13, no. 4) and recurred at irregular intervals. Notable among these are "New Voices in Russian Writing: An Anthology" (20, no. 4) and "Jorge Luis Borges: An Anthology" (32, no. 4). In October 1969 a "Special History Book Section" (32, no. 4) appeared, and has been followed intermittently through the 1980s by other book sections on "Literature and Criticism," "History and Archeology," "Sociology," "Education," and the like. The thirtieth anniversary issue features Jeane Kirkpatrick, United States Ambassador to the United Nations, in a twenty-five-page "conversation" with George Urban, "American Foreign Policy in a Cold Climate" (61, no. 3).

Those who share *Encounter*'s fervently pro-American, anticommunist stance found and still find it highly stimulating, and the literary criticism also has often elicited spirited response. An article in the *Manchester Guardian* noted, on the appearance of the 100th number in January 1962, "When a British intellectual monthly sells close on thirty thousand copies something is happening which we thought had gone out with the decline of the great Victorian reviews."[7] (In 1964 *Encounter* reached a circulation peak of 40,000.) Criticism of Koestler's *Suicide of a Nation?* number ran from "formidably written" through "lively and provoking" to "lightweight." Nancy Mitford's "The English Aristocracy" (5, no. 3), in which she expatiated upon Alan Ross's division of British society into "U" (upper-class) and "non-U" speakers, provoked not only a rebuttal by Evelyn Waugh but also self-conscious U and non-U cults. Sometimes contributors attacked one another: Trevor-Roper employed devastating irony in "Arnold Toynbee's Millennium" (8, no. 6); Herbert L. Matthews, criticized for his views on Fidel Castro by Theodore Draper, counterattacked in "Dissent over Cuba" (23, no. 1); Richard Aldington replied to K. A. Porter's disparaging article on D. H. Lawrence, "A Wreath for the Gamekeeper" (14, no. 2) with "A Wreath for Lawrence?" (14, no. 4). Walter Allen wrote in 1963 that "*Encounter* has been much more successful in the field of high-brow journalism, polemics and the ventilation of ideas than in discovering new writing,"[8] and the subsequent history of the magazine has borne out his judgment. Among the best elements in *Encounter* have been the autobiographical and critical essays: selections from the journals and diaries of Camus, Giorgio de Chirico, Ionesco, Mary McCarthy, Goronwy Rees, and Spender; essays by Trilling on Santayana (7, no. 6), Auden on Falstaff (13, no. 5), Bellow on "Recent American Fiction" (21, no. 5).

Sometimes the encounters which give the magazine its name were face to face as well as intellectual: André Malraux's "Malraux & de Gaulle" (37, no. 4), Edmund Wilson's "Meetings with Max Beerbohm" (21, no. 6), Golo Mann's recollections of Auden (42, no. 1). A few interviews with such figures as Grass, Sartre, and Aleksandr Solzhenitsyn have appeared. *Encounter* has periodically dipped into the recent past to print selections of previously unpublished letters by D. H. Lawrence, Thomas Mann, George Orwell, Ezra Pound, and W. B. Yeats, and also a short story, "The Torque," by E. M. Forster (39, no. 1). In recent years obituary articles and memoirs on important past contributors have become significant features.

The one major controversy over the magazine did not arise because of anything published in *Encounter* or because of any policy of its editors, but due to the revelation in 1967 that it had been funded, at least in part, by the Central Intelligence Agency (CIA) from its inception through June 1964. There had been rumors to this effect for several years, including one published in the *New York Times* for 27 April 1966, all of them denied, disingenuously by Lasky and somewhat naïvely by Spender. Then solid evidence for CIA backing of the CCF was printed in *Ramparts* magazine (March 1967), naming the conduits for CIA funds. Spender, who had previously believed the claim of Julius Fleischmann that he was the sole benefactor of *Encounter*, resigned his post as U.S. corresponding editor. Kermode, who had succeeded Spender as main English editor in 1966, also resigned. Lasky stayed on as American editor, and Nigel Dennis took over from Kermode. A statement by the trustees of *Encounter*, Sir William Hayter, Schlesinger, Schonfield, and Shils, announced the resignations as due to unexplained "serious differences of viewpoint," and included an avowal of editorial independence: "The main point is that *Encounter* has, since it was established in 1953, enjoyed complete independence in its editorial policy. . . . This was so both before 1964, when the magazine was financially supported by the Congress for Cultural Freedom, and subsequently when the financial sponsorship has been provided—as it is at present—by the International Publishing Corporation" (29, no. 1:[96]). Spender's testimony casts doubt on some of this statement:

> It would be untrue to write that the Congress never tried to influence the editorial policy of *Encounter*, although the influence it attempted to exercise was by no means always political: simply, the people in Paris had bright ideas about the kind of articles we should put in. They also, in the early stages, wanted us to be an organ for Congress activities, with a column devoted to them. Irving Kristol and I resisted this pressure and *Encounter* became an independent magazine.[9]

There had been complaints, however, that *Encounter* was quick to run articles on repression inside the Soviet Union while it virtually ignored racial injustice in South Africa, and did not accord the Third World in general adequate representation. Other critics, even before the CIA disclosures, simply regarded the magazine as a semi-official apologist for American geopolitics.

Whatever pragmatic justifications there may have been for CIA funding of the CCF, damage was done to *Encounter* by the disclosure: a hitherto highly respected voice in literature, the arts, and politics became discredited in many circles. Various prominent contributors ceased appearing in its pages, among them Alfred Alvarez, David Daiches, Richard Ellmann, V. S. Naipaul, Sartre, Trilling, and the two editors who had resigned over the scandal. With Spender's departure went a host of important poets: Auden, John Betjeman, Robert Creeley, Richard Eberhart, Ted Hughes, Day Lewis, Robert Lowell, W. S. Merwin, and Christopher Middleton. By the early 1970s *Encounter* could not claim the same importance in the literary field it had held before. For instance, a comparison of the writers of primary literary importance in volume 20, four years before the resignation of Spender, against those in volume 36, an equal amount of time after it, reveals a definite decline in the number of widely recognized literary figures. In the earlier volume appear Auden, Borges, Michael Butor, Nicola Chiaromonte, Daiches, Eberhart, Gordimer, Graves, Greene, John Lehmann, Doris Lessing, C. S. Lewis, Mary McCarthy, V. S. Naipaul, Kathleen Nott, Plomer, Herbert Read, Alan Ross, Spender, Solzhenitsyn, John Wain, Arnold Wesker, Angus Wilson, and Yevgeny Yevtushenko. Although most of these were still actively writing eight years later, of this group only Wain appears in volume 36, and there are but a few writers of arguably comparable creative stature in the later volume, such as Böll, Paul Theroux, Anthony Thwaite, and the very posthumous Ivan Goncharov. Clearly, from a purely literary standpoint, *Encounter* did not survive the CIA funding disclosure and Spender's departure, but as a magazine of politics, history, and criticism of all the arts with a circulation still close to 20,000, it continues to have considerable value.

Notes

1. C.L.R. James, "Britain's New Monthlies," *Saturday Review*, 22 May 1954, p. 13.
2. Christopher Lasch, "The Cultural Cold War," *Nation*, 11 September 1967, p. 200.
3. John Lehmann, *The Ample Proposition* (London, 1966), p. 75.
4. "*Encounter* across the Seas," *Time*, 5 October 1953, p. 48.
5. Stephen Spender, *The Thirties and After: Poetry, Politics, People (1933–75)* (London, 1978), p. 157.
6. Ibid., p. 163.
7. Quoted by Melvin J. Lasky, "Preface," in *Encounters: An Anthology from the First Ten Years of Encounter Magazine*, ed. Stephen Spender, Irving Kristol, and Melvin J. Lasky (New York, 1963), p. xii.
8. Walter Allen, "From the First It Was a Successful Anglo-American Encounter," *New York Times Book Review*, 10 November 1963, p. 22.
9. Spender, *The Thirties and After*, p. 163.

Information Sources

BIBLIOGRAPHY

Alvarez, A. "Light Is Dark Enough." *New Statesman and Nation*, 29 December 1961, pp. 990–91.

Brogan, D. W. "The Intellectual Review." *Encounter* 21, no. 5 (November 1963):7–15.

Hartley, Anthony. "Review of Reviews." *Spectator* 193 (2 July 1954):36, 38.

James, C.L.R. "Britain's New Monthlies." *Saturday Review*, 22 May 1954, pp. 13, 38.

Kristol, Irving. "Memoirs of a 'Cold Warrior.' " In *Reflections of a Neoconservative: Looking Back, Looking Ahead*. New York, 1983.

Lasch, Christopher. "The Cultural Cold War." *Nation*, 11 September 1967, pp. 198–212.

O'Brien, Conor Cruise. "Journal de Combat." In *Writers and Politics*. New York, 1965.

Spender, Stephen. "Background to the Fifties." In *The Thirties and After: Poetry, Politics, People (1933–75)*. London, 1978.

Anthologies

Brief Encounters. Edited by Goronwy Rees. London, 1974.

Encounters: An Anthology from the First Ten Years of Encounter Magazine. Edited by Stephen Spender, Irving Kristol, and Melvin J. Lasky. Selected by Melvin J. Lasky. New York, 1963.

Encounters with Kennan: The Great Debate. Introduction by Daniel P. Moynihan. London, 1979.

Issue Published Separately as Book

Suicide of a Nation? An Enquiry into the State of Britain Today. Edited by Arthur Koestler. London, 1963.

Encounter *Pamphlet Series*

[While most of the fourteen *Encounter* pamphlets are original publications, five consist of material reprinted from the magazine.]

Chalfont, Alun. *The Great Unilateralist Illusion*. Encounter Pamphlet Series, no. 13. London, 1983.

Crosland, C.A.R. *The Future of the Left*. Encounter Pamphlet Series, no. 4. London, 1960.

Cunliffe, Marcus, and Melvin J. Lasky. *America and Europe: Transatlantic Images*. Encounter Pamphlet Series, no. 7. London, 1961.

Kirkpatrick, Jeane, with George Urban. *Do the Americans Have a Foreign Policy?* Encounter Pamphlet Series, no. 14. London, 1983.

Lowenthal, Richard. *The Points of the Compass*. Encounter Pamphlet Series, no. 2. London, 1960.

INDEXES

Each volume (six monthly issues) indexed.

REPRINT EDITIONS

AMS Press Inc., 56 East 13th Street, New York, N.Y. 10003. (Available in combined reprint/original editions through 1969.)

Microform: Microfilm Ltd., Main Street, East Ardsley, Wakefield, West Yorkshire WF3 2AT, England (North American distributor: Clearwater Publishing Co., Room 400, 1995 Broadway, New York, N.Y. 10023).

LOCATION SOURCES
American
>Widely available.

British
>Widely available.

Publication History

MAGAZINE TITLE AND TITLE CHANGES
>*Encounter.*

VOLUME AND ISSUE DATA
>Volume 1, numbers 1–3, October-December 1953. Volumes 2–57, numbers 1–6 in each volume, 1954–1981. Volume 58, numbers 1–5, January-May 1982. Volume 59, five numbers, with single issues dated June/July (58:6 and 59:1) and September/October (59:3 and 59:4) but carrying the double volume:number designations shown here. Volumes 60–, numbers 1–5 in each volume, 1983–; second volume for each year begins with June issue, with single issues dated July-August and September-October respectively, and carrying a single number designation each.

FREQUENCY OF PUBLICATION
>Monthly through 1981; thereafter ten issues per year, spaced as described above.

PUBLISHERS
>October 1953–June 1964: Martin Secker and Warburg Ltd., published for the Congress for Cultural Freedom. July 1964–: Encounter Ltd.

EDITORS
>Stephen Spender, October 1953–January 1966; thereafter corresponding editor, United States, through June 1967. Irving Kristol, October 1953–November 1958. Melvin J. Lasky, December 1958–. Frank Kermode, January 1966–June 1967. Nigel Dennis, August 1967–October 1970. D. J. Enright, December 1970–February 1973. Anthony Thwaite, March 1973–.

Ian S. MacNiven

ENEMY, THE

Wyndham Lewis took his epigraph for the first issue of the *Enemy* for January 1927 from Plutarch's *Moralia*: "A man of understanding is to benefit by his enemies. . . . He that knoweth he has an enemy will look circumspectly about him to all matters, ordering his life and behaviour in better sort" (no. 1:iv). As he explained in the first editorial, he did not want the *Enemy* to "arrive under the misleading colours of friendship or of a universal benevolence," but to galvanize contemporary artists and writers into order by means of its penetrating opposition (no. 1:ix). Most magazines, according to Lewis, succumbed to the two main diseases of the age—the reference of individual thought to "mass psychology" and a philosophy of "Time," a fidelity to the superficialities of the age (no. 1:x, xi). The three issues of the *Enemy* would escape.

Despite the suggestion that "no politics" might be an appropriate motto for the *Enemy* (no. 1:xiv), its editorial contents immediately recalled Lewis's political preoccupations in *The Art of Being Ruled*, published the previous year. There Lewis had presented his case against liberal-democratic capitalism, which he saw as destructive of the rights of the intellect by virtue of its mass market values. What such a system produced, he argued, was an "enlightened, despairing, liberal intelligence" which is "futile."[1] Later he was to extend this critique, arguing for federalism as an alternative to capitalism and communism alike; it provided the only system that allowed a healthy balance between proper authority and decentralized thought.

The *Enemy*, whatever its political interest, was emphatically a one-man campaign: "There is no 'movement' gathered here (thank heaven!), merely a person: a solitary outlaw and not a gang" (no. 1:ix). Most of the three issues were taken up with long critical works by Lewis himself. In the first *Enemy* T. S. Eliot's "Note on Poetry and Belief" is overshadowed by Lewis's *The Revolutionary Simpleton*, a book-length attack on "the time-mind" as exemplified by James Joyce and Gertrude Stein in literature and A. N. Whitehead, Albert Einstein, and others in science (no. 1:27). The thesis is largely a rehearsal for Lewis's *Time and Western Man*, which was to be published concurrently with the second issue in September 1927. Again a politics is implicit, continuous with that of *The Art of Being Ruled*. For Lewis the time-mind, along with all the other modish European influences, was a "standardized form" of thinking, imposed on the people through various media: "We are the *changed* too much; we are not enough the *changers*" (no. 2:xxxiii).

This editorial is a lucid and (for Lewis) brief distillation of his anger, not against personalities, a wasteful and irrelevant concern in his view, but against an ideology and so a political system: "Standardized thought, or rather information, must in the end result in the disappearance of the individual altogether, and of all spontaneous thinking, except on the part of the controlling sect" (no. 2:xxxvii). Lewis detects a massive conspiracy among educationalists, politicians, journalists, artists, and philosophers to foist onto the people a facile faith in what he calls "the world as history" and "history as truth" (no. 2:xxiv).

In order to provide such a brief, coherent critique, Lewis is himself in danger of ignoring history, a lapse inconsistent with his recurrent insistence elsewhere on the need of the critical intellect to comprehend time and to analyze the present without succumbing to it. But in the *Enemy* Lewis is not eager to burden his argument with particulars, and it is not his intention to credit the class war with an importance equal to the war he is fighting singlehandedly:

That I cannot make myself into a declared "Enemy" of all these vested and intellectual interests, and proclaim myself a champion of all those outside the evolutionist canon, menacing with my bull's-eye, the very vulnerable communications of the pashas of "Time"—without movements

of some kind against my outlaw position, is a foregone conclusion.
[No. 2:xxxix]

The remainder of the second *Enemy* consists almost entirely of the book
Paleface, published separately in May 1929. Known popularly as an attack on
D. H. Lawrence, the work is, in fact, a defense of an ideal: the sovereignty of
the mind. Any celebration of emotion, unconsciousness, and flux in contemporary American and English letters is condemned, whether it takes the form of
a novel by Lawrence, a cult of African art, or the form of the ubiquitous jazz.
Though Lewis spends most of *Paleface* criticizing fiction, he insists, in the
preface, that the essays are not literary criticism. They are

> investigations into contemporary states of mind, as these are displayed for
> us by imaginative writers pretending to give us a picture of current life
> "as it is lived" but who in fact give us much more a picture of life as,
> according to them, it *should* be lived. In the process they slip in, or thrust
> in, an entire philosophy." [No. 2:5]

For Lewis, a central function of the critical mind was to identify and weed out
politics in art, where it has no place. Politics is largely a matter of ideology:
Lawrence is a political writer, and so a bad writer, because he attempts to "slip
in, or thrust in, an entire philosophy," one antagonistic to the autonomy of the
intellect.

The third *Enemy*, published in March 1929, consists almost entirely of *The
Diabolical Principle*, which was to appear as a book in April 1931. Lewis repeats
and extends his critique of Joyce and Stein, begun in the first *Enemy* and in
Time and Western Man, that these writers, in their obsession with time-philosophy,
are not really innovators at all, but Romantics in disguise. In the third and last
Enemy he provides a more detailed critique, the burden of which is that the two
writers' specific affinity is with the diabolism of the 1890s. This prompted the
avant-garde *Transition*, which had been publishing work in progress by Joyce
and Stein regularly, to attack Lewis in an editorial article. The debate did not
continue, for the third *Enemy* was the last, and *Transition* was itself discontinued
well before *The Diabolical Principle* appeared as a book. The three issues of
the *Enemy* span Wyndham Lewis's most vital critical period, which had begun
with *The Art of Being Ruled* and reached its conclusion with *The Diabolical
Principle*.

Note

1. Wyndham Lewis, *The Art of Being Ruled* (London, 1926), p. 84.

Information Sources

BIBLIOGRAPHY

Grigson, Geoffrey. *A Master of Our Time*. London, 1951.

Lewis, Wyndham. *Blasting and Bombardiering*. London, 1937.

Meyers, Jeffrey. *The Enemy: A Biography of Wyndham Lewis*. London, 1980.

Rickword, Edgell. "Wyndham Lewis," in *Essays and Opinions 1921–1931*. Edited by Alan Young. Cheadle, Eng., 1974.

Wagner, Geoffrey. *Wyndham Lewis: A Portrait of the Artist as Enemy*. London, 1957.

INDEXES

> *Comprehensive Index to English Language Little Magazines 1890–1970*, series 1, ed. Marion Sader (Millwood, N.Y., 1976).

REPRINT EDITIONS

> Kraus Reprint, Millwood, N.Y.

LOCATION SOURCES

American

> Complete runs: Boston Athenaeum; Brown University Library; New York Public Library; Ohio State University Library; University of Washington Library; Yale University Library.
>
> Partial runs: Princeton University Library; U.S. Library of Congress; Vassar College Library; Wesleyan University Library.

British

> Complete runs: Birmingham Public Library; British Museum; Victoria and Albert Museum Library.
>
> Partial runs: Bodleian Library; Cambridge University Library.

Publication History

MAGAZINE TITLE AND TITLE CHANGES

> *The Enemy: A Review of Art and Literature.*

VOLUME AND ISSUE DATA

> Numbers 1–3, January 1927, September 1927, March 1929.

FREQUENCY OF PUBLICATION

> Irregular.

PUBLISHER

> The Arthur Press, 113a Westbourne Grove, London W. 2.

EDITOR

> Wyndham Lewis.

Laurence Coupe

ENGLISH

The English Association was founded in 1906 at the instigation of E. S. Valentine, who was then head of the English department at Dundee High School. Its aims were both academic and educational, and it swiftly attracted to its membership many of the better-known names in English scholarship and teaching. From quite early in its history the association embarked on a series of occasional and regular publications—mainly the "Presidential Address"; the *Bulletin*, which kept members and branches of the association in touch with each other; and various pamphlets containing critical essays concerned with literary scholarship or teaching. It was not until 1935, however, that a proposal for a regular journal was mooted. In June 1935 a special subcommittee of the association was set up to look into the problems of falling membership and to suggest ways of revitalizing the association. One of its recommendations was that a special magazine should be started. Although there was some disquiet on the part of the executive at this suggestion, the idea was, nevertheless, put forward by Guy Boas at the Annual Association Dinner on 11 October 1935 and in a leaflet sent to all members. Following this, *Bulletin* no. 81 for November 1935 announced that the first number of *English* would be issued in January 1936, that it would replace the *Bulletin*, and that it would

> record the activities and voice the policy of the Association, and . . . contain literary, university and scholastic features, with special sections devoted to Drama, Broadcasting, Correspondence, and the Association's work in the Empire and Overseas.[1]

The first issue of *English* was duly published early in 1936. Its price was "half-a-crown net," or 12½ pence. By modern standards the magazine was a thick one, containing ninety pages, including a small number of advertisements, all of them from publishers. Though he had been instrumental in launching *English*, Guy Boas was at this time headmaster of the Sloane School, Chelsea, and rather heavily engaged in other activities. So it was that George Cookson, who had retired from the Board of Education Inspectorate a few years earlier, was invited to be editor and Guy Boas became associate editor. Cookson had had a distinguished career in the service of education both at home and abroad, and at the age of sixty-five he agreed to take on this new editorial post and steer the magazine through its formative years. He remained editor until his death in 1949, when he was seventy-seven.

In his editorial in the first number Cookson discussed the scope of the magazine: to encourage an interest in "Drama, Broadcasting, Music, and Art as well as general literature"; to provide a medium for teachers to express their views about the teaching and study of English; and to act as a bond of union between branches of the association. He hoped that in following these aims *English* would attract new members for "an Association that was founded to bring the best attention to the Language and Literature most widely known among men."

Cookson continued to edit the magazine until his death on 24 September 1949; the last number for 1949 came out under the acting editorship of Guy Boas. Boas never felt himself to be more than a temporary editor. For number 48 (1951) he appointed poet and critic Margaret Willy as associate editor, and with the publication of number 56 (1954), she became editor and Boas reverted to the position of associate editor. There were no further editorial changes until 1965 when, owing to the illness of Boas, Willy assumed sole editorial responsibility. Though she followed the general policy of the magazine's previous editors, Margaret Willy introduced a number of editorial changes, particularly that of "Special Numbers." She also introduced a volume index, and it was under her editorship that in 1968 *English* changed to annual volumes. In 1973, though *English* was still under the editorship of Margaret Willy, an editorial advisory panel, composed of William Armstrong, Francis Berry, R. A. Foakes, and Roger Sherrock, was established. With the final number of 1975 (no. 120) Martin Dodsworth became editor, and the following year the panel was disbanded.

A magazine which has survived for nearly fifty years is more than likely to have made shifts in direction during that time. *English* began as, and continues to be, the journal of the English Association; thus, as long as the association itself survives, it has a ready-made readership, for the price of the magazine is included in the annual subscription. *English* has not always had a smooth passage, however. In 1937, its second year of publication, at a conference held in London *English* was attacked on the grounds that it was "lowering the standards and the prestige of the Association"; critics argued that editors should be "promoting English scholarship rather than indulging in journalism" (11 [1956]:62). Considering the contents of the first volume of *English*, this was an extraordinary accusation. While it is true that the magazine was not devoted exclusively to literary scholarship, the standard of most of the contributions was high, and the reviews particularly were of sterling quality. The first number was generally well received, and the *Times* for 28 February 1936 gave six and a half column inches to reviewing it, assering that "it is a well-printed and dignified quarto; and, not content with being a medium of communication for teachers of English and a bond between the many branches of the Association, it makes very good reading for the general." The review ended by describing *English* as "a magazine that is worthy of its origin."

While he was editor, Guy Boas reaffirmed the aims of *English* (8 [1951]:46), particularly emphasizing the role it had to play in publishing work which might otherwise be difficult to place, especially light verse. He reminded his readers that *English* should "give special attention to the subject of English teaching" but pointed out that there was generally a dearth of good articles from practicing teachers. Under his editorship, and for a while under that of Margaret Willy, a small section of the magazine entitled "English Symposium" was dedicated to dealing with questions mainly, though not exclusively, of special interest to teachers; this section died out quietly, without remark, in 1955. Since then there has been little emphasis on teaching; and articles concerned with it, never a very substantial part of the magazine, have under the most recent editor disappeared, either by deliberate editorial policy or for sheer lack of contributions.

Among the innovations introduced by Margaret Willy during the 1960s and early 1970s were the "Special Numbers," an average of one a year appearing from 1964 to 1974. They began with the "Shakespeare Quatercentenary Number" in Summer 1964 (number 86) and concluded with an issue on the "Twentieth Century Novel" for Autumn 1974 (number 117). W. B. Yeats, T. S. Eliot, William Wordsworth, and Thomas Hardy were individually celebrated, and issues were dedicated to Commonwealth, Scottish, and Irish writing. An especially interesting number was the 100th, published in the spring of 1969 (volume 18). Entitled "Centenary Issue: The Contemporary Scene," it contained poems by C. Day Lewis, R. S. Thomas, Norman Nicholson, Thomas Blackburn, D. J. Enright, John Holloway, and Vernon Scannell, and excellent essays on the three main genres in English literature. Walter Allen contributed "Recent Trends in the English Novel," Martin Esslin "Contemporary English Drama and the Mass Media," and Thomas Blackburn "Poetry Today." The editor herself surveyed the magazine during the thirty-four years of its life in a short piece entitled "English: 1936–1969."

When Martin Dodsworth became editor in 1975 he made a number of sweeping changes, which he discussed in the editorial of the issue for Spring 1976 (25, no. 121). The change in format was intended "to put more into each number of *English*," but it was decided that the "more" should also be different. *English* was becoming, perhaps, too much like other journals, and so certain deliberate changes in policy were brought about. A major proportion of the available space was allotted to more substantial reviews: 79 of 127 pages in the first new issue. The review section also contained an "Editorial Miscellany," a briefer "survey of recent editions, reprints and so on." The other innovation was to give space to the longer essay on a major work of English literature, and the first such essay was "*Middlemarch*: Public and Private Worlds" by Barbara Hardy. The shape of today's *English* is much the same.

From the outset *English* was healthily catholic and attracted a number of distinguished contributors. The first issue contained a short story by Sean O'Casey, poems by Laurence Binyon, John Drinkwater, T. Sturge Moore, and others, and critical essays by Dorothy L. Sayers and Edmund Blunden. In addition, there were two short articles concerned with the teaching of English and reviews both of theater performances and books; among them there was a review of the first commercial production of T. S. Eliot's *Murder in the Cathedral* at the Mercury Theatre, London, in November 1935. The last twenty pages of the magazine contained association news—a report of speeches at the annual dinner and the "Proceedings of Branches"—and correspondence.

From the beginning, *English* received and published a considerable number of poems, though it never became a popular vehicle for the short story. While the poets who published in *English* subscribed to no "school," many works had a faintly Georgian flavor. This perhaps reflected the interests and age of the editor, George Cookson, who was himself an occasional writer of poems, such as "The Moth," which appeared in the first number. There is a noticeable absence of poems from the left-wing political writers of the 1930s such as W. H. Auden, C. Day Lewis, Louis MacNeice, and Stephen Spender, as well as from the major elder poets of the time, W. B. Yeats and T. S. Eliot.[2] Nevertheless, a good number of the poets published in the early volumes of *English* are well known, at least as anthology poets: W. W. Gibson, Edmund Blunden, Phoebe Hesketh, Walter De la Mare, Patric Dickinson, Robin Atthill, Geoffrey Johnson, Alfred Noyes, and many others appeared in its pages. The Scottish number (96), under Willy's editorship, contained poems by most of the major Scottish poets of the day: George Mackay Brown, Robert Garioch, Norman MacCaig, Hugh MacDiarmid, Iain Crichton Smith, and Sydney Goodsir Smith. During recent years, however, most of the poetry published has been by part-time poets, the better-known choosing not to contribute to *English*.

Over the years, *English* has avoided falling into the trap of catering to a small coterie by publishing only articles with a particular slant or by writers belonging to one critical school. A great variety of scholars and critics have contributed essays to *English*, and no one contributor could be called "frequent" in that, over almost fifty years of publication, most have contributed only once or twice and very few more than three or four times. The magazine also serves the whole field of English literature, and no priority appears to have been given to one chronological period over another. Thus, scholars and critics of widely differing interests and loyalties have made contributions, some of the better known being Harold Brooks, William Cooke, Ifor Evans, K. J. Fielding, Barbara Hardy, A. N. Jeffares, G. Wilson Knight, Pat Rogers, George Steiner, Kathleen and Geoffrey Tillotson, and Beatrice White.

Apart from Una Ellis-Fermor, who reviewed drama for *English*'s first seven years, the most frequent reviewers have been the first editor George Cookson, Vivian de Sola Pinto, R. A. Foakes, and Timothy Rogers. A large number of reviewers have been employed, and the substantial reviews of the past few years have helped *English* to maintain its special strength as a critical journal.

Notes

1. *English* "replaced" the *Bulletin* in the sense that the *Bulletin* was no longer necessary: information about the association could be placed in *English* instead. However, the *Bulletin* was not a literary magazine and was in no serious way the forerunner of *English*.

2. Much later, in 1969, Day Lewis contributed to the Centenary Number, presumably by invitation.

Information Sources

BIBLIOGRAPHY

Boas, Guy. "The Association: 1906–1956." *English* 11 (1956).

———. "*English* and Its Contributors." *English* 8 (1951).

Esdaile, Arundell. "A Half-Century of the English Association." *Essays and Studies*, n.s. 9 (1956):1–31.

Smith, Nowell. *The Origin and History of the Association*. London, 1942.

Willy, Margaret. "*English*: 1936–1969." *English* 17 (1969).

INDEXES
> Volumes 1–14: separate numbers indexed. Volumes 15–: each volumes indexed.

REPRINT EDITIONS
> William Dawson & Sons Ltd., Kent, England.

LOCATION SOURCES
> *American*
>> Complete runs: Widely available.
>
> *British*
>> Complete runs: Widely available.

Publication History

MAGAZINE TITLE AND TITLE CHANGES
> *English.*

VOLUME AND ISSUE DATA
> Volumes 1–16, numbers 1–96, Spring 1936–Autumn 1967 (2 years per volume).
> Volume 17–, numbers 97–, Spring 1968– (1 year per volume).

FREQUENCY OF PUBLICATION
> Three times a year: Spring, Summer, Autumn. Summer/Autumn 1978 is a double issue.

PUBLISHER
> 1936–: Oxford University Press for the English Association.

EDITORS
> George Cookson, 1936–1949. Guy Boas, 1949–1954. Margaret Willy, 1954–1975. Martin Dodsworth, 1975–.

Hilda D. Spear

ENGLISH ASSOCIATION BULLETIN. See ENGLISH

ENQUIRY

When the first regular number of *Enquiry: A Journal of Modern Thought*, edited by Alfred Ridgway and Nigel Cox, appeared in April 1948, the list of distinguished academicians and intellectuals on the editorial advisory panel was clearly intended to lend respectability to a publication that could easily have been misconstrued as sensational, since it was founded for the express purpose of inquiring into psychic phenomena. The first four numbers contained forewords by members of that advisory board. In the first, Professor C. D. Broad, Knight-bridge Professor of Moral Philosophy at Cambridge, stressed the credentials of other members of the panel, described telepathy as an established fact, and suggested that science had produced "excellent evidence" of the survival of the personality after death. He emphasized the "extreme importance" for philosophy and psychology of the results of psychical research. G.N.M. Tyrrell, another member of the panel, in the first article, "A New Task for Science," made a similar point.

In the second number Professor Habberley Price, Wykeham Professor of Logic at Oxford, suggested that a publication such as *Enquiry* was a response to modern disillusionment with both scientific materialism and the "traditional religious outlook, with its sharp dualism of Soul and Body." Another member of the panel, C.E.M. Joad, University Reader in Philosophy, London, in number 3, most clearly stated the editorial policy as an interest in those speculations that "lie on the borderland between science and philosophy" and that *Enquiry* would print articles on philosophy, psychology, physics, and theology. In the fourth issue, William Brown, a former director of the Institute of Experimental Psychology at Oxford, discussed the impact of the new science of parapsychology on philosophy and science. J. B. Rhine, the pioneer of the science of parapsychology, was also a member of the editorial advisory panel, which included three ex-presidents of the Society for Psychical Research and its research officer, as well as Carl Jung, who was interviewed in the third number. The brother of A. E. Housman, Laurence Housman, submitted an article, "The All-Seeing Eye," in which he argued that there is infinitely more of life than we know about.

These first four numbers were devoted almost entirely to articles on parapsychology and psychic phenomena, but with the fifth number there was an indication of broadening interests. It included the first foreword by someone not on the advisory panel, Sir Arthur Keith, Fellow of the Royal Anthropological Institute, who cited the evidence uncovered by L.S.B. Leakey and others that Africa, not Asia, was the cradle of humanity. In this foreword, there is no mention of *Enquiry*'s concern with psychic phenomena. The widening of interests was suddenly quite apparent in the sixth number, with an editorial by the poet and scholar John Gawsworth, who had been writing reviews for *Enquiry* on books concerned with psychic matters. Gawsworth quoted Gerald Heard's description of *Enquiry* as a " 'liaison centre' for converging enquiries" and went on to argue for the inclusion of poetry as one of the subjects for enquiry, citing recent explorations of the connection between poetry and dream and the possible signs of "something of a Romantic Revival" after thirty years of increasingly cerebral poetry. The new interest in literature was apparent in the publication of a poem by Walter De la Mare, a study of Goethe's *Faust*, and a new "Literary Section," including reviews of two books on Henry James and a book on Napoleon at St. Helena. From this time on, many books were reviewed that had no connection with psychic experience.

The literary interests continued with the publication in August 1949 (2, no. 2) of Robert Graves's poem "The White Goddess," which had first appeared in the 4 December 1948 issue of the *New Statesman and Nation** (see *VEA*). The same number included an unsigned editorial announcing that *Enquiry* was continuing to widen its field of investigation to embrace "politics, art, the theatre, broadcasting, sport and even gastronomy," as well as the "philosophies and humanities which at the outset it fostered particularly and still maintains.'' While the interest in psychic phenomena continued until the expiration of the magazine with the July 1950 issue, the subjects of enquiry became sufficiently broad to include a series of cartoons on hypnotism in the December 1949 issue and articles seemingly intended to be more entertaining than serious, such as "Concerning Cats" in the April 1950 issue.

Despite Gawsworth's statement that *Enquiry* would explore the relations between poetry and psychic phenomena, literary interests were confined for the most part to book reviews and only occasional publications of literary criticism, fiction, or poetry. The September 1949 number contained Siegfried Sassoon's poem "Ultimate Values," with its striking first line: "The hour grows late, and I outlive my friends." Such distinguished figures as Frank Swinnerton, Eden Phillpotts, and Havelock Ellis had also contributed, but *Enquiry* remained a journal of ideas rather than a literary magazine. Furthermore, the quality of literature published was very uneven; the same issue that contained "The White Goddess" also included an undistinguished poem by R. H. Mottram, "The Churchyard Path," and the December 1949 number contained a rather pedestrian story by John Symonds.

An interest in politics was not extensively developed in *Enquiry*, but there was a trend toward conservatism, in politics as well as in other areas. Vigorously antisocialist articles appeared in the August and September 1949 numbers, and an attack by T. C. Dugdale on modern art for its lack of technique was published in the August 1949 issue. This same issue, however, contained a poem and an autobiographical article, "I Am a Highbrow," by the sometime communist Hugh MacDiarmid, and a review of John Gawsworth's *Collected Poems* by Roy Campbell, who used the occasion to express strongly anti-Marxist views.

Enquiry's unwillingness to commit itself to a doctrinaire political position was perhaps consistent with the open-minded attitude toward psychic experience expressed from the very beginning. The third number, for instance, included a serious treatment of the subject of dowsing, which caused Aldous Huxley to write a letter (1, no. 6) suggesting that ESP might help explain the phenomenon. The editors reported in the third number that Huxley, who announced that he was studying oriental mysticism, had promised to contribute something to *Enquiry*, but the promise never materialized. Indeed, the magazine always showed an interest in any type of spiritual experience, from orthodox Christianity and Far Eastern religions to ghosts and flying saucers. In the September 1949 number (2, no. 3) the editors described *Enquiry* as a magazine that asked questions "because we believe in the spirit of Wonder and of wondering," but the following number (October/November 1949) emphasized that not all questions can be answered and that "the spirit of interrogation keeps alive the sense of mystery" (2, no. 4). It is perhaps significant that this was the last issue to contain an editorial statement. Nevertheless, despite the increasingly vague focus, the magazine was never unduly credulous or naïve in its enquiry into psychic experience. The October/November 1949 issue also contained a wry, ironic article by John

Symonds entitled "The Mind and the Mask of Aleister Crowley," which was not an especially complimentary portrait of the eccentric spiritualist.

A recurrent theme in *Enquiry* was a rejection of the scientific materialism that denies the spiritual and mysterious aspects of experience. This denial of spirit was seen as affecting all areas of modern life. In editorials, Laura Riding and William Wordsworth were cited for their wisdom in identifying the depersonalization of modern life. The limits of a narrowly mechanistic science were repeatedly pointed out. In the issue for September 1949 (2, no. 3), for example, H. J. Masingham questioned the value of a "scientific progress" that was rapidly reducing the world to starvation; and in the same issue J. Middleton Murry argued that modern democracy has made an abstraction of the state, which evokes from its citizens no sense of moral obligation or duty. Murry's book *The Free Society*, with its Orwellian portrayal of a society without a sense of moral purpose, was favorably reviewed in the fifth number of volume 1. In one of the last issues (April 1950) Gerald Heard wrote a comic description of the excesses of California, which he said ran the gamut from physical to spiritual experience, but concluded, "Indeed it may be that it is only out of such a welter of conflicting credulity that profound creation can arise."

Some readers might have found a great deal of credulity, some of it conflicting, in the articles published in *Enquiry* during its little more than two years of existence, but its earnest search for some alternative to the extremes of mechanistic scientific materialism, on the one hand, and moribund traditional religion, on the other, focused on a problem that has continued to challenge thinkers in the second half of the twentieth century.

Information Sources

INDEXES
>   None.

REPRINT EDITIONS
>   Microform: Harvard University. New York Public Library. U.S. Library of Congress. University of Virginia.

LOCATION SOURCES

American
>   Complete runs: Harvard University Library; Los Angeles Public Library; New York Public Library; Northwestern University Library; U.S. Library of Congress. Partial run: University of Virginia Library.

British
>   Complete runs: British Museum; London University Library; University College of North Wales Library, Bangor.
>   Partial runs: Glasgow University Library; Institute of Education, University of London; Science Museum Library, London.

Publication History

MAGAZINE TITLE AND TITLE CHANGES
>   *Enquiry: A Journal of Modern Thought*

VOLUME AND ISSUE DATA

Volume 1, numbers 1–6, April 1948–? (nos. 2–6 undated). Volume 2, numbers 1–5: number 1 undated; number 2, August 1949; number 3, September 1949; number 4, October/November 1949; number 5, December 1949. Volume 3, numbers 1–7, monthly, March-July 1950.

FREQUENCY OF PUBLICATION

Irregular.

PUBLISHER

Horace Cox, Ltd., 239–241 Shaftesbury Avenue, London, W.C.2.

EDITORS

Alfred Ridgway and Nigel Cox.

Terence L. Grimes

EUROPEAN QUARTERLY, THE

The *European Quarterly* (1934–1935) had its origins in the early 1920s in the offices of the London *New Age** (see *VEA*), where Edwin Muir and Janko Lavrin, the two editors, and Stanley Nott, the publisher, began the friendship which led to its publication. Edwin Muir, a native of the Orkney Islands, was then beginning his career as a professional writer; he soon became known as a critic, novelist, and poet, and he and his wife Willa were considered two of the best translators of German. In the early 1920s Muir was a subeditor for the *New Age* and a frequent contributor, as was Janko Lavrin, a Russian who had worked as a journalist during the war and who had settled in England after the Russian Revolution. In 1923 he was named professor of Slavic languages at the University of Nottingham, and in future years he produced a steady stream of books— before and after his retirement in 1953. When Muir and Lavrin met at the *New Age*, the weekly had become a voice for Guild socialism and the economic theory of Social Credit put forward by Major C. H. Douglas, whose writings appeared under the imprint of the publisher Stanley Nott.

Edwin and Willa Muir left London in 1922 to live on the Continent, and their growing involvement with European literature (they were the translators of— among other writers—Franz Kafka and Hermann Broch) was accompanied by an increasing awareness of the political unrest in Europe. This awareness reached a highpoint in 1933 when Muir attended the P.E.N. conference in Dubrovnik and saw at first hand the effects of the new Nazi regime. He realized that the English public was either unaware of or indifferent to the world situation and that this traditional English insularity was responsible for editors turning away from political writings and advanced intellectual ideas emanating from the Continent. Hoping to overcome such restrictions, Muir and Lavrin decided to publish a journal which would provide a platform for ideas unavailable to the English public. Their outlook was shared by Stanley Nott, who agreed to be publisher of the new journal.

The first issue of the *European Quarterly* for May 1934 began with an unsigned, two-page "Comment," in which the editors declared that instead of an improvement in the world situation since the war ("Not a single promise of the self-appointed 'makers of a new world' has been fulfilled") there was rather "a growing political, economic and cultural chaos, with the prospect of new and even more terrible disasters to come." They noted that while the means of communication were better than ever before, "the actual distance between the various nations has never been greater than it is at present." The "object of the present review," they stated, was to attempt to bridge this gap by establishing

a sympathetic contact between the intellectual life of this country and that of the Continent by the publication of contemporary work drawn from the various literatures. [The *Quarterly*] will also try to supply material from the work of great writers and thinkers of an earlier generation who are still comparatively unknown in this country. Explanatory and critical articles will deal with contemporary European movements in literature and the arts. [1:1–2]

Looking at this first issue—as well as at the other three—from a fifty-year perspective, one appreciates a selection of material that was truly in advance of its time and not merely novel or meretricious. The editors' own work figured largely in the *Quarterly*: the first issue contained Muir's essay "Bolshevism and Calvinism" and Lavrin's on Sergei Essenin, the writer of revolutionary Russia, followed by a translation by R. M. Hewitt of Essenin's "Poem." Other poems included works by George Barker, Otokar Březina (translated from the Czech by Dora Round), and C. M. Grieve; and there were stories by Franz Kafka (translated from the German by Willa Muir) and by R. M. del Valle Inclán (translated from the Spanish by Edward Richardson). There were also studies by M. O. Gershenzon (translated from the Russian by R. Gill), Maxwell Fry, and A. T. Cunninghame—the latter contributing a review of the Hogarth Press anthologies, *New Signatures* and *New Country*. Here, too, appeared recollections of D. H. Lawrence; the first three issues contained selections from *D. H. Lawrence, A Personal Record* by Jessie Chambers. The presence of these selections in the *Quarterly* may be explained by the fact that her younger brother was a faculty member at Nottingham, although of course Muir's connections with London publishers put him in a position to know about forthcoming books. These selections are significant evidence of the editors' appreciation of Lawrence, who, in 1934, had not begun to gain his literary reputation.

The second issue of the *Quarterly* came out in August 1934, prefaced by a brief statement by the editors in which they repeated their aim of helping the different nations to understand one another ("the magazine . . . will be a valuable link between the culture of the Anglo-Saxon world and of Europe") and their wish to "produce work that is lucid as well as intelligent." They gave another installment of Chambers's memoir and two stories by Zofja Nalkowska and by

G. Bozhovitch, both translated (from the Polish and the Serbian, respectively) by N. B. Jopson. There was an unsigned book review and four essays: an anonymous "Analysis of Hitlerism"; a sketch of London ("Baal: Impressions of London") by Dostoevsky, translated by R. Gill; an essay by Lavrin entitled "Sex and Eros (On Rozanov, Weininger, and D. H. Lawrence)"; and "A Personal Confession" by Søren Kierkegaard, translated by A. Dru. This last piece is yet a further indication of Muir's and Lavrin's intellectual sophistication, for while post–World War II intellectuals came to regard Kierkegaard as one of the most important influences on modern philosophy, Muir and Lavrin were among the first editors to make his work accessible to the English reading public. (The first major translation of Kierkegaard—that of *The Journals*—by Alexander Dru was not published until 1938.) This interest in the Danish philosopher and theologian was evidently shared by Stanley Nott, for in October 1935 he published E. L. Allen's *Kierkegaard: His Life and Thought*. The appearance of Kierkegaard in the *European Quarterly* is perhaps the clearest indication of the intellectual awareness of the two editors and their publisher.

The third issue of the *Quarterly* contained an equally avant-garde if less influential publication, "The Martyrdom of Saint Eulalia," a poem in three parts by Federico García Lorca, in the translation of A. L. Lloyd. Lorca, one of the most important of the twentieth-century Spanish poets, was just beginning to be known in England, and his appearance here in November 1934 is additional evidence that Muir and Lavrin were aware of significant European cultural developments. This issue also included a poem in English by Emily Holmes Coleman and stories by Ivan Vazov (translated from the Bulgarian by Lavrin) and Antonio Fogazzaro (translated from the Italian by Edward Richardson). There was a final installment of Chambers's memoir, as well as a wide range of essays: a political survey, "Great Britain and Europe," by "A Continental"; essays by Muir on Oswald Spengler and by Lavrin on Rimbaud; and a translation of Alexander Blok's "The Downfall of Humanism" by R. Gill.

The last issue of the *Quarterly* came out in February 1935, and essays again predominated: there was another translation of Kierkegaard by Dru ("The Public and the Press"); a political study by Arsen Wenzelides; literary studies by M. Levidov (of Shakespeare) and by Muir (of Hölderlin's *Patmos*); a study entitled "Niko Pirosmanishvili" which included two leaves of photographs; and an essay by Frank Granger, "The Fiend in Our Universities." The poets in this issue were David Gascoyne, A. L. Morton, and Tadeusz Micinski, the latter's "Lucifer" being translated from the Polish by Paul Selver. There were also stories by Lavrin and by Georg Britting (translated by R. H. Hull) and an unsigned book review—but there was no indication that this was to be the last issue of the journal.

In all, the *European Quarterly* contained 276 pages, and there have probably been few other journals of this—or any other—period which published more recondite and, from the point of view of the English public, more esoteric material. Yet it was generally writing of lasting importance which had an important influence on the cultural life of the twentieth century. If the *European Quarterly* was not a primary vehicle for the dissemination of this material, at least the editors and their publisher helped to bring these names before the public, and to that extent assisted in their popularization. Peter Butter, Edwin Muir's biographer, remarks that the *Quarterly* "contained writing of high quality. It aroused some interest abroad, but very little in Britain, where almost the only subscribers were Jews and Germans. There was not enough support to enable them to keep going beyond the one year."[1] The facts in this comment, shaped though they are by Butter's own prejudices, are probably true; but in 1961 Willa Muir told the present writer (upon his inquiring about the *Quarterly*) that her husband and Lavrin really had no intention of founding a long-lived journal: they had certain ideas and certain writers which they wished to put before the English public, and the *Quarterly* allowed them to attain these goals. In any event, it stands as a highpoint of the intellectually advanced periodicals of the 1930s.

Note

1. Peter Butter, *Edwin Muir Man and Poet* (Edinburgh, 1966), p. 130.

Information Sources

BIBLIOGRAPHY
Butter, Peter. *Edwin Muir Man and Poet*. Edinburgh, 1966.
Mellown, Elgin W. *Edwin Muir*. Boston, 1979.
INDEXES
> Table of contents for each issue. *An Author Index to Selected British Little Magazines*, ed. B. C. Bloomfield (London, 1976).

REPRINT EDITIONS
> Kraus Reprint, Nendeln, Liechtenstein. Scholars' Facsimiles and Reprints, Delmar, N.Y.

LOCATION SOURCES
> *American*
>> Complete runs: New York Public Library; Princeton University Library.
>> Partial runs: University of Texas Library; Vassar College Library; Yale University Library.
>
> *British*
>> Complete runs: British Museum; National Library of Scotland, Edinburgh.
>> Partial run: Cambridge University Library.

Publication History

MAGAZINE TITLE AND TITLE CHANGES
> *The European Quarterly.*

VOLUME AND ISSUE DATA
> Volume 1, numbers 1–4, May 1934–February 1935.

FREQUENCY OF PUBLICATION
> Quarterly.

PUBLISHER
    Stanley Nott Ltd., 69 Grafton Street, Fitzroy Square, London W 1.
EDITORS
    Edwin Muir and Janko Lavrin.

Elgin W. Mellown

EXPERIMENT

Experiment began in 1928 at the same time another Cambridge magazine, the *Venture*, was born. A comparison of the two reveals the differences between the magazines and indicates the transition taking place in English poetry: the *Venture*,

> tastefully produced, adorned with woodcuts and filled with neo-Georgian poems and stories, was in reality an undergraduate heir to Sir John Squire's *London Mercury**; but *Experiment*, claiming to be youthful, rebellious, provocative, and to be concerned with "all the intellectual interests of undergraduates", contained articles on science as well as literature, stills from modernist films, photographs of surrealistic paintings, much obscure poetry and experimental prose.[1]

As one of the contributors to *Experiment*, John Lehmann, recalls: "A furious battle raged (in our minds at any rate) between the protagonists of the two magazines. *Experiment* disdained wood or lino-cuts, but had reproductions of paintings by abstract and surrealist artists. There were surrealist and imagist poems, many pieces in which the influence of Eliot was glaringly evident."[2] Remarkably, *Experiment* and *Venture* had similar lifespans: while both started in the autumn of 1928, *Venture* died after its sixth issue in June 1930, and *Experiment* expired after its seventh issue in May 1931.

Under the initial editorship of William Empson, *Experiment* espoused modernism and experimentation from its first issue. Empson proclaimed contributions from "degreeless students or young graduates" and defined the editorial policy of *Experiment*: "to gather all and none but the not yet too ripe fruits of art, science and philosophy in the university." Empson's background in mathematics and (later editor) Jacob Bronowski's training in science probably gave *Experiment* a wider range of interests than many other literary magazines. Empson's opening editorial concludes that Cambridge may be suffering symptoms of "anxiety neurosis" (no. 1:1). Bronowski, who became coeditor in October 1929 with Hugh Sykes, changed the editorial policy of *Experiment* with the sixth issue (October 1930). They decided that as the magazine matured it could represent non-Cambridge writers or "writers whom English literary society taboos or neglects"; furthermore, they proposed to investigate "the neglect as well as the taboo of considerable writers" and to question "literary societies" (no. 6).

Despite this potential reform movement, much of the interest in *Experiment* derives from the contributors to the early issues of the magazine.

The editors were the major contributors to *Experiment*. In addition to publishing about two poems per issue, Empson contributed chapters of *Seven Types of Ambiguity* and review essays, such as his prescient review of W. H. Auden's *Paid on Both Sides* (no. 7). Bronowski contributed nearly as much verse as Empson, but his essays were less inclined to be strictly literary. The other two editors, Hugh Sykes and Humphrey Jennings, were less prolific; Sykes contributed some free verse, and Jennings produced some critical essays on museum exhibits and theater design.

The range of contributors and topics for this magazine went beyond its editors and their interests, however. Poets who contributed to *Experiment* included T. H. White, Basil Wright, Christopher Saltmarshe, Richard Eberhart, Kathleen Raine, J. M. Reeves, John Davenport, and Conrad Aiken. Elsie Phare, Basil Wright, T. H. White, Richard Aldington, George Reavey, Louis Le Breton, R. A. Alcock, and J. D. Solomon all contributed essays. As indicative of the range of *Experiment*, G. F. Noxon contributed essays on cinema and J. O. Girsavicius submitted an essay entitled "Biochemistry" to the first issue. Prose fiction came from James Joyce and Basil Wright. However, true to its name, *Experiment* included a variety of other entries: portraits by Henri Cartier-Bresson, translations (including George Reavey's translations of Boris Pasternak), Nikhil N. Sen's "Scenario" (no. 3) and his "L'Etoile de Mer: A Poem as Seen by Man Ray" (no. 1), O. W. Reynolds's "The Dansant: Moment," a free association sketch (no. 2), and Malcolm Grigg's "Sonata for a Young Man," a narration for a drama (no. 1).

Perhaps the most interesting selection in the brief life of *Experiment* is "Wyndham Lewis's 'Enemy,' " which appears in the third issue and is attributed to "Five." This "attack" on Lewis is more a defense of modern writers and trends in contemporary literature. The authors accuse Lewis of oversimplification, and argue most strenuously against Lewis's claim that the artist must "banish his political sensations altogether." Instead, they conclude that "theology and politics are implicit in all significant art," and that Lewis has unfairly labeled some writers with differing aesthetic views as communist and has associated this "pretty Bohemian communism" with a definite political doctrine. T. S. Eliot's developing conservatism is also mentioned in passing. The "Five" conclude that Lewis, who does not really offer a system, is a "wistful" figure "desperately cherishing a set of beliefs." Despite this bold response from the "Five," *Experiment* lasted for only one more issue, its demise corresponding with Empson's departure for the Orient in 1931.

Notes

1. James Reeves, "Cambridge Twenty Years Ago," ed. R. March and Tambimuttu, 1948. As quoted in A. T. Tolley, *The Poetry of the Thirties* (New York, 1975), p. 59.

2. John Lehmann, *In My Own Time: Memoirs of a Literary Life* (Boston, 1969), pp. 96–97.

Information Sources

BIBLIOGRAPHY

Hoffman, Frederick J., Charles Allen, and Carolyn F. Ulrich. *The Little Magazine: A History and a Bibliography.* 2nd ed. Princeton, 1947.

Hynes, Samuel. *The Auden Generation: Literature and Politics in England in the 1930's.* New York, 1977.

Lehmann, John. *In My Own Time: Memoirs of a Literary Life.* Boston, 1969.

Tolley, A. T. *The Poetry of the Thirties.* New York, 1975.

INDEXES

Each issue indexed. Numbers 5–7 in *An Author Index to Selected British Little Magazines*, ed. B. C. Bloomfield (London, 1976).

REPRINT EDITIONS

Microform: Brookhaven Press, La Crosse, Wis.

LOCATION SOURCES

American

Partial runs: Poetry Collection, State University of New York at Buffalo; University of California at Berkeley Library; University of Kansas Library; Yale University Library.

British

Complete run: British Museum.

Partial runs: Cambridge University Library; National Library of Scotland, Edinburgh; St. John's College, Cambridge.

Publication History

MAGAZINE TITLE AND TITLE CHANGES

Experiment.

VOLUME AND ISSUE DATA

Numbers 1–7, November 1928–Spring 1931.

FREQUENCY OF PUBLICATION

Irregular.

PUBLISHERS

William Empson and G. F. Noxon, Magdalene College, Cambridge University, Cambridge (1928–1929)/68a St. Andrews St., Cambridge (1930–1931).

EDITORS

William Empson, 1928–1929. Jacob Bronowski, 1929–1931. Hugh Sykes, 1929–1931. Humphrey Jennings, 1929–1931.

Thomas M. Sawyer

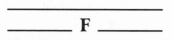

F

FOLIOS OF NEW WRITING. See NEW WRITING

FORTNIGHTLY REVIEW, THE

During the years of World War I and for a decade after, editor William Leonard Courtney maintained the reputation of the *Fortnightly Review*, first published in 1865, for coverage of political affairs, literature, and general intellectual life. The many articles on the war covered a wide range of subjects. Some dealt with weapons, tactics, military education and history, or particular battles, while others treated the general economic, political, and social effects of the war. The issues for the first six months of 1915 can be taken as typical. There were discussions of the effect of the military struggle on wages, the Vatican, the national character, manufacturing, the Boy Scouts, and diplomacy. Also covered were the defenses of Constantinople, the campaigns in the Caucasus and the Dardanelles, the morality of war, and Shakespeare and war. Among the chief writers on war-related subjects were J. B. Firth, Archibald Hurd, Sidney Low, J.A.R. Marriott, Julius Price, Charles H. Woods, John R.C. Kershaw, George Aston, H. H. Maxwell, Robert Crozier Long, Thomas Barclay, Arthur Baumann, John H. Harris, J. G. Swift McNeill, James D. Whelpley, Elizabeth Holdane, Joseph Gollomb, Lewis Melville, Harold Spender, E. J. Dillon, John Bell, W. L. George, Sisley Huddleston, M. F. O'Dwyer, Janet Courtney, Holford Knight, Hugh F. Spender, Robert Machray, James Corbett, J. Ellis Barker, and Anthony M. Ludovici. Quite a few of the writers on the more sensitive military and political subjects remained anonymous.

Second in emphasis to coverage of war and political affairs during the period 1914–1928 was coverage of literature. Shakespeare, Milton, and classical Greek and Latin literature received important attention. Arthur Waugh, W. J. Lawrence,

F. S. Boas, William Archer, Edmund Gosse, Arthur Quiller-Couch, and others contributed work on Shakespeare. H. G. Wells wrote on classical literature. There were articles on Thomas Carlyle, Charles Dickens, William Hazlitt, and John Clare. But the most valuable literary content during this period was in contemporary literature. Thomas Hardy was a regular contributor of poetry. Ezra Pound wrote on vorticism and Remy de Gourmont. Among those who wrote about literature were Frederic Harrison, Robert Graves, John Palmer, Harley Granville-Barker, George Moore, J. B. Priestley, D. H. Lawrence, G. Wilson Knight, Hilaire Belloc, Ivor Brown, S. M. Ellis, and Lucie Simpson. Rabindranath Tagore contributed original work, as did John Masefield and John Drinkwater. There were serialized novels and a large number of short stories, including Henry James's "Within the Rim" (posthumously published). Every issue carried reviews of new books.

The important elements in Courtney's success as editor of the *Fortnightly* were his energy and the breadth of his interests and acquaintances. He published studies in philosophy and literature, and wrote plays. He maintained his early academic connections at Oxford all his life and was a longtime member of the Garrick and Beefsteak clubs. He was chief dramatic critic and literary editor of the *Daily Telegraph* during much of the time he edited the *Fortnightly*, and he served for years as chairman of the publishing firm of Chapman and Hall.

Following Courtney's death in 1928, the quality of the *Fortnightly* dropped off sharply. None of the subsequent editors had Courtney's stature. Standard sources name no chief editor for nineteen of the twenty-six years that the magazine continued to be published after Courtney's death. Most of the old writers stopped contributing, and the new writers who replaced them were not as good. The emphasis on political, intellectual, and foreign affairs continued.

The primary emphasis in the years just before and after World War II was on international politics. The 1937 volume can be regarded as typical. It included articles on the United States, Germany, Newfoundland, Korea and Japan, Japan and Hong Kong, India, Czechoslovakia, Ireland, Portugal, Brazil, Hungary, Switzerland, Russia and Stalin, Palestine, Africa, and Europe in general. There was a lesser emphasis on domestic (British) politics and education. The articles dealing directly with the military aspects of World War II were fewer and less substantial than those appearing in the *Fortnightly* during World War I.

The coverage of literature was much diminished after Courtney. The *Fortnightly* continued to publish short stories and poetry, but these were fewer and poorer in quality than those appearing earlier. Of the approximately 750 pages making up the issues for the year 1938, fewer than twenty pages were devoted to essays on literature, and the only writer of any reputation was B. Ifor Evans. The issues of 1943 contained not a single essay on literature. Those of 1952 included only two. By comparison, under Courtney the issues of the *Fortnightly* in 1928 contained more than 100 pages of literary material, including two important longer essays by John Drinkwater and Harley Granville-Barker.

When the *Fortnightly* went out of existence in 1954, there was not a single important notice of its passing, perhaps because it had outlived its own reputation, continuing in mediocre fashion as it did for so many years after its great successes. The reasons for its cessation are several. There was a paper shortage from 1939 to the years just after the war, and production costs in general rose. The *Fortnightly* lacked the large number of subscribers necessary to finance production and attract more lucrative advertising. A large number of illustrated magazines appeared and drew away some readers, as did cheap paperback books. Increasing specialization among magazines drew away others, as did television and radio, both of which grew rapidly during the last years of the *Fortnightly*'s existence. The *Fortnightly* and a fairly large number of other magazines simply did not survive the changed conditions, and in 1955 the *Fortnightly* was absorbed by the *Contemporary Review** (see *VEA, MA*). [See also the article on the *Fortnightly Review* in *VEA*.]

Information Sources

BIBLIOGRAPHY

Courtney, Janet. *The Making of an Editor, W. L. Courtney, 1850–1928*. London, 1930.
Waugh, Arthur. "The Biography of a Periodical." *Fortnightly Review*, n.s. 126 (1929):512–24.
————. *A Hundred Years of Publishing*. London, 1930.

INDEXES

Each volume indexed.

REPRINT EDITIONS

Microform: Bell and Howell Co., Wooster, Ohio. 1900–1934 in Early British Periodicals (UMI), reels 797–799, 857–868. Princeton Microfilm Corp., Princeton, N. J.

LOCATION SOURCES

American

Widely available.

British

Widely available.

Publication History

MAGAZINE TITLE AND TITLE CHANGES

The Fortnightly Review, 15 May 1865–July 1934.
The Fortnightly, August 1934–December 1954. (Absorbed by the *Contemporary Review*, January 1955.)

VOLUME AND ISSUE DATA

Continuous series (old series), volumes 1–182, 15 May 1865–December 1954.
New series, volumes 1 (vol. 7, o.s.)–175 (vols. 181/182, o.s.), 1 January 1867–December 1954.

FREQUENCY OF PUBLICATION

Monthly (November 1866–December 1954).

PUBLISHERS
>   January 1881–June 1931: Chapman and Hall, 11 Henrietta Street, Covent Garden, London. July 1931–December 1954: Horace Marshall, Temple House, Tallis Street, London.

EDITORS
>   William Leonard Courtney, December 1894–October 1928. Unknown, November 1928–June 1947. John Armitage, July 1947–December 1954.

Dickie A. Spurgeon

G

GAMBIT

Founded in 1963 by Robert Rietty, *Gambit* was established to bring a new internationalism and a new perspective to contemporary drama by making available—for the first time in English—the texts of plays by noteworthy playwrights from throughout the world. Unlike *Plays and Players*,* which regularly featured the texts of plays currently being produced in London, *Gambit* set out to publish plays that were, in the view of its editors, worthy of production; the selection of plays to be offered in its pages was not to be contingent on the already established success of productions in London or elsewhere. As an editorial in the first issue made clear, the mere publication of international drama was insufficient, however, and the magazine clearly held greater ambitions: "A play is only complete on the stage. Our chief hope is that while we are doing the best possible for people who are cut off from opportunities for seeing or taking part in performances, we may also stimulate productions—both professional and amateur—of . . . plays we shall be offering" (no. 1:3). Frequently, *Gambit* even served as a direct intermediary between prospective producers and the authors or their agents. Although its format has changed considerably in the years since its first appearance, *Gambit* remains the foremost journal on international theater published in England.

"Drama probably suffers more than any other form of writing from being too much written about and too little experienced directly," the editorial in the first issue contended, adding that "at a time when serious writers in every part of the world are turning to the theatre, it is becoming increasingly necessary to redress the balance by making original works accessible" (no. 1:3). With editorial advisers in the United States, Italy, France, Spain, Israel, Austria, India, Australia, Ireland, and Yugoslavia (and others soon added in Germany, Holland, Belgium, Poland, Canada, Czechoslovakia, Sweden, and Bulgaria as well),

Gambit offered the first English publication (and sometimes the first English translation) of numerous modern plays. The first issue, for example, contained the full text of *Vasco* by Georges Schehadé, whom the editor described as "one of the most subtle and poetic of modern dramatists, and . . . perhaps the gentlest satirist of our time" (no. 1:3); *Gambit*'s publication of this controversial play, which was written in 1956 and first staged in Paris in 1957, was its first appearance in English. Other early issues featured *Edward and Agrippina* by René de Obaldia (the first publication of any of his works in English) and *Philipp Hotz's Fury* by Max Frisch.

Not all of the noteworthy plays published in the early issues of *Gambit* were contemporary, however; the seventh issue offered two plays from the 1930s by Giovacchino Forzano, *To Live in Peace* and *A Gust of Wind*, while other issues featured *The Little Saint* by Roberto Bracco and *Dawn, Day, Night* by Dario Niccodemi. In addition to the plays published in the pages of *Gambit* itself, the magazine also maintained a list of unpublished translations of Italian plays that were available on request. Published in the second issue, which was devoted exclusively to Italian theater, the list contained thirty works by seventeen authors, including Nicolo Machiavelli's *Il Cucchiaio Lungo* (The Long Spoon); twelve of the plays had been translated by Rietty himself.

With justifiable pride, the editors announced that, among the seven plays that had been published in the first three issues, forty-one theater, radio, and television productions had been brought about in twelve different countries (no. 4:2); by the end of the second year, there had been fifty-three productions of the thirteen plays that had appeared in *Gambit*. A stock of "hire copies" had been established for subscribers who were interested in staging or offering readings of the plays, and initial interest had been expressed in forming a Gambit Theatre to produce plays in London on a regular basis as well. Clearly, in a remarkably short time, *Gambit* was achieving its goals, making available to the public original, provocative, and unusual plays that brought new perspectives to contemporary drama.

Beginning with the eighth issue, *Gambit* was published in association with Calder and Boyars in a new format that included notices and previews of forthcoming productions in London and elsewhere, as well as reviews of new plays and " 'declarations' by people dedicated or opposed to the theatre of today" (no. 8:2). The magazine's international interests (and advisers) were maintained, of course, and they were reflected in the features included in this issue: Jack MacGowran's "Working with Samuel Beckett" (from *Beckett at Sixty,* also published by Calder and Boyars); Eugene Ionesco's "Have I Written Anti-Theatre?" (reprinted from his "Reply to an Inquiry," which had first been published in *L'Express* in 1961); and reviews of the Glasgow production of Beckett's *Happy Days* and the Royal Court Theatre's production of Wole Soyinka's *The Lion and the Jewel* in London. The following issue included the first publication in English of Jean-Paul Sartre's "Myth and Reality in the Theater," a lecture given in Bonn and reprinted from *Le Point*. The "back-of-the-book" section was divided into "News," "News of Forthcoming Presentations," "Reviews," "Reviews of Recent Productions," and "World Premieres"—and its interests expanded to include works as diverse as *Volpone*, Aleksey Arbuzov's *The Promise*, and *Fiddler on the Roof*. Synopses and one-sentence highlights of press reviews on productions from nine countries on four continents were featured.

Subsequent issues continued to show major transformations in the nature and scope of the magazine. Initial plans to publish it bimonthly (as *Encore** had been issued) were not carried through, though the subtitle of the magazine was changed to reflect the planned change in frequency. An editorial in the tenth issue effectively embodied the shift in its emphasis, observing the centenary of John Galsworthy and Arnold Bennett in 1967. The editors lamented that "the British stage—ever ready to revive those of recent memory and the unneglected—[has] almost totally ignored this opportunity of paying homage to their own" as well as to Luigi Pirandello, who was also born in the same year (no. 10:89). In the following issue, Robert Rietty was listed as the executive editor, while the "magazine editor" was Tony Vivis; the editorial board (John Calder, Marion Boyars, John Grillo, and Geoffrey Skelsey) was added to the masthead of the next issue (no. 12). Throughout this period of transition, *Gambit* continued to present the full texts of plays by prominent international writers, including Fernando Arrabal's *The Solemn Communion*, Tadeuscz Rozewicz's *An Interrupted Act*, and Partap Sharma's *A Touch of Brightness*—a play that had been scheduled for the first Commonwealth Arts Festival, though the company had been prevented from leaving India because of official charges that the play was "set in one of the most infamous localities of Bombay" and depicted "matters which it is highly undesirable to [have] show[n] on stage" (no. 9:2).

With the fourteenth issue, *Gambit* began devoting each issue to a single topic, nationality, or author—a practice which has been continued to the present day. Its first such number, on children's theater, was the first magazine issue to be wholly devoted to this topic. Number 15 was given over to Swiss theater (though its reviews were international, as always); number 16 featured aspects of London's "fringe" theaters and contained the text and manuscript of Samuel Beckett's *Breath*, the world's shortest play—a "dramaticule" lasting only thirty-five seconds and having neither plot nor dialogue nor the presence of an actor at the time of the performance. *Gambit*'s publication of it was, in fact, the first publication of the original, uncorrupted version of the text, which had been altered when it was used as the prologue to the American production of *Oh! Calcutta*.[1] Number 16 also included a valuable survey of the "fringe" theaters by Brendan Hennessy, listing the title, location, artistic director, stage size, and seating capacity of each.

When Irving Wardle, drama critic for the *Times*, became the editor of *Gambit* with issue 17, two additional changes in the magazine's format were made: play texts were relegated to the back half of the magazine, and a series of extended discussions with prominent playwrights was begun. In his first editorial, Wardle acknowledged that *Gambit* had provided Britain's "only regular outlet . . . for unfamiliar new work," but he also contended that the nation lacked a "platform for serious theatrical discussion" (no. 17:3) of the sort that had formerly been found in *Encore*. Accordingly, this issue was devoted primarily to the works of Edward Bond, featuring a lengthy discussion among Bond, Harold Hobson, Jane Howell, John Calder, and Wardle himself; it also offered the texts of several of the playwright's previously unpublished works, including the short story "Mr. Dog," several poems, and the brief play *Black Mass*, which had been written for the anti-apartheid cause. The same issue featured an interview with William Gaskill of the Royal Court Theatre, who had directed two of Bond's earliest plays, and it also contained the text of David Hare's first play, *How Brophy Made Good*.

The following issue (no. 18–19, the first of *Gambit*'s occasional double issues) contained the full text of Heathcote Williams's *AC/DC*, which had been widely acclaimed as the most promising play of 1970 when it was first produced at the Royal Court. Illustrated with numerous photographs from the production, the text was printed in a wide variety of type fonts to reflect "its exploration of the interlocking psychic vibrations of a group of 'heads', only one of whom is genuine, the rest, in a sense, sparking off him" (no. 18:cover 4). Though normal printing costs were quadrupled in order to accommodate the demands of the text, "Williams's original idea of printing the text in hollow letters which fill in with colour according to the characters' influence on one another" was not carried out, though Wardle insisted that "this version does relate the verbal structure to its source imagery and uses separate type faces both as an index of character and an aid to reading without constant reference to the speakers' names" (no. 18:3). The issue also contained an interview with the author as well as accounts of European political theater and of the first productions of *Hair* in Amsterdam and Rome. *Gambit*'s traditional international interests were again evident in the next two issues. Number 20 contained the full text of *1789: The French Revolution, Year One* by Sophie Lemasson and Jean-Claude Penchenat, with illustrations of Le Théâtre du Soleil's production. Issue 21 examined contemporary German theater and featured the text of Rainer Werner Fassbinder's *Pre-Paradise Sorry Now*, the editors noting that "the scene order is left to the discretion of the director" and that the cast can consist of five actors, thirty, or any number in between (no. 21:6). Amid the seemingly limitless experimentation and technical innovation that characterized the avant-garde theater of the early seventies, *Gambit*'s commitment to bringing such works to the attention of a wider public was second to none.

In subsequent issues, *Gambit* continued to focus on "neglected" aspects of the theater, though its topics became increasingly English or (when international at all) European: number 22 commemorated the quatercentenary of Ben Jonson, "undoubtedly the most neglected of our great dramatists" (no. 22:cover 4) despite his acknowledged influence on modern repertory (no. 22:3). That such attention would be given a classical author marked a clear departure from *Gam-*

bit's usual interests, though the issue did feature a discussion with Peter Barnes, author of *The Ruling Class*—one of the most Jonsonian of contemporary satires— and an essay on Jonson by the playwright John Arden. This issue also included three early short plays by Bernard Pomerance: *Hospital, Thanksgiving Before Detroit*, and *High in Vietnam, Hot Damn*. The twenty-third issue was devoted to London's fringe theaters and featured an interview with Howard Brenton entitled "Messages First," and number 24 (the first to be edited by Chris Barlas) examined the issues surrounding subsidies for the theater and related problems of financing productions.

Though its international emphasis has remained relatively strong, particularly in comparison to coverage in other magazines, the range of interests in *Gambit* has changed considerably in recent years: topical issues have been devoted to subjects as diverse as television drama (double issue no. 26–27), political theater (nos. 31 and 36), and theater and music (no. 38). English theater has been represented increasingly often (no. 29 on the opening of the National Theatre complex, no. 29 on young British dramatists, no. 32 on Steven Berkoff's London Theatre Group, no. 37 on Tom Stoppard), but entire issues have also been given over to French theater (no. 30), Polish theater (double issue no. 33–34, which, as a result of technical and financial difficulties, caused a one-year hiatus in the publication schedule), and German theater (double issue no. 39–40). Having at one point even invited readers' suggestions about the magazine's "policy, content, and what we should be doing" (no. 30:6), *Gambit* remains deliberately unpredictable in its topicality—a fact that gives it a tremendous potential that has not yet been fully achieved.

Firm in its commitment to "what is *really* happening in the interesting theatre internationally" (no. 30:6), *Gambit* remains the foremost magazine on world theater, and the flexibility of its format provides unique opportunities for coverage of trends and movements that receive such attention virtually nowhere else. Yet in many ways, Anglo-American conceptions of world theater continue to resemble antique maps: vast territories remain simply unknown, their outlines being at best only vaguely charted, their treasures unappreciated and their wonders unseen. In devoting entire issues to the drama of France, Germany, and Poland, among others, *Gambit*'s efforts to widen theatrical horizons are laudable indeed, though non-European drama of the Commonwealth and the Third World might afford equally rich lodes, as the magazine's earliest issues proved they could do. Though more "localized" or autochthonous subjects may prove to be of more topical interest (London's fringe theaters, television, subsidy), and though issues on such well-established figures as Stoppard and Bond undoubtedly have greater sales appeal, *Gambit*'s original commitment to truly "international"— rather than merely English and European—theater remains its greatest potential. Despite the various changes in publishing and international theater since the magazine's founding in 1963, the availability of notable plays from throughout the world has not markedly improved, and much of *Gambit*'s initial editorial statement remains equally true today. Having long been the most courageous explorer of largely unknown theatrical realms, *Gambit* is as valuable as it is unique, with its continuing capacity for growth equal to its potential to startle, to provoke, and to astound.

Note

1. For an account of the controversy surrounding the text of *Breath*, see Deirdre Bair, *Samuel Beckett: A Biography* (New York, 1978), pp. 602–3, and John Calder's brief introduction to the play in *Gambit*, no. 16:6–7.

Information Sources

INDEXES
>   None.

REPRINT EDITIONS
>   Kraus Reprint, FL–9491 Nendeln, Liechtenstein. Scholars' Facsimiles and Reprints, Delmar, N.Y. 12054 (bound reprint of nos. 1–11, 1963–1968 only).

LOCATION SOURCES

American
>   Widely available.

British
>   Complete runs: Bodleian Library; University of Edinburgh Library; University of Glasgow Library.
>   Partial runs: Widely available.

Publication History

MAGAZINE TITLE AND TITLE CHANGES
>   *Gambit: An International Drama Quarterly*, 1963–1967. *Gambit: An International Drama Bi-Monthly*, 1967. *Gambit International*, 1968. *Gambit: International Theatre Review*, 1968–.

VOLUME AND ISSUE DATA
>   Number 1, 1963–. Issues are numbered but undated.

FREQUENCY OF PUBLICATION
>   Quarterly. (Plans for bimonthly issuance, reflected in the title change in 1967, were not carried out.)

PUBLISHERS
>   1963–1967: Robert Rietty, 40 Old Church Lane, London, NW9. 1967–1976: Calder & Boyars, Ltd., 18 Brewer St., London W1R 4AS. 1976–: John Calder (Publishers) Ltd., 18 Brewer St., London W1R 4AS.

EDITORS
>   Robert Rietty, Cav., 1963–1968 (and executive editor thereafter). Tony Vivis, 1968–1970. Irving Wardle, 1970–1973. Chris Barlas, 1974–1975. John Calder, 1976–1981. John Calder and David Roper, 1981–.

William Hutchings

GANGREL

J. B. Pick introduced *Gangrel*, a title derived from the Scottish term for "tramp," in 1945 with a letter to his assistant (later associate editor) Charles

Neill. In his "Editorial Letter," Pick acknowledges the difficulty of starting a "small review" with the large number that already exist, but he argues that "literary reviews are in the front-line against the world-wide advance towards totalitarianism" (no. 1). Although Pick and Neill attracted such contributors as George Orwell, Henry Miller, Richard Wright, Lawrence Durrell, George Wood-cock, and others, *Gangrel* lasted for only four issues, until 1946, perhaps because of the high price (because it paid its contributors) and competition from other small reviews or because of its championing of Scottish literature. In any event, its eclectic blend of poetry, literary essays, personal reminiscences, and essays on philosophers and media never developed under Pick's somewhat tangled editorial policies.

Of the two editors, (Stephen) Charles Neill is probably better known, but as a religious scholar, professor, and Anglican minister. He was apparently a member of the theological faculty at Cambridge during the publication of *Gangrel*. Pick, whose family owned a knitwear business, left Cambridge without a degree to help with the war effort by serving in an ambulance unit, in hospitals, and in air raid shelters. He also volunteered for the coal mines and served for eighteen months as a miner before moving to Scotland at the end of the war.[1] Perhaps the experience of working as a miner led to Pick's emphasis on the vocational work of the poet, which served as an editorial policy.

Pick explained his editorial philosophy in a letter to the authors of *The Little Magazine*. He saw the world as "suffering from the disease of self-consciousness, . . . its crisis in egoism." The response was to have *Gangrel* provide *"moral* criticism," which Pick apparently hoped would lead writers to replace "extreme theoretical idealism" with a concern with the function of the writer as a member of society.[2] In the first issue, Pick declares, "I want to demonstrate the writer as a man with a vocation; to point the way to a free, vocational society." Although he says he does not have space to apply "the vocational argument" to nonin-tellectual activities such as "coal-mining, dock-labouring, sailoring," he summarizes his vocational argument in his "Manifesto on Poetry" in the third issue, in which he says: "Vocational work is the only salvation and happiness which an individual thinking man who has honestly stripped himself of egoistic illusions can hope to discover in the modern world." By adhering to the "vocational approach," an artist, in search of truth, will strip away all illusions, and "the greatest illusion is that of Romanticism." Another egoistic illusion, according to Pick, is disillusioning introspection, which is the result of living in "an age of the intellect." Pick's solution is to be concerned with *"implication"* or *"a* poetry which is marginal notation to the main flow of thought."

In terms of the function of the writer within a society, Pick, on the one hand, sees society in a "state of disintegration" as the result of the "development of the ego." On the other hand, he perceives as dangerous "centralisation, mass-production, [and] large-scale planning," which eliminate the "sense of individual responsibility for the quality of work." Consequently, Pick argues in the last issue of *Gangrel* that we must reestablish "a vocational basis for society," and that the writer must be able "to justify himself vocationally."

Of the prose contributors, the most frequent was Alfred Perles, who contributed three essays, including one on Louis-Ferdinand Céline. Frederick Lohr contributed two essays under the heading of "Philosophy," and Henry Miller submitted two essays; one, "Vive La France," in the second number, was submitted as a part of "The Air-Conditioned Nightmare." Ross Nichols and J. B. Pick also contributed two essays, though that might indicate the narrow range of *Gangrel*, for they and Lohr also contributed poems. Other contributors of individual essays included Charles Neill, John Atkins, Denise Levertov, and, as part of the "Why I Write" section of the fourth issue, Neil Gunn, Rayner Heppenstall, and George Orwell. By the last issue the pattern of including one cultural or media essay in each issue had been abandoned, and Pick grouped three unrelated essays together under the heading of "General."

Orwell's contribution of "Why I Write" to *Gangrel* may seem surprising in view of his stature in England at the time, having just published *Animal Farm*. Neither of the two biographies of Orwell mentions the publication of this essay, which is identical (except for an abridged version of Orwell's early poem) to the version found in the 1968 edition of *The Collected Essays, Journalism, and Letters of George Orwell*. However, according to George Woodcock, one of the poets published in *Gangrel*, Orwell "characteristically" wrote his essay "for his friend John Atkins to publish in a little magazine called *Gangrel* that made at best a token payment."[3]

Pick and Neill attracted a much wider range of contributing poets for *Gangrel*, and several published in more than one issue. Arthur Vivian was the most frequent contributor of poetry with six poems in the second and third issues. T. W. Ramsey and J. G. Braine (John Braine of *Room at the Top*) each contributed a poem to the last three issues. John Atkins also published three poems, two in heroic couplets as parts of "Birth of Military Hierarchy." Two poems were contributed by Thomas Good, A. J. Bull, James Kirkup, Muriel Granger, Ross Nichols, Frederick Lohr, and Denise Levertov. The contributors of single poems included Lawrence Durrell, Kenneth Patchen, George Woodcock, Ronald Bottrall, and Richard Wright. Despite this interesting collection of contributors, *Gangrel* survived for only four issues.

Notes

1. *Contemporary Authors,* New Revision Series, ed. Ann Evory (Detroit, 1979), 7: 359, 5:420, respectively.

2. Letter from J. B. Pick as quoted in Frederick J. Hoffman, Charles Allen, and Carolyn F. Ulrich, *The Little Magazine: A History and a Bibliography*, 2nd ed. (Princeton, 1947), p. 371.

3. George Woodcock, *The Crystal Spirit: A Study of George Orwell* (Boston, 1966), p. 295. John Atkins later collaborated with J. B. Pick on a novel, *A Land Fit for Eros* (1956).

Information Sources

BIBLIOGRAPHY

Contemporary Authors. New Revision Series. Detroit, 1979.

Crick, Bernard. *George Orwell: A Life.* New York, 1982.

Hoffman, Frederick J., Charles Allen, and Carolyn F. Ulrich. *The Little Magazine: A History and a Bibliography.* 2nd ed. Princeton, 1947.

Orwell, George. *The Collected Essays, Journalism and Letters of George Orwell.* New York, 1968.

Stansky, Peter, and William Abraham. *The Unknown Orwell.* London, 1972.

Woodcock, George. *The Crystal Spirit: A Study of George Orwell.* Boston, 1966.

INDEXES

   None.

REPRINT EDITIONS

   None.

LOCATION SOURCES

   American

      Complete runs: Harvard University Library; State University of New York at Buffalo, Poetry Collection.

   British

      Complete run: British Museum.

Publication History

MAGAZINE TITLE AND TITLE CHANGES

   Gangrel.

VOLUME AND ISSUE DATA

   Numbers 1–4, 1945–1946.

FREQUENCY OF PUBLICATION

   Irregular.

PUBLISHER

   J. B. Pick, 170 Westbourne Terrace, London.

EDITORS

   J. B. Pick and Charles Neill.

Thomas M. Sawyer

GOLDEN HIND, THE

The *Golden Hind*, first published in 1922, was the creation of two men, one a writer who had trained as an artist and the other an artist who was also a writer. Clifford Bax had studied at the Slade and Heatherley's before achieving some distinction as a man of letters. He was a poet, playwright, novelist, and ballad opera collaborator. He studied Eastern philosophy and claimed to be a Buddhist. His longtime friend Alec Waugh wrote that Bax suffered from having entered a world he did not consider himself a legitimate citizen of: he inherited money enough to pursue a career in letters and to satisfy his gentlemanly tastes, but he could not dismiss as unimportant the fact that he was not university educated.[1] Austin O. Spare, the son of a London policeman, trained at the Lambeth School of Art and the Royal Academy of Art. At the age of sixteen he exhibited at the Royal Academy and received the special praise of John Singer Sargent.[2] He developed into what Mario Praz called a "satanic occultist," whose drawings were "inspired by the New Aesthetic, the New Sexuality," and who had a recognizable talent for evoking in his work phallic spirits, demons, and voluptuous females nudes.[3] In the decade preceding the appearance of the *Golden Hind* he published two extraordinary books, *The Book of Pleasure* (1913), on the psychology of ecstasy and self-love, and *The Focus of Life* (1921), purportedly the murmurings of Spare's psychic familiar. The *Golden Hind* must have evoked in early subscribers the dream of treasures from more remote places than Drake ever imaged.

Coeditors Bax and Spare may have known one another as young art students: both were born in the late 1880s. Certainly they were acquainted before their collaboration on the *Golden Hind*. Bax had contributed to *Form*, a magazine remarkably similar to the *Golden Hind*, which Spare had coedited first with Francis Marsden and later with W. H. Davies.[4] The *Golden Hind* began publication in October 1922—just a few months after the demise of *Form*—and it attracted to its pages a number of contributors to *Form*, including writers Richard Church, Laurence Housman, Edith Sitwell, Havelock Ellis, Aldous Huxley, and W. H. Davies, as well as artist and poet Cecil French, and artists Nora Wright and Laura Knight. Like *Form*, the *Golden Hind* is most memorable as a visual delight, both for its graphics and for its richly various and ornamented typography. What was observed of the *Golden Hind* applied equally to *Form*: "The magazine is beautifully got-up; and if it has no other special charm or attraction, the lithographs and wood-engravings are a very good excuse for its existence."[5]

During its first year of publication, the *Golden Hind* was published in folio. During its second and last year of publication, the quarterly abandoned the large page "because few people have shelves that are high enough to accommodate folios, and because (according to a well-known authority in the book trade) most people, if a magazine contains large pictures, disregard its literary contents."[6] In its reviews of the first and second numbers of the *Golden Hind*, the *Times Literary Supplement* judged the quarterly to be "stronger in the graphic art than in the literary,"[7] a judgment which Bax cited with some misgiving as reason for reducing the *Golden Hind* to quarto: "Even the Times Literary Supplement, I think, has underrated our literary contents because they have been overwhelmed by our pictures" (1, no. 4:cover 3).

The reduction of page size seems to have affected only the layout: fewer pieces were printed in large and spacious type, and virtually eliminated were color printing and underprinting. What the *Golden Hind* lost in visual appeal it did not compensate for with enhanced literary quality. In terms of the relative amount of space devoted to art and literature, the first and second years of publication are practically indistinguishable. In each issue of forty-eight pages, ten to fifteen are devoted entirely to art. Except for the second issue, each issue contains one or two reproductions extending over two full facing pages. Each issue contains, on the average, more than a dozen smaller reproductions of artwork plus another dozen or so quite small reproductions. By far the most frequently represented artist in the *Golden Hind* is Spare, whose nude figures—often reminiscent of Rubens and often grotesquely informed by animal features—comprise perhaps the single most striking feature of the quarterly: a double-page color lithograph of a nude (3:36–37), a tour de force of intricate design and open space, "The Blasé Bacchante" (5:40–41); the double-page "The New Eden" (1:44–45); and a series of color-printed studies of nudes (1:5–8,10). Apparently Spare's nudes excited controversy among critics, for Bax acknowledged the end of one stage of the life of the magazine and the beginning of another with a clear insistence on the distinction between aesthetic and nonaesthetic realms when contemplating Spare's work:

> Our passage has been somewhat squally. Some of our pictures have been roundly abused. . . . I want, however, to assure our adverse critics that we have no desire to shock anyone, and to remind them of the familiar doctrine that in looking at a picture we ought rather to ask ourselves "Is it well done?" than "Do I like the subject?" [1, no. 4:cover 3]

Each issue of the quarterly includes literary pieces in roughly this distribution: about half a dozen poems; one to three pieces of of short fiction; somewhat fewer pieces of nonfiction; brief reviews—often no longer than a paragraph—of about ten recent publications of art and literature; and, occasionally, a translation of a foreign literary work. Of all literary contributions in the quarterly the poems are perhaps the least distinguished. If Spare established a level of graphic excellence that other contributors could happily aspire to, Bax established a level of poetic mediocrity other contributors of poetry seldom exceeded, with his "Trinacria" (1:30), "At the Turn of the Year" (2:13), "Shipton Gorge" (6:30), "The Dew of a Dream" (7:3), and "Migration" (8:17). Typical of poetic contributions in the *Golden Hind* are Cecil French's "Port de France: Tunis" (1:14) and "London: Monastir" (6:3); G. M. Hort's "Consummation" (1:22) and "The Accusers" (5:42); E. L. Grant Watson's "Dragon-Flies" (1:22); Stanley Snaith's "Old Man in Spring" (5:4); Victor Black's "You Love Me at Your Peril" (5:6); Richard Church's "The Past" (1:34), "The Last Summer" (2:13), and "Worship" (7:31); and Peter Renny's sonnet sequence (2:22–23). Noteworthy for their psychological aspect if not for their technical skill are two poems: W. H. Davies's "Down Underground" (3:3) and L.A.G. Strong's "Talk at the Inn" (7:5–8).

Strong also contributed one of about a dozen short stories appearing in this quarterly: "Storm" is a first-person account of a man tormented by his violent nature and his lover's acceptance of physical abuse, which concludes with a statement that is not certainly ironic: "Perhaps no woman had more imagination than that: perhaps they were all as ready to take anything, cruelty, violence even, from the man they loved" (8:15). Ethel Colburn Mayne, whose publishing career began in the late nineteenth century with a short story that appeared under the pseudonym "Frances E. Huntley" in John Lane's *Yellow Book** (see *VEA*), contributed three pieces of short fiction to the *Golden Hind*: "Stripes" (1:31–34), "The Shirt of Nessus" (5:15–20), and "Humour" (8:19–20) explore the effects of failed sentimental relationships. Greek scholar Kathleen Freeman, who wrote detective fiction under the pen name "Mary Fitt," provided the quarterly with a delicately conceived but finally ineffectual account of an Englishman's recollection in France of his past in his native land ("Nostalgia," 7:9–12). Freeman also contributed poems, including "Candour" and "Liberation" (8:17). Naomi Mitchison, who was just beginning a career as a historical novelist—her first novel, *The Conquered*, is favorably reviewed in the *Golden Hind* (4:34)— contributed a first-person account of piratical life ("The Wine Merchant," 3:5–8). Edith Sitwell—goddaughter of Bax—contributed "Undergrowth," a short story more remarkable for its sensational plot than for its mode of presentation (6:5–16). K. Arnold Price contributed a short story in which are brought into conflict a young couple's Victorian and post-Victorian attitudes toward sex ("Resolution," 6:17–21). Phyllis Mégroz's "The Wolf Man of Rouen" is the confession of a possessed murderer (3:19–22). Several of the pieces of short fiction in this magazine exploit the sensational possibilities of violence and mental derangement, but few with greater control than Herbert Farjeon's account of the progressive movement toward insanity in "Maria Pasinato" (4:26–31).

There appear in this quarterly a few translations of poetry: for example, Havelock Ellis's translations of Spanish folk songs ("Cantares Populares," 1:21); T. Sturge Moore's verse translation of Nobel Prize winner Rabindranath Tagore's "The Foundling Hero" (2:9–12); Harold Harding's translation of a prose poem by Ou-Yang-Hsiu ("Hatred of Flies," 3:31); and Dorothy Una Ratcliffe's prose translations of a sequence of love lyrics by V. Sylvanus ("Seven Letters to Circe," 4:23–25).

Contributions of nonfiction, including literary criticism, figure more prominently in the early issues of the *Golden Hind* than in later ones. In fact, as much nonfiction appears in the first two issues as in all subsequent ones together. In the first issue there appear three substantial pieces of art criticism: Louis N. Parker's "Wagner Reconsidered" (1:5–13); J. Thomas Looney's tracing of Shakespeare's writings to Edward de Vere ("The Earl of Oxford as Shakespeare," 1:23–30); and Ford Madox Hueffer's [Ford Madox Ford] solicited defense of a remark made to Bax years before that Shelley's achievement is diminished by its political motivation ("A Third Rate Poet," 1:15–20). In the second issue appear two essays, one an architectural commentary on the German city of Würzburg by H. J. Birnstingl ("Würzburg," 2:3–8), the other a romantic appreciation of English landscape by E. L. Grant Watson ("Twilight," 2:15–19). Watson later contributed another essay, which comes as close as any literary piece in the magazine to evoking the spirit of Spare's drawings: "In that towering phallic presentation [of the temple at Madura] was symbolized all the deep secrets of the unconscious, the sexual origin of the soul, the rich, unlimited sea of primordial being, all the terrors and the mysteries from which our western life is so cautiously shielded" ("My Own Country," 6:31–38). Other nonfiction pieces include Alec Waugh's essay on the difficulties confronting the artist in a communist society ("The Artist," 4:5–9); Samuel Hoare's appreciative assessment of Chekhov's fiction ("Anton Tchehov," 5:9–14); a historical and critical view of criticism based on Benedetto Croce (Norman Davey, "In Defense of Criticism," 5:21–35); and Cecil French's assessment of the poetry of Arthur Symons compared to his contemporaries' ("The Poetry of Arthur Symons," 7:13–22).

In addition to Ford Madox Ford, Sitwell, Havelock Ellis, and Evelyn Waugh, well-known contributors to the *Golden Hind* include Dorothy Richardson and H. Graham Greene. Each contributed a poem to the next-to-last issue: Richardson, "Helen" (7:31), and Greene, "The Coming" (7:31). Aldous Huxley contributed two brief dramas, one a technical experiment involving a cinematic projection on stage of the unverbalized thoughts of characters ("The Ambassador of Capripedia," 3:9–13), the other a biographical comedy on Albert and Victoria ("Albert: Prince Consort," 4:13–19). It bears mentioning, perhaps, that none of the contributions from these distinguished writers suggests the distinctive qualities or modes of expression for which they are now remembered.

Bax and other contributors of major pieces to the *Golden Hind* wrote a good number of reviews. Bax reviewed recently published volumes of poetry, such as *An Anthology of Italian Poems* (1:35–36); drama; and even a textbook on astrology, Vivian Robson's *A Student's Textbook of Astrology* (3:39). Alec Waugh discussed a recent translation of Flaubert's *Three Tales* (6:47); Birnstingl reviewed Charles Marriott's *Modern English Architecture* (8:35–36). Victor Black reviewed poetry, for example, an edition of Keats's odes with decorations by Vivien Gribble (6:45); drama (Una Ratcliffe, *Dale Dramas*, 7:39); graphics (E. Gordon Craig, *Woodcuts and Some Words*, 8:36); painting (C. Lewis Hind, *Landscape Painting*, 8:36); and nonfiction (Helen Jerome, *The Secret of Woman*, a rejoinder to H. L. Mencken's *In Defense of Women*, 6:45). Purportedly as a substitute for a contribution that failed to appear, there is "The Miniature Review," a brief and lighthearted spoof of such a magazine as the *Golden Hind*, "edited by" Victor Black (7:35–37), and including "An Essay on Women" (7:35). Eric Gillett also served as one of the magazine's most faithful literary reviewers: of poetry by E. A. Robinson, Gwen John, and E. F. Edgett (2:38); a translation of Aeschylus by George Trevelyan (3:28–29); Bax's *Midsummer Madness: A Play for Music* (6:39–42); and *Myself When Young* by Alec Waugh, who "has joined the ranks of . . . inspired gossips" (6:43). Peter Renny reviewed two publications by Ford Madox Ford, *Mister Bosphorus and the Muses* (7:39–42) and *Some Do Not* (8:39), as well as Richard Church's volume of poems, *Philip* (4:34), and Ethel Colburn Mayne's *Nine of Hearts*, a volume of short stories characterized as having "the shadowy beauty of a perfect mezzotint" (3:30).

After two years and eight handsome issues, the *Golden Hind* abruptly announced that it would cease publication, "owing to insufficient support" (8:1).

Notes

1. Alec Waugh, *The Early Years of Alec Waugh* (New York, 1962), pp. 101, 178–79.
2. Kenneth Grant, *The Magical Revival* (New York, 1973), pp. 180–208.
3. Mario Praz, *The Romantic Agony*, trans. Angus Davidson (London, 1933), pp. 18, 196.
4. Richard J. Stonesifer, *W. H. Davies: A Critical Biography* (Middletown, Conn., 1963), pp. 172–76.
5. *Times Literary Supplement*, 1 February 1923, p. 79.
6. Clifford Bax, "A Note," prospectus inserted inside the back cover of the *Golden Hind* (July 1923). Subsequent references to the *Golden Hind* will be indicated in the text within parentheses by issue and page numbers.
7. *Times Literary Supplement*, 9 November 1922, p. 730; 1 February 1923, p. 794.

Information Sources

BIBLIOGRAPHY
Grant, Kenneth. *The Magical Revival*. New York, 1973.
Praz, Mario. *The Romantic Agony*. Translated by Angus Davidson. London, 1933.
Stonesifer, Richard J. *W. H. Davies: A Critical Biography*. Middletown, Conn., 1963.
Sykes, Christopher. *Evelyn Waugh: A Biography*. Boston, 1975.
Waugh, Alec. *The Early Years of Alec Waugh*. New York, 1962.
Waugh, Evelyn. *Diaries of Evelyn Waugh*. Edited by Michael Davie. Boston, 1976.
INDEXES
    None.
REPRINT EDITIONS
    Kraus Reprint, Nendeln, Liechtenstein. Scholars' Facsimiles and Reprints, Delmar, N.Y.
LOCATION SOURCES
American
    Widely available.
British
    Complete runs: Bodleian Library; British Museum; Cambridge University Library; Leeds Public Library; Victoria and Albert Museum Library.
    Partial run: Edinburgh Public Library.

Publication History

MAGAZINE TITLE AND TITLE CHANGES
    The Golden Hind: A Quarterly Magazine of Art and Literature.
VOLUME AND ISSUE DATA
    Volumes 1 and 2, numbers 1–8, October 1922–July 1924.

FREQUENCY OF PUBLICATION
    Quarterly.
PUBLISHER
    Chapman and Hall, Ltd., 11, Henrietta Street, Covent Garden, London, W. C. 2.
EDITORS
    Clifford Bax and Austin O. Spare.

Carol de Saint Victor

H

HORIZON

Cyril Connolly, the founder and editor of *Horizon*, once referred to his magazine of literature and art as a "child of war": it was, in fact, planned in the summer of 1939 and began publication in January 1940, during that period of quiet on the Western front known as the Phoney War. The magazine came to an end ten years later with the double issue of December 1949–January 1950. A practical reason for the magazine's birth in wartime evidently lay in the opening created for *Horizon* by the demise of a number of literary publications. T. S. Eliot's *Criterion** had suspended publication in January 1939 and had been followed by a chain of closings: the *London Mercury** in April, *New Verse** in May, and *Twentieth Century Verse** in June.[1] The departure of some leading British writers to America, including W. H. Auden and Christopher Isherwood, also contributed to the sense of a literary era closing in Britain as well as a political one.

At its wartime inception *Horizon* was intended to be a statement in itself of the value of literary and artistic culture and a defiance of the totalitarian enemy. Other principals who joined with Connolly in making this gesture were Peter Watson, the proprietor, and Stephen Spender, coeditor, whose flat in Lansdowne Terrace, Bloomsbury, served as the magazine's first office. Spender was in a state of personal unhappiness at the time, and his memoir of the period stresses the therapeutic value of the appearance every weekday "of Cyril Connolly, Peter Watson—the adored, handsome and rather enigmatic young man who paid for the magazine and was its art editor—and of the editorial secretaries, Sonia, Lys and Diana."[2] William Makins was the business manager, and it is a sign of the house style of *Horizon* that he, too, wrote and occasionally advised Connolly on the quality of contributions.[3]

In relation to other literary journals of the period that were committed to political causes or specific interests—as in the declared intent of *New Writing*'s* title—the stance taken by Connolly was distinctly ivory tower. In his opening editorial for January 1940 he declared that the magazine would avoid the "brightness" of journalism, would publish no reviews of the cinema or theater, and would eschew the delights of a correspondence page. *Horizon* would publish good writing and further "an appreciation of delicate poetry and fine prose," he announced in February 1940. In a side-comment, Connolly welcomed the end of social realism. The break with the committed literature of the 1930s was unmistakable, and Connolly expressed the change in a much-quoted phrase: "Our standards are aesthetic and our politics are in abeyance."

This manifesto gave *Horizon* a direction and brought it notoriety. But highbrow artistic detachment proved difficult to maintain as the war came closer. Connolly had argued the case for artistic withdrawal in the face of war in an article wittily entitled "Ivory Shelter" in the *New Stateman** (see *VEA*) for October 1939. Continuing to maintain this attitude in the pages of *Horizon*, Connolly asserted in the issue for May 1940 that "the war is the enemy of creative activity and the writers and the painters are wise to ignore it" (1, no. 5). The timing for such a pronouncement could not have been worse. The Germans attacked on the Western front on 10 May and achieved a breakthrough with staggering speed which brought the fall of France and the occupation of the Low Countries. Britain seemed next. Connolly was neither defeatist nor pacifist and was consequently caught off balance. A writer in uniform, Goronwy Rees, chose to take Connolly to task for his statement, pointing out that the war would not be ignored, and should not be if soldiers were to be given a voice. Connolly published the objection prominently in the issue for June 1940, and in his own reply modified his aesthetic position. He continued to remain divided in his ideas, and this division may be read in the intermittent attention given to the war in the pages of *Horizon*.

Its political attitudes, Connolly had declared, were in abeyance. But here, too, the demanding times forced commitment. "Fascism is the enemy of art," he had written (in *Enemies of Promise*) in 1937, when Republican Spain was a cause generally adopted by many writers of left or liberal inclination. Disillusion in the wake of the Republican defeat brought Connolly to the point where, in his "Ivory Shelter" article, he welcomed the freeing of the writer from both "the burden of anti-Fascist activities . . . [and] the subtler burden of pro-Communist opinions." Under the pressure of Nazi triumphs in war, Connolly's antifascism revived and he adopted a wartime species of independent socialism close to that of his friend George Orwell. The only thing which can defeat German National Socialism, he declares in *Horizon* for November 1940, is "international socialism." Later, Connolly would support the postwar Labour government, despite the impingement of its austerity program upon his style of good living. This display of principle aside, Connolly's politics appear to have been generally an extension of his aesthetic interests. The left was friendlier to art, and this gave him a political position when positions had to be taken. But his art was also international and not narrowly political, and Connolly's declaration to his critics, in January 1946, that *Horizon* was a magazine of "international humanism" appears to be the broadest and also the truest description of the political views which guided it. (The phrase recurs in his editorial in the 100th issue, for April 1948.)

Goronwy Rees proved right in his assertion that the war would not be ignored. Connolly published articles by leading intellectuals on the war aims of the Allies, and George Orwell reviewed books by generals on military strategy. But some of these signs of war appeared in the guise of belles lettres and even fiction. France's defeat and occupation are recorded in a contributor's personal journal; Russia's entry into the war is signaled by a memoir of life in Moscow before the German attack. "The Mixed Transport," in the issue for October 1943, a powerful, impressionistic short story by Arthur Koestler, describes the shipping of Jews and others across Europe by train to their deaths in concentration camps. Two months later *Horizon* published a letter from Koestler emphasizing the factual truth of his story.

The historical growth in the role of the United States, first in the European war and then in postwar Europe, can also be read in the increased space given by *Horizon* to American material. The work of a group of contemporary American poets, Karl Shapiro, Allan Tate, Delmore Schwartz, and Randall Jarrell, was published in the issue for February 1944, and Jarrell's war poem "The Death of the Ball-Turret Gunner" received its first publication in *Horizon* for April 1945. The October 1947 issue was a special double number, "The Arts in America." In this postwar period Connolly gave *Horizon* the role of maintaining Britain's cultural tradition in the face of the country's decline in world power. This did not translate into anti-Americanism, and, in fact, from its earliest days, *Horizon* kept an opening to the United States, partly through the journals of English literary travelers and partly through its connection with *Partisan Review*, the left-wing American journal of the arts. From this source came noteworthy articles by the art critic Clement Greenberg.

Naturally, during the war years Europe provided only a thin nourishment of contemporary work. Such refugees in England as Koestler and the Spanish writer and critic Arturo Barea contributed to *Horizon*, and some material came out through the enclave of Switzerland. The Allied invasions of 1943–1944 reconnected this vital line. The liberation of much of Italy was marked by the publication of specially commissioned work from Benedetto Croce and the novelist Alberto Moravia. But it was France that held the secret hoard of developments in philosophy and literature, developments exposed to view in critical articles and in the publication of selected representative gems from the summer of liberation of 1944 onward. Philip Toynbee's "The Literary Situation in France," in the issue for October 1944, broke the news of incomparable gains during the occupation which placed French literature far ahead of English writing. (This claim brought a letter of protest from John Lehmann, editor of *New Writing*, at its alleged undervaluing of English writers.)

The main evidence of French achievement came with the issue for May 1945. Connolly had followed Toynbee to France to gather material. The leading feature was Jean-Paul Sartre's statement of the necessity for an "engaged" literature, an article which had not then been published even in France, though it was widely known by repute. The issue included critical articles on existentialist theater and on French poetry and prose by John Russell, Stephen Spender, and Toynbee, and a prose poem, in French, by a newly discovered writer, François Ponge. The French thunder rumbled on through the next year or so, with commentary on Sartre as philosopher by A. J. Ayer (July 1945), and an issue for October 1945 heavily devoted to André Malraux. With this issue *Horizon* also announced that it was available to French subscribers at a rate of 500 francs a year. Attempts to open up the Mediterranean generally can be discerned in the appearance of travel pieces on Italy and Greece and the discussion of the work of Ghika, a Greek painter, in the March 1946 issue.

Germany was to remain essentially unknown in its literary and artistic features, though not otherwise unobserved. The publication, in April 1944, of specially commissioned translations of Friedrich Hölderlin on the eve of an expected Allied invasion of Europe may be seen as a typical gesture of *Horizon*'s belief in a European culture above war and politics. Attempts were made to tease out the condition of literary and artistic life—"Art Life under Hitler" (March 1944), "Broken Minds" (April 1946), "German Writers of Today" (January 1947)— but the reports of a shattered cultural life merge with the general reportage of ruined cities and of death camps, which conveys the dominant impression of that country at the end of the war. Spender contributed to this higher journalism with a series of pieces in *Horizon* in 1945 on his travels in the British-occupied zone (later reprinted in *European Witness*). Alan Moorehead described in July 1945 the opening of the camp at Belsen. *Horizon*, in its own way, provided a witness to war and its horrors.

At home, *Horizon* offered unquestioned prestige to the writers who entered its pages. Connolly set high standards, published writers of established status, and was not intimidated by reputations. *Horizon* was not a magazine devoted to unearthing new talent, but it did creditably in this area, publishing for the first time the fiction of William Sansom, Philip Toynbee, and Angus Wilson. J. Maclaren-Ross has given an account of being discovered by *Horizon* which demonstrates Connolly's tenacity in pursuit of him, still an unknown. In the same episode Maclaren-Ross saw his editor rejecting an article by a writer of international note because the work in question, in Connolly's phrase, "was good enough to be accepted for *Horizon* but not quite good enough for me to publish."[4] Connolly himself liked to repeat this story.

Horizon published the leading poets of the 1930s alongside poets of Georgian reputation or manner. In the first number, for instance, work by Walter De la Mare, the poet laureate, and John Betjeman, always eccentrically behind the fashion, appears with poems by W. H. Auden and Louis MacNeice. These two, with Cecil Day Lewis and Stephen Spender, appeared all through the ten-year span of *Horizon*, and at the magazine's close Connolly referred to Auden and MacNeice as figures of continuity in its history. Auden, in fact, dropped away from *Horizon* during the war years when he was living in the United States and submitting his poetry to American magazines. In the postwar years the connection was restored; curiously, Auden had fallen silent after publication of his poem "At the Grave of Henry James" in the issue for June 1941, and reappeared with a prose essay on Henry James in February 1947. Connolly is said to have asked Auden about this time for a poem that would make him cry: the result was "The Fall of Rome," published in April 1947, judged by Connolly to be "moving but careless."[5] The much-anthologized "In Praise of Limestone" appeared in *Horizon* in July 1948 and "Memorial for the City" in November 1949.

Dylan Thomas, whose reputation was just emerging, differed from the Auden circle. He had no public-school-and-Oxbridge background and his poetic manner was deplored by the critic Geoffrey Grigson for its Romantic excess of feeling. Thomas's uncertain and bohemian life marks the history of his connection with *Horizon*. His poems were bought "spot cash . . . like buying cocaine," reported Connolly.[6] The setting of a 200–line poem, "The Long-Legged Bait," in small type because of paper shortage, was badly received by the poet, who refused to go to the office to correct the proofs. Stephen Spender had encouraged Thomas when his work first appeared and in 1940 launched an appeal fund for the poet, whose domestic cupboard was bare.[7] "Deaths and Entrances," Thomas's first war poem, made a timely appearance in *Horizon* in January 1941 at the height of the Blitz. Some of Thomas's best work—"Fern Hill," "Refusal to Mourn the Death by Fire," and "Poem in October"—appeared in *Horizon* in the last year of the war, and the poet was awarded the *Horizon* Prize for 1945. An uncertainly defined honor, the prize was apparently only awarded to one other writer, Mary McCarthy, for her short novel *The Oasis* in February 1949. Other poets who published with some frequency in *Horizon* included Conrad Aiken, George Barker, Norman Cameron, William Empson, Patrick Kavanagh, Anne Ridler, Francis Scarfe, Ruthven Todd, and Laurie Lee.

In prose fiction, Connolly published the work of established writers such as H. E. Bates and Elizabeth Bowen alongside that of his young discoveries, William Sansom, J. Maclaren-Ross, and Philip Toynbee. Angus Wilson's first published story, "Mother's Sense of Fun," appeared in *Horizon* in November 1947. Wilson, then employed at the Reading Room of the British Museum, and writing on weekends, showed his stories to Robin Ironside, an author of critical articles for *Horizon*, who passed them on to Connolly. Two of the pieces published in *Horizon* were reprinted in Wilson's collection *The Wrong Set* (1949), which was well received and inaugurated his career as "one of the best half-dozen novelists writing in England at mid-century."[8] *Horizon*'s fiction was distinctly good. Even an abbreviated list of contributors includes such names as V. S. Pritchett, Graham Greene, Sean O'Faolain, Frank O'Connor, Nancy Mitford, and Evelyn Waugh, and an impressive American contingent: Truman Capote, Henry Miller, Eudora Welty, and James Thurber.

The link with high culture was maintained through critical articles, many of them by leading academics and literary critics, including Edmund Wilson, Edwin Muir, and Lionel Trilling, the historians A.J.P. Taylor and H.R. Trevor-Roper, and the philosophers Bertrand Russell and A. J. Ayer. The best issues of *Horizon* brought together works of style and intelligence in a number of fields. The issue for March 1941, for example, offers essays by J. B. Priestley, H. G. Wells, and T. S. Eliot (on the *Times* obituary notice of Joyce); a war diary from France; a travel journal from Louis MacNeice in America; and reproductions of Henry Moore's drawings from the London Underground. Reviews by Graham Greene, George Orwell, and William Empson complete the issue.

Dedicated though it was said to be to the imaginative arts, *Horizon* published the work of two of the most socially conscious, and politically skeptical, writers of the day: George Orwell and Arthur Koestler. Orwell and Connolly had known each other at preparatory school, and their friendship continued through the thirties and the war years. (In his war diary Orwell recalls watching the great fires engulfing the dockland of East London from Connolly's Bloomsbury flat: "Connolly . . . took us up to the roof and, after gazing for some time at the fires, said 'It's the end of capitalism. It's a judgment on us.' ")[9] Orwell's contributions to *Horizon* were varied, for Connolly used him as an eclectic reviewer. His major pieces for the magazine were essays on the social meaning and context of literature (and not high literature), as in "Boys' Weeklies" (February 1940), "Rudyard Kipling" (February 1942), and "Raffles and Miss Blandish" (October 1944). A number of these *Horizon* pieces were to be reprinted later in Orwell's various collections of critical essays. Orwell's *Animal Farm* was reviewed favorably by Connolly in September 1945 as marking a rebirth of the political fable, and *1984* was treated by Connolly in *Horizon* for September 1949. Koestler's contributions were less frequent, but some of his best-known work first appeared in *Horizon*, notably his essays "The Yogi and the Commissar" (June 1942) and "The Intelligentsia" (March 1944).

Horizon gave nurture to another social writer of unusual distinction, Tom Harrisson, who in 1937 had founded Mass Observation, a movement, or institution, of social observation to find out what ordinary people were really thinking— and not what the popular press said they were thinking—and to describe the activities of ordinary life. Harrisson and his colleague, the poet Charles Madge, used their literary and social connections to recruit some distinguished Mass Observers to carry out their studies, including the poet William Empson and the columnist Tom Driberg.[10] *Horizon* published Mass Observation articles on public attitudes to the war, workshop and factory life, and the Allied invasion of Europe. Harrisson also wrote searching articles on the Beaverbrook Press and on popular war books.

Connolly might have cited some of this journalism, which was distinctly on the nonconformist wing of British letters, against those critics who complained of *Horizon*'s bland and cultured tone. Julian Symons, for instance, described it as a "neo-Georgian literary paper with modernist overtones" in the anarchist periodical *Now*; and he was even more severe toward Connolly in a piece in *Partisan Review*, charging that he printed "odd fag-ends of the Twenties bound together by no organised view of Life or Society, no stronger thread than his own erratic intelligence." Connolly chose to deflect the criticism with wit. Symons was evidently correct, however, in registering the personal style of Connolly's editing, which friends and colleagues also noted. John Lehmann, who was quite a different sort of editor, thought *Horizon* enjoyed a "chancy brilliance" related to Connolly's expenditure of effort.[11] *Horizon*'s proprietor, Peter Watson, told Stephen Spender, "Cyril's a brilliant editor because he's like a brothel keeper, offering his writers to the public as though they were the girls, and himself carrying on a flirtation with them."[12]

Horizon enjoyed great prestige during its ten years of life. But the labor of carrying it through the difficulties of wartime paper shortages and dislocation caused by enemy action, and then through the austerity of the postwar years, evidently told on the editor. Writing in 1941, Orwell noted that *Horizon*, although a "modern and democratized version" of the old highbrow literary magazine, was having difficulty in surviving.[13] The magazine's circulation never rose above 10,000 and was just below 9,000 in its final months.[14] In addition, Connolly cited the continuing difficulty of finding good writers and extracting good contributions, along with his own feeling of staleness as editor, as reason for closing. *Horizon* was a magazine driven, to an exceptional degree, by the personal energy and enthusiasm of its editor. Connolly had written in *The Enemies of Promise*: "The vocabulary of a writer is his currency but it is a paper currency and its value depends upon the reserves of mind and heart which back it."[15] By late 1949 the reserves were exhausted, and the last issue of *Horizon* appeared—a double number (December 1949–January 1950) that greeted the new decade as it drew a cover over the old.

Notes

1. Samuel Hynes, *The Auden Generation: Literature and Politics in England in the 1930s* (London, 1976), p. 340.

2. Stephen Spender, *The Thirties and After* (London, 1967), p. 68.

3. J. Maclaren-Ross, *Memoirs of the Forties* (London, 1965), p. 73.

4. Ibid, pp. 77–80.

5. Humphrey Carpenter, *W. H. Auden: A Biography* (New York, 1981), p. 342n.

6. Constantine Fitzgibbon, *Life of Dylan Thomas* (London, 1968), p. 278.

7. Constantine Fitzgibbon, ed., *Selected Letters of Dylan Thomas* (London, 1966), pp. 94, 248.

8. Jay Halio, *Angus Wilson* (Edinburgh, 1964), pp. 8–9.

9. George Orwell, *Collected Essays, Journalism and Letters*, ed. Sonia Orwell and Ian Angus (London, 1968), 2:444.

10. Anthony Burgess, "People's Voice," *Observer* (London), 18 March 1984.

11. John Lehmann, *In My Own Time* (London, 1955), p. 323.

12. Spender, *The Thirties and After*, p. 66.

13. Orwell, "London Letter," in *Collected Essays*, 2:72.

14. Robert Hewison, "Cyril Connolly," in *Makers of Modern Culture: A Biographical Dictionary*, ed. J. Wintle (London, 1981); Lehmann, *In My Own Time*, p. 473.

15. Cyril Connolly, *The Enemies of Promise* (London, 1938), p. 43.

Information Sources

BIBLIOGRAPHY

Hewison, Robert. *Under Siege: Literary Life in London 1939–45*. London, 1977.

Lehmann, John. *In My Own Time*. London, 1955.

Maclaren-Ross, Julian. *Memoirs of the Forties*. London, 1965.

Orwell, George. *Collected Essays, Journalism and Letters*. Edited by Sonia Orwell and Ian Angus. London, 1968.

Pryce-Jones, David, ed. *Cyril Connolly: Journal and Memoir*. London, 1984.

Sinfield, Alan, ed. *Society and Literature 1945–1970*. London, 1983.

Spender, Stephen. *The Thirties and After*. London, 1967.

INDEXES

Volumes 1–19, numbers 1–108, January 1940–December 1948, external index. Volume 20, January 1949–January 1950, indexed at end. *Comprehensive Index to English Language Little Magazines 1890–1970*, series 1, ed. Marion Sader (Millwood, N.Y., 1976).

REPRINT EDITIONS

Johnson Reprint Corp. New York, N.Y.

Microform: New York Public Library; KTO Microform, Route 100, Millwood, N.Y.

LOCATION SOURCES

American

Widely available.

British

Widely available.

Publication History

MAGAZINE TITLE AND TITLE CHANGES

Horizon: A Review of Literature and Art.

VOLUME AND ISSUE DATA

Volumes 1–20, numbers 1–121, January 1940–December 1949/January 1950 (double number). Special number 1945: *La littérature anglaise pendant la guerre.*

FREQUENCY OF PUBLICATION

Monthly.

PUBLISHER

Peter Watson, 53 Bedford Square, London WC1.

EDITORS

Cyril Connolly; Stephen Spender (coeditor), 1940.

Alan C. Thomas

HUMANIST. See LITERARY GUIDE (VEA)

I

INTERIM DRAMA. See DRAMA

K

KINGDOM COME

Kingdom Come announced itself in November 1939 as "The Magazine of War-Time Oxford." It had a large format (slightly larger than that of *Encounter**) and thick card covers decorated with what has been described as "an atrociously ugly neo-expressionist" design by the extravagantly named Baptista Gilleat-Smith.[1] Between its arresting covers lay thirty-two pages of articles, stories, and poems edited by John Waller, then an undergraduate at Worcester College, and Kenneth Harris from Wadham. Financial backing for the magazine was provided by Dr. Marie C. Stopes, more famous for her work concerning contraception and her book *Married Love* than for her less than distinguished poetry. Her patronage of *Kingdom Come*, however, was well placed, for Waller and Harris produced a lively, invigorating magazine, as free of coteries and cliques as it was of determinedly highbrow pretensions. Julian Symons has written appreciatively of the periodical: "It is impossible to convey the rich confusion of *Kingdom Come*: I doubt if any odder magazine has appeared since its extinction after eight issues."[2] The only point in need of correction here is a matter of fact: *Kingdom Come* was not extinct after eight issues; there were a further four. But Symons may be forgiven his error, for the magazine changed its editors, format, and style completely when Waller left England to serve in the Middle East at the end of 1941. With the removal of Waller, Marie Stopes approached Symons with the editorial job. But despite his proven ability as an editor, demonstrated in the pages of *Twentieth Century Verse,** he was unable to take on *Kingdom Come* due to personal circumstances. Instead the job was undertaken by Henry Treece, Stefan Schimanski, and Alan Rook. With their accession the magazine lost its fresh, if slightly undergraduate, flavor and gained a sobriety which sometimes became portentous. Treece also brought with him a fondness for the overblown rhetoric associated with the Apocalypse movement, of which he was a founder.

Despite the Apocalyptic resonances of its title, in its inception and for the first eight issues *Kingdom Come* had little if anything in common with the Apocalypse movement. Indeed, it stood on no aesthetic platform, did not declare any literary principles upon which material would be selected, and did not confine itself entirely to publishing younger writers. The first five editorials were wholly concerned with the political implications of the war. Written in Waller's light and lively style, they nevertheless demonstrate the profound difficulties and uncertainties encountered by the young intelligentsia in trying to formulate a viable progressive political position. It had been possible in the 1930s for the young to find in communism a naïve redemptive vision; it provided a clear corrective to the evils of capitalism that they so plainly perceived. In 1939, with communism and Russia discredited by the internecine strife within the left during the Spanish Civil War, the Stalinist purges, and finally the Nazi-Soviet pact, socialists were in an awkward position. They could either fight fascism in defense of a capitalist state in which they did not believe, or they could adopt an uneasy pacifism.

Without overt polemics *Kingdom Come* initially advocated the latter position. In his opening editorial, Waller reiterated with approval John Middleton Murry's remarks made in the *Adelphi** for November 1939. The main point of these was that "the overthrow of Hitlerism" would be fatal to Europe and to England and that "peace negotiation" was a "condition precedent of the overthrow of Hitlerism." In the following issue of *Kingdom Come* Murry was given space to speak for himself and Waller expanded his parties-above-politics thesis. Murry expressed the view that the war was being fought to preserve imperialist power, that England should accept the fact that it was a second-class state and should leave the issue of power in Europe to be fought out by Germany, Italy, and Russia. Waller, on the other hand, decided that "in the early days of war" the hedonist "has a faith only a little below the pacifist" since pleasure is not the "chief good, but the only good." He advised his contemporaries to make the most of festivities; "not to be content to have a party" when they could "have a blind" and "not to be content with a flirtation" when they could "achieve love" (1:35).

As the war progressed, however, and the Germans advanced through France, both hedonism and pacifism were abandoned by Waller, to be replaced by vague, almost desperate hopes and pleas that the war should give rise to a new order of things. After the fall of France he explicitly stated that pacifism was no longer a viable attitude on the grounds that "allied victory or defeat may decide the fate of the intellectual" (1:103). In the next issue of the magazine Waller declared that England needed new generals, new leaders, and new ideals to fight for. He presumed to speak for his generation when he said, "We are not again willing to fight for the old ineffective order of things" (2:3). Waller's most impressive and impassioned remarks not unnaturally appeared in the last editorial he wrote for the magazine in the spring of 1941. But for all the weight of feeling that informed his prose, he could only speak in imprecise abstractions against "the old" and in favor of "the new": "It is a new world that we must fight for, a new way of life, a time without fear and without reproach" (2:68).

Other writers published in *Kingdom Come* offered more detailed critiques of the past and aspirations for the future. A. L. Rowse analyzed the disillusion arising from the left's failure in the 1930s to provide effective, positive solutions to the problems it had so accurately diagnosed. He warned that this made a reaction to the right all too tempting (1:75–76). In another essay, on Bertrand Russell and André Gide, Rowse concluded that "the considerations they urge necessitate a Socialist society" (2:75–77). The Duke of Bedford, in the same issue of the magazine, attacked the far left and past politicians for a "lack of ability, principle, imagination and moral courage." He went on to outline a moderately progressive plan for the economic future of England after the war (2:69–70). Philip Toynbee revealed similarly moderate beliefs when he discussed the clash of liberal bourgeois morality and the communist belief in the class war. His humanism clung to the former at the expense of the latter (1:115–17).

In the eight issues edited by Waller no fewer than sixty-five poets contributed to the magazine. Traditional forms were favored by the bulk of these poets; sonnets, ballads, and lyrics written in quatrains prevailed as writers sought viable attitudes toward the war. The relatively simple ethical positions of the World War I poets and of many poets in the thirties were not available to the young men of 1939 and 1940. There was little confidence in who was right or wrong, no certainty as to what was being fought for. Such attitudes are expressed in early work by Keith Douglas: "Haydn Clock Symphony," "Russians," "Search for a God." Other notable poems are Anne Ridler's ballad "Geordie," Norman Nicholson's "Carol for Holy Innocents Day," Herbert Read's "Ode without Rhetoric," and two of C. Day Lewis's translations from the "Georgics." G. S. Fraser's translations of André Breton, Paul Eluard, and Giorgio de Chirico added an awareness of European modernism, while Alan Rook's several contributions augured the fine war poems he wrote from his war experiences. Edmund Blunden, Lawrence Durrell, Roy Fuller, David Gascoyne, Norman MacCaig, Ruth Pitter, and Hugh MacDiarmid also made single contributions to the first eight issues of *Kingdom Come*, ensuring that writing of the highest quality was always present; while Christopher Hassall, John Short, Gervase Stewart, and George Woodcock produced work which testifies to the fact that fine occasional poems may be written by poets who lack a sustained impulse.

The prose fiction was rarely less than entertaining and renders useful insight into the social and sexual mores of the times. The bulk of the prose was naturalistic and dealt with the social and psychological complexities of postadolescent lovemaking. Andrew Murray's "Arthur's Evening Out" and "Don Juan," Ruth Gray's "Chagrin," and Gordon Geoffrey's "It's Good to be Young" showed their writers to be acutely aware of class and culturally transmitted Puritanism as barriers to sexual fulfillment. S. G. Watts and Woodrow Wyatt obliquely showed the influence of Freud as they dealt with savage power struggles in domestic, familial situations. H. E. Bates provided some leaven to earnest undergraduate writings with a brilliantly comic piece, "Mademoiselle."

When *Kingdom Come* changed hands and was taken over by Treece, Schimanski, and Rook, prose fiction was the largest casualty. In an announcement on the inside cover of the new, smaller-format magazine, the editors declared that *Kingdom Come* would "continue to offer a platform to the best contemporary writers, artists and political theorists both European and American," but fiction was not high in their priorities. Only William Sansom's story "Kiss," published in the last issue of the magazine, is worth attention. The majority of space was reserved for discursive prose about literature and politics, some if not all of which bore the rhetorical sententiousness associated with the Apocalypse movement.

In the second number of *Kingdom Come* under its new editors, Treece explicitly aligned the magazine's "poetic policy" with the Apocalypse movement. Treece began his "Statement on Poetry Today" by outlining his antipathies. Geoffrey Grigson, the influential editor of *New Verse** in the thirties, is attacked for propounding "the dance of images" which, according to Treece, gave sanction to "impersonal word columns . . . as safely dead as stuffed trout" (3:21). Treece went on to castigate John Lehmann, editor of *New Writing** and *Penguin New Writing,** for judging everything by "degrees of poverty," and lastly dismissed surrealism and Georgianism. What was left, he suggested, was the Apocalypse, and he supported this contention with quotations from theoretical essays by G. S. Fraser and J. F. Hendry.

In practice the poetry contributors to the Apocalypse anthologies, no less than to the last four issues of *Kingdom Come*, shared little if any coherent aesthetic doctrine. Certainly they reacted against lists of images, the "bourgeois objectivism" advocated by Grigson, but otherwise there was a multiplicity of styles, ranging between the obscure and clotted symbolism which informed the deliberately mythopoeic work of Treece, and the socially concerned, overly public and political poetry of Hendry.

After Treece, Schimanski, and Rook became editors, the general standard of the poetry declined. But there remained notable contributions from Alan Rook and Herbert Read, and newcomers Alun Lewis, Sidney Keyes, and John Heath-Stubbs.

The nonfictional prose published by the later editors bears more of the Apocalyptic taint than the poetry. Schimanski established the tone in his opening editorial. Drawing heavily upon Herbert Read's *Poetry and Anarchism* for his definition of progress as the gradual strengthening of the differentiation of individuals within a society, he went on to argue, with a bombast verging on hysteria, that the purpose of *Kingdom Come* was "to help in bringing about a spiritual union to supplement the material alliance now united to defeat the philosophy of slavery." He went on to announce that "Our Kingdom to come is not the Kingdom of the Church or State but . . . the Kingdom of the spirit . . . when man shall rule himself in righteousness" (3:5–8).

Many of Schimanski's sentiments were reiterated in the first two essays in a series of six entitled "Art and Democracy," to which an inordinate amount of space was devoted (nos. 9, 10, 11). Herbert Read contributed an entirely muddled digest of his ideas as he attempted to reconcile the irreconcilable by arguing that the artist both was and was not a "separatist individual" (3:9–12). Kingsley Martin, editor of the *New Statesman and Nation** (see *VEA*), followed in a similar vein, when he remarked with little sense of embarrassment that "it is the artist's business to remain an individual and so, one of the herd, prevent the herd from being a herd" (3:15). Further unremarkable contributions to this series came from Leonard Woolf, Eric Newton, Norman Demuth, and Paul Bloomfield. With the exception of the dissenting Newton, who propounded the view that art had nothing to do with democracy, the others used their space to advocate the unexceptionable position that democracy was more conducive to artistic endeavor than totalitarianism.

Despite the rather mixed quality of the material appearing in the last four issues of *Kingdom Come*, the magazine as a whole remains a considerable achievement for its young editors and contributors in wartime circumstances. Unlike the more famous *Horizon** and *Penguin New Writing*, *Kingdom Come* was edited by men who were at undergraduate age when war broke out; they were members of what Sidney Keyes called the "O.C.T.U. [Oxford Christian Temperance Union] generation."[3] Cyril Connolly and John Lehmann both had been heavily involved in the literature and politics of the 1930s; their tastes had been formed in that troubled decade and inevitably affected the editorial policy of their respective magazines in the forties. *Kingdom Come* is of importance, then, not only because of the intrinsic merit of the work it printed, but also because it reflects the mood of the younger intelligentsia: their confused and desperate attempts to hang on to progressive political ideals, their determination to forge their own poetry and poetics. The first eight issues of the magazine capture something of the frenetic gaiety of Oxford during the earlier part of the war. The last four issues show the intensity and earnestness with which the debate on politics and literature was carried from the thirties into the forties. The magazine is thus invaluable to literary historians of the period both as it was involved in the fashionable movements of the day like anarchism and the Apocalypse, and as it stood outside them.

Notes

1. Julian Symons, *Notes from Another Country* (London, 1972), p. 67.
2. Ibid., p. 68.
3. Sidney Keyes, "The Artist in Society," in *Minos of Crete*, ed. Michael Meyer (London, 1948), p. 140.

Information Sources

BIBLIOGRAPHY

Hewison, Robert. *Under Siege: Literary Life in London 1939–45*. London, 1977.

Schimanski, Stefan, and Henry Treece, eds. *War Time Harvest: An Anthology of Poetry and Prose from the Magazine "Kingdom Come."* London, 1944.

Skelton, Robin. *Poetry of the Forties*. Harmondsworth, Eng., 1968.

Stanford, Derek. *Inside the Forties: Literary Memoirs 1937–1957*. London, 1977.

Symons, Julian. *Notes from Another Country*. London, 1972.

INDEXES

Volume 1, number 1 in *An Author Index to Selected British Little Magazines*, ed. B. C. Bloomfield (London, 1976).

REPRINT EDITIONS

None.

LOCATION SOURCES

American

Complete runs: Harvard University Library; U.S. Library of Congress; University of Chicago Library.

Partial run: University of Buffalo Library.

British

Complete runs: Bodleian Library; British Museum; Cambridge University Library.

Partial runs: Birmingham Public Library; National Library of Scotland, Edinburgh.

Publication History

MAGAZINE TITLE AND TITLE CHANGES

Kingdom Come, The Magazine of War-Time Oxford, Autumn 1939–Summer 1940. *Kingdom Come, Founded in War-Time Oxford*, Autumn 1940–Summer 1941. *Kingdom Come, The First Literary Magazine to Appear in War-Time*, Autumn 1941–Autumn 1943.

VOLUME AND ISSUE DATA

Volume 1, numbers 1–4, Autumn 1939–Summer 1940. Volume 2, numbers 1–4 [5–8], Autumn 1940–Summer 1941. Volume 3, numbers 9–12, Autumn 1941–Autumn 1943.

FREQUENCY OF PUBLICATION

Volumes 1 and 2: quarterly. Volume 3 was advertised as a bimonthly but the issues actually appeared in Autumn 1941, Spring 1942, Winter 1942, and Autumn 1943.

PUBLISHERS

Volumes 1 and 2: The Alden Press, Oxford. Volume 3, numbers 9, 10: Galil Publishing Company, Oxford. Volume 3, number 11: The Grey Walls Press, Billericay, Essex. Volume 3, number 12: published for the proprietors by the editor.

EDITORS

John Waller and Kenneth Harris, Autumn 1939–Winter 1939–1940. John Waller and Kenneth Harris; subeditor, Mildred Clinkard, Spring 1941. John Waller, Kenneth Harris, Miles Vaughan Williams, and Mildred Clinkard, Summer 1941. John Waller and Miles Vaughan Williams; subeditor, Elizabeth Waller, Autumn 1940–Summer 1941. Alan Rook, Stefan Schimanski, and Henry Treece; Oxford editor, Elizabeth Waller; art editor, Robert Melville, Autumn 1941–Autumn 1943.

A. D. Caesar

LEFT REVIEW

From October 1934, when it succeeded *Viewpoint* as the organ of the British section of the Writers' International, until its demise in May 1938, *Left Review* provided the leading voice for the "art as propaganda" school of leftist literary thought. As a result, critics frequently dismiss the magazine as politically simplistic and aesthetically unsatisfying, echoing Julian Symons's charge that the "editorial stance of *Left Review* [was] . . . You are either with us or against us: and if you are with us you will recognize that the principal function of writers today is to reject war and support the Soviet Union. . . . the effect of its conscious party line was to make its contributors write so uncommonly badly."[1] Most attacks, however, dismiss without close examination the underlying aesthetic premises of *Left Review*. Edgell Rickword, who edited the magazine during its middle period, described its commitment to

> literature that expressed and reflected the actual struggle of the down-trodden, as it were, or could convey by realistic treatment, reportage, their actual conditions of work and communicate their humanity and the plight of their position in a flourishing society—you know, a society that was bilious with riches at the top.[2]

Although some of this "revolutionary literature" certainly demonstrates what Bernard Bergonzi calls a "simplistic sentimental Russophilia," *Left Review* attempted to confront seriously the aesthetic issues raised by political art.[3] As Philip Henderson commented in 1939, "Articles have appeared in *Left Review* from time to time which encourage one to believe that at least some English Marxists realize that literature cannot be treated in quite the same way as a collection of statistics."[4]

The history of *Left Review* can be divided into three major periods corresponding to the tenure of the editors or editorial team. From October 1934 (1, no. 1) through December 1935 (2, no. 3), the monthly was edited by Montagu Slater, Amabel Williams-Ellis, T. H. Wintringham, and—after May 1935—Alick West. This period was devoted primarily to defining the magazine's role and published work primarily by British writers. Although the magazine appealed for 250 pounds to cover debts accumulated during the first year (1, no. 12:487), it also claimed the second highest circulation of any contemporary literary periodical (1, no. 9:359). From January 1936 (2, no. 4) through June 1937 (3, no. 5), it was edited by Rickword, who encouraged more penetrating criticism and published work by a number of important international writers. From July 1937 (3, no. 6) through the final issue of May 1938 (3, no. 16), it was edited by Randall Swingler and turned increasingly to purely political commentary as the international situation worsened.

Rickword traced the origins of *Left Review* to a meeting in Fitzrovia attended by a group which, while revolutionary in sympathies, was not explicitly linked to the Communist Party. Nevertheless, *Left Review*, like its short-lived predecessor *Viewpoint*, was closely allied to the pro-Soviet Writers' International. Wintringham, who had served a prison term, visited Russia, and later suffered a serious wound in Spain, was secretary of the organization; and Williams-Ellis was married to Executive Committee member John Strachey. A Writers' International statement published in the first issue (1, no. 1:38) defines the basic editorial stance of *Left Review* under the original editorial team. It condemns "the decadence of the past twenty years of English literature and the theatre" which reflects "the collapse of a culture, accompanying the collapse of an economic system." The statement concludes with a call for writers to oppose fascism, express the struggle of the working class, and defend the Soviet Union by exposing the "hidden forms" of imperialist war. Slater, this period's dominant editorial voice (Williams-Ellis handled correspondence with aspiring proletarian writers, while Wintringham was more directly involved with the political events and groups surrounding the journal),[5] reiterated these ideas in essays such as "The Purpose of a Left Review" (1, no. 9:359–65) and "Art and Right and Left" (2, no. 2:83–87). While calling for more rigorous intellectual engagement because "theoretical knowledge is one of the conditions of literary advance," the first essay also asserts that "to describe things as they are is a revolutionary act in itself." *Left Review* on occasion published straightforward reportage, such as "Nine Workers Describe a Shift at Work" (1, no. 6:201–16). But the second essay, published near the end of Slater's editorship, warns against overextending this approach and demands a refinement of British leftist aesthetics. Responding to an essay by Herbert Read, Slater writes, "Mr. Read's idea that socialist realism intends a mere transcript of the commonplace is simply mistaken." He quotes Maxim Gorky: "If to the idea extracted from the given reality we add, completing the idea, the desired, the possible, we obtain that romanticism which is at the basis of myth and which provokes a revolutionary attitude to reality, an attitude that changes the world" (2, no. 2:85).

The most serious discussions and applications of these ideas occurred under the editorship of Rickword, who had edited the influential *Calendar of Modern Letters** in the 1920s and served as treasurer of the Writers' International. Although several prominent writers, including W. H. Auden and Edward Upward (1, nos. 4, 5), had already been published by *Left Review*, Rickword expanded the range of contributors markedly. He convinced Stephen Spender and C. Day Lewis, both of whom had also previously written for the magazine, to become regular contributors (2, no. 13:667) and published a much greater amount of international writing. Some of the international material consisted of statements and manifestoes from writers such as André Malraux and Bertolt Brecht (2, no. 10), Gorky (2, no. 12), and Alexei Tolstoy (3, no. 3), and politicians such as Jawaharlal Nehru (2, no. 12). But it also included fiction by Ignazio Silone (2, no. 11) and poetry by Federico García Lorca (3, no. 2), Pablo Neruda (3, nos. 3, 7), and Vladimir Mayakovski (2, no. 13). The expansion of the focus of *Left Review* reflected Rickword's commitment to the Popular Front and his dedication, reiterated almost monthly in his editorials, to linking the British left with the international left, particularly in the defense of Republican Spain.[6] Lewis's essay "English WRITERS & a People's Front" states the basic political stance of *Left Review* under Rickword's guidance:

> As literature draws its nourishment from the life of the people and as its ideology is deeply affected by the social conditions of its age, so it is in the interest of the writer to establish connections with this life and to fight for conditions more favourable to his art. [2, no. 13:671]

During this period, *Left Review* by no means parroted a simple party line concerning the political role of the artist. A special supplement on surrealism (2, no. 10) included essays by West, Read, and Anthony Blunt, and paintings by Joan Miró and René Magritte. Read broke from the "party line" and directly attacked the official Soviet version of social realism as a formally reactionary "flirtation with the ideology of capitalism." In turn West defended the social realists, claiming that the surrealists "pretend to free language and thought from all conventions, but take no account of the fact that they are using bourgeois conventions, in a negative form all the time." West's call for an internal reorientation (rather than simple rejection) of surrealism shows an aesthetic openness which the magazine's critics rarely concede. Similarly, Rickword published a series of critical articles reassessing major literary figures (Blake, Dickens, Spenser, Hopkins, Ibsen, Swift, and Shakespeare) in relation to leftist aesthetics. Swingler's essay on Blake (3, no. 1), Lewis's review of Hopkins's papers (3, no. 3), and Rex Warner's essay on Swift (3, no. 5) concentrate on identifying structural similarities between the artistic vision and leftist theory. They rarely invoke simplistic ideological formulas.

Under Swingler *Left Review* went into a decline that Hugh Ford attributes to "a combination of unreasonable party control and a gradual exhaustion of funds. ...During Swingler's tenure, the party gradually assumed full control of the journal, including the purely mechanical details of size and shape, with an eye primarily on increasing its sale."[7] There are several obvious indications of direct party control. Swingler's first issue (3, no. 6) includes articles such as "The New Moscow" and "Life in the U.S.S.R." The November 1937 issue (3, no. 10) celebrates Soviet culture in nearly a dozen articles. The aesthetic focus of the magazine rapidly shifts from the evaluation of tradition to the direct consideration of propagandistic technique, as typified by Jack Lindsay's "Plea for Mass Declamation" (3, no. 9:511–16). Swingler's essay "What Is the Artist's Job?" (3, no. 15:930) contrasts sharply with the discussion of surrealism during Rickword's editorship. Swingler claims that the surrealists "are betrayed by their very vociferation, the pretentious flourish of any pseudo-philosophical, pseudo-psychological, pseudo-literary pseudo-phraseology which has nothing to do with painting, as people with a complete despair and sterility as regards the practice of Art." The polemical dismissal typifies the aesthetics of the final half-year of *Left Review*.

Swingler assessed the legacy of *Left Review* in an editorial at the beginning of the final issue (3, no. 16:957–60). Claiming that the magazine's history "has been the consistent and unwavering development of a principle," he credits *Left Review* with "mobilising a group of writers to express their common aim" and "tapping a source of writing which previously had found no means of expression." From the beginning, *Left Review* had in fact sought to discover working-class writers and bring them into contact with more traditional literary circles. Simon Blumenfeld (1, no. 7; 2, no. 9; 3, nos. 6, 7), Lewis Jones (3, nos. 3, 7), B. L. Coombes (3, no. 14), and Idris Davies (2, nos. 1, 16) could be classified as such discoveries, but the vast majority of *Left Review* was written by intellectuals with bourgeois backgrounds. Slater and Rickword, for example, both attended Oxford. Rickword, like Swingler, believed that "the real triumph was the drawing into the cultural ambit of a significant number of men and women who were barricaded out from participation in what was regarded as a middle-class preserve."[8] But he also admitted that the magazine's demise resulted in large part from the fact that they "couldn't get the quality that would have justified [their] carrying on."[9] More than Swingler's glowing editorial, this reflects the atmosphere and contents of the final issues of *Left Review*.

Several of the editors planned successors to *Left Review*. The final issue announced a new review tentatively titled *Art and Science* which would seek "to sharpen and direct our experience, to mobilise our powers *for action*" (3, no. 16:967). Allen Lane and Swingler had hoped to turn *Penguin New Writing**into a revolutionary review, a hope which was thwarted when John Lehmann became editor. Only Rickword's *Our Time** actually inherited what Arnold Rattenbury called the "worker-writer ideology."[10] Fittingly, Rickword, who guided the magazine at its peak, provides the best summation of the legacy of *Left Review*:

I think on its literary side it demonstrated that there could be a fruitful relationship between literature and politics, which in academic and conventional circles at that time were consciously kept separate. The Review, as consciously, regarded them as inseparable—as had always been recognised at times of social stress. Of course we weren't always successful in what we set out to do.[11]

Notes

1. Julian Symons, *The Thirties: A Dream Revolved* (London, 1960), pp. 74–75.
2. John Lucas, "An Interview with Edgell Rickword," in *The 1930s: A Challenge to Orthodoxy*, ed. John Lucas (New York, 1978), p. 5.
3. Bernard Bergonzi, *Reading the Thirties* (Pittsburgh, 1978), p. 135.
4. Philip Henderson, *The Poet and Society* (London, 1939), pp. 43–44.
5. Arnold Rattenbury, "Total Attainder and the Helots," in Lucas, *The 1930s*, p. 154.
6. A. T. Tolley, *The Poetry of the Thirties* (New York, 1975), p. 317.
7. Hugh D. Ford, *A Poets' War: British Poets and the Spanish Civil War* (Philadelphia, 1965), p. 81.
8. Quoted in Tolley, *Poetry of the Thirties*, p. 320.
9. Lucas, *The 1930s*, p. 5.
10. Rattenbury, "Total Attainder," p. 154.
11. Lucas, *The 1930s*, p. 12.

Information Sources

BIBLIOGRAPHY

Ford, Hugh D. *A Poets' War: British Poets and the Spanish Civil War*. Philadelphia, 1965.
Lewis, Cecil Day, ed. *The Mind in Chains*. London, 1937.
Lucas, John. "An Interview with Edgell Rickword." In *The 1930s: A Challenge to Orthodoxy*. Edited by John Lucas. New York, 1978.
Rattenbury, Arnold. "Total Attainder and the Helots." In *The 1930s: A Challenge to Orthodoxy*. Edited by John Lucas. New York, 1978.
Symons, Julian. *The Thirties: A Dream Revolved*. London, 1960.
Tolley, A. T. *The Poetry of the Thirties*. New York, 1975.

INDEXES

An *Author Index to Selected British Little Magazines*, ed. B. C. Bloomfield (London, 1976).

REPRINT EDITIONS

Frank Cass and Company Limited, London, 1968.

LOCATION SOURCES

American

Complete runs: Harvard University Library; New York Public Library; Pennsylvania State University Library; Smith College Library; University of Buffalo

Library; University of Kansas Library; University of Michigan Library; Yale
University Library.

British

Complete run: British Museum.

Partial run: Birmingham Public Library.

Publication History

MAGAZINE TITLE AND TITLE CHANGES

Left Review.

VOLUME AND ISSUE DATA

Volume 1, numbers 1–12, October 1934–September 1935. Volume 2, numbers
1–16, October 1935–January 1937. Volume 3, numbers 1–16, February 1937–
May 1938.

FREQUENCY OF PUBLICATION

Monthly.

PUBLISHERS

No publisher listed. Editorial address c/o Collet's Bookshop at various addresses.
Volume 1, numbers 1–5: 66 Charing Cross Road, London, W. C. 1. Volume 1,
numbers 6–11: 3 Red Lion Passage, Holborn, W. C. 1. Volume 1, number 12–
volume 2, number 6: 7 John Street, Theobald's Road, London, W. C. 1. Volume
2, number 7–volume 3, number 16: 2 Parton Street, Red Lion Square, London
W. C. 1.

EDITORS

Montagu Slater, Amabel Williams-Ellis, T. H. Wintringham, volume 1, numbers
1–8. Slater, Williams-Ellis, Wintringham, Alick West, volume 1, number 9–
volume 2, number 3. Edgell Rickword, volume 2, number 4–volume 3, number
5. Randall Swingler, volume 3, numbers 6–16.

Craig Werner

LIFE AND LETTERS

In 1928, with the financial support of Oliver Brett (later Third Viscount Esher),
Desmond MacCarthy began *Life and Letters*. MacCarthy had already gained
prominence as a critic of literature and drama as editor of *New Quarterly* (1907–
1910), and as literary editor of *New Statesman** (see *VEA*). As he admitted
somewhat ruefully in his first editorial in September 1928, he was a man in the
midst of middle age. As such, though MacCarthy was not so quick to admit
this, his tastes were to a large degree already determined; his editorial policy
reflected his interests in recording contemporary trends rather than introducing
new approaches. As a result, for the nearly six years that he edited it, *Life and
Letters* generally published pieces appealing to contemporary British interests,
and it gave attention to writers and topics outside the British Isles only in relation
to those concerns.

Much of the early success of *Life and Letters* must be attributed not only to Desmond MacCarthy's enormous personal talent but also to his close ties with many of the prominent intellectual figures of the day, in many cases dating from his university days. As a member of the prestigious Cambridge Conversazione Society (the Apostles), MacCarthy first came to know Bertrand Russell, Lytton Strachey, Leonard Woolf, and John Maynard Keynes. When *Life and Letters* was being formed, MacCarthy did not hesitate to press these men, and a number of other figures in the Bloomsbury set, to contribute pieces for early numbers of the magazine.[1] In a 22 March 1928 entry in her diary, Virginia Woolf made note of MacCarthy's efforts to solicit the help of his friends. "All his blandishments are now active to get articles for 'Life & Letters' which comes out in May. I am scarcely flattered now to be asked."[2] His activities met with fine success, and in the early volumes of the magazine most of the prominent individuals associated with Bloomsbury published at least one piece and often several.

In the opening editorial MacCarthy sought to emphasize the openness of his magazine by assuring that "readers of *Life and Letters* cannot expect to perceive any marked tendency in its pages and may anticipate that they will be given a varied diet." From MacCarthy's perspective this was probably an accurate statement. In the early volumes the magazine showed a broad, apolitical concern for the arts and the affairs of the day. A retrospective analysis permits one to see the marked influence of Bloomsbury figures and the distinct preference for Bloomsbury enthusiasms. Pieces by Virginia Woolf (October 1928), Vita Sackville-West (December 1928), Bertrand Russell (November 1928), Clive Bell (June 1928), and Peter Quennell (July 1928) appeared in the first volume, as did contributions from writers of previous generations like Max Beerbohm and Thomas Hardy (June 1928).

After the first few volumes, certain characterizing features began to emerge. Figures associated with modernism received a great deal of space, either as subjects of essays or as contributors themselves. Cyril Connolly regularly presented his views on James Joyce (April 1929), D. H. Lawrence, Aldous Huxley (December 1931), and others. E. M. Forster (May, June 1928), A.J.A. Symons (March 1929), and George Santayana (June 1929) all wrote on contemporary artists, while Sir Kenneth Clark wrote on Leonardo da Vinci and Lytton Strachey offered sketches of eighteenth- and nineteenth-century figures. In fiction MacCarthy was equally careful to bulwark each number with established figures. He published short stories by Sherwood Anderson (January, March 1931), Lord Dunsany (February 1934), Enid Bagnold (May 1930), and Sean O'Casey (February 1934), and various pieces by D. H. Lawrence (July 1930, March 1932). He devoted an entire issue to an abridged version of Richard Hughes's *A High Wind in Jamaica* (August 1929), and he printed a prepublication extract from Evelyn Waugh's *Black Mischief*. In early numbers MacCarthy published with some frequency "Reader Bibliographies" on a range of topics: recent Shakespearean investigations (January 1929); Ibsen (June 1928); life and letters after the Restoration (compiled by John Haywood) (June 1930). Although some might feel that MacCarthy gave an inordinate amount of space to detective fiction, despite its admitted popularity at the time, book reviews generally reflected the interests and tastes of the period. Like most journals, for example, *Life and Letters* savagely attacked William Faulkner's *The Sound and the Fury* when it reviewed the novel in July 1931, while a March 1933 review of *Light in August*, appearing after Faulkner had begun to gain some acceptance, asserted that "the book makes Mr. Faulkner's position as high as that of anyone writing in America to-day."

In March 1932, beginning with volume 9, *Life and Letters* shifted from monthly to quarterly publication. The change apparently reflected the magazine's difficulties, for in a 12 December 1933 letter to Quentin Bell, Virginia Woolf bluntly stated, "Life and Letters is dying."[3] The journal survived, but MacCarthy left his position as editor after the publication of volume 10. In April 1934 Hamish Miles took over as editor. Monthly publication resumed, and the basic format remained the same. The editorial slant, however, shifted markedly away from Bloomsbury writers. His approach was more daring than the one that MacCarthy followed when he had begun editing *Life and Letters*, devoting attention to emerging writers rather than to established figures, including W. H. Auden (May 1934), Stephen Spender (April 1934), C. Day Lewis (August 1934), Louis MacNeice (June 1934), Frank O'Connor (May, August 1934), and Graham Greene (August 1934). Miles balanced these pieces by relatively new talents with those from established writers of previous generations: Herbert Read, Siegfried Sassoon (September 1934), Osbert Sitwell (August 1934), George Santayana (August 1934), and Wyndham Lewis (April, June 1934). Miles, however, did not repeat MacCarthy's success, and he left his position after completing only one volume.

In September 1934 Constable and Company acquired the magazine, and R. Ellis Roberts became its editor. In an editorial in the October issue, Roberts asserted that he would maintain traditions established over the first six years. In addition, he introduced certain features that in varying forms became part of the magazine's permanent format: a monthly commentary on world affairs, reviews of theater and cinema productions and of gallery exhibitions, essays on "governing ideas of the day in science and politics," and "articles on prominent and notorious persons of the past and, sometimes, the present." Despite the high aspirations of the editorial, the volumes that Roberts edited, 11 and 12 (a single issue), proved if anything to be revisionist, drawing heavily on well-established writers such as W. B. Yeats (November 1934), G. K. Chesterton (December 1934), Clive Bell (October 1934), and St. John Ervine (March 1935).

The Bredin Publishing Company acquired *Life and Letters* in September 1935, beginning an association with Robert Herring that would continue for the duration of the magazine's existence. The name was changed to *Life and Letters To-Day*, and volumes 13–15 (September 1935–Winter 1936) appeared under the joint editorship of Herring and Petrie Townshend. The magazine reverted to quarterly publication, and Herring and Townshend announced in their inaugural editorial, "We incline to young writers, more for what they may do, given outlet than for what they have done." Subsequent editorials disavowed an interest in specific critical theory and declared the aim to be to produce "an international review in the Anglo-Saxon tongue." Generally the magazine still favored authors who had already gained some recognition, and it included some very famous writers, presumably to demonstrate its substance—Havelock Ellis (September 1935), Gertrude Stein (September 1935), Osbert Sitwell, H[ilda] D[oolittle] (September, December 1935), Edith Sitwell (December 1935). A number of the pieces that appeared at this time were from writers just beginning to establish themselves. Dylan Thomas published what was to become the first poem in his sonnet sequence, "Altarwise by Owl Light" (December 1935), and poems by Ruthven Todd (December 1935, Spring 1936) and John Pudney (September 1934) also appeared. The editors printed a rare critical piece by Wallace Stevens on Marianne Moore (December 1935) as well as a number of essays by more established figures: Sergei Eisenstein on film (September-December 1935), Bertolt Brecht on Chinese theater (Winter 1936), and Thomas Mann on Freud (Autumn 1936). With volume 16 Herring assumed sole editorship, and he continued in that position until publication ceased in 1950.

An editorial in the first issue of volume 15 signaled a significant shift in policy. Although for its first eight years *Life and Letters* had eschewed giving notice to the political and social turmoil in England and on the Continent, in its Autumn 1936 number it announced support for the Republican forces in the Spanish Civil War. While its editorials never attained the fervent polemical pitch of pieces in contemporary journals such as *New Verse** or *Left Review,** this move marked the beginning of a period of activity that would continue as long as the magazine existed. Julian Symons remembered the general attitude among intellectuals toward the conflict. "To those uncertain of their course . . . and feeling above all a need to identify themselves with some cause unquestionably good, it seemed that the future of Europe was being drawn on the map of Spain."[4] Herring made clear the depth of his feeling on the turmoil in Spain by contributing succeeding editorials on the topic and by printing a number of pieces dealing with the war and the havoc it created.

Concern for international politics coincided with increased interest in literary figures outside the British Isles. Essays examined a range of well-known Continental writers, contributions from non-English authors increased, and a succession of articles appeared on contemporary poetry. Several figures began to emerge as frequent contributors. H. D. and her close friend Bryher (Winifred Ellerman) often published their work. Herring showed scant interest in the Auden generation, but he published at regular intervals the work of Dylan Thomas, and Vernon Watkins, and other poets who would later come to be associated with the neo-Romantic movement. Thomas Mann, Osbert Sitwell, and Dorothy Richardson contributed a number of essays.

In March 1939 the *London Mercury and Bookman* ceased publication, and in April it was amalgamated into *Life and Letters To-Day* with no noticeable change in the latter's format or editorial policy. Editorials commented on the growing tension in Europe, but contributions followed much the same pattern that had characterized the magazine since its inception. In the last volume to be published before the outbreak of World War II, Dorothy Richardson wrote a long review essay of James Joyce's *Finnegans Wake*, and Herring devoted the August number to articles, fiction, and poems from Baltic countries.

The war exerted a pronounced change on *Life and Letters*, as it did on every aspect of English life. While many would question J. B. Priestley's dour assessment that World War II "marked the end of literary society," the feeling of crisis that produced those sentiments was clearly present in the wartime numbers of *Life and Letters*.[5] During the conflict Herring devoted a great deal of editorial space to the impact of the fighting on civilians in England, the role of artists in war, and the devastation that Europe was being forced to endure. If at times these pieces seemed to take on apparently shrill or strident tones, they served to reflect the tremendous stress continual fighting must have placed on the civilian population. Herring's editorials showed no lack of spirit, but they did convey a sense of the appalling waste that the conflict created. The London Blitz forced a temporary displacement of editorial offices to Derbyshire from early in 1941 until July 1942, when the London offices reopened with a staff greatly reduced because of conscription.

Life and Letters survived what Robert Hewison has termed "a grand slaughter of magazines" brought on by the shortages and uncertainties of the war in 1939 and 1940, but it did undergo significant modifications. (The war did not bring new magazine publication to a standstill. Cyril Connolly began *Horizon*,* a direct competitor of *Life and Letters*, in 1940, and a number of other new journals appeared as well.)[6] While the format generally remained the same, the circumstances of the war exerted a marked influence on its breadth and scope. During this period many of the contributors dealt, naturally enough, with subjects directly related to wartime experiences. Shortages of paper and ink limited the length of individual numbers, and disruptions in day to day activities brought the attenuation or disappearance of certain features. Film reviews, which had received a great deal of space during the mid and late thirties, appeared less and less frequently and finally were dropped. Theater reviews also disappeared as German bombing forced many companies out of London and into the provinces on tours. For a time Herring's editorials, essays, and poems increasingly dominated the magazine, possibly to compensate for the difficulty during the early years of the war in acquiring contributions to meet deadlines. After the London offices reopened in 1942, the quality and the range of contributions generally matched prewar standards. Even during the turbulence of the war, *Life and Letters* proved well attuned to prevailing tastes. Poetry of the Apocalyptic writers, for example, was strongly represented, as it was in most literary magazines of the period.[7] Herring, in fact, seemed greatly taken with the movement, for as Derek Stanford noted, "*Life and Letters*, . . . through the welcome extended by its editor Robert Herring, became the nearest thing to a Neo-Romantic periodical we were able to find."[8]

As the conflict in Europe drew to a close and England prepared for peace, the tone of the magazine reflected a slow recovery from the trauma of war and a growing pessimism for the future. In an editorial in the first issue of volume 44 (January 1945), Herring drew a stark picture of the society emerging from the conflict. "I see in all fields, from international relationships to literary politics, the familiar jockeying into position whose selfishness results in dissipation of energy and halted achievement."[9]

Despite the grim tone of the editorials, the character of the magazine and its structure continued much along the lines set down by Desmond MacCarthy when it was first established. Its essays reflected a continuing interest in the development of contemporary poetry, the work of established writers, the state of international literature, and world affairs. H. D. published a series of articles on Freud that subsequently formed the basis for her *Tribute to Freud*, which appeared in 1956. Special postwar numbers were devoted to writers of Italy, Sweden, Persia, China, India, Jamaica, Scotland, and Wales. Theater reviews again became a regular feature, and film reviews were restored. The journal, in fact, reflected the general stability that had characterized its existence. Consequently, its cessation of publication came abruptly and unexpectedly. A brief announcement, in the penultimate number, of plans to discontinue publication was the first hint that problems existed. In the final issue, for June 1950, Herring expanded the explanation, citing rising costs and limited circulation as the reason for its demise.

Notes

1. David Gadd, *The Loving Friends: A Portrait of Bloomsbury* (New York, 1974), p. 21.
2. Virginia Woolf, *The Diary of Virginia Woolf*, ed. Anne Olivier Bell assisted by Andrew McNeillie (New York, 1980), 3:178.
3. Virginia Woolf, *The Letters of Virginia Woolf*, ed. Nigel Nicolson and Joanne Trautmann (New York, 1979), 5:259.
4. Julian Symons, *The Thirties: A Dream Revolved* (London, 1960), p. 118.
5. Robert Hewison, *Under Siege: Literary Life in London 1939–1945* (London, 1977), p. ix.
6. Ibid., pp. 11–12.
7. Ibid., p. 113.
8. Derek Stanford, *Inside the Forties: Literary Memoirs 1937–1957* (London, 1977), p. 81.
9. Quoted in Hewison, *Under Siege*, p. 172.

Information Sources

BIBLIOGRAPHY

Gadd, David. *The Loving Friends: A Portrait of Bloomsbury*. New York, 1974.
Hewison, Robert. *Under Siege: Literary Life in London 1939–1945*. London, 1977.
Hoffman, Frederick J., Charles Allen, and Carolyn F. Ulrich. *The Little Magazine: A History and a Bibliography*. 2nd ed. Princeton, 1947.

MacCarthy, Desmond. *Memories*. London, 1953.

Stanford, Derek. *Inside the Forties: Literary Memoirs 1937–1957*. London, 1977.

Symons, Julian. *A.J.A. Symons: His Life and Speculations*. London, 1950.

––––––. *The Thirties: A Dream Revolved*. London, 1960.

Woolf, Virginia. *The Diary of Virginia Woolf*, vol. 3. Edited by Anne Olivier Bell assisted by Andrew McNeillie. New York, 1980.

––––––. *The Letters of Virginia Woolf*, vol. 5. Edited by Nigel Nicolson and Joanne Trautmann. New York, 1979.

INDEXES

Each volume indexed. *Comprehensive Index to English Language Little Magazines 1890–1970*, series 1, ed. Marion Sader (Millwood, N.Y., 1976).

REPRINT EDITIONS

Kraus Reprint, Millwood, N.Y.

LOCATION SOURCES

American

Widely available.

British

Complete runs: Birmingham Public Library; Bodleian Library; British Museum; Cambridge University Library; Liverpool University Library; Manchester Public Library; University of London Library.

Partial runs: Widely available.

Publication History

MAGAZINE TITLE AND TITLE CHANGES

Life and Letters, 1928–1935. *Life and Letters To-Day*, 1935–1939. *Life and Letters To-Day continuing The London Mercury and Bookman*, 1939–1945. *Life and Letters and The London Mercury and Bookman*, 1945. *Life and Letters and The London Mercury*, 1946–1950.

VOLUME AND ISSUE DATA

Volumes 1–12, numbers 1–64, June 1928–April 1935. Volumes 13–64, numbers 1–154, September 1935–June 1950.

FREQUENCY OF PUBLICATION

Monthly, June 1928–December 1931. Quarterly, March 1932–February 1934. Monthly, April 1934–April 1935. Quarterly, September 1935–June 1938. Monthly, September 1938–June 1950.

PUBLISHERS

1928–1934: The Statesman Publishing Co., 10 Great Queen Street, London, W.C. 2. 1934: Life and Letters, 30 Bedford Square, London, W.C. 1. 1934–1935: Constable & Co. Ltd., 10–12 Orange St., London, W.C. 2. 1935–1950: The Bredin Publishing Co., 26 Maiden Lane, London, W.C. 2 (1935–1940); 41 Upper Town Road, Greenfield, Middlesex (1941–1942); 26 Maiden Lane, London, W.C. 2 (1942–1943); 430 Strand, London, W.C. 2 (1943–1950).

EDITORS

Desmond MacCarthy, 1928–1934. Hamish Miles, 1934. R. Ellis Roberts, 1934–1935. Robert Herring and Petrie Townshend, 1935–1936. Robert Herring, 1937–1950.

Michael Patrick Gillespie

LIFE OF THE SPIRIT, THE. See BLACKFRIARS

LILLIPUT

Started in London in 1937 by Stefan Lorant, a refugee from Hitler's Germany, *Lilliput* bore the marks at birth of its origins in the smart, assured world of European journalism. Lorant was said to have borrowed from a lady-friend the 1,200 pounds in capital necessary to start the magazine. It was an immediate success. A thick, pocket-sized monthly selling at the low price of six pence, it created an impression of offering much in little. (The first issue boasted fifty full-page photographs, a center section of color reproductions of art, ten articles, and ten short stories.) From an initial print order of 75,000 the magazine rose to 175,000 by October 1938 and in the following year approached a quarter of a million. This desirable property was bought by Edward Hulton, the publisher, in the summer of 1938; he promptly introduced advertising, which Lorant had done without. Lorant continued as editor and began the publication, for Hulton Press, of another very successful periodical, the illustrated weekly *Picture Post*.

Lorant, a Hungarian born in Budapest in 1901, was a superb picture editor who had at one time worked as a cameraman in European films before he began his career in journalism. In 1933 he had been the editor of the *Münchner Illustrierte Presse*, an illustrated weekly. When the Nazis came to power he was arrested immediately, held without trial for six months, and then deported to Hungary. The story is told in his book *I Was Hitler's Prisoner* (1935). He made his way to England and was working for Odhams Press, in London, when he began the magazine whose success established him as one of the most sought-after editors in Fleet Street.

Lorant had proved able to capitalize on his European experience and contacts. Above all, he knew how to employ the relatively sophisticated, and recently developed, forms of photojournalism, and drew for his material upon the photo agencies of continental Europe as well as of Britain and America. His facing-page juxtapositions of images became famous: Hitler, arm upraised in the Nazi salute, opposite a friendly dog lifting a paw; a British statesman's face opposed to a close-up photograph of a pear.

The focus of the magazine was contemporary and international. Although perhaps best known for its photographs, which today make it a collector's item, *Lilliput* also published humorous writers of worldwide reputation. In the prewar years, American contributors included James Thurber, Manuel Komroff, Leonard Q. Ross, and William Saroyan; the Europeans, Ferenc Molnar, Hasse Zetterstrom, and Sandor Hunyedi; British and Irish writers providing stories included Liam O'Flaherty, Monica Dickens, and Lord Dunsany. Light verse came from Stevie Smith and Ogden Nash. Celebrated writers of a generally heavier manner and subject were not excluded; they provided personal anecdotes. Arthur Koestler, for instance, wrote "The Foulest Christmas I Ever Had" for the December

1942 number. Only very occasionally the antifascist stance of the magazine became explicit in dark and even despairing words, as in an article by Ernst Toller, the German playwright, on Nazi oppression, published shortly before his death. The general tone of the magazine was light and the articles and stories were short, rarely more than 1,000 words.

When Britain, in turn, was threatened by invasion, Lorant, who had good reason, personally, to expect the worst from the Nazis, left for America. He traveled on the S.S. *Britannic*, making the last voyage of a trans-Atlantic liner carrying fare-paying passengers for the duration of the war. One of his fellow passengers was Noel Coward. After the war, Lorant continued to live and work in the United States, where he published a number of picture books.

In wartime Britain, *Lilliput* continued to flourish, its good humor suiting the national mood of jaunty defiance of the enemy. Tom Hopkinson, who was Lorant's assistant, became editor of both *Picture Post* and *Lilliput*. Of the two, the pocket magazine of humor made fewer demands. "*Lilliput*," he has written, "was an easy magazine to sell. It did not attack or criticize. It simply made one laugh. . . . Sales soared into the hundreds of thousands." His assistant editor, Kaye Webb, continued the prewar practice of attracting big names to provide personal anecdotes or opinion pieces. G. B. Shaw, for instance, wrote an article for relatively small pay. A generally high quality of comic fiction continued to be published, largely by British writers; in 1941 contributors included V. S. Pritchett, Wyndham Lewis, Evelyn Waugh, J. Maclaren-Ross, and the duo of Caryl Brahms and S. J. Simon.

In the postwar years Richard Bennett, succeeding Hopkinson, developed a strongly British humor in the magazine. The leading spirits were Patrick Campbell and Maurice Richardson, the first providing an adroit comedy of wit and the second being notable for stories of surrealist humor involving a series of adventures of the Id, Dwarf Engelbrecht by name. Short story writers John Pudney, L.A.G. Strong, and Sylvia Townsend Warner were among the British writers contributing to a magazine that was now a rival to *Punch** (see *VEA*) in its brand of English humor and definitely a cut above general interest periodicals in its literary contributions. *Lilliput* had not generally maintained its prewar international range of contributors, although the work of Belgian crime writer Georges Simenon regularly appeared in 1948 in a series of 1,500–word stories.

In the early 1950s, in a climate of uncertainty common to many periodicals with the arrival of television in Britain, *Lilliput* abandoned its formula of short, light stories and began to print longer stories (up to 10,000 words) which, in 1951, included Doris Lessing's "A Home for the Highland Cattle." The magazine had become thicker, to accommodate the longer work, and enlarged its octavo page size; photographically, the magazine published more nudes. (In April 1960 the entire shipment of the magazine to Malta was seized on the grounds of indecency.) The circulation had dwindled to 73,000, and in July 1960 *Lilliput* ceased publication when it was incorporated into another pocket magazine of more evident salacious content, *Men Only*.

The best period of the magazine's existence had been its first dozen years, when it filled the prescription of Lorant's editorial of March 1939. *Lilliput's* success, he explained, owed to the need for a low-priced magazine for intelligent readers, for "a magazine which would mingle humor and information, which would be both funny and thought-provoking, a magazine with no axe to grind, which would have the courage to present an undistorted, unbiased picture of our times."

Note

1. Tom Hopkinson, *Of This Our Time* (London, 1982), p. 57.

Information Sources

INDEXES
> None.

REPRINT EDITIONS
> None.

LOCATION SOURCES

American
> Partial runs: New York Public Library; U.S. Library of Congress; University of Oklahoma Library, Norman.

British
> Complete runs: British Museum; National Library of Scotland, Edinburgh.

Publication History

MAGAZINE TITLE AND TITLE CHANGES
> *Lilliput: The Pocket Magazine for Everyone.*

VOLUME AND ISSUE DATA
> Volume 1, number 1–volume 46, number 7, 1 July 1937–July 1960.

FREQUENCY OF PUBLICATION
> Monthly.

PUBLISHER
> Pocket Publications, 43–44 Shoe Lane, London, E.C. 4.

EDITORS
> Stefan Lorant; Sydney Jacobson, assistant editor, 1937–1940. Tom Hopkinson; Kaye Webb, assistant editor, 1940–1947. Richard Bennett, 1947–1950. Jack Hargreaves; Patrick Campbell, associate editor; Maurice Richardson, literary consultant, 1951–1955. Unknown (no staff listed), November 1955–. June 1959. William Richardson, executive editor; Denis Pitts, assistant editor, July-December 1959. Denis Pitts, editor; Walter Clapham, assistant editor, January-July 1960.

Alan C. Thomas

LINES. NEW POETRY, SCOTLAND. See LINES REVIEW

LINES REVIEW

During the Edinburgh Festival of 1952 an eight-page poetry broadsheet was offered to the public. It sold for one shilling or five new pence, and contained just eight poems by five Scottish poets. This was the first number of what has since become the prestigious *Lines Review*. Then entitled *Lines*, only the fact that it was described as "A Quarterly Broadsheet of Poetry" suggested that anything beyond a single issue was contemplated; it had no title page, listed no editor or editorial board, and made no policy statement. Its original *raison d'être*, however, was a peculiarly Scottish one, for it was printed "in honour of Hugh MacDiarmid's 60th Birthday." The five poets whose work appeared were Norman MacCaig, George Kay, Sydney Goodsir Smith, Hamish Henderson, and Alan Riddell. (Long since sold out, this first issue is now a collector's item.)

New Year 1953 passed without a further number of *Lines* appearing, and it began to look as though the promised quarterly was not to continue. Spring, however, brought forth *Lines* number 2, no longer described as a broadsheet but subtitled *New Poetry, Scotland*. Still priced at one shilling, it had twice as many pages as the previous issue, though the pages were somewhat reduced in size. There was now a title page; Alan Riddell was listed as editor, assisted by Bill Hall, George Oliver, and Ivor Turnbull. A journalist and minor poet with several volumes of published verse to his name, Riddell's enthusiasm for poetry helped to launch *Lines Review* successfully. He remained editor for the first six numbers, until September 1954, when he left to visit his native Australia, and returned as editor from 1962 to Spring 1967 (nos. 18–23). The scope of the magazine had been enlarged: besides poems by nine poets, there was a black-and-white line drawing as frontispiece and a page of biographical notes; advertisements were also included, presumably to help make *Lines* financially viable. Four of the poets who had appeared in the first number were again represented, and among the newcomers, one, Derick Thomson, published one of his Gaelic poems, together with his own translation.

Lines 3 appeared, on time, in Summer 1953, extended to twenty-eight pages. In a page of editorial comment Alan Riddell stated clearly and succinctly that the policy aim of *Lines* was "to present the best products of living Scots writers, without regard to their intellectual basis." Works by fourteen poets, including all of the original five, were printed in this number, as well as a critical article on Robert Fergusson and Sydney Goodsir Smith by the academic poet Alexander Scott. Space was also given for the first time to a review. The three assistants to the editor named in *Lines* 2 were no longer mentioned, but M. Macdonald was named as managing editor.

After a gap of some six months, the successor of *Lines* 3 was published in January 1954. Its title was changed to *Lines Review*, but its heredity was acknowledged in the sequential numbering; though it was given a new title and a new format, it was number 4. Alan Riddell was assisted by an editorial board, comprising Hugh MacDiarmid, Sydney Goodsir Smith, Norman MacCaig, and Somhairle MacLean (Sorley MacLean); Denis Peploe was art editor. Physically, the format was reduced to A5 size, as it remains today. Despite the three numbers of *Lines*, this issue may be seen as the true beginning of *Lines Review*. It contained poems, a critical article on the Scottish Renaissance movement, an obituary on

Dylan Thomas, who had died the previous year, an editorial "Comment," and a picture as frontispiece.

For two years the magazine appeared fairly regularly, but after the publication of number 10 in December 1955 difficulties began to arise; a double number 11/12 was issued in 1956, and thereafter, until number 22 for Winter 1966, there was an average of only one a year. Since number 23 (Spring 1967) *Lines Review* has again appeared fairly regularly, three, four, or five times a year. However, the numbers do not correspond to a quarterly issue from the magazine's inception, and it is not possible to be sure of the number of any particular magazine from its date of issue. Also, there has been no attempt as yet to impose volume numbers; thus, the bound volumes may vary in content, according to the practice of the library responsible for the binding.

Between 1954 and 1962 there were several editors. The four numbers published in 1955 and the double number of 1956 were edited in ebullient fashion by Sydney Goodsir Smith. Also antipodean by birth (in Wellington, New Zealand), Smith attended the universities of Edinburgh and Oxford. A poet and journalist, he had absorbed Scottish culture fully and was for some years one of the most highly respected of Scottish poets. *Lines Review* 13 (Summer 1957) was edited by the Glaswegian poet Tom Scott. The next two numbers (14 and 15; Spring 1958, Summer 1959) were edited by J. K. Annand, numbers 16 and 17 (Winter 1960, Summer 1961) by Albert Mackie, both poets who had previously published in the magazine. In Summer 1967, beginning with number 24, Robin Fulton took over as permanent editor. Born on the Isle of Arran, Fulton, like several of the earlier editors, attended Edinburgh University; there he was awarded his M.A. in 1959 and his Ph.D. in 1972. He is a sensitive and delicate poet, and he has an increasing body of verse published in regularly produced volumes since 1963.

Numbers 61 and 62 (June and September 1977) were edited by Robert Calder, the first editor not himself a poet. With number 63 (December 1977) William Montgomerie became editor. One of the elder statesmen of Scottish literature, Montgomerie has published widely, both poetry and other works, mainly with a Scottish flavor. The present editor, Trevor Royle, succeeded to the editorial position in June 1982 with number 81. A well-known figure on the Scottish literary scene, he was for some years literature director of the Scottish Arts Council, a position which he resigned in order to become a full-time writer and broadcaster.

At the outset, *Lines* was no more than the vehicle for presenting to the public new poems by Scottish poets. *Lines* 3 suggested a concern not solely with poetry, but with Scottish writing in general, including the reviewing of books on Scottish literature new and old; significantly, its policy was one of noncommitment to any particular school or movement. Before he gave up the editorship for the first time, Alan Riddell, in his editorial "Comment" in number 6, emphasized the neutrality of *Lines Review* and reaffirmed its intention of publishing "the best poetry of whatever school we can find in Scotland." In the next number Sydney

Goodsir Smith gave an assurance that, although the editorial board had been shuffled, the policy remained unchanged. Two slight shifts in direction occurred under Smith's editorship: more prose was published and a long "Editorial" replaced Alan Riddell's page of "Comment." The lively editorials reflected not only Smith's personality but the cut and thrust of critical argument which almost always looms large in the somewhat enclosed Scottish literary world. The magazine continued, however, to take a fairly independent line, though some of the reviews began to have a bipartisan look.

With the publication of number 13 in the summer of 1957, Tom Scott became editor, and *Lines Review* appeared to be a different magazine. There were an aggressively Scots-oriented editorial and a new statement of policy. The magazine would concentrate on "essays in Scots criticism" and encourage long poems. This number contained two essays, one by Robert Garioch and the other by Hugh MacDiarmid, and a long poem by the editor himself. This new look, however, died almost at inception. The next number, 14, which appeared in the spring of 1958, was edited by the Scots poet J. K. Annand, who reaffirmed in his editorial the original policy "to publish verse, produced in Scotland or by Scottish writers furth of the country, of as wide a range as possible, and in any medium, so long as it is good of its kind"; he also promised prose articles with a "point of view" to express and reviews by writers "who display disinterestedness, experience and maturity." What had looked like a takeover by a Scots faction had been averted, and the magazine had once more reasserted its independence of coterie control. Number 21 for Summer 1965 announced that an Arts Council guarantee would enable *Lines Review* "to come out regularly twice a year—summer and winter—in future!"

The next change of policy occurred in the third number edited by Robin Fulton (no. 26). He gave notice that there would be a reduction in the number of contributors in order to allow each of them more space; the second and more significant change was the decision to include "a foreign item" in each edition, making the magazine no longer exclusively Scottish. The changes under Fulton's editorship were, in fact, more radical than at first appeared, for the whole character of *Lines Review* began to alter. The "foreign" items appeared regularly, often as major contributions to the magazine and on several occasions comprising the whole of an edition. Number 35 (December 1970) was a Swedish issue, while the double number 52/53 for May 1975 was devoted to Irish writing and number 59 for September 1976 to Hungarian poetry. Additionally, special numbers were devoted to the work of one writer, making a kind of minor *festschrift* for several well-known poets and novelists, mainly, but not exclusively, Scottish: Iain Crichton Smith (no. 29, June 1969), Sorley MacLean (no. 34, September 1970), Robert Nye (no. 38, September 1971), Derick Thomson (no. 39, December 1971), and David Lindsay (no. 40, March 1972) were honored in this way. Number 37 for June 1971 was entirely given over to a long article by Alan Jackson, "The Knitted Claymore: An Essay on Culture and Nationalism," in which he argued against the view that literary nationalism should be encouraged and that writers are heirs only to their own national literary heritage. The following number carried a supplement of letters responding to this essay, most of them attempting to defend Scottish national culture against what the writers saw as Jackson's strictures. Number 58 for June 1976 was also given up to one long essay, this time a critical appraisal of the poetry of Robert Lowell by the academic critic and poet Philip Hobsbaum.

When Fulton gave up the editorship in 1977, *Lines Review* reverted to a more general, broadly based quarterly, publishing in each issue a good selection of poems and reviews and, occasionally, short stories and critical essays. The foreign flavor introduced by Fulton was maintained, but as a minor contribution, with the Scottishness of the magazine reasserting itself. In his editorial for June 1978 (no. 65), William Montgomerie commented on the appearance of several Aberdeen poets and of a number of women poets in recent issues; he also took the opportunity of restating the general policy: "Our primary purpose is to print the best in poetry and criticism, and to explore new country in these two media." This the magazine continues to do.

Originally intended as an outlet for new poetry in Scotland, *Lines Review* remains primarily a poetry and review magazine, though it publishes some prose and, at odd moments in its history, has appeared to have very diverse interests. Since its inception in 1952 it has published the work of well over 200 poets and continues to attract the famous as well as the unknown. Half of the poets have been published in only one issue, but a number of writers have appeared many times. The poet most frequently published is one of the founders, Norman MacCaig, with Iain Crichton Smith running him a close second. However, most of the better-known names in contemporary Scottish poetry have appeared regularly in the pages of *Lines Review*. The late Sydney Goodsir Smith, Hugh MacDiarmid, and Robert Garioch were all contributors; Alan Riddell ceased to contribute only when he left for London; George Mackay Brown, Sorley MacLean, Edwin Morgan, William Montgomerie, Alexander Scott, and Derick Thomson continue to publish in the magazine.

Other well-known figures—Scottish, English, American, and other—who have made occasional appearances in the magazine's pages are Douglas Dunn, G. S. Fraser, Carson McCullers, Maurice Lindsay, Naomi Mitchison, Robert Nye, Peter Porter, Alistair Reid, Jon Silkin, Burns Singer (the young Scottish poet who, sadly, died at the age of thirty-six), and Anne Stevenson. Under the two most recent editors, *Lines Review* has broadened its scope to include a large number of new writers; we may hope to see more of many of these, but among the more regular contributors are Ian Abbot, Robin Hamilton, Christopher Rush, and Robert Preston Wells. The most recent young poet to come to the fore is Iain Bamforth, who received a Scottish Arts Council Award in 1982.

Through its independent stance in printing poetry in English, Scots, and Gaelic without commitment to any particular faction, and through its widely spread reviewing policy, *Lines Review* has become a significant voice on the contemporary Scottish literary scene.

Information Sources

BIBLIOGRAPHY
Fulton, Robin, comp. *Lines Review Index*. Loanhead, Midlothian, Scotland, 1977.
INDEXES
   Each number indexed. Numbers 24–41 in *Lines Review* 42/43. Numbers 1–60 in
   Lines Review Index, comp. Robin Fulton, Loanhead, Midlothian, Scotland, 1977.
REPRINT EDITIONS
   Kraus Reprint, Millwood, N.Y. (*Lines* nos. 1–6 in one volume). Johnson Reprint
   Corp., New York (*Lines Review* nos. 1–25, 1952–1967/1968).
LOCATION SOURCES
   American
   Partial runs: New York Public Library; University of Akron Library.
   British
   Complete run: National Library of Scotland, Edinburgh (no. 1 is a photocopy).
   Partial runs: Aberdeen University Library; Bodleian Library; British Museum;
   Cambridge University Library; Mitchell Library, Glasgow; St. Andrews University
   Library.

Publication History

MAGAZINE TITLE AND TITLE CHANGES
   Lines, 1952–53. *Lines: New Poetry, Scotland*, number 2, 1953. *Lines Review*,
   1954–.
VOLUME AND ISSUE DATA
   Number 1–. Numbers 11/12, 42/43, 52/53, and 55/56 are double issues.
FREQUENCY OF PUBLICATION
   Numbers 1–27, 1953–1968, issued irregularly. Number 28–, March 1968–, four
   times a year, usually March, June, September, December.
PUBLISHERS
   1952: "Poetry Edinburgh." Spring 1953: "New Poetry Scotland." Summer
   1953–: M. Macdonald, Edgefield Road, Loanhead, Midlothian, Scotland.
EDITORS
   Alan Riddell, 1953–1954. Sydney Goodsir Smith, 1955–1956. Tom Scott, 1957.
   J. K. Annand, 1958–1959. Albert Mackie, 1960–1961. Alan Riddell, 1962–1967.
   Robin Fulton, 1967–1977. Robert Calder, 1977. William Montgomerie, 1977–
   1982. Trevor Royle, 1982–.

Hilda D. Spear

LONDON APHRODITE, THE

The *London Aphrodite* appeared in August 1928 with the clear intent of causing
a stir. Its editors, Jack Lindsay and P[ercy] R[eginald] Stephensen, acquaintances
at Queensland University in Australia, had decided that their recently established
Fanfrolico Press was stable enough to launch their answer to J. C. Squire's
London Mercury,* complete with a masthead depicting a Pan astride Pegasus

and a reproduction of their Aphrodite, a nude by contemporary painter Lionel Ellis. Lindsay explains in his autobiography:

> The name was a joke, though a serious one. If there was room for a *London Mercury*, why not for a London Goddess of Beauty? (Mercury, we recalled, was a patron of businessmen and a guide of the dead; we wanted a deity who damned all profitable prudences and who guided the quick.) The publicist work of Wyndham Lewis, which was having a considerable success, also spurred us on.[1]

Profit was not a primary motive, the editors indicated on the masthead: they intended to bring out only six numbers "for the fun of the thing, obviously." After repeating this statement in each number with variations, they confessed in the last to having had their "joke."

Editorial "Manifestos" in the first number self-consciously blast the enemies of artistic and intellectual vitality in the late twenties. In the first and longer salvo, Lindsay proclaimed:

> We stand for a point of view which equally outrages the modernist and the reactionary. . . . We affirm Beauty . . . a sensual harmony, a homogeneous ecstasy, which constructing intellectually, yet hates nothing so much as the dry cogs of the objectified and objectifying intellect. [No. 1:2]

P. R. Stephensen added that "you cannot get blood from a Stein" and "Freud means Joy and not Joyce." Lindsay's views were further expounded in the opening number's first selection, "The Modern Consciousness: An Essay towards an Integration." Admitting an "avowedly personal" approach, he attacked the modernists as purveyors of disintegration. Having dismissed "modernity" as a "smug term," like another vogue word, *transition* (a potshot at the magazine, one assumes), he drew upon his intellectual hero, Nietzsche, for a more appropriate definition of transition; it is Nietzsche who teaches us to "submit incessantly our Apollonian intellect to the Dionysian tumult of experience . . . to escape the static abstraction, we must be for ever dynamically transitional."

The first enemy of a synthesis of sensibility is Wyndham Lewis, whose attacks upon Nietzsche were on the "moron-level." Lewis represents the "dissatisfied element of self-conscious modernity." Other enemies belong to a "school of verse, almost completely American in origin, which is doing its best to sterilise the effort of English poetry to reknit its thews"—Gertrude Stein, Laura Riding, but preeminently T. S. Eliot, in whom Lindsay sees "barren intellectuality" and "lassitude of the will." Of Joyce, he comments: "A depressed Irishman, a very fine realist of minutiae," whose work is a "neurotic upheaval he vomited up."[2] Ezra Pound, a "literary amateur," and e. e. cummings, whose vers libre may be seen "dwindling into snatches of zigzag impressionism under the excuse of 'psychology,' " fare no better. Misreading D. H. Lawrence as a primitivist, Lindsay dismissed him also for an "itch to get back to the night of the unconscious, the primal plasm of instinct, the dark pit of the blood." Finally, Bernard Shaw was pilloried as the "worst obstructive mind of the decade," because he "devitalized" Nietzsche. In modernism, then, Lindsay saw the human spirit breaking down into its components—the "chaos of the senses" and the "dead geometry of the intellect."

Surveying the six numbers of *Aphrodite*, one is impressed by the editorial comments, entitled "Ex Cathedra," and the editors' selection of material. The six numbers contain Lindsay's own poems, plays, and fiction; fiction and poetry by his brother Philip; stories by his father, the Australian painter Norman Lindsay; a poem and a story by his mistress Elza de Locre; poems by Australian friend and coeditor of *Vision* (1923–1924) Kenneth Slessor; poems by friends Thomas Earp, Robert Nichols, Powys Mathers, Edgell Rickword (editor of the *Calendar of Modern Letters**), Stanley Snaith, and a dozen others, most of whom have settled into obscurity.[3] Indeed, the only writers included whose reputations endure are Liam O'Flaherty (two stories), Sacheverell Sitwell (one poem), Karel Capek (one story), and Aldous Huxley (two sonnets).[4]

The power of any magazine in the 1920s to ignore or denigrate a recently published work or famous figure is demonstrated in both the *Aphrodite* and its archrival *London Mercury*. One notes, for example, the *Mercury*'s reviewer Edward Shanks dismissing Virginia Woolf's *To the Lighthouse* thus: "There are several brilliancies here, but this minute breaking-up of the psychological processes, when it is persevered in for more than three hundred pages, ends by conveying nothing."[5] J. C. Squire dubbed Isadora Duncan "The Apotheosis of the Half-Baked" and asserted, "She was not a great dancer and not a very beautiful woman; and she had just the small amount of brain that is a dangerous thing."[6] In his article "Waste of Time: Or, T. S. Eliot of Boston, A Yawn," Lindsay calls Eliot "frightened of life, desperately but unconsciously expressing this fear in an effort to castrate life of its dangers by the blade of intellectualism." Lambasting the *Mercury* editor for attacking Aldous Huxley, Stephensen calls Squire the "Apotheosis of the Average," the mold from which all criticism comes out uniformly bland. In the "Ex Cathedra" sections Lindsay satirizes the smug pontificating of fellow editors whose views are seldom questioned. All settles into blandness: "All the *Criterions*,[*] *Coteries*,[*] *Blasts*,[*] *Damns* and *Dials* are now no more alive than that wonderful old standby, the *London Mercury*."

Setting out to "draw blood even from the bloodless," the editors seemed very willing to bring their magazine's year to a close, despite their readers' pleas not to be abandoned to the "Squire—MacCarthy—Eliot—Lewis—Transition" crowd once again, since they could point to no literary magazine that had escaped dullness after six numbers. They anticipated an "unlimited field of attack among the muddlepates of modernity," but, halfway through, they were already growing tired of the attack, one suspects because they saw no blood. Squire noted the appearance of *Aphrodite*, but publicly ignored its frontal assault.[7] In his auto-biography, Lindsay speculates about that silence: "We remained at root an Australian explosion in the English scene, which politely ignored the noise, held its nose, and went on with its business."[8]

Lindsay proceeds in his autobiography to assess *Aphrodite*'s role in the late twenties. Unable to recall exactly how many copies were printed, he guesses at 3,500, with a reprint in bound form of 1,500. He laments the decision to cease publication, since they were "building a strong support." Fanfrolico, however, was in the "fine-book market," and *Aphrodite* departed from the "Fanfrolico aesthetic." Although the press achieved nothing, he feels, the magazine had a "wider impact," not so much among English critics "strangled by the public-school tie" as among American scholars, like Frederick J. Hoffman, who were more impressed.[9]

Lindsay points out, too, that *Aphrodite* was out of step with the sexual re-pressiveness that London experienced during the magazine's short life. Praising Stephensen's polemic against Squire in *Aphrodite* number 2, he claims that his partner's article "opened the fight in defense of free expression against the dominant Philistine puritans represented by Squire among the intellectuals and James Douglas [editor of the *Sunday Express*] among the journalists." It is no coincidence that Stephensen was defending Lascelles Abercrombie's *Phoenix*, which Lindsay had jeered at Squire for attacking when Lindsay was writing for the *Sydney Bulletin*. During this period, Lindsay reminds us, Eric Partridge had copies of a book seized by the police, merely because "buggers" appears in its dialogue; and James Douglas denounced Huxley's *Antic Hay* as "ordure and blasphemy" and joined the pack that condemned Radclyffe Hall's *Well of Lo-neliness*, which Lindsay found merely "dull." Meanwhile, the London police were raiding the exhibition of Lawrence's paintings got up by Stephensen.

It is impossible to see any direct effect upon the thirties, Lindsay concludes, because "there was an almost clean break in the intellectual scene." Soon Huxley would be dismissed as a "petty-liberal," and debates would rage over how much of a fascist Lawrence was, and no one would recall that "P.R.S. had founded Marxist literary criticism in 1928–29."[10]

Notes

1. Jack Lindsay, *Fanfrolico and After* (London, 1962), p. 117.

2. The emetic image is a curious anticipation of Judge John M. Woolsey's comment that *Ulysses* was not erotic but emetic.

3. Lindsay's own poems, plays, and fiction occur in numbers 1:54–64; 2:66–77, 151–59; 3:162–66; 4:234–45, 298–313; 5:321–36; 6:402–20. Philip Lindsay's fiction and poetry occur in nos. 1:50–53; nos. 3:215–21, 246–59; no. 6:433. Norman Lindsay's stories occur in numbers 2:99–105; 3:183–93. Elza de Locre's fiction and poetry occur in numbers 2:113–15; 5:384. Friends and associates appear as follows: Slessor, numbers 1:25 and 2:125; Earp, numbers 2:77 and 3:193; Nichols, numbers 1:28a–28b, 2:115, and 3:167–80, 222–23; Mathers, number 1:47; Rickword, number 5:337; Snaith, numbers 2:97–98, 3:180, 5:390–92.

4. O'Flaherty appears in numbers 1:29–34 and 2:78–83. Sitwell appears in number 2:84; Capek in number 2:105–10; and Huxley in number 3:166.

5. *London Mercury* 16 (July 1927): 324.

6. *London Mercury* 18 (June 1928): 121.

7. *London Mercury* 18 (August 1928): 348.

8. Lindsay, *Fanfrolico and After*, pp. 182–83.

9. Ibid., p. 182. Lindsay quotes from Hoffman's *Freudianism and the Literary Mind* (Baton Rouge, La., 1945).

10. Lindsay, *Fanfrolico and After*, p. 183. Lindsay has published over 100 works. Stephensen, who left Fanfrolico shortly before its bankruptcy, returned to Australia in 1936 to edit a Sydney monthly, the *Publicist*. When World War II broke out, he advocated neutrality for Australia and, as a result, was interned without trial in a concentration camp for the duration of the war.

Information Sources

BIBLIOGRAPHY

Hoffman, Frederick J., Charles Allen, and Carolyn F. Ulrich. *The Little Magazine: A History and a Bibliography*. 2nd ed. Princeton, 1947.

Lindsay, Jack. *Fanfrolico and After*. London, 1962.

INDEXES

Table of contents for end numbers.

REPRINT EDITIONS

Johnson Reprint Corp., New York, 1968.

LOCATION SOURCES

American

Complete runs: Widely available.

Partial runs: Northwestern University Library; Ohio State University Library.

British

Complete runs: Birmingham Public Library; Bodleian Library; British Museum; Cambridge University Library; London University Library; National Library of Scotland, Edinburgh.

Publication History

MAGAZINE TITLE AND TITLE CHANGES

The London Aphrodite.

VOLUME AND ISSUE DATA

Numbers 1–6, August 1928–July 1929.

FREQUENCY OF PUBLICATION

Bimonthly.

PUBLISHER

The Fanfrolico Press, 5 Bloomsbury Square, London, W.C.1.

EDITORS

Jack Lindsay and P. R. Stephensen.

Earl G. Ingersoll

LONDON BULLETIN

The *London Bulletin* was begun in April 1938 by E.L.T. Mesens to introduce readers to surrealist and other avant-garde works being exhibited at the London Gallery, where Mesens had become director. In England, surrealism had "seeped" in, according to William York Tindall, influencing T. S. Eliot, and later Dylan Thomas, Lawrence Durrell, and others.[1] Interest in surrealism had been developing over the previous several years due to André Breton and his group of surrealists in France. Their first review, *La révolution surréaliste* (1924–1929), contained "dreams, automatic texts and a number of illustrations by Giorgio De Chirico, Max Ernst, Andre Masson, Picasso, and Man Ray." The more political *Le surréalisme au service de la révolution* appeared from 1930 to 1933, and in 1933 Breton and fellow artists shared the publishing costs of *Minotaure*, which later became their official publication. In 1936 they published the London issue of the *International Bulletin of Surrealism.*[2] *This Quarter* had a surrealist number in 1932. Roger Roughton's journal, *Contemporary Poetry and Prose*, introduced the French writers to the British public.[3] David Gascoyne's *Short Survey of Surrealism* (1935) and Herbert Read's *Surrealism* (1936) spread the message.

Most important was the June 1936 London Exhibition organized by Mesens, Roland Penrose, and Herbert Read. At the exhibition, according to Tindall, surrealism "emerged at last. . . . Breton attended the opening with Mme. Breton, who had blue hair. Sheila Legge's face was smothered in red roses. The principal address, delivered by Dali from within a diver's helmet, was inaudible." The exhibition was a scandalous success, and public interest grew.

Although *London Bulletin* ran for twenty numbers, it was not until the sixth issue, for October 1938, that Mesens explained some of its history and orientation:

Since its appearance in April of this year *London Bulletin* has assumed the position of the only *avant-garde* publication in this country concerned with contemporary poetry and art. Although its first number was practically a monograph, by various hands, concentrated on the work of the surrealist René Magritte, it has rapidly extended its range, reflecting besides exhibits of painting, other activities of living interest in its pages. [P. 1]

The issues featured general essays by Breton and Read, followed by catalogues of the works of artists currently being exhibited. Then Paul Eluard, Paul Nougé, or Benjamin Peret or others would have poems based on their experience of the painters' work. There were also poems, short prose sketches, or critiques by Read, Ruthven Todd, Samuel Beckett, Djuna Barnes, Ithell Colquhoun, Gordon Onslow-Ford, and Conroy Maddox.

Special issues were organized differently. "Man and Machine" (no. 4/5, July 1938) had thematic articles and illustrations. Oliver Elton wrote the lead article, "The Gods Move House," while Breton discussed the machines of Marcel

Duchamp and the paintings of Yves Tanguy. "Living Art in England" (no. 8/9, January-February 1939), an illustrated catalogue of London Gallery's exhibit of surrealist and avant-garde art works, listed the artists alphabetically, giving each a page containing a photo of the artist and one of his works, and a biographical sketch. The list of constructivists, expressionists, and independents included Eileen Agar, John Heartfield, the "inventor of montage," Naum Gabo, Oskar Kokoschka, Mondrian, Henry Moore, and Ben Nicholson. "Picasso in English Collections" published poems by Picasso, and opinions by R. H. Wilenski, Gertrude Stein, Gabo, Siegfried Giedion, and Robert Melville (no. 15/16, 15 May 1939).

Breton suggested the surrealist poetic experience in the *Second Manifesto*: it involves the "belief that there exists a certain spiritual plane on which life and death, the real and the imaginary, the past and the future, the communicable and the incommunicable, the high and low are not conceived as opposites."[4] In the first number of *London Bulletin* Mesens's own stance is similar: "In 1924 I abandoned music for moral reasons and decided to concentrate on poetical expression whose manifestations will conquer all the domain of human activity" (p. 19). This issue was devoted to Magritte, who, Paul Nougé explained, lived the surrealist mission as "a man who uses painting to perfect astonishing experiences in which all forms of our existence are taking part" (p. 6).

Artists exhibited and discussed were John Piper, Joan Miró, Bram Van Velde, Paul Delvaux, Picasso, Tanguy, De Chirico, Humphrey Jennings, Max Ernst, Man Ray, Wolfgang Paalen, Paul Klee, F. E. McWilliams, Ben Nicholson, John Tunnard, Charles Howard, Louis Marcoussis, Ithell Colquhoun, and Roland Penrose.

These works inspired a variety of essays and poems. Samuel Beckett characterized Van Velde as a painter who stressed color. Jean Scutenaire described the world of Delvaux where "giant virgins of sleep reign over the countries whose details are of singular precision" (no. 1:7). In his poem on Tanguy, Eluard responds to the painter's work with the line "nothing can withstand my desolate images" (no. 4/5:36). Herbert Read announces in number 6 that Picasso's *Guernica* is "a modern Calvary" and that it is an immortal work because it combines the "widest commonplaces with the intensest passion" (p. 6). De Chirico's essay, "Mystery and Creation," echoes this idea when he writes that an immortal work of art has to exceed human limits, going beyond "logic and common sense." That area is one of revelation which means "absolutely nothing from the logical point of view" (no. 6:14).

Surrealist aesthetics were never far from politics or psychoanalysis. "Poem" by Hugh Sykes Davies in number 2, for May 1938, concludes that "anything you see will be used against you" (p. 7). Of Breton's many essays the most important is his joint manifesto with Diego Rivera, "Towards an Independent Revolutionary Art," in which he proposes that in the socialist society of the future art should be given complete anarchistic freedom (no. 7, December 1938–January 1939). In the same issue Grace Pailthorpe, in the "Scientific Aspect of

Surrealism," suggests that surrealist art is therapeutic for mental patients. Werner Von Alvinsleben, in "Automatische Kunst," objects that "pure automatism" in art produces not the expression of feeling, but "free objectivity, literal representation" (no. 13:24). Parker Tyler disagrees that unconscious painting by insane people liberates them. They remain insane. For him "it is conscience that liberates" (no. 17:82).

The final issue, number 18/20, was published in June 1940, not by the gallery, for it closed that year, but by the Surrealist Group in England. The issue was related to an exhibit at the Zwemmer Gallery.[5] Most striking is the contrast between the hopes for the future, making it a sort of time capsule, and the militant cry to "FIGHT HITLER" in large letters on the first page. Pierre Mabille's essay on Monk Lewis is the last in the volume and restates the surrealist hope that humanity will develop greater sensitivity and imagination, realizing that "the marvelous is everywhere." He predicts a synthesis of science and emotion to create "a language accessible to communal emotion. This language will create the new lyric and collective poetry, a poetry freed at last from the shudders, the illusive tricks, the obsolete images" (pp. 48–49).

Notes

1. William York Tyndall, *Forces in Modern British Literature, 1885–1956* (New York, 1956), pp. 236–50.

2. David Gascoyne, *A Short History of Surrealism*, 2nd ed. (San Francisco, 1982), pp. 68–72; René Passeron, *Phaidon Encyclopedia of Surrealism* (New York, 1978), p. 14. Mesens had contributed to the Belgian journals *Oesophage* and *Documents 34*. See *The Oxford Companion to Twentieth Century Art* (Oxford, 1981), p. 530; Paul C. Ray, *The Surrealist Movement in England* (Ithaca, N.Y., 1971), p. 218.

3. A. D. Tolley, *Poetry of the Thirties* (London, 1975), pp. 222–25.

4. *Surrealists on Art*, ed. Lucy Lippard (Englewood Cliffs, N.J., 1970), p. 28.

5. Ray, *The Surrealist Movement in England*, p. 228.

Information Sources

BIBLIOGRAPHY

Alquié, Ferdinand. *The Philosophy of Surrealism*. Ann Arbor, 1965.

Balakian, Anna. *Surrealism: The Road to the Absolute*. New York, 1959.

De Chirico, Giorgio. *Memoirs*. Coral Gables, Fla., 1971.

Hynes, Samuel. *The Auden Generation*. New York, 1976.

Matthews, J. H. *The Custom House of Desire*. Berkeley, 1975.

Wilson, Simon. *The Surrealists*. London, 1974.

INDEXES

Numbers 1–9 indexed in numbers 10 and 11. Cumulative index in Arno reprint. Numbers 1–17 in *An Author Index to Selected British Little Magazines*, ed. B. C. Bloomfield (London, 1976).

REPRINT EDITIONS

Arno Press, New York, 1970.

Microform: Chadwyck-Healey; New York Public Library; Kraus Microform, Millwood, N.Y.

LOCATION SOURCES
American
  Widely available.
British
  Complete run: Victoria and Albert Museum.

Publication History

MAGAZINE TITLE AND TITLE CHANGES
  London Gallery Bulletin, number 1, April 1938. *London Bulletin*, numbers 2–20, May 1938–June 1940.
VOLUME AND ISSUE DATA
  Numbers 1–20, April 1938–June 1940.
FREQUENCY OF PUBLICATION
  Claimed monthly, but actually irregular.
PUBLISHERS
  London Gallery, Ltd.; Surrealist Group in England. (April 1938–15 June 1939): 28 Cork Street, London, W. 1. (June 1940): 21 Downshire Hill, London, N.W.
EDITORS
  E.L.T. Mesens, April 1938–June 1940. Humphrey Jennings, assistant editor, June 1938–July 1938. Roland Penrose, assistant editor, October 1938–January 1939; 15 April 1939–June 1940. George Reavy, assistant editor, 1 March 1939–15 March 1939. Gordon Onslow-Ford, assistant editor with Penrose, June 1940.

Thomas J. Kenny

LONDON MAGAZINE

Taking its name from the famous *London Magazine** (1820–1829; see *RA*) that featured works by William Hazlitt and Charles Lamb, the twentieth-century title began publication in February 1954 under the editorship of John Lehmann, the former editor of the defunct *Penguin New Writing.** That magazine (under the earlier title *New Writing**) had been the resounding success among literary magazines during the years of World War II. Its cessation, along with that of Cyril Connolly's *Horizon,** in 1950, had meant that for a period there was no purely literary magazine publishing in London in which young writers could place their work. The newspaper group publishing the popular tabloid, the *Daily Mirror*, provided the money to start *London Magazine*. Cecil King, the chairman of the *Mirror* group at the time, has recalled that he was approached for support by Lehmann's sister, the novelist Rosamond Lehmann, and that it "seemed a useful piece of do-gooding" to back the magazine.[1]

London Magazine began with good prospects of success, secure finances, and an experienced and successful editor. Lehmann adopted a central position for the magazine between "the academic and the popular sensational," as he was later to describe it (no. 87:7). He sought to publish both established British writers and the new ones coming into prominence in the literary transformations of the early and mid-fifties; a broad international purview for the magazine was also asserted by Lehmann's introduction to the British scene of new European and American writers.

Some of the finest prose writers of midcentury were available to Lehmann. Stories by L. P. Hartley, Graham Greene, V. S. Pritchett, William Sansom, and Paul Bowles appeared in the early years of *London Magazine* alongside the work of distinguished poets whose names included Edwin Muir, Edith Sitwell, Robert Graves, William Plomer, Louis MacNeice, Roy Fuller, and John Betjeman. Publishing the best-known writers of the day, *London Magazine* enjoyed an undoubted prestige.

In the early 1950s the correspondence pages of magazines with literary interests were loud with the sound of controversy generated by a new group of so-called university wits—graduates of Oxford and Cambridge who had gone on to become lecturers at provincial universities and who were to be labeled the "Movement." (The phrase had first been publicly used in a dismissive article in the *Spectator* for 1 October 1954, entitled "In the Movement.")[2] As editor of the BBC radio program *New Soundings*, Lehmann had encountered their work in 1952–1953. Although he was later to characterize the provincial chauvinism associated with the Movement as "squalid" (no. 87:7), Lehmann brought their work into the magazine. An issue devoted to "New Poets of 1956" (May 1956) presented to the public the work of Kingsley Amis, Thom Gunn, Elizabeth Jennings, Philip Larkin, and John Wain—virtually a roll call of leading members of the Movement; two others, D. J. Enright and John Holloway, were added in "New Poets II" (November 1956).

The voice of the Movement had actually been heard earlier in *London Magazine* in a letter from Donald Davie protesting the "fulsome ballyhoo," as he described it, surrounding the death of Dylan Thomas (no. 2:74). Thomas's *Collected Poems* had appeared in 1952, the year before his death, to widespread approval; and this towering reputation clearly had to be set aside by a new generation intent upon different poetic goals. Both in life and poetry, it seemed, the Movement recommended the avoidance of excess and the maintenance of a sense of proportion: "keeping the keen equipoise between always and never," as John Wain put it in "Poem without a Main Verb" (no. 47:22–23). Movement poets were often to express dismay, sometimes in the form of parodies, at the loose verbal free-for-all and enraptured emotional tones, in a word, the Romanticism, of Thomas's verse. Davie had provided an alternative set of poetic values in his *Purity of Diction in English Verse*, a critical work which applauded the decorum of language and economy of metaphor characteristic of the Augustan poets.

The energy of Movement prose writers went into novels rather than short stories, but *London Magazine* offered an outlet for opinion both in its letters section and in the series of articles and symposia it published on the role of the writer in society. Movement writers, and Amis and Wain in particular, liked to adopt a blunt, no-nonsense manner in such discussions. "Why," asked Amis in a typical voice of scorn, "do people talk as if having a job is bad (even though economically necessary) for a novelist? It's lack of a job that can be bad" (no. 44:76). And Wain, while arguing for the writer to be seen as a self-conscious intellectual, might be seen to be drawing on his work-gloves as he writes, "The fact is that a grip on contemporary literary history is a necessity for anyone wishing to know what can usefully be done *next*" (no. 34:60). The general attitude of the Movement to art was workmanlike. However, this did not mean that the group took the side, as so many thirties writers had, of "the workers," or approved of any strong sociopolitical leanings. On the question of the writer's "engagement," it emerged that both Larkin and Enright took the view that writing was the writer's first and only necessary engagement (no. 40:41–47). Thom Gunn followed this with a letter in the issue for June 1957, asserting that, in any case, "political engagement has nothing to do with literary merit" (no. 41:65–66).

After 1957 the polemical voices associated with the Movement fell silent. An antimodernism implicit in some of the group members' attitudes persisted and can be seen, for instance, in Robert Conquest's challenging of the reputation of Ezra Pound in April 1963 (n.s. no. 25:33–49). But the group's unity of opinion was in dissolution, and further, new poets were stirring in the late fifties. Ted Hughes's *Hawk in the Rain* was published in 1957, and the author was welcomed as a powerful new Romantic voice. Hughes himself regarded the Movement poets as belonging to an earlier generation than himself, touched by war and wanting no more heroics: "They'd seen it all turn into death-camps and atomic bombs" (no. 118:10–11). Hughes's poems and stories, and those of his wife, Sylvia Plath, were linked by the British critic Alfred Alvarez with the work of the Americans Robert Lowell, John Berryman, and Anne Sexton as a new school of extremism—a term which well illustrates the degree of departure from the Movement line.[3]

Lehmann left the editorship of the magazine in 1961. Looking back over the decade of the fifties, he wondered aloud at how remote had become the Movement and anti-Movement polemics of just a few years earlier (no. 86:9). In his leave-taking, Lehmann indicated three developments of great moment to the literature of the period, developments which had made more difficult the publication of a literary magazine. In the first place, he saw the success of the new British novelists—Amis's *Lucky Jim* (1954), Wain's *Hurry On Down* (1953), Iris Murdoch's *Under the Net* (1954)—as strengthening the pull of the novel away from the short story. Secondly, he cited the revival of contemporary dramatic writing, following the success of the English Stage Society's season of 1956, which had seen the performance of John Osborne's *Look Back in Anger*. Here opportunities for success had opened for young writers in a field that had hitherto appeared unrewarding. Finally, Lehmann saw a gradual altering of the balance between creative and critical writing, possibly as a result of the expansion of the universities in Britain and America. In a clear allusion to F. R. Leavis's *Scrutiny*,* Lehmann wrote that literature had experienced "a puritan reign of terror" established by leading academic critics "from whose cold-eyed scrutiny" few were able to escape censure, and concluded that such a critical reign of terror was not helpful to young writers or to the editors seeking to publish new writing (no. 87:9).

Lehmann had steered a careful course in the midstream of English letters. He had undoubtedly also been percipient and bold in his attentiveness to foreign developments in literature. A list of leading Continental writers published in the fifties includes Marguerite Duras (2, no. 4); Alain Robbe-Grillet, who contributed an article on the *nouveau roman* (6, no. 2); Michel Butor (5, no. 10); Jean Ferry (1, no. 4); Eugene Ionesco (4, no. 6); Friedrich Dürrenmatt (6, no. 6); Mario Soldati (6, no. 11); and Italo Calvino (2, no. 1). From the English-speaking world Lehmann published the West Indian Samuel Selvon (7, no. 8) and the young Americans Bianca Van Orden (3, no. 3), Janice Warnke (4, no. 8), and David Condé (4, no. 4). He had maintained this opening to the world during a period when Little England sentiments and hostility to foreign intellectuals had become a popular pose among some leading young writers.

Lehmann explained his departure as arising from a desire to have time to write and a weariness with the constant material cares involved in editing a literary magazine. Financial difficulties had in fact surfaced earlier, in 1956, when the *Mirror* group had announced its discontinuance of support due to the *London Magazine*'s weak circulation. Lehmann had responded vigorously that the real reason for the *Mirror*'s withdrawal was a loss of interest on the part of Cecil King, for *London Magazine*'s circulation had held steady at between eight and nine thousand. "In my opinion," he told a *Times* reporter, "that is a good circulation for any literary magazine."[4] New financing was found (from the publishing company William Heinemann), but the magazine was in difficulties again in 1960 when Lehmann took a year off. During his absence the magazine was edited by Maurice Cranston and Alan Ross, both members of the advisory board. Lehmann's formal connection with *London Magazine* ended in March 1961, and the editorship was taken over by Alan Ross.

Ross, a poet, and at that time a writer on soccer and cricket for the *Observer*, was able to restore *London Magazine*'s financial health with the aid of a trust fund left by his father-in-law, Sir Geoffrey Fry (once secretary to Prime Minister Stanley Baldwin).[5] As a poet, he had been publishing since his wartime service in the navy, on Arctic convoy duty, and had been awarded a postwar Atlantic Award. His work had appeared in *Horizon* and *New Writing*. By 1960 he had published several collections of poetry, much of which had appeared first in *London Magazine*, and written a number of travel books.

The magazine experienced a face-lift under Ross. He wished to open it up to "living in a broader sense" and transformed it from a purely literary magazine to a review of the arts.[6] Sections on art, architecture, cinema, and drama were introduced, and the discreet, bookish appearance of the magazine became radically altered through the design of front covers using glossy photographs and graphics. Photographs also appeared inside, as did reproductions of paintings and drawings, as part of the attention to the visual arts which was to become a hallmark of Ross's editorship. With these changes, Ross produced a magazine in tune with the stylistic innovations of the sixties in England, bright, visual, and flavored with sexuality. For more than two decades the magazine has maintained a smartness of style which has led Douglas Dunn (himself a frequent contributor) to write of its "glamourous metropolitan image." The contents, according to Dunn, have been in keeping with the image, featuring a "wide range of interests: soft-core pornography, architecture, music, design, fine art (often well illustrated) as well as poetry and reviews."[7]

Along with a declared aim of high-quality production, Ross has asserted over the years a seriousness of broadly humanistic purpose which has been quite religious in its tones. Literature nourishes fastidiousness and irony of perception, he has written, and provides a medium for "belonging and sharing, lowering aggression and raising involvement" (n.s. no. 120:5–6). There is reason to trace here the influence of *New Writing*, which in its formative years of the forties gave Ross a model for a literary magazine "at the service of human [values] rather than narrowly doctrinaire ones."[8]

The sustaining of this faith through difficult times for literary magazines has been assisted by the Arts Council for Great Britain. In consistently receiving the largest single grant in the country for a magazine, *London Magazine* has demonstrated its status as a "respectable and respected creature of the literary mainstream."[9] In 1969–1970 the magazine received 2,000 pounds; by 1978–1979 this had risen to 24,000 pounds.[10] But rising costs appear to have kept the magazine financially vulnerable. In the 1970s Ross experimented with bimonthly publication. This had editorial advantages, allowing him, for example, to publish longer works without throwing the magazine into imbalances of content. A further reason lay in the demonstrated success of the sales of double numbers. In recent years the magazine has reverted to monthly publication, but with double numbers in the spring, autumn, and winter. An index of the magazine's financial weakness was provided when, in 1981, the costs of a libel suit brought a real threat of closing; the magazine was saved by a fund established with a target of 10,000 pounds.

Two traditions have been maintained by Ross which go back to Lehmann's years as editor: the openness of the magazine to world literature and its refusal to be dogmatic about the nature of art or to follow a particular group or movement. In an interview in 1971 Ross said that the magazine's purpose was to unite rather than divide.[11] Nor, despite its brighter look under Ross, has the magazine practiced generationism. In the early sixties it published the work of Jean Rhys on her return to writing after years of silence. L. P. Hartley and Graham Greene continued to be published in years when the magazine was also paying attention to Beatle music and Pop art. Another tradition, perhaps stemming from *Horizon*, was the awarding of a prize annually for the most distinguished contributions; in 1961 and 1962 magnums of champagne went to the poets Bernard Spencer and Peter Porter and to prose writers James Kennaway and Brigid Brophy; after this, the practice ceased.

Under Ross, the magazine has been regarded as especially strong in its support of young poets.[12] While the magazine has continued to find space for the work of Roy Fuller, Gavin Ewart, Philip Larkin, and Ted Hughes, it has also published many younger British poets, including Seamus Heaney (n.s. 19, no. 1), Tony Harrison (n.s. 9, nos. 1, 2, 7), and Brian Jones (n.s. 10, no. 11). *London Magazine* has published world-famous Europeans, such as Eugenio Montale, and Natalia Ginzberg (the Italian connection has always been strong), and has also searched out the corners of the Commonwealth and crossed political borders to present poetry from Malaysia and Singapore, Vietnam and East Germany. Derek Walcott, whose own work has frequently appeared, selected the West Indian entries for a Commonwealth poetry number for the issue for September 1965. In the late sixties Ross published short stores by Frank Tuohy (n.s. 5, no. 1), William Trevor (n.s. 7, no. 2), Julia O'Faolain, Ruth Prawer Jhabvala, A. E. Ellis, and Nadine Gordimer (all in the short-story number, n.s. 6, number 6), and Caroline Blackwood (n.s. 10, no. 1), all of whom became better known a decade later. Ross has not demonstrated any marked fondness for new American poetry, but he has published a number of new prose writers, including Charles Bukowski (n.s. 13, no. 6:5–16), John Rechy (n.s. 8, no. 3:36–56), and Raymond Carver (n.s. 23, no. 11:3–18).

Critically, the magazine has produced material which interests the practicing writer rather than the academic. William Sansom, V. S. Pritchett, and Francis King attempt, for instance, to define the short story form, and in doing so bring in their own pre-occupations with its market economics (n.s. no. 66). In an interview in the issue for January 1971 Ted Hughes responds to the question of his alleged Nietzscheanism; Philip Larkin, now an aging man of the Movement, continues to advocate sanity in writing (April/May 1980). These are small panels of tiles in the broad mosaic of an international and interrelated culture of the arts which the magazine seeks to foster.

A book-publishing house, London Magazine Editions, has been run by Ross alongside the magazine to accommodate writers moving from magazines to books, and to deal adequately with the large amount of foreign material which the magazine receives. Anthologies of individual authors and also of genres have been published; a collection of concrete poetry was particularly successful. Due to pressures on staff and to rising costs, an announcement of the closing of the publishing house was made in May 1978, but some titles have been published since that date.

Notes

1. Cecil King, *Strictly Personal* (London, 1969), p. 133.

2. Blake Morrison, *The Movement: English Poetry and Fiction of the 1950's* (Oxford, 1980), p. 1.

3. Alfred Alvarez, "Poetry of the Fifties," in *International Library Annual*, ed. John Wain (London, 1958), p. 99.

4. *Times* (London), 14 May 1956, p. 12.

5. Hugh Hebert, "The Years with Ross," *Guardian*, 18 April 1971, p. 8.
6. Interview with Ross, *The Review*, no. 25 (Spring 1971):34–50.
7. Douglas Dunn, "Coteries and Commitments," *Encounter* 48 (June 1977):58–65.
8. Alan Ross, "Literary Magazines," *Times Literary Supplement*, 16 June 1978, p. 666.
9. Hebert, "Years with Ross," p. 8.
10. "London Magazine," *Times Literary Supplement*, 6 June 1980, p. 646.
11. Interview in the *Review*, p. 39.
12. Dunn, "Coteries and Commitments," p. 60.

Information Sources

BIBLIOGRAPHY
Lehmann, John. *The Ample Proposition: Autobiography 3*. London, 1966.
Morrison, Blake. *The Movement: English Poetry and Fiction of the 1950's*. Oxford, 1980.
Williams, Hugo. *London Magazine Poems, 1961–66*. London, 1966.

INDEXES
Each volume indexed.

REPRINT EDITIONS
Kraus Reprint, Nendeln, Liechtenstein. Scholars' Facsimiles and Reprints, Delmar, N.Y.

LOCATION SOURCES
American
Widely available.
British
Widely available.

Publication History

MAGAZINE TITLE AND TITLE CHANGES
London Magazine.

VOLUME AND ISSUE DATA
Volume 1–8, numbers 1–87, February 1954–March 1961. New series, volume 1–, number 1–, April 1961–.

FREQUENCY OF PUBLICATION
Monthly, February 1954–March 1971; bimonthly, April/May 1971–November/December 1978; monthly, January 1979–.

PUBLISHERS
1954–1956: Chatto and Windus, 42 William St., London W.C. 2. 1957–1960: William Heinemann, The Windmill Press, Kingsworth, Tadworth, Surrey. 1961–1970: Shenval Press, 58 Firth Street, London, W. 1. 1971–: London Magazine, 30 Thurloe Place, London, S.W. 7.

EDITORS
John Lehmann, 1954–1961. Alan Ross, 1961–.

Alan C. Thomas

LONDON MERCURY, THE

In the twenty years of its life, 1919–1939, the *London Mercury* had two very distinct personalities. The first, under the editorship of J. C. Squire, was Georgian, even late Victorian. The second, under R. A. Scott-James, from November 1934 to its demise in April 1939, was leftist in politics and progressive in literature. The two personalities must be treated separately.

Before the founding of the *Mercury* in 1919, Squire had been developing a considerable reputation as a parodist, serious poet, reviewer, and literary journalist. Kept out of the war by poor eyesight, he used his time in London to develop a great many powerful literary connections (Edmund Gosse saw him as something of a personal protégé), so that he moved into the post of editor of the *New Statesman** (see *VEA*) in 1917. When he inaugurated the *Mercury* two years later, he was able to drum up over 1,000 subscribers in advance of the first issue; by 1921 circulation was up to 10,000. That level of success was maintained through most of the next decade.[1] Few literary magazines could boast such auspicious beginnings, and the credit must all go to Squire—his personality, and his contacts.

The *Mercury* came out as a monthly of 128 pages, with only three pages of advertisements. The look of the magazine was very important to Squire: it was printed in a rich and attractive format by the Field Press and enhanced, increasingly over the next few years, by woodcuts and drawings. Until 1924 Squire's assistant editor was Edward Shanks, a poet and critic whose impulses were close to his own.

Throughout the *Mercury*'s life, each issue began with "Editorial Notes," a two- to four-page column in which Squire treated diverse topics, ranging from modern poetry to cruelty to animals. The first issue's column describes what the magazine was to be: a combination of original poetry and fiction, book reviews, and criticism and belles lettres. It was to avoid political controversy altogether, and would follow no literary or critical school: diversity and inclusiveness were to be the aims, and the young and unknown were to be published alongside the well established. But that first column makes it clear that not everything would be represented. There had been, Squire wrote, an "orgy of undirected abnormality" of late in literature, and he attacked the "young simpletons" who "have discovered that they have only to become incoherent, incomprehensible, and unmetrical to be taken seriously." The new magazine would have done its part "if some of the rubbish can be cleared away." For all his talk about diversity and openness to the new, Squire was clearly taking from the start a firm stand against the major new movements—the intentionally obscure, vers libre, the experimental.

The poets in the first issue reveal this bias: Thomas Hardy, Rupert Brooke, W. H. Davies, Walter De la Mare. Squire was siding with the poetic modes of the older generation, and insuring that his magazine would be seen as the prime symbol of the philistine and reactionary by the major talents of the younger. Still, the *Mercury* under Squire published a stunning array of work by major authors: Robert Frost appeared several times (vols. 3, 5, 6), as did W. B. Yeats (vols. 3, 5, 7), Thomas Hardy (vols. 1, 5, 7), Vachel Lindsay (vols. 1, 3), Hilaire Belloc (vol. 7), Edmund Blunden (vol. 2), and Conrad Aiken (vols. 2,

3). There were poems by the young Dorothy Sayers (vol. 3), C. K. Scott Moncrieff (Proust's translator) (vol. 6), Owen Barfield (vol. 5), F. L. Lucas (vol. 24), Vita Sackville-West (vol. 21), John Betjeman (vol. 22), and Graham Greene (vol. 18). D. H. Lawrence made several appearances (almost alone among the names we now associate with the avant-garde of the era); his "The Snake" first appeared in the *Mercury* (vol. 4). Squire and Shanks frequently printed their own poetry also.

Squire printed fiction by Virginia Woolf (vol. 2), Katherine Mansfield (vol. 5), Walter De la Mare (vols. 5, 6), Elizabeth Bowen (vol. 12), Max Beerbohm (vol. 15), Lawrence (vol. 16), and Graham Greene (vol. 25). Toward the end of Squire's tenure as editor, the names become less illustrious: Yvonne Ffrench (vols. 25, 26), Huw Menai (vols. 25, 26), James Stern (vol. 26), and Helen Moran (vol. 25). The poetry toward the end seems pale (rather than grand) Georgian, and the fiction is increasingly light and humorous, without the intellectual toughness of the early years.

The essayists represented are likewise a parade of major names: Gosse wrote on George Eliot (vol. 1), Robert Bridges on George Santayana (vol. 2), G. K. Chesterton on Milton (vol. 5). Yeats and Arnold Bennett contributed memoirs (vols. 2, 4, 6). More academic writers like R. W. Chapman (vol. 22) and Geoffrey Tillotson (vols. 24, 27) were also printed.

In his critical pronouncements on contemporary literature in the book review sections, Squire sounds much like a modern Francis Jeffrey (see *Edinburgh Review* [RA]), damning with great confidence much of the work that we now call major. T. S. Eliot in particular had a rough time of it in the *Mercury*. Squire's review of *The Waste Land* has the dubious honor of vying with Jeffrey's reviews of Wordsworth for sheer obtuseness: Eliot is not so much exploring a new avenue as a "dark cul-de-sac." Of the poem's ending, Squire says, "conceivably, what is attempted here is a faithful transcript, after Mr. Joyce's obscurer manner, of the poet's wandering thoughts when in a state of erudite depression. A grunt would serve equally well" (8:655–56). He concludes that "the printing of the book is scarcely worthy of the Hogarth Press." Shanks had earlier reviewed *The Sacred Wood* and found Eliot wasting his intelligence in vagueness (3:447–50). In 1932 Pryce-Jones reviewed Eliot's *Poems 1909–1925* and found Eliot's brand of obscurity becoming common among all the second-rate poets. This "will not be very good for Mr. Eliot's reputation, for when all can understand him, all will realize how very little he has to say" (26:455–56).

William Faulkner's *Light in August*, Helen Moran wrote, is a novel "whose sordidness does not serve any useful purpose," Faulkner being dismissed as "one of those ru-ged [*sic*] and confused writers like Theodore Dreiser" (27:470). Squire did find considerable promise in Wallace Stevens, though he would be better off if he could "persuade himself that writing was meant to be a means of communication" (12:657). The experimentalism of Virginia Woolf, on the other hand, was always well received by the *Mercury*, but that of W. H. Auden merely showed that he was "devoid of wit and frequently boring" (29:259).

The new critical work of William Empson was also damned as "irritating and self-conscious" (23:507). Clearly, in its critical outlook the *Mercury* was not prepared to welcome the new; and, as the new became the established norm, it is not surprising to see the magazine's contributors becoming a list of now-forgotten names.

The *Mercury* included a number of columns besides its reviews. Mario Praz contributed a regular "Letter from Italy," Alfred Thibaudet one from France, Aiken one from America; there were also "Letters" from Ireland and Germany. "Bibliographies of Modern Writers" was a less-regular feature as the 1920s wore on, but did include bibliographies of contributors such as Gosse, De la Mare, Hardy, and some others. There were also regular columns on architecture, films, and book production techniques (the latter often richly illustrated). And there were columns of literary gossip—the founding and passing of other magazines, notices of upcoming events, and a column on rare-book sales. From the latter one learns that a first edition of *Queen Mab*, with Shelley's own corrections, sold in 1920 for a mere $6,000, and, in 1921, the only known blackletter copy of *Everyman* went for 1,080 pounds.

By the end of the twenties, the *Mercury*'s status was beginning to droop, leading quickly into a full-speed descent toward disaster. The Great Depression was taking its toll on all publishing, of course, but Squire's own personal battle with alcoholism led to increasing disorganization in running the magazine, and his pool of contributors was shrinking rapidly. It is perhaps more than a morbid coincidence that Squire and his staff were increasingly filling the pages with eulogies for the recently deceased: Moncrieff, Lawrence, Bridges, Lytton Strachey, George Saintsbury, George Moore. Poignantly enough, one of the best essays printed during these last years was Wynyard Browne's "The Culture-Brokers" (28:436–45), an attack on F. R. Leavis and the then-new *Scrutiny** enterprise for its arrogance and cliquish elitism. Encountering this essay at this point in the *Mercury*'s history is like witnessing the death of the old order and the birth of the new.

R. A. Scott-James took over the editorship with the November 1934 issue; his inaugural "Editorial Notes" stressed how he would maintain the *Mercury*'s tradition of excellence rather than mere novelty. Squire, however, wrote to a friend in November that "the *Mercury* is dead and something else is bearing its name."[2] He was correct, for Scott-James's "Editorial Notes" went on, in that first issue, to say that the magazine would widen its scope to take in discussions of economics and politics—which Squire had taken pains to avoid—and that it would be welcoming the work of new young poets like Stephen Spender and Michael Roberts.

In the November issue, Edwin Muir—who was to be frequent contributor thenceforth—printed an essay on poetic diction explaining the inevitability of a change in idiom from one generation to the next. He quoted Eliot approvingly as having a style "perfectly free of hackneyed romantic associations, completely contemporary, and at the same time with no mark of class idiom'' (31:37). Clearly, the ''young simpletons'' Squire had battled against were now in control.

In January 1935 Scott-James announced that the *Mercury* was incorporating the *Bookman** (see *VEA*), which had been founded in 1891 and was most recently edited by Reginald Pole Ross Williamson. The *Bookman* too had been plagued by recent financial problems and by a too assiduous cultivation of old-guard literature. The only major change the incorporation made in the *Mercury* was in the number of photographs—but far less lavishly produced than in the *Bookman*'s heyday.

Scott-James also made some changes in format. The lengthy reviews of books under numerous special headings (poetry, history, typography) were now compressed into a single section headed ''New Literature,'' composed of numerous unsigned, one-paragraph reviews. There were also a few full-scale reviews in each issue, but far fewer than in Squire's day.

The new editor's emphasis on politics changed the tone of the magazine and opened the gates to many of the major young leftist writers of the day: Yeats continued to contribute, but now there were also C. Day Lewis, Spender, Auden, Louis MacNeice, George Barker, and Muir. Stevie Smith wrote several reviews, and there was poetry by May Sarton and fiction by Kay Boyle, Christopher Fry, Frank O'Connor, Richmond Lattimore, Jack Lindsay, and Mervyn Peake (who also contributed a fine series of drawings of contemporary authors).

The *Mercury*'s old audience perceived the change readily enough, and there were a number of shocked and saddened letters to the editor. Scott-James replied to one of them in his ''Editorial Notes'' for February 1935: ''Literary criticism would be in a bad way indeed if it were fixed in the tastes and habits of the world of three decades ago—even if it were true, as perhaps it is, that a majority of men and women are still spiritually housed in that distant, diminishing past'' (31:324). This was hardly conciliatory, but it did signal the *Mercury*'s commitment.

That commitment was not enough to ensure solvency, however, and in April 1939 Scott-James announced that the *Mercury* had been sold to *Life and Letters.** His tone in the announcement is quite bleak, and he speculates that the larger causes of the *Mercury*'s failure are the rise of cheap mass culture and lowbrow reading matter, and even the apparent suspension of civilization—in 1939 not an extreme set of ideas.

If we can speak of two distinct *London Mercury* magazines, we can also speculate that the failure of each was a matter of timing. Squire's *Mercury*, which has been called, with a touch of justifiable derision, the ''home of Georgianism and good fellowship,'' really should have been launched a decade or so before 1919.[3] And if Scott-James's *Mercury* could have begun in 1920 or so, it could have had the impact of a combined *Blast** and *Criterion**. Perhaps cursed by its historical moment, the *Mercury* was nonetheless blessed by an extraordinary set of contributors: the magazine is a phenomenon which must be of lasting interest to the literary historian of our century.

Notes

1. Detailed information about the financing and circulation of the *Mercury* is in Patrick Howarth's biography, *Squire: Most Generous of Men* (London, 1963).
2. Ibid., p. 233.
3. Francis Mulhern, *The Moment of "Scrutiny"* (London, 1979), p. 16.

Information Sources

BIBLIOGRAPHY
Howarth, Patrick. *Squire: Most Generous of Men.* London, 1963.
Mulhern, Francis. *The Moment of "Scrutiny."* London, 1979.
INDEXES
Each volume indexed.
REPRINT EDITIONS
Kraus Reprint, Millwood, N.Y.
LOCATION SOURCES
American
Widely available.
British
Widely available.

Publication History

MAGAZINE TITLE AND TITLE CHANGES
The London Mercury.
VOLUME AND ISSUE DATA
Volumes 1–39, numbers 1–234, November 1919–April 1939.
FREQUENCY OF PUBLICATION
Monthly.
PUBLISHER
The Field Press, Windsor House, Bream's Buildings, London, E.C. 4.
EDITORS
J. C. Squire, 1919–1934. R. A. Scott-James, 1934–1939.

Raymond N. MacKenzie

LONDON MERCURY AND BOOKMAN, THE. See LIFE AND LETTERS

LONDON QUARTERLY AND HOLBORN REVIEW, THE. See VEA

LOVAT DICKSON'S MAGAZINE

In recalling the literary world of the late 1920s—just a few years prior to beginning, in 1933, the magazine bearing his name—Lovat Dickson noted that it was "little changed from what it had been in [George] Saintsbury's and Edmund Gosse's time. The quarterlies still flourished, the serious monthlies had had no important casualties in their ranks, and under formidable titles like the *Nineteenth Century and After* [see *Twentieth Century*], the *Contemporary* [*Review**], and the *Fortnightly* [*Review** (for both, see *VEA*, *MA*)], they still appeared in the same forbidding formats in which they had originally made their bows to the world."[1] Yet despite this air of permanence, Dickson soon concluded that these journals were doomed; frustrated by his limited opportunities in changing the *Fortnightly*, for which he was assistant editor, he began to dream of creating a new magazine for the modern reader. To this end, he became editor and proprietor of the *Review of Reviews** (see *VEA*). By 1931, once again dissatisfied, he resigned both his editorships and became a publisher and managing director of Lovat Dickson Ltd.

The new publishing firm moved into offices at 38 Bedford Street, Strand, London, soon to become the mailing address of yet another periodical, a short story magazine initiated solely to benefit Dickson's publishing house. To succeed, he had to make his house well known. His autobiography is very candid on this point: "I liked editing magazines and I knew now how it was done, so I decided to start a magazine the sole object of which would be to feed my publishing list with authors."[2] In the grand if somewhat immodest tradition of Macmillan, Scribner, and Harper, the magazine was named after himself, *Lovat Dickson's Magazine*. What better way to publicize his firm? Dickson anticipated a two-way benefit: liking the quality of work in his magazine, writers would send their material to his publishing house; as a publisher, too, he could promote his own list through the magazine.

Dickson's motives were not just self-serving, but aesthetic as well. He objected to the restrictions of the popular magazines with their concerns about advertisers' and readers' biases. Their fear promoted formula work and "was death to the art of the short story."[3] In the editorials and essays on the short story that appear in *Lovat Dickson's Magazine*, this self-definition through contrast to the popular magazines, the abhorred "glossies," is a constant refrain. Not surprisingly, the magazine was very short-lived, only twenty months. Although it began with a 10,000–copy run and its circulation rose steadily, the magazine never made any money. Nevertheless, despite the 1,500–pound net loss yearly, Dickson still felt that it was a success, for it made his firm known, and when he printed excerpts from a novel he was publishing, such as Jules Romains's *Quinette's Crime*, the demand for the complete work significantly increased.

The magazine began under the editorship of P. Gilchrist Thompson, who defended the venture in his first editorial by asserting that *Lovat Dickson's Magazine* was interested in the short story as an art form, with no particular political slant. As well as publishing the work of well-known writers when their work did not suit the requirements of popular magazines, he hoped to publish many new writers. Later editorials admitted that the magazine failed in this objective and concluded that writers too improve with practice and that often the best stories are written by experienced craftsmen. Instead of an editorial, the next issue opened with an essay by Edward J. O'Brien, for years editor of *The Best British Short Stories* and *The Best American Short Stories*. In "A Word About the Short Story," O'Brien began by remarking that twenty years earlier a magazine "devoted entirely to the short story as a form of art would have been impossible" (1, no. 2:1). He suggested that this change was due to the little magazines, which welcomed the serious writer and allowed him to educate his public. The successful American magazine *Story* offered a model for England, where there were few short story magazines but a definite revival of interest in the serious short story. Praising *Lovat Dickson's Magazine* as a necessary English experiment, his only advice was that the editors abandon class consciousness and look beyond the universities for new writers.

This sense that *Lovat Dickson's Magazine* was part of a wonderful experiment, at the center of an astonishing development of the short story, pervades the comments on the short story. While Thompson's brief editorials usually restricted themselves to noting the plenitude of manuscripts and subscribers, or asking why so few comic stories were written, H. E. Bates's essay, "A Note on the English Short Story," was more characteristic of the magazine's sense of mission. Bates began by declaring, "The history of the English short story is a melancholy one" (2:145). Except for the rare and usually non-English exception (Anton Chekhov, Guy de Maupassant), there were no nineteenth-century short story writers. Until after World War I, there was only contempt for the form, but since then a "renaissance" had occurred (2:147). Not only was the short story distinct from the novel, but in the last ten years even newspapers had revised their former objections, and Bates counted ten newspapers that published a short story a day. He even predicted that the short story would soon replace the novel in popularity. It seems fitting that Bates's optimistic piece was followed by "Welcome to a Rival," in which *New Stories** was hailed for following the example set by *Lovat Dickson's Magazine*. The new magazine's editorial board included several contributors to *Dickson's*: H. E. Bates, Arthur Calder-Marshall, and Edward J. O'Brien.

Not all the theoretical essays were as complimentary as Bates's. In the next issue, L.A.G. Strong challenged the uncritical regard for the serious short story. In "The Short Story: Notes at Random," he acknowledged the many developments in the short story, but argued that "the serious short story is now as full of clichés as the commercial" (2:285). At the expense of plot, the short story emphasized characterization, atmosphere, and psychological unity. Ironically, the serious short story became more restricted than the commercial story, for it limited itself to certain themes and was preoccupied with technique. Strong argued for a revival of narrative, and offered an analysis of a Jack London story, "The House of Mapuhi," as an example. He was really arguing for a widening of the definition of the short story, a recognition that a short story was just "a short piece of prose fiction" (2:291), not necessarily what its modern practitioners limited it to.

With the July 1934 issue, *Lovat Dickson's Magazine* adopted a subtitle, "Devoted Solely to the Short Story." Essentially a recognition of what its policy had been in the first eight issues, the new name did not exclude further discussions on the nature of the short story, and the July issue contained a polemical article, "Fiction and the Short Story," by R. Ellis Roberts. Like L.A.G. Strong, Roberts objected to the direction of the new short story. With his obsession with technique, the short story writer failed to recognize that the story must be about something. Roberts was arguing for a recognition that stories are about people, although his three propositions did not initially mention people. He proposed: "There must be a story. The story must be the author's. The story must be written" (3:2). He lamented the popularity of the thesis story: "Only a narrow line separates some modern stories by Soviet authors from *Jessica's First Prayer* or *Froggie's Little Brother*" (3:3). He criticized writers such as D. H. Lawrence for not understanding the social conditions of the world that they portrayed, and for turning the short story into an essay. In his conclusion, offering the work of Rudyard Kipling and H. G. Wells as models to the young writer, he echoed the conservative ideals of Matthew Arnold in his 1853 "Preface": "Young, comparatively inexperienced authors will go less astray, if they follow some formula, than if they insist on the delight and dangers of licence" (3:9).

Three months later, Roberts's essay saw a rebuttal, "What Is the Short Story?" by Edwin Muir. Although Muir purported to agree "with almost everything" Roberts wrote (3:463), his essay proceeded to reject most of it. Muir accepted Roberts's three propositions, but noted that they apply equally well to any form of narrative. He essentially rejected the value of critical theory: "All purely technical theories of the short story help only to stereotype it" (3:465). Social and economic theories tended to emphasize the role of magazine conditions in determining the nature of the short story, allowing for no explanation of the short stories written before there were magazines. In place of Roberts's Kipling, Muir praised Chekhov and Katherine Mansfield. He disagreed with Roberts on the significance of plot: "A story is not more completely a story because it contains a great number of incidents: for essentially a story is a description, not of things happening, but of how things happen" (3:467). Rather than bemoan an emphasis on technique, he saw a healthy movement away from technique "to a naturalness and unobtrusiveness so complete that sometimes the story hardly seems a story at all" (3:467).

Muir's was the only essay on the nature of the short story to appear during Lovat Dickson's term as editor. In *English Literary Journals 1900–1950*, Michael N. Stanton has stated that under Dickson's tenure there was more critical material,[4] but his statement does not accurately reflect the critical debate on the short story that existed throughout the magazine's run. In one of his last issues as editor, Thompson expanded the magazine's interest in reader participation by "An Invitation." Wanting readers' opinions on their selection of stories, he offered a twelve-month subscription for the best article on the contents of the August 1934 issue, and any two books published by Lovat Dickson for the best article explaining one's preference for one story from each of the first ten issues. The winner of both contests, Giles Wing, was announced in the October 1934 issue, and his essay, "Talking of the August Number," appeared in that issue. Wing's essay raised several objections to the magazine's format, but his primary one, what a serial was doing in a magazine that claimed to be devoted to the short story, was never answered, since the true answer was hardly aesthetic: serialization promoted Dickson's publishing list.

The main change under Lovat Dickson's tenure was the shift from the original policy of short stories only, a change indicated by the new subtitle, "A Magazine for Thoughtful People." In his introductory editorial, "Looking Forward," Dickson explained this deviation as an attempt to increase the range of interest of the magazine. While concentrating on the innovative short story, he planned to include more literary features because no other magazine was doing so. Repeating his belief that the magazine was aimed at "a reading public capable of thinking and eager to think" (3:376), he hoped to make it "the most important and the most interesting periodical in the English-speaking world" (3:377). But perhaps the special subscription offer that followed indicates the real motivation. By late 1934, there were several short story magazines; Dickson was once again trying to capture more of the market.

In its new and final format, *Lovat Dickson's Magazine* contained several "Amiable Confessions," writers' explanations of their first literary attempts; essays on writers' childhoods; memoirs of foreign correspondents; a philosophical inquisition on the nature of intention in murder; a discussion of the philosophy in Jules Romains's Men of Good Will series (novels published by Lovat Dickson); and an essay by Humbert Wolfe, "Art and a Sense of Humour." In addition, Dickson expanded the "End Pages" to include several story competitions: the best short story by a writer who had not published short stories before; the best short story written to a predetermined pattern; the best short story by a university student. He also used the section to review and recommend books (not all published by his own firm), to comment on the success of his writers, and to answer readers' complaints. When L.A.G. Strong became editor for the last three issues, the format remained basically the same. Strong announced that he would welcome stories of all kinds, but emphasized that *Lovat Dickson's Magazine* was primarily still a forum for the "serious, non-commercial short story" (4:468).

In its brief history, *Lovat Dickson's Magazine* published many well-known writers, for example, Ernest Hemingway, Henry Handel Richardson, H. E. Bates, Sean O'Faolain, V. S. Pritchett, Luigi Pirandello, D. H. Lawrence, V. Nabokov, William Saroyan, Grey Owl, Vera Brittain, Erskine Caldwell, Pearl Buck, André Maurois, and John Steinbeck. But the story that perhaps best exemplifies the spirit of its endeavor and one of the few to be singled out for praise by Lovat Dickson in his "End Pages" was William Saroyan's "Seventy Thousand Assyrians." In its defiance of commercial interests and disdain for commercial success, it explains both the success and failure of *Lovat Dickson's Magazine*:

"Nothing is going to happen in this work. I am not using a slick style of writing. ... I have no desire to sell this story ... to *The Saturday Evening Post* or to *Cosmopolitan* or to *Harper's*" (4:99).

Notes

1. Lovat Dickson, *The House of Words* (Toronto, 1963), p. 20.
2. Ibid., p. 121.
3. Ibid., p. 122.
4. Michael N. Stanton, *English Literary Journals 1900–1950: A Guide to Information Sources* (Detroit, 1982), p. 40.

Information Sources

BIBLIOGRAPHY

Dickson, Lovat. *The House of Words*. Toronto, 1963.

Stanton, Michael N. *English Literary Journals 1900–1950: A Guide to Information Sources*. Detroit, 1982.

INDEXES

Volume 3 indexed (pp. 721–23). *Comprehensive Index to English Language Little Magazines 1890–1970*, series 1, ed. Marion Sader (Millwood, N.Y., 1976).

REPRINT EDITIONS

Kraus Reprint, Millwood, N.Y., 1967.

LOCATION SOURCES

American

Complete runs: Harvard University Library; New York Public Library; Xavier University Library.

Partial run: Yale University Library.

British

Complete run: National Library of Scotland, Edinburgh.

Partial runs: British Museum; Cambridge University Library.

Publication History

MAGAZINE TITLE AND TITLE CHANGES

Lovat Dickson's Magazine, November 1933–June 1934. *Lovat Dickson's Magazine: Devoted Solely to the Short Story*, July 1934–September 1934. *Lovat Dickson's Magazine: A Magazine for Thoughtful People*, October 1934–June 1935.

VOLUME AND ISSUE DATA

Volume 1, numbers 1–2, November 1933–December 1933. Volume 2, numbers 1–6, January 1934–June 1934. Volume 3, numbers 1–6, July 1934–December 1934. Volume 4, numbers 1–6, January 1935–June 1935.

FREQUENCY OF PUBLICATION

Monthly.

PUBLISHER

Lovat Dickson Ltd., 38 Bedford Street, Strand, London.

EDITORS

P. Gilchrist Thompson, November 1933–September 1934. Lovat Dickson, October 1934–March 1935. L.A.G. Strong, April–June 1935.

Adrienne E. Kertzer

M

MANDRAKE

Mandrake was begun in 1945 by John Wain, then an undergraduate at St. John's College, Oxford, as a literary vehicle for undergraduates and others associated with the university. His signed editorial in the first number for May 1945 claimed, "This miscellany [is] representative of its kind and it has the freshness of variety" (no. 1:3). Except for some poems by Edward William Harry Meyerstein, the poet and biographer of Thomas Chatterton, the writers were undergraduates, and the "timid blue pamphlet" (no. 1:3) was frankly put forth as a venture.

The second number appeared a year later with a cover bearing a large number 2 as well as dozens of quotations about the mandrake and its sleep- and death-inducing qualities. This design was not repeated: later issues used a drawing of the mandrake root. James Blair Leishman, a senior lecturer in English at Oxford, who would become an outstanding commentator on John Donne and the metaphysical poets, contributed three poems, and Roger Lancelyn Green wrote "Stevenson Fifty Years After" (no. 2:15–22). Green had taken his B.A. and B.Litt. degrees and was acting as deputy librarian of his undergraduate college, Merton. His essay displayed an empathy with those Victorian writers popular with young people. The other contributor of note to the second number was Arthur Boyars, then an undergraduate at Wadham. By the fourth number Boyars had become coeditor with Audrey M. Arnold and soon had elevated *Mandrake* into "an international review of the arts" in contradistinction to *Isis*, the official undergraduate magazine that reported on life at Oxford and which Boyars accused of a "snobbish attitude," especially in its "Comments" section: "a mixture of cheap wit, pomposity and snobbery" (no. 4:3). Boyars later wrote that the university displayed toward *Mandrake* "hostility" and "an unbelievably petty and mean indifference" (no. 6:3).

In the fourth number, for Winter 1946, Boyars declared his wish "to oppose sham and cant (not by irritable polemic but by quietly fostering honest workmanship) and to stand as a testimony against the fraud and fear of the days we live in" (no. 4:3). In this attitude *Mandrake* predated *Nine,** which was similar in tone but more strident. Like *Nine*, *Mandrake* was interested in Continental literature and complained of the dearth of good poets writing in England immediately after the war (no. 7:1).

The pages of *Mandrake* reveal some of the earliest work of poets and critics now established as major figures of the post–World War II period. John Wain reviewed Cleanth Brooks's *Modern Poetry and the Tradition* in 1952, and in the same issue Alfred Alvarez took on William Empson's *Structure of Complex Words* (no. 8:174–78). Early poetry by Kingsley Amis appeared along with his review of Philip Larkin's *A Girl in Winter* (no. 5:48, 85–86). Michael Hamburger, now a poet and translator of worldwide reputation, was in 1946 a Christ Church undergraduate serving with the Army of Occupation in Austria; he published in *Mandrake* the first translation into English of Georg Buchner's *Lenz*. The issue was devoted to the theme of "self-consciousness," which the editor saw as an element contributing to the "chaos in artistic standards" and "irresponsibility in social attitudes" characteristic of the postwar period (no. 5:6). "In *Lenz*," wrote Boyars, "we see sincerity at the point of madness, and for a few uncorrupted artists this stage has been tragically reached" (no. 5:7).

Mandrake saw itself rather self-consciously as a "little magazine" which was probably doomed to a brief and impecunious existence but selflessly devoted to the promotion of new talent (no. 4:3). John Wain remained a steady contributor, and writers as diverse as Roy Campbell and Wolf Mankowitz can be found in the same issue.[1] In 1949 Wain edited a symposium on drama in the universities. Along with contributions by Neville Coghill and Bertram Josephs is a long piece by "Ken" Tynan on his production of *Samson Agonistes* at the University Church of St. Mary's, Oxford, in 1947. In this piece the church intimately associated with John Henry Newman intersects the career of the creator of *O! Calcutta* as Tynan described how he turned Milton into a dynamic theatrical experience.

From the fourth issue on Arthur Boyars contributed long record reviews under the heading "Gramophone Notes." He continued to publish and edit *Mandrake* after moving to London sometime before the sixth number appeared in 1949. By then the magazine was looking increasingly abroad, with reviews on non-English writers and translations. The seventh number, for example, for December 1950–April 1951, was devoted to "modern Italian arts" and carried both translations and critical articles by Mario Praz, Lionello Venturi, Salvatore Quasimodo, Eugenio Montale, and Emilio Cecchi. As did Peter Russell, the editor of *Nine*, Boyars periodically bewailed the lack of English poetic talent: "The United States and Central America," he proclaimed, "have absorbed all that is best in the European tradition, and are busily producing young writers whose achievements have already eclipsed those of our own soi-disant 'promising young men' of forty-five" (no. 7:2).

Issues appeared at intervals of nearly a year between 1947 and 1956, and Boyars continued to view the magazine as a fragile enterprise. He noted in 1949 that most English people had little spare money and if any was available, "greyhound racing [was] less exacting" than spending an evening reading *Mandrake* (no. 6:3). As with so many little magazines, *Mandrake* had no public announcement of its demise; it expired with the eleventh number, for Autumn/Winter 1955–1956. While its reviews and articles toward the last were well done and included pieces by Wain, W. W. Robson, and Marius Bewley, by then *Mandrake* had given up both its associations with Oxford and, to all evidences, its posture as an "outsider." There remained little to distinguish it from other, better-financed, serious critical journals. In the fifth number, Boyars had written that *Mandrake* would justify itself if it could make "some unknown and promising writer less unsure of his talent" (no. 5:6). By printing some of the earliest work of Wain, Alvarez, Hamburger, and Amis, *Mandrake* more than fulfilled its own hopes.

Note

1. See Roy Campbell's translation of García Lorca's "Ballad of the Spanish Civil War" and Wolf Mankowitz's story, "Account of a Visit to a Local Sanitorium," *Mandrake*, no. 4 (1946).

Information Sources

BIBLIOGRAPHY

Contemporary Poets of the English Language, ed. Rosalie Murphy (London, 1970). A very brief note on Arthur Boyars appears in this edition, but not in subsequent editions.

INDEXES

None.

REPRINT EDITIONS

None.

LOCATION SOURCES

American

Complete runs: Harvard University Library; Yale University Library.

Partial runs: Columbia University Library; Cornell University Library; Enoch Pratt Library; New York Public Library; University of Buffalo Library; University of California Library, Los Angeles; University of Pittsburgh Library; University of Texas Library; University of Wisconsin Library.

British

Complete runs: British Museum; London University Library.

Partial run: National Library of Scotland, Edinburgh.

Publication History

MAGAZINE TITLE AND TITLE CHANGES

Mandrake.

VOLUME AND ISSUE DATA
>Volumes 1–2, numbers 1–11, May 1945–Autumn/Winter 1955–1956.

FREQUENCY OF PUBLICATION
>Irregular. Volume 1, numbers 1–6 appeared between May 1945 and 1949; volume 2, numbers 7–11 appeared between April 1951 and Winter 1956.

PUBLISHER
>1945–1947: Arthur Boyars, Wadham College, Oxford. 1949–1956: Arthur Boyars, 44 Cholmley Gardens, London, N.W. 6.

EDITORS
>John Wain (with assistance from Valmai Adams), 1945. Arthur Boyars and Audrey M. Arnold, 1946. Arthur Boyars and John Wain, 1947. Arthur Boyars, 1949–1956.

>*Barbara J. Dunlap*

MINT, THE

Only two numbers of the *Mint* appeared: one in 1946, the other in 1948. Its editor, Geoffrey Grigson,[1] intended the *Mint* to be a genuine miscellany, a comparatively apolitical magazine that would attempt to collect good fiction, poetry, and criticism. The "Foreword" (signed by "G.") to the first number (pp. vii-viii), in fact, warns in an Orwellian vein against the corrosive effects that propaganda and political expendience will have on language. It also suggests that too many magazines were enforcing some kind of party line.[2] With the postwar *Mint*, then, Grigson seems to have been trying to create a magazine similar in intent to his prewar *New Verse*.* In both magazines he expresses to some extent a wish to escape politics.

The list of contributors to this short-lived magazine is impressive, to say the least, for it includes W. H. Auden, Sean O'Casey, Graham Greene, Rhys Davies, Owen Barfield, Peter Taylor, James T. Farrell, Simone Weil, and Douglas Bush. The magazine cannot have failed for want of recognized names or for not achieving the breadth of subject matter and point of view that one would expect from a miscellany. Weil writes on the *Iliad* (no. 2:84–112); Auden on "Criticism in a Mass Society" (no. 2:1–14); Farrell on "The Language of Hollywood" (no. 1:195–206); Grigson on William Barnes (no. 1:72–102); and Nikolaus Pevsner on the architecture of mannerism (no. 1:116–39).

This remarkable roster of writers and range of topics must have impressed those interested in little magazines at the time, even if some of the names are more familiar now than they may have been in the 1940s. To younger writers of the time, however, the magazine must have seemed not just impressive but imposing. For while Grigson in the forewords to both volumes invites newer writers to submit their work, the magazine itself looks very much like a forbidding anthology, not a miscellany seeking new work. Furthermore, Grigson seems to have been so intent on the "negative identity" of the magazine—on its *not* being politically or critically focused—that the *Mint* lacks a personality, a center. In its very impressiveness, therefore, and in Grigson's editorial attitude, we might find at least part of the reason for the *Mint*'s not having endured. In the 1940s, even as now, a little magazine, to have a chance of surviving, must have had to seem more available to newer talent and to possess a more positive identity.

The *Mint* was not without a recurring theme, though, if a miscellany of only two numbers can be said to have such a thing. Obviously, Grigson himself in his forewords is concerned with the effects of censorship and propaganda on language, and a number of the other contributors echo this concern. Auden's "Criticism in a Mass Society,"[3] Christopher Salmon's "Broadcasting, Speech, and Writing" (no. 1:206–20), and Farrell's essay on the language of Hollywood vary widely in their announced topics, but they are linked by an implicit question: What will happen to language in the postwar world?

The *Mint* also contained pieces that were not primarily concerned with the fate of language and that are more in keeping with a miscellany. Graham Greene's "Convoy to West Africa" is such a piece. It gathers several journal entries from December 1941 and January 1942, and though Greene is too modest in his prefatory note, he is at least partially correct in saying that "if they are of any interest at all, [the entries] are of interest as an indication of the kind of raw material a novelist stores" (no. 1:40). The passages are indeed full of the exotic characters, the curious bits of dialogue, and the sense of imminent danger that one finds in many of his novels. The excerpts also show Greene to be a far colder, less sentimental analyst of the war than was America's chief war journalist, Ernie Pyle.

From our perspective, several decades later, the *Mint* may have needed more of such unusual pieces, whether they were written by well-known writers or not. For, in a sense, the *Mint* was not what it stated itself to be, despite Grigson's insistence to the contrary in the first foreword. Rather than being a true miscellany, it was for the most part an anthology that took few chances with inexperienced writers and that sprang from Grigson's reluctance to be political. The magazine is in many ways too careful. Because it did publish and reprint the work of established writers, however, and because it concentrated on the fate of language, the *Mint* will endure as an interesting shard of post–World War II British literary history. It will also endure as the less successful sibling of *New Verse*, demonstrating Grigson's stubborn determination to distinguish between literature and politics.

Notes

1. Identified by Richard Hoggart, in *Auden: An Introductory Essay* (London, 1961), p. 253n.
2. The first and last sentences of Grigson's foreword to the first number exemplify this Orwellian concern for honest language: "*The Mint* is what it states itself to be—a

miscellany of literature, art and criticism." "Contributions need not be short and they will not be censored" (pp. vii-viii).

3. This essay originally appeared in *The Intent of the Critic*, ed. Donald A. Stauffer (Princeton, 1941). The poetry that Auden contributed to the first volume had also been published earlier, giving some indication of the extent to which Grigson viewed the *Mint* as an anthology, rather than as a miscellany that would publish new work by established writers or even work by new writers.

Information Sources

BIBLIOGRAPHY

Beach, Joseph Warren. *The Making of the Auden Canon*. 1957. Reprint. New York, 1972.

Bloomfield, B. C., and Edward Mendelson. *W. H. Auden: A Bibliography*. 2nd ed. Charlottesville, Va., 1972.

Grigson, Geoffrey. *The Crest on the Silver: An Autobiography*. London, 1950.

Hamilton, Ian. *The Little Magazines: A Study of Six Editors*. London, 1976.

Hoggart, Richard. *Auden: An Introductory Essay*. London, 1961.

Osborne, Charles. *W. H. Auden: The Life of a Poet*. New York, 1979.

Sullivan, Alvin. *New Verse: A Critical Survey and Index*. Ph.D. dissertation, Saint Louis University, 1972.

INDEXES
None.

REPRINT EDITIONS
None.

LOCATION SOURCES

American

Complete runs: Amherst College Library; Harvard University Library; Lehigh University Library; Northwestern University Library; University of Chicago Library; University of Michigan Library; University of Pennsylvania Library; University of Texas Library.

Partial runs: Joint University Libraries, Tennessee; U.S. Library of Congress; University of Kansas Library.

British

Complete runs: British Museum; Cambridge University Library; Leeds Public Library; University College of South Wales Library.

Partial run: Victoria and Albert Museum Library.

Publication History

MAGAZINE TITLE AND TITLE CHANGES
The Mint.

VOLUME AND ISSUE DATA
Number 1, 1946; number 2, 1948.

FREQUENCY OF PUBLICATION
Irregular.

PUBLISHERS
    1946: George Routledge and Sons, Limited, 68 Carter Lane, London, E. C. 4.
    1948: Routledge and Kegan Paul Limited, 68 Carter Lane, London, E. C. 4.
EDITOR
    Geoffrey Grigson.

                                                            Hans Ostrom

MONTHLY CRITERION, THE. See CRITERION, THE

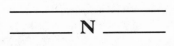

NATIONAL REVIEW. See VEA

NATION AND ATHENAEUM, THE

In 1921, the *Nation* was a highly respected publication. Henry William Massingham, a distinguished British journalist, had been editor of the *Nation* since 1907, when the Liberal weekly developed out of another periodical, the *Speaker*. Previously, Massingham had written for the *Eastern Daily Press*, the *Manchester Guardian*, and the *Daily News*, and had edited the *National Press Agency*, the *Star*, *Labour World*, and the *Daily Chronicle*.[1] Although Massingham had made the publication a powerful organ of Liberal opinion, the *Nation* never reached a high degree of financial success. The Rowntree family, the weekly's financial backers, lost several thousand pounds on it each year.[2]

The financial situation probably influenced the decision to merge the *Nation* and *Athenaeum* in February 1921. Too, while the *Nation* had appeal as a political organ, it was anticipated that the addition of *Athenaeum* would allow the editors "to devote a far greater space to science, musical and dramatic art, and literature" (28, no. 20:1), thus, in theory, widening the audience. From the number for 26 February 1921 until that for 5 May 1923, the *Nation and Athenaeum* was a two-section weekly, each section carrying one-half of the title.

One of the names on the list of distinguished contributors to the *Nation and Athenaeum* was John Maynard Keynes. When, in 1921, Keynes, Ramsay Muir, and other important Liberals met at Grasmere to discuss the future direction of party policy, an immediate need was perceived for a weekly publication to disseminate the political, social, and economic views of the group. The *Nation* was seen as being close to fitting the bill, but not entirely. It had a "smell of its own," as Leonard Woolf put it, because of the influence of Massingham's personality.[3] Massingham's brand of Liberalism was looked upon as being old-fashioned and, in some respects, closer to the Labour Party than to the Liberal. Too, the Grasmere group was seeking fresh ideas which, they hoped, would pump new life into the party. Keynes and the others decided to enquire into the possibility of acquiring *Nation and Athenaeum*, and in 1923, after consultation with the Rowntree family, the group put up some money to get control of the publication.[4] Massingham refused to go along with the plan, and the new board, under Keynes's chairmanship, accepted his resignation. Massingham thereupon accepted a position with the *New Statesman** (see *VEA*).

In the search for a new editor, Ramsay Muir was first considered. However, both Muir and Keynes decided that the possibility existed for personality or ideology clashes, so the idea of Muir's editorship was abandoned. Instead, Keynes turned to Hubert Douglas Henderson, a lecturer at Cambridge and a Liberal whose ideas were close to those of Keynes. Henderson remained as editor until 1930. Although Henderson had never worked as a journalist, he was very successful as editor. The periodical's reputation continued under his leadership as one of the foremost weeklies in the country. Keynes consulted with his colleague, but did not dictate editorial policy, which was left to Henderson. Keynes did, however, recruit writers of the first rank to the *Nation and Athenaeum*, including Lytton Strachey, Virginia Woolf, Gilbert Murray, Maxim Gorky, and others.[5] He also continued to contribute articles of his own.

With his training in politics and economics, Henderson was an able editor for the *Nation* section of the publication, but Keynes and the board felt that a literary editor was needed as well. T. S. Eliot was approached, but he was not able to accept the position. Leonard Woolf subsequently became editor of the literary pages. Woolf had been hired in 1922 and had worked under H. M. Tomlinson, Massingham's literary editor. Woolf had autonomy in editing the section for which he was responsible, and at times the imprint of his political views, obviously to the left of Henderson's, is discernible in the literary pages.[6]

Henderson left the editorship in 1930, when he was appointed to the staff of the Economic Advisory Council by Ramsay MacDonald. He was succeeded by Harold Wright. Woolf continued as literary editor and Keynes remained chairman of the board of The Nation, Ltd., until 1931. At that time, the publication was merged with the *New Statesman* to become the *New Statesman and Nation*. Woolf continued on the staff and Keynes sat on the board of the new periodical for a time.

"Events of the Week," a column of political commentary, was the lead article for the life of the periodical. News of Parliament was prominently featured there, as were significant international happenings. Another weekly feature was the financial news, including items from the stock exchanges and the insurance companies. From time to time the editor included "A Hundred Years Ago," an item outlining significant news events from a century before. The periodical commented on most of the major political issues of the era, including World

War I reparations, foreign commerce, the return to the gold standard, the spread of economic depression, and proportional representation.

Literature and the arts were prominently featured as well; essays entitled "The Drama," "Poetry," "Exhibitions of the Week," "Art," and "Foreign Literature" appeared weekly. Some verse was published from time to time, as were reviews of new gramophone records. Reviews and notices of books were published, and much of the advertising in the weekly was placed by the London book trade. The weekly also carried notices of forthcoming meetings and lectures. The "Science" feature carried news and information from the world of science couched in layman's terms.

Notes

1. *The Dictionary of National Biography*, s.v. "Massingham, Henry William."
2. R. F. Harrod, *The Life of John Maynard Keynes* (London, 1951), p. 335.
3. Leonard Woolf, *Downhill All the Way: An Autobiography of the Years 1919–1939* (New York, 1967), p. 93.
4. For a discussion of the acquisition of the publication by the Keynes group, see Harrod, *Life of John Maynard Keynes*, pp. 335–37.
5. Harrod, *Life of John Maynard Keynes*, p. 337.
6. Woolf, *Downhill*, pp. 92–98.

Information Sources

BIBLIOGRAPHY
Harrod, R. F. *The Life of John Maynard Keynes*. London, 1951.
Lea, F. A. *The Life of John Middleton Murray*. London, 1959.
INDEXES
    Each volume indexed.
REPRINT EDITIONS
    Microform: British Library Newspaper Library. Datamics, Inc., New York.
    Library of Congress Photoduplication Service, Washington, D.C.
LOCATION SOURCES
    American
        Widely available.
    British
        Widely available.

Publication History

MAGAZINE TITLE AND TITLE CHANGES
    The Nation and The Athenaeum, 1921–1926. *The Nation and Athenaeum*, 1926–1931.
VOLUME AND ISSUE DATA
    The Nation, volume 28, number 21–volume 39, number 12, 19 February 1921–26 June 1926. *The Athenaeum*, number 4738–number 5017, 19 February 1921–26 June 1926. *The Nation and Athenaeum*, volume 39, number 13–volume 48, number 21, 3 July 1926–21 February 1931.

FREQUENCY OF PUBLICATION
    Weekly.
PUBLISHERS
    1921–1923: British Periodicals, Ltd. 1923–1931: The Nation, Ltd.
EDITORS
    Henry William Massingham, 1921–1923. Hubert Douglas Henderson, 1923–1930.
    Harold Wright, 1930–1931.

James W. Parins
Marilyn Parins

NEW ADELPHI, THE. See ADELPHI, THE

NEW AGE, THE. See VEA

NEW BLACKFRIARS. See BLACKFRIARS

NEW COTERIE. See COTERIE

NEW CRITERION, THE. See CRITERION, THE

NEW DEPARTURES

New Departures, founded by Michael Horovitz in 1959, was originally to
have been called *Spasm*. "Spasm," it seems, would have been a true description,
judging by the spasmodic assault of the magazine during its adolescent life, thus
far, of twenty-six irregular years. In the past, publication of issues has been as
close together as five months and as far apart as five years. Advertisements for
publishing companies and other angels have not been sufficient to allow more
regular publication. Faber and Faber, and Zwemmer's Book Shop, along with
jazz records and albums, have not been enough to subsidize the little magazine.
In the double issue 2/3, Horovitz projected fifteen issues. The last one to appear
(1984) was, however, number 16. Several issues contain begging pleas by the
publisher. Size differs from quarto to octavo; some printing is mimeographed,
some offset; some bindings are fastened with a spiral, others are more conventional. Another route to publication was chosen in publishing the fifth issue with
volume 2, number 12 of *Resurgence* in the spring of 1970. In addition, earlier
issues have later numbers in some cases.

To make poetry live for the masses, Horovitz has directed and performed in more than 2,000 "Live New Departure Roadshows." An Albert Hall poetry reading in 1965 supported Horovitz's dream of taking the poetry to the people and the pub. This was carried further in the 1980s with the Poetry Olympics, surfacing in Poets' Corner of Westminster Abbey and repeated two years later, a further attempt to involve the public with the poet.

Horovitz's credo in the first issue of *New Departures* states, "Two ways of changing people's minds without resort to violence" are to show agreement with the "principles, but not necessarily the style, or [with] those opinions reasonably held." He continues affirming "the avant garde of all ages" and remarks that one of the ways of repairing a cathedral is building a new cathedral. In another metaphor, he says that the audience's obligation to the actor should be to understand that some silences are intentional, while the actors' responsibility is to be audible. "A spasm seen simply as a literary event would be an attempt to rejuvenate, perpetual task, by the usual means of shock, originality, and reformulation of the ideas of the rheumaticky muses and their confidantes." A spasm, he continues, is read as a reaction.

Contributors to the first issue, for Summer 1959, include Samuel Beckett, Alan Brownjohn (spoken of in a congratulatory advertisement as the editor of "The old Departure"), Patrick Bowles, Cornelius Cardew, Peter Ferguson, Charles Lamblett, Bernard Kops, John McGrath, Philip O'Connor, David Slayden, Stevie Smith, and others. Virtually the same list of contributors was to appear in each issue, with some additions, and many of the contributions were selected for inclusion in *Children of Albion*, the Penguin book subtitled "Poetry of the Underground in Britain," which Horovitz edited in 1969. Of interest with regard to *New Departures* is the editor's sixty-page "After Words"; Horovitz quotes the *Times Literary Supplement* as finding *New Departures* "the most substantial avant-garde magazine in Britain." He says, "*New Departures* was a preview of life." His aim was "that taste be refined, responses sharpened."[1] The first issue of the magazine was a melange of all the arts: poetry, painting, cartooning, photography, music, explaining the works of Horovitz's master, William Blake.

Subsequent issues have pictures of the contributors, drawings by David Hockney, and various cartoons, illustrative of the text or independent. One cartoon, for example, illustrates a festival for the 300th birthday of Purcell: a small orchestra of only a flautist and chairs for other members of the orchestra. Another musical entry in the third issue is Cardew's "Piano Piece February 1959," covering seven pages, which consists of codes dealing with musical signs and printed instructions for playing a musical game. An accompanying cartoon shows five men around a baby grand piano. Emphasized along with musical space and its unity is an explanation of Schoenberg, followed by several pages continuing the use of the terminology of music. In subsequent issues (nos. 4, 5), jokes are made using the language referring to music.

The fifteen contributors to the combined number 2/3 included Gregory Corso, Donald Davie, Allen Ginsberg, Eugene Ionesco, Jack Kerouac, John McGrath, and Jon Silkin. Photographs of Corso, Ionesco, Robert Creeley, and Alan Davie on the inside front cover were topped by a cartoon of a man with a banner, crudely drawn, and the words, "Like Help!" inscribed. Following closely was the rubric that was to become commonplace: if the financial plea made in this issue is not heeded, the magazine will be forced to close. In the second issue, Faber and Faber advertised books by Wallace Stevens, Samuel Beckett, John Golding, Ezra Pound, Edwin Muir, Lawrence Durrell, Jean Genet, and Ted Hughes. In the first issue Horovitz had blamed the dire state of poetry on Eliotic dessication; nevertheless, Eliot's publishing company remained one of his supporters. Other advertisements appeared from Weidenfeld and Nicolson, Zwemmer's New Bookshop, and *Big Table*, an American quarterly. Music entries for number 2/3 included various staffs running vertically, not horizontally, entitled "Winter Music for Bob Rauschenberg and Jasper Johns," by John Cage. Set up on its spine, the issue reads left to right.

Subsequent issues followed in intervals of years. Number 4 appeared in London in the spring of 1963 and featured "News About Time" by Horovitz. Seven years later, a fifth issue appeared in combination with *Resurgence*. In a note Horovitz regretted the delay in printing and pointed out that all preceding issues were sold out. Announcing number 6, for 1971, Horovitz revealed that it would be *The High Tower*, the second booklet of poems by Frances Horovitz. Number 7 for 1975 was to be the long-awaited bumper issue celebrating eleven years of new poetry, prose, and graphics. It promised to internationalize and bring up to date *Children of Albion*, and to "catch up and to make amends." Those plans came to fruition with a fourfold effort, *New Departures* numbers 7/8 and 10/11. Poets included W. H. Auden, John Berryman, Paul Celan, Austin Clarke, Langston Hughes, Jack Kerouac, Pablo Neruda, Ken Patchen, Charles Olson, Pablo Picasso, Ezra Pound, Anne Sexton, and Stevie Smith. David Hockney contributed drawings and paintings. (Number 9 preceded numbers 7/8 and 10/11 by two years, and appeared as *19 Poems of Love, Lust, and Spirit* by Michael Horovitz.)

The eccentric publication style saw number 12 for 1980 in quarto size, mimeographed, with plastic ring spine, and featuring such poets as Ted Hughes, Stephen Spender, Seamus Heaney, Beckett, and Corso. Number 13 for 1981 appears to be typed, then offset, with a saddle-stitched binding; David Hockney's drawing of Horovitz was among the graphics included. In 1982 number 14 reported on the "Second International Poetry Olympics." Priced at one pound, fifty pence, it returned to the type of contents that characterized the fifties and sixties issues. The last item in the issue is Samuel Beckett's "PSS." Andrei Voznesensky's "Troubadors and Buyers" and "Apple Fall," translated by Richard McKane, accompany work by Michael Horovitz and Mara Amata. Heathcote Williams contributes a Blakean page, "Death is Unspeakable," and Yevgeny Yevtushenko's three poems, translated by R. Millner-Cullard and Peter Levi.

The editor's notes pointed out that for survival the magazine published material that was "multi-racial, anti-arms race, anti-war with the hope that poetry might do something towards healing the nations, too."

Number 15 appeared in 1983. The format reflected the multimedia approach of number 1. Number 16 was published in two editions in 1984 as a special volume honoring Horovitz's former wife, poet Frances Horovitz. It contained poems by Mrs. Horovitz, her son Adam, Michael Horovitz, and many of her friends, including Ted Hughes. The Arts Council subsidized both editions with 250 pounds. The size of both editions is octavo, with fifty-six pages; the second edition is distinguished from the first by a black border around the cover photograph of Mrs. Horovitz.

Note

1. Michael Horovitz, ed., *Children of Albion: Poetry of the Underground in Britain* (London, 1969), p. 32.

Information Sources

BIBLIOGRAPHY
Horovitz, Michael, ed., *Children of Albion: Poetry of the Underground in Britain.* London, 1969.
INDEXES
Two numbers (1, 2/3) indexed.
REPRINT EDITIONS
None.
LOCATION SOURCES
American
Complete runs: New York Public Library; Stanford University Library.
Partial runs: Cornell University Library; Indiana University Library; U.S. Library of Congress; University of California Library; University of Georgia Library; Vanderbilt University Library.
British
Complete runs: Bodleian Library; National Library of Scotland, Edinburgh.

Publication History

MAGAZINE TITLE AND TITLE CHANGES
New Departures.
VOLUME AND ISSUE DATA
Number 1, 1959. Number 2/3 (double issue), 1960. Number 4, 1963. Number 5, 1970 (joint issue with *Resurgence*, volume 2, number 12). Number 6, 1971? (booklet of poems, *The High Tower*). Number 7/8–10/11, 1975 (called "huge anthology" issue). Number 9, 1973? (book of poems, *19 Poems of Love, Lust & Spirit*). Number 12, 1980. Number 13, 1981. Number 14, 1982. Number 15, 1983. Number 16, 1984.
FREQUENCY OF PUBLICATION
Irregular.

PUBLISHERS
   Number 1: Hinksey, Oxon. Numbers 2/3–11: 29 Colville Terrace, London, W.
   11. Numbers 12–16: Piedmont, Bisley, Stroud, Glos.
EDITORS
   Michael Horovitz. Roger Franklin and Michael Horovitz (joint issue no. 5).

Johnnie Wade Burns

NEW ENGLISH WEEKLY, THE

   At the time of the British financial crisis of 1931, Alfred Richard Orage, best
known for his editing of the *New Age** (see VEA) from 1907 to 1922, decided
to publish his own journal, conceiving it first as a monthly but then as a weekly.[1]
On 21 April 1932 the *New English Weekly: A Review of Public Affairs, Literature,
and the Arts* began publication. Revealing much of what the paper was all about,
political and economic "Notes of the Week" and the "Review of Public Affairs," mentioned first in the subtitle, began each issue. These notes were written
by the editors, Orage, and then Philip Mairet: "Orage had not intended to write
the weekly political notes, but when the first number was due to appear, no
other pen could satisfy him."[2]
   What the title does not reveal, a survey of the contents or a knowledge of
Orage, a proponent of the Social Credit movement, does. The journal was an
organ for Social Credit, a theory first proposed by Major C. H. Douglas that
suggested that "modern economics suffer from a deficiency of purchasing power"
and that the remedy was "to increase purchasing power by controlling prices
and creating 'social credit' which would be distributed to consumers by discounts
paid to retailers, and also by 'dividends' paid to citizens for the heritage of
earlier generations."[3] In his "Notes of the Week" for the inaugural issue, Orage
wrote, "The fundamental problem . . . is one of Money since Science has settled
every other; and there is no problem of the world to-day whose solution does
not depend on it" (1:2). Although former readers from the *New Age* days had
greeted the new journal in letters to the editor, many were alienated by the
"nagging social credit propaganda which from the first made it [the *New English
Weekly*] seem eccentric" and by the lack of the freshness of the earlier periodical,
"for Orage was much more ready to give space to established names, whether
they wrote well or not, provided they supported his ideas."[4] But Orage was
attempting to get a propaganda value by using "contributors distinguished in
affairs . . . to insinuate persuasion into more influential circles, even those of
financiers and industrial magnates, from which effective action might originate.
. . . he wanted new ideas in the heads of the people best able to carry them into
practice."[5]
   Though he disagreed with some technical generalizations of Social Credit
advocates and did not believe the implementation of credit reforms could by
itself create a complete regeneration of society, Orage did believe the main

conclusions of the Social Credit theory—that the economic problem was essentially financial—and agreed with the main proposals of Major Douglas to reduce prices, augment incomes, or both. Not surprisingly, Orage and the *New English Weekly* were significant factors in the growth of the Social Credit movement.

Orage's and Mairet's "Notes of the Week" were followed typically in each issue by "The Credit Forum," signed "Pontifex" and later called "Forum"; "Current Cant," signed "A.F.T." and dropped after the early volumes; and then a continuing series in 1935 and 1936 on the American economic scene by Ezra Pound. Under the heading "American Notes," signed "E. P.," Pound often wrote on the "Nude Eel," his name for the New Deal. Later columns of "American Notes" were written by David Warren Ryder. Pound contributed to the *New English Weekly* many articles and letters to the editor until he turned in 1937 and 1938 more to *Action* and *Townsman** for publication of his prose; he contributed more than the editors were prepared to print, especially when his views became embarrassing in their stridency and partisan nature.[6]

Other articles related to economics, politics, and current events appeared in the first few pages of each issue or received special emphasis. For example, in the 23 March 1933 issue (2, no. 23) appeared the first article printed with double-size titles as well as a bold listing in the table of contents: "A Draft Social Credit Scheme [Scotland]. By Major C. H. Douglas, with a commentary by the Credit Study Group" (brackets in the original), a collection of ten clauses with comments on each. Articles with similar bold headings were scattered through the issues until the demise of the paper, all—with notable exceptions—related to economics: "Petition to H.M. the King" (8, no. 1 [1935]); "Bankers in Italy. By Odon Por" (8, no. 24 [1936]); "Social Credit Looks Ahead—The Opening Address to the York Conference on Social Credit. By Maurice B. Reckitt" (10, no. 1 [1936]); "The Credit Forum: Ten Points for a Social Credit Programme" by Pontifex (10, no. 4 [1936]); "Will Dyson: In Memoriam" (12, no. 16 [1938]); "Crown Credit Vouchers" (12, no. 17 [1938]); "The First of a Weekly Series by Yvette Guilbert," in extra bold type and boxed (12, no. 17; this series appeared in this volume only, in the original French); "Soil Fertility: A National Health Policy. I" by Sir Albert Howard (14, no. 22 [1939]; part 2, also titled boldly, appeared in the following issue); "Social Credit To-day and To-Morrow—I" by Maurice B. Reckitt, and "The Salvage of Agriculture" by Sir Albert Howard, C. I. E. (16, no. 11 [1940], followed in the next issue by part 2 of the Social Credit piece); "*Little Gidding*. A Poem by T. S. Eliot" (21, no. 11 [1942]); "Views and Reviews. *The Science of Power*. By Maurice B. Reckitt" (25, no. 1 [1944]); "*The Pax Americana*. By T. M. Heron" (26, no. 5 [1944]). In the second half of the thirty-five volumes of the *New English Weekly*, articles on agriculture, hydroponics, and agricultural revival appeared frequently, supplying another approach to economic reform. Every several issues Ronald Duncan then supplied a column called "Husbandry Notes" with tips for the home farmer.

Prominent contributors of articles related to the public affairs aspect of the paper include J. P. Angold (cf. vols. 6, 7, 16–23), Major C. H. Douglas (vols.

1,2), Lt.-Commander A. S. Elwell-Sutton (vols. 7, 8, 10–13, 15, 23), Sir Albert Howard (14, nos 22, 23; 16, no. 11), Anthony M. Ludovici (vols. 23–26), Hugh MacDiarmid (vols. 1–4), Philip Mairet (vols. 1–6), Gorham Munson (vols. 2, 12–14), Ezra Pound (vols. 1–10), Maurice B. Reckitt (10, no. 1: 12; 16, nos. 11–12), Major E. Glasbrook Richards (vols. 1, 2), C. E. Bechhofer Roberts (vols. 1, 4, 7, 29), and E. W. F. Tomlin (vols. 10, 12).

To Orage, "art, religion and culture, education and sociology generally, world-peace, internationalism, the whole future of mankind on this planet, all alike depend on our ability to face up to and practically solve the problem [of applying Social Credit] presented to the race for the first time in its history" (1:2); thus, economics had first place in his paper. After the primary emphasis on Social Credit and public affairs, nevertheless, came the portion of the paper devoted to literature and the arts. Columns regularly reviewed literature, drama, cinema, music, ballet, and art. More important, however, original works of literature, as well as a handful of cartoons and translations of original works, also were published.

Typically, Paul Banks wrote reviews of plays under the heading "The Drama," later written by Michael Sayers, P. T. [Pamela Travers], and then Henry Adler; and of current films under "The Cinema," later taken over by Betty Dyson, Clifford Dyment, Henry Adler, and Roland Loewe. In early issues, Rayner Heppenstall reviewed poetry and the ballet, also done in later issues by Ross Nichols. Hugh Gordon Porteus contributed the column "Art," later written by Joseph Bard and Terence Denis; Arnold C. Haskell began "Art Notes" in volume 1. For volumes 1 to 28 concert reviewer Kaikhosru Shapurji Sorabji contributed essays on music. A column on recent novels had a variety of authors: Storm Jameson (cf. vol. 1), George Orwell (vols. 8, 9), Oswell Blakeston (vols. 11, 12), Dylan Thomas (vols. 12–15), Wynyard Browne (vol. 14).

More important to Orage than the various reviews were the "Views and Reviews," drawing on a current work for a more substantial essay developing ideas beyond a mere review. Mairet comments that at the time of his editorship of the *New English Weekly* Orage found fewer original writers than when he was editing the *New Age*: "His new contributors seemed always to be writing reviews instead of views."[7] Notable or frequent contributors of "Views and Reviews" and other literary commentary were T. S. Eliot, George Orwell, A. Desmond Hawkins, H. G. Porteus, Ezra Pound, E.W.F. Tomlin, Julian Symons, Brother George Every, Maurice B. Reckitt, Herbert Read, Upton Sinclair, Dylan Thomas, Henry G. Finlayson, and Llewelyn Powys.

During the first six years of the *New English Weekly*, Will Dyson contributed political cartoons as well as articles. But after his death, the pages of the paper were devoid of illustration until volumes 29 and 30. In issue 12 of volume 29, for 4 July 1946, two glossy reproductions of the paintings *La Femme à sa Toilette* (1942) and *Intérieur* (1942) by Georges Braque were printed to accompany an article on the artist, and issue 3 of volume 30 (31 October 1946) displayed a small "One-line Drawing" of a bird by N. Dudley Short.

Translations, at times, also found space in the pages of the periodical. Most significantly in this respect, parts of W.H.D. Rouse's translation *The Story of the Odyssey* ran in volumes 7 and 12, and four sections of his *Iliad* in volume 12. In volume 13, three poems by Rainer Maria Rilke were translated to appear together; a short translation of Franz Kafka's "Him" appeared in volume 3.

From a literary point of view, the most important portion of the paper was that devoted to poetry and stories. Often they were slight or soon forgotten. An early department titled "Pastiche" gave way to "Poems"; Orage found more poets wishing to publish than in his days as editor of the *New Age*, but "their work was mostly of idiosyncratic or merely technical interest."[8] While most of the names have lost significance, one does find notable exceptions. Pound, who contributed more prose than poetry to the paper, here published *Canto 38* (3, no. 4 [1934]) and many slight poems signed Alf or Alfie Venison, such as "The Charge of the Bread Brigade," or signed Ez.P., "Glory and Yet Again Glory" (8, no. 2 [1935]). E. E. Cummings reprinted three poems in 1935; Marianne Moore was represented by "Smooth Gnarled Crape Myrtle" in 1935; and James Laughlin, better known now as the publisher of New Directions Press, had several poems in volumes 7 and 8. Lawrence Durrell contributed "The Prince and Hamlet" to volume 10 in 1937 and several poems to volume 14.

The *New English Weekly* is significant also for having published the first poem by Dylan Thomas to appear in a London literary magazine, "And Death Shall Have No Dominion," on 18 May 1933. After this first publication he generally published poetry in the *Adelphi** at the urging of J. Middleton Murry,[9] but more than half a dozen other poems by Thomas appeared during the years 1934 through 1938, as well as essays on "Recent Novels," "Recent Fiction," and other topics.

Most important, the *New English Weekly* was distinguished by being the first place of publication for three of T. S. Eliot's *Four Quartets*; all but "Burnt Norton" appeared in the journal. Verse regularly appeared in the standard two columns of the paper, but when "East Coker," "The Dry Salvages," and "Little Gidding" were printed (16, no. 22:325–28; 18, no. 19:217–20; 21, no. 26: 213–17), they were given one column per page with larger type, the only pieces accorded such a distinction in the history of the journal. "East Coker" was published in a special supplement, and the final poem, "Little Gidding," was given a bold title in the table of contents as well as prominent single-column pages. Eliot published here several minor poems also, "Rannoch, by Glencoe" and "Words for an Old Man," as well as essays and letters.

The era of the *New English Weekly* was one in which writers were virtually required to have strong political, economic, and social views. Thus, one is not surprised to find here the first publication of T. S. Eliot's *Notes Towards a Definition of Culture*, serialized in January and February 1943. Eliot and Pound also engaged in a long exchange of review articles and letters to the editor, beginning in 1934 with Pound's review of Eliot's *After Strange Gods* and concluding after his review of *The Use of Poetry and the Use of Criticism*.[10] Pound, as is well known, was extremely vocal in his opinions; and in February 1946, in a two-part article, Reginald Snell warned Pound of danger, were he ever to be found sane and convicted of treason.

Beyond his policy of publishing articles by the well known and influential when their ideas followed his own, Orage actively recruited submissions for the paper, an unusual step in those days. He also typically sent out 100 complimentary copies of each issue to those he wished to interest in publishing in the journal.[11] Two and half years after the founding of the paper, however, Orage suddenly died, on 5 November 1934, and Philip Mairet stepped in as acting editor and then editor until the weekly ceased publication in 1949. The issue following Orage's death was a memorial to him, filled with tributes from the literary world. Ironically, the last words Orage wrote for the *New English Weekly* were "The reports of our death have been much exaggerated"; he had once observed about the periodical, "This paper is my epitaph."[12]

After her husband's death, Jesse R. Orage continued as sole proprietress of the journal. Not until 1942, in the middle of volume 21, was an editorial committee listed: Maurice B. Reckitt, Pamela Travers, T. S. Eliot, Rowland Kenny, and W. T. Symons. In volume 23, T. M. Heron was added to the list, and by the end of the journal Rowland Kenny had been dropped and Jesse R. Orage and her son Richard Orage added to the editorial committee. Beginning with twenty pages an issue, by volume 14 (13 October 1938–13 April 1939) most issues were sixteen pages long. With the advent of World War II and the shortage of paper, length dropped to twelve and then eight pages of reduced print, first on browning cheap paper and then very thin, but white, paper. After the war, print size returned to normal.

When the first issue of volume 30 came out on 7 October 1946, a notice to the readers advised them that the volume was being started without the funds required to pay for it, that "the *New English Weekly* has been dependent upon its supporters, each year since its beginning, for direct financial aid amounting to five or six hundred [pounds] a year" (30:3). For three more years the paper lingered and then, with a notice in the last issue (35, no. 22), ceased publication.

Notes

1. Philip Mairet, *A. R. Orage: A Memoir* (London, 1936), p. 109; John Carswell, *Lives and Letters: A. R. Orage, Beatrice Hastings, Katherine Mansfield, John Middleton Murry, S. S. Koteliansky, 1906–1957* (New York, 1978), p. 216.

2. Mairet, *A. R. Orage*, p. 111.

3. Alan Bullock and Oliver Stallybrass, eds., *The Harper Dictionary of Modern Thought* (New York, 1977), p. 578.

4. Carswell, *Lives and Letters*, pp. 216–217. Mairet comments that Orage obtained articles from various public men of distinction whose ideas in any way corroborated those he was popularizing. Writers such as Vincent Vickers and Sir William Blackett— both quondam directors of the Bank of England—Sir Harold Bowden, and Walter Elliot appeared from time to time in the paper, when they were expressing views that gave incidental support to editorial policy (p. 113).

5. Mairet, *A. R. Orage*, pp. 113–114.

6. Earle Davis, *Vision Fugitive: Ezra Pound and Economics* (Lawrence, Kans., 1968), pp. 107, 188–89.

7. Mairet, *A. R. Orage*, p. 114.

8. Ibid.

9. Carswell, *Lives and Letters*, p. 217 n.

10. See Christina C. Stough, "The Skirmish of Pound and Eliot in *The New English Weekly*: A Glimpse at Their Later Literary Relationship," *Journal of Modern Literature* 10 (1983):231–46.

11. Wallace Martin, *"The New Age" under Orage: Chapters in English Cultural History* (Manchester, Eng., 1967), p. 34.

12. Mairet, *A. R. Orage*, p. 121.

Information Sources

BIBLIOGRAPHY

Carswell, John. *Lives and Letters: A. R. Orage, Beatrice Hastings, Katherine Mansfield, John Middleton Murry, S. S. Koteliansky, 1906–1957*. New York, 1978.

Davis, Earle. *Vision Fugitive: Ezra Pound and Economics*. Lawrence, Kans., 1968.

Mairet, Philip. *A. R. Orage: A Memoir*. London, 1936.

Martin, Wallace. *"The New Age" under Orage: Chapters in English Cultural History*. Manchester, Eng., 1967.

Stough, Christina C. "The Skirmish of Pound and Eliot in *The New English Weekly*: A Glimpse at Their Later Literary Relationship." *Journal of Modern Literature* 10 (1983):231–46.

INDEXES
Volumes 1–16: each volume indexed.

REPRINT EDITIONS
Microform: Datamics, Inc., New York.

LOCATION SOURCES

American
Widely available.

British
Complete runs: Birmingham Public Library; British Museum; Cambridge University Library.

Partial runs: Bristol Public Library; Liverpool Public Library; London University Library; National Library of Scotland, Edinburgh.

Publication History

MAGAZINE TITLE AND TITLE CHANGES
New English Weekly: A Review of Public Affairs, Literature, and the Arts, 1932–1939. *The New English Weekly and the New Age: A Review of Public Affairs, Literature, and the Arts*, 1939–1947. *The New English Weekly: A Review of Public Affairs, Literature, and the Arts*, 1947–1949.

VOLUME AND ISSUE DATA
Volumes 1–35, 21 April–September 1949.

FREQUENCY OF PUBLICATION
Weekly.

PUBLISHERS
    1932–1934: Alfred R. Orage. 1934–1949: Jesse R. Orage.
EDITORS
    A. R. Orage, 1932–1934. Philip Mairet, 1934–1949.

Christina C. Stough

NEW HUMANIST. See LITERARY GUIDE (VEA)

NEW MEASURE

New Measure began publication at Oxford in the fall of 1965, about the same time that one of its editors, Peter Jay, won the Newdigate Prize for Poetry. Throughout its existence its central concern remained contemporary British verse, and Michael Schmidt and Grevel Lindop, writing on the state of poetry in Britain in the sixties, called it a "notable magazine for new poets."[1] Jay and John Aczel jointly edited *New Measure* 1, but with the second number Jay, still an undergraduate, assumed sole editorship. After three numbers loss of financial backing forced Jay to take over the duties of publisher and to limit the magazine's run to a total of ten numbers. In an editorial in *New Measure* 4, Jay alluded indirectly to the circumstances which contributed to the journal's economic problems. "*New Measure* is not a popular magazine. It neither expected nor intended to be so. . . . We have printed material which has displeased many; equally, we have been rewarded by the appreciation of others." Arts Council grants enabled Jay to fulfill his commitment to produce ten numbers, and after the publication of *New Measure* 10 he turned his energy to the little press he had founded, Anvil Press Poetry.

The inaugural issue of *New Measure* offered the following description of its format: "It is . . . our intention always to try and choose poetry which enables us to see objects, ideas and actions more clearly. In the future we shall print translations from foreign poets, contemporary and otherwise, reviews, critical articles, special issues, and possibly contributions on the other arts and non-artistic subjects." Despite its short run, *New Measure* very nearly met all of these goals, and it remained faithful to the policy articulated in *New Measure* 2 of judging "each poem submitted as far as possible on its own merits rather than on any preconceived notion of what the magazine's poems ought to be." The editorial went on to eschew "partisan" attitudes, affirming its intention to be "catholic in taste." In fact, despite the close Oxbridge connections which Jay maintained throughout the life of *New Measure*, the magazine offered the work of a range of poets from established writers to unknowns, presenting a cross-section of the state of British poetry in the mid to late sixties.

Early issues reflected some vacillation as to precisely how *New Measure* should structure itself. Its first number contained contributions from established poets—

W. H. Auden, Alan Brownjohn, and Christopher Middleton—as well as those establishing a reputation, such as Anselm Hollo and Tom Raworth, and many unknown writers. The second number featured translations from Greek, Italian, German, French, and Russian poets (including Boris Pasternak and Yevgeny Yevtushenko), and poems by Englishmen Jack Clemo, Christopher Middleton, and Matthew Mead. *New Measure* 3 was devoted to three Oxford poets: Gavin Bantock, John Wheway, and Adrian Husain.

With the decision to suspend publication after the tenth number, *New Measure* settled into a format that would be maintained for the remainder of its issues. Contributors remained basically British artists, many with university affiliation, but Jay also published some Canadians and translations of Russian, German, and Austrian poets. Matthew Mead and a number of writers associated with Anvil Press Poetry were frequent contributors. *New Measure* 6, with guest editor Stuart Montgomery, was devoted to American poets, and it included the work of Gary Snyder and Joel Oppenheimer. *New Measure* 9 featured poets associated with Anvil Press Poetry. Reviews of books of poetry appeared in numbers 2, 4–8, and 10. In *New Measure* 10, Jay announced that with the cessation of publication of the magazine he would devote his energy to Anvil Press Poetry.

Note

1. Michael Schmidt and Grevel Lindop, eds. *British Poetry since 1960: A Critical Survey* (Oxford, 1972), p. 5.

Information Sources

BIBLIOGRAPHY

Jones, Peter, and Michael Schmidt, eds. *British Poetry since 1970: A Critical Survey.* Manchester, 1980.

Schmidt, Michael, and Grevel Lindop, eds. *British Poetry since 1960: A Critical Survey.* Oxford, 1972.

INDEXES

None.

REPRINT EDITIONS

None.

LOCATION SOURCES

American

Widely available.

British

Complete runs: Manchester Public Libraries (Central Library); National Public Library of Scotland, Edinburgh; University of London (Goldsmith Library). Partial run: University of Strathclyde Library.

Publication History

MAGAZINE TITLE AND TITLE CHANGES

New Measure.

VOLUME AND ISSUE DATA
  Numbers 1–10, Autumn 1965–Winter 1969.
FREQUENCY OF PUBLICATION
  Three times a year.
PUBLISHERS
  1965–1966: Donald Parsons and Co., Ltd., 1a, Littlegate Street, Oxford. 1966–
  1969: Peter Jay, Lincoln College, Oxford (1966–1967); 5 Carew Road, North-
  wood, Middlesex (1968–1969).
EDITORS
  Peter Jay and John Aczel, 1965. Peter Jay, 1966–1969.

Michael Patrick Gillespie

NEW POETRY (1945)

New Poetry was a literary magazine of the purest sort: it devoted virtually
every inch of its thirty-two pages to poetry and nothing else. It had a life of two
issues, the first in 1945, the second in late 1946. Nicholas Moore edited it and
contributed poems to both issues.[1] Other contributors included Conrad Aiken,
Kenneth Allott, Elizabeth Bishop, Lawrence Durrell, Paul Goodman, Horace
Gregory, Howard Nemerov, Wallace Stevens, and Allen Tate.

Moore's connection with the Fortune Press, which published *New Poetry*,
involved several other anthologies and editions. His connection with the contributors to *New Poetry*, however, is more difficult to pinpoint—except in the
case of Aiken. In a letter to Malcolm Cowley on 22 January 1946, Aiken observes
that he has reached a certain status in the literary world without "ever at any
point being treated to a full-dress consideration as This or That." "What I got
of this sort," he wrote, "was wholly private: from my English pupil Malcolm
Lowry, and through him from a still continuing line of Cambridge (Eng.) University young writers—John Davenport, Gerald Noxon, Julian Symons, Nicholas
Moore, *et al.*"[2] Davenport, Noxon, and Symons did not contribute work to *New
Poetry*; aside from Moore's association with Aiken, then, the influence of Cambridge on the magazine is unclear.

As with the best and worst of little magazines devoted to poetry, the quality
and the style of the verse in *New Poetry* varies greatly. The magazine does
exhibit elements of consistency and coherence from page to page, however;
generally, the poetry shows the expected influence of modernism and New
Criticism—and little of the influence of surrealism, which Moore had experimented with some years before *New Poetry*. Stylistically, most of the poems
show a respect for the advice of T. S. Eliot and Ezra Pound, even if they do
not follow their precise example. The poets are poised, civilized, ironic, thoughtful, and allusive—all standard characteristics for poetry of the mid-forties. Occasionally, one even senses that a poet was writing something that he expected
a New Critic to explicate almost immediately.

One surprise that will greet many readers of *New Poetry* is the comparative lack of references to World War II. Certainly, a magazine of the mid-forties need not have achieved a quota of war poetry. One suspects, though, that most readers would simply expect such a magazine to reveal—in a variety of ways—the influence of the war. This expectation would seem even more natural if one were to consider the success with which poets like Randall Jarrell, Richard Eberhart, and Karl Shapiro were linking a similar poetic manner to the matter of the war at roughly the same time. The ahistorical bias of New Criticism, in other words, reveals itself in this magazine.

Aside from the apparent avoidance of the war as a topic and the general influence of formalism, Moore's editorial intent is hard to determine. How or why he went about soliciting and selecting the poems is not clear. Ironically, he seems to have achieved by default the kind of magazine that Geoffrey Grigson deliberately set out to create with the *Mint**—a magazine relatively free of politics. The "new" in *New Poetry* had virtually nothing to do with either historical immediacy or experimental poetics. Rather, Moore seems to have set out to gather the fairly recent work of established poets he liked and of acquaintances who may or may not have been publishing regularly elsewhere.

The design of the magazine was as straightforward as any purist could expect. In addition to the poems, the only other material included was a "Selective List of Volumes by Those Authors Represented in This Collection" and a one-paragraph obituary notice for John Peale Bishop, who died on 4 April 1945. The notice predicts that Bishop "will seem one of the four or five most wonderful lyric poets of our age." Both the "List" and the obituary appear on the last page (32) of the first issue.

As one might expect, the poems by Stevens—"The Bed of Old John Zeller" and "Less and Less Human, O Savage Spirit" (1:1)—and Elizabeth Bishop—"The Gentleman of Shallot" (1:16)—are far and away the most inventive and memorable ones in the magazine. Aiken's "Blind Date" (2:14) is an interesting if not entirely successful attempt to mix contemporary and more traditional poetic diction. Otherwise, the poetry Moore collected was generally competent but often mannered and occasionally dull. Few such short-lived magazines, however, contain so many enduring names: *New Poetry*'s roster clearly outdoes its actual contents.

Notes

1. Moore's own books of poetry include *A Book for Priscilla* (London, 1941), *The Cabaret, the Dancer, and the Gentleman* (London, 1942), and *The Glass Tower* (London, 1942). In the thirties, Moore had also been part of the group of poets calling themselves the "New Apocalypse." The group, which consisted of Henry Treece, John Bayliss, George Barker, and J. F. Hendry, saw itself in part as a reaction against surrealism. None of these poets appeared in *New Poetry*. For a discussion of Moore's connection with this group and his earlier experimentation with surrealism (including "chain poems"),

see *English and American Surrealist Poetry*, ed. Edward B. Germain (New York, 1978), pp. 40–41, 160, 169–70.

2. *Selected Letters of Conrad Aiken*, ed. Joseph Killorin (New Haven, 1978), p. 268.

Information Sources

BIBLIOGRAPHY

Aiken, Conrad. *Selected Letters of Conrad Aiken*. Edited by Joseph Killorin. New Haven, 1978.

Bishop, Elizabeth. *The Complete Poems: 1927–1979*. New York, 1983.

Durrell, Lawrence. *Collected Poems*. New York, 1960.

Germain, Edward B., ed. *English and American Surrealist Poetry*. New York, 1978.

Stevens, Wallace. *The Collected Poems of Wallace Stevens*. New York, 1975.

INDEXES

None.

REPRINT EDITIONS

None.

LOCATION SOURCES

American

Complete run: U.S. Library of Congress.

Partial runs: Columbia University Library; Newberry Library; New York Public Library; Northwestern University Library; University of Texas Library.

British

Complete run: British Museum.

Publication History

MAGAZINE TITLE AND TITLE CHANGES

New Poetry.

VOLUME AND ISSUE DATA

Volume 1, 1945; volume 2, 1946.

FREQUENCY OF PUBLICATION

Yearly.

PUBLISHER

Fortune Press, London (now an allied company of Charles Skilton, Ltd., 2–4 Abbeymount, Edinburgh).

EDITOR

Nicholas Moore.

Hans Ostrom

NEW POETRY (1967). See WORKSHOP

NEW ROAD

Two recent Cambridge graduates—Alex Comfort was twenty-three, John Bayliss a year older— came together in 1943 to edit *New Road: New Directions in*

European Arts and Letters, an annual miscellany of poetry, fiction, criticism, and the visual arts. For neither editor was *New Road* an all-absorbing or essential enterprise; for Comfort, indeed, who was in the forties balancing a medical career with the writing of poetry and novels, it was perhaps no more than a convenient outlet and occasional forum. Rather than the tastes (or ideologies) of individuals, *New Road* expressed the taste of an ill-defined group of young, vaguely internationalist, left-leaning writers toward the end of the war. The "crowd who are grouped around *New Road*, *Now* [*] and *Poetry London* [*]" constitute "the movement," wrote George Orwell in a fall 1944 "London Letter" to the *Partisan Review*, adding that the movement gave him the impression of fleas hopping among the ruins of a civilization.[1]

The editors and other writers associated with *New Road* undoubtedly would have resented being placed in a single group almost as much as being associated with fleas. The introduction to the poetry section in the first issue emphasizes an eclectic principle of selection. Older writers, whose reputations had become fully established before the war, were not to be published ("as in the case of *Lyra*," which Comfort had edited with Robert Greacen in 1942), but younger writers in several different varieties were to be welcomed—poets of the Apocalypse school; poets associated with the group of Anne Ridler, Kathleen Raine, and Norman Nicholson; the Oxford poets (Sidney Keyes and James Kirkup); poets not belonging to any group (David Gascoyne, Vernon Watkins, Fred Marnau). The first issue is in fact chiefly devoted to poetry by Wrey Gardiner, Marnau, Raine, G. S. Fraser, Comfort, and Bayliss (Bayliss's five poems appear here under his own name; elsewhere he published under the pseudonym John Clifford). Derek Stanford and Raine contribute critical statements on contemporary poetry.

The remaining sections of the first issue are devoted to political writing, including excerpts from Orwell's "Looking Back on the Spanish War," the plastic arts, and surrealism. The last is the most European section, as one would expect, with work from Toni del Renzio, Max Ernst, André Breton, and Nicolas Calas, whose surrealist proverbs—"A woman who is ashamed is a crown to her husband's rottenness"—are an unintentionally comic comment on the period.

The four later issues of *New Road* include fiction but otherwise hold to the editorial policies established by Comfort and Bayliss. Sections of American and South American writing keep the 1944 annual from being too parochially European (Henry Miller, Kay Boyle, Elizabeth Bishop, Paul Goodman, and Delmore Schwartz all appear); the 1945 issue, edited by Fred Marnau, has a lengthy Slavonic section, in keeping with Marnau's central European antecedents and determinedly pan-European perspective. The 1946 *New Road*, again edited by Marnau, begins with a florid statement of purpose: "We must transform the fire into light and warmth. The poet-man in us is called upon to perform the change: an alchemical creation. . . . This is the mystery, the sacramental act of the twentieth-century" (no. 4:11); it is perhaps the most interesting of all the issues, with writing by John Heath-Stubbs, George Takl, Ignazio Silone, Oskar Kokoschka,

Hugh MacDiarmid, Ernst Juenger, Paul Eluard, and others. After three years, in 1949, the last *New Road* appeared, edited now by Wrey Gardiner, and including poems from England, Ireland, and France.

Note

1. George Orwell, *Collected Essays, Journalism and Letters*, ed. Sonia Orwell and Ian Angus (New York, 1968), 3:195. In 1943, Orwell had conducted a public quarrel with Comfort, in poems exchanged in *Tribune*, and this may have colored his judgment; he did, however, compliment Comfort on the "quantity and the general level of the verse" in *New Road*, and thought well enough of the annual to contribute an essay to it (2:303).

Information Sources

BIBLIOGRAPHY

Comfort, Alex. *Art and Social Responsibility: Lectures on the Ideology of Romanticism*. London, 1946.
Comfort, Alex, and Robert Greacen. *Lyra: An Anthology of New Lyric*. Billericay, Eng., 1942.
Hoffman, Frederick J., Charles Allen, and Carolyn F. Ulrich. *The Little Magazine: A History and a Bibliography*. 2nd ed. Princeton, 1947.
Stanford, Derek. *The Freedom of Poetry*. London, 1947.

INDEXES
None.

REPRINT EDITIONS
Kraus Reprint, Nendeln, Liechtenstein, 1969. Scholars' Facsimiles and Reprints, Delmar, N.Y.

LOCATION SOURCES
American
Widely available.
British
Complete runs: Birmingham Public Library; British Museum; Liverpool Public Library; National Library of Scotland, Edinburgh; University of London Library. Partial runs: Glasgow University Library; Manchester Public Library.

Publication History

MAGAZINE TITLE AND TITLE CHANGES
New Road: New Directions in European Art and Letters, 1943–1944. *New Road: Directions in European Art and Letters*, 1945–1946. *New Road*, 1949.

VOLUME AND ISSUE DATA
Numbers 1–4, 1943–1946. Number 5, 1949.

FREQUENCY OF PUBLICATION
Annually.

PUBLISHER
Grey Walls Press, Billericay, Essex, and 4 Vernon Place, London.

EDITORS
Alex Comfort and John Bayliss, 1943–1944. Fred Marnau, 1945–1946. Wrey
Gardiner, 1949.

Jefferson Hunter

NEW SALTIRE. See SALTIRE REVIEW, THE

NEW STATESMAN (AND NATION). See VEA

NEW STORIES

In the first issue of *New Stories*, for February-March 1934, "A Prefatory
Note" traced the reasons for the new magazine. The success of the American
periodical *Story*, with the publication of short stories in Great Britain in the
Manchester Guardian, the *London Mercury*,* *Life and Letters*,* the *Adelphi*,*
and *Lovat Dickson's Magazine*,* and the appearance of several volumes of stories
from English publishers were evidence that "interest in the short story as a
literary form is markedly reviving, amongst both readers and writers" (1, no.
1:1). The editorial board—H. E. Bates, Arthur Calder-Marshall, Hamish Miles,
Edward J. O'Brien, L. A. Pavey, and Geoffrey West—felt that still "a large
body of fine and uncommon work" was being "overlooked, neglected, or under-
estimated" (1, no. 1:2); *New Stories* would provide a channel for the publication
of some of these works and focus attention on writing of "accomplished and
original quality," irrespective of the fame or obscurity of its author.[1] The editors
did not confine publication to a particular school, and they refused even to define
the genre to which writers would have to conform. Publishing "representative
work of very varied, but always vital, character" was its goal. The only limitation
imposed was that the contents would be confined to "stories originally written
in English," though it was acknowledged that exceptions might be made for
foreign pieces "likely to have a fertilizing influence," an option that was never
exercised.

The board planned to produce the magazine in facsimile typescript, but by
the first number (February-March 1934), advance support from readers in England and abroad was sufficient to justify a printed issue. By the publication of
number 4 the journal's circulation had grown so "burdensome" that the editors
accepted Basil Blackwell's offer to take over the production of the magazine.
As an editorial pointed out, Blackwell had an established reputation as the
publisher of "original and experimental work," and its participation would
enhance the journal's reputation and allow the editors to devote more time to
reading manuscripts. Even though contributors were not paid for their work,
during the first six months of *New Stories*' existence, approximately 1,250 man-

uscripts had been submitted for consideration (from four continents). Almost 900 of the stories had survived a first reading and were evaluated further by the editorial board; 43 of these had already been published, and an additional 20 had been selected for publication in future issues.

Volume 1 of *New Stories* contained six numbers, each measuring four by eight inches with an average of eighty pages per issue. For volume 1, fifty-five authors contributed sixty-two short stories. Averaging just over seven and a half pages per selection, the stories actually ran from one page to more than twenty-eight, the longest piece being poet Stephen Spender's "By the Lake" in the first number. Besides Spender, there were several other writers who would become noteworthy—Benjamin Appel, H. S. Manhood, Ronald Tansley, Romer Wilson, T. C. Worsley (who became a drama critic), and August W. Derleth (who become important in the field of science fiction) among them. Most famous was Dylan Thomas, whose allegorical "The Enemies" appeared in the third number. The first volume also included Elita Morris's "Mrs. Lancaster-Jones," a tale about a widowed nanny who does not fit in contemporary society; editor Arthur Calder-Marshall's "The Swan," which describes the killing of the bird by three boys; Gavin Ewart's "Inner Circle," a short psychological study of an adolescent; and Ruth O'Brien's "An Accident," a fable about a little devil and a little child. Louis Mamet's "Episode from Life," a six-page radio program scenario, is the most experimental piece in the volume.

The eight numbers that constitute volume 2 published seventy-nine stories, of which Barrington Gates's "Bateman's," a five-page slice of life sketch about mundane events in a bicycle repair shop, is typical. Alfred H. Mendes's thirty-one page "Lulu Gets Married," in number 5, was the longest story to be published in *New Stories*. In addition to the authors whose writing appeared in volume 1, another forty-eight writers are represented in the second volume. With the third number of volume 2, for June-July 1935, book reviews became a feature of *New Stories*. Written by members of the editorial board, the essays ran from half a page to three and a half pages in length; some reviews dealt with single volumes, but most covered several collections. In the six remaining issues, a total of twenty pages was allotted to thirty-five reviews of books by authors such as John Galsworthy, William Saroyan, Anatole France, P. G. Wodehouse, Frank O'Connor, Laura Riding, A. E. Coppard, and Theodore F. Powys. In general the reviews are short and not especially distinguished.

New Stories ceased publication, without advance notice, with the April-May 1936 number. In the fourteen issues of the magazine, 139 short stories by 103 authors were published. Although no individual piece published in *New Stories* has become a recognized classic of the genre, most of the short stories printed were well written and insightful, and the journal served its purpose well.

Note

1. Bates had published pieces in other little magazines such as the *Adelphi*, *Life and Letters*, the *Whirl*, the *New Coterie** (see *Coterie*), *Story*, *Lovat Dickson's Magazine*,

and *Programme*. O'Brien edited *Best Short Stories of 1930*, served as editor of the *Westminster Magazine* (1935–1944), and wrote a history of the short story over the previous twenty years, published in the December 1933 issue of *Lovat Dickson's Magazine*. Miles spent a short term (March-August) as editor of *Life and Letters* in 1934.

Information Sources

BIBLIOGRAPHY
Hoffman, Frederick J., Charles Allen, and Carolyn F. Ulrich. *The Little Magazine: A History and a Bibliography*. Princeton, 1946.
INDEXES
Each volume indexed. *An Author Index to Selected British Little Magazines*, ed. B. C. Bloomfield (London, 1976).
REPRINT EDITIONS
None.
LOCATION SOURCES
American
Complete runs: Harvard University Library; New York Public Library; Ohio State University Library; Princeton University Library; University of California Library, Berkeley; University of Chicago Library; University of Kansas Library.
Partial runs: University of Buffalo Library; University of Washington Library; Xavier University Library; Yale University Library.
British
Complete runs: Birmingham Public Library; British Museum; Cambridge University Library; National Library of Scotland, Edinburgh.
Partial run: Leeds University Library.

Publication History

MAGAZINE TITLE AND TITLE CHANGES
New Stories.
VOLUME AND ISSUE DATA
Volume 1, numbers 1–6, February-March, 1934–December-January, 1934–1935.
Volume 2, numbers 1–8, February-March, 1935–April-May, 1936.
FREQUENCY OF PUBLICATION
Bimonthly.
PUBLISHER
Basil Blackwell, 118 Banbury Road, Oxford.
EDITORS
H. E. Bates, Arthur Calder-Marshall, Hamish Miles, Edward J. O'Brien, L. A. Pavey, and Geoffrey West.

Steven Gale

NEW VERSE

In 1932, when he founded *New Verse*, Geoffrey Grigson was the twenty-seven-year-old literary editor of the London *Morning Post*. He admired Wyndham Lewis' *Blast** and started his own magazine as a "major-counterpoise" against Georgianism, imagism, and "Pure Poetryism," "what [was] left of the nineteenth under the name of the twentieth century."[1] In 1932 no London journal published poetry exclusively, and there would not be any besides *New Verse* until 1937, when Julian Symons would begin *Twentieth Century Verse.** But in 1932 there did appear a self-proclaimed "new" Marxist poetry anthology: Michael Roberts's *New Signatures*. The poets whom Roberts published—W. H. Auden, Stephen Spender, C. Day Lewis—would also appear in *New Verse*, lending an appearance of group solidarity and giving the magazine a leftist, socially conscious air. Throughout its seven years of bimonthly issues Grigson resisted the labeling of *New Verse* as activist or propagandistic of either social or literary aims. In the first issue for January 1933 he eschewed any doctrine but revealed the influence of I. A. Richards as he claimed the dominance of poetry:

> [*New Verse*] favors only its time, belonging to no literary or politico-literary cabal. . . . There is no "poetic" and therefore no supplementary experience. . . . If the poem is only one organism in the creation of which experiences are collected, concentrated, transmitted, it is the chief organism.

Keeping poetry independent of politics in the 1930s was to prove impossible; separating the relative merits of the "Group" poets was somewhat easier. Grigson denounced Day Lewis because his poems were propagandistic, Spender because his poems were Romantic (see no. 2:15; no. 12:14; no. 15:18). Louis MacNeice and Auden produced the model poems for which *New Verse* would be known, a style that one critic has called "British Objectivism" and another critic has labeled "poetry of addition."[2] Some poets merely listed or catalogued objects or events; but the more successful ones, like Auden or MacNeice, could "see objects as themselves and as symbols, all at once" and "impart ideas through objects." Their works revealed a "moral sense" in that the poets were "ever careful to convey the inner by the outer shape of things."[3] In the beginning Grigson did not intend that the magazine would foster one kind of poem, but near the end of *New Verse*, when he collected the most notable poems for an anthology, he admitted that "his intellectual and perceptive fault" had been "not joining up symptoms into a pattern as early and as understandingly as others." His only criterion for accepting or rejecting a poem, he maintained, had been "the degree to which it takes notice, for ends not purely individual, of the universe of objects and events."[4]

Except for Grigson, who published under such pseudonyms as "Martin Boldero" (his mother's maiden name), Auden was the most frequent contributor of poems to *New Verse*. Prolific as he was, his early work appeared in several other journals as well—The *Listener*, the *Criterion*,* and *New Statesman and Nation** (see *VEA*)—but twenty-one of his poems made their way to *New Verse*. Among them are poems that were never anthologized before the posthumous *English*

Auden (New York, 1977) and others written before 1927 that have never been republished: the untitled five-poem sequence, of which he retained only the last, revised and entitled "Meiosis"; "The Carter's Funeral"; and "Allendale." Equally as important as the publication of those poems is the almost constant critical acclaim *New Verse* gave Auden. Grigson hailed him as a standard-bearer, not just for a new poetry, but for a new culture. In 1937, when critics began to detect an "opacity" and "dullness" in Auden's poetry, Grigson published a special double issue (no. 26–27) for Auden.[5] He solicited encomiums from twenty-two fellow poets and published the first bibliography of Auden's work. In the last issue of the magazine, for May 1939, Grigson lavishly praised *In Time of War* and issued one last paean; people might say of Auden: "To you I owe the first development of my imagination; to you I owe the withdrawing of my mind from the low brutal part of my nature, to the lofty, the pure and the perpetual" (n.s. no. 2:49).

After Auden and MacNeice, the most frequently published poets were Bernard Spencer, Kenneth Allott, Gavin Ewart, Charles Madge, Norman Cameron, David Gascoyne, and Dylan Thomas. The first three certainly qualified as "objectivist" poets of the mold Grigson derived from Auden. Spencer's "Allotments: April" (no. 21) was described by Kenneth Allott, for a while an assistant editor, as "the kind of poem for which *New Verse* stood."[6] Gavin Ewart was still a student at Wellington when he began contributing to *New Verse* such poems as "Phallus in Wonderland," "Audenesque for an Initiation," and "Journey," which concludes: "All those roads are Auden's. . . . / I've been over them once, following his tracks" (no. 8). Other *New Verse* poets were less Audenesque. Cameron offered an alternative (as another contributor, Roy Fuller, noted) to "the clotted style that was the epoch's bane."[7] Grigson praised his friend's work as "natural . . . with all the virtues, and all the illumination, of the spontaneous amateur" (no. 19:17). For Gascoyne and Thomas there was less admiration; they pursued, not objects, but forms and mysticism. In Thomas's first work Grigson detected "a rhetorical toughness . . . not infrequent excellences of imaginative statement" (no. 13: 22). He urged Thomas in 1935 to cultivate "severity from himself," and in 1969 he reaffirmed his earlier judgment and bemoaned Thomas's "failure."[8]

The importance of *New Verse* lies not only in its advocacy of one dominant poetic style but in its critical involvement with all the movements and most of the major figures of the 1930s. Two far-reaching experiments recorded there are surrealism and the concomitant phenomenon Mass Observation. *New Verse* became the vehicle for the latter pop-sociological experiment because of Charles Madge, whose poems and reviews appeared there frequently. Madge and an anthropologist, Tom Harrisson, organized teams of reporters in cities throughout England to write about the ordinary details of their lives and of such special occasions as the coronation of George VI. To *Left Review** Madge contributed essays explaining the Marxist side of the experiment; in *New Verse* he discussed the aesthetic interests. By recording events and impressions, the "Observers" would bring into consciousness all their "concealed wishes"; they would consciously interpret symbols as a first step toward changing institutions that were embodiments of symbols. In *New Verse* Madge juxtaposed a passage from a novel, a historical account, and a Mass Observation report to prove that the last was "(i) scientific, (ii) human, and therefore by implication, (iii) poetic." It was also more objective "because the subjectivity of the observer is one of the facts under observation" (no. 24: 2).

The involvement of *New Verse* with Mass Observation culminated in the publication of the "Oxford Collective Poem" in the next issue. Under the supervision of Herbert Howarth, twelve undergraduates spent a month to produce a single poem that Madge termed "virtually a 'landscape' for their Oxford environment." It was, he noted, "another angle on a possible connection between Mass Observation and poetry" (no. 25: 16). For three weeks each observer recorded daily a single dominant image; from twelve lists dominant, similar, or recurring images were drawn. Each observer then composed a single pentameter line for each of the images, and collectively the best was chosen. Finally, one weekend each observer integrated the lines into a poem; collectively each poem was revised and one of them chosen.

Mass Observation has been explained as reverse surrealism: "whereas the surrealist sees in his object—found or made—an objectification of inner states or desires, Mass Observation assumes that the objects and images of our worlds are the concretization of inner states and seeks to recover those inner states by using the objects and images as signposts."[9] Both produced, as Kathleen Raine observed, "a kind of poetic (or pictorial) imagery at once irrational and objective."[10] It is the latter quality that perhaps accounts for the range of surrealist poets in *New Verse*: Gascoyne, Raine, Philip O'Connor, Ruthven Todd, Hans Arp, Paul Eluard. While it published their poems, the magazine also traced in a series of essays the growth of the movement. Madge attempted to show the historicism of surrealism in such a work as "Night Thoughts" (no. 6), while Hugh Sykes Davies, a classicist, traced its origin to primitivism in Homer (no. 8) and argued for a psychoanalytic approach (no. 20). In 1936, at the height of the movement in England, Auden, signing himself as "J. B." for "John Bull," questioned such assumptions. He argued that most surrealistic writing was "the work of highly repressed individuals in a society with very strong taboos" and speculated whether surrealism might flourish only among peoples ignorant of psychoanalysis or repressed by "strong sexual or political censorship" (no. 21: 15–16).

New Verse thus became the only magazine to address the issues raised by surrealism. Julian Symons announced that *Twentieth Century Verse* would publish an entire issue on surrealism, but he soon reported that the issue would not appear and rejected all surrealist verse. Roger Roughton began a magazine of surrealist verse and fiction, *Contemporary Poetry and Prose*,* but it lasted only ten issues, from May 1936 to Autumn 1937, and never attempted to define or characterize the movement whose works it published.

New Verse is remembered almost as much for its acerbic criticism as for the poetry it published. Grigson recalls:

> It is rather more than I can bear to look now in old numbers of *New Verse*.
> . . . But the public assault to which young poets were treated in those days
> . . . [was] an irritant to a reply in kind, to a slash with the billhook, which
> was far too much my weapon and which I endeavored to keep sharp.[11]

One prominent victim of the billhook was Edith Sitwell. When she attacked *New Verse* in her *Aspects of Modern Poetry*, Grigson replied by characterizing her family as eels that wrapped themselves in their own mud. In subsequent issues he dubbed her "old Jane" and exhibited her in his column, "Private Zoo." When Roy Campbell came to Sitwell's defense, Grigson reviewed his *Flowering Rifle* as "a hyena, ambitious to be lion, howling away to itself . . . in the middle of a lonely and extensive sewage farm" (n.s. no. 1). Others who suffered Grigson's vituperative wit were Laura Riding, "Queen-bore among all the poets"; Robert Graves, "an archaeological indulgence"; and Edwin Muir, "the Amateur Poet attached to the Professional Man of Letters."

Grigson's quarrels extended to editors of other magazines. When F. R. Leavis treated *New Verse* condescendingly in *Scrutiny*,* Grigson characterized that magazine as "too adolescent, too self-righteous, too ready to accept the naivetes of ledger-criticism" (no. 4: 1–2). Morton Zabel, writing in *Poetry* in April 1936, called Grigson's criticism "slap-dash impertinence." Grigson replied that *Poetry* was "almost corpse, prints for preference corpse poetry" (no. 21: 21). Two years later D. S. Savage laid the same charge against *New Verse*. Writing in *Poetry* late in 1938, he called Grigson's causes "passé" and accused him of promoting an Oxbridge clique. The second charge bothered Grigson most, since he had used the same taunt against establishment figures when *New Verse* began. Accordingly, he wrote to *Poetry* a letter which the editors printed in the issue for April 1939: "I should like Mr. Savage to tell me what good 'non-bourgeois' poet is ringing the doorbell of *New Verse* without getting an answer."

No one could blame Grigson for righteous indignation against the charge that there was a *New Verse* clique. At the very end the magazine was "discovering" new poets—Theodore Roethke, Keith Douglas, Lawrence Little—and planning a "new series." The magazine regularized at two signatures; first cover ads disappeared; photographs were used more frequently; and the price was raised from six pence to a shilling. *New Verse* was also becoming more political. Grigson ended 1938 with a double issue on "Commitments" and announced "the end of political isolation." But such a concern was almost ludicrously late: war replaced both politics and poetry; *New Verse* and other magazines ended abruptly. Symons's epitaph for the 1930s journals is apt:

> The war would produce a flood of subjective flatulently emotional verse.
> . . . The decision to pack up the magazine was right, even though some of

the reasons were wrong. The little magazines of the period—*New Verse*, *Left Review* and the rest—were, more than are most such magazines, an image of their time: and in September 1939 that time was over.[12]

Notes

1. Geoffrey Grigson, "Notes on Contemporary Poetry," *The Bookman* 83 (September 1932): 287.

2. Kenneth Rexroth, *The New British Poets* (Norfolk, Conn., 1947), p. viii; Martin Dodsworth, "Bernard Spencer: The Poet of Addition," *The Review*, no. 11–12 (1964): 72–73.

3. Geoffrey Grigson, comp., *New Verse: An Anthology of Poems Which Have Appeared in the First Thirty Numbers of New Verse* (London, 1939), p. 22.

4. Ibid., p. 34.

5. See, e.g., Francois Duchene, *The Case of the Helmeted Airman: A Study of W. H. Auden's Poetry* (Totowa, N.J., 1972), p. 111.

6. Quoted by Dodsworth, p. 72.

7. "Norman Cameron: Four Views," ed. James Reeves, *The Review*, no. 27–28 (1971–72): 15.

8. "Poet of Over-Poetry," in *Poems and Poets*, ed. Geoffrey Grigson (London, 1969), p. 198.

9. Paul Ray, *The Surrealist Movement in England* (Ithaca, N.Y., 1971), pp. 177–78.

10. Kathleen Raine, *Defending Ancient Springs* (London, 1967), pp. 48–49.

11. Geoffrey Grigson, *The Crest on the Silver: An Autobiography* (London, 1950), p. 162.

12. "Twentieth Century Verse," *The Review*, no. 11–12 (1964): 24.

Information Sources

BIBLIOGRAPHY

Grigson, Geoffrey. "Coming to London." In *Coming to London*. Edited by John Lehmann. London, 1957.

———. *The Crest on the Silver: An Autobiography*. London, 1950.

———. *Poetry of the Present: An Anthology of the Thirties and After*. London, 1949.

———, comp. *New Verse: An Anthology of Poems Which Have Appeared in the First Thirty Numbers of New Verse*. London, 1939.

Hamilton, Ian. *The Little Magazines: A Study of Six Editors*. London, 1976.

Hoffman, Frederick J., Charles Allen, and Carolyn F. Ulrich. *The Little Magazine: A History and a Bibliography*. 2nd ed. Princeton, 1947.

Sullivan, Alvin. *New Verse: A Critical Survey and an Index*. Ph.D. dissertation, Saint Louis University, 1972.

Symons, Julian. *The Thirties: A Dream Revolved*. London, 1960.

———. "Twentieth Century Verse." *The Review*, no. 11–12 (1964): 22–24.

INDEXES

Alvin Sullivan. *New Verse: A Critical Survey and an Index*, Ph.D. dissertation, Saint Louis University, 1972. *An Author Index to Selected British Little Magazines*, ed. B. C. Bloomfield (London, 1976). Numbers 1–32 in *Comprehensive Index*

to English Language Little Magazines 1890–1970, series 1, ed. Marion Sader
(Millwood, N.Y., 1976).
REPRINT EDITIONS
   Kraus Reprint, New York, 1966.
   Microform: Brookhaven Press, La Crosse, Wis.
LOCATION SOURCES
American
   Complete runs: Harvard University Library; New York Public Library; University
   of Buffalo Library; Yale University Library.
   Partial runs: Columbia University Library; Hamilton College Library; Loyola
   University Library; Princeton University Library; University of Michigan Library.
British
   Complete runs: National Library of Scotland, Edinburgh; University of Hull Library.
   Partial runs: Birmingham Public Library; British Museum; Leeds Public Library;
   Queen's University of Belfast Library; University College of Swansea Library.

Publication History

MAGAZINE TITLE AND TITLE CHANGES
   New Verse.
VOLUME AND ISSUE DATA
   Numbers 1–32, January 1933–Autumn 1938. New series, numbers 1–2, January–
   May 1939. 26/27 and 31/32 are double issues.
FREQUENCY OF PUBLICATION
   Bimonthly.
PUBLISHER
   January 1933–September 1936: Frances Franklin Grigson, 4A Keats Grove, Lon-
   don NW 3. Christmas 1936–May 1939: no publisher listed; editorial address is 3
   Wildwood Terrace, London NW 3.
EDITOR
   Geoffrey Grigson.

Alvin Sullivan

NEW WRITERS

In 1961 John Calder began to introduce European and American prose writers
to a British audience. Before the appearance of *New Writers*, longer fiction had
only appeared in anthologies, the yearly collection *Winter's Tales* of St. Martin's
Press, individual translations, and occasional work in literary magazines such
as the *Dial* and the *Evergeen Review*, which Calder had imported to England.[1]

New Writers was published irregularly from 1961 to 1976, and the volumes
were numbered 1 through 12. It showcased about forty-two writers, usually three
or four per volume, including some important but seldom translated foreign
writers, promising younger writers, and complete unknowns. A special issue,

New Writers 4, the "Happenings" volume, was an exception, as it had a variety of works about this art form by six artists and an introduction by Calder.

In *New Writers* 1, Calder uses the space on the dust jacket to announce works by Dino Buzzati, Monique Lange, and Alan Burns, and to explain the purpose of the series:

> This volume is the first of a series to bring dynamic and unusually inter-esting creative writing to the reader at an economic price and according to an international formula. The three writers presented here are quite new to the English reader and we believe that all three are destined to become familiar names in the near future.

The novelists in this volume, picked so that they could contrast as much as possible with each other, were soon published in longer works by Calder's press. The degree of Calder's success may be seen in the reaction of critics and reviewers to these new works and writers. Buzzati, whom Calder describes on the dust jacket as "the outstanding short story writer of the present day" in Italy, was reviewed in the *Times Literary Supplement* for 5 January 1962 as "much the best of the three. . . . it can be enjoyed as the work of a competent, subtly observant craftsman." Simon Vestdijk, whom Calder called the "best known contemporary Dutch novelist," and whom he published in *New Writers* 2, was praised in the *Times* for 25 January 1963. In issue 2 Calder also printed a play by Robert Pinget, translated by Samuel Beckett, and work by novelist Alexander Trocchi, "a major literary force [since] his novel *Cain's Book*." Trocchi's stories were called "splendid stuff" in the *Guardian Weekly* for 28 August 1969.

Critics also applauded the "Happenings" volume, *New Writers* 4, which Calder organized around the theme of decline in the theater. Arguing that "there is a purpose in going to the theatre to participate in an event that will add significantly to living, to thinking, to feeling," Calder commissioned happenings to be staged at the Edinburgh Festival in 1963. A *Times* reviewer of *New Writing* 4 liked the fact that it was "not by writers at all but by painters. One is made aware of the continuity of these Happenings with the antiart of the Dadaists, with its attempt at the direct involvement of the spectator." Ervin Gaines, in the *Library Journal* for December 1967, praised Jean Jacques Lebel's explanation of the happenings for helping "us unreconstructed squares to understand the worldwide literary and artistic revolution."

Other *New Writers* featured Carol Burns's "An Infatuation" and F. W. Wil-lets's "Cunard in the Desert" (no. 6); David Galloway's "Melody Jones" (no. 12); Alex Nersh's "Before the Undertaker Comes" (no. 5); Edmund Crocke-nedge's "Modd" and Karval Sundar's "A Strange Tale" (no. 7). While all of those contributions earned praise from various review journals, not all of Calder's protégés fared as well.

Unusual styles and approaches sometimes resulted in bad reviews. Joyce Mansour's "The Contented Effigies" in *New Writers* 12 was attacked by Stephen

Clark in the *Times Literary Supplement* (17 September 1976) as a "tripartite agony," and he criticized the language of her work without any mention of her position as a published French surrealist writer. He complains that "if this is what creative writing does for you, God help us all, for our creative writing will not." Ray Mathews explained the difficulties of publishing experimental short stories in that "the kind of short stories that tend to get into volume form tend to be experimental and they eschew plot and tend to stress a single mood or a verbal experiment and therefore become unrewarding to the general reader."[2]

By the end of 1976, with number 12, Calder decided that the project had become too expensive and planned a different series to accomplish his goal of drawing attention to new writers. With its twelve numbers, *New Writers* "forms an anthology of creative writing of some avant-garde writers" and provides a record of "the new scene" of the 1960s and 1970s.[3]

Notes

1. Denys Val Baker, "The Small Voices of Sanity," in *International Guide, 1961* (Los Angeles, 1961), p. 31.
2. *London Magazine*, n.s.5 (February 1966): 94.
3. *Library Journal* 92 (December 1967): 48.

Information Sources

BIBLIOGRAPHY

Kaprow, Allan. *Assemblages, Environments, and Happenings*. New York, 1966.
Kostelanetz, Richard, ed. *Breakthrough Fictioneers*. Barton, Vt., 1973.
Matthews, J. A., ed. *Custom House of Desire*. Berkeley, 1975.
Meijer, Reinder P. *Literature of the Low Countries*. London, 1978.
Robbe-Grillet, Alain. *For a New Novel*. New York, 1965.

INDEXES

    New Writers 12 contains a cumulative list of contributors, excluding translators.

REPRINT EDITIONS

    Transatlantic Arts, New York (Calder & Boyars). *Red Dust 1* and *2* (Calder & Boyars). Humanities Press, Atlantic Highlands, N.J. Riverrun, N.Y., 1980.

LOCATION SOURCES

  American
    Widely available.
  British
    Complete run: National Library of Scotland, Edinburgh.

Publication History

MAGAZINE TITLE AND TITLE CHANGES
    New Writers. Continued by *New Writing and Writers*.
VOLUME AND ISSUE DATA
    Numbers 1–12, 1961–1976.
FREQUENCY OF PUBLICATION
    Irregular.

PUBLISHER
   John Calder, Calder & Boyars. 1961–1962: 17 Sackville St., London, W. 1.
   1965–1976: 18 Brewer Street, London, W.1.
EDITOR
   John Calder.

Thomas J. Kenny

NEW WRITING

New Writing and its successors, *Folios of New Writing* and *New Writing and Daylight*, provide an excellent perspective on the shift in the British literary mainstream from the political concerns of the 1930s to the eclecticism of the postwar years. Its central place stems, in part, from the fact that the magazine was one of the few which published without substantial hiatus throughout World War II, and in part from the sensibility of its editor, John Lehmann, who founded the journal in 1936. Lehmann had made his literary debut in *New Signatures* and *New Country*, where his work appeared alongside that of W. H. Auden, C. Day Lewis, and Stephen Spender. These three, along with Christopher Isherwood, were largely responsible for both the leftist political orientation and the high literary quality of the prewar *New Writing*. By 1946, when the last issue of *New Writing and Daylight* appeared, however, Auden and Isherwood had emigrated to the United States, and only Spender was still contributing to the magazine. Lehmann, never as politically oriented as his friends, had published writers as diverse as Virginia Woolf, George Orwell, Lawrence Durrell, Dylan Thomas, and Elizabeth Bowen in his attempt to maintain the high literary standards for which the magazine is remembered.

Even in its early days *New Writing* was a less doctrinaire magazine than the thirties Marxist platforms typified by *Left Review*.* In fact, the magazine originated in part as a reaction against dogmatic literary politics. After discussing the project with Spender, Isherwood, William Plomer, and his sister Rosamond, Lehmann determined to found "a magazine in England round which people who held the same ideas about fascism and war could assemble without having to prove their Marxist purity."[1] The "Manifesto" published in the first number echoes this position: "NEW WRITING is first and foremost interested in literature, and though it does not intend to open its pages to writers of reactionary or Fascist sentiments, it is independent of any political party." In addition, the manifesto indicates that *New Writing* would seek out work by foreign and colonial writers and concentrate on prose rather than poetry. The final statement reflects both Lehmann's respect for Geoffrey Grigson's *New Verse** and his belief that prose was

   much more important for my purpose than poetry. It was in prose that the
   idea of "an effective brotherhood born between victims of oppression"

and the "sense of broader comradeship" was most clearly to be traced, especially in its international parallels; modern English poetry, at that moment, seemed to me to be following a more complex ideal, in which the champion influences of Eliot, Hopkins and Rilke fought against the transparency I looked for (and found) in prose.[2]

The contents of the first number, published by the Bodley Head with financial support from Lehmann's mother, typify the immediate results. In addition to work by Isherwood, Plomer, and Spender, the volume includes writing by English leftists Edward Upward and T. H. Wintringham; Russians Nikolai Tikhonov and Boris Pasternak; Chinese writer Tchang T'Ien-Yih; Frenchman André Chamson; and a section titled "Workers All: A Symposium." "Workers All" is the first of many sequences published in *New Writing* which were part fiction and part journalism. These "reportages," which Julian Symons dismissed as "documentary propaganda" condescending to the working class, nonetheless provide the clearest indication of *New Writing*'s political sympathies.[3] Despite their intention, however, the stories only rarely succeeded as political statements. As Lehmann observed, "The aim of this kind of story was to arouse pity and indignation; and yet owing to a certain flatness and too monotonous an insistence on dejection and misery the examples that had come my way all too often failed to arouse any reaction except boredom."[4]

If the reportage frequently fell short of Lehmann's aesthetic standards, the remainder of the prose frequently fulfilled it. Among the important works first published in *New Writing* and its successors were several sections of Isherwood's *Goodbye to Berlin* (nos. 1, 3, 5); George Orwell's "Shooting an Elephant" (no. 2), which Lehmann specifically commissioned; the first English translation of Jean-Paul Sartre's "The Room" (n.s. no. 2); and Virginia Woolf's "The Leaning Tree" (*Folios*, no. 2), which appeared shortly before her death. Lehmann's interest in foreign writing resulted in translations of stories by writers such as Ignazio Silone (nos. 2, 4), Mikhail Sholokhov (no. 4), André Gide and Antoine de Saint Exupéry (*New Writing and Daylight*, nos. 5, 7). *New Writing* also published fiction by E. M. Forster, V. S. Pritchett, Peter Yates, Elizabeth Bowen, and Henry Green. Like many editors of the thirties, Lehmann attempted to seek out working-class writers in order to "break down the barrier between these and the other team [writers with a background of middle-class education], to provide a place of cross-fertilization of their talents."[5] While it did publish the work of several working-class writers, including Lehmann's personal favorite, B. L. Coombes, *New Writing* was largely unsuccessful in this attempt; its best domestic prose reflects the well-established literary mainstream.

Despite Lehmann's emphasis on prose, *New Writing* also published a substantial amount of good poetry. Auden contributed numerous poems (nos. 2, 3, 4; n.s. nos. 1, 2, 3) including "Lay Your Sleeping Head" and "Palais des Beaux Arts." Spender, Federico García Lorca (no. 4; n.s. no. 1), Dylan Thomas (*Folios*, no. 4), and Odysseus Elytis (*Folios*, no. 3; *New Writing and Daylight*, nos. 6,7) were also among the contributors. Nonetheless, *New Writing* served primarily as a second outlet for poets associated with *New Verse* rather than as a creative force in the development of English poetry.[6]

After the second number, Lehmann moved *New Writing* from the Bodley Head to the communist publishing firm of Lawrence and Wishart, hoping to initiate a "New Writing Library" of novels, autobiographies, and poems. When the project failed to develop, Lehmann, who had been associated with the Hogarth Press prior to founding *New Writing*, bought out Virginia Woolf's half-interest in that venture. Moving *New Writing* to Hogarth in 1938, Lehmann convinced Isherwood and Spender to accept formal roles as advisory editors for a new series. Except for the final number of *New Writing and Daylight*, the magazine would remain at Hogarth through its subsequent publication history.

No drastic changes are evident in the new series of *New Writing*. The Christmas 1939 number (n.s. 3) reveals its close affinity with the original series. In addition to stories and sketches by Orwell, E. Sackville-West, V. S. Pritchett, and Rex Warner, the number includes three special sections. The first, titled "The English Muse," includes poems by Auden, Spender, the surrealist David Gascoyne, and Louis MacNeice, alongside several critical essays, including one by *Left Review* editor Randall Swingler. The second special section, "Workers All," is another example of Lehmann's emphasis on documentary material. The third, "Russian Pattern," reflecting *New Writing*'s cosmopolitanism and its leftist sympathies, consists of three translations and an original essay, "The Russian Cinema."

The coming of World War II brought substantial changes in *New Writing*. Isherwood and Auden had moved to the United States. Spender, though remaining a contributor, disappointed Lehmann by devoting his energies to *Horizon** at a time when the future of *New Writing* was very much in doubt. In addition, the Spanish Civil War had shaken Lehmann's faith in the Soviet Union. As a result, *Folios of New Writing*, first published in the spring of 1940, largely abandoned leftist politics while maintaining an antifascist stance. Lehmann explained the change:

> It seemed to me that the spirit of *New Writing* was in fact very far from confined to the association of left-wing politics and literature, whatever might be said by the detractors and those who, silent in their hostility before, were now eagerly gathering round the burial ground they had marked out for it. The belief in literature as a part of life, the belief in the power of the creative imagination to give meaning to life; these were surely going to be as important as ever in the times we were about to enter.[7]

Lehmann's introductory message in *Folios of New Writing* assured its audience that "our guiding principle remains the same: to create a laboratory where the writers of the future may experiment, and where the literary movement may find itself." Nevertheless, he realized that the magazine was in fact moving rapidly toward a new stance in response to the altered social context: "If *New Writing* was to go on, it must avoid the political, yes, but emphasize the human, be committed to the human scene even more completely; it could be a laboratory, an experimental ground for the development of a new consciousness; it would probably find itself moving towards something more lyrical and individual."[8] Lehmann implemented these ideas in both *Folios of New Writing*, which maintained the original *New Writing* format (though the number of pages was reduced by half because of the wartime paper shortage), and *Penguin New Writing*,* which appeared in a paperback book format and attained a wartime circulation of nearly 100,000.

As Lehmann recognized, *Folios of New Writing* was more a miscellany than a literary magazine with a strong central purpose. In part, this shift reflected the increasing difficulty of finding high-quality writing during the early years of the war. Lehmann's British collaborators were fighting or in America, and communication with his Continental sources was difficult or impossible. With the third number of *Folios of New Writing* (Spring 1941), he attempted to counteract the problem by announcing a new emphasis on critical writing; the issue also includes replies to Woolf's "The Leaning Tree" by Upward, Coombes, MacNeice, and Lehmann. *New Writing and Daylight* similarly emphasized critical writing, publishing essays by Helen Gardner (no. 1), Raymond Williams (no. 2), Robert Graves (no. 3), and Philip Toynbee (no. 4), and a symposium on "The Future of Fiction" (no. 7) which included statements by Pritchett, Arthur Koestler, and Walter Allen.

Lehmann's sympathy with the difficulties of *Daylight*, a magazine edited by exiled Czech writer Jiři Mucha and threatened by the paper shortage, resulted in a merger which restored some of the focus missing in *Folios of New Writing*. Lehmann later commented on the change: "The new contacts I had made with the exiled European writers in London, the new scope in articles on the theatre, ballet and the plastic arts that the preparation of *Daylight* had suggested, restored to *New Writing* something it had lost since the outbreak of the war."[9] The first number of *New Writing and Daylight* (Summer 1942) opened with Edwin Muir's essay "The Natural Man and the Political Man," which Lehmann considered among the most significant wartime defenses of culture. Subsequent numbers included "reports from the front," stylistically resembling reportages such as "Workers All" and intended to "reveal a truth more authentic, more intimate in detail than the propaganda to which we were (ever so gently) subjected could admit."[10] A strong concern with traditional humanistic ideals typifies the wartime numbers.

The end of the war brought with it a new paper shortage and marked the demise of *New Writing* in its original format. Lehmann, who had been reprinting the best pieces from *New Writing and Daylight* in *Penguin New Writing* for several years, sold his interest in the Hogarth Press and founded a new firm, John Lehmann, Ltd., which published the final number of *New Writing and Daylight* in 1946. Rather than continue with a "formula [that was] wearing a little thin," Lehmann discontinued the magazine and replaced it with *Orpheus*, which differed radically in both form and aesthetic emphasis.[11]

While it did not survive in its original form into the postwar era (*Penguin New Writing* continued publication), *New Writing* played a substantial role in establishing a cultural continuity between the 1930s and the 1950s. Commenting on letters he had received from British pilots during the war, Spender summed up the achievement of the magazine in its final years: "For these young men, *Horizon, New Writing* and one or two other literary reviews, were the means whereby they felt they, as well as we, survived the war."[12]

Notes

1. John Lehmann, *The Whispering Gallery* (London, 1955), p. 232.

2. Ibid., p. 253.

3. Julian Symons, *The Thirties: A Dream Revolved* (London, 1960), p. 63. For the contemporary response to *New Writing*'s political position, see Samuel Hynes, *The Auden Generation: Literature and Politics in England in the 1930s* (New York, 1976), p. 198.

4. John Lehmann, *I Am My Brother* (London, 1960), p. 17.

5. Lehmann, *The Whispering Gallery*, p. 257.

6. For commentary on *New Writing*'s poetry, see A. T. Tolley, *The Poetry of the Thirties* (New York, 1975), pp. 320–23. Lehmann examines the poetic achievement of the early numbers in "Without My Files," *Penguin New Writing* 21 (1944): 137–48.

7. Lehmann, *I Am My Brother*, p. 41.

8. Ibid., p. 42.

9. Ibid., p. 205.

10. Ibid.

11. John Lehmann, *The Ample Proposition* (London, 1966), p. 35.

12. Stephen Spender, *World Within Worlds* (New York, 1951), p. 265.

Information Sources

BIBLIOGRAPHY

Ford, Hugh D. *A Poets' War: British Poets and the Spanish Civil War*. Philadelphia, 1965.

Hewison, Robert. *Under Siege: Literary Life in London 1939–1945*. London, 1977.

Hynes, Samuel. *The Auden Generation: Literature and Politics in England in the 1930s*. New York, 1976.

Lehmann, John. *The Ample Proposition*. London, 1966.

———. *I Am My Brother*. London, 1960.

———. *The Whispering Gallery*. London, 1955.

———. "Without My Files." *Penguin New Writing* 21 (1944): 137–48.

Symons, Julian. *The Thirties: A Dream Revolved*. London, 1960.

Tolley, A. T. *The Poetry of the Thirties*. New York, 1975.

INDEXES

   Comprehensive Index to English Language Little Magazines 1890–1970, series 1, ed. Marion Sader (Millwood, N.Y., 1976). Numbers 1–5, n.s. 1–3 in *An Author Index to Selected British Little Magazines*, ed. B. C. Bloomfield (London, 1976).

REPRINT EDITIONS
   Johnson Reprint Corp., New York.
LOCATION SOURCES
   American
      Widely available.
   British
      Widely available.

Publication History

MAGAZINE TITLE AND TITLE CHANGES
   New Writing; New Writing (new series); *Folios of New Writing*; *New Writing and Daylight*.
VOLUME AND ISSUE DATA
   New Writing, numbers 1–5, Spring 1936–Spring 1938. *New Writing* (new series), numbers 1–3, Autumn 1938–Christmas 1939. *Folios of New Writing*, four un-numbered issues, Spring 1940–Autumn 1941. *New Writing and Daylight*, six unnumbered issues, Summer 1942–1945; number 7, 1946.
FREQUENCY OF PUBLICATION
   Irregular.
PUBLISHERS
   John Lane, The Bodley Head, London (*New Writing*, nos. 1–2, Spring 1936–Autumn 1936); Lawrence and Wishart, 2 Parton Street, London, W.C. 1 (*New Writing* nos. 3–5, Spring 1937–Spring 1938); The Hogarth Press, 52 Tavistock Square, London, W.C. 1 (*New Writing*, n.s. nos. 1–2, Autumn 1938–Spring 1939); The Hogarth Press, 37 Mecklenburgh Square, London, W.C. 1 (*New Writing*, n.s. no. 3, Christmas 1939; *Folios of New Writing*, nos. 1–4, Spring 1940–Autumn 1941; *New Writing and Daylight*, nos. 1–6, Summer 1942–1945); John Lehmann, London (*New Writing and Daylight*, no. 7, 1946).
EDITOR
   John Lehmann.

Craig Werner

NEW WRITING AND DAYLIGHT. See NEW WRITING

NIMBUS

   The first issue of the quarterly *Nimbus* appeared in December 1951, a fifteen-page offering of seven poems, four stories, and a single brief essay. Tristram Hull, its editor, expressed his faith in a realism that could rise above "slum dwellings" and "aging prostitutes," and explained that the "unknown" contributors to *Nimbus* would try to give new life to the "fading interest" in modern literature. Hull's hopes were realized to a degree: *Nimbus* published twelve more issues in the next six years, expanding to an average of sixty-eight pages and printing work by many distinguished writers. Well-known poets published in *Nimbus* included Vernon Watkins (1, no. 3; 3, no. 2), Bertolt Brecht (2, no. 1), Hugh MacDiarmid (2, no. 3), George Barker (1, no. 2; 3, no. 1), Patrick Kavanagh (2, no. 4; 3, no. 4), Roy Campbell (3, no. 1), Geoffrey Hill (3, nos. 1, 2), Stevie Smith (3, no. 2), Richard Wilbur (3, no. 2), W. H. Auden (3, no. 2), David Wright (1, no. 2; 2, no. 4; 3, no. 2), and Pablo Neruda (4, no. 2). Ernst Kaiser (2, no. 2; 3, no. 1), J. P. Donleavy (4, no. 1), and Italo Svevo (3, no. 1) contributed stories, and William Empson (3, no. 2), C. G. Jung (2, nos. 1, 2), J. M. Tambimuttu (2, no. 4), Joyce Cary (3, no. 2), Jean Genet (3, no. 1), and D. J. Enright (2, no. 2) were among those who wrote criticism and commentary.

No "school" emerges in the pages of *Nimbus*. In the fourth issue (2, no. 1), where Ivo Jarosy's name appears for the first time as coeditor, the editors disavow identification with any specific literary group or movement. Its last two issues were published with no editor's name listed, and the easy assumption is that, despite the high quality of many of its issues, *Nimbus* succumbed partly because it could not settle into a comfortable sense of its own nature and purpose.

Even though it lacked a pronounced program, *Nimbus* probably came to see itself as unsympathetic to the stance of the so-called Movement in British poetry of the fifties. Of the nine Movement writers—D. J. Enright, Kingsley Amis, Robert Conquest, Donald Davie, John Holloway, Elizabeth Jennings, Philip Larkin, John Wain, and Thom Gunn—only Enright appears in *Nimbus*, with two poems and an essay in the second volume. A clear sense of the distance between *Nimbus* and the Movement emerges in David Wright's account of his editorial involvement with *Nimbus*. Speaking of George Barker, Vernon Watkins, and Patrick Kavanagh, all of whom appeared in *Nimbus*, Wright praises their "undiluted dedication to the vocation" of poetry "in a society where material benefit was becoming a *sine qua non*, and where the Arts Council and the universities were beginning to rig trampolines for the daring young men on the flying trochees."[1]

Wright also quotes Kavanagh's complaint that much criticism has as its purpose the trumpeting of mediocrity, and asserts that the charge is justified by the difficulties many poets had getting into print in the fifties, when the literary magazines were "awash with sub-Empsonian villanelles and the like." Wright then points to the publication under his coeditorship of fourteen pages of poems by Stevie Smith and nineteen poems—in the same issue—by Kavanagh. But, explains Wright, "Almost immediately after the Kavanagh issue, Christopher Logue took my place on the editorial board of *Nimbus*, which thereafter concerned itself with Sicilian politics."[2] This last remark needs some discounting, since *Nimbus* published but two more issues and in those included only "Sicilian Documents" as evidence of Logue's obsession. In summary, Wright seems to have had a clear notion of what poetry should be, and perhaps if he had had a longer tenure on the editorial board he could have shaped *Nimbus* into a genuine counter-movement and given the journal a longer life.

True to its promise not to be parochial, *Nimbus* frequently offered translations and reprints of work by foreign writers (seven poems by Tristan Corbière [3, no. 2], for instance, and a generous spread of sketches from Pablo Neruda's *The Earth Is Called John* [4, no. 2]); and some of its finest stories are by Continental writers. The editors were especially sympathetic to Ernst Kaiser, publishing not only his long story ''The City'' (2, no. 2) but also an excerpt from his huge, dense novel, *The Murder Story* (3, no. 1). Italo Svevo is represented by an excerpt from *Confessions of Zeno* (3, no. 1), and the last issue of *Nimbus* features Bertolt Brecht's ''The Private Life of Mister Julius Caesar'' (4, no. 2). One of the more interesting of the fiction writers who are reprinted is the little-known Afrikaner H. C. Bosman (3, no. 2). Two of his witty, sad stories, ''Makapan's Caves'' and ''The Rooinek,'' are included, along with a brief appreciation of his work by Wright. All in all, the fiction is not exciting, but it probably remains as readable as what was appearing in most periodicals of the time.

The essays and review pieces in *Nimbus* offer the most variety and the greatest number of surprises. William Empson's discussion of *The Spanish Tragedy* is vigorous literary criticism, as is Jung's essay on Joyce's *Ulysses*. Joyce's work, Jung says, ''belongs to the class of cold-blooded animals,'' and the eighteen sections of *Ulysses* are ''eighteen alchemical retorts ranged the one behind the other in which acids, poisonous fumes, cold, and heat are used to distil the homunculus of a new world-consciousness!'' (2, no. 1:20).

New work is discussed, and most issues carry one or more substantial review essays, such as Ronald Hayman's evaluation (2, no. 3:50–58) of John Whiting's play *Marching Song* and David Wright's analyses of the poetry of George Barker (2, no. 3:59–65) and Vernon Watkins (3, no. 1:12–17). Anthony Cronin's review (3, no. 2:3–9) of the first novels by John Wain and Kingsley Amis is still worth reading for the strength of its attack on those two writers. Cronin perceives that the world of *Lucky Jim* is the same world depicted in the verse of the Movement poets, and he judges both severely: ''It would be a pity if this widespread dissatisfaction were to give rise to a new class, the professional pedant-cum-writer, who looks on the activity of letters simply as a way of reconciling himself to a position he dislikes.'' (3, no. 2:9).

Hostility to the Movement emerges in the later issues of *Nimbus*; but before that little stir in literary politics *Nimbus* had printed its brief contribution to a much more notorious feud—that between Jean-Paul Sartre and Albert Camus over the issue of engagement. The subject came up when Alexander Trocchi published ''Letter from Paris'' and compared the ''dynamic'' Sartre to Samuel Johnson and in passing sneered at the writer's situation in London in the fifties (1, no. 3). Ivo Jarosy replied bitterly and spoke contemptuously of Trocchi's ''Marxist sociological arguments'' (2, no. 1:53–55). The affair concluded with the wounded Trocchi's reply in the next issue, which also added an editorial remarking that ''commitment'' had run its course as a doctrine and that ''there is something to be said for a periodic return to those primal human realities symbolised by the great myths'' (2, no. 2:2, 67–68).

Most of the nonfiction prose focuses on literary issues, but there are several exceptions in the early issues. Stetson Kennedy's essay "The Re-emergence of the Ku Klux Klan" (2, no. 1) is an engrossing narrative of his penetration in 1946 of both the Ku Klux Klan and the Georgia Bureau of Investigation. The essay seems strangely out of place in *Nimbus*, but it must have been a journalistic coup in 1953. The Rev. Michael Scott's "African Episode" (2, no. 2) treats racial injustice in Nyasaland and is thus a sort of companion piece to the Kennedy essay, but later issues reveal none of this direct interest in social questions.

Thumbing through the issues of *Nimbus* today, a reader senses the improvisation to which its editors seem to have been driven. After an amateurish first issue, *Nimbus* became in a year a journal that many readers must have often found provocative and exciting. In its second year it adopted as its cover illustration the depiction by Vitruvius of a human figure with arms and legs outspread within a circle; and at the same time it began describing itself as "A Magazine of Literature, the Arts, and New Ideas." Its last two issues, however, dropped the Vitruvian man in favor of a livelier cover layout suitable to its rebirth as a "New English Review." After two issues in this format it quietly gave in to the identity problems that had bedeviled it from the start.

Notes

1. David Wright, "Another Part of the Wood," *Poetry Nation* 4 (1975):124.
2. Ibid., p. 125.

Information Sources

BIBLIOGRAPHY
Wright, David. "Another Part of the Wood." *Poetry Nation* 4 (1975):121–28.
INDEXES
    None.
REPRINT EDITIONS
    Kraus Reprint, Nendeln, Liechtenstein, 1971. Scholars' Facsimiles and Reprints, Delmar, N.Y.
LOCATION SOURCES
    American
        Widely available.
    British
        Complete run: London University Library.

Publication History

MAGAZINE TITLE AND TITLE CHANGES
    Nimbus, 1951–1952. *Nimbus: A Magazine of Literature, the Arts and New Ideas*, 1952–1957. *Nimbus: New English Review*, 1957–1958.
VOLUME AND ISSUE DATA
    Volume 1, numbers 1–3, December 1951–Summer 1952. Volume 2, numbers 1–4, June/August 1953–Winter 1954. Volume 3, numbers 1–4, Spring 1955–Winter 1956. Volume 4, numbers 1–2, Summer 1957–February 1958.

FREQUENCY OF PUBLICATION
   Quarterly (irregular).
PUBLISHERS
   1951–1952: None listed. 1953–1958: John Trafford.
EDITORS
   Tristram Hull, 1951–1952. Tristram Hull and Ivo Jarosy, 1953–1954. Tristram
   Hull and David Wright, 1955–1956. None listed, 1957–1958.

Frank Day

NINE

Nine, which debuted in 1949, was very much the creation of Peter Russell, a young London poet and bookseller. In common with Arthur Boyars, editor of *Mandrake*,* Russell experienced a strong sense of intellectual alienation from the England of the late 1940s. In the pages of *Nine* he sought not only to publish new work, but, through critical articles on a wide range of historically important writers, to "establish a *new* relation to the past" and help the contemporary writer to escape from "our long confinement in the prison of the *Zeitgeist*" (no. 5:269). The editors, all men in their twenties, had clear artistic and critical preferences, but avoided manifestoes. In responding to Russell's request that he write a "message" for the first number, T. S. Eliot had "noted with pleasure that your circular does not contain a manifesto" (no. 1:7). Eliot's "message" mainly spoke of the important role little magazines had played and should continue to play in fostering new talent and urged Russell "to use distinguished seniors sparingly" (no. 1:6). Russell's strong allegiance to one such senior— Ezra Pound—was evident from the first number, which printed Pound's postscript to *Kulchur*, "As Sextant," which lists seven works vital for a civilized man to know. Russell was at this time printing Pound's "Money Pamphlets," and he continued to print works by and about Pound and to advertise them in *Nine* throughout the life of the magazine.

Russell's first coeditors were George Sutherland Fraser and Iain Fletcher. By the fourth number they had been joined by D. S. Carne-Ross, who had a strong interest in translation and wrote the lengthy "Editorial Statement" in the fifth number (pp. 269–78). While *Nine* had at first rather scornfully eschewed regular book reviews, it began to carry short ones in the second number and later even reviewed other literary magazines. The editors requested readers to call attention to worthwhile new titles in poetry and criticism. At the same time they announced their delight at having discovered that the original Chinese form of the figure 9 was "intended to represent the unwinding, transforming, mutation of the Yang (male) principle, as exhibited in the course of rivers." "Also culled from very olde Chinese dictionary" were such meanings for "nine" as "perfect, highest and best." The editors concluded: "This tendency of the male to turn outwards towards something bigger and better than 'the self' suggests the objective attitude in literature which is, broadly speaking, favoured by NINE—the extrovert mentality rather than the introvert in fact" (no. 2:6). This meaning for "nine" reinforced the original reason for naming the magazine for "a magical force, the Nine Muses, all the arts and sciences" (no. 8:205).

The preference for the "objective attitude" was further developed in the editorial for the second issue, in which G. S. Fraser praised "writing which has a marked objective constituent—or writing, as one might say, that is about something—over writing which merely projects a mood" (p. 7). As the editors claimed to find insufficient new work which met their requirements, they turned to new translations of both older and modern poetry which exemplified the qualities they admired. Translations ranged from Robert Payne's version of two poems written by Mao-Tse-Tung during the Long march of 1934–1935 to versions of Rainer Maria Rilke. Ian Scott-Kilvert's editorial in the fourth number defended the practice of publishing numerous new translations as a means of "throw[ing] a fresh light upon our own literature." *Nine* favored "poetic versions" of short poems in renderings which "illustrate the technical problems of poetic translation and . . . convey something of the intensity of the original; together with the text and notes they offer a study of a foreign poet which should engage the whole sensibility of the reader" (no. 4:174). Among translations which met the editors' standards were "Five Romanceros of Lorca," translated by Roy Campbell; lyrics by Walther von de Vogelweide, translated by Michael Hamburger; and Giovanni Meli's "Summer" from *La Bucolica*, translated by D. S. Carne-Ross.

Nine did indeed publish a substantial amount of new work in the course of its eleven numbers. Contributors included Anne Ridler, Roy Campbell, Charles Tomlinson, Richard Eberhart, C. H. Sisson, Neville Coghill, and Allen Tate. Notable essayists included Bernard Bergonzi and Hugh Kenner in addition to Russell himself. While *Nine* printed little fiction, among that little was Jorge Luis Borges's "The Library of Babel" (no. 6:47–52), a key story in the Borges canon, and "Death and the Compass" (no. 4:193–200). The translator in each case was G. R. Coulthard. One of the earliest appreciations of Charles Williams's fiction appeared in the Summer-Autumn 1952 number as a long article by Antony Borrow (no. 9:325–53).

With the fifth number, for Autumn 1950, *Nine* came perilously close to issuing the manifesto Eliot had been glad not to read. D. S. Carne-Ross's statement is really a defense of *Nine*'s policies. While the editors, and especially Russell, clearly recognized the genius and importance of the pioneers of modernism—Yeats, Joyce, Wyndham Lewis, Pound and Eliot—they found the postwar literary landscape peopled with writers for whom the essence of these artists had been reduced to a series of techniques and attitudes. The new writers, moreover, lacked the deep, true literary culture of the older men—the knowledge of medieval, Renaissance, and seventeenth-century literature which had nourished them and made their departures possible. The postwar writers ("their literary roots go no deeper than 1800") had narrowed the subject matter of modern poetry to the documentation and analysis of their own psyches. Carne-Ross protested that "even today a tormented subjectivity is not the only possible attitude for a writer to adopt. Nor are boredom, neurosis, fear, disgust and guilt the only kinds of experience to which we have access" (no. 5:7).

The same editorial noted that political and religious conservatism could "imperil" creativity, and *Nine* was not even totally uncritical of Eliot and Pound. The editors avoided any direct statement of the conservative political views associated with these two writers until the ninth number for Autumn 1952. In this issue, Russell's editorial inveighed against the "bureaucratic society" of postwar England as "degraded . . . and uninspired" (no. 9:301), and praised Pound as a keen analyst of the faults of an overly centralized government concerned only to level down (no. 9:302).

Russell's views were expanded in this same issue in his long joint review of the autobiographies which Stephen Spender and Roy Campbell had published in 1951. Russell made Campbell into an emblem of much that he admired in life and in literature and felt that Campbell's work was not sufficiently appreciated. Moreover, he had written a substantial article on Campbell's poetry in the third number in which he had pilloried "the attempts made by left-wing intellectuals to have Campbell's books banished at the time of the Civil War in Spain" (no. 3:85), but praised Spender for his testimony "to the quality of Cambpell's poetry." Russell admired Campbell's "healthy masculinity, the absence of morbid introspection, and the rough, honest humour" (no. 3:83). He asserted that when Campbell used the word "Philistines" in his poetry he "evidently means . . . the Godless, the free thinkers and the half-baked reformers, the guilt obsessed neurotics who are too dizzy with their Central European psychoanalysts to bother about God, and the left-wing 'intellectuals' with their shorts and spectacles" (no. 3:85). In writing about Campbell, Russell wrote the manifesto he scrupulously avoided placing in the editorial columns.

In reviewing Campbell's *Light on a Dark Horse*, Russell pitted it against Spender's *World Within Worlds*. While recognizing the value of Spender's book as the testament of one who had participated in the left-wing politics of the 1930s, Russell attacked the book in every other way. "Spender's writing has an unctuous self-righteousness about it which disgusts me just as much as the sloppiness of his poetry" (no. 9:363). His prose lacked "beauty and distinction." Beyond Spender, Russell's target was the literary journalists who rushed to praise the book because of its fashionable political stance. Spender's autobiography, like his poetry, Russell saw as a hymn to his weaknesses; indeed, he pointed to portions of the text in which Spender could be said to nurse and capitalize on his defects. By contrast, Campbell's book was, according to Russell, passed over by the reviewers because, Russell implied, his political attitudes and love of form were not fashionable. Campbell's poetry and prose exhibited "vigour and humour"; he had "grand eloquence . . . wonderful powers of observation and humour." Most important, Campbell had a "courtly and ritual attitude towards life" (no. 9:365) which takes him out of himself and makes him responsive to others and to the natural world.

Russell's analysis and preferences illustrate G. S. Fraser's editorial remark of 1950:

> Of three poems, the first expressing an inexplicable sadness, the second still not explaining the sadness but embodying it in some outer scene, such as a rainy landscape, the third presenting the experience which has made the poet sad, we would tend to prefer—other things being equal—the second to the first, and the third to the second. [No. 2:7]

From the second number on, *Nine* responded in its editorial columns to readers' comments and criticisms in order to refine further its point of view. The essays in its Autumn 1951 issue on European Renaissance epic and lyric poetry were attacked for resembling "those that intelligent undergraduates provide weekly for Dr. Leavis" (no. 8:[297]), and it was suggested that rather than taking backward looks, *Nine* should give more space to current work. The editors' response lamented the lack of new poetry which met their standards. Another little magazine of the era, *Mandrake*, also bemoaned the lack of good poetry being written in England.[1] The second number published favorable remarks about the magazine by Edith Sitwell, Henry Treece, Marianne Moore, and Walter Allen, among others, but they are all of an exceedingly polite blandness. John Sanders found in *Nine* "a refreshing lack of waffle" and Richard Aldington advised: "I think Tom Eliot's advice about NINE very sound—keep out everyone over forty—over thirty, I should say" (no. 2:6). While admitting the older generation of poets to its pages, *Nine*'s literary criticism tended to be written by men who met Aldington's standards.

As did so many little magazines, *Nine* endured vicissitudes and delays during its brief existence. While still keeping the London address, Russell announced in the seventh number that he had moved the magazine and its effects to a cottage in Sussex which had then burned down. Burnt with the cottage were a number of unacknowledged manuscripts. Though it called itself a quarterly, *Nine* appeared on a quarterly schedule only for volumes 2 and 3, which were issued between January 1950 and Summer/Autumn 1952. There was a gap of almost three years between numbers 1 and 2 of volume 4; and when the latter appeared in April 1956, Russell had moved to Tunbridge Wells and was operating the Grosvenor Bookshop. His editorial spoke of "making a new start with NINE" (no. 11:6), and the magazine carried an announcement that the next issue would contain work by Campbell and Kathleen Raine. Russell now described the printing of new poetry as the new *Nine*'s "first ambition," with second place to be given to critical articles and translations. Writing now as sole editor, he declared that the tendency of the modern age to attribute all developments to economic causes "had debased the status of the creative artist." Little magazines, published out of a true love for literature and with no expectation of economic gain for those associated with them, bore the responsibility for keeping letters alive (no. 11:5). Future issues were announced on Latin, medieval, and modern poetry as well as a number devoted to Ford Madox Ford. Despite such promising plans for the future, *Nine* did not appear again.

Various devices had been tried to help the magazine's finances. In the Autumn 1951 issue Russell noted that the costs of printing had doubled in the past year. In order to fund the magazine, he asked for outright donations, but also proposed to issue vellum copies to be sold at a premium and to act as the agent for a bookmart in which readers would trade wants and offerings (no. 7: cover 2).

Peter Russell has been praised by Hugh MacDiarmid for his "disinterested, many-sided service to poetry."[2] Certainly in *Nine* he and his fellow editors chose many of their contributors with prescience. If the bracingly astringent tone of *Nine*'s critical essays and reviews sometimes degenerated into waspishness, it did fulfill its mission of avoiding critical flaccidity. After the demise of *Nine*, Russell continued until 1963 to run bookshops in England that both printed and sold the work of new poets. His own particular poetic interests lie in translating the elegies of Quintilus and, more recently, Arabic and Persian poetry. Since 1964 Russell has made his home in Venice, but he has lectured widely in North America and Europe. In 1977 he went to Iran as a lecturer and barely escaped with his family during the revolution of 1979.[3] His own poetry has appeared primarily through the medium of small and private presses.

Notes

1. [Arthur Boyars], ["Editorial"], *Mandrake*, no. 7 (1950–1951): 15.

2. William Oxley, "Peter Russell," in *Contemporary Poets of the English Language*, 3rd ed., ed. James Vinson (New York, 1980), pp. 1316–18.

3. "[Irwin] Peter Russell," in *Contemporary Authors*, 97–100 (Detroit, 1981), pp. 474–75.

Information Sources

INDEXES
   None.
REPRINT EDITIONS
   None.
LOCATION SOURCES
   American
      Complete runs: Bryn Mawr College Library; Catholic University of America Library; Columbia University Library; Cornell University Library; Harvard University Library; New York Public Library.
   British
      Complete runs: Birmingham Public Library; Edinburgh University Library; Glasgow University Library; Leeds University Library; National Library of Scotland, Edinburgh; University of Cambridge Library; University of London Library.

Publication History

MAGAZINE TITLE AND TITLE CHANGES

Nine: A Magazine of Poetry and Criticism, 1949–1950. *Nine: A Magazine of Literature and the Arts*, 1951. *Nine: A Magazine of Literature and Criticism*, 1952 (Spring). *Nine: A Magazine of Literature and the Arts*, 1952 (Summer/ Autumn 1956).

VOLUME AND ISSUE DATA

Volume 1, number 1, Autumn 1949. Volumes 2–3, numbers 2–9, January 1950– Summer/Autumn 1952. Volume 4, numbers 10–11, Winter 1953/1954–April 1956. The contents page numbered each whole volume (vol. 2, nos. 1–4; vol. 3, nos. 1–4; vol. 4, nos. 1–2). Large arabic numerals in a continuous sequence appear on the cover, and this sequence, clearly more important to the editors, has been used in the references.

FREQUENCY OF PUBLICATION

Quarterly. Irregular—there was a gap of nearly three years between numbers 10 and 11.

PUBLISHER

Peter Russell. Autumn 1949: 43 Duke Street, London, W. 2. January 1950– Winter 1953/1954: 114B Queens Gate, London, S.W. 7. April 1956: 69 Grosvenor Road, Tunbridge Wells, Kent.

EDITORS

Peter Russell, G. S. Fraser, and Iain Fletcher, Autumn 1949–Spring 1950. Peter Russell, Iain Fletcher, Ian Scott-Kilvert, and D. S. Carne-Ross, August 1950– Autumn 1951. Peter Russell, April 1952–April 1956.

Barbara J. Dunlap

NINETEENTH CENTURY AND AFTER. See
TWENTIETH CENTURY

NORTHERN REVIEW, THE

The *Northern Review, A Progressive Monthly of Life and Letters*, was a short-lived venture of Hugh MacDiarmid (Christopher Murray Grieve), a successor to journals that MacDiarmid had introduced into Scotland in the early postwar period. Unlike its predecessors, however, the *Northern Review*, which was published from May to September 1924, extended its boundaries beyond Scotland to include the whole area north of London. The magazine took as its stand the case for "literary devolution," breaking the hold of London publishers and editors on the rest of the nation's literary life. The attack on centralization was part of MacDiarmid's concern with the fate of regional literature and local dialects under the prevailing idea of standard or "correct" English, an attack he had already begun with the publication of his poetry in Scots, poetry which rejected the English model and tradition in favor of the free-flowing and rhythmically richer vernacular. MacDiarmid recognized that unless he was able to spread the interest in working in the vernacular outside of Scotland, his own literary movement was likely to be seen as no more than a parochial event. The *Northern Review* was an attempt to enlist the help of those faced with similar linguistic and literary difficulties by encouraging them to begin experimenting and publishing in their own dialects.

MacDiarmid understood that massive social and cultural changes were under way in postwar Britain; indeed, as an early champion of socialist ideals, he had helped shape those changes. His war experience in the Royal Army Medical Corps in Greece, Italy, and France only confirmed his belief that the breakup of the British Empire was inevitable. Eager to reject the old ways, he looked forward to the task of "reconstruction," a process which he saw extending to language and literature:

> The chaos the war caused in the physical world has been replaced in intenser form in the spiritual and all our theatrics and all our forms are either survivals or experiments. Those who retain the old are those whom the war passed over. [No. 4:234]

MacDiarmid rejected what he was later to describe as the "English Ascendency" in literature, directing would-be writers to look to Europe and America for literary models. As part of this program he asked Edwin Muir to contribute articles on German poetry and French scholar Denis Saurat to write on French literature.

A friend and early champion of MacDiarmid's work in the vernacular, Saurat wrote an article, "La Renaissance écossaise," defending MacDiarmid's "synthetic Scots" (no. 2:116–17). MacDiarmid had been attacked for his habit of using words and idioms with little regard to the fact that he was mixing time periods and dialects of different locations. Like any good poet, MacDiarmid simply used language which best fitted the perceptions he wanted to express, and he ably defended himself against the purists:

> If I write in a language I invent wholly myself and insist upon calling it Scots in defiance of all precedents, nothing you can do can prevent my ultimate success—if I write well enough! And on the other hand nothing you can do with all your industry can revive the Vernacular, until you can enlist a creative artist to put the breath of life into it once more. [No. 4:277]

In addition to publishing his own poetry in the *Northern Review*, MacDiarmid also encouraged the work of other experimenters in dialect, like Neil Gunn, whose short stories appeared regularly. Other contributors included Walter De la Mare, John Buchan, Cunningham Graham, George Reston Malloch, and MacDiarmid's musician friend, Francis George Scott, so that the coloring of the periodical remained decidedly Scottish. Although there were articles on James Joyce, Joseph Conrad, and others, the content too reflected Scottish concerns—"Religion and the Scottish Renaissance," "The Future of Scottish Liberalism," and a regular feature, "Little Scots Theatre," in which MacDiarmid, following the Irish lead, urged the establishment of a Scottish Players Movement and published plays in the vernacular, including his own, *The Purple Patch* (no. 1:16–21).

Beset by financial and publication problems, MacDiarmid published only four issues of the *Northern Review*. Nevertheless, it was an interesting, if unsuccessful, attempt to change the face of literary publication in Britain.

Information Sources

BIBLIOGRAPHY

Buthlay, Kenneth. *Hugh MacDiarmid*. Writers and Critics Series. Edinburgh, 1964.

Glen, Duncan. *Hugh MacDiarmid and the Scottish Renaissance*. Edinburgh, 1964.

Kerrigan, Catherine. *"Whaur Extremes Meet": The Poetry of Hugh MacDiarmid, 1920–1934*. Edinburgh, 1983.

Watson, R. B. *Hugh MacDiarmid*. Milton Keynes, Eng., 1976.

INDEXES
  None.

REPRINT EDITIONS
  None.

LOCATION SOURCES
  American
    Complete run: New York Public Library.
    Partial runs: Northwestern University Library; University of Chicago Library; Yale University Library.
  British
    Complete runs: Aberdeen University Library; British Museum.
    Partial runs: Edinburgh University Library; National Library of Scotland, Edinburgh.

Publication History

MAGAZINE TITLE AND TITLE CHANGES
  The Northern Review, A Progressive Monthly of Life and Letters.

VOLUME AND ISSUE DATA
  Volume 1, numbers 1–4, May–September 1924.

FREQUENCY OF PUBLICATION
  Monthly, except for the June/July 1924 double issue.

PUBLISHER
  C. M. Grieve.

EDITOR
Hugh MacDiarmid.

Catherine Kerrigan

NOTES AND QUERIES. See VEA

NOW

In 1940 George Woodcock, a pacifist and proponent of anarchy, began *Now* with two purposes: "to publish the best writing we can obtain, and to proclaim our opposition to all war" (no. 2:1). Woodcock considered the first purpose more important; therefore, he vowed *Now* would not discriminate against writers who voiced opinions different from the editor's. In the sixth issue, Julian Symons, a frequent contributor and London editor of issue number 5, objected to Woodcock's policy of nondiscrimination, saying that *Now* could not be forceful unless it uniformly promoted anarchy, the ideology favored by Woodcock. In the first volume of the new series begun in 1943, Woodcock conceded that Symons was right: *Now* would not be a proponent of any literary school, but it would "be edited from an anarchist point of view" (n.s. no. 1:2). The very next issue, though, contained a note stating that *Now* "represents no political sect" (n.s. no. 2:4). Woodcock's anarchic beliefs, which made him distrust any well-organized political group (anarchists included), apparently prevented him from deliberately editing a politically unified work.

From the beginning, *Now* failed to have the necessary financial backing to appear consistently. Seven issues were published in 1940 and 1941; in the new series nine issues appeared from 1943 to mid-1947. In more than one editorial commentary, Woodcock wrote of his conviction that *Now* would be appearing regularly, but his hopes were never realized. The first seven issues contained thirty to forty pages of poetry, essays, reviews, and stories. In the new series the issues doubled in length and also included political cartoons and reproductions.

George Woodcock dominated *Now.* He wrote essays for every issue and poetry for many. Repeatedly his work reflected his three major interests— his hatred of World War II, his belief in anarcho-syndicalism, and his concept of the artist in society.[1]

Woodcock was an anarchist, basing his beliefs on Peter Kropotkin's anarchic theory of cooperation.[2] Although Woodcock believed that destruction is a necessary prelude to creation, he felt that World War II was senseless because it promoted totalitarian ends and did not further the anarchists' cause. What had to be destroyed was man's notion that government is good (n.s. no. 3:1–3). He disliked capitalism, fascism, and communism, and strongly disagreed with those writers in the thirties who saw dictatorship as a necessary step to anarchy. "No better world . . . can come except by the economic and social revolution which brings the abolition of authority, class and property, the destruction of the wages system and money relationships, and the end of the domination of man by man" (n.s. no. 1:8).

Feeling as he did about government, Woodcock objected to any effort on its part to censor or subsidize artists. He bitterly called those artists who worked for the government during the war "collaborationists" (n.s. no. 2:3); artists, and people in general, must act individually and not from external authority. Woodcock, glad that W. H. Auden forsook communism, perceived anarchist tendencies in "September 1, 1939" a poem Auden wrote for 1941 (n.s. no. 1:4).

Woodcock kept his original promise to publish opposing views. For example, he published Julian Huxley's essay "Art as a Social Function," which proposed that the state be a patron of the arts (no. 5:4–7). However, most of the works appearing in *Now* generally supported Woodcock's opinions. In "The Paradox of Anarchism" (no. 7:3–9) and "The Cult of Leadership" (n.s. no. 1:9–19), Herbert Read wrote about his anarchist beliefs. Hugh Ross Williamson in "Bread and Circuses" criticized democracy, capitalism, and socialism (no. 6:16–18). Alex Comfort wrote "Art and Social Responsibility," which Arthur Edward Salmon calls a "manifest of Neo-Romanticism."[3] According to Comfort's essay, people in the war era went from a classical view of the world where they felt in charge of their destiny to a Romantic one where they were victims. The artist, Comfort maintained, must be a detached observer of humanity while at the same time recognizing his responsibility to others (n.s. no. 2:39–50).

Both concerned with the role of the artist, Julian Symons and D. S. Savage were two of the most frequent contributors to *Now*. Symons wrote that there are three artist types—the extrovert (for example, Anthony Trollope), the introvert (A. E. Housman), and the mentally unbalanced (William Blake). For him art is a reflection of the time in which it is created. Jane Austen and Henry James, for example, wrote good works because their novels keenly reflect their society. This does not mean, however, that an artist intentionally creates a reflection of society. Even if he deceives himself to the contrary, he writes autobiographically, not socially or politically (n.s. no. 3:14–21). An artist should have no political involvement. Thus, Symons felt that the artist should divorce himself from the war effort and concentrate on his technical skill.[4]

One of Symons's most interesting essays was his evaluation of art produced during World War II. *Horizon** reflected writing during the war—it was "bland and cultured" (n.s. no. 5:6). Little magazines tended to publish poetry that was depleted Romanticism. Poetry, with the exception of some poems by Stephen Spender, Alun Lewis, and Roy Fuller, tended to be deliberately obscure or simplistic. Graham Greene and Evelyn Waugh were the only English writers who produced novels approaching art, but compared to works by Hardy or James, they were "fifth-rate" (n.s. no. 5:7). Art had disintegrated because, without a belief in free will or even moral determinism, man had no moral problems:

"There are no moral problems in Hemingway, Faulkner, or Dos Passos—their characters live at too low a plane of perception, and the force of events is too great, for moral problems to exist" (n.s. no. 5:11). Symons concluded that change would come and with it new forces, most notably in radio and film.

Savage agreed with Symons and Woodcock that the artist should not be associated with a political organization. According to him, men like Auden in the 1930s wrongly embraced social responsibility in order to forget themselves. One must, he wrote, be responsible to oneself first (n.s. no. 9:52–60). Savage, though, disagreed with Symons's belief that the artist should ignore the war. The artist needs to understand the social issues of his world; specifically, he should protest conscription and the rise of totalitarianism. He need not use his art as a medium for his views, but he cannot forget his responsibilities as an individual (no. 1:8–9). Salmon describes Savage as a "Christian Personalist."[5] Apart from the social issues of art, Savage wrote that art cannot be vital unless the artist maintains physical "immediacy" with the world (no. 7:22).

Other important prose contributors to *Now* were George Orwell, who in "How the Poor Die" (n.s. no. 6:1–8) recounted his experiences in a French hospital; and Henry Miller, who wrote about censorship of *Tropic of Cancer* (n.s. no. 5:26–35).

Much of the poetry in *Now* concerned the war. Most of the poems were stale, formulaically expressing unmitigated gloom or despair until the obligatory final stanza of hope. However, for such a short-lived magazine, *Now* published a remarkable number of poems by outstanding poets, including Roy Fuller, Kathleen Raine, E. E. Cummings, Kenneth Rexroth, Richard Eberhart, and Denise Levertov. Richard Eberhart's "At the End of the War" (n.s. no. 8:28–30) was "essentially unimaginative," but other poems by these poets were more successful.[6] Two of the better war poems were "what if a much of a which of a wind" by E. E. Cummings (n.s. no. 3:40–41) and "October 1940" by Roy Fuller (no. 4:15). Kathleen Raine's poems in *Now* were not usually about topical events; but in the Romantic tradition, they explored the relationship between humanity and the natural world. With remarkable clarity, Denise Levertov, in "Folding a Shirt" (n.s. no. 8:33), linked the simple act of a woman folding a shirt to the love she has for the man who wears it.

The greatest flaw in *Now* was its fiction. Most of it was intensely sincere but utterly lacking in characterization and subtlety of technique. In one allegorical tale, "The Warehouse" by Mary Harris (n.s. no. 8:49–53), the manager in a warehouse is God and the young foreman who replaces him is Jesus. In "The Choice" by Patricia Johnson (n.s. no. 9:60–65), the devil, with tail and all, rides a train with five passengers. The best story is Louis Adeane's "A Visit to Madame Zena" (n.s. no. 7:25–33) because the title character is a full-blooded person: a victim of the government, a charlatan fortune teller, and a heroine to a little boy.

Now's importance rests in its essays on politics and art. Although eccentric and idealistic, the lucid arguments of Woodcock and Read lend respectability to anarchy. And with its contributors' dislike of World War II, distrust of Churchill's government, and rejection of the artistic views of the thirties, it preserves a view of the war era not always remembered today.

Notes

1. Besides the articles cited in the text, see Woodcock's articles in no. 7:34–36, n.s. nos. 2:1–4, 4:1–11, and 5:1–5.
2. Arthur Edward Salmon, *Poets of the Apocalypse* (Boston, 1983), p. 92.
3. Ibid., p. 105.
4. Symons's articles appear in nos. 2:12–14, 3:15–16, and n.s. no. 3:14–21.
5. Salmon, *Poets of the Apocalypse*, p. 88.
6. Bernard F. Engel, *Richard Eberhart* (New York, 1971), p. 79.

Information Sources

BIBLIOGRAPHY

Engel, Bernard F. *Richard Eberhart*. New York, 1971.
Hewison, Robert. *Under Siege: Literary Life in London 1939–1945*. London, 1971.
Hoffman, Frederick J., Charles Allen, and Carolyn F. Ulrich. *The Little Magazine: A History and a Bibliography*. Princeton, 1946.
Salmon, Arthur Edward. *Poets of the Apocalypse*. Boston, 1983.
Scarfe, Francis. *Auden and After: The Liberation of Poetry*. London, 1969.
Vinson, James, ed. *Great Writers of the English Language: Poets*. New York, 1979.

INDEXES
    None.

REPRINT EDITIONS
    Kraus Reprint, Nendeln, Liechtenstein, 1968.

LOCATION SOURCES

American
    Complete runs: State University of New York at Buffalo, Lockwood Memorial Library; University of Iowa Library.
    Partial runs: Widely available.

British
    Complete run: British Museum.
    Partial run: National Library of Scotland, Edinburgh.

Publication History

MAGAZINE TITLE AND TITLE CHANGES
    Now, numbers 1–4, new series 1–9. *Now: A Journal of Good Writing*, numbers 5–7.

VOLUME AND ISSUE DATA
    Old series, numbers 1–7, Easter 1940–Fall 1941. New series, numbers 1–9, 1943–July/August 1947.

FREQUENCY OF PUBLICATION
    Irregular.

PUBLISHERS

Number 1: Printed and published by M. C. Pitts, Dry Cottage, Cookham Dean, Maidenhead, Berks, England. Number 2: Published by George Woodcock, Dry Cottage, Maidenhead; printed by John W. Gait & Sons, Boar Lane, Shipley, Yorks. Number 3: Published by George Woodcock, 38 Queen's Avenue; printed by John W. Gait & Sons. Numbers 4–7: Published by the Proprietors, 66, Huntington Road, Cambridge; printed by John W. Gait & Sons. New series numbers 1–3: Published by George Woodcock, c/o Freedom Press, 27 Belsize Road, London; printed by Express Printers, London. New series numbers 4–6: Published by George Woodcock, c/o 27 Red Lion Street, London; distributed by Freedom Press, 27 Red Lion St., London. New series numbers 7–9: Published by George and Ingeborg Woodcock, 24 Highgate West Hill, London; printed by Express Printers, London.

EDITOR

George Woodcock.

Margaret Ann Baker Graham

O

ORION

Orion originated in the spring of 1945 with Denys Kilham Roberts, a solicitor with literary ambitions who was secretary-general of the Society of Authors. During World War II and afterward in the "austerity" period, the British government tightly controlled the use of paper. Only publishers established before the war received allotments, and the founding of new periodicals was forbidden. A number of enterprising editors followed the lead of John Lehmann with his miscellany *New Writing and Daylight** (see *New Writing*); they too turned to the established publishers and persuaded them to bring out volumes which were issued, either in paper or in hardcover, as books, even though they were dated and were produced with a certain degree of regularity. *Orion* was one of several such miscellanies issued at this time.[1]

Roberts was an author and had edited for Penguin the *Penguin Parade** anthologies and *The Century's Poetry* in the Pelican series. According to Sean Day-Lewis, Roberts "raised some money to start a new literary journal and recruited Cecil [Day Lewis] and Rosamond [Lehmann], and Edwin Muir, as his co-editors."[2] C. Day Lewis was well known as a poet and, under his pseudonym "Nicholas Blake," as a writer of detective fiction; Rosamond Lehmann gained her reputation as a novelist in the late 1920s. Both were active members of the professional literary world of London, as was Edwin Muir, even though at this time he was living in Edinburgh, where he was working for the British Council. He had been a literary journalist since the early 1920s and was widely known as a critic, translator, and poet. In the 1940s most general readers would have identified him as the author of the fortnightly reviews of new novels published in the BBC's *Listener*.

The "Editors' Foreword" to the first volume of *Orion* perhaps inevitably reflects the professional orientation of the four editors. Disavowing attachments to any "group or movement," the editors suggest their predisposition for the

> "written" and away from the improvised, toward the imaginative and away from reportage. ORION will publish experimental work, if the particular experiment seems to the editors a successful one: it is equally open to traditional work, provided the work has character. ORION welcomes the contributions of young or unknown writers. But it hopes to devote considerable space to those whose work has reached maturity. [1:3]

The first volume was priced at five shillings (somewhat less than the cost of the average novel) and was issued in gray paper covers printed in maroon and white, the names of the twenty-two contributors being given on the front cover. There were poems by Walter De la Mare (1:5–6), Edith Sitwell (1:28–29), Edwin Muir (1:41–42), Andrew Young (1:70–71), William Plomer (1:60–62), Margiad Evans (1:76), John Lehmann (1:87–88), and Henry Reed (1:103–4), as well as translations by C. Day Lewis of Paul Valéry (1:16–19), and by Maurice Bowra of Boris Pasternak (1:48–50). There was no fiction as such, but there were personal essays, memoirs, letters, and essays by Rose Macaulay (1:6–16), Ivy Compton-Burnett (1:20–28), Mary MacRae (1:51–59), Frank O'Connor (1:62–69), Walter Allen (1:71–75), Leonard Woolf (1:76–87), and Franz Kafka (selections from the *Diaries* translated by Willa Muir [1:104–15]). Essays by John Piper, on Seaton Delaval (1:43–47), and by John Russell, on Courbet (1:88–102), were illustrated, that by Piper including a full-page color reproduction of his painting of Seaton Delaval. Almost all of these writers were well-established literary figures; and many of the selections attempt to provide literary contacts between Britain and the Continent.

The second volume of *Orion*, considerably expanded in page size and length, was issued in orange-cloth boards in the autumn of 1945, and again established writers were in the majority. Indeed, three selections were extracted from forthcoming books, and one was from an already published work. In this volume the editors printed two short stories, by V. S. Pritchett (2:10–17) and Irene Nicholson (2:40–52), as well as translations: R.F.C. Hull's versions of Rilke's Orpheus Sonnets (2:52–54), already in print from the Hogarth Press. As in the first volume, the selection of poems represented a conventional, middle-of-the-road taste, Muir's long poem "The Voyage" appearing first and setting the tone for the pieces that followed. Other contributions appeared by Edmund Blunden (2:17), Anthony Rye (2:29–31), Laurie Lee (2:39–40), Stevie Smith (2:62), Lilian Bowes-Lyon (2:72–75), Alexander Henderson (2:87–92), Roy Fuller (2:100), Patric Dickinson (2:108–9), and Walter De la Mare (2:118–19). The nonfiction prose writers included Elizabeth Bowen (2:18–29), R. D. Smith (2:55–61), Edwin Muir (2:92–100), Rayner Heppenstall (2:110–17), Eric Bligh (2:32–39), John Strachey (2:63–72), Logan Pearsall Smith (presenting his exchange of letters with Virginia Woolf [2:73–86]), Margaret Lane (2:101–8), and Osbert Sitwell (2:120–54), whose memoir of Walter Sickert (later included in *Noble Essences* [1950]) was illustrated by five full-page reproductions of Sickert's drawings.

While there had been two issues of *Orion* in 1945, the third volume was not published until the autumn of 1946, by which time Muir had gone to Prague for the British Council and had resigned from the editorial board. The three remaining editors brought together in this volume writers whose work was not significantly different from that in the first two volumes, although the writers themselves were perhaps not as well known, and there was also a greater emphasis on the literary essay. Thus Elizabeth Bowen discussed the writing of fiction (3:10–14), E. C. Pettet wrote "Milton and the Modern Reader" (3:68–81), D. A. Shaw offered "Reflections on Rimbaud" (3:89–104), and S. Gorley Putt contributed a twenty-one-page essay on Henry James's *The Wings of the Dove* (3:120–43). Again there was an essay on art, a consideration by Michael Ayrton of contemporary British painters (3:84–89), accompanied by reproductions of six paintings. Elsewhere in the volume was a full-page reproduction of a portrait of Day Lewis, followed by his poem "The Sitting," which was addressed to the painter Laurence Gowing (3:6–91). There were memoirs or essays by Edward Sackville-West (3:51–58), William Samson (3:14–16), Cecily Mackworth (3:62–68), and Laurie Lee (3:104–113), and short stories by Stevie Smith (3:114–17) and Jean Howard, the latter's twenty-five pages in length (3:23–48). Poets ranged from Louis MacNeice (3:81–82) to James Kirkup, presented here as the translator of Guillaume Apollinaire (3:17–22); from Edith Sitwell (3:59–61) to her recent discovery, Denton Welch (3:119); as well as A.S.J. Tessimond (3:16), G. Rostrevor Hamilton (3:48–49), Elizabeth Cluer (3:50), Jack R. Clemo (3:83), Frances Bellerby (3:117–18), and Helen Spalding (3:119).

With the appearance of the third volume Cecil Day Lewis decided to resign. His son Sean points out that "Cecil was never a very enthusiastic or committed editor, partly due to his other work and partly to his antipathy to Kilham Roberts," and he quotes a 29 January 1946 letter from his father to Roberts in which Day Lewis writes: "I have decided not to continue with *Orion* after number three—I've really got too much on my plate to be able to give it all the attention I ought to."[3] Since at this time Day Lewis was debating whether permanently to leave his wife for Rosamond Lehmann, his resignation also implied the resignation of Lehmann. There was, however, to be yet one further issue of *Orion* in the autumn of 1947 with Kilham Roberts as the sole editor.

This final issue, printed in a smaller type, was the largest of the four, but the selection of entries shows a taste not radically different from that of the previous issues and may indicate that Kilham Roberts had always had the major role on the editorial board. Representation of Continental literature continued unabated: there was an essay in French by René Dumesnil, "La Tragédie de Guy de Maupassant" (4:30–39), a translation by Frances Cornford of poems by Louis Aragon (4:72–74), and Rimbaud's "Drunken Ship" in an English version by George Duncan Painter (4:147–49). Again literary criticism was the focus of several essays: David Cecil on Dorothy Osborne (4:22–26), S. Gorley Putt on Henry James (4:53–71), Margaret Lane on Dr. Johnson (4:105–116), and—a remarkably advanced selection for *Orion*—Henry Reed on James Joyce with quotations from *Finnegans Wake* (4:131–46). Kilham Roberts continued to print authors whose work had appeared in earlier issues: Edward Sackville-West (4:7–16), William Sansom (4:16–21), Edith Sitwell (4:26–29), Walter De la Mare (4:47–49), and Osbert Sitwell, the latter being represented by yet another extract from his forthcoming autobiography, *Great Morning!* (4:74–88). As in earlier issues there was an essay on art: Stephen Bone wrote on the late eighteenth-century artists and the brothers Daniell, and illustrated his piece with four reproductions. Yet for all these similarities there is a certain breaking away from the more established writers found in previous issues: the editor included a long poem by George Barker (4:21–22) and a short story by Graham Greene (4:50–53), as well as stories by Philip O'Connor (4:39–47) and Ethel Wilson (4:121–30) and poems by Joseph Chiari (4:102–4), Anthony Rye (4:88–90), Geoffrey Parsons (4:116–18), and W. H. Osborne (4:118–21).

Sean Day-Lewis, offering reasons for the demise of *Orion*, noted that the "compilers lacked John Lehmann's single-mindedness [as shown in the periodicals he edited], and publication was neither sufficiently frequent nor consistent to build a following."[4] Actually, however, the four volumes of *Orion* were published to meet the needs of a particular time and situation, and there is little or no indication that the editors thought or even desired that their new publication would continue indefinitely. They intended to publish writers who, having established their reputations before and during the war, now needed an outlet for their work. The editors received the cooperation of publishers who wished to keep their authors' names before the public, as well as to create interest in forthcoming books. Although there were new writers in the final volume, *Orion* was essentially an outlet for the literary establishment of the late 1930s and mid–1940s and, as such, could be said to represent some of the forces against which the younger writers of the 1950s and 1960s were in revolt.

Notes

1. John Lehmann, *I Am My Brother* (New York, 1960), p. 310.
2. Sean Day-Lewis, *C. Day Lewis: An English Literary Life* (London, 1980), p. 149.
3. Ibid., pp. 160–61.
4. Ibid., p. 150.

Information Sources

BIBLIOGRAPHY
Day-Lewis, Sean. *C. Day Lewis: An English Literary Life*. London, 1980.
Lehmann, John. *I Am My Brother*. New York, 1960.
INDEXES
     Table of contents for each volume.
REPRINT EDITIONS
     None.

LOCATION SOURCES
American
> Complete runs: Amherst College Library; Columbia University Library; Cornell University Library; Dartmouth College Library; Indiana University Library; New York Public Library; Ohio State University Library; Princeton University Library. Partial runs: Widely available.

British
> Complete runs: Birmingham Public Library; London University Library; National Library of Scotland, Edinburgh; University College of Swansea Library. Partial runs: Birmingham University Library; Leeds Public Library; University of Bristol Library.

Publication History

MAGAZINE TITLE AND TITLE CHANGES
> *Orion: A Miscellany*, volume 1. *Orion*, volumes 2–4.

VOLUME AND ISSUE DATA
> Volume 1, [Spring] 1945; volume 2, Autumn 1945; volume 3, Autumn 1946; volume 4, Autumn 1947.

FREQUENCY OF PUBLICATION
> Irregular.

PUBLISHER
> Nicholson and Watson, 26 Manchester Square, London W. 1.

EDITORS
> Cecil Day Lewis, Rosamond Lehmann, Edwin Muir, and Denys Kilham Roberts, volumes 1–2. Cecil Day Lewis, Rosamond Lehmann, and Denys Kilham Roberts, volume 3. Denys Kilham Roberts, volume 4.

Elgin W. Mellown

OUR TIME

Our Time, begun in 1941 as a populist magazine, was officially the continuation of *Poetry and the People*, a small occasional pamphlet of verse which had flourished briefly at the end of the 1930s under the control of Jack Lindsay and Janet Watson. But from its first issue for February 1941 *Our Time* addressed itself to more ambitious matters. Its field would include "theatre, graphic art, music, architecture and literature." It provided also a vehicle for such newly flourishing organizations as the British Drama League, the Council for the Encouragement of Music and the Arts, the Workers' Music Association, the Workers' Film Association, and the Unity Theatre. *Our Time* was intended to signify that World War II was, in England, truly a people's war. Workers were encouraged to write about their jobs, and they produced a number of fascinating anonymous contributions, such as "A Tour with C.E.M.A." by "A Violinist" (1, no. 7:16–18) or "The Army Has Its Say: The Private; The Captain" (1, no. 9:18–19).

Populism did not in the long run amount to total inclusiveness. Two and a half years later the magazine adopted a large format that made it one of the best "glossy" publications of its day, and changed its focus. Artistic standards were being encouraged by a body of eminent critics. The issue for August 1943, which saw the change of format, carried, for example, T. A. Jackson on Charles Dickens, and F. D. Klingender's "The Problems of Realism" (3, no. 1:8–9, 10–11). But the two most influential voices were those of Edgell Rickword and Lindsay. Indeed, literary history associates *Our Time* almost exclusively with Rickword (former editor of the *Calendar of Modern Letters** and *Left Review**), despite the fact that he had editorial control of the magazine for only three of its seven and a half years. Apart from a series of typically astute reviews, he contributed major articles on the radical English tradition, such as "William Hazlitt—An English Jacobin" and "William Hone—Parodist for Progress" (3, no. 6:10–11; 4, no. 2:8–9). In this way he maintained an impressive continuity with the pioneering anthology *A Handbook of Freedom*, which he had edited with his friend Lindsay.[1] It was Lindsay who persuaded Rickword to take over *Our Time* in 1944: as chief director of Fore Publications he was, he later recollected, looking for someone who shared his own desire to "record and stimulate the Cultural Upsurge"[2]—and thought immediately of Rickword. Lindsay himself reviewed the Apocalyptics (3, no. 4:17–18) and reflected on the contemporary significance of William Blake (3, no. 11:10–12) and John Bunyan (3, no. 8:13–15). It was in these writings that populism and erudition met perhaps the most impressively.

The goal of *Our Time* was to present art as real, concrete practice: to show that it was not the expression of solitary genius but that it resulted from a specific mode of production. It had its own forces of production—film and stage equipment, paper, artists and writers and performers—and specific relations of production; it was the latter which the magazine would be revealing, and seeking to question.

Rickword set himself two tasks. The first was to foster and sustain a sense of the radical English tradition. The second was to demonstrate the relevance of what was happening in contemporary European art: his first issue as editor, for November 1944, carried on its front cover a photograph of Pablo Picasso, whose *Guernica* he regarded as a major revolutionary work, and printed an article by Nancy Cunard entitled "Intellectuals in the French Resistance."

Apart from expressing a personal conviction, Rickword was showing himself to be shrewdly in tune with a growing consensus. This was late 1944: the peace and the ensuing Labour victory, with the singing of Blake's "Jerusalem" outside the headquarters of the Trades Union Congress, would be a reflection of a new kind of national consciousness, a new conviction of the necessity for true democracy; nor would the spirit be an insular one, based as it was on the experience of men who were to return home from the Europe they had been fighting to save. (A frequent acquaintance of Rickword's from 1942 had been E. P. Thompson, later famous as a social historian and peace campaigner, who when on leave used to keep him informed of the mood of the army.)

The first half of *Our Time* spans the period of a genuine people's war; the second half was the period of another conflict, the Cold War. Rickword's editorship from 1944 to 1947 therefore has a crucial and tense interest. The key year is, of course, 1945. With the end of the war and the Labour victory in the general election, *Our Time* was expressive of a second wave of popular feeling: this time one of political confidence as well as cultural excitement. Rickword, alert to the moment, managed to bring circulation up to an unprecedented 15,000 copies a month— and still at six pence each. During this year and the next he gave space to Jack Lindsay, F. D. Klingender, Randall Swingler, and David Holbrook for articles and reviews of considerable weight but also of appealing vitality.

Rickword's editorial comments of June 1945 suggest a mind already well prepared for the specific demands of the peace. Speaking of the need for a "workable policy" for the collectivization of artistic practice, he attacks the "hostile beings" who are "asking the electorate to renounce the cooperation to which, imperfect as it has been, we owe the progress we have demonstrably made in these past five years": a return to the spirit of "individual enterprise" would be disastrous for art (4, no. 11:3).

But the postwar forces antagonistic to an extension of the wartime progress were too great. One clue is there in 1945 itself: the replacement of the Council for the Encouragement of Music and the Arts by the Arts Council and the consequent shift from diversity and national populism to divisiveness and metropolitan bureaucracy, the effectively official quashing of the cultural upsurge which *Our Time* had been founded to encourage. More generally, the Labour victory was the beginning of an end: disillusionment with governmental socialism set in early as reform after reform was averted or compromised on economic grounds. Of course, this could have meant a renewed Marxist initiative, but the Cold War was already beginning, and the Communist Party was soon more suspect than it had been in the twenties.

It is not surprising, therefore, that *Our Time* ran into difficulties again in 1947. The circulation of 15,000 that Rickword had achieved in 1945 fell to half that by 1947. Though it was never an official party publication, *Our Time* was strongly influenced by the communist headquarters at King Street. In the summer of 1947, Rickword was summoned to a meeting by Emile Burns, cultural spokesman, and Douglas Garman, his former friend from the *Calendar*: the magazine's decline was naturally the editor's responsibility and he had better resign. This Rickword quietly agreed to do.

Perhaps it was not simply a matter of circulation. It seems just as likely that the calm, practical authority of Rickword's voice, though ideally suited to the realistic optimism of the mid-forties, was found increasingly unacceptable by a party needing to assert a straight and simple Soviet line. Certainly such pronouncements as those in the 1945 article on Hazlitt could not have worn very well: "He did not approach politics in a formal, party-spirited way. . . . But he understood the mixed nature of men as they actually are and did not believe that the alteration of political institutions would automatically usher in the Millennium" (3, no. 6:10–11). Perhaps, too, Burns would have felt uneasy about the influence the editor was having on the younger contributors, such as David Holbrook. In June 1947, not long before Rickword's resignation, Holbrook was rejecting, implicitly at least, the crude sovietization of British socialist art and arguing, in a spirit dangerously reminiscent of the *Calendar*, for a proper "critical atmosphere" which would foster a "currency of values" more subtle than "bad or good" (6, no. 5:240).

Rickword was gone from *Our Time* by September 1947, for which month no issue appeared. Thereafter even lively and competent minds such as Randall Swingler's could not save the magazine. *Our Time* was over by the summer of 1949.

Notes

1. Jack Lindsay and Edgell Rickword, eds., *A Handbook of Freedom* (London, 1937).
2. Jack Lindsay, *Life Rarely Tells* (Harmondsworth, Eng., 1982), p. 799.

Information Sources

BIBLIOGRAPHY

Coupe, Laurence. "Edgell Rickword: Modernist or Marxist?" *Stand* 22, no. 3 (1981):38–42.
Hewison, Robert. *Under Siege: Literary Life in London 1939–1945*. London, 1977.
Munton, Alan, ed. "Edgell Rickword: A Celebration." *PN Review*, no. 9 (1979):supplement 1–32.
Rickword, Edgell. *Literature in Society*. Edited by Alan Young. Manchester, 1978.
INDEXES
    None.
REPRINT EDITIONS
    Kraus Reprint, Nendeln, Liechtenstein. Scholars' Facsimiles and Reprints, Delmar, N.Y.
LOCATION SOURCES
    American
        Complete runs: University of Buffalo Library; University of Kansas Library. Partial run: University of Minnesota Library.
    British
        Complete runs: British Museum; Cambridge University Library. Partial run: National Library of Scotland, Edinburgh.

Publication History

MAGAZINE TITLE AND TITLE CHANGES
    Our Time: Incorporating "Poetry and the People," 1941–1949 (from November 1944: . . . and "New Theatre").

VOLUME AND ISSUE DATA
Volumes 1–7, February 1941–July/August 1949.
FREQUENCY OF PUBLICATION
Monthly, except for volumes 4, 6, and 7, which appeared irregularly.
PUBLISHERS
February 1941–January 1943: Newport Publications, Leicester Square, London W.C. 2. February 1943–August 1949: Fore Publications, 28–29 Southampton Street, London W.C. 2.
EDITORS
Beatrix Lehmann, John Banting, Birkin Howard, Ben Frankel, and Randall Swingler, 1941–1942. Alfred Sharp, 1942–1943. Peter Philips and Honor Arundel, 1943. R. Vernon Beste, 1943–1944. Edgell Rickword, 1944–1947. Jack Beeching, George Martin, Montagu Slater, Arnold Rattenbury, John Summerfield, and C. H. Hobday, 1947–1948. Frank Jellinek, 1948. Randall Swingler, 1949.

Laurence Coupe

OUTPOSTS

In 1943, when he started *Outposts*, Howard Sergeant was on wartime service, attached to the Air Ministry. He was

> concerned not only with the publication of outstanding poetry at a reasonable price, but also in assembling those poets, recognized and unrecognized, who, by reason of the particular outposts they occupy, were able to visualize the dangers which confront the individual and the whole of humanity, now and after the war. [No. 1:1]

The preface to the third number asserted that "*Outposts* will continue to provide an open platform, entirely free from the restrictive influence of schools and cliques; and the only standard we shall impose will be that of quality" (no. 3:1). Although from the fifth number onward reviews of recently published poetry were included, the main substance of the magazine has always been individual poems. Editorial comment has been kept to a minimum.[1]

From the beginning, *Outposts* encouraged aspiring poets. Eschewing ideologies, nationalities, and poetry politics, Sergeant has devoted his life to editing, publishing, criticizing, and disseminating poetry. In addition to *Outposts*, he has published a series of several hundred booklets, collections by individual poets under the title Outposts Modern Poets Series, four books of his own poetry, and three critical books; and he has edited innumerable poetry anthologies. In 1978 Sergeant was awarded the M.B.E. for his services to literature. *Outposts* and the Outposts Modern Poets Series have played a significant role in the formation of contemporary British poetry by providing platforms for the first work of such authors as D. M. Thomas, Alan Sillitoe, Ruth Fainlight, Kingsley Amis, Muriel Spark, Peter Redgrove, Elizabeth Jennings, Dannie Abse, and Anthony Thwaite, to mention but a small number. The list of contributors to the fortieth anniversary number—extending from well-known literary figures and men of letters to hospital pharmacists in southern Africa and those institutionalized in psychiatric hospitals—reflects a loyalty and indebtedness to the magazine and its editor. Dannie Abse writes of the "enormous encouragement" and elation felt and remembered thirty-six years after the acceptance of one of his poems in *Outposts* (no. 40:11). Contributors drew attention to the sole criterion of quality and to the avoidance of specific poetic fashions, trends, schools, and groups. Nevertheless, although eclecticism has been the dominating ideology, the poetry represented in *Outposts* has tended to favor "the broadly traditional" rather than the *"avant garde"* (no. 40:15).

The flavor of the magazine is suggested by a representative issue. Number 62 for Autumn 1964 consists of thirty-two pages within stiff paper wrappers. Advertising is restricted to the back endpapers and consists of publishers' announcements for new poetry volumes, the Society of Authors' announcement of "The Eric Gregory Trust Fund Awards for 1964," and notices of poetry readings. The inside back wrapper contains a listing of some of *Outposts'* poetry pamphlet collections. Twenty-two poems by twenty-two poets appear, with few exceeding a single page. Poems extend from the seventeen-line "The Rock Pool," by Philip Hobsbaum, to a twenty-four-line poem (with no line longer than seven syllables) by Helen Shaw, "Bonestone and Spirit." Other contents include Nissim Ezekiel's powerful symbolic poem "Marriage" and an early poem by Seamus Heaney, "The Play Way." A review section includes a substantial piece by Zulfikar Ghose, "A Further Consideration of Syllabics" on B. S. Johnson's *Poems*, Philip Hobsbaum's *The Place's Fault*, and Michael Bullock's *World without Beginning*.

Outposts has played a significant role in post–1945 British poetry. The eclectic nature of its poems, poets, and reviews has served to make the British poetry scene less rigid and clique-ridden than it would otherwise have been. The pages of Sergeant's magazine have been available to all, irrespective of class, social and educational connections, or religious orientation. In the words of Sir John Betjeman, in a prospectus sent to possible subscribers, *Outposts* has been a quarterly "in which young poets can try their wings and older ones can keep flying and half dead ones like yours truly can profit."

Note

1. Howard Sergeant has helpfully provided information to the author for this profile.

Information Sources

REPRINT EDITIONS
    Numbers 1–75, 1944–1967, Kraus Reprint, Liechtenstein, 1972. Scholars' Facsimiles and Reprints, Delmar, N.Y.
INDEXES
    None.

LOCATION SOURCES

American

Partial runs: Widely available.

British

Complete runs: Bodleian Library; British Museum; Cambridge University Library; National Library of Scotland, Edinburgh; Trinity College Library; University of Hull Library.

Partial runs: Widely available.

Publication History

MAGAZINE TITLE AND TITLE CHANGES

Outposts, numbers 1–132, October 1943–Spring 1982; *Outposts Poetry Quarterly*, number 133,–Summer 1982–.

VOLUME AND ISSUE DATA

Number 1, October 1943. Special centennial issue 1974. Separately published supplement on new poets, number 138, Autumn 1983.

FREQUENCY OF PUBLICATION

Number 1, October 1943–number 31, Winter 1956: irregular. Numbers 32–, 1957–:quarterly.

PUBLISHERS

Numbers 1–2: Howard Sergeant, 59 Orchard Avenue, Squires Gate, Blackpool. Numbers 2–3: Favil Press, London. Numbers 4–13/14: Meridian Press Ltd., 27 Brazenose Street, Manchester. Numbers 15–22: Howard Sergeant, 31 Dulwich Village, London SE21. Numbers 23–78: Howard Sergeant, 209 East Dulwich Grove, Dulwich Village, London SE22. Number 79–: Howard Sergeant, Outposts Publications, 72 Burwood Road, Walton-on-Thames, Surrey, KT 12 4AL.

EDITOR

Howard Sergeant.

William Baker

OWL, THE

During his editorship of the *Owl* in the years immediately after World War I, Robert Graves followed an unfashionable policy of eclecticism. In a period when the trend was literary journals with definite ideological bents, Graves took no doctrinaire editorial stance, which may explain the short run of the *Owl*— only two numbers in 1919 and a one-number revival issue in 1923 that was entitled the *Winter Owl*.

The foreword to the first volume of the magazine, which Graves probably wrote, stated the editorial policy: "*The Owl* has no politics, leads no new movement and is not even the organ of any particular generation. . . . But we find in common a love for honest work well done, and a distaste for short cuts to popular success." Thus the aims of the *Owl* seem to leave out much that would have appealed to contemporary interests and literary trends. Graves's sanguine expectations for the success of the journal are revealed in a quotation that he takes from an essay on owls by Lewis Carroll, "all owls are satisfactory," a line the editor gratefully accepts as an omen. A large (13" x 10"), eye-catching publication with softbacked, purplish-red tinted covers, the magazine featured a woodcut of a whimsical looking owl surrounded by six owlets decorating the front cover. On the back cover there was another smaller owl, centered over a motto.

In getting out the magazine Graves was helped by W. J. Turner and J. C. Squire, the latter a political conservative and a champion of Georgian poetry. Financial support for the *Owl* was provided by Graves's father-in-law, Sir William Nicholson, who also drew the owl cover design.[1] The first issue was published in May 1919 and carried an impressive number of works by well-known writers. Among the more famous were John Masefield (Graves's landlord at the time), who provided a sonnet; Thomas Hardy, who submitted a four-stanza poem, "The Master and the Leaves"; John Galsworthy, who contributed a dramatic dialogue; and Max Beerbohm, who had an interesting article about Dr. Johnson. Graves published two of his own poems, "Ghost-Raddled" and "A Frosty Night." His wife Nancy, an artist, was represented by an illustration to a doggerel rime about a careless lady who gives her baby to a beggar man. In addition, there was a series of full-page illustrations by F. Vincent Brooks done in a wryly humorous vein.

The second number of the *Owl*, which came out in October 1919, was subtitled "A Miscellany" and was identical to the first number except that it was done in hardback covers and that, at fifty-four pages, it was somewhat longer in length. It again featured notable contributors; Walter De la Mare, Siegfried Sassoon, and Graves had poems. There were a chant for recitation by Vachel Lindsay, a story by Edmund Blunden, and an essay by Beerbohm. Artwork by Rockwell Kent, Pamela Bianco, Nancy Nicholson, and DerWent Wood completed the magazine's layout.

Graves had hoped to publish the *Owl* on a quarterly basis, or at least as often as enough suitable material was in the hands of the editors, but the magazine did not catch on. It died after a futile effort to keep it going with a name change in 1923, when the last volume came out in November as the *Winter Owl*. The final number was the same size and format as the earlier volumes, but featured blue covers. The masthead indicated that Graves and William Nicholson were the editors. Some new contributors appeared in the *Winter Owl*, such as T. E. Lawrence, whose chapter "Massacre" from his *Arab Revolt* was published here. Two poems by John Crowe Ransom, "Winter Remembered" and "Philomela," were his first verse publications in England. There were again poems by Graves and Sassoon, a short story by Thomas Hardy, "The Missed Train," and assorted artwork in the form of woodcuts by William Nicholson, prints by Pamela Bianco, and an illustrated letter by Sir Edward Burne-Jones.

Despite Graves's large hopes, the *Winter Owl* did not survive the cold reception it received from the public, and there were no further volumes of the journal. It had never been Graves's intention to make money from this publishing venture, but he had wished to gain some publicity for himself, not as a popular poet in the Georgian mode, but as a writer of what he called "true poetry."[2] The short-lived *Owl* unfortunately did not do much to expand his literary reputation or his financial resources. It did afford, however briefly, the publication of a variety of interesting and important writers, some of whom were already established, like Masefield and Hardy, and others who were just then establishing themselves, like Ransom, Sassoon, and Graves himself.

Notes

1. Martin Seymour-Smith, *Robert Graves* (London, 1983), p. 105.
2. Ibid., p. 106.

Information Sources

INDEXES
    None.
REPRINT EDITIONS
    None.
LOCATION SOURCES
    American
        Complete runs: Harvard University Library; New York Public Library; Princeton University Library; United States Library of Congress; University of Chicago Library; University of Georgia Library; University of Michigan Library; University of Minnesota Library.
        Partial runs: Cincinnati Public Library; Cleveland Public Library; Johns Hopkins University Library; Oberlin College Library; Ohio State University Library; University of California at Los Angeles Library; University of Kentucky Library; University of Southern California Library.
    British
        Compete runs: British Library; University of London Library.
        Partial runs: Bodleian Library; Cambridge University Library; Oxford University Library; Victoria and Albert Museum Library.

Publication History

MAGAZINE TITLE AND TITLE CHANGES
    The Owl, May 1919–October 1919. *The Winter Owl*, November 1923.
VOLUME AND ISSUE DATA
    Volume 1, number 1, May 1919–number 2, October 1919. Volume 2, number 3, November 1923.
FREQUENCY OF PUBLICATION
    Quarterly and occasional.

PUBLISHERS
Gerard T. Meynell, The Westminster Press, 11 Henrietta Street, Covent Garden, London, England. Cecil Palmer, 49 Chandos Street, Covent Garden, London, England.

EDITORS
Robert Graves, volume 1. Robert Graves and William Nicholson, volume 2.

Hallman Bell Bryant

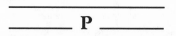

P

PEARSON'S MAGAZINE. See VEA

PENGUIN NEW WRITING

Penguin New Writing is one of four magazines—along with *New Writing**
and its successors, *Folios of New Writing* and *New Writing and Daylight*—edited
solely by John Lehmann. In May 1940, when many leading British literary
magazines, among them the *Criterion*,* the *London Mercury*,* and *New Verse*,*
either had ceased publication or were faltering due to wartime conditions, Allen
Lane of Penguin Books responded to an earlier proposal from Lehmann by
inviting him to follow up his *New Writing in Europe* anthology with a selection
of prose reprinted from *New Writing*. "I immediately saw the possibilities in
this suggestion for reviving the influence and usefulness of *New Writing*," wrote
Lehmann.[1] Before the appearance of the first number of *Penguin New Writing*
in December 1940, he had convinced Lane to sponsor a monthly magazine.
Lehmann had originally intended simply to reprint the best of *New Writing* in a
quantity and format which could be sold for six pence (the price climbed gradually
to one shilling, six pence by 1948) and therefore reach a larger audience than
the six–shilling *New Writing*, but when he decided upon monthly publication he
planned, beginning with volume 2, to include new material as well and to print,
besides fiction, critical articles, reviews, and verse.

Lehmann's experience in publishing included an intermittent association from
1931 with Leonard and Virginia Woolf's Hogarth Press; he bought out Virginia's
half-share in 1938. He had founded *New Writing* in 1936, and thus brought to
Penguin New Writing a profound sensitivity and creative talent. A widely published poet himself, Lehmann questioned the viability of loosely structured verse,
which he thought often dissolved into prose, and preferred the tighter traditional

forms. On content, he thought that "a magazine of creative literature" should try to supply "the more permanent truths that no military emergency, however urgent, can make nonsense of" (11:7).

In his Foreword to the first number of *Penguin New Writing*, Lehmann implied that he would continue the practices of *New Writing*: careful printing, avoidance of editorials (although his forewords to each issue, collectively, constitute a statement of editorial policy), a wide variety of material, prose in "the realistic tradition of Defoe and Fielding," and a generous representation of foreign writers. The volume opens with George Orwell's "Shooting an Elephant," commissioned for *New Writing*, and contains a strong international contingent: Tchang T'ien-Yih (from China), Mulk Rah Anand (India), William Plomer (South Africa), Alfred Kantorowicz (Germany), André Chamson and Louis Gilloux (France), Morton Freedgood (United States), and Nikolai Ognev (Russia). Among the seven British writers are Christopher Isherwood and V. S. Pritchett, and, in keeping with Lehmann's practice of encouraging proletarian authors, Leslie Halward and George Garrett, manual laborers who both began to write while unemployed.

Volume 2 is the first of the regular monthly issues of *Penguin New Writing*, and in his foreword Lehmann proclaimed the freedom of his editorial stance, equating it with his governing principles for *New Writing*:

> I have always felt that if a magazine . . . is properly edited, it will reveal its character best in the reading, and will not be helped by any special boost or apology. . . . I should like, however, to think that it was helping towards a reaffirmation of human values, in a world suffering from the triumph of inhuman ideals and the pursuit of values which are unreal and destructive.

Lehmann tried to maintain an apolitical position, but made exceptions for fascists and for those writers he saw as reactionary: *Penguin New Writing* was closed to them. He was often directly involved in the creative process, both in commissioning about a third of the works published, and in advising on the rewriting of many unassigned contributions.

Volume 2 introduced the recurring special features, published several of the authors who would appear frequently throughout the war years, and went beyond the original anthology plan by including, besides reprints from *New Writing*, five stories and critical articles commissioned especially for *Penguin New Writing*. The most significant of the special features is "Books and the War," a series of reviews and criticism written by Stephen Spender through volume 12, with the exception of the essay by Walter Allen in volume 9. Lehmann envisioned Spender's articles to be not primarily reviews but "a continuing discussion on the relations between literature (and the other arts) and life, especially those aspects which the war made to seem so important."[2] With volume 13 for June 1942 Lehmann began a separate section, "Book Front," which was to continue through volume 24 (1945) and usually included articles by three critics. It was superseded by a section entitled "The Critical View," which appeared irregularly, although every issue of *Penguin New Writing* contains important criticism. Another feature, "The Way We Live Now," ran for eleven issues beginning with the second number, and included essays by Louis MacNeice and Pritchett, among others. It was succeeded by "Report on Today" and finally by "The Living Moment," which continued through volume 34 (1948). Lehmann asked his novelist sister Rosamond to contribute a series of short stories exploring the past against the present; only five of these were to appear, although she wrote on other themes for seven later volumes. Two light features became highly popular: Plomer's satires, written under the pseudonym "Robert Pagan," and George Stonier's regular "Shaving through the Blitz," also signed with a pseudonym, "Fanfarlo." When the Blitz itself ended, Stonier contributed to *Penguin New Writing* under another pseudonym, "Joseph Gurnard." Volume 2 contains a short story by Chamson, who would appear in eight volumes (1, 2, 4, 6, 9, 11, 12, 31), while poetry by C. Day Lewis and MacNeice initiated their long association with *Penguin New Writing*. One of Lehmann's favorites among proletarian writers, B. L. Coombes (vols. 2, 4, 9, 21), was also represented. In layout and content, volume 2 represents faithfully what *Penguin New Writing* would be like through volume 12, and, with periodic, relatively slight alterations, for its entire career.

In the order of frequency of their contributions, the prose authors who best characterize *Penguin New Writing* are Plomer, Stonier, Pritchett, and Rosamond Lehmann; the poets are Day Lewis, MacNeice, William Sansom, and Terence Tiller; the critical voices are Spender and John Lehmann. All these appeared in ten or more issues, with Spender the most consistent, contributing to twenty–five of the first twenty–seven. Other contributors of significant amounts of fiction and nonfiction include Sid Chaplin (vols. 6, 12, 15, 17, 22, 31, 37), J. Maclaren-Ross (15, 26, 27, 29, 30), Jim Phelan (4, 11, 23, 27, 32), Frank Sargeson (5, 8, 13, 17, 18, 19, 27, 28, 29), John Sommerfield (4, 8, 14, 17, 21, 26), and James Stern (5, 20, 23, 29, 31, 34, 38). Contributors primarily of poetry who belong on a similar list are W. H. Auden (3, 5, 7, 10, 12, 14, 19), George Barker (15, 18, 20, 25, 33, 34, 36, 40), Roy Fuller (13, 16, 17, 18, 19), John Heath-Stubbs (18, 21, 27), Federico García Lorca (5, 7, 9, 11), Alan Ross (17, 25, 28, 33, 35, 40), and Edith Sitwell (19, 20, 23, 27, 32, 34, 38, 40). Literary criticism by Walter Allen (9, 14, 18, 25, 29, 34, 36) and Kenneth Muir (24, 26, 28, 31) is important, as is the writing on art by Keith Vaughan (22, 31, 34, plus various articles he signed simply as "Art Critic"). Many of these writers contributed in one or more genres besides those for which they are listed above, for instance, Heath-Stubbs in criticism (23, 25, 32) and Vaughan in fiction (12, 26). Lehmann recognized important new critical voices by publishing David Magarshack on Anton Chekhov (37), Philip Toynbee's "The Decline and Future of the English Novel" (23), and John Wain's "Ambiguous Gifts" on William Empson (40).

Many established writers, among them Elizabeth Bowen (20), Henry Green (4, 14), Graham Greene (9, 30), Frank O'Connor (37), and Osbert Sitwell (21, 27, 29), appeared in *Penguin New Writing*, often marking the first publication in England of the work printed. Toward the end of the magazine's run, Lehmann was able to publish more American authors. This was something he had been eager to do before, but he lacked suitable offerings until he received three stories from Nelson Algren (34, 35, 36) and one each from Saul Bellow (38), Paul Bowles (39), Eudora Welty (36), and Tennessee Williams (40). The final number of the magazine contains photographs of seven American authors. Lehmann's appreciation of European writers is shown by the inclusion of Bertolt Brecht (6), Jean Giono (3, 10), André Gide (33), Boris Pasternak (30), Jean-Paul Sartre (7, 16), Mikhail Sholokhov (3), Ignazio Silone (2, 10), and Jules Supervielle (37). Through his coeditorship with Jiři Mucha of the single-issue periodical *Daylight*, Lehmann located and published several Czech authors. He also admired a number of Greeks, and printed poems by Odysseus Elytis (31, 35, 37) and Angelos Sikelianos (33), the latter in Lawrence Durrell's translations, as well as criticism and the first poems written in English by Demetrios Capetanakis (13, 16, 19, 20), a personal friend who died at a young age in England during the war. An article by Robert Liddell on Sikelianos (39) helped give the Greek poet the reputation he deserved in England.

The major changes in *Penguin New Writing* are marked by volumes 2, 13, and 27. With volume 2 the magazine became a monthly with the features normally associated with a literary journal; with 13, Lane insisted on quarterly publication, citing paper shortages, but he allowed Lehmann to begin printing artwork in each issue. Lehmann also introduced at this time "A Reader's Notebook," reviews and essays on literature which he wrote under the pseudonym "Jack Marlowe." Most important about the art reproductions was the exposure given many young English painters of a rather neo–Romantic bent, especially Michael Ayrton, John Craxton, Leslie Hurry, John Minton, Leonard Rosoman, and Keith Vaughan. Lehmann also regularly printed illustrations of ballet, film, and theater productions, and occasionally portfolios of photographs of *Penguin New Writing* authors. Volume 27 began postwar publication in April 1946 with a new, larger format (up from around 144 pages to 192), new typography, a new cover design by John Minton, and four color plates, apart from those in volume 23 the first to appear in the magazine. Lehmann proclaimed:

Penguin New Writing had at last become what we had always hoped it could be: a magazine primarily devoted to literature—and offering opportunities to young writers above all—but also covering the other arts, with articles on the theatre, the ballet, music, cinema, radio, as well as on literary themes, and illustrations to complement these articles. All this, of course, on an international, not merely British scale.[3]

Volumes 27–30 represent a high plateau for *Penguin New Writing*. By volume 31 in 1947, the color plates had disappeared and the printing runs had dropped from 100,000 to 40,000.

The importance of *Penguin New Writing* to contemporary readers was due in part to wartime conditions. Spender described the sense of mission imposed upon magazine editors, seen through his coeditorship of Cyril Connolly's *Horizon**: "It could make us feel humble that there were pilots in the Battle of Britain who came into our offices to say that they felt they were fighting for whatever *Horizon* represented. (There were still more who were ready to fight for John Lehmann's more widely circulated *New Writing*.)"[4] And, by extension, for *Penguin New Writing*. The sizeable percentage of Continental writers in Lehmann's magazines served the triple purpose of "keep[ing] alive the awareness of a great modern literature in Europe" (6:8); of reminding the embattled Britons that they had valuable literary friends abroad, even in those countries with whom they were at war; and of giving European writers an outlet in the free nonfascist world. Lehmann mentioned in the foreword to volume 29 (1947) that it was equally important for understanding Europe to renew artistic and literary contact with Austria, Germany, and Italy as with the wartime allies. Quite as relevant was his plea in volume 37 (1949) for more cultural contact with the U.S.S.R. and other nations to the east. While Lehmann was concerned over the effects of too little contact between European and British writers, he worried that Dominion literature was too much "under the enormous shadows of England and America" (5:8), and gave the New Zealander Frank Sargeson an English public he would probably otherwise have lacked.

Penguin New Writing encouraged new writers, printing early work by Chaplin, Coombes, Hamish Henderson, Laurie Lee, Sansom, and others, as well as the first stories ever published by Patrick Boyle and Alec Guinness. The magazine performed a service by keeping Auden and Isherwood before the English public, despite their often-condemned wartime residence in the United States. Pritchett acknowledged the importance of being consistently published by Lehmann. In his constant search for new talent, Lehmann discovered that two poets he admired, Alun Lewis and Dylan Thomas, both wrote excellent prose, and he set himself the task of cajoling Thomas into writing fiction. However, Thomas merely drank down the pounds advanced him and thereafter tried to avoid Lehmann. "I deeply regretted this, not only for the loss of *Adventures in the Skin Trade* but also because it put a spoke of embarrassment into our relationship for many years, during which I should only have been too happy to publish his poems."[5] Another of Lehmann's acknowledged failures, which was not for want of trying, was his inability to discover many genuine working-class writers of high caliber.

Lehmann deliberately avoided the quarrels common among the more controversial magazine editors of the period. A satire on contemporary poets came from one of Lehmann's regulars, Stonier (writing as "Joseph Gurnard"): in "Poets' Excursion" he mocks, among others, "Stephen Spendlove," "Louis

('Borzoi') MacNoose,'' ''Kitty Rainy,'' and even the editor himself as ''Don Layman'' (18). Apparently no one was seriously offended. Lehmann fared differently with his own ''State Art and Scepticism'' (24), however: he criticized his old friend and contributor to *Penguin New Writing* (5, 11) Nikolai Tikhonov, then chairman of the Union of Soviet Writers, for ''dogmatic earnestness,'' for advocating strict conformity to state propaganda aims on the part of all creative writers, and compared this unfavorably to ''the sceptical British temperament.'' A vituperative campaign, which was to continue for years, was launched against Lehmann in the *Literaturnaya Gazeta* and other Soviet magazines.

The only magazine of the period which can be meaningfully compared to *Penguin New Writing* is Connolly's *Horizon*. Both covered literature and art with illustrations and in all genres; and they were nearly contemporaneous: January 1940 through January 1950 for *Horizon*, December 1940 through July 1950 for *Penguin New Writing*. A significant link between the two magazines was Spender's connections with both; clearly, his literary taste coincided with and perhaps helped form Lehmann's. Many authors appeared in both magazines, including Auden, Barker, Day Lewis, MacNeice, Plomer, and Edith Sitwell. As an editor, Lehmann showed a preference for rather more orderly writing than Connolly, but the latter's critique of Lehmann, with the corrective on his wartime shift away from most political biases, is probably fair: ''There is no doubt that John Lehmann was the outstanding British editor of the [prewar] period, capable of selecting poetry, fiction, reportage and reviews—provided they were Left-wing—with both flair and discrimination. . . . the war-time *Penguin New Writing* was an eclectic magazine. . . . The Left-wing dynamism had departed.''[6]

Lehmann's early difficulties—the night rides on blacked-out trains with a suitcase of proofs he couldn't see to correct, the paper rations and shortages, the bomb holes in the roof of the printshop, postal delays in the handling of correspondence and manuscripts—were vicissitudes common to most contemporary editors, and they were to some extent compensated for by the avidity of the public for reading matter. Lehmann's standard runs of 75,000 copies, all he could print on his five-ton paper allotment (equal to a year's ration for the Hogarth Press), usually sold out within weeks, as did occasional printings of 100,000 when he could manage them. This situation obtained through the end of the war, but in the years immediately following 1946 the drop in circulation was substantial, although the quality of material remained high. In 1949 Penguin insisted on cutting the number of pages from 160 back to 128, and on reducing the frequency to twice a year. Rather than continue under such terms, Lehmann decided to cease publication with volume 40 in 1950, after the demise of *Horizon* in January and of *Life and Letters Today** (see *Life and Letters*) in June. *Penguin New Writing*, ''a 'little magazine' that had had the public of a very big magazine indeed,'' came to an end.[7]

Notes

1. John Lehmann, *I Am My Brother* (London, 1960), p. 91.
2. Ibid., p. 94.

3. John Lehmann, *In My Own Time* (Boston, 1969), p. 449.

4. Stephen Spender, *The Thirties and After: Poetry, Politics, People (1933–75)* (London, 1978), p. 88.

5. Lehmann, *I Am My Brother*, p. 98.

6. Cyril Connolly, *The Evening Colonnade* (New York, 1975), pp. 384–85.

7. Lehmann, *In My Own Time*, p. 448.

Information Sources

BIBLIOGRAPHY

Connolly, Cyril. *The Evening Colonnade*. New York, 1975.

Hewison, Robert. *Under Siege: Literary Life in London, 1939–1945*. London, 1977.

Hoffman, Frederick J., Charles Allen, and Carolyn F. Ulrich. *The Little Magazine: A History and a Bibliography*. Princeton, 1946.

Lehmann, John. *The Ample Proposition*. London, 1966.

————. *I Am My Brother*. London, 1960.

————. *In My Own Time*. London, 1969.

————. *The Whispering Gallery*. London, 1955.

————. "Without My Files." *Penguin New Writing* 21 (1944):137–48.

Spender, Stephen. *The Thirties and After: Poetry, Politics, People (1933–75)*. London, 1978.

Tolley, A. Trevor. *The Poetry of the Thirties*. London, 1975.

Anthologies

[*Penguin New Writing* is itself in part an anthology of work originally published in *New Writing*, and while there is no specific *Penguin New Writing* anthology, the various *New Writing* anthologies reprint some of the prose and verse found in *Penguin New Writing*.]

English Stories from New Writing. Edited by John Lehmann. London, 1951. (Published in America under the title *Best Stories from New Writing*, New York, 1951.)

Pleasures of New Writing. Edited by John Lehmann. London, 1952.

Poems from New Writing, 1936–1946. Edited by John Lehmann. London, 1946.

INDEXES.

None.

REPRINT EDITIONS

Kraus Reprint, Nendeln, Liechtenstein. Scholars' Facsimiles and Reprints, Delmar, N.Y.

LOCATION SOURCES

American

Complete run: Princeton University Library.

Partial runs: Widely available.

British

Complete run: British Museum.

Partial runs: Birmingham University Library; Leeds Public Library; London University Library.

Publication History

MAGAZINE TITLE AND TITLE CHANGES

Penguin New Writing.

VOLUME AND ISSUE DATA
> Volumes 1–8, December 1940–July 1941. Volume 9, September 1941. Volumes 10 and 11, November 1941. Volume 12, April 1942. Volume 13, April–June 1942. Volume 14, September 1942. Volume 15, October–December 1942. Volume 16, January–March 1943. Volume 17, April–June 1943. Volume 18, July–September 1943. Volume 19, October–December 1943. Volumes 20–22, 1944. Volumes 23–26, 1945. Volume 27, April 1946. Volume 28, July 1946. Volumes 29–32, 1947. Volumes 33–35, 1948. Volumes 36–38, 1949. Volumes 39 and 40, 1950.

FREQUENCY OF PUBLICATION
> Monthly, then quarterly and irregularly.

PUBLISHER
> Penguin Books Ltd., Harmondsworth, Middlesex, England.

EDITOR
> John Lehmann.

Ian S. MacNiven

PENGUIN PARADE

Penguin Parade, first published in 1937, had its origins in the general burgeoning of the publishing firm of Penguin Books Ltd. late in that decade. The company was eager to branch out beyond its paperback reprint series and so naturally turned to the magazine market. Allen Lane, the founder of Penguin Books, was tempted to make this venture into periodical publication because he was "gulled by the past, by a half-understood memory of *'The Yellow Book'* [*see *VEA*] . . . and by some dim glimpse of a future in which he was the master of every mode of disseminating the printed word."[1]

Under the direction of Lane, Penguin would succeed at almost every sort of printing enterprise, but the company was not, with the exception of *Penguin New Writing** and two scientific periodicals, *New Biology* and *Science News*, a successful magazine publisher.[2] An astute and inventive publisher, Lane was always on the lookout for new markets and challenges. He was also guided by a belief that he could influence public taste and stimulate the life of the mind in England, and had found sudden and sensational success with Penguin Books. The paperback series found readers for intelligent and high-quality writing of all types in a market that was larger than anyone had suspected. Optimistically, he believed that Penguin's accomplishments in book publishing might be repeated in periodical publishing. While *Penguin Parade* did not fulfill expectations, it was nonetheless an innovation of some consequence, the first of several ventures by Penguin into journalism, periodicals, and magazines.

The miscellany was launched as a quarterly in December 1937 to test the waters of the magazine market. Appearing in a plain but cheerful format of red paper covers, the magazine fit the standard four-by-seven-inch Penguin size and sold at the usual six-penny price for paperbacks. The first number of *Penguin*

Parade featured the table of contents on the cover with the title carried on a white band across the top; the sole ornament, the Penguin colophon, appeared at the foot of the cover page. Subsequent issues in the first series would follow this format with only the color of the cover being changed from number to number. Number 1 was red, 2 blue, 3 yellow, 4 green, and so on. Had the run of *Penguin Parade* been longer, the color scheme would have become redundant; as it was, by number 11 the standard colors had all been used. The prevalence of red for the jacket color might have been seen by some of Penguin's detractors as a signal of the journal's political sympathies, but an inspection of the contents of *Parade* would have laid to rest any suspicion that the editor was trying to further any causes, and for a journal of that period *Parade* is remarkably free of politics.[3]

Although the first editor, Denys Kilham Roberts, primarily sought contributions in the form of short stories of any length, essays, poems, and woodcuts, wood engravings and line drawings were also invited. The typical issue (which ran to 200 pages) carried more short stories than anything else, as the editor attempted to publish a series of collections of new short stories "different in character from most of the stories printed in popular magazines" (no. 4:vii). Roberts admits to having had some apprehension about the British public's indifference to short fiction that demanded "a sustained mental effort and digestive energy" (no. 4:vii) and to an uncertainty about whether the quality of the material forthcoming from contributors would be of the high standard that *Penguin Parade* had set for itself. But on the latter score the editors had no need to worry; manuscripts arrived at first at the rate of ten per day and rose to thirty per day by 1938, according to Roberts (no. 4:vii). All contributions were "over the transom," as the editors decided not to be respecters of names, reputations, or persons in their policy of acceptance or rejection of manuscripts. All contributors were on the same footing with regard to treatment and payment; established authors were dealt with in the same way as amateurs.

The initial success of *Penguin Parade*, which went through two reprints, was substantial enough to convince the publishers to continue with the venture, and ten more numbers appeared until the end of the first series in 1945. Having a run of eight years through depression and war was no mean feat. *Parade* was in competition with *Penguin New Writing*, under the brilliant editorial leadership of John Lehmann, and it was crimped by Lane's reluctance to create an adequate organization to support a magazine through either subscription or distribution.

It is not possible to say if Denys Roberts was ever given a brief from his superiors at Penguin as to what editorial policy he should follow. More likely he was given no specific mandate; Lane liked to leave an editor to follow his instincts once a project was launched. Roberts may have set his sights by comparing his task to Lehmann's at *Penguin New Writing*, which was to widen the range of Penguin's readership by operating "at the higher echelons of literary endeavor."[4] The difference between the two Penguin-sponsored journals was that *Penguin New Writing* was a deliberately highbrow periodical that drew its material, mainly poetry, from an elite corps of regular contributors, paying considerable attention to Continental writers, whereas *Penguin Parade* drew most of its submissions from English authors, was much more egalitarian in its submission policy for contributors, and published primarily fiction. Though the avowed purpose of *Parade* was to publish short stories different in character from those printed in popular magazines, it nevertheless had a target audience that was more middlebrow and populist than *Penguin New Writing*'s readers. Surprisingly, the quality of *Penguin Parade* was comparable to *Penguin New Writing* in the fiction it published. Its cover proudly claims "the first English publication" of writing by British, American, and Commonwealth authors, and among those represented in its pages were writers such as Faith Baldwin, H. E. Bates, Stephen Vincent Benet, Sherwood Anderson, James Gould Cozzens, Sean O'Faolain, Herbert Read, Irwin Shaw, and Katherine Anne Porter.

Benet's familiar story, "The Devil and Daniel Webster," appeared in *Penguin Parade* number 1, along with Sherwood Anderson's "The Corn Planting." There were poems by Herbert Read and woodcut illustrations by Gwen Raverat, J. R. Biggs, and Percy Bliss, who later launched the well-known series of Penguin Illustrated Classics. Taken together, contributors of this quality made for an auspicious start of the magazine. In later numbers Benet would appear again with more fiction, such as "Johnny Pye and the Fool Killer" (no. 2), "The Last of the Legions" (no. 3), and "O'Hara's Luck" (no. 4). In the early 1940s *Parade* published Irwin Shaw's stories: "Weep in Years to Come" (no. 8) and his more famous "Main Currents of American Thought" (no. 9). Perhaps more notable was the publication of Katherine Anne Porter's "Pale Horse, Pale Rider" (no. 5) long before the story had become an anthology piece in American textbooks.

An interesting feature of the first series of *Penguin Parade* was the section in the end-pages of each number devoted to biographical sketches of each contributor. These entries are surprisingly chatty and expansive, going far beyond the terse notes about authors that most journals run. For example, over 500 words are devoted to Benet in which is revealed that his family name is Minorcan and that he is of Spanish origin. As war rationing enforced paper conservation, there was a noticeable decline in the size of the biographical notes during the war years, and the contributors section was dropped altogether with the second series of *Parade*.

The exigencies of wartime publishing were obvious in other ways: the hiatuses between numbers grew longer; number 10 was issued in 1943, and number 11 did not appear until 1945, a lapse of nearly two years. Other harbingers of the hard times facing *Penguin Parade* were the increasing advertisements for candy bars, shaving soaps, and aspirin that appeared in the files for the war years. A more ominous sign was an item entitled "The Editor Says" that appeared in number 7, the first issue to be published after the outbreak of war. Here it is indicated that the magazine was considering "widening its scope by including a section consisting of articles on questions of immediate interest and sacrificing a corresponding amount of short story space" (p. vii). It was decided, however, to let newspapers and journals of opinion comment on current affairs. *Parade* would continue to develop the field that it had to itself, the short story, because, as the editor writes, "We do not believe that in wartime imaginative literature has or should have no place." Unfortunately, there was a decline in the quality of fiction being published by *Parade*, as a glance at the table of contents for the last numbers reveals; many more amateurs were contributing to the magazine, and short stories of real quality were rare indeed.

While *Parade* tried to go on publishing serious and intelligent fiction, rather than reportage, the combined wartime pressure of material shortages and the public's engrossment in more topical, superficial, and entertaining writing led to the eventual closedown of the initial series of *Penguin Parade*.

The revival of the periodical was attempted in 1947 with J. E. Morpurgo assuming the editor's chair of the second series. In outward form *Parade* was only slightly revised. It still featured gaily colored covers, but with stylized penguins now enclosing the title. Also different was the removal of the table of contents from the jacket. But in other ways the revived *Parade* was similar to the first series; it still bore marks of the comparative emanicipation evidenced by the slimmed-down pagination and closed-up type forced on the magazine by wartime paper shortages, and, more unhappily, it was "predestined to the irregularity of issue" that had to beset the original run of *Parade*.

But at least one major change was made in the journal: its editorial design. While the second series continued to be a miscellany, it did not devote itself principally to the publication of short stories and poems. Under Morpurgo's editorial policy *Parade* emphasized critical and informative writing "without prejudice of school or subject" that paid more attention to "up-to-the-minute articles." Furthermore, the new editorial policy did not accept much from hopefuls; instead, topics were devised by the editor for future issues, and authors who were appropriate to the subject were found.[5] The revived *Parade* made an express attempt to "achieve topicality," insofar as any editor can forecast several months in advance of a number what the topics of the moment will be (ser. 2, no. 1:5).

The new direction of *Parade* was immediately apparent from the first number of the second series. Several articles dealt with events taking place in England at the time of publication. The lead essay was devoted to a comparison of the procedures of literary criticism and book reviewing. Other articles were concerned with the advent of television and the problems facing schools as revealed by the Fleming Report on Education in Post-War Britain. In addition, there were informative pieces on the endeavors of the Edinburgh Festival Committee, the Shakespeare Memorial Theatre, and the Trustees of the Victoria and Albert Museum.

Later numbers of *Parade* attempted the same emphasis on contemporaneity with an expanded focus. Through a special section on overseas backgrounds called "Distant Correspondence," which started with number 2, an attempt was made to reveal the state of the arts, cinema, music, and literature in Australia,

Canada, South Africa, and New Zealand and to give "some idea of the cultural temperature of all these member states in the intellectual Commonwealth" (p. 6). In this vein of covering events in English-speaking nations, Morpurgo himself wrote a perceptive essay on the 1948 American presidential election, in which he tried to explain for British readers the differences between the Democratic, Dixiecrat, and Republican parties.

Another noticeable change in the format of *Parade* was the introduction of more illustrations. The black-and-white woodcuts that decorated the first series were dropped for more numerous color plates and photogravure illustrations that made for a more expensive-looking magazine and probably accounts for the increase in price to a shilling and two pence for each number.

Although there were several breaks from the tradition of the original *Parade*, the magazine continued to set itself against publishing writing aimed at other writers and to include the work of contemporary creative artists; the editor noted that "any periodical that purports to reflect some aspects of life today must include the work of poets and fiction writers." Because good short fiction was scarce, Morpurgo published few stories, but he scored a coup by being the first British editor to accept a story by Eudora Welty, "Hello and Good-bye," which appeared in the third and final number of *Parade*'s second series.

By number 3 of the second series the editor's foreword showed signs that the revival of *Parade* was not as robust as had been hoped. It speaks of the frustration of its "occasional" publication schedule to both readers and writers, asks for patience over publication delays, pleads for loyalty from the readers, and gives thanks for the patience shown by the literary establishment for its critical tolerance of *Parade* as a "casual" publication that was outside of any political and party affiliations.

Despite the editor's hope to fill the pockets and minds of the reading public with a "thoughtful" periodical, the second *Parade* fell victim to the same set of circumstances as the original *Parade*. While Penguin's other publishing wings— Penguin Guides, Handbooks, Poets, Classics, Plays—were growing, the increasing competition in the postwar magazine market was crimping Penguin's *Parade*. But what was finally fatal for the magazine was internal rather than external: the inability to maintain a regular publishing schedule and the lack of an adequate system for sales and distribution. The sales methods for book publishing and periodical publication were totally different, and Penguin's *Parade* representatives "were bookmen, not periodical peddlers."[6] The demise of *Penguin Parade* came in 1948 after the third number of the second series.

Notes

1. J. E. Morpurgo, *Allen Lane: King Penguin* (London, 1980), p. 130.
2. Ibid., p. 129.
3. Although Allen Lane was an entrepreneur and arch-capitalist, he was accused of being a fellow traveler whose publishing list was made up to further the Marxist line. While Allen employed editors who were from the political left wing, like John Lehmann

and Krishna Mennon, he himself was not particularly political, and though he did vote with the Labour Party, he did not allow trade unions to deal with Penguin. Apparently his reason for a socialist tilt in his firm's publications was due less to ideological convictions than to an assumption that most intellectuals and book dealers were liberals or radicals who would be better buyers of Penguin books; see Morpurgo, pp. 131–32.

4. Letter in the *Times Literary Supplement* received from J. E. Morpurgo, 30 December 1983.

5. Ibid.

6. Jack Morpurgo, who took over the editorship of *Penguin Parade* in 1946, was still in uniform when employed by Lane to work as head of Penguin's public relations department and possibly as a contributor to *Transatlantic*. Instead he was made an ancillary editor of *Parade* and was charged with reviving the magazine; see Morpurgo, p. 206. According to Morpurgo, he was the only editor of a journal who was an "in-house," working member of the staff at Penguin (*Times Literary Supplement*, 30 December 1983).

Information Sources

BIBLIOGRAPHY

Hoffman, Frederick J., Charles Allen, and Carolyn F. Ulrich. *The Little Magazine: A History and a Bibliography*. 2nd ed. Princeton, 1947.

Morpurgo, J. E. *Allen Lane: King Penguin*. London, 1980.

INDEXES

Numbers 1–6 in *An Author Index to Selected British Little Magazines*, ed. B. C. Bloomfield (London, 1976).

REPRINT EDITIONS

None.

LOCATION SOURCES

American

Complete runs: Duke University Library; U.S. Library of Congress; University of California Library, Berkeley.

Partial runs: Catholic University Library; Massachusetts State Library, Boston; New York Public Library; University of Minnesota Library; University of Pennsylvania Library; Yale University Library.

British

Complete runs: British Museum; National Library of Scotland, Edinburgh.

Partial runs: Birmingham Public Library; London University Library; Victoria and Albert Museum Library.

Publication History

MAGAZINE TITLE AND TITLE CHANGES

Penguin Parade

VOLUME AND ISSUE DATA

Volume 1, numbers 1–3, December 1937–(?) 1938. Volume 2, numbers 4–6, (?) 1938–1939. Volume 3, numbers 7–11, (?) 1940–1945. Volume 4, second series, numbers 1–3, (?) 1947–1948.

FREQUENCY OF PUBLICATION

Quarterly, irregular.

PUBLISHERS
  Penguin Books Ltd., Harmondsworth, Middlesex, England. Penguin Books, Inc.,
  245 Fifth Avenue, New York.
EDITORS
  Denys Kilham Roberts, 1937–1945. Jack Eric Morpurgo, 1947–1948.

Hallman Bell Bryant

PLAYS AND PLAYERS

First published in October 1953, just four months after the coronation, *Plays and Players* provides the most comprehensive record of the English theater of the second Elizabethan age. Like the other magazines issued by its publisher in a similar format—*Art and Artists, Books and Bookmen, Dance and Dancers, Films and Filming, Music and Musicians*—it is primarily a popular rather than strictly literary or scholarly magazine. Alongside various features designed for the immediate, practical use of London's theater-goers, *Plays and Players* also contains abundant materials of more permanent value: its reviews are typically more substantial than those appearing in the daily and weekly press; its featured interviews and profiles of playwrights, directors, and designers are among the most thorough to have been published anywhere; its numerous production photographs provide the most widely available archival record of performances on the modern English stage; and its long-standing (though recently abandoned) practice of printing the full texts of newly produced plays has made available works that would otherwise be virtually inaccessible. For all of these reasons, *Plays and Players* is an indispensable resource for the study of contemporary English theater.

Unlike more specialized drama magazines such as *Encore** and *Gambit,* Plays and Players* has consistently devoted itself to the most comprehensive coverage possible of contemporary theater in all of its forms—commercial, subsidized, underground, festival, and "fringe." From the commercial hits of Shaftesbury Avenue to the assertive plays of the "Angry Young Men" at the Royal Court Theatre in Sloane Square, from the classic revivals at the National Theatre and Stratford to the most antiestablishment "happenings" in converted Soho lofts, *Plays and Players* has provided extraordinarily thorough coverage and (with remarkable consistency) incisive and fair-minded reviews from such critics as Martin Esslin, John Russell Taylor, Richard Findlater, Michael Billington, Peter Ansorge, Robert Brustein, and many others.

The magazine's deliberate catholicity of interests has inevitably invited unmitigated scorn from partisans of every style and type of theater. Many complained about the detailed coverage given "dirty plays"—and (especially) about the equally explicit photographs that often accompanied reviews of *Oh! Calcutta* and other plays of its kind. A number shared *Encore* magazine's contempt for the bland popular fare and standard revivals that were often featured on the covers of *Plays and Players*; and still others objected to the regular coverage given even the most outrageously iconoclastic of the Angry Young Men. Nevertheless, with what one of its editors, Philip Roberts, once described as the magazine's "limited budgetary and staff conditions [which] make an adjective like 'shoestring' conjure up resources of gargantuan proportions" (19, no. 2:18), it continued to expand and adjust its scope, giving serious attention even to regional theater, television and radio drama, pub theater, "club" theater, and (on rare occasions) amateur interests as well; foreign productions from throughout the world are covered regularly in a briefer "Newsletter" format. Although the search for the proper balance among such varied types of coverage has led inevitably to an ongoing series of revisions and adjustments in the magazine's format, it has continued throughout its long history to offer thorough coverage of new plays both in and out of London (with feature reviews often as long as 1,500 to 2,000 words), accompanied by the unabridged text of "the month's most widely discussed play" (13, no. 5:6). Often, such works would have had an extremely limited audience otherwise, since many were offered only in short runs in small theaters such as the Royal Court, the Arts Theatre Club, the Traverse Theatre Club, and others.

During the late 1960s and early 1970s the texts of the plays were printed in full in a single issue; in the earlier years—and again from the mid- to late seventies—they were presented in two consecutive issues. Almost always, publication in *Plays and Players* preceded the play's appearance in book form, and the magazine was often the first publisher for many unknown playwrights who would later achieve considerable renown and acclaim. The most prominent of these is Edward Bond, whose controversial play *Saved* appeared in full in the January 1966 issue, accompanied "by way of introduction" by Laurence Olivier's classic letter to the *Observer* in its defense. Invoking Chekhov, Shakespeare, and Shaw in a defense that applies not only to Bond's works but to those of countless other contemporary authors, Olivier contended that

> the theatre is concerned . . . with the teaching of the human heart the knowledge of itself and [hence] sometimes, when it is necessary—and we are obviously going through such a time—with the study, understanding, and recognition of that most dreaded and dangerous eccentricity in the human design, the tripartite conspiracy between the sexual, the excretal, and the cruel. [13, no. 4:28]

Yet, reflecting the magazine's diversity of opinions, the same issue contained a review of *Saved* by John Russell Taylor, who remarked of the play's most controversial scene (in which an infant is viciously defiled before being stoned to death in its pram), "I can't really see how anybody could be seriously offended by something so feebly written and inertly directed" (13, no. 4:22). Characteristically, *Plays and Players* brought its readers the full text of the most controversial play of its time, undaunted by its notoriety; yet it was equally open to critical censure of the work, championing no particular ideology and advocating no single style or type of theater over others, as the cover of the issue makes clear in a particularly ironic way. Though the magazine contains the first publication of what is arguably the most significant play of its decade—a work having an impact that may be considered historically as important as that of *Look Back in Anger* ten years earlier—its cover featured a portrait of Mary Martin, who had just opened in *Hello, Dolly*.

Nevertheless, *Plays and Players* devotes remarkably little space to celebrity profiles and promotional features on cast members of various plays; instead, it has focused attention on the authors, directors, and stage designers, whose work, though vital, remains too often unheralded in the popular press. Of particular importance was the series of profiles by John Russell Taylor, "British Dramatists: The New Arrivals," which appeared between April 1970 (17, no. 7) and March 1971 (18, no. 6); it offered the earliest major critical assessment of such aspiring authors as Edward Bond, Joe Orton, David Storey, Tom Stoppard, Simon Gray, and David Hare.[1] A similar series by Martin Esslin, "Drama in Europe: New Writing," appeared from April 1971 (18, no. 7) through October 1971 (19, no. 1) with early evaluations of such authors as Peter Handke and Peter Weiss. More recently, in early 1983, the magazine has even featured a series on the practice of theater criticism itself, with contributions by J. C. Trewin, David Nathan, and Clive Barnes, and new profiles of promising playwrights such as Terry Johnson, Louise Page, Stephen Fagan, Tony Marchant, and Kevin Elyot. By providing a platform for such new authors to express their views as well as a medium for serious critical consideration of their works, *Plays and Players* has performed an invaluable service in bringing them to the attention of the general public as only a "popular" magazine can.

Alongside the scripts, interviews, and profiles, each issue of *Plays and Players* contains a number of features designed for the more practical use of its general readership—the theater-going public. These have typically included the "Playguide" (including recommendations of "The Best in Town" and the longest-running "Ten at the Top"), the list of forthcoming "First Nights" (with cast listings, opening date, director, and the address of the theater), "Playbills" ("casts and credits of first nights reviewed this month"), "Cues" ("new plays and casting" announcements), and reviews of theater-related books and records. The ongoing effort to balance the interests of the magazine's various constituencies (theatrical professionals, the literary avant-garde, and the general public seeking the occasional "good night out") has led to a series of adjustments in the amount and kind of coverage of "practical" ("consumer-oriented") concerns. Virtually every editor has changed the format and amount of space allotted to such matters. In the early 1970s, as many as five pages per issue were allocated to a thirty-three part series, "Quick Theatre Guides," which included not only seating charts for each major theater in London (and many of the regionals) but suggestions about nearby restaurants, advice on the availability of parking, assessments of the programs ("informative, repetitious and didactic . . . printed on quality paper and nicely planned'') and even reviews of the loos (''palatial and well maintained; acres of mirrors''). The series was abandoned in July 1972 when Peter Buckley became the magazine's editor.

In establishing itself as the foremost chronicler of contemporary drama, *Plays and Players* absorbed four other magazines: *Shows Illustrated*, *Play Pictorial*, *Theatre World*, and *Encore*. Publication of *Plays and Players* was itself suspended in June 1980 (27, no. 9) and resumed with a new publisher in October 1981. Though many of its features remain the same (and though Peter Roberts resumed the position of editor), the most notable change in the magazine's format is the discontinuation of its long-established practice of publishing the texts of new plays. Defending the new policy in response to a letter to the editor in the February 1984 issue, the editor, David Roper, explained that ''since it is now common for theatres to sell a playscript quite cheaply for their new productions (e.g., The Royal Court, the RSC) it seems pointless for *P&P* to try to compete'' (no. 365:5). With the relatively recent appearance of such series as Methuen's new paperback ''Theatrescripts,'' designed to close the gap between the production of a play and publication of its script, more new and innovative scripts will be more quickly available to theater-goers than ever before; yet it seems inevitable that such publications will reach a far narrower audience than the worldwide circulation of *Plays and Players* afforded and will be far less readily available in libraries and specialized collections.

In its new, leaner format, *Plays and Players* more nearly resembles *Drama*,* the quarterly publication of the British Theatre Association—though its coverage remains by far the most comprehensive of any magazine available today. Now entering its fourth decade of existence, *Plays and Players* remains a vital resource for anyone seriously interested in the contemporary English stage.

Note

1. This series later appeared (in a slightly expanded form) as *The Second Wave: British Drama of the Sixties* (London, 1971; repr. in paperback with a new bibliography in 1978). The book contains no acknowledgment of any kind that the contents first appeared in *Plays and Players*. In a review of it in the October 1971 issue, editor Peter Roberts complained that ''Methuen . . . are not above systematically blocking the magazine publication of scripts by young authors in these pages—contrary to the wishes of both author and agent . . . whilst happily grabbing a series from the magazine without so much as an acknowledgment'' (19, no. 1:18).

Information Sources

INDEXES

Annual indexes in the January issues of some years but not others; indexes refer to the previous calendar year, not to volume numbers (October through September).

REPRINT EDITIONS

None.

LOCATION SOURCES

American

Complete runs: Detroit Public Library; New York Public Library; Los Angeles Public Library; Stanford University Library; University of Alabama Library. Partial runs: Widely available.

British

Complete runs: Bodleian Library; British Museum; Liverpool Public Libraries; National Library of Scotland, Edinburgh; University of Cambridge Library. Partial runs: Widely available.

Publication History

MAGAZINE TITLE AND TITLE CHANGES

Plays and Players, 1953–1965. *Plays and Players, Incorporating Theatre World and Encore*, 1965–1980. *Plays and Players*, 1981–.

VOLUME AND ISSUE DATA

Volume 1, number 1–volume 27, number 9, numbers 1–321, October 1953–June 1980. Volume 29, number 1–, [number 337–,] October 1981–.

FREQUENCY OF PUBLICATION

Monthly.

PUBLISHERS

1953–1980: Hansom Books, Ltd., Buckingham Palace Road, London SW1. 1981–1982: Brevet Publishing Ltd., 2 Old Pye St., London SW1P 2LD. 1982–: Brevet Publishing, Ltd., 445 Brighton Road, South Croydon, Surrey CR2 6EU.

EDITORS

Ronald Barker, October 1953–October 1955. Frank Granville-Barker, November 1955–April 1962. Philip Roberts, May 1962–June 1972. Peter Buckley, July 1972–January 1973. Peter Ansorge, February 1973–January 1975. Michael Coveney, February 1975–June 1978. Simon Jones, July 1978–February 1979. Robin Bean, March 1979–June 1980. Peter Roberts, October 1981–November 1983. David Roper, December 1983–.

William Hutchings

PN REVIEW. See POETRY NATION

POETRY COMMONWEALTH

When Lionel Monteith founded *Poetry Commonwealth* in 1948, he was twenty-seven years old, a relatively young man with a decided interest in the spiritual side of life. That interest was to lead him, later, to read in divinity at the University of London, where he earned a degree in theology in 1957; and at New College, London, where in 1958 he was ordained. Subsequently, he studied psychotherapy with P. L. Backus and L. Haas and pursued, after that, a triple career—as man of letters, minister of religion, and psychotherapist. Since the

1970s, he has served as director of the Lincoln Memorial Clinic for Psychotherapy in London. Monteith's career is worthy of mention in relation to the history of *Poetry Commonwealth* if only because the direction his life took might well have been predicted from the contents of the little magazine to which he devoted his efforts after the war.

Although it purported to have the "simple aim" of providing British readers with "the best poetry currently written in the countries of the British Commonwealth," *Poetry Commonwealth* reflects a very strong editorial commitment to publishing poetry about inner states of being. The deeply disturbing ideological conflicts that swept the world in the 1930s and 1940s produced a strong reaction in Western philosophy and the arts: the radical subjectivity of existentialism. And traces of the existential attitude may be felt in most of the poetry in *Poetry Commonwealth*. If historical circumstances clearly contributed to the subjective orientation among Britons living in the Commonwealth after World War II, it was Lionel Monteith's special combination of interests—in literature, religion, and psychology—that endowed him with the sensitivity to recognize the trend and to value it sufficiently to bring it to the world's attention. Just so, *Poetry Commonwealth* represents, for the most part, the work of poets with Anglo-Saxon roots seeking to discover their authentic voices in lands remote from their ancestral homes and doing so at that very significant if often innominate moment in literary history, the period which immediately precedes the transforming discovery of a more comprehensive national consciousness.

While *Poetry Commonwealth* seems to reflect his particular sensibility, Monteith did not produce the magazine singlehandedly. He was in close communication with other avid readers of Commonwealth poetry—among them Howard Sergeant, Roy Macnab (from South Africa), T. Inglis Moore (Australia), Earle Birney (Canada), Louis Johnson (New Zealand), and Michael Redgrove, all of whom contributed editorially, in one way or another, to the venture. Indeed, Macnab, Birney, and Johnson are among the most distinguished poets of their respective countries and are still writing today. Howard Sergeant, the magazine's primary book reviewer, went on to distinguish himself among critics of Commonwealth poetry as the author of several critical studies and the editor of numerous excellent anthologies, some published only recently. In short, these contributors shared an important trait, their intimate awareness of white people's postcolonial frame of mind.

Even though the magazine ran for only three years and lasted but eight numbers, by the fourth issue Monteith could already boast that in its first year, "we have printed the work of nearly fifty poets—some of them the most outstanding in their own countries, others almost unknown" (no. 4:1). The first issue had just sixteen pages; by the fourth issue, the magazine was twenty pages long, the size it was to stay for the duration of its run. Despite its small size, *Poetry Commonwealth* fulfilled its primary purpose well: to be a "first step in promoting two-way exchange of ideas, and in developing a more intimate cultural relationship between the countries concerned" (no. 4:1). Contributions of a remarkably high quality came from Canada, Australia, New Zealand, South Africa, Ireland, and the United Kingdom. The first issue included an impressive sheaf of short works by eighteen poets, including Australians Judith Wright, Robert D. Fitzgerald, and Rosemary Dobson; Canadians Earle Birney, Dorothy Livesay, and P. K. Page; New Zealanders James K. Baxter, Kendrick Smythyman, and Hubert Witheford; and South Africans R. K. Cope, Annette Maxwell, and R. F. Tronson. Fortified by the success of the first folio, Monteith determined to devote a section of each subsequent issue to a group of poems by a single author, or to dedicate the major portion of the number to poems from a single country. Thus, numbers 2 and 7 feature poems by Judith Wright; numbers 4 and 5, poems by New Zealand poets Louis Johnson and Kendrick Smythyman, respectively; and number 6 showcases two new poems by Canadian poet Anne Wilkinson. In accord with the general plan, Roy Macnab served as guest editor for the third issue, a South African number; and, in the final issue, a special number compiled by Earle Birney, *Poetry Commonwealth* published fourteen exciting new poems by Canadians. After the first issue, too, Monteith incorporated a section of book reviews, which serve as excellent introductions to the volumes of verse and verse anthologies produced during that period, many of them published in the Dominions.

The poems in *Poetry Commonwealth* are as diverse as the personalities of the poets who composed them. But in comparison with Commonwealth poetry produced a generation later, the poems which Lionel Monteith selected for publication in *Poetry Commonwealth* evince a curious resemblance to each other and a distinct difference from the newer, emerging trend. The major characteristic of the poems in *Poetry Commonwealth* is their almost overcharged subjectivity, which contrasts markedly with the rich nationalistic and communal character of more recent poetry written by members of the indigenous populations. *Poetry Commonwealth* contains nothing like the poetry of the Ghanaian Kwesi Brew, which so often voices the feelings of a whole people. In fact, even local color, an important element in the colonial ballads that Rudyard Kipling and others made famous, is almost entirely missing from the soul-searching private meditations of the *Poetry Commonwealth* poems. Many of the poems are elaborate efforts to situate the speaker in a comfortable space or, failing that, to sublimate the reality of the actual places he inhabits by creating the verbal equivalent of a dream. Differences of expression aside, many of the poems in *Poetry Commonwealth* merely suggest the disturbing emotions which are their true subjects; they do not account historically for them. The net result of such a poetic procedure is to force the reader to attempt to solve the cultural riddles for himself. It would be far more productive to read *Poetry Commonwealth* as a gloss on W. H. Auden's *The Age of Anxiety*, which was published the same year the magazine was founded, than to read it as a gloss on events occurring in the British Dominions during that period; for although the poems are genuine and reflect the spirit of the age, they are set, by and large, in symbolic landscapes—not the real world of social and political struggles.

One comes away from *Poetry Commonwealth* feeling that he has been in the presence of a group of apocalyptic poets, sophisticated visionaries who have experienced private revelations of their tragic condition. The leader of the "New Apocalypse" movement himself, Henry Treece, is represented in two issues (no. 3:13 and no. 7:8–9), and one of Treece's henchmen, G. S. Fraser, appears in another (no. 2:8). The catchwords of the Apocalypse movement were myth, imagination, and liberation, but in *How I See Apocalypse*, Treece emphasized the most narrowly personal versions of these concepts. Like the poems in *The White Horseman*, an anthology that Treece compiled in 1941, the poems in *Poetry Commonwealth* are nearly always provocative psychologically and often sound religious. They are, even more obviously, almost entirely asocial and apolitical, not the sort of writing one would expect to get from some of the world's most racially troubled areas.

A salient feature of the articles and reviews published in *Poetry Commonwealth* is their common explanation for the somewhat bizarre mix of morality and eroticism that permeates the works of Dominion poets. Particular cases are too numerous and too redundant to cite, but what Louis Johnson said of his fellow poets in New Zealand he might as readily have said of white Commonwealth poets everywhere else: "There is an element of the displaced person in much of their work, whereas the earlier writers here had inherited the concept of colonizing small Britains all over the earth, and the Victorian belief in the divine right of the Englishman" (letter to the editor, no. 8:13).

It may well be that subscriptions to the magazine tailed off as readers began to see how insular were the poems it published. Despite his "most assiduous efforts" to keep the publication afloat, Monteith decided in the spring of 1951 that those efforts were not worthwhile. "The average response to our publicity activities in the past eighteen months has been about two and a half percent," he explained in his farewell editorial (no. 8:1). But he added, "We believe that poetry audiences are transferring their interest more and more from the written to the spoken word. At the branches of the British Poetry Association and at diverse other meetings scores of people have paid more than the price of a 'little review' to hear Commonwealth poetry read. We think this trend will continue." Monteith expected to carry on his work in behalf of Commonwealth poetry "in his capacity as Chairman of the Council of the British Poetry Association," but there is very little hard evidence that he actually did.

Much has transpired in Commonwealth literature since 1951. To gain an appreciation of just how much, one could hardly begin more pleasantly than by reading the six anthologies compiled by Howard Sergeant since 1967. They offer poems by hundreds of poets—among them Derek Walcott, Kwesi Brew, Gabriel Okara, Wole Soyinka, and A. K. Ramanujan—who, in recent years, have radically transformed the meaning of the phrase "Commonwealth poetry."

Information Sources

BIBLIOGRAPHY

Commire, Anne, ed. "Wright, Judith. 1915–." In *Something About the Author*. Volume 14. Detroit, 1978.

Miller, G. M., and Howard Sergeant. *A Critical Survey of South African Poetry in English*. Cape Town, 1957.

Sergeant, Howard, ed. *African Voices*. London, 1973.

———. *African Voices*. New ed. London, 1978.

———. *Commonwealth Poems of Today*. London, 1967.

———. *New Voices of the Commonwealth*. London, 1968.

———. *Poetry from Australia*. Pergamon Poets 6. Oxford, 1969.

INDEXES

    None.

REPRINT EDITIONS

    None.

LOCATION SOURCES

    American

        Complete runs: Harvard University Library; Northwestern University Library; University of California Library, Los Angeles; State University of New York Library, Buffalo.

        Partial runs: New York Public Library; Yale University Library.

    British

        Complete run: British Museum.

Publication History

MAGAZINE TITLE AND TITLE CHANGES

    Poetry Commonwealth.

VOLUME AND ISSUE DATA

    Numbers 1–8, Summer 1948–Spring 1951.

FREQUENCY OF PUBLICATION

    Quarterly, numbers 1–4. Biannually, numbers 5–8: 5 (Summer 1949), 6 (Winter 1949–1950), 7 (Summer 1950), 8 (Spring 1951).

PUBLISHER

    Lionel Monteith/*Poetry Commonwealth*. Number 1: 155, Croxted Road, West Dulwich, London, S.E. 21. Numbers 2–8: The College Press, 31, Dulwich Village, London, S.W. 21, England.

EDITOR

    Lionel Monteith.

R. Victoria Arana

POETRY (LONDON)

Poetry (London) was "started uncertainly" in 1939 by J. M. Tambimuttu and continued its erratic course until 1951.[1] Although Tambimuttu advertised *Poetry*

(London) as a bimonthly, between 1939 and 1943 only nine issues appeared; in 1944 issue 10 was a hardcover edition of 264 pages, a compendium of poetry and prose by everyone to whom Tambimuttu had promised publication. *Poetry (London)* then lapsed into silence for three years, reappearing in 1947 when its editor optimistically and somewhat disingenuously declared in his editorial that with this issue the magazine would "resume" its bimonthly publication. In fact, it continued as unpredictably as ever, with a further four issues to May 1949. In September of that year the sixteenth issue of the magazine appeared under the editorship of Nicholas Moore and Richard March, Tambimuttu having left England for America. The magazine then entered its only period of brief stability, operating as a quarterly until it finally succumbed to financial exigencies in the winter of 1951.

The pressures imposed by wartime economy undoubtedly contributed to the sporadic appearance of *Poetry (London)*, but Tambimuttu was not blameless in this regard. Although gifted with editorial and entrepreneurial flair, he possessed no great sense of urgency and contracted a "disease" against which he warned other writers: "Sohoitis." Robert Hewison has described this debilitating ailment, an overfondness for the ambience of Fitzrovia, that area on the fringes of Soho in and around Fitzroy Square where the literati met and drank during the war. "Tambi" was a regular presence here with his "entourage of males and females who journeyed with him," most of whom aspired to the publication of verse.[2] Despite, or perhaps because of, this lackadaisical attitude, *Poetry (London)* was undoubtedly the foremost periodical devoted solely to poetry in the 1940s. With a few notable exceptions—W. H. Auden, C. Day Lewis, Roy Fuller, and Charles Causley—most young poets appeared in its pages.

Catholicity was Tambimuttu's creed, pronounced at some length and occasional depth in the "Letters" that opened each number of the magazine. The "First Letter" comprised a series of aphorisms in which Tambimuttu expressed his all-encompassing, holistic view of poetry. "Every man," he declared, "has poetry within him. Poetry is the awareness of the mind to the universe. It embraces everything in the world." Poetry is also "religion," "a descent to the roots of life." The only anathema was "pure intellectualization," which should be subordinated to "Life, Being, Poetry." Tambimuttu's sensibility led him willingly to accept, even rejoice in, contradiction: "contrast . . . teaches us the nature of truth." The only indication that the editor would exercise any editorial discrimination was expressed in a typically equivocal manner: "No man is small enough to be neglected as a poet. Every healthy man is a full vessel, though vessels are of different sizes. In a poetry magazine we can only take account of those sizes of vessels which represent humanity as a whole" (no. 1:1–4). Some "vessels" were clearly to be neglected more than others.

Given such flouting of rationality and insistence on poetry as an ethereal abstraction, it is not difficult to see how *Poetry (London)* became identified with neo-Romanticism and its apotheosis in the 1940s, the Apocalypse movement. Derek Stanford notes that Tambimuttu's "Letters" in *Poetry (London)* "did more to popularise the New Romanticism than the critical and philosophical lucubrations of Henry Treece and J. F. Henry." Robert Hewison concurs:

> The Apocalyptics . . . carried out a remarkable putsch against the literary establishment. *New Writing*[*] held out, *Horizon*[*] stopped short at Dylan Thomas, George Barker, W. S. Graham and Norman Nicholson (these were Connolly's chosen 'new romantics' not Apocalyptics), but *Poetry (London)*, *Kingdom Come*,[*] *Now*,[*] *The Adelphi*,[*] and *Life and Letters Today* [see *Life and Letters*] all fell under the Neo-Romantic spell.[3]

Tambimuttu shared with the Apocalyptics certain beliefs: the origin of poetry in the irrational, the need in British culture for spontaneity and vitality, and the importance of transcendental, spiritual values. But he insisted that his editorial policy was to eschew all "movements," including the neo-Romantic. He reiterated in the second issue of *Poetry (London)* that the paper was a platform for those who wished to escape cliques and stated his belief in a catholicity which "was not a party and . . . has no policy" (no. 2:34). Other protestations of independence appeared in the ninth, tenth, and eleventh numbers. Tambimuttu regarded the distinction between classical and Romantic as a "rationalist conceit," categorically denied even the existence of a contemporary Romantic movement (no. 7:6), and later protested that *Poetry (London)* was not "intended as the organ of a new Romantic revival" (no. 11:8; no. 10:219).

Tambimuttu identified the direction of his magazine only by saying that he was sympathetic to the reaction against the "objective reportage" of the 1930s. He admitted that this "reaction" was to be seen within the pages of *Poetry (London)* but argued that it had taken place in the minds of the poets first; he was merely publishing what was being written (no. 6:164). Temperamentally and ideologically antipathetic to Geoffrey Grigson, editor of *New Verse*[*] and a major proponent of "objectivism," Tambimuttu defended Dylan Thomas against Grigson's venomous *New Verse* critique (no. 11:5–8). It is to Tambimuttu's credit that he printed Grigson's riposte, which among other barbs made mention of "that faith in muddle and contradiction which has made *Poetry (London)* the most foolish (if representative) periodical of its time" (no. 13:46).

A survey of the poetry in *Poetry (London)* reveals not only a consistently high quality of work, but a range of styles that belies endeavors to attach the magazine to any one particular school. In the first issue Tambimuttu asserted that he had tried to include every kind of poetry being written at the time, and a perusal of the contributors to this number shows that he largely succeeded. The Georgian interest was represented by Laurence Whistler, Walter De la Mare, Laurence Clark, and Audrey Beecham, while contributions from Stephen Spender, Louis MacNeice, and Gavin Ewart demonstrated Tambimuttu's openness toward contributors to Grigson's *New Verse*. George Barker and Dylan Thomas, who had resisted the dominant ethos of *New Verse* and thus called forth dismissive criticism from Grigson, also contributed, along with the Apocalyptics Henry Treece and Nicholas Moore. Lawrence Durrell, Herbert Read, and Keidrych Rhys also contributed poems.

Subsequent issues of *Poetry (London)*—at least until Nicholas Moore and Richard March assumed the editorship—maintained the standard and diversity of the opening number. Contributors included Audrey Beecham, Whistler, De la Mare, Clark, MacNeice, Spender, and Gavin Ewart. Other poets associated with *New Verse* in the 1930s were also published, Kenneth Allott and Charles Madge among them. George Barker published his "Six Poems from America," which included his tribute "To My Mother," and part of the distinguished "True Confession of George Barker." Dylan Thomas continued to benefit from Tambimuttu's editorial patronage, appearing regularly in the wartime issues of the magazine. David Gascoyne, Kathleen Raine, W. S. Graham, Anne Ridler, and David Wright, all of whom had in their different ways been in honorable opposition to Auden and his acolytes in the 1930s, found a regular outlet for their work in *Poetry (London)*. Other contributors included Robert Grecean, Michael Hamburger, Patrick Kavanagh, Alan Ross, Stevie Smith and R. S. Thomas, John Heath-Stubbs, Norman Nicholson, Vernon Watkins, Charles Williams, and Ronald Bottrall.

Another group of poets who found an English audience through the pages of *Poetry (London)* was that fascinating set of exiles who, through the exigencies of war, found themselves keeping company in Cairo and Alexandria. Some of these writers were civilians, others servicemen; some had committed themselves to living in exile before the war, others not. Together they comprised the most outstanding group of interacting talents to emerge in English letters during the war years. They produced their own magazines in the Middle East—*Oasis, Personal Landscape, Salamander*—and most of them also contributed to *Poetry (London)*: Lawrence Durrell, Keith Douglas, Bernard Spencer, G. S. Fraser, Ian Fletcher, John Waller, Dorian Cooke, Terence Tiller, Ruth Speirs, Hugh Gordon Porteus, and John Gawsworth (Terence Ian Fytton-Armstrong). Tambimuttu and John Waller were responsible for the first book publication of Douglas's poems, the majority of which had already appeared (many posthumously) in *Poetry (London)*. Of the other poems from the Middle East to be printed in the magazine, the translations from the Chinese by H. G. Porteus and Ruth Speirs's accomplished versions of Rainer Maria Rilke's *Duino Elegies* deserve particular mention.

Apart from Keith Douglas, several other poets in uniform were represented in *Poetry (London)*. Nine of Alun Lewis's poems grace the magazine, including "The Public Gardens," "To Edward Thomas," "Postscript for Gweno," and "In Hospital Poona." Alan Rook, who wrote three volumes of poetry dominated by his war experiences but whom the muse deserted after the war, contributed several poems, including the much-anthologized "Dunkirk Pier," "The Retreat," and "Lager." "Soldiers Bathing" by F. T. Prince, one of the finest war poems, was also first printed in *Poetry (London)*. Sidney Keyes, who was killed at the end of the North African campaign in 1943 and whose published work predates his battle experience, published four of his poems, including "Rome Remember" and "Seascape."

Complementing the impressive array of poetry were many critical reviews. Tambimuttu revealed his opposition to willfully destructive criticism of the kind that Grigson reveled in. Reviews by H. G. Porteus, G. S. Fraser, Francis Scarfe, Kathleen Raine, Terence Tiller, James Kirkup, and Stephen Spender upheld their editor's viewpoint, exhibiting a lively discrimination that, if sometimes tough, was never unfair. During the postwar years Fraser became increasingly well known for his critical writings, some of which he wrote for *Poetry (London)*; "Syntax and Imagery in Poetry," "Auden up to Date," and "Mr. Empson's Approach and Method" prefigure his reputation and amply repay today's reader. George Orwell, Kathleen Raine, and H. G. Porteus contributed useful essays on Eliot's *Four Quartets*, John Heath-Stubbs a lucid explanatory essay about challenging and idiosyncratic Charles Williams. David Gascoyne wrote about recent French poetry and translated Pierre Jean-Jouve's weighty essay, "The Unconscious: Spirituality: Catastrophe." Francis Scarfe and Herbert Read contributed "Letters" to complement those of Tambimuttu. Scarfe's was in the mold of his book *Auden and After* (1942), an intelligent piece upon the state of contemporary poetry, in which he cogently argued that every poet since the nineteenth century had been writing in the Romantic tradition. Read used his space to propagate the notions expressed most fully in *Poetry and Anarchism*. His arguments not unnaturally enjoyed a vogue in the 1940s, since they constituted a sophisticated attempt to reconcile the individualist artist with a progressive, collectivized economy. John Waller's "Biographical Introduction to the Collected Poems of Keith Douglas" provided the first invaluable account of that poet's life as well as an advertisement for the book itself.

Poetry (London) was enhanced by the work of several fine artists. Henry Moore provided the famous "Lyre Bird" painting that appeared on the covers of many issues; Graham Sutherland provided a "Lyre-Bird" cover. Some of Mervyn Peake's etchings for *The Ancient Mariner* appeared in *Poetry (London)* number 10, as did Gerald Wilde's interpretation of Eliot's "Rhapsody on a Windy Night." Ceri Richards provided small drawings depicting the comedy of manners, and John Caxton contributed several pieces heavily influenced by Picasso.

When Tambimuttu left England and *Poetry (London)* in 1949, the magazine lost much of its character and energy. How much of this was due to the loss of his talents and how much to the faintly *fin de siècle* air with which the decade closed is difficult to tell; certainly both were contributory. The new editors caught something of the mood of the time, wishing "to see poets turn their attention more to satirical verse, or occasional poems with a bite and an edge to them" (no. 17:4). But *Poetry (London)* took little part in the establishment of the new poetic fashion. "Movement" poets Donald Davie and Bernard Bergonzi appeared in the closing issues of the magazine, but most of the notable poetry was provided by older contributors. Although financial necessity brought about the demise of the magazine, its ending was peculiarly appropriate. *Poetry (London)* belonged to the 1940s, and neither Moore nor March had the editorial panache to carry the magazine into the fifties with any conviction.

Robert Hewison has written that the importance of *Poetry (London)* "was almost entirely accidental . . . . A gap had been left by the collapse of Geoffrey Grigson's *New Verse* and Julian Symons's *Twentieth Century Verse*[*]; the demand for poetry caused circulation to expand."[4] But the loss of competition and a boom in poetry do not and cannot explain the quality of the poetry published in *Poetry (London)*. Julian Symons describes the magazine as "a vast junk shop, or oriental bazaar, in which you may pick up among the curios—odd bargains, simple pots and genuine Birmingham brass." But Symons is describing the ambience created by Tambimuttu's editorial "Letters" rather than that created by the poetry he published.[5] While the magazine has never received the critical acclaim afforded Grigson's *New Verse*, its denigration owes more to a mistaken identification with the literary cliques and schools that Tambimuttu so determinedly and productively avoided than it does to an objective judgment of the poetry published in each issue. A belief in catholicity and a commitment to the value of minor poetry, together with Tambimuttu's ability to recognise a wide range of high-quality writing, made *Poetry (London)* a magazine which deserves fuller recognition than it has been afforded hitherto.

Notes

1. Robert Hewison, *Under Siege: Literary Life in London 1939–45* (London, 1977), p. 12.
2. Ibid., pp. 57–58.
3. Derek Stanford, *Inside the Forties* (London, 1977), pp. 154–55; Hewison, *Under Siege*, pp. 112–13. J. F. Hendry and Henry Treece brought the "Apocalypse" movement into being with their anthology of prose and verse, *The New Apocalpyse* (London, 1940). They went on to edit two further anthologies, *The White Horseman* (London, 1941) and *The Crown and the Sickle* (London, 1945).
4. Hewison, *Under Siege*, p. 99.
5. Julian Symons, *Notes from Another Country* (London, 1972), p. 65.

Information Sources

BIBLIOGRAPHY

Fletcher, Ian, and A. D. Caesar, eds. *White Light and Sand: An Exhibition of Poetry from the Middle–East, 1940–45*. Reading, Eng., 1981.
Hewison, Robert. *Under Siege: Literary Life in London 1939–45*. London, 1977.
Skelton, Robin. *Poetry of the Forties*. Harmondsworth, Eng., 1968.
Symons, Julian. *Notes from Another Country*. London, 1972.
Tambimuttu, J. M. *Out of This War*. London, 1942.

INDEXES

Numbers 1–2 in *An Author Index to Selected British Little Magazines*, ed. B. C. Bloomfield (London, 1976).

REPRINT EDITIONS
None.
LOCATION SOURCES
American
Complete runs: Harvard University Library; University of Buffalo Library; Yale
University Library.
Partial run: University of Michigan Library.
British
Complete run: British Library.
Partial runs: Birmingham Public Library; Cambridge University Library; Glouces-
ter City Library; Kensington Public Library; Leeds University Library; London
University Library; National Library of Scotland, Edinburgh.

Publication History

MAGAZINE TITLE AND TITLE CHANGES
Poetry (London).
VOLUME AND ISSUE DATA
Volume 1, numbers 1–6, February 1939–May/June 1941. Volume 2, numbers 7–
9, October/November 1942–1943. (Number 9 carries no date.) Volume 3, numbers
11–12, September/October–November/ December 1947. Volume 4, numbers 13–
16, June/July 1948–September 1949. Volume 5, numbers 17–21, January 1950–
February 1951. Volume 6, numbers 22–23, Summer–Winter 1951. The pagination
of the magazine is somewhat eccentric. No page numbers were printed on the
first two issues; issues 3–6 are paginated consecutively to the end of the volume;
volume 2 is paginated consecutively; each following issue is paginated individually.
FREQUENCY OF PUBLICATION
The magazine was advertised as a bimonthly, but it appeared at irregular intervals
until issue 17. Numbers 17–23 appeared quarterly.
PUBLISHERS
1939–1940 (numbers 1–2): J. M. Tambimuttu and Anthony Dickens, 64, Grafton
Way, London, W. 1. 1940–1951 (numbers 3–22): Nicholson and Watson/Editions
Poetry London (1940–1942: 25, Marchmont Street, London W. C. 1; 1942–1943:
Craven House, Kingsway, London, W. C. 2; 1943–1948: 26, Manchester Square,
London W. 1; 1948–1951: 55, Victoria Street, London S.W. 1). 1951 (number
23): Mandeville Publications, 45, Great Russell Street, London W.C. 1.
EDITORS
General editor, Anthony Dickens; literary editor, J. M. Tambimuttu, 1939–1940
(numbers 1–2). J. M. Tambimuttu, 1940–July 1949. Richard March and Nicholas
Moore, September 1949–1951.

A. D. Caesar

POETRY NATION

Poetry Nation began in 1973 as a hardbound biannual, edited at the English
Department of the University of Manchester by C. B. Cox and his younger

colleague, Michael Schmidt. Their intention was to serve Schmidt's generation the way that the *Critical Quarterly*,* also at Manchester, had served Cox's.[1] *Poetry Nation* ran six issues, into 1976, before expanding to a quarterly and then to a bimonthly publication, retitled *PN Review*. The first issue considered the potentially dissonant resonances of "nation": would this be the tribal drumbeat of British rustication, away from London's hegemony, or the authoritative voice of a BBC broadcast? Tracing the criticism of John Bayley, Donald Davie, and Terry Eagleton and the poetry of Charles Tomlinson, Geoffrey Hill, C. H. Sisson, and Philip Larkin, the editors found "a renewed popularity and practice of clearly formal writing, a common bridling at vacuous public and private rhetoric, and at the same time a refusal . . . to surrender catholicity" (*PN* no. 1:3–5).

Tomlinson's poem "The Way In" expressed editorial fears, with images of bulldozers gobbling up streets and a future already seething in the crevices: "a race in transit, a nomad hierarchy." In that first issue, Schmidt and Donald Davie discussed the "politics of form," partly in answer to a recent *Partisan Review* symposium. Terry Eagleton, in his sole appearance, wrote on Marxism and form, where literary form is a second-order structure of history's form.

Throughout its first six issues, *Poetry Nation* maintained its generous selection of contemporary poetry, offering at least twenty poets in each issue. Some of the many poets featured included Tomlinson, Davie, Douglas Dunn, Sisson, and Geoffrey Hill, as well as younger poets like Tom Paulin. The early issues also reviewed poetic theory and other magazines. A review in the second number argued that Donald Davie's "The Varsity Match" marked the limits of the *Review** and the Movement, whose style of judging poetry was "mostly *impatience*," full of such phrases as "One has to bear with," and "one gets slightly weary of " (*PN* 2:78; see also "Obituaries and Births," *PN* 3:44–48; "A Failed Humanism," *PN* 5:38–43). Although it changed title, editors, format, and frequency, these first six issues set the standard for the next nine years: a lively, pointed selection of poetry, and strong, skeptical reviews of recent publications in poetry and criticism.

In 1977, *Poetry Nation* became *PN Review*, changed its format to an oversized paperback quarterly, and added C. H. Sisson and Donald Davie as editors, with Schmidt as general editor. The greater size and frequency enabled the review to give the most sustained attention to British poetry; anyone considering British literary history of the 1970s and 1980s will have to consult virtually every issue of *PN Review*. In its enlarged format—including "News and Notes," reports of two months of awards, readings, publications, and deaths—editors and publishers were often asked to look back over the history of their work. John Cotton for example, wrote on the Priapus Press (*PNR* no. 21:8) and William Cookson on *Agenda** (*PNR* no. 18:6). Authors were encouraged to respond to reviews of their work. One controversial figure, Marjorie Perloff, was invited to review *British Poetry since 1970*, a critical survey by Peter Jones and Michael Schmidt of poets associated with *PN Review*. Their introduction quarreled with Perloff's distinction of "two poetries," American and British. Perloff argued that contemporary British poets had forsaken the monumental moderns and taken minor British poets as models. British critics simply reiterated unexamined positions held over from F. R. Leavis (*PNR* no. 19:47–51; cf. *PNR* nos. 20:6–8, 21:22–23). When Nicolas Tredell's "The Politicization of English" reviewed the influential *Re-Reading English*, he was answered in detail in numbers 38 and 40. The high energy of each issue's notes, letters, and reviews also allows risks for special issues: on Lionel Trilling (*PNR* no. 10), I. A. Richards (*PNR* no. 16), and, more daringly, Adrian Stokes (*PNR* no. 15) and Sylvia Townsend Warner (*PNR* no. 36).

In the 1980s *PN Review* attempted to remain the arbiter of taste in British poetry, carrying on vigorous debates between Sisson and Davie over such figures as John Ashbery and Yvor Winters (*PNR* nos. 7, 9, 15, 34).

Note

1. Michael Schmidt, *PN Review: Tenth Year Index* (London, 1982).

Information Sources

INDEXES
  PN Review: Tenth Year Index (London, 1982).
REPRINT EDITIONS
  None.
LOCATION SOURCES
  American
    Complete runs: Harvard University Library; Indiana University Library; Purdue University Library; University of California Library, Los Angeles.
    Partial runs: Widely available.
  British
    Complete runs: British Library; University of Aberdeen Library; University College Library, London.
    Partial runs: Widely available.

Publication History

MAGAZINE TITLE AND TITLE CHANGES
  Poetry Nation, 1973–1976. *PN Review*, 1977–.
VOLUME AND ISSUE DATA
  Poetry Nation, numbers 1–6, 1973–1976. *PN Review*, number 1, 1977–.
FREQUENCY OF PUBLICATION
  1973–1976: biannual; 1977–1981: quarterly; 1982–: bimonthly.
PUBLISHER
  Carcanet Press, Cheadle Hulme, Cheshire.

EDITORS
  Michael Schmidt, 1973–. C. B. Cox, 1973–1976. Donald Davie, 1977–1984.
  C. H. Sisson, 1977–1984.

W. A. Johnsen

POETRY QUARTERLY

Although *Poetry Quarterly* began life in 1933 as *Poetry Studies*, it was effectively a magazine of the 1940s. Launched (or relaunched) in 1939 by Katherine Hunter Coe, it had within a year come under the control of C. Wrey Gardiner and the Grey Walls Press of Essex, England, who saw it through the decade and beyond. The obvious comparison for *Poetry Quarterly* is with Tambimuttu's *Poetry (London)*,* also launched in 1939. Put starkly, the latter has a reputation as the vehicle for the New Apocalypse; the former has very little reputation at all. In fact, C. Wrey Gardiner was as keen to encourage new movements in poetry as was Tambimuttu, but his longer-running magazine includes an amount of safe, traditional poetry which seems to outweigh the progressive.

The first two volumes of *Poetry Quarterly* are composed mainly of verse rather than criticism. Posterity has not been kind to the poets represented there: Mabel Posegate, Doreen C. Watts, Bertram Day, Dulcie Warwick, and Vivan D'Wit are all now largely unknown. The initial tone, as set by their contributions, is rather smug and sanctimonious; and the small amount of critical writing of that period only substantiates that tone.

Gardiner did not recognize that World War II might affect or even prescribe one kind of poetic utterance. His editorial for the Spring 1940 issue affirmed that "the lyric muse has many voices when she speaks to the world" and that the task set the editor of a poetry magazine, that of "preventing all those voices from speaking at once," is an "unenviable" one (2, no. 1:3). Wishing to accommodate as many voices as possible, he set no limits on editorial choices. In the Winter 1940 issue he refused to put his literary journal to any political cause, reaffirmed the priority of poetry, and announced his intention "to continue our policy of making good writing the only rule for appearance in our pages" (2, no. 4:87).

Such eclecticism did not make an exciting poetry magazine, such as Geoffrey Grigson's *New Verse*,* for example. Nevertheless, the magazine did, especially with the adoption of its smaller format in the Spring 1942 issue, accommodate some distinctive voices of the time. To that issue Norman Nicholson contributed "Songs of the Island," and the New Apocalyptics G. S. Fraser, "Elegy for Certain Resolutions," and Henry Treece, "Ophelia." Nor were the voices always insular: subsequent issues published Wallace Stevens and Kenneth Rexroth, Paul Eluard and Louis Aragon. Indeed, so consistent was Gardiner's recognition of new, frequently neglected poetry that by the winter of 1943 he was having to defend himself from charges of exclusive modernity: "In spite of erroneous impressions to the contrary, we have never narrowed our appeal to one school, apocalyptic or other" (5, no. 4:123). One can see how such "impressions" arose by turning to an earlier editorial statement in the issue for Autumn 1942: "Neo-Romanticism and the Apocalyptics . . . are not afraid to show that they have feelings. They stand in absolute and irreconcilable contrast to the dessicated despair, dishonest niggling and brazen rather bawdy cynicism of the prewar decade" (4, no. 3:83).

In reacting against the 1930s, Gardiner was inevitably suggesting a sympathy with Tambimuttu's magazine. Both *Poetry Quarterly* and *Poetry (London)* show neo-Romantic tendencies and opposed the cleverness and political opportunism of the 1930s. Some of the critical articles included in *Poetry Quarterly*, in number increasing from 1943, were crucial to the Apocalypse: Margaret Crosland on Nicholas Moore, Moore himself on Dylan Thomas, Lionel Monteith on Howard Sargeant, Geoffrey Wagner on J. C. Hall. But Gardiner's magazine was more eclectic than Tambimuttu's. The same issue that included Nicholson, Fraser, and Treece also contained Diana Gardner's "My Heart Is Like a Little Pellet," a whimsical, unremarkable meditation which just happens to be in free verse and may have struck Gardiner as daring and modern. The neo-Romanticism of *Poetry Quarterly* is more diffuse than that of *Poetry (London)*.

Gardiner also appears less certain than Tambimuttu about the state of contemporary culture. Indicative of this uncertainty is an essay by Gardiner in the issue for Spring 1945. Noting the threat to poetic creativity posed by big business, Gardiner saw a conspiracy afoot in London to condemn poetry to obscurity. His defense, he asserted, would be to rely on what he vaguely calls "the devoted labour of the few"; he would not support or associate his magazine with any literary provocation or controversy. And Tambimuttu's magazine should appear "more frequently" but "less fantastically" (7, no. 1:3).

The lasting impression given by *Poetry Quarterly* is one of generalized Romanticism and open lyricism, rather than that of a forum for creative innovation and critical debate, in spite of the proportion of new poets it published. *Poetry Quarterly* reflected its age rather than shaped it. In the 1950s it began to flounder. In the last issue, for Spring-Summer 1953, Gardiner bewailed the "glib flatness" of up-and-coming English poets: "There have always been glib, flat poets but it is not necessary to encourage them" (14, no. 5:3). Clearly, Gardiner was referring to the rise of the Movement poets like Philip Larkin, Donald Davie, and John Wain. Dedicated to restraint, sensibleness, and exactitude, they discredited the neo-Romanticism of the forties. *Poetry Quarterly*, whatever else it might have tolerated, Gardiner seems here to say, could not and would not tolerate the Movement.

Information Sources

BIBLIOGRAPHY

Hoffman, Frederick J., Charles Allen, and Carolyn F. Ulrich. *The Little Magazine: A History and a Bibliography*. 2nd ed. Princeton, 1947.

Press, John. *A Map of Modern English Verse*. London, 1969.

Skelton, John. *Poetry of the Forties*. Harmondsworth, Eng., 1968.

Treece, Henry. *How I See Apocalypse*. London, 1946.

INDEXES

Volume 1, numbers 1–2 in *An Author Index to Selected British Little Magazines*, ed. B. C. Bloomfield (London, 1976). *Comprehensive Index to English Language Little Magazines 1890–1970*, series 1, ed. Marion Sader (Millwood, N.Y., 1976).

REPRINT EDITIONS

Kraus Reprint, Nendeln, Liechtenstein. Scholars' Facsimiles and Reprints, Delmar, N.Y.

LOCATION SOURCES

American

Complete runs: Brown University Library; Harvard University Library.

Partial runs: Cornell University Library; University of Buffalo Library.

British

Complete runs: British Museum; National Library of Scotland, Edinburgh; Trinity College Library, Dublin.

Publication History

MAGAZINE TITLE AND TITLE CHANGES

Poetry Quarterly.

VOLUME AND ISSUE DATA

Volume 1, number 1–volume 14, number 5, Summer 1939–Spring-Summer 1953.

FREQUENCY OF PUBLICATION

Quarterly.

PUBLISHERS

1939–1940: The Channing Press, Dawlish, Devon, England. 1940–1953: Grey Walls Press, Billericay, Essex (1940–1943); 4 Vernon Place (1943–1945); 7 Crown Passage, Pall Mall (1945–1953).

EDITORS

Katherine Hunter Coe, 1939–1940. C. Wrey Gardiner, 1940–1953.

Laurence Coupe

POETRY STUDIES. See POETRY QUARTERLY

POETRY WALES

In the 1967–1968 winter issue of *Poetry Wales* Meic Stephens, founder and editor, recounts the circumstances of the origin of the magazine three years before (3, no. 3). Stephens relates that when he was preparing the first number in early 1965 he had believed there were then about a dozen Anglo-Welsh poets all told; and, as a member of Plaid Cymru and committed to the nationalist cause, he had wanted "to satisfy a personal preoccupation with the psychology of English-speaking Welshmen, particularly the writers, by enquiring how much and what standard of verse was being written in English about Wales." Of course, he also thought that there was a need for this kind of journal because *Wales** had folded and the recently begun *Welsh Outlook* was experiencing financial difficulties; he knew that the *London Welshman* was based in England and for some reason thought the *Anglo-Welsh Review** was headquartered there as well. Moreover, during the time he was reading the proofs for his first number he also read a lecture by Gwyn Jones that included a call for some enterprising Welshman to create a journal as a vehicle for the young writers of Wales. The times seemed to be falling happily in with his own interests and to be perfect for launching *Poetry Wales*.

By the end of its second year, the magazine had 100 subscribers, financial support from the Welsh Committee of the Arts Council, and abundant submissions. Anglo-Welsh poets now seemed "as numerous as blackberries in the woods." Stephens had found, however, a group of regular contributors to rely on for each issue, occasionally adding a new writer or two. Among his regulars were old friends and acquaintances and writers who had given him encouragement, all staunchly nationalist though not necessarily Plaid Cymru. Stephens wanted *Poetry Wales* to be a nationalist publication; he believed "political questions must be asked in any consideration of Anglo-Welsh verse these days." To his readers, therefore, some of whom were probably aspiring contributors, the same names seemed to appear in every issue: Harri Webb, Gerald Morgan, Roland Mathias, Raymond Garlick, Vernon Watkins, and later, when the office was moved to Cardiff, John Stuart Williams, Cyril Hodges, and Herbert Williams. Poems and encouragement had come from London from John Tripp, Sally Roberts, Leslie Norris, Tom Earley, Robert Morgan, and Bryn Griffiths, chairman of the Guild of Welsh Writers. Other writers whose work readers saw frequently were Alison J. Bielski, Bruton Connors, Anthony Conran, Aneirin Talfan Davies, Richard Evans, Peter Gruffydd, Bobi Jones, John Idris Jones, Robert Nye, John Ormond, Douglas Phillips, Peter Preece, Alun Rees, and R. S. Thomas. Stephens also printed much of his own material.

Complaints of this practice may have accumulated in the normal course of affairs, but not until the Autumn 1972 number did anyone respond. In that issue (8, no. 2) review editor Sam Adams, who wrote editorials now and then, was moved to mock the accusations: "It is a magazine for a 'clique' [and publishes] the editors' friends, the Anglo-Welsh Establishment . . . members of Plaid Cymru or the Welsh Council, Calvinistic Methodists or left-handed academics with aunties in the BBC, and so on *ad absurdum*." Adams assumes these objections have come from disgruntled poets whose work *Poetry Wales* had rejected. He goes on to justify printing the same poets again and again by quoting the magazine's credo published in the third number (2, no. 1) in 1966, which said, "Our business is to publish the best available poems by young men and women who are writing now, in and about Wales." Youth, of course, is a relative term; in 1972 Raymond Garlick was forty-six, John Ormond was forty-nine, and R. S. Thomas was fifty-nine. To an aspiring poet of twenty all these would seem old codgers of a previous generation. Adams continues his explanation: "Of all the poems submitted to *Poetry Wales* it is generally the work of these poets which seems . . . *the most accomplished in literary terms*." Whether the editors had a guilty conscience or not, the number in which this editorial appeared was a special issue devoted to the work of new or young poets, only four of whom the editors claimed to know personally.

Despite some truth to the charge of catering to a clique, *Poetry Wales* almost always includes at least one young poet in an issue and always prints a few poems in Welsh. It usually lives up to its title and emphasizes poems over articles about poems. Anyone looking at the early numbers of the magazine will find in its fifty or sixty pages an average of twenty-five pages devoted to poems. The third number (2, no. 1), for example—along with reviews by John Stuart Williams and Meic Stephens, a five-page article by Peter Gruffydd on R. S. Thomas, a four-page article by Aneirin Talfan Davies on David Jones, and a somewhat longer article by Gerallt Jones on Welsh literature in the twentieth century—has poems by sixteen poets. Poems held center stage in that issue and continue to be the magazine's reason for existence.

In its early issues the magazine also lives up to its title by restricting itself to Welsh subjects and concerns, a mixed blessing occasionally, when its editorials sound a bit shrill over some discernible failure of the nationalist movement. The editors are indeed concerned about the usefulness and meaning of the term "Anglo-Welsh" and, of course, about the political status of Wales as a nation. When they respond in their editorials to the political scene with name-calling and ridicule, and to minor skirmishes about whether the Anglo-Welsh are really Welsh with elaborate defenses, they may exasperate the seeker of good poems and interpretive essays; but by and large they are faithful to the mission they have assigned themselves of producing a journal that can help the Welsh people to a sense of what it means to be Welsh.

Meic Stephens returned as editor in 1969 for the spring issue when Gerald Morgan resigned because of "the pressure of his duties as headmaster of a large comprehensive school." In his first editorial he summarized developments in Anglo-Welsh literature during 1968 (4, no. 3). He listed volumes of verse by R. S. Thomas, Vernon Watkins, and Raymond Garlick; books on Anglo-Welsh literature, such as *The Dragon Has Two Tongues* by Glyn Jones and *This World of Wales* by Gerald Morgan; and a series of BBC programs entitled *The First Fifty Years*. Subsequently, Stephens continued his previous editorial policies, mildly militant, strongly nationalistic, and staunchly faithful to his regular contributors. In an editorial protesting the middle age of Anglo-Welsh poets (7, no. 1), he told younger poets, "Don't despair but go on writing." He maintained his practice of printing twenty-five or so pages of poetry each issue and began a series of special issues to appear approximately every other number. In the magazine's twenty-first number Stephens supplied more statistics. *Poetry Wales*, he said, had published 550 poems by 130 poets (thirty-five of them Welsh-language poets) and had reviewed 148 books. He included a checklist of all the poets printed in the twenty-one numbers, among whose names are those of Dannie Abse, Robert Graves, and Vernon Watkins (7, no. 3). Notable special issues during Stephens's editorship are those on R. S. Thomas (7, no. 4), new poets (8, no. 2), David Jones (8, no. 3), and Dafydd ap Gwilym (8, no. 4). In this last special number Stephens announced his resignation and Sam Adams as his successor.

When Sam Adams took his seat in the editor's chair in 1973 he promised that there would be no changes other than superficial ones. The magazine would begin a regular series of side-by-side translations of Welsh poems with Gilbert Ruddock of University College, Cardiff, as translator. But he perhaps inadvertently opened the magazine's editorial policy to further change when he expanded the review section to include non-Welsh books. Otherwise he kept his promise. His second issue was a special number on Dylan Thomas, his third on Sir T. H. Parry Williams (in which Cary Archard became review editor), and his fifth on Alun Lewis. Adams's last issue (10, no. 4) announced that the new editor would be J. P. Ward. Cary Archard stayed on to edit the reviews.

Ward made no mention of change, but his Summer 1975 issue (11, no. 1) included poems by Seamus Heaney, Alastair MacLean, and an American, Ellen Levine. From this time the magazine published more and more work by writers outside Wales (Roy Fisher and C. H. Sisson, for example); and on what had been a controversial matter, the meaning of the term "Anglo-Welsh," Ward commented, "Why not just write it, not define it?" Indeed, in his Summer 1977 issue (13, no. 1) he implies that the controversy is over, saying that "the sense of identity sought a decade back is now adequate" and poets can take risks without thinking they will weaken "any tradition of Welsh poetry in English." This issue also began a practice of printing more poems by fewer poets. During his editorship Ward brought out special numbers on Henry Vaughan (11, no. 2), poetry and translation (11, no. 3), poetry and education (12, no. 2), Vernon Watkins (12, no. 4), Edward Thomas (13, no. 4), Welsh traditional forms (14, no. 1), and critical issues (15, nos. 2 and 3). In two of his regular numbers he printed special sections on Dannie Abse (13, no. 2) and a United States miscellany (14, no. 3). Ward's last issue (16, no. 1) has Cary Archard as coeditor, and together they make an interesting comment to justify Ward's expansion policy. In their editorial they say that *Poetry Wales*'s main concern is with Welsh poets, "poets living and writing in Wales," but as part of an educative purpose they must publish non-Welsh poets as well. Subsequently, Cary Archard became sole editor.

Highlights of *Poetry Wales* under the editorship of Archard include a special feature on John Ormond (16, no. 2), a special Idris Davies number (16, no. 4), a special feature on the achievement of David Jones (17, no. 4), a W. H. Davies number (18, no. 2), and a special feature on James Kitchener Davies (17, no. 3), who wrote a verse drama in Welsh, *Meini Gwagedd*, which Pennar Davies argues is greater than *Under Milk Wood* and which Ioan Williams thinks is superior to any of the plays by T. S. Eliot.

Thus, despite the opening of its pages to non-Welsh concerns, *Poetry Wales*, as its title promises, continues its emphasis on poetry and Wales.

Information Sources

INDEXES
> None.

REPRINT EDITIONS
> None.

LOCATION SOURCES
> *American*
>> Complete runs: Harvard University Library; Russell Sage College Library (Troy, N.Y.); U.S. Library of Congress.
>> Partial runs: Northwestern University Library; University of California Library, San Diego; University of Colorado Library; University of Michigan Library.
>
> *British*
>> Complete runs: National Library of Scotland, Edinburgh; University College of Swansea Library.
>> Partial runs: University College Library, London; University of Manchester Library.

Publication History

MAGAZINE TITLE AND TITLE CHANGES
> *Poetry Wales*.

VOLUME AND ISSUE DATA
> Volume 1, number 1–, April 1965–.

FREQUENCY OF PUBLICATION
> Quarterly, but occasionally fewer issues in a year.

PUBLISHERS
> 1965–1968: Triskell Press. 1968–1980: Christopher Davies Ltd. 1980–: Poetry Wales Press, 56 Parcau Avenue, Bridgend, Mid-Glamorgan.

EDITORS
> Meic Stephens, 1965–1967. Gerald Morgan, 1967–1968. Meic Stephens, 1969–1973. Sam Adams, 1973–1975. J. P. Ward, 1975–1980. Cary Archard and J. P. Ward, 1980 (for one issue). Cary Archard, 1980–.

Martin E. Gingerich

POOR. OLD. TIRED. HORSE.

Poor. Old. Tired. Horse. is one of "the short lived periodicals" that the Scottish Renaissance "has run from time in the face of opposition from all the forces of reaction.''[1] A poetry magazine published in Scotland, it appeared irregularly from 1961–1962 to 1967; its twenty-five numbers contribute a sense of playfulness, internationalism, and graphic experiment to modern world poetry. The title itself is a poem made from four separate words, exemplifying the editors' aesthetic and showing their debt to Louis Zukofsky, the Brooklyn poet-critic, and Eugen Gomringer, the Swiss concrete poet. Zukofsky, in his essay ''An Objective (1931),'' asserts that ''each word in itself is an arrangement'' and that poetry involves ''the isolation of each noun so that in itself it is an image, the grouping of nouns so that they partake of the quality of things being together without violence to their individual, intact, natures.''[2] Gomringer introduced the idea of the ''constellation, the word group which replaces the verse. Instead of syntax it is sufficient to allow two, three or more words to achieve their full effect.''[3] These experimental ideas helped the editors in their selection of poems and also in the design of the magazine.

The first issue shows its playfulness. Featured on the front page is a humorous poem in Scots' Gaelic and an Edwin Morgan translation of a poem by Fyodor Tyutchev, a nineteenth-century Russian poet. Above the poems, two editors' names are listed, those of J. McGuffie and P. Pond, which never appear again. There is no editorial comment except for Augusto de Campos's introduction to Edgard Braga's concrete poetry in number 21. Ian Hamilton Finlay, the most active contributor, is generally considered to be the editor and publisher.

As the issues follow in succession, there emerges a growing sense of design that includes both poetry and graphics. While the earlier issues simply printed poems, later ones began to explore the relations of the words to the typography and graphics, and tended to develop each issue as a unified work of art. Number 8 gave homage to modern Russian writers and artists, with translations by Edwin Morgan of Iurĭ Ivanovich Pankratov's ''Slow Song'' and Andrei Voznesensky's ''Parabolic Ballad.'' J. F. Hendry translated Velimir Khlebnikov's ''From a Zoological Garden'' and a poem by Aleksandr Tvardovsky. It was decorated by drawings by Vladimir Mayakovsky with layout by El Lissitsky. Number 9 was half filled with the ''Sports & Divertissements'' of Ronald Johnson of the United States, explained as ''Eric Satie's notes to the music,'' and ''Autumn,'' a poetry sequence by American Lorine Niedecker. Number 10, a ''Concrete Number,'' featured the drawings of Robert Frame and included ''the port'' by Robert Lax. The next one, the ''lollipop number,'' kept its high spirits through John Picking's graphics and Edwin Morgan's translation of Guillaume Apollinaire's *Bestiary*. For number 12, on the ''Optical-Concrete,'' the designs of Jeffrey Steele highlighted the work of Ernst Jandl of Austria in ''schützengraben [trenches]'' and Mary Ellen Solt's ''E PLURIBUS UNUM.''

By number 14, the ''Visual-Semiotic'' issue, the poems of Mary Ellen Solt, Heinz Gappmayr, John Furnival, Finlay, and Pedro Xiste explored concrete forms. The theme of number 15 was the seacoast; it featured work under the categories of ''Boats, Shores, Tides, Fish.'' Sketches by Margot Sandeman illuminated the poems of George Mackay Brown, Eli Siegel, Hamish Maclaren, and Ted Enslin. Finlay and Morgan used the names and numbers of fishing trawlers as found objects. Number 17 combined a concrete style poem by Robert Lax with graphics by Emil Antonucci. Lax's poem arranges nouns vertically, one under the other as "the stone/ the vine// the water/ the sun." The eighteenth issue combines drawings by Bridget Riley and Ad Reinhardt with a text stating that only one art can exist. Number 19 unites the concrete poems of Ronald Johnson with the artwork of Furnival to create the sculptured letters in a sequence called "Io and the Ox Eye Daisy," while number 20 is entirely Finlay's experiment with constellations of words in "the tug, the water, the sky," interacting with the drawings of Peter Lyle.

Brazilian concrete poetry is the subject for issue 21, in which Augusto de Campos introduces the work of his fellow Brazilian artist, Edgard Braga: "In these 'tactilograms' Dr. Braga develops a sort of ideographic handwriting where letters and drawings inter-relate into a gestation of form which has something to do with his professional activity as a surgeon" (p. 2). Number 22, entitled "Charles Biederman: An Art Credo," combines photos with his poem beginning "art is an evolution of vision." Photos and typography are by Philip Steadman. Number 23 lightly plays with the theme of teapots. Furnival's designs are mixed with poems by Enslin, Finlay, Eli Siegel, and Gael Turnbull. The next issue offers a photo essay on "Concrete Poetry at the Brighton ('67) Festival." The last number, on "One Word Poems," with design and calligraphy by Jim Nicholson, brings back many writers previously published, including Edwin Morgan, Siegel, Jerome Rothenberg, and Xiste, and adds such new ones as Dick Sheeler and Aram Saroyan of the United States and Astrid Gillis of Scotland.

Finlay published the work of over 130 writers and artists, including Zukofsky and Gomringer. Aside from Finlay's own work, the most frequently published were the poetry and translations of Edwin Morgan (Scotland), with 26; Ronald Johnson, 18; Anselm Hollo (Finland), 16; George Mackay Brown (Scotland), 12; and Apollinaire, 7. There were six each by J. F. Hendry (Scotland), Rothenberg and Eli Siegel (United States). Ernst Jandl contributed five, and there were four each from Spike Hawkins and Libby Houston of England and the Russians Voznesensky and Mayakovsky.

While *Poor. Old. Tired. Horse.* influenced the international poetry scene, it was generally attacked or ignored in Scotland. Even Duncan Glen, editor of the well-known poetry magazine *Akros,** writes benevolently in 1966 of "the passingly interesting lively 'visual' work of Mr Finlay, but although no one could be as bravely exposed as Finlay, I see no future for these adventurous games."[4] He admits, however, that *Poor. Old. Tired. Horse.* was the only poetry magazine actually being published in Scotland at that time. Less restrained was the well-known poet Norman MacCaig, who stated in 1968 that "Concrete is unspeakable."[5] Two years later, however, he and Alexander Scott, in the introduction to their anthology *Contemporary Scottish Verse 1959–1969*, acknowledged that "the Scots . . . have produced in Morgan and Ian Hamilton Finlay two of the more noteworthy of the concretists."[6]

Internationally, *Poor. Old. Tired. Horse.* succeeded in introducing many new poets as well as providing a medium for Finlay's experiments. M. L. Rosenthal praises Finlay's success in spreading the recognition of the international concretist movement. Rosenthal's first impression of Finlay's work is of "trivial though charming playfulness, or a type of harmless madness, compulsive, repetitive." Yet there is an order here: since ordinary syntax is rejected, "the words must be allowed to determine their own small but intense and tightly bound system of relationship." These free words have the ability to suggest the real world.[7] Fergus Dunn finds that "characteristically in Finlay's work, words form and distill things in the world; thus defined, things exist in terms of each other. The words, as objects of meditation on the page or standing on a hillside, begin to yield the tension and attraction between such things. By taking poems into the garden and the landscape, Finlay is completing the logic of the poems."[8] The best explanation of Finlay's work and affirmation for his magazine was provided by Edwin Morgan, who explained that Finlay was carefully searching for a new lyricism, "basically verbal," that would take into account constructivist aesthetic and developments in the visual arts: "If Scotland seems traditionally cast as Kokoschka country, there is surely reason to welcome a touch of Mondrian."[9]

Notes

1. Hugh MacDiarmid, "Scottish Poetry 1923–1953," *Lines Review* 5 (June 1954):15. (I am grateful to the Humanities Research Center, Austin, Texas, for access to this review.)

2. Louis Zukovsky, *Prepositions* (London, 1967), p. 21. (I am grateful to Serge Brethé, New Sorbonne, for this information.)

3. "Eugen Gomringer," in *An Anthology of Concrete Poetry*, ed. Emmet Williams (New York, 1967), n.p.

4. "Scottish Poetry Now," *Akros* 1, no. 3 (August 1966): 27ff.

5. Quoted by Alexander Scott, "Scottish Poetry in 1968," *Studies in Scottish Literature* 6, no. 4 (1969):202.

6. Norman MacCaig and Alexander Scott, eds., *Contemporary Scottish Verse 1959–1969* (London, 1970), p. 21.

7. M. L. Rosenthal, *The New Poets: American and British Poets since World War II* (New York, 1967), pp. 195ff.

8. Fergus Dunn, in *Scottish International* (1968), p. 58.

9. Edwin Morgan, "Scottish Poetry of the 1960s," in *British Poetry since 1960: A Critical Survey*, ed. Michael Schmidt and Grevel Lindop (Oxford, 1972), p. 138.

Information Sources

BIBLIOGRAPHY

Morgan, Edwin. "Scottish Poetry of the 1960s." In *British Poetry since 1960: A Critical Survey*. Edited by Michael Schmidt and Grevel Lindop. Oxford, 1972.

Rosenthal, M. L. *The New Poets: American and British Poets since World War II*. New York, 1967.

Tait, James. "The Wild Hawthorne Press." *Scottish International Review*, no. 5 (1969):64–67.

Williams, Emmet, ed. *An Anthology of Concrete Poetry*. New York, 1967.

INDEXES

Comprehensive Index to English Language Little Magazines 1890–1970, series 1, ed. Marion Sader (Millwood, N.Y., 1976).

REPRINT EDITIONS

Microform: AMS Press, New York. New York Public Library.

LOCATION SOURCES

American

Complete runs: New York Public Library; Northwestern University General Library; Stanford University Libraries; State University of New York at Buffalo, Poetry Collection; University of California at Berkeley, Bancroft Library; University of Texas at Austin, Humanities Research Center.

Partial run: Ohio State University Library.

British

Complete runs: Bodleian Library; National Library of Scotland, Edinburgh.

Partial run: University College Library, London.

Publication History

MAGAZINE TITLE AND TITLE CHANGES

POOR. OLD. TIRED. HORSE., volumes 1–16, 21. P.O.T.H., volumes 17–19. POOR. OLD. TIRED. HORSE. POTH2O, volume 20. POTH 22, volume 22. teapoth 23, volume 23. Poor Old Tired Horse 24, volume 24. POOR OLD TIRED HORSE, volume 25.

VOLUME AND ISSUE DATA

Volumes 1–25, issues undated, 1961–1962 to end of 1967.

FREQUENCY OF PUBLICATION

Announced monthly, but irregular.

PUBLISHER

Ian Hamilton Finlay, Wild Hawthorne Press. Volumes 1–14: 24 Fettes Row, Edinburgh. Volumes 15–18: Gledfield Farmhouse, Ardgay, Ross-shire. Volume 19: Coaltown of Callange, Ceres, Fife. Volume 20: Coaltown of Callange, Ceres, by Cupar Fife. Volumes 21–25: Stonypath, Dunsyre, Lanark.

EDITORS

J. McGuffie and P. Pond, volume 1. Ian Hamilton Finlay, volumes 2–25.

Thomas J. Kenny

PRIAPUS

The small magazine *Priapus* was started in the winter of 1962 in Southall (then Middlesex) by John Cotton and Ted Walker, the first number appearing in August of that year and the twenty-second and last appearing in the winter of 1971. In the farewell issue, John Cotton, the editor and publisher, stated proudly that the magazine had maintained its independence for just short of ten years by refusing outside financial support, and went on to say:

> We began at a time when Al Alvarez's Penguin "The New Poetry" announced its attack on the "gentility principle." It seems apt to end at a time when that principle seems to have reasserted itself in a new romanticism—a new sentimentalism even—if, indeed, it had ever been overcome.

He then cited examples of this decline in the revised edition of *New Poetry** itself. Although *Priapus* published many types of poems on a wide range of subjects, there seems to have been a continuing effort to avoid anything ordinary or hackneyed. This search for the new and fresh sometimes resulted in uneven quality.

Although it gave most of its space to poems, *Priapus* regularly included book notices and a review section entitled "New Poetry." There were occasional prose selections, such as excerpts from a forthcoming biography of Tom Deakin or the script of a BBC interview by George Macbeth with the octogenarian clergyman-poet Andrew Young, selections from whose book of prose nature descriptions, *The New Poly Olbion*, appeared in *Priapus* number 4. Each issue ordinarily contained a number of woodcut illustrations by Oscar Mellor, Rigby Graham, Heinke Jenkins, or Richard Hearsey. Although the quality of the artwork was not as fine as that in Rigby Graham's short-lived magazine *Enigma*, it was of sufficient quality to bring praise from Derwent May in the *Times Literary Supplement*.[1] There were some special issues, such as the one devoted entirely to the poetry of John Cotton and the "linographics" of Heinke Jenkins (no. 17), the Oxford poetry issue (no. 10), or the supplement to Autumn 1966 (no. 6), an anthology of the recent Fantasy Press poems edited by Oscar Mellor and including Thom Gunn, Kingsley Amis, Philip Larkin, and other writers of the Movement. One number was devoted entirely to translations of poetry (no. 6).

In an early number John Cotton announced that *Priapus* would publish some of the best modern poetry and would not become a critical review. However, having apparently received some strong letters of protest and realizing that an indication of critical principles would be inevitable in the "New Poetry" section, he retracted the earlier statement and acknowledged that certain critical principles would emerge. For example, in a review of Ted Walker's *Fox on a Barn Door* he favorably noted the influence of Ted Hughes's unsentimental nature poetry (no. 4), and he later invoked Matthew Arnold's touchstones principle when he cited the poems of Norman Jackson as examples of the magazine's standards (no. 6). He praised Andrew Young's poems for clear observation and lucidity of expression (no. 9), and he gave a mixed review to Gary Snyder's *The Back Country* and *Six Sections from Mountains and Rivers*, praising those poems in the books that capture sense experience in relaxed, conversational language (no. 14). In a study of the poems of Leslie Norris in a double issue, Ted Walker praised Norris for precision and accuracy of observation (no. 11-12). Repeatedly,

Cotton stated that the magazine published poetry that said something and that what it said ought to mean something. There seems, then, to have been a heavy emphasis on lucid and accurate description, a sense of the importance of direct engagement with experience.

Ted Hughes's *Wodwo* and *Crow* were given very favorable reviews, and a large number of poems published in *Priapus* were nature poems in the mode of Hughes. For instance, a poem by Paddy Webb (no. 6) is a very unsentimental description of a dead skate on the beach. The realism in these poems is sometimes stridently harsh. As Derwent May pointed out in the *Times Literary Supplement* review, *Priapus* seemed to be catholic in its taste for poems, but it is possible to group the poems published in the magazine into categories. A number of poems give a wry or ironic treatment to traditional mythological or historical subjects, such as Roy Bennett's "Xanthippe" (no. 13) or the dramatic monologue by Jesus's disgruntled illegitimate son in B. S. Johnson's "The Son of Jesus" (no. 16). There are several science fiction poems by D. M. Thomas and John Cotton, a few war protest poems, and a number of poems dealing very realistically with sex, such as "Lay-By" by John Mole, about the discomforts of sex in the back seat of an automobile (no. 13). "Ballsgame," a satire on a ruthless businessman by Peter Cundall, is typical of the magazine's tone of hostility toward conventionality (no. 13). The criterion consistently applied seems to have been the search for work that was fresh and authentic, even if it was in traditional forms or on traditional subjects. In one of the few really unfavorable reviews, John Fuller's *The Tree That Walked* and Thom Gunn's *Touch* were criticized as being largely a repetition of Movement verse of the 1950s (no. 13). Penelope Shuttle's early comment on *Priapus* remained more or less accurate throughout its lifetime: "It is reminiscent of the poems found in *Poetry and Audience*, the Leeds University magazine. Many of the poems deal with the physical world, with weather, landscapes and seascapes which are compared to either the world of humanity or the personal intricate world of the poet."[2]

A number of writers who published work in *Priapus* appeared in the Penguin Modern Poets series of the 1960s: Edward Lucie-Smith, D. M. Thomas, George Macbeth, and Kingsley Amis. Frequent contributors, in addition to Lucie-Smith and Thomas, included Leslie Norris, Ted Walker, Paddy Webb, Norman Jackson, Philip Hobsbaum, and Alan Golightly. Paddy Webb, Ted Walker, and John Cotton also appeared in the P.E.N. anthology *New Poems, 1965*.

Announcing the demise of *Priapus* in number 22, John Cotton stated that he preferred to end the magazine rather than let it die a lingering death. For just under ten years, *Priapus*, with its inexpensive mimeographed duplication and a circulation of only 360 in 1969, had been a vehicle for the publication of a wide range of poems by new or recently discovered poets. But with the discontinuation of the Penguin Modern Poets series in 1970 and the retreat into sentimentality that Cotton detected, the magazine no longer seemed necessary and therefore was allowed to die with dignity.

Notes

1. *Times Literary Supplement*, January 1968, cited in *Priapus* 11 and 14.
2. *Aylesford Review* (Winter 1964/1965), quoted in *Priapus* 4.

Information Sources

INDEXES
   None.
REPRINT EDITIONS
   None.
LOCATION SOURCES
   Complete runs: Cornell University; Harvard University.
   Partial runs: Arizona State University; Duke University; Northwestern University; San Francisco Public Library; U.S. Library of Congress; University of California, Berkeley; University of California, Santa Barbara; University of Pittsburgh.
   British
   Complete run: University College, London.

Publication History

MAGAZINE TITLE AND TITLE CHANGES
   Priapus.
VOLUME AND ISSUE DATA
   Volume 1, numbers 1–22, Autumn 1962–Winter 1971.
FREQUENCY OF PUBLICATION
   Usually three times a year, but irregular.
PUBLISHER
   John Cotton.
EDITOR
   John Cotton.

Terence L. Grimes

PURPOSE

Purpose was created in 1929 by a group of London writers who perceived important philosophical connections between two theoretical systems that had emerged during the first two decades of this century. These two systems derived from two men who probably never met, who were of different nationalities and social milieux, and whose interests were to lead them into very different arenas of personal endeavor. One was the Austrian psychologist Alfred Adler and the other was the originator of Social Credit, C. H. Douglas. Though *Purpose* appeared only during the twelve years preceding the outbreak of World War II, the story of its intellectual and journalistic antecedents begins in the last years of the nineteenth century, and its publication history stands as a curious document on the interplay of politics and literature during the 1930s.

Purpose was created as an avowed replacement of *Focus*, a magazine founded in the mid-1920s to further a number of causes, including the nature movement, and to oppose a number of others, including capitalistic economics.[1] Before its cessation in 1928, *Focus* had published a series of articles advocating Social Credit, a monetary system which opposed capitalistic supply and demand and favored instead a government-controlled economy and clearly established profit levels and guaranteed subsidies, particularly for consumers. *Purpose* was also closely allied to another magazine, the *New Age** (see *VEA*), which began publication in the late nineteenth century as an anti-imperialist weekly.[2] In 1907 Richard Orage, an early translator of Friedrich Nietzsche, took over the editorship of the *New Age* and made it an influential periodical. It claimed among its contributors Havelock Ellis, Katherine Mansfield, T. E. Hulme, Wyndham Lewis, G. B. Shaw, G. K. Chesterton, and—of particular interest to readers of *Purpose*—Ezra Pound, Herbert Read, W. Travers Symons, Philip Mairet, and Anthony Ludovici. The year that World War I ended, Douglas converted to his theory of economic reform a number of individuals who, in various ways, proselytized on behalf of Social Credit during the years leading to World War II. The range of Douglas's influence is indicated by the work of two of his early apostles, Orage and Pound. The former was to try unsuccessfully to convince the British Labour Party to adopt Douglas's principles and was to spend many years as editor of Social Credit organs. The latter, in his assessment of fascism, in his devotion to Mussolini, and in the writing of his most famous poems, was to preach and sing Social Credit.[3]

Among Orage's favored political contributors to *New Age* during the early 1920s, when it was known as the journal of Guild socialism and Social Credit, was D. Mitrinovic, a Serbian writer with mystical leanings and problems with English expression: in the *New Age* his articles appeared over the name of M. M. Cosmoi.[4] When Orage left the *New Age* in 1922, Mitrinovic found his contributions to be less appreciated than they had been earlier. During this time Mitrinovic and a few other Bloomsbury thinkers formed a discussion club called the Chandos Group (so named for the restaurant where they regularly met). Included in this group were Maurice Reckitt, Travers Symons, and Philip Mairet, all Social Creditors and all important forces in the founding of *Purpose*.

Adler came to England first in 1923 and again in 1926. Certainly during his second visit and possibly during his first one, Mitrinovic, who had taken a great interest in Adler's theory of individual psychology, met the controversial Austrian and played an important part in arranging meetings between Adler and Mairet, Symons, the American Alan Porter, and others associated with the Gower Street Lecture Club of Individual Psychology.[5] (In time, Adler disassociated himself from the Bloomsbury Group, apparently out of disdain for Mitrinovic as well as because of his abiding reluctance to forge an alliance with any group with political interests.)[6] During its lifetime *Purpose* published translations of a few of Adler's lectures, but Adler seems not to have offered the quarterly any writing intended especially for it. *Purpose* was to serve Social Credit and individual psychology through the publication of articles written by apostles—most of them selfappointed—of Douglas and Adler.

One connection that Mitrinovic and his friends perceived in both Social Credit and individual psychology is the acknowledgement in both systems of the subordination of individual demands to larger social purposes—what Adler called *Gemeinschaftsgefühl*, or *social interest*. In order to escape neurosis, Adler asserted, the individual should conceive of his life as a contribution to the perfection of society rather than fall prey to egocentric and finally inadequate goals of personal success or pleasure.[7] Rather than engage in competition with one another, Douglas said, individuals should unite in a social system which structurally will not accommodate control of one group of persons by another.[8] It appeared to Mitrinovic, Mairet, and others that Douglas and Adler had made the same discovery in different spheres: that purpose rather than force—that the demands of healthful evolution rather than the personal ambitions of a few vested with power—should determine behavior. The name of the magazine was to suggest that which should shape behavior and, by implication, to call into question all efforts which interfere with a natural developmental pattern that ideally informs all action (1, no. 1:5–6). The founders of *Purpose* perceived, too, that Adler and Douglas shared a certain disdain for those—such as British capitalists and Sigmund Freud—who insisted on understanding the past in order to explain and even justify the present. Society can be changed, and so can the life of the individual, by conscious effort. Attention is better focused, therefore, on effecting change than on looking back in time to uncover causes.

The papers that appear in the first issue of *Purpose* reaffirm the resoluteness suggested in the magazine's title, and together they define the range of concerns and genres to be represented in the next several issues. Dorothy M. Richardson's uniquely personal essay, "Resolution," contemplates the use to which we put the days between Christmas and New Year's Day, when we customarily commit ourselves to purposeful life choices (1, no. 1:7–9). Other articles in the first issue were provided by Gower Street Club members. Alan Porter, who, according to Adler's English biographer, "gave a brilliant follow-up course of lectures on Individual Psychology" to the Gower Street Club after Adler's departure from England in 1926,[9] argues for willful control over one's life in "Will and Purpose" (pp. 10–12). Symons proclaims Adler's contribution to the supreme achievement of modern science, which is the declaration that man "*is* what he is *doing*, and nothing else" ("Purpose and Responsibility," pp. 13–16). Mairet discusses the function of Britain in the community of nations in "The Purpose of England" (pp. 26–31). A. Rabagliati, author of a number of books on health and nutrition and perhaps a contributor to *Focus*, applied Adler's theory to biology in "Has Nature a Purpose?" (pp. 17–25). Purpose is everywhere: the word *purpose* is a part of most titles and of every contribution in the first issue. The tautology is unavoidable: the purpose of *Purpose* is to articulate purpose, whether in nature, society, the sciences, or the arts.

In its twelve years of publication *Purpose* served as a forum for writers whose beliefs allied them to one or the other of the systems of thought the quarterly was created to serve. The most prescient reader could not have foreseen how, between 1929 and 1940, Adler's and Douglas's views on the mutual responsibility of society and the individual were to prove to be relevant, if not sufficient, in explaining what was happening throughout the Western world. The publication history of *Purpose* is most easily traced through four distinct periods of editorship: 1929, 1930–1934, 1935, and 1936 to the last issue in 1940.

During its first year John Marlow served as editor and established *Purpose* as a lean and narrowly focused quarterly. Each issue consisted of about forty pages and about six essays, nearly all of which pertained to Adler's psychology or the need for Social Credit. Two notable exceptions were essays by the only women contributing to *Purpose* in 1929: Dorothy M. Richardson's second essay, on the British tradition of fair play ("Law," 1, no. 2:67–68), and Winifred E. Fish's second contribution, a review article on Ortega y Gasset's *The Task of Our Times* (1, no. 2:50–56). About three-fourths of the articles published in 1929 were contributed by those writers represented in the first issue. Other contributors include V. A. Demant, later professor of moral philosophy at Oxford and author of *Religion and the Decline of Capitalism* ("Purpose—or Plan," 1, no. 2:45–49), and Mitrinovic, who accuses Freud of wanting to destroy Western culture in "Freud *versus* Adler" (1, no. 2:69–81). During the next five years, from 1930 through 1934, Symons and Mairet served as coeditors. Under these experienced journalists *Purpose* gave up its aura as a quarterly anthology and assumed the appearance of a more orthodox periodical. The two men changed the format of the magazine by adding two set articles, one at the beginning and the other at the end of each issue. The first of these additions, which were to characterize *Purpose* until its cessation, is "In the Human Interest," a series of several paragraphs on political and cultural matters of the time and the relevance of Social Credit and Social Interest to them. The second addition is a series of brief reviews of recently published books. The editors assumed much responsibility as contributors during this period. "In the Human Interest" and reviews, though normally unsigned, probably represent in large part the work of the editors: "In the Human Interest" first appears over the initials "W.T.S." Symons and Mairet each contributed, also, about one article to each issue.

In addition to Reckitt and Porter, who continued to contribute to *Purpose* in the early 1930s, other writers continued to expound Douglas's and Adler's principles. F. G. Crookshank, "the most convinced and clearest exponent of Adler's psychology in England,"[10] contributed a lecture on illness as a patient's statement ("Organ-States and Emotional Correlatives," 1, no. 1:12–21), and an argument for incorporating psychology in medical studies rather than defining it as a specialty ("The New Psychology and the Health of the People," 4, no. 2:122–27). Psychotherapist Georg Grodeck provided *Purpose* with at least three articles before his death in 1934, all of which reveal his Freudian sympathies: "Psychology in Parable" (2, no. 1:6–11; 2, no. 2:60–64); "Repression and

Release'' (3, no. 3:96–103); and "Man's Double-Sexed Nature" (4, no. 1:21–28).

The greatest number of articles on psychology proffer a strict Adlerian stance, and this period of *Purpose* is remarkable for the appearance of two pieces by Adler, both of them translations of lectures: "Tricks of Neurosis" (5, no. 1:19–27) and "Individual Psychology" (6, no. 3:99–110), on how, by way of the Stoics and Auguste Comte, Adler came to his theories and methods. Of particular interest are two articles on women in psychology. One is Mairet's discussion of the contributions of Adler, Freud, and Carl Jung to the new understanding of sexual differences ("Feminism and Twentieth-Century Psychology," 5, no. 3:104–10); the other is A. M. Ludovici's argument that one of the meanings of maleness is sadism as one of the meanings of femaleness is masochism ("Man and Woman," 5, no. 4:158–63).

During this period, there appear in *Purpose* more articles on politics than on psychology, though, as Europe moved through the early 1930s, the magazine's insistence on theoretical connections between Social Credit and individual psychology took on a larger and deeper meaning: "The leadership [of England appears to us to exhibit a divided, and largely] disintegrated mind; it is evidence of a state of national civilization lacking in will and purpose" ("In the Human Interest," 2, no. 1:3). Many articles address problems posed by the times and theoretically dealt with in Douglas's monetary system, among them articles by Symons: "Leisure: Its Necessity and Meaning in This Age of Abundance" (2, no. 1:22–27) and "The Financial Order as Will to Power" (3, no. 4:149–58). Particularly valuable for its backward look at the development of Social Credit since the publication in 1919 of Douglas's principal work, *Economic Democracy*, is "The Approach to Social Credit" (5, no. 3:93–98). *Purpose*'s vision extended beyond Britain: Russia inspired hope among Social Creditors (see 2, no. 3:122–32; 4, no. 4:146–51; 6, no. 1:43–46), whereas fascism did not (see 6, no. 1: 6–12, 38–42; 2, no. 4: 160–64).

Another significant change in *Purpose* effected by Symons and Mairet was the inclusion of a few articles in each issue on the arts, particularly literature. Neil Montgomery, one of Symons' and Mairet's most faithful contributors, provided several critical pieces, including ones on Joseph Conrad's *The Arrow of Gold* (4, no. 4:164–68), another on mythology in James Barrie's writings (3, no. 1:29–32), another on Denis Saurat's *L'Actuel*—which he finds more convincing than *Paradise Lost* because of its expression of universal purpose (5, no. 2:65–72), as well as an essay on creativity as an attempt to reconcile opposing ideas, with examples from Nietzsche, Fyodor Dostoevsky, and Marcel Proust ("Multiple Personality," 6, no. 1:20–27), and pieces on tragedy and comedy deriving from Nietzsche and George Meredith: "The Growth of Tragedy" (6, no. 1:14–20) and " 'Risit Apollo' " (4, no. 2:75–82).

From the first issues of *Purpose* Nietzsche figures as an important intellectual antecedent of individual psychology, as in "Marx and Nietzsche: As the Historic Background of Adler" by "Scribe," (1, no. 4:145–58); and James Carruthers

Young's lecture to the Individual Psychology Club on views shared by Adler and Nietzsche, "Individualism and Individuation" (6, no. 2:79–85). Nietzsche provided contributors with ideas useful to *Purpose*'s other main concern: an article on Nietzsche's political influence in Spain (2, no. 4:165–67); one on Nietzsche's and Marx's theoretical ties to Adler (6, no. 1:28–37). Mairet, too, contributed a number of essays on literary subjects as they are informed by Adlerian psychology and Social Credit: an Adlerian reading of Hamlet's indecision (4, no. 3:100–117), and an essay on the place of literary criticism in the battle for freedom (6, no. 2:53–58).

Effective with the first issue of 1935, Mairet resigned from *Purpose* because of the editorial demands of *New English Weekly*,* but he was to remain as an unofficial collaborator with the quarterly he had helped create.[11] Left with full responsibility as editor, Symons began the seventh year of *Purpose* with a plea to readers for their financial support during a difficult period. In return he promised to continue the important work *Purpose* had always been devoted to: "to increase psychological and economic enlightenment" (7, no. 1:3). Symons sustained the loyalty of a number of *Purpose*'s earlier contributors, including Montgomery, Le Gros Clark, and Erich Gutkind. And he attracted such new contributors as the anthropologist J. D. Unwin, Norrie Fraser, and Marjorie Gabain. By far the greatest number of articles published this year concerned economics and international finance (cf. 7, no. 2:57–64, 75–81; 7, no. 3:105–12, 113–16). Perhaps the most important contribution relating to Social Credit is an excerpt from A. R. Orage's *Apologia*, a survey of social problems of the last twenty years and a testimony to Douglas's influence on Orage as expressed in the *New Age* and *New English Weekly* ("A. R. Orage," 7, no. 1:33–44). Among the few articles devoted to Adlerian psychology the most important is a translation of an article that originally appeared in a collection edited by Adler: Alexander Neuer, "Courage and Discouragement: The Principle of Alfred Adler's Psychology" (7, no. 1:16–24). Two articles on the arts lament the destructive influence on art and music of political institutions: Kaikhosru Shapurji Sorabji, "The Decline of Musical Standards" (7, no. 3:117–22), and Claude Flight, "The Art Standard" (7, no. 3:123–28).

The third issue of 1935 welcomes A. Desmond Hawkins as an editorial collaborator and with him the contributions of a number of writers not before published in *Purpose* (7, no. 3:104). With that issue, reviews assume an importance they had not hitherto enjoyed, with contributions from Ashley Sampson, K. D. Barlow, Wynyard Browne, and—in subsequent issues—David Gascoyne and Elizabeth Bowen, as well as Hawkins himself. And so was introduced the last and, literarily, the most distinguished period of *Purpose*—its last five years, when Hawkins served as literary editor.

Even through this last period, from 1936 through 1940, the contributions of "M. B. Oxon," Montgomery, Reckitt, Mairet, and Symons assured the quarterly its reputation as an indefatigable advocate of Social Credit and Social Interest. But during this period, *Purpose* underwent its most pronounced change. Hawkins's appointment as literary editor coincided with the enlargement of each issue by about sixteen pages and the accommodation thereby of more literary pieces than before. Hawkins's intention was not simply to publish criticism and poetry. It seems to have been, rather, to present examples of such writings which confronted political and largely cultural issues of the time. In an unsigned "In the Human Interest" segment, poetry of the last twenty years is named "the vehicle of the intense struggle to pass from one historical epoch to another" (9, no. 4:194). Possibly this article was written by Hawkins, for it identifies an attitude that pervades much of the criticism published in *Purpose*'s last period. Several issues of *Purpose* are organized around subjects which focus on the interplay of culture and politics—and more particularly, of poetry and political doctrine. One issue (9, no. 2) considers Marxist thought, especially as it finds expression in poetry. Another issue on and of modern poetry is intended "to detect and foster 'conviction' and faith amongst 'the best,' wherever it may be found" (10, no. 1:4)—conviction and faith that poetry can affect the world.

Another innovation of Hawkins's is the organization of a literary "Symposium." The plan was to present a series of articles by writers whose interests were primarily literary, either as critics or poets, on the condition of Western culture and what it likely or ideally will become.

The "Symposium" begins with the third issue of 1938 and continues through the last issue of 1940. The first contributor is Pound, whose "Consegna" argues that Marx's teachings are not to be found in the Russian Revolution but in the thought of C. H. Douglas and the government of Mussolini (10, no. 3: 164–68). Michael Roberts's "The Critic and the Public" follows, on the impoverished state of popular criticism (10, no. 4:213–24). E.W.F. Tomlin, in "Art and Culture," proposes that the social purpose of art is to tell us the truth about our feelings, which, in the modern world, are diseased (11, no. 1:38–49). T. S. Eliot's "The Idea of a Christian Society" is perhaps the most distinguished contribution to the "Symposium" (11, no. 3:162–73). This plea for a return to Christian community is responded to in the next "Symposium" article, Herbert Read's "A Community of Individuals," which argues for an egalitarianism derived from global control of economic wealth (12, no. 1:22–28). It bears mentioning that at least three of the six contributors to the "Symposium" had declared their belief in Social Credit: Pound, Eliot, and Read.[12]

In the beginning, *Purpose* was remarkable for its dependence on a few contributors, many of whom are now forgotten. In the end *Purpose* is remarkable for its publication of so many distinguished men and women of letters. Dylan Thomas contributed poems—"Fine Meats on Bones That Soon Have None" (8, no. 2:102–3), "Then Was My Neophyte" (8, no. 4:230–31), "Today, This Insect, and the World I Breathe" (8, no. 4:231–32)—as did Lawrence Durrell: "Egyptian Pastiche" (10, no. 3:168), "In Crisis" (12, no. 2:90–91). Henry Miller provided *Purpose* with an essay on D. H. Lawrence ("Creative Death," 10, no. 2:67–75), Eliot on "The Poetry of W. B. Yeats" (12, no. 3/4:155–26) and on Pound, ("On a Recent Piece of Criticism," 10, no. 2:90–94) the latter in response to G. W. Stonier's unsympathetic article on Pound that had appeared earlier in *Purpose*. Auden contributed an essay on Hardy's poetry ("A Literary Transference," 12, no. 3/4:127–34). Anaïs Nin wrote on Otto Rank's theory of the neurotic as a creative force in "Creative Principle in Analysis" (10, no. 2:147–51). Stephen Spender contributed "Some Notes on Being a Poet Today" (12, no. 3/4:135–41), and Elizabeth Bowen provided *Purpose* with many novel reviews: on Durrell and John Steinbeck (11, no. 2:116–19), on Franz Kafka and John Dos Passos (11, no. 1:51–55), on James Joyce (11, no. 3:177–80), and on Henry Green (12, no. 2:92–95).

If monetary and psychological theories gave birth to *Purpose*, historical events destroyed it. By late 1940 the Twilight War was over and Germany had invaded the Low Countries. That which *Purpose* had been created to forestall had occurred. The quarterly had begun in the hope of articulating the sane and just purpose in all human endeavor and working for its realization. Twelve years later it announced: "*Purpose* falls victim to the circumstances of the time" (12, no. 3/4:100). *Purpose*'s "Symposium" had begun with Hawkins's hope for a resolution of the paradox of political optimism, which still prevailed, and literary pessimism, which characterized the best writing of the post–World War I period. Historical events resolved that paradox as they proved the optimistic theories of Social Credit and Social Interest virtually irrelevant, at least for the time being.

Notes

1. John L. Finlay, *Social Credit: The English Origins* (Montreal, 1972), pp. 180–81, 251.
2. Ibid., pp. 63–74.
3. Earle Davis, *Vision Fugitive: Ezra Pound and Economics* (Lawrence, Kans., 1968), pp 23–26, 52–71, 103–6.
4. Finlay, *Social Credit*, pp. 57–76, 168.
5. Phyllis Bottome, *Alfred Adler: A Biography* (New York, 1939), pp. 240–54.
6. Phyllis Bottome, *The Goal* (New York, 1962), pp. 262ff.
7. Bottome, *Alfred Adler*, pp. 62ff.
8. Finlay, *Social Credit*, pp. 57ff.
9. Bottome, *The Goal*, p. 262.
10. Bottome, *Alfred Adler*, p. 243.
11. Eric Homberger, *Ezra Pound: The Critical Heritage* (London, 1972), p. 332.
12. See Bonamy Dobrée, "T. S. Eliot: A Personal Reminiscence," in *T. S. Eliot: The Man and His Work*, ed. Allen Tate (New York, 1966), p. 82; and Davis, *Vision Fugitive*, p. 20.

Information Sources

BIBLIOGRAPHY

Bottome, Phyllis. *Alfred Adler: A Biography*. New York, 1939.
———. *The Goal*. New York, 1962.
Chace, William C. *The Political Identities of Ezra Pound and T. S. Eliot*. Stanford, Calif., 1973.

Davis, Earle. *Vision Fugitive: Ezra Pound and Economics*. Lawrence, Kans., 1968.

Dobrée, Bonamy. "T. S. Eliot: A Personal Reminiscence." In *T. S. Eliot: The Man and His Work*. Edited by Allen Tate. New York, 1966.

Finlay, John L. *Social Credit: The English Origins*. Montreal, 1972.

Hawkins, Desmond. "The Pope of Russell Street." In *T. S. Eliot: A Symposium*. Edited by Richard March. New York, 1965.

Homberger, Eric. *Ezra Pound: The Critical Heritage*. London, 1972.

Howarth, Herbert. *Notes on Some Figures behind T. S. Eliot*. Boston, 1964.

Kermode, Frank, ed. *Selected Prose of T. S. Eliot*. New York, 1975.

Mairet, Philip. *A. R. Orage: A Memoir*. New Hyde Park, N.Y., 1966.

———. *John Middleton Murry*. London, 1958.

Margolis, John D. *T. S. Eliot's Intellectual Development, 1922–39*. Chicago, 1972.

INDEXES

Volume 9 prefaced with index to subjects and index to authors of this volume only, both alphabetically arranged.

REPRINT EDITIONS

Microform: Kraus Microform, Millwood, N.Y. New York Public Library.

LOCATION SOURCES

American

Complete runs: University of Chicago Library; University of Kansas Library.

Partial runs: New York Public Library; Princeton University Library; University of Buffalo Library; Vanderbilt University Library.

British

Complete runs: British Museum; Cambridge University Library; Trinity College Library, Dublin.

Partial run: National Library of Scotland, Edinburgh.

Publication History

MAGAZINE TITLE AND TITLE CHANGES

Purpose: A Quarterly Magazine.

VOLUME AND ISSUE DATA

Volumes 1–12, with four numbers each through volume 11; with three numbers (the third one a double number) for volume 12, January/March 1929–July/December 1940.

FREQUENCY OF PUBLICATION

Quarterly.

PUBLISHER

C. W. Daniel, 46 Bernard St., London, W.C. 1.

EDITORS

John Marlow, January/March 1929–October/December 1929. W. T. Symons and Philip Mairet, January/March 1930–October/December 1934. W. T. Symons, January/March 1935–October/December 1935. W. T. Symons, general editor, and A. Desmond Hawkins, literary editor, January/March 1936–July/December 1940.

Carol de Saint Victor

—— Q ——

QUARTERLY REVIEW, THE

The twentieth-century *Quarterly Review* was a far less formidable presence than its nineteenth-century forbear, established in 1809 (see *RA*). Its tone was less harsh and its criticism far less malicious, and the literary world had changed: reputations in the twentieth century were less likely to be made or destroyed by a single anonymous review in a pontifical magazine. But if it was less dramatic than in the days of William Gifford and John Gibson Lockhart, the twentieth-century *Quarterly* nonetheless contained work by some of the best-known names of the literary world.

The outlook was conservative, of course, in keeping with the *Quarterly*'s long tradition, but there were many articles whose aim was to introduce new or less familiar authors. Such were Percy Lubbock's enthusiastic survey of Edith Wharton's work (223:182–201), and John Middleton Murry's review of the first four volumes of Marcel Proust's *A la recherche du temps perdu* (238:86–100), which compared Proust's advent in our era with Jean Jacques Rousseau's in his. These and similar essays are sensitive and critically generous.

But the *Quarterly* did not always manage to open its arms to the significantly new in literature. Arthur Waugh's 1916 article, "The New Poetry" (226:365–86), for example, found little to praise and much to lament: poetry, he felt, was becoming "democratized" (which is to say, vulgarized) by its insistence on everyday language and realistic subject matters. Waugh also lamented the passing of traditional forms and the healthy restraint they helped foster. The poems of D. H. Lawrence, for example, "illustrate a degree of self-abandonment which is so invertebrate as to be practically abnormal" (p. 381). Ezra Pound's line, "I have gone half-cracked," should serve as his epitaph, Waugh suggested. He went on to quote parts of T.S. Eliot's *Prufrock*, without naming its author, to show the depths to which literary license can sink a writer. Waugh's essay, though, is not a mere hatchet-job: though history has proven his judgments wrong, the essay is closely and intelligently argued, the sort of document which can help the modern student of Pound and Eliot better understand how they were perceived, and how they perceived themselves and their audience.

Shane Leslie's review of *Ulysses* in 1922 (238:219–34) is even more negative and more emphatically so; it is worth preserving as a most interesting piece of critical hysteria. James Joyce's novel is seen as "literary Bolshevism," an "Odyssey of the sewer," a profanation of Homer, chaotic and unreadable. American and French critics will praise it, Leslie predicts, in keeping with their habit of lauding whatever they cannot understand. Finally, he notes that the *Quarterly*'s staff hesitated in reviewing *Ulysses* at all, fearing it might only bring the book to the attention of the prurient-minded; Leslie was apparently unaware of what that fear said about the *Quarterly*'s readers. It is curious that so hidebound and dogmatic a piece should appear in the very same volume as Murry's enthusiastic introduction of Proust.

But the *Quarterly*'s literary conservatism was not uniformly in evidence. One can see a softening in the hard-line rejection of modernism when Edward Shanks (who had recently left his post as assistant editor of the conservative *London Mercury**) contributed, in 1926, "The New Poetry, 1911–1925: A Survey" (246:139–53). Shanks regretted what he saw as the formal looseness of Lawrence, Eliot, and the others, but did admit that Eliot was the "most able of the critics" and saw him as a powerful agent of deep changes in modern poetry. Shanks disliked what he called the crossword-puzzle quality of *The Waste Land*, but chiefly criticized the modernists for their major theme of disillusionment; it is, Shanks warned, a sterile source for poetic inspiration. Modern poetry's best hopes, be felt, were with the work of Edmund Blunden and Robert Graves.

The bulk of material in the *Quarterly*, however, was not literary but social, political, and historical. Much patriotic and anti-German writing appeared during both wars. But there was also a disturbing step into the darkness with the publication, in 1919, of the Count de Soissons's "The Jews as Revolutionary Leaven," where for a moment the *Quarterly*'s conservatism threatened to ally itself with the anti-Semitic new right. The article argued, in an ugly tone, that Jews were natural allies of anarchist and leftist movements. One is relieved to see the *Quarterly* print an anonymous reply in the very next issue which treated the Soissons piece as it deserved. There were no more anti-Semitic essays; in fact, several essays were printed which solicited active sympathy for the Jewish plight. An unsigned article in the 500th issue for July 1929, titled "A Retrospect: Numbers 1–500" (253:1–17), argued that the *Quarterly* had always been in the forefront of real social progress and reforms, having taken the progressive side on the major nineteenth-century issues of slavery, the Corn Laws, and child labor. This was often the case, though not always: in the 1820s, for example, the magazine printed a great deal of vicious anti-Catholic material in an effort to stave off Catholic toleration. Still, one could characterize the politics of both the nineteenth- and twentieth-century runs of the *Quarterly* as generally enlightened conservatism. The Soissons article is one glaring exception; another, printed in 1958, is an essay defending apartheid (296:367–78).

The list of writers on historical topics is impressive: J. B. Bury on the Trojan War (vol. 226), T. Sturge Moore on Gustave Flaubert (221), Evelyn Underhill on Plotinus (231), Edmund Gosse on Austin Dobson (237), Sir James G. Frazer on Joseph Addison's London (237). The *Quarterly* printed a great many articles on Lord Byron, nearly all of them biographical studies. Rowland Prothero, the editor of Byron's letters and journals, and his brother, Sir George Prothero, were editors of the *Quarterly* (respectively, from 1893 to 1899, and from 1899 to 1922), so the Byron connection was well established. Much of the groundbreaking work in our century on Byron's biography was printed in the *Quarterly*; of special note is Rowland Prothero's untangling of the facts regarding "Lady Byron and Her Separation" in 1930 (254:15–36). Articles about Byron continued to appear into the 1960s.

The *Quarterly* also printed some early, and still valuable, film criticism. Its first article on the subject was Bertram Clayton's "The Cinema" (234:177–87), which, appearing in 1920, found the new medium itself less entertaining than its promoters, and ridiculed the superficial moralizing that was becoming common in films. Five years later, Carleton Kemp Allen also raised the issue of " 'Movies' and Morals" (245:313–30), making a sophisticated argument against the movies' ethic of violence. Allen's article also contains much statistical material about the state and quantity of British film-making, and it laments the American ascendancy in the new genre. Other studies of popular culture include Horace G. Hutchinson's "Detective Fiction" in 1929 (253:148–60) and I. F. Clarke's excellent survey, "Science Fiction: Past and Present," in 1957 (295:260–70).

In the 1940s and later, the *Quarterly* began publishing a great many articles relating to its own history and to its nineteenth-century editors and contributors. Malcolm Elwin wrote on the "The Founder of the *Quarterly* Review," John Murray II (281:1–15), and on Robert Southey (281:187–200). W. M. Parker wrote some ten articles, printed from 1954 to 1967, on Lockhart, Gifford, and others from the early *Quarterly* circles. These article are valuable to the student of the nineteenth-century *Quarterly*, but they also point up the fact that the magazine was becoming a relic rather than a vital center of critical discussion. The old *Quarterly* had been a production of the old-style man of letters. But by the 1960s, historical work was being done with more precision (or, perhaps, with more pedantry) in the dozens of academic journals, and social criticism and literary reviews were being done in the newer fast-paced, slick formats. The *Quarterly*, neither academic nor slick, belonged to a different era. [See also the article on the *Quarterly Review* in *RA*.]

Information Sources

INDEXES
Volumes 200–220 in volume 221; volumes 221–241 in volume 242. Thereafter, each volume indexed.

REPRINT EDITIONS
    Microform: UMI.
LOCATION SOURCES
American
    Widely available.
British
    Widely available.

Publication History

MAGAZINE TITLE AND TITLE CHANGES
    The Quarterly Review.
VOLUME AND ISSUE DATA
    1809–1914: See entry in *RA*. Volumes 220–305, numbers 438–654, January 1914–
    October 1967.
FREQUENCY OF PUBLICATION
    Quarterly.
PUBLISHERS
    1808–1914: See entry in *RA*. 1914–1967: John Murray Publishers, Ltd., 50 Al-
    bermarle Street, London W1X 4BD.
EDITORS
    1809–1899: See entry in *RA*. Sir George Prothero, 1899–1922. John Murray IV
    and C. E. Lawrence, 1922–1928. John Murray V and C. E. Lawrence, 1928–
    1967.

Raymond N. MacKenzie

QUIVER, THE. See VEA

R

REVIEW, THE

The first issue of the *Review* appeared in London in April 1962. Although its editor, Ian Hamilton, set forth no editorial policies, it was clear from the contents what the magazine stood for. Of its forty-two pages, fifteen were given to a long conversation between Alfred Alvarez and Donald Davie about the nature of contemporary poetry (no. 1:10–25). Alvarez and Davie contributed also a poem each, as did Peter Redgrove, Roy Fuller, and Michael Fried. There were translation of poems by Zbigniew Herbert and Vladimir Mayakovsky. The rest of the issue, fourteen pages, was given to reviews, almost all of them deprecating the recent works of Apocalyptic or neo-Romantic poets. Not since *New Verse** had battle lines been so clearly drawn in British poetry wars; the objective, true-to-fact poetry, which Geoffrey Grigson's magazine from the 1930s had promoted, opposed again the rhetorical, fraudulent and "genteel": in the 1960s such poets as the Group and their Liverpudlian counterparts.

The two opposing camps of poetic theory were the substance of the conversation between Alvarez and Davie in the first issue. Davie qualified for Alvarez his position on a "new aestheticism": seeing all art as the relationship between the artist and his medium. Alvarez objected to what he regarded as Davie's "academic point of view" that only styles from the past could be "tarted up for our use now . . . and expanded." Davie denied such a view, and expressed his fear that such attempts as Alvarez's to use new styles might "write off our past." Alvarez cited the work of *Review* contributor Zbigniew Herbert as an example of "factuality [which] makes his poetry good and at the same time very involved, commited." Davie replied that such Eastern poets were not "embarrassed" to speak of art; Alvarez concluded that their aestheticism worked on a "much more serious level" (no. 1:23–25). The *Times Literary Supplement*, in reviewing the first issue of the *Review*, singled out Alvarez and Davie's essay as the most valuable part of a contemporary poetry magazine. While there were "some admirable poems" in the *Review*, its "novelty" was to have such "really intelligent discussion and criticism of contemporary poetry."[1]

Hamilton regarded criticism as a vital part of his mission, to "clear the air ... be rigorous and polemical ... rap dunces and hound charlatans. ... What was needed was a new poetry, or a new sense of the poetic."[2] In its bimonthly issues, the *Review* promoted in fairly long lead reviews the poets whose work Hamilton admired, and relegated to biting brief reviews at the back of the magazine the others. The second issue, for example, continued the arguments of Alvarez in a review by Colin Falck of Alvarez's seminal *The New Poetry*. Falck, a twenty-eight-year-old university lecturer who would soon become associate editor, tried in his reviews to place the "weight of our major poetic tradition" behind the work of new poets (no. 29/30:70)—in this review, behind John Berryman, Robert Lowell, Philip Larkin, and Charles Tomlinson. In another review in that issue, entitled "An Unconvincing Handful," Hamilton, using the pseudonym "Peter Marsh," dismissed the work of Robert Conquest, Derek Walcott, John Heath-Stubbs, and Ewart Milne. In that same issue Hamilton assumed another pseudonym, "Edward Pygge," and castigated as "Tedium" Dannie Abse's *Poems, Golders Green*.

By the fifth issue Pygge had his own column at the back of every issue. Just as Grigson's "Martin Boldero" had taken on Edith Sitwell and Edmund Blunden in *New Verse*, so Hamilton's Pygge baited G. S. Fraser, R. P. Blackmur, Edward Lucie-Smith, and the establishment press (cf. no. 5:51; no. 16:50; no. 17:2; no. 18:69). But Pygge's real forte was the creation of satirical figures with names like "B. F. Razor," "Gorge Macdeth," and "John Stain," respectively, B. F. Ivor, George MacBeth, and John Wain. A conversation between Razor and Stain in issue 8 (p. 59), for example, had Stain bemoaning the lack of critical attention paid him; the conversation was recalled ten years later, with Wain's elevation to Oxford Professor of Poetry. Pygge, nosing around Oxford, finds the only copy of Stain's inaugural poem, *Letters to Five More Artists*, in which Stain compares himself to Michelangelo, Mozart, and Rilke, and thumbs his nose at his competitor for the chair, Stephen Spender (*NR* no. 2:4). Throughout the run of the *Review*, devastating satirical tricks accomplished more in a phrase than a serious review could in a paragraph. C. Day Lewis is "A Poet Nearly Anonymous" (no. 3:31); Vernon Scannell a "Pulp Poet" (no. 3:39); Vernon Watkins a "Visionary Drear" (no. 5:35). The review of Denis Donoghue's *Connoisseurs of Chaos* was entitled "Base Infection," while the work of Seamus Heaney, J. C. Hall, and Elizabeth Jennings was that of "Gummidge and Others" (no. 16:40, 43). In some issues, a barb might follow a longer serious treatment of the subject: after Derwent May's four-page review of Geoffrey Hill's *King Log*, Pygge "discovered" a lost poem by the overly rhetorical Hill in a bombed-out shrine in a mythical, pristine English village (no. 20:53–56, 67). A series of unfavorable reviews might follow the career of one from whom the *Review* expected better: an interview with Stephen Spender was sandwiched in between

"Bare Bones," a review by Francis Hope of *The Struggle of the Modern*, and "A Generous Daze," David Harsent's review of *The Generous Days* (no. 8:46; no. 23:19–32; *NR* no. 10:65).

The short snippet reviews were balanced by the long, serious essays that discussed the work of more deserving poets. The most frequent reviewers included three poets whose work appeared regularly in the *Review*—Colin Falck, Roy Fuller, and John Fuller—and three critics, Martin Dodsworth, Clive James, and Gabriel Pearson. When a poet was considered frequently, it was seldom by the same reviewer. Thom Gunn, for example, was reviewed three times—by John Fuller, Dodsworth, and Michael Fried (no. 1:29; no. 18:46; no. 25:59); Robert Lowell was the subject of reviews and interviews by Alvarez, Pearson, Hamilton, John Fuller, and others (no. 8:36; no. 18:62; no. 20:3; no. 26:10). Reviewers' works were themselves frequent topics for discussion: John Fuller's *The Tree That Walked* (no. 18:65), Roy Fuller's *Collected Poems, New Poems* and *A Reader's Guide to W. H. Auden* (no. 3:3; no. 20:57; no. 22:57), Davie's *Essex Poems* (no. 22:46), James's *The Metropolitan Critic* (*NR* no. 3:76), and Peter Porter's *Last of England* (no. 24:53), for example. One of the most unusual exchanges appeared in the last issue of the *Review*, when John Fuller reviewed James Fenton's *Terminal Moraine* and Fenton, immediately following, wrote on Fuller's *Cannibals and Missionaries*. Each review was a poem (stanzas of triplet/tercet in tetrameter and trimeter) satirizing the work of the other (no. 29/30:90, 97).

The *Review* aimed to be the most comprehensive survey of modern poetry, and it succeeded. When Hamilton culled from the first fifteen numbers of the *Review* an anthology of review-essays, *The Modern Poet*, the subjects included Alvarez (no. 2), Gunn (no. 1), Roy Fuller, Lowell (no. 3), Edwin Muir (no. 4), William Empson (no. 6/7), Yvor Winters (no. 8), Sylvia Plath (no. 9), poets of the 1930s (no. 11/12), Philip Larkin (no. 14), John Berryman, Marianne Moore, poets of World War I (no. 15), Alun Lewis (no. 17), and Randall Jarrell (no. 16).[3] The *Times* reviewer of the volume quibbled over a few choices (the inclusion of thirties poet Bernard Spencer rather than Louis MacNeice), pointed out the "confused or evasive language" of essays by Falck, and singled out the "most clear and coherent writing" of John Fuller and Francis Hope before concluding that the anthology was "the best guide available to recent poetry."[4]

The critical success of the *Review*, as Roy Fuller sees it, lay in the editorial acumen of its editor. Hamilton's "distinguishing method of approach, and one which pays off again and again, is the historical."[5] When Hamilton reviewed William Carlos Williams's work in 1964, he discussed Williams's imagist phase; he remembered Berryman's work from the thirties as well as from the 1960s.[6] Reviews by other hands in Hamilton's magazine reflect the same historical concern; usually the essays are retrospectives of a figure's entire canon as well as an evaluation of his or her recent work. Graham Martin traced all of Roy Fuller's works before concluding that he "had never found a wholly personal voice" (no. 3:4). John Fuller noted that Randall Jarrell never outgrew the influences of Robert Frost and John Crowe Ransom (no. 16:5) and that Thom Gunn's poems were marked by a "growing indistinctness and abstraction of language" that betrayed his origins (no. 1:29).

If the most important mission of the *Review* was to sort out genuine poetry from the disingenuous, scarcely less important was its function to print as models the poetry it admired. Unlike *New Verse*, which had Auden as its mascot, no single figure served as the epitome of the *Review* poet. Hamilton singled out Michael Fried, Hugo Williams, David Harsent, Falck, and Douglas Dunn as representative of the *Review*'s standards, but he admitted that they had at times written "badly, self-parodically [and] . . . erred in the direction of the minimal." Every commentator, according to Hamilton, had "seized on" that error in attempting to construct a *Review* school.[7] All the poets were contemporaries of Hamilton—Falck four years older than he, Dunn and Harsent four years younger. All had bookish professions—Harsent was a bookseller and publisher, Falck a university lecturer, Dunn a librarian. In their frequency of publication, if not their achievement, some of the poets might constitute a *Review* "coterie." Fried, for example, contributed poems to eight of the first twenty-seven issues, along with two reviews; Williams contributed thirty short poems to almost consecutive issues (nos. 17, 18, 20, 22, 23, 26, 27/28, 29/30); Falck's work, most of it reviews, appeared in nearly every issue. But other contributors appeared even more frequently than Dunn or Harsent: John Fuller's poems, for example, appeared in issues 1, 2, 4, 8, 14, 16, 18, 24, and 27; Dunn's first work did not appear until the twentieth issue. Given the variety of poetic styles in the *Review*, it is impossible to accept the minimalist work by a handful of young poets as the advocacy of the editor. The shorter poems were only one expression of what Hamilton "was after: a new lyricism, direct, personal, concentrated, a poetry that would prove whatever it promised."[8]

The revival of English poetry remained a concern, even after the efforts of magazines like the *Review*. Increasingly, the British looked to the Americans and measured English lethargy against what seemed to be American vitality. The pages of the *Review* are filled with laments, like Peter Porter's, about British "colonial status, and rule from America." Innovative British poets—Porter names Tom Raworth and Lee Harwood—felt they must wait to get "the Good Housekeeping seal by their American mentors." For Porter, the state of poetry in Britain was a function of the class system: good poets automatically became "Establishment figures," therefore reactionaries; bad poets rushed in (no. 29/30:42). Alan Brownjohn complained of a "crisis of purpose," a neurosis wished on [English poets]," presumably by Americans, that produced a "failure to seize chances, tackle the big themes, and face up to brute realities." He urged British poets not to succumb to the ploy (no. 24:41).

The Americans were given their own space in reply. Dan Jacobson, in "Vurry Amurk'n," reminded readers of the American poets who a few decades earlier had gained acceptance in their own country only after the British had approved of them. It "really shouldn't follow," he argued, "that because Britain has lost an empire, her literary men should be compelled to lose their nerve and their self-regard as well" (no. 25:10). In the next issue Louis Simpson compared the American William Carlos Williams to the British D. H. Lawrence. Both seemed to say the same thing, that one must find the language and form for each particular experience; but the British did not listen to Lawrence. They were concerned not so much with poetry as with literary movements; they wanted a group to send against the Black Mountain poets, and the Mersey Sound couldn't compete (no. 26:19–31). Three issues later, Donald Hall compared the relationships of poets in America—including British poets living in the United States—to those in England. In America there was a "spirit of *detente*," while in England there were a "million particles. . . . so much anger, so much bitchery, so much attention to reviews, to the Arts Council, to allegiances and betrayal." He cited his own favorite British poet, Geoffrey Hill, whom Hamilton did not care for, and despaired of Hill's relative neglect in England (no. 29/30:39).

While American-British poetic interdependence had existed long before Hamilton's magazine, the *Review* nevertheless played a major role by securing the reputations of such American poets as John Berryman and Robert Lowell in England, and from the beginning the *Review* included discussions on American poets. The third issue contained Hamilton's first essay on Lowell (pp. 15–23). The lead essay for issue 8 focused on Yvor Winters (pp. 3–12). Issue 9 began with poems by Sylvia Plath, printing for the first time in England "Daddy" and "Ariel"; a seven-page essay on Plath by Alvarez followed (pp. 20–27). In issue 11/12 Eric Mottram discussed "American Poetry in the Thirties" (pp. 25–41). In issue 18 the longest feature was a symposium on poetic response to the Vietnam War (pp. 28–44). In number 20 Clive James discussed E. E. Cummings (pp. 38–48), and Gabriel Pearson led the issue with the longest essay, a paean to Lowell: "He reaffirms the power of literature to order the chaos of society, personality, with its own history, its own order, its own virtue" (pp. 3–34). Subsequent issues dealt again with Lowell (no. 23:3; no. 26:3), Berryman (no. 27/28:77), Frost (no. 25:3), and Elizabeth Bishop (no. 25:51). To be sure, not all American poets who were reviewed fared well; James Merrill was dismissed as "a clever technician [who] quickly becomes tiresome, trivializing, and twentyish" (no. 17:48). Laura Riding was the subject of an essay by Roy Fuller. He doubted that readers who made it to the end of a Riding work would have "any experience other than the arduous climb itself through the rarified logical air." But he praised the early work of Riding and demonstrated its influence on Auden (no. 23:6). When Riding took exception to the review, characterizing a part of it as "complication of admixtures of misknowledge," the magazine printed her letter, and Fuller's apologetic reply, in the next issue (no. 24:7).

While the reputation of the *Review* rests, in the main, on its coverage of British and American poetry, more attention needs to be given to the other national literatures that it featured. From its first issue, with poems by the Polish Zbigniew Herbert and the Russian Vladimir Mayakovsky, the *Review* continued to promote non-English contemporary poetry. In the second issue Patrick Bridgwater reviewed Michael Hamburger and Christopher Middleton's *Modern German Poetry* (pp. 37–43); the third issue printed Hamburger's poem "The Search" (p. 24). The most impressive German feature was Hamburger's essay in number 24 on the influence of Bertolt Brecht and minimalism on poets Gunter Kunert, Johannes Bobrowski, Wolf Biermann, Kurt Bartsch, Volker Braun, Bernd Jentzsch, Karl Mickel, and Heinz Kahlau. The review also contained three poems by Brecht and four by Peter Huchel, translated by Hamburger ("Brecht and His Successors," pp. 9–40). Issue 5 contained Hamburger's translation, with notes, of eleven poems by Friedrich Hölderlin (pp. 18–31) and Falck's translation of one poem each by Juan Jiminez, Antonio Machado, and Federico García Lorca (p. 16). A longer section of Machado's work, translated by Falck, appeared in number 13; and Falck's translations of poems by Cavafy were featured in issue 22 (p. 32). In number 17 the poems of Zbigniew Herbert were featured again, preceded by a discussion by Alvarez (pp. 4–21). Issue 9 contained poems from the T'ang Dynasty, translated by A. C. Graham (pp. 27–38).

In its ten-year run the *Review* broke the monotony of format with special issues. The first, on T. S. Eliot, came as early as issue 4. With that number the little magazine, with its pocket-size format (5 × 7 1/4) began to print photographs of the lead subject on the front cover. The issue was organized by specific works by Eliot, each with its prominent essayist: John Bayley wrote on the *Complete Plays*, F. W. Bateson on "Burbank with a Baedeker," Martin Dodsworth on "Gerontion," John Fuller on "Five-Finger Exercises," W. W. Robson on *On Poetry and Poets*, and Colin Falck on *Notes towards a Definition of Culture*. Michael Hamburger contributed "The Unity of Eliot's Poetry." Two issues later the *Review* introduced its first double issue, number 6/7 with contents devoted to William Empson; an interview by Christopher Ricks and a bibliography by Peter Lowbridge were featured. Number 11/12 was one of the most valuable the *Review* ever published; its subject was poetry of the 1930s. The cover photograph of the youthful trio Auden, Stephen Spender, and Christopher Isherwood caught the spirit of the age, and the contents made it live again: Julian Symons on his *Twentieth Century Verse*,* Peter Lowbridge on the Spanish Civil War, Martin Dodsworth evaluating the obscure but excellent Bernard Spencer, interviews with Edward Upward and James Reeves. The 1930s was a subject the *Review* would return to again in number 27/28 with a four-part essay on poet Norman Cameron by Geoffrey Grigson, Reeves, Roy Fuller, and even G. S. Fraser (pp. 9–21)

With the next issue there was an even more radical departure; the number consisted of three small anthologies: Antonio Machado's *The Garden in the Evening*, Michael Fried's *Appetites*, and Hamilton's *Pretending Not To Sleep* (no. 13). Number 19 was also a three-part anthology: *Twelve Poems* by Alvarez, *Tonight's Lover* by David Harsent, and *The Art of Love* by John Fuller.

The last special issue was also to be the last of the *Review*: its tenth anniversary double number. There was no parting announcement in the *Review*, but in a retrospective in the *Times* Hamilton confessed disappointment in the magazine's inefficacy to change the practice of poetry and criticism. He pointed also to the stagnant sales that such little magazines as the *Review* almost inevitably endured, while costs kept spiraling up. The *Review*'s circulation had reached what Hamilton believed to be the ceiling: an average of 1,000. Its costs had trebled.[9] Even Arts Council support of 300 pounds a quarter, awarded in 1971,[10] and price increases (from two shillings, six pence, to three shillings, to five, even to seventy-five new pence for the last double issue) could not meet rising costs.

In the last issue, almost all of the contributors were *Review* regulars; Fried, Roy Fuller, John Fuller, Hugo Williams, Harsent, Dunn, and Falck all contributed poems. Along with twenty-seven other poets, they contributed also to a major symposium, "The State of Poetry." Hamilton posed two questions: What were the most encouraging and discouraging elements of the "poetry scene" during the past decade? What encouraging developments lay ahead? Answers predictably ranged from dislike about American dominance (even some American respondents commented) to complaints about insularity and standard anthologies such as Penguin editions. Several traced the influences of major contemporary poets, especially Lowell, and others mentioned their favorite "new" poets who were neglected.[11] So ended the *Review*, which was universally acknowledged as the best poetry magazine in Britain, fulfilling Hamilton's comment that magazines should last only ten years: each decade needed its magazine, each magazine its decade.[12]

If the *Review* was the magazine for the 1960s, Hamilton clearly had something else in mind for the 1970s. The *New Review* did not appear until nearly two years later, in April 1974. Although Hamilton described the new magazine as "incorporat[ing] the *Review*," it was a venture radically more comprehensive than the early poetry magazine. Its format was a slick hundred pages measuring around 7 1/2 by 11 inches; it had outgrown poetry as a single interest and included fiction, drama, biographies of novelists, histories of other magazines, "letters" from foreign cities, and columns on science fiction and crime novels. "Anyone afraid that Ian Hamilton's monthly was going to err on the side of ragged-trousered frugality," the *Times* noted, would be "pleasantly surprised." Its format matched its "first-rate material. . . . To say that in many ways it is the old *Review* writ large" was a recommendation, "a guarantee of high standards."[13] Echoes of the *Review* survived: "Edward Pygge" returned from time to time, and many of the *Review* contributors continued to appear: notably, Falck, Dunn, Harsent, Alvarez, Hugo Williams, and John Fuller. Some of the interests and features of the *Review* surfaced to remind readers of the early magazine. Interest in Lowell continued, with five issues featuring his work (*NR* nos. 1:5; 18:11; 26:10; 34:10; 43:3). Interest in Berryman strengthened, with an essay, "Berryman's Fate," and a two-part study, "Berryman in the Forties" (*NR* nos. 47:3; 30:7; 31:25). Upon the death of John Crowe Ransom in 1974, Lowell, Roy Fuller, Richard Ellmann, and Denis Donoghue each supplied a tribute (*NR* no. 5:3–8). Falck pursued his interest in Alun Lewis from the *Review* (no. 17:22–31) with a new essay, "Lewis and Twentieth Century Romanticism"

(*NR* no. 25:53–59). A column of invited commentary, entitled "Opinion," which had appeared for the first time in the twenty-second issue of the *Review* for June 1970, was continued sporadically in the new magazine. Hamilton also expanded his editorial observations into a lead column, "Greek Street," in which he continued to take on other publishers and their authors. New targets included, for example, Robin Skelton and the *Malahat Review*, Chatto and Windus for their republication of Arnold Bennett's *Evening Standard* columns, and the *Times* for its reviewing policies (*NR* nos. 2:3; 4:4; 43:1). He continued to parody new works, such as Auden's *Thank You, Fog*, which became *Frog*, accompanied with a mildly obscene parody of Auden's mildly obscene limericks (*NR* no. 4:4).

But these familiar features were less apparent in the plethora of new genres and artists in the widened *New Review*. The number of new contributors was staggeringly impressive, including, among others, William Stafford (*NR* no. 20:53), Martin Amis (*NR* no. 20:55), David Lodge (*NR* no. 20:3), Joan Didion (*NR* no. 36:11), D. M. Thomas (*NR* no. 30:47), Frank Kermode (*NR* no. 22:57), Malcolm Bradbury (*NR* no. 33:39), M. L. Rosenthal (*NR* no. 31:5), Margaret Drabble (*NR* no. 11:25), Saul Bellow (*NR* no. 28:53), Paul Theroux (*NR* no. 9:23), Alan Sillitoe (*NR* no. 17:39), Bernard Bergonzi (*NR* no. 8:50), Gavin Ewart (*NR* no. 17:14), Peter Taylor (*NR* no. 6:15), Joyce Carol Oates (*NR* no. 14:3), Christopher Ricks (*NR* no. 6:49), Melvyn Bragg (*NR* no. 1:75), Alison Lurie (*NR* no. 2:33), Nadine Gordimer (*NR* no. 5:63), Irvin Ehrenpreis (*NR* no. 4:38), Alan Williamson (*NR* no. 5:11), and Ronald Hayman (*NR* no. 5:25).[14] With their contributions of plays, short stories, poems, novels-in-progress, essays, profiles, and columns, the *New Review* resembled not so much its single-minded predecessor as a cross between the *New Yorker* and the American *Saturday Review*.

Especially noticeable in the *New Review* was the attention given to fiction. Nearly every issue contained a short story or an excerpt from a novel. The first issue contained a chapter from Dan Jacobson's *The Maturity of Josef Baise* (pp. 60–63). The second printed part of Thomas Hinde's *Agent* (pp. 61–65), the third Jean Rhys's "Sleep It Off Lady" (pp. 45–49), the fifth Nadine Gordimer's "The Dogs" (pp. 63–68), the sixth two stories by Shiva Naipaul and Peter Taylor (pp. 15–20, 55–59). And the quality of fiction continued to be equally high throughout the run of the *New Review*; two years later it was publishing John Cheever's *Falconer*, and other short stories by Gordimer (*NR* no. 38:23; no. 34:47).

The criticism of fiction was vigorous, but in no way contentious, as that of poetry had been for the *Review*. Most of the discussions were relegated to a section of brief reviews at the end of each issue. The few that were given article status—such as Russell Davies's essay on Malcolm Lowry, cruelly titled "Bottle Baby," Derek Mahon's analysis of Brian Moore, or Malcolm Bradbury's essay-review of Kingsley Amis's *Alterations* and *I Want It Now* (*NR* nos. 2:81; 3:32; 33:39)—were not as substantive, or provocative, as other features in the issues. As Bradbury observed, the magazine had a "good number of good young critics" but it did not push them "to any real ambitiousness," and as a consequence the *New Review* could not sustain the critical level of the first *Review*[15]

More important than the reviews were the profiles of leading novelists that appeared almost as frequently as their fiction, providing (in some cases) criticism about works that were too new to be examined in much detail elsewhere: Angus Wilson, Kingsley Amis, Anthony Powell, John Fowles, Doris Lessing, Christopher Isherwood, John Hawkes, and William Burroughs (*NR* nos. 1:16; 4:21; 6:21; 7:31; 8:17; 17:17; 12:23; 25:37). None of the profiles were humdrum academic exercises, but few matched the inventiveness of Victor Bockris's portrait of Burroughs. Entitled "Information about the Operation," the piece adumbrated the style of the subject, weaving earlier interviews and recollections into its own dizzy structure. "Chapter 1" contained "answers," but readers had to wait until "2" to get the question, "Is he a drug addict?" (*NR* no. 25:37–46). In addition to the profiles, the *New Review* featured a series of interviews under the rubric, first, of "In Conversation With," changed in later issues to "Talks With . . . ": Philip Roth with Joyce Carol Oates (*NR* no. 14:3), Irwin Shaw with David Harsent (*NR* no. 22:52), Joseph Heller with Martin Amis (*NR* no. 20:55), Italo Calvino with Guido Almansi (*NR* no. 45:25), Dan Jacobson with Ian Hamilton (*NR* no. 40:25), and others.

Not all of the profiles were of novelists; dramatists Tom Stoppard, Arnold Wesker, and Simon Gray, and performers Liv Ullman and Marcel Marceau were interviewed (*NR* nos. 9:15; 11:25; 31:63; 37:60; 36:21). John Osborne's *Look Back in Anger* was treated as the pivotal modern play in "*Look Back* Looked Back On" by J. H. Huizinga (*NR* no. 29:59). Short plays, many of them for television, appeared in their entirety: Martin Amis's *It's Disgusting at Your Age*, Simon Gray's *Two Sundays* and *Dog Days*, Harold Pinter's *No Man's Land*, and Dennis Potter's *Brimstone and Treacle* (*NR* nos. 30:19; 20:8; 13:3; 26:34). An investigative piece on "The 'Lost Plays' of BBC TV" tried to determine what happened to plays after their television performance (*NR* no. 27:45). The *New Review* sent Alison Lurie to cover rehearsals of *Hamlet* for a Greenwich Theatre production and published her account in the first issue (pp. 33–42); in the thirty-third issue Bernard Crick reported on a Royal Shakespeare production of *Lear* (pp. 58–60).

Covering major novelists, poets, and dramatists was not, however, what gave the *New Review* its spark. Hamilton had a keen appreciation for journalistic topics, even offbeat ones, that could be handled wittily, but in depth. So one finds Melvyn Bragg writing about election canvassing techniques in Derby (*NR* no. 2:65); Irvin Ehrenpreis reporting on the Nixon tapes as "Yucktalk: Literary Style in the Oval Circus" (*NR* no. 6:5) and on the American Bicentennial celebration (*NR* no. 27:3). Philip Whitehead reviewed Carl Bernstein and Bob Woodward's *The Final Days* (*NR* no. 27:55). Caroline Blackwood talked about lesbianism in the feminist movement (*NR* no. 1:43). Ian McEwan defined pornography (*NR* no. 23:48). The art world was not ignored: subjects ranged from Christo's fence in California, to a National Portrait Gallery showing of portraits from the 1930s, to an examination of "Art Nouveau in America," and an interview with David Hockney (*NR* nos. 31:19; 28:57; 32:63; 34/35:75). Thomas Szasz and Anthony Clare argued about Ronald Laing's psychoanalytic theories in "Antipsychiatry: The Paradigm of the Plundered Mind" and "An Alternate View" (*NR* nos. 29:3; 33:25). Mary Kay Wilmers "reviewed" the *Times* obituary column (*NR* no. 25:19).

Some of the essays picked a particular historical moment that produced consequences of which most people were unaware. Jon Stallworthy wrote on the meeting of Wilfred Owen and Siegfried Sassoon at a war hospital and how it affected Owen's poem "Anthem for Doomed Youth" (*NR* no. 4:5). Diana Davenport related, in "The Malting House Summer," how John Davenport and Dylan Thomas came to write *The Death of the King's Canary* (*NR* no. 31:66). On the political front, Hans Keller showed how the Soviets used a soccer game for sinister ends (*NR* no. 30:49). His essay balanced the opening feature of the issue, on British soccer, which led Malcolm Bradbury to comment that the only thing the *New Review* "managed in the realm of stylistic synaesthesia to link" was literature and football.[16] Bradbury might also have noted other synaesthetic linkages in the descriptive pieces of American cities like Boston or Buffalo or San Francisco (*NR* nos. 3:29; 34/35:51).

No essay, however offbeat or well-executed, ever engendered as much excitement as a verse "epic" by the *New Review*'s frequently published critic, Clive James. "Peregrine Prykke's Pilgrimage through the London Literary World: A Tragedy in Heroic Couplets" had its premiere, a dramatic reading by Russell Davies, Martin Amis, and the author, on 3 June 1974, and its first publication in the *New Review* for August 1974. "Prykke's Pilgrimage" was the ultimate satire of the London literary scene, devastating in one performance many of the figures that Hamilton had swiped at for years in his role of "Pygge." This time Hamilton himself was parodied as "Hammerhead," while Falck was "Fluck," Dunn "Dunge," and Harsent "Harsfried." "Pygge, a satirist" was also one of the characters, joining other loosely disguised literary figures N. T. Thweet (Anthony Thwaite), Stephen Spindle (Spender), Mitch L. Adrian (Adrian Mitchell), the original "Anna Pest, poet, model, and vamp," and a cast of "many more." Hammerhead is, of course, the first editor that Prykke calls on when he gets to London, and Hammerhead in his other role as a reviewer for the *Times* assigns him a stack of books to review; he's not ready for the rarified air of his most prestigious *Review*. The "tragedy" of the farce is that Prykke dares ultimately to criticize his new literary mentors, has his work summarily destroyed by their reviews, is scorned by all of them, and hangs himself. The next few issues of the *New Review*, needless to say, touted first publication of James's *succès d'estime* and advertised its appearance as a monograph by a London publisher.

If the London literary world was indicted by James as an incestuous fraternity, the *New Review* certainly overcompensated for the sins of its fellows. Almost every issue abandoned traditional British insularity, with letters from Paris,

Vienna, Rome, even Rumania (cf. *NR* nos. 1:73; 18:57; 33:55; 28:62; 23:70); with profiles of foreign artists like Louis Céline, Thomas Mann, and Claude Chabrol (*NR* nos. 14:37; 16:15; 5:25); poems by Tadeusz Rozewicz, Osip Mandelstam, and Miroslav Holub (*NR* nos. 5:25; 18:37; 23:7); plays by Slawomir Mrozek and Bertolt Brecht (*NR* nos. 28:28; 33:11); Hans Keller's "Prague Diary" (*NR* no. 17:3); reports on Italo Calvino and Jean Genet (*NR* nos. 39:13; 37:9); and coverage of a television interview of Yevgeny Yevtushenko, and a German production of *Waiting for Godot* (*NR* nos. 32:67; 26:66). Four accounts, sensitive both politically and emotionally, dealt with South Africa: one recorded Afrikaans poet Breyten Breytenbach's struggle against conviction under the Terrorism Act (*NR* no. 25:3); another was the memoir of H. M. Jacobson of Johannesburg, published a year after his death (*NR* no. 30:25); and Norman Bromberger's "South Africa Journal" appeared in two parts (*NR* nos. 7:41; 18:23).

In its variety of content, seeming always to present the unexpected, the *New Review* tried to balance surprise with continuity in several ways. One was the regularity of its format, with a full front cover photograph; a first page for contents below another half-page photograph or cartoon; reviews and letters at the back; and, in volumes 1 and 4, the editorial "Greek Street" at the front. Additionally, the reader's expectation of such features as profiles or interviews was seldom disappointed. Another effort at continuity was a series of columns, in addition to "Greek Street," that appeared in many early issues: "SF," a review by Brian Aldiss of science fiction; "Media," authored first by Alan Brownjohn, then by Melvyn Bragg; and reviews of detective fiction, "Criminal Activities," the purview for a year of mystery novelist and poet Julian Symons and thereafter of David Craig. Only the last column survived the run of the *New Review*. "SF" did not survive the first year, and in the second the "Media" column briefly became "Television," authored by David Harsent. Appearing for only two consecutive issues (*NR* nos. 16, 17) were columns on cinema by Michael Mason and on theater by D.A.N. Jones. An untitled series was Hamilton's collection of essays that would lead eventually to a separate book on six little magazines. Essays appeared in the *New Review* on four of the six: the *Little Review, New Verse, Poetry,* and *Horizon** (*NR* nos. 2:43; 5:50; 8:39; 9:3).[17]

Unfortunately, the extraordinary efforts that made the *New Review* a critical success did not make it cost-effective in a country ravaged by economic hard times. The *Times* once suggested that the magazine would "probably become a collector's item, and might offer a useful hedge against inflation."[18] But few apparently invested in back issues of literary magazines. In July 1976 the magazine dropped its per copy price to seventy-five pence from ninety. At the beginning of its fourth year, the *New Review* revamped its contents page to a single one-third page column, made other minor format changes, shortened its length by a signature, and went to a lighter cover stock. Over a quarter of its subscription income had gone to mailing costs, the editor explained, and its lighter weight would put the *New Review* in a cheaper mail category. Hamilton admitted that within a year new postal rates would probably wipe out the savings, but he liked the magazine's "more workmanlike appearance" anyway (*NR* no. 37:1). Two issues later the editor resorted to using double issues, and four issues later he increased the cover price to its former ninety pence; the subscription price rose from eight pounds to ten (for institutions from twelve pounds to fifteen). At the end of its fourth year the *New Review* became quarterly. In his "Greek Street" column Hamilton pointed out that for two years the magazine had been losing money, and predicted that a reduced publication schedule would "stabilize our position once and for all, and also permit us the option of resuming on a monthly basis later on" (*NR* no. 48:1). Such an option never materialized, and after two more quarterly issues, the *New Review* stopped publication.

Notes

1. *Times Literary Supplement*, 29 June 1962, p. 477.
2. Ian Hamilton, "Viewpoint," *Times Literary Supplement*, 11 August 1972, p. 842.
3. *The Modern Poet: Essays from "The Review,"* ed. Ian Hamilton (London, 1968).
4. "Detectives of the Spurious" [review of *The Modern Poet*, ed. Ian Hamilton], *Times Literary Supplement*, 30 January 1969, p. 107.
5. Roy Fuller, "Who Needs a Poetry Reviewer?" *Encounter* 40, no. 5 (May 1973):74.
6. See Ian Hamilton, *A Poetry Chronicle: Essays and Reviews* (London, 1972). Not all agreed with Fuller about Hamilton's reviewing skills; see, e.g., "What's Good Is Well Made" [review of *A Poetry Chronicle*], *Times Literary Supplement*, 23 March 1973, p. 319.
7. Hamilton, "Viewpoint," p. 842.
8. Ibid.
9. Ibid.
10. "Commentary," *Times Literary Supplement*, 18 June 1971, p. 704.
11. Poets and critics who contributed to the symposium were Dannie Abse, Alvarez, John Bayley, Kingsley Amis, Richard Eberhart, Martin Dodsworth, Clive James, Douglas Dunn, Anthony Thwaite, Peter Levi, Elizabeth Jennings, Richard Wilbur, Julian Symons, John Fuller, Roy Fuller, George MacBeth, David Harsent, Donald Hall, Vernon Scannell, Peter Porter, Gavin Ewart, Michael Longley, Charles Tomlinson, Alan Brownjohn, Jonathan Raban, Philip Larkin, Jeff Nuttall, John Carey, and Peter Redgrove.
12. See the preface to Hamilton's *The Little Magazine: A Study of Six Editors* (London, 1976). For a sample of the encomia from other little magazines, see the back cover of issue 21 of the *Review*.
13. "Commentary," *Times Literary Supplement*, 5 April 1974, p. 366.
14. The issue numbers do not indicate the first or the only appearance of the authors in the *New Review*.
15. Malcolm Bradbury, "The Shock Troops of Modernism," *Times Literary Supplement*, 15 October 1976, p. 1297.
16. Ibid.
17. Hamilton, *The Little Magazines*, p. vii.
18. "Commentary," *Times Literary Supplement*, 5 April 1974, p. 366.

Information Sources

BIBLIOGRAPHY

Bergonzi, Bernard. Review of *The Little Magazines*, ed. Ian Hamilton. *Modern Language Review* 74, no. 4 (October 1979):932–33.

Bradbury, Malcolm. "The Shock Troops of Modernism." *Times Literary Supplement*, 15 October 1976, p. 1297.

"Commentary." *Times Literary Supplement*, 18 June 1971, p. 704.

"Commentary." *Times Literary Supplement*, 5 April 1974, p. 366.

"Detectives of the Spurious." *Times Literary Supplement*, 30 January 1969, p. 10.

Fuller, Roy. "Who Needs a Poetry Reviewer?" *Encounter* 40, no. 5 (May 1973):74.

Hamilton, Ian. *The Little Magazines: A Study of Six Editors*. London, 1976.

————. *The Modern Poet: Essays from "The Review."* London, 1968.

————. *A Poetry Chronicle: Essays and Reviews*. London, 1972.

————. "Viewpoint." *Times Literary Supplement*, 11 August 1972, p. 842.

May, Derwent. "London Magazines." *Times Literary Supplement*, 11 January 1968, p. 41.

Morrison, Blake. "A Place for Poetry." *Times Literary Supplement*, 16 June 1968, p. 665.

INDEXES

The New Review, volumes 1–3, indexed.

REPRINT EDITIONS

The Review: Kraus Reprint, Nendeln, Liechtenstein; Scholars' Facsimiles and Reprints, Delmar, N.Y.

LOCATION SOURCES

American

Widely available.

British

Widely available.

Publication History

MAGAZINE TITLE AND TITLE CHANGES

The Review, April/May 1962–Spring/Summer 1972. *The New Review*, April 1974–September 1978.

VOLUME AND ISSUE DATA

The Review: Number 1, April/May 1962–number 29/30, Spring-Summer 1972. *The New Review*: Volume 1, number 1, April 1974–volume 5, number 2, September 1978. *New Review* volumes 1–4 are consecutively numbered, numbers 1–48; volume 5 begins as number 1. *Review* numbers 6/7, 11/12, 27/28, and 29/30 are double issues. *New Review* numbers 34/35, 39/40, and 45/46 are double issues.

FREQUENCY OF PUBLICATION

The Review announced as bimonthly; irregular. *The New Review*, volumes 1–4, monthly; volume 5 quarterly.

PUBLISHERS

The Review: Nexus Publications. *The New Review*: New Review Limited, 11 Greek Street, London, W1V 5LE.

EDITORS

The Review: Ian Hamilton. Colin Falck, associate editor, *Review*, numbers 22–30, with editorial board members Michael Fried, John Fuller, Francis Hope, Clive James, Gabriel Pearson, and Stephen Wall. *The New Review*: Ian Hamilton. Elizabeth Ogilvie, Charis Ryder, deputy editors, volume 1, numbers 1–6. Charis Ryder, volume 1, number 7–volume 5, number 2. Karl Miller, associate editor, volume 2, number 14–volume 5, number 2. Jeanette Dixon, associate editor, volume 2, number 13–volume 3, number 36. Amanda Radice, assistant editor, volume 4, number 43–volume 5, number 2.

Alvin Sullivan

REVIEW OF ENGLISH LITERATURE, A

During its eight years of existence, from January 1960 to October 1967, *A Review of English Literature* was edited by A. Norman Jeffares, an established scholar-critic who was then professor of English literature at the University of Leeds. Each of the thirty-two numbers began with a two-page editorial; in the first of them Jeffares sketched a *raison d'être* for the journal. It was addressed to "general readers" as well as to "those who are professionally engaged in the study and teaching of literature." Its contributors would write "clearly and with zest" and and avoid the pretentious "pseudo-scientific air of over-specialized criticism." For literature was "a thing to be enjoyed," and the critic must be "a person of lively and penetrating mind who adds to our enjoyment of what we read by writing about it in a stimulating and appreciative way." The critic's role was to "communicate his enjoyment . . . to illuminate, to help us to understand what we read, to elucidate, to modify and develop taste" (1, no. 1:3).

Jeffares also announced that his journal would not restrict its gaze to the British Isles. Literature in English transcended national and political boundaries, and the *Review* was especially interested in "the spreading and burgeoning of the parent stock" in the countries of the Commonwealth (1, no. 1:4). Poems by Earle Birney (of Canada), Derek Walcott (West Indies), R. Parthasarathy (India), and Nizim Ezekiel (India) appeared in subsequent issues, as did articles on the novels of Hugh MacLennan (Canada), R. K. Narayan (India), and Patrick White (Australia), on Chinus Achebe's *Things Fall Apart* (Nigeria), on the beginnings of Nigerian literature in English, on a new English of Africa, and on the poetry of A. D. Hope (Australia). In the final 1965 number the editor announced with satisfaction that "the rapidly increasing amount of material in Commonwealth literature of high quality arriving for consideration" had helped lead to the establishment of a new publication also edited at Leeds, the *Journal of Commonwealth Literature* (6, no. 4:7).

Published in London by Longmans, *A Review of English Literature* was attractively designed and attractively priced at four shillings an issue. Its average length was 80 (later 100) pages, and contributors were advised not to submit articles of more than 3,600 words or poems of more than twenty-four lines. Another attractive feature was that issues usually featured a group of articles on a particular subject: examples are American literature, literary magazines, Yeats, drama, the contemporary novel, Macaulay, and Swift. Particularly noteworthy were the clusters devoted to John Cowper Powys, Coleridge, Dickens (guest edited by John Butt), and Shakespeare (guest edited by Kenneth Muir).

These clusters, however, did not keep the *Review* from remaining a wide-ranging and eclectic journal. The special focus numbers usually contained other material as well; an interview with C. P. Snow, for example, is included in the Swift issue. From time to time the bill of fare also included unusual entrées like "The Scientific Textbook as a Work of Art," Quentin Bell on Leslie Stephen's "Mausoleum Book," "The Australian Folk-Song and the Origin of the Folk-Song," and Edmund Blunden's verse translation of Aeschylus' *Prometheus Bound*. Contributors to *A Review of English Literature* were as varied as the contents, and few appeared more than once or twice. The majority were academics at British universities and (to cite only the best known) ranged from older figures like E.M.W. Tillyard and William Empson, through Graham Hough and Frank Kermode, to younger critics like Tony Tanner and Malcolm Bradbury. Nonacademic contributors included David Garnett, Edmund Blunden, George Woodcock, Frank O'Connor, John Wain, and (on two notable occasions) Angus Wilson.

How influential was *A Review of English Literature*? How deep did it bite? The answer to both these questions is "not very." In coming to understand why, the first place to turn is to Jeffares's editorials; perhaps their most noticeable feature is the consistently belletristic tone, which ranges from postprandial sonority to bluff fatuity: "In an age when the level of technique has risen," the editor wrote at the beginning of an issue devoted to the contemporary novel, "we must beware of whoring after mere novelty. The gimmick in the flood may be but a haystack carrying the writer to oblivion; the raft which can land lesser as well as greater writers among the ever-living is made of integrity of purpose as well as sheer skill in writing" (1, no. 2:6).

A second place to turn for understanding is the *Critical Quarterly*,* which began publication the year before *A Review of English Literature* at a university not far from Leeds and which was similarly committed to the belief that literature should be enjoyed, and similarly concerned to address the general as well as the professional reader through the medium of an eclectic and lively journal. The reasons why the *Critical Quarterly* became the more penetrating and influential literary magazine include the fact that its editors were more *au fait* with contemporary critical trends, made more attempt to identify and to provide useful commentary on contemporary writers of emerging distinction, had a number of more or less regular contributors, and paid particular attention to the critical needs of schools and universities.

Jeffares began his editorial to the October 1967 issue by discussing his journal's increased production costs. *A Review of English Literature* had done very well, "handsomely exceed[ing] the circulation target initially set" and reaching a comparatively wide audience. But this audience would diminish as the selling price of the journal rose and, therefore, Jeffares surprisingly concluded, "This . . . is the last number of *A Review of English Literature*." He went on to reaffirm his commitment to a criticism that carries "the mark of style rather than the style sheet, . . . creates while criticising, and generally communicates an over-flowing enthusiasm and enjoyment of life itself'' (8, no. 4:7–8). Such an over-flowing enthusiast as A. Norman Jeffares could not be contained for long: three years later he became the first editor of *ARIEL: A Review of International English Literature* (published by the University of Calgary in Alberta, Canada), the trans-Atlantic successor to *A Review of English Literature*.

Information Sources

INDEXES
    None.
REPRINT EDITIONS
    None.
LOCATION SOURCES
    American
        Widely available.
    British
        Widely available.

Publication History

MAGAZINE TITLE AND TITLE CHANGES
    A Review of English Literature.
VOLUME AND ISSUE DATA
    Volume 1, number 1–volume 8, number 4, January 1960–October 1967.
FREQUENCY OF PUBLICATION
    Quarterly.
PUBLISHER
    Longmans, Green and Co., Ltd., 6 and 7 Clifford Street (later 48 Grosvenor Street), London, W. 1.
EDITORS
    A. Norman Jeffares. John Butt was guest editor for volume 2, number 3; Kenneth Muir for volume 5, number 2.

Kerry McSweeney

REVIEW OF REVIEWS, THE. See VEA

RIGHT REVIEW

Right Review, established in October 1936, is less a literary journal than an offensive and blatant political diatribe presented by a Polish Royalist, Count Potocki of Montalk. The magazine sold for six pence, measured 6 1/4 by 9 inches, and sported red covers (later purple) and a woodcut of an eagle looking to its left and adorned with a shield. Additional decorations, such as the number 44, a globe, and representation of the zodiac or a horoscope, became part of the cover design in subsequent issues; cover art for the final number was simply an enlargement of the horoscope.[1] Most numbers of the magazine carried a table of contents on the inside front cover; only the last three issues were paginated. According to Potocki's editorial statement in that first number, *Right Review* was printed "entirely by hand," as its rough quality attests. The editor intended for the journal to appear monthly, but his goal was never realized; he soon advertised the magazine as a bimonthly, but publication was always irregular.

To some extent *Right Review* was meant to counter another journal being published in England contemporaneously, *Left Review* (1934–1938), and Potocki, who called it "the Wrong Review," celebrated the passing of the rival periodical. "The LEFT REVIEW having found itself unable to sustain comparison with The Right Review, has ceased publication," he gloated in his July 1938 issue. Still, it was only happenstance that the two journals existed at the same time, and Potocki's editorial statement makes it clear that there were motivations other than *Left Review* that led to his creation of *Right Review*. "The principle [*sic*] aims of this review," he declared, "are to voice the opinions and the works of the editor, to carry out a frontal counter-attack against the noisy and misleading propaganda of the communists . . . and to harbour any Poets and other men of real genius whom the Editor can come across." The use of the adjective "noisy" in this pejorative sense is particularly revealing. Potocki was a firm believer in strict adherence to social class, and he considered common men rabble. Thus, "noisy" implies his perception of the lower classes as rude and offensive to his sense of taste and decorum. This attitude is reinforced in the next paragraph of the editorial statement when he explains how his staunchly Royalist political beliefs will be served by the magazine: "It is our aim to show that the Divine Right of Kings is the sanest and best form of government. . . . We intend to prove that such government is ultimately beneficial to the whole human race including the lowest classes of mankind."

The contents of *Right Review* reflect the editor's strong beliefs. Some poetry was published, much of it written by the editor or translated from Polish or French authors by him.[2] A few mediocre pieces by right-wing poets Maxwell Billens Rudd, Charles Maurras of the Action Française, Roy Campbell, and others were also included, and a previously unpublished quatrain purportedly by Lord Byron appeared in the inaugural issue. Amusingly, there is even an "Ode to Hypocrisy" by Comrade (ci-devant Prince) Bobowski, who is identified as the "Poet Laureate to the Bank of Poland." In addition, there were woodcuts by Georg Hann and Marguerite Salle, a gossipy column entitled "Parish Notes," astrological information, constant requests for money and information, and advertisements—primarily for Potocki's own works. He requests that "communists and racial enemies please abstain from calling" at the Right Review Bookshop, and slogans similar in tone to this request are interspersed throughout the journal: "Workers of the World Unite to Crush Communism!" is a typical example. There were also occasional letters from people such as Lawrence Durrell (January 1939) and Aldous Huxley (December 1939).[3] Even book and music reviews obviously reflect the editor's biases. Potocki openly avowed that he liked novels, but not modern novels. Similarly, when Margaret Townshend reviewed several concerts in glowing terms, she reported that the only blemishes were two modern pieces (June 1939). A fine example of Potocki's reactionary political views— and how those affected his stance on social issues—is his declaration that women who question the right of male sexual dominance are guilty of creating gross perversions of the natural order of things. The material in *Right Review* that best expressed the editor's prejudices, lack of logic, and self-serving, paranoiac, and vengeful charges was the serialized autobiography, "Whited Sepulchres," an account of Potocki's trial and imprisonment for a parody of obscene poetry by Verlaine.

Certain themes recur throughout the contents of *Right Review*: royal geneal-ogies, Polish history, and a glorification of all monarchies, with particular at-tention being paid to France, England, and above all Poland. Politically, Potocki preferred fascism to democracy. Indeed, democracy was the reason that fascism had to be created. Many of these subjects appear in a series of essays, "Social Climbers in Bloomsbury," which is almost literary and social history at times. Potocki recounts his meetings with Virginia Woolf and the members of the Bloomsbury group, several of whom had served as his legal defense.[4] In the essays Potocki takes advantage of every opportunity to blame various religions for the world's woes. Christians, he proclaims, "stink in the nostrils of men of good will," and in October 1938 he calls for "more religion and less Christi-anity." His favorite hobbyhorse is Judaism. He records, for instance, that he acquainted Virginia Woolf with the fact that "Jews are not civilised even now." Elsewhere, in his defense of British fascist leader Sir Oswald Mosely, and in pieces such as "The Jewry Disagrees" (October 1938), "Jewish Genealogies," "Gentile Defense," and, in fact, on practically every page of *Right Review*, Potocki shrilly and adamantly declaims against long-nosed "jews and their Aryan slaves." These "loathsome" creatures, he declares, are traitors bent on con-trolling the world while simultaneously perverting noble blood lines and dis-rupting honest society through the use of "every device" imaginable.

Potocki, who signed one of his essays "Senior Polish co-heir general of the Kings of Poland and the Grand Dukes of Lithuania," seems to have been par-ticularly proud of two things. In January 1939 the *Criterion** called *Right Review* "the only only uncompromisingly right review in this country"; this quote appeared under the masthead on the inside front cover in every subsequent issue.[5] Secondly, beginning in March 1940, *Right Review* labeled itself "The Official Organ of the Royal House of Poland." *Right Review* was an interesting exper-iment. It lived a short life, and appears to have inflicted little influence on English literature or society.

Notes

1. Actually, due to the poor quality of the printing, it is impossible to determine whether this is an exact enlarged replica of the small zodiac that appears on the cover of the earlier issues.

2. Although poems or essays occasionally were published in Polish, the journal's contents were primarily in English.

3. Durrell writes that while he does not agree with what Potocki says, he does find the editor's style appealing.

4. Others among the Bloomsbury group whom Potocki writes about include Virginia Woolf's husband, Leonard, Kingsley Martin, William Plomer, and Douglas Glass. Potocki goes so far in his attempt to discredit the group in any way that he can that he even derides their accents—which he tries to reproduce.

5. The quotation is included in a review of British Journals (18, no. 71:400–401). Interestingly, the ideas and tone contained in *Right Review* were not uncommon in England and on the Continent during the 1930s. As shrill and offensive as Potocki's proclamations are, the *Criterion* reviewer's admiration of *Right Review* and his contention that its October 1938 number would "widen . . . its circle of readers" is evidence that Potocki's journal was derivative and merely reflected the popular concepts of the radical fringe of the far right in Great Britain and Europe.

Information Sources

INDEXES
   None.
REPRINT EDITIONS
   None.
LOCATION SOURCES
   American
      Complete runs: University of Buffalo Library; University of Wisconsin Library; Yale University Library.
      Partial run: University of Kansas Library.
   British
      Partial run: British Museum.

Publication History

MAGAZINE TITLE AND TITLE CHANGES
   Right Review.
VOLUME AND ISSUE DATA
   Volume 1, numbers 1–17, October 1936–June 1947.
FREQUENCY OF PUBLICATION
   Irregular.
PUBLISHER
   Count Potocki of Montalk, 1936–1939: 39 Lambs Conduit Street, London, W.C. 1. 1939: 12 Winchester Street, London, W.C. 1. 1939–1940: 16 Claverton Street, London, W.C. 1. 1943: Half Moon Cottage, Little Bookham, Surrey. 1946: 10 St. Peter's St., London, N.1. 1946–1947: 22 Devonia Road, London, N.1.
EDITORS
   Count Potocki of Montalk. Nigel Heseltine, coeditor of issue 2, 1936.

Steven Gale

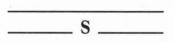

S

ST. MARTIN'S (IN-THE-FIELD) REVIEW. See VEA

SALTIRE REVIEW

Founded in 1936, the Saltire Society was one of the results of the nationalist movement in culture and politics usually referred to as the twentieth-century Scottish Renaissance. "The Society is concerned with all things Scottish, past, present, and future. It seeks to preserve all that is best in Scottish tradition and to encourage developments which can strengthen and enrich the country's cultural life."[1] This sweeping statement from a recent handbook could have served as a manifesto for the two periodicals published by the society between 1954 and 1964: despite changes of editorship, style, emphasis, and physical appearance, the *Saltire Review* and its successor *New Saltire* were essentially faithful to the breadth of concern of their parent organization. They were never conceived as narrowly literary periodicals, though they were always valuable outlets for the new Scottish writing of their day. New poetry and fiction, however, were juxtaposed with essays on the other arts, with antiquarian material, with discussions of politics and economics, with explorations of the Scottish character and way of life, and with comment on world events—always with an attempt to provide a distinctively Scottish angle of vision. Fueled as they were by a strong commitment to a nationalistic viewpoint, they never finally succumbed to the temptation to restrict their literary offerings to the work of a nationalistic coterie.

Before the *Saltire Review*, the Scottish Renaissance movement had spawned a large number of periodicals, but their mortality rate had been high. When the *Saltire* first appeared in April 1954, it was possible to detect a new optimism in the cultural life of Scotland: as the first editorial pointed out, the previous ten years had seen "fresh developments in every branch of artistic activity." Especially noteworthy were the establishment in 1947 of the Edinburgh Festival, the creation of a new Edinburgh theater, recent developments in the Scottish organization of the British Broadcasting Corporation, and the establishment of *Lines Review*,* a poetry journal which has survived to this day. In the longer perspective, all these were symptoms of Britain's postwar recovery in the 1950s.

The founding editor of *Saltire Review*, Alexander Scott, was a writer and academic with several works of poetry and scholarship already to his credit. Behind him stood an advisory board of senior figures in the Scottish cultural world, covering between them all the fine arts, and combining authority and respectability with vitality. They included the novelists Neil Gunn, Eric Linklater, Naomi Mitchison, and Sir Compton Mackenzie, and the poet Edwin Muir, with representatives of the worlds of historiography, folklore, and the fine arts. Such a board was the clearest possible indication of the periodical's aim to perform a central role in the artistic life of Scotland. From the beginning, the emphasis was very much on the arts: even when the journal's focus was turned on the world furth of Scotland, it was with aspects of foreign artistic life that it dealt. The comparison with Scotland was usually very much in mind, as in Jack House's account of theater in Russia and Gordon Chapman's discussion of contemporary Spanish writing, both in the second issue for August 1954. The early numbers, in fact, have the air of a determined internationalism. The first number, for instance, featured an essay on the poetry of Dylan Thomas, as well as a defiantly intellectual discussion entitled "Carlyle and the Germans" by John Holloway. The third issue had an account of contemporary Italian politics and writing. A small but regular amount of space was thus devoted in each issue to exploring what was happening overseas.

One can detect in the early issues, however, a developing tendency—indeed, a desire—to get beyond the confines of the world of the arts, and to comment more broadly on Scottish life and world affairs. This impulse came to full fruition with the appointment of James M. Reid as coeditor with Alexander Scott from the eighth number (Autumn 1956). Reid was an experienced and well-respected journalist, and his interests included literature. His outlook was, if anything, left-wing and nationalist, and he was, for a time, president of the Saltire Society. His first appearance had been in the second issue, to which he contributed an article to counteract some assumptions about the United States. Prior to his appointment, a section entitled "Quarterly Comment" had been instituted in the seventh number, but on his appointment this became a column of considerable weight and bite, discussing the crisis-laden international scene and the local issues of Scottish life. With the joint editorship, the *Saltire Review* came of age, and two issues later it became a true quarterly, having hitherto appeared three times a year.

The literary dimension of the periodical under Alexander Scott's editorship was valuable and distinguished. Few Scottish poets of note failed to be represented in its pages, and a wide range of unknown writers were given their chance. Especially significant, with hindsight, was the encouragement given to certain major figures at the outset of their careers, most notably Edwin Morgan, George Mackay

Brown, and Iain Crichton Smith. Lesser, but still worthwhile, talents which were similarly nurtured included Burns Singer, W. Price Turner, and Alastair Mackie. Frequently to be found enriching the pages of *Saltire Review* from its earliest days were poems by Norman MacCaig, Maurice Lindsay, George Bruce, Derick Thomson, Sydney Tremayne, Sydney Goodsir Smith, and Alexander Scott himself, all of whom had begun publishing in the forties, and who were coming to be thought of as the second generation of Scottish Renaissance poets.

Among the most significant items published in *Saltire Review* were the extracts, in the first number, from the diaries of William Soutar (an important young Scots poet who died in 1943 after years of illness), Sydney Goodsir Smith's long poem "Gowdsmith in Reekie" and David Daiches's seminal paper, "The Writing of Scottish Literary History," both in the fifth number, and the extracts from Hugh MacDiarmid's work in progress in the tenth. From the later numbers, after Scott and Reid had relinquished the editorship, one might pick out as especially significant the extract in number 16 from the work in progress of Robin Jenkins, a novelist whose body of work, in number, range, and weight, is arguably the most significant in modern Scottish writing after Neil Gunn. The periodical would regularly attract "star" names, such as Daiches, MacDiarmid, Muir, and Gunn, and received contributions from major scholars such as John Holloway, James Kinsley, and Helena Mennie Shire. Yet the essential character of the journal— and the credit for its success—was due to Scott and Reid and their associates, such as Walter Keir, a university lecturer whose book reviews were among the liveliest and most valuable of the regular items in its pages.

In numbers 14 and 15, no editors' names are listed, though Scott and Reid still contribute. But with the sixteenth number for Autumn 1958, Alexander Reid took over as editor. Reid had been a journalist, bookseller, accountant, and broadcaster, as well as a poet and dramatist. No very clear change in character came over the periodical with the new editor, though with issue 19 it published only three times a year. With number 21 for Summer 1960, the editorship passed to David Cleghorn Thomson. The weight of J. M. Reid's journalistic expertise was lacking, and the buoyant urgency which propelled the publication in its best years had gone with Scott's zest and flair. After number 23 *Saltire Review* ceased publication: the Saltire Society was unable to continue the annual subsidy it had been providing.[2]

Within months, however, a new quarterly publication appeared, entitled *New Saltire* and edited jointly by Giles Gordon and Michael Scott-Moncrieff. Some external funding had been made available,[3] and further steps to secure the financial future of the new publication were taken when the Scottish Committee of the Arts Council of Great Britain provided a further grant from the fourth issue onwards. Number 6 announced that a new company had been formed, New Saltire Ltd., to relieve the Saltire Society of the financial burden. When the journal finally folded after the eleventh number, however, it was clear that the financial problems of such a publication had still not been solved. Although the immediate cause of *New Saltire*'s demise was given as the resignation of its editor, Magnus Magnusson, and the difficulty of finding a replacement, it was also admitted that despite "a healthy and growing circulation," it had proved difficult to "secure enough advertising revenue to support the production of a magazine of the standards at which it aimed."

In its eleven issues *New Saltire* had three editors. The editorship, at the outset shared, was reduced to Giles Gordon alone for the fourth number; he and Scott-Moncrieff had quarrelled over an article by Hugh MacDiarmid on David Hume.[4] From the fifth issue, editor Magnus Magnusson changed both the format and the scope of the publication. The larger page size and glossy paper gave it a refreshingly up-to-date image, and it now set out to discuss current affairs to an extent new to its pages.

Under both editorial regimes, the literary content of *New Saltire* was distinguished. Hugh MacDiarmid, Goodsir Smith, Morgan, Gunn, Lindsay, and Bruce continued to support it. And the period of *New Saltire*'s publication coincided with the coming to full maturity of Iain Crichton Smith and George Mackay Brown. New names were increasingly associated with *New Saltire*. David Craig contributed poetry and discussion from a radical standpoint; several poets at the outset of their careers appeared in its pages, such as James Rankin, Robin Fulton, and James Aitchison; and Alexander Trocchi contributed a long article to number 8. Glasgow-born Trocchi was the author of *Cain's Book*, a novel set in the New York drug scene, which became one of the *causes célèbres* of sixties Britain.

The departure of *New Saltire* was a real loss. It is true that *Lines Review* continued to act as an important outlet for new Scottish poetry, and in 1965 Duncan Glen launched *Akros*,* his influential magazine of poetry and poetry criticism. The loss of the *Saltire* combination of creative writing, artistic criticism, and informed comment on politics and society was keenly felt in Scotland, and there have started up, from the later sixties onwards, several new publications with variations on that formula. It is pleasant to note that they include the *Scottish Review*, partly supported by the Saltire Society, and with Alexander Scott as a joint editor.

Notes

1. *The Scottish Companion 1985*, ed. Kenneth Roy (Ayr, 1985), p. 130.
2. Duncan Glen, *Hugh MacDiarmid and the Scottish Renaissance* (Edinburgh, 1964), p. 222.
3. Ibid.
4. Ibid.

Information Sources

BIBLIOGRAPHY
Glen, Duncan. *Hugh MacDiarmid and the Scottish Renaissance*. Edinburgh, 1964.
Royle, Trevor. *The Macmillan Companion to Scottish Literature*. London, 1983.
Wilson, Norman, ed. *Scottish Writing and Writers*. Edinburgh, 1977.
INDEXES
None.
REPRINT EDITIONS
None.

LOCATION SOURCES

Saltire Review

American

Complete runs: Buffalo and Erie County Public Library; Kansas State University Library; Los Angeles Public Library; New York Public Library; University of California at Los Angeles Library; University of Chicago Library; University of Kentucky at Lexington Library; University of Wisconsin at Madison Library.

British

Complete runs: Aberdeen University Library; Birmingham Public Library; British Museum; Cambridge University Library; Glasgow University Library; London University Library; Mitchell Library, Glasgow; National Library of Scotland, Edinburgh.

New Saltire

American

Complete runs: New York Public Library; U.S. Library of Congress; University of California at Los Angeles Library; University of Chicago Library; University of Kentucky at Lexington Library.

British

Complete runs: Bodleian Library; Edinburgh Public Library; Edinburgh University Library; Glasgow University Library; National Library of Scotland, Edinburgh; University College Library; University of London, Goldsmith's Library.

Publication History

MAGAZINE TITLE AND TITLE CHANGES

Saltire Review of Arts, Letters and Life, 1954–1961. *New Saltire*, 1961–1964.

VOLUME AND ISSUE DATA

Saltire Review: Volumes 1–6, numbers 1–23, April 1954–Winter 1961. *New Saltire*: Numbers 1–11, Summer 1961–April 1964.

FREQUENCY OF PUBLICATION

Saltire Review: Numbers 1–9: three times a year. Numbers 10–18: quarterly. Numbers 19–23: three times a year. *New Saltire*: quarterly.

PUBLISHERS

Saltire Review: The Saltire Society, Gladstone's Land, 483 Lawnmarket, Edinburgh 1. *New Saltire*: Numbers 1–5: The Saltire Society; numbers 6–11: New Saltire Ltd., Gladstone's Land, 483 Lawnmarket, Edinburgh 1.

EDITORS

Saltire Review: Alexander Scott, 1954–1958. James M. Reid, 1956–1958. Alexander Reid, 1958–1960. David Cleghorn Thomson, 1960–1961. *New Saltire*: Giles Gordon, 1961–Summer 1962. Michael Scott-Moncrieff, 1961–Spring 1962. Magnus Magnusson, August 1962–1964.

David S. Robb

SAMPHIRE

Samphire, a small poetry magazine published in Ipswich from 1968 to 1981, took its title, referring to an edible sea plant, from *King Lear*: "Half way down

hangs / one that gathers Samphire / dreadful trade!'' Coeditors Michael Butler
and Kemble Williams were poets themselves, authors, respectively, of *Nails and
Other Poems* and *The Kind Woman and Other Poems*. Although they published
a few of their poems in *Samphire*, they never used their magazine to promote
their own poetry or personal viewpoints. Their contribution to *Samphire* and to
poetry in general lay in their judicious publication of poetry from other, usually
new, authors and in their even-tempered reviews of poetry collections.

The magazine's purpose, according to Butler, was to reach that audience
(which the editors believed was larger than many supposed) interested in the
''exciting experiments [that] are going on—concrete poetry[,] sound poetry, jazz
poetry'' (1, no. 1:21). They did not detest conventional rhythm and rhyme but
believed that contemporary poetry demanded ''a subtle use of rhyme'' and a
change from iambic rhythm (2, no. 14:14). They were also aware of the limitations of contemporary verse: ''Too much contemporary poetry is disfigured by
self-indulgence, cliché, 'cleverness' or plain sentimentality'' (1, no. 7:21). At
first they perceived their audience as those readers in East Anglia (1, no. 5:22),
but this seemed to cease to be important as people subscribed to *Samphire* from
as far away as the United States, Australia, and Hong Kong.

The editors' reviews made up the bulk of their writing for *Samphire*. Butler's
special interest was in perceiving contrasts. In his review of Jeff Nutall's work,
he observed that the ''ironic tone of *Sixties Christmas* . . . contrasts sharply with
the pervading atmosphere of violence'' (1, no. 13:27). Butler's review of David
Jaffin's *The Half of a Circle* pointed out the tension between the objective and
subjective (3, no. 1:47). Concerning Anne Sexton's posthumously published
collection, *45 Mercy Street*, he mentioned the contrasting subjects of ''perse-
cutors and victims'' (2, no. 16:30). Williams, on the other hand, analyzed form,
discussing, for example, the irregular rhythm of Gael Turnbull's poetry in *Scantlings* (1, no. 14:10) and the sprung rhythm of poetry in Geoffrey Holloway's
Rhine Jump (2, no. 11:30).

Butler and Williams believed that they should encourage new writers. Therefore, their reviews were usually favorable. When they did criticize the work of
a lesser-known poet, it was gently done. For example, Michael Butler said of
Erica Jong, ''What the poet lacks in exactness, she makes up for in energy''
(2, no. 16:29). Probably because he was well-established, Auden was treated
less kindly than other poets. Kemble Williams did not like Auden's latest collection, *An Epistle to a Godson*, finding it left ''little more than what often seems
like donnish cleverness and whimsy'' (2, no. 3:10). He also objected to Auden
as an old man removing from his collection poetry written when he was young.

Letters to the editors suggested that a major criticism leveled against *Samphire*
was that, in the social and political unrest of the late 1960s and early 1970s, it
lacked political poetry. The editors replied much as Geoffrey Grigson had in the
1930s in *New Verse**: they did not object to political poetry, but they demanded
that it also be good poetry. This they felt was nearly impossible. According to
Butler, ''Propaganda, unfortunately, has very little to do with poetry, for when

successful it is simple, exaggerated, slanted, whereas poetry is (among other things) complex, tentative, multivalent'' (1, no. 3:22).

Widely known poets who published in *Samphire* included Donald Davie, whose ''January'' appeared in the second issue (1, no. 2:6); Roy Fisher, who published ''Discovering Form'' (3, no. 1:28); and Martin Booth, Gavin Ewart, Michael Horovitz, John Mole, Peter Redgrove, Vernon Scannell, and D. M. Thomas. Because many contributors were not well known when they began publishing in *Samphire*, one of the most valuable parts of *Samphire* is the brief biographies of its contributors. The tenth anniversary issue also included three previously unpublished letters from D. H. Lawrence: one expressing regret about not having children; another the difficulty of working with publishers and making money by writing (3, no. 1:22–24). This tenth anniversary issue, Williams believed, ''was perhaps the best issue we ever published.''[1]

Samphire exceeded the editors' expectations. All 250 copies of the first issue were sold, and the subscription list rose steadily until at the end 750 copies of each issue were sold. The journal ceased primarily because it was too successful for the two editors to handle without a larger staff—something Butler and Williams did not want because ''the personal relationship between editor and contributors—always the magazine's distinctive feature—would be drastically modified'' (3, no. 8:3). Since the end of *Samphire*, the coeditors have pursued separate interests. Butler, head of the German department at the University of Birmingham, will soon publish his third book on Max Frisch. Kemble Williams is writing a book on the poetry of Rimbaud. From 1968 to 1981, though, they worked together to make an important contribution to contemporary literature; as the *Times Literary Supplement* wrote near the end of the magazine's run, ''*Samphire* has gradually established itself as one of the best outlets for contemporary poetry in the country.''[2]

Notes

1. Kemble Williams, to the author, 16 July 1984.
2. *Times Literary Supplement*, 3 July 1981, p. 746.

Information Sources

INDEXES
   Volumes 1–2 in volume 2; volume 3 in 3.
REPRINT EDITIONS
   None.
LOCATION SOURCES
   American
      Complete runs: Los Angeles Public Library; University of Iowa Library; University of Tennessee Library, Knoxville; Yale University Library.
   British
      Complete runs: London School of Economics and Political Science Library; University of London, Senate House.

Publication History

MAGAZINE TITLE AND TITLE CHANGES
> *Samphire*, volume 1, numbers 1–4; volume 2, numbers 5–6, 11, 14, 15; volume
> 3, numbers 7–8. *Samphire: New Poetry. East Anglia*, volume 1, number 5.
> *Samphire: New Poetry*, volume 1, numbers 6–16; volume 2, numbers 1–4, 7–10,
> 12–13, 16; volume 3, numbers 1–6.

VOLUME AND ISSUE DATA
> Volume 1, numbers 1–16, January 1968–Summer 1972. Volume 2, numbers 1–
> 16, Autumn 1972–Autumn/Winter 1977. Volume 3, numbers 1–8, Spring 1978–
> Spring 1981.

FREQUENCY OF PUBLICATION
> Alternating three, then four times a year, from 1968 through 1974; then two or
> three times a year until 1981, when one issue was published.

PUBLISHERS
> Michael Butler (15, Phillips Road, Barham/Ipswich [1968–1970]; 45 Westfield,
> Catshill, Bromesgrove, Worcs. [1970–1981]) and Kemble Williams (S. Bank,
> Spring Road, Ipswich [1968–1973]; Heronshaw, Fishpond Lane, Holbrook, Ips-
> wich [1973–1981]).

EDITORS
> Michael Butler and Kemble Williams.

Margaret Ann Baker Graham

SATURDAY REVIEW, THE. See VEA

SCOTTISH CHAPBOOK, THE

When Hugh MacDiarmid (Christopher Murray Grieve) launched the *Scottish
Chapbook* in August 1922 he gave voice to the idea of a Scottish cultural
renaissance. Since his release from the army in 1919, MacDiarmid had been
determined to make his mark as a writer and had published several poems in
English in *Northern Numbers*, the series of poetry anthologies which he had
edited. But the *Scottish Chapbook* was MacDiarmid's outlet for his early work
in the vernacular, poetry which was to declare at once the break with the English
literary and political tradition and which was to establish MacDiarmid, not only
as a great poet in Scots dialect, but as a force in the modern literary world.

The *Scottish Chapbook* was seen by MacDiarmid as a radical literary magazine,
a Scottish equivalent to such publications as *Blast*,* a periodical much admired
by MacDiarmid; the influence is evident in the literary manifesto of the first
issue of the *Chapbook* where the policy of the periodical was declared to be:

> To report, support, and stimulate, in particular, the activities of the Franco-
> Scottish, Scottish-Italian, and kindred Associations; the campaign of the

Vernacular Circle of the London Burns Club for the revival of the Numbers'
movement in contemporary Scottish poetry. . . . To bring Scottish literature
into closer touch with current European tendencies in technique and ideation.

Touting the slogan, "Not traditions—precedents," the direction set by the *Chapbook* was toward new developments in all areas of cultural life, but the emphasis
was indisputably on new literary expression. The editorials urged the need for
a thriving literary criticism in Scotland and at the same time directed aspiring
writers in "English, Gaelic, or Braid Scots" to familiarize themselves with the
latest European modernist movements.

The postwar spirit in Scotland was one of hope and expectation, a marked
contrast to the pessimism which characterized postwar England. With the example of Irish independence on their doorstep, many leading Scots felt that the
time was at hand for a new political stand on the old issue of Home Rule. To
this spirit MacDiarmid brought, through the pages of the *Chapbook*, a new
intellectual and literary dimension. MacDiarmid early recognized that if there
was to be a true national independence it could only come through a cultural
movement which emphasized the distinctiveness of Scottish life, letters, and
language.

The *Chapbook* was very much a one-man effort. While other contributors
included Edwin Muir, Neil Gunn, William Soutar, and a number of other Scottish
poets and writers of the day, the contents—editorials, book reviews, bibliographies, as well as his own poetry and prose—were labors divided among the
many personas of the Grieve/MacDiarmid complex. For the most part the editorials and poems in English were written under the name Grieve, while the
poetry in Scots was always signed with the pseudonymous MacDiarmid by which
he is now best known. Apart from being the chief contributor, MacDiarmid also
arranged the printing, publication, and distribution of the periodical from his
home in the small east coast town of Montrose, where he worked as a reporter
on the local newspaper.

In the editorials of the *Chapbook* MacDiarmid quickly set his sights on some
of the entrenched traditions of Scottish culture—in particular, the cult which
surrounded the national poet, Robert Burns. "The time has come," he wrote,
"for a drastic re-orientation of the Burns movement. The struggle is really
between those whose allegiance is to the letter of Burnsiana: and those who are
filled with the spirit of Burns" (1, no.2:48). While never undermining Burns's
achievement as a poet of the populace, MacDiarmid did criticize the way in
which his imitators over the past two centuries had debased the vernacular (1,
no. 6). MacDiarmid wanted to reclaim for Scottish poetry its earlier traditions.
He wanted new poetry in Scots to look back to the work of William Dunbar,
Robert Henryson, and Gavin Douglas, to a time when experimentation had
flourished and when Douglas's great translation of *Aeneid* had set standards. He
wanted to see a Scottish literature and culture take the very best of its old traditions
and move forward into the modern world.

In a series of articles he wrote for the *Chapbook*, "A Theory of Scots Letters," MacDiarmid tried to evolve a theoretical base for the proposed new literary movement. Drawing on the ideas of Spengler and Nietzsche, he developed a dialectical view of history in which he explored the relationship between literary revivals and national movements. MacDiarmid argued that the war had marked the end of Western civilization as it had been known, but that new, more humane orders would arise. It was his contention that these new orders would come from countries previously seen as culturally backward. In fact, he claimed that the process was already under way and cited as examples of his "theory" the work of Dostoevsky in Russia and Joyce in Ireland, two writers whose work was completely antipathetic to the English tradition. MacDiarmid compared Joyce's "tremendous outpouring" and the "uncanny spiritual and pathological perceptions" of Dostoevsky's novels to Scots vernacular, claiming that the "vast unutilized mass of lapsed observation" which was to be found in Scots could be the foundation of a great modern vernacular movement (1, no. 8:210).

MacDiarmid had already begun experimenting with the vernacular before the first issue of the *Chapbook*. Possibly influenced by some of the new work in Scots which he had published in *Northern Numbers*, he began producing short lyrics and was to use the *Chapbook* as the showcase for this work. The rich rhythmic language, the cosmogonical perspective, and the abundance of images drawn from science immediately marked this work as the most distinctive verse in dialect to emerge in over 200 years. Using, for the most part, the traditional ballad form, and drawing his language from what was still a lively oral tradition, MacDiarmid created such classics of his early style as "Empty Vessel," "The Eemis Stane," "The Watergaw," "Bonnie Broukit Bairn," "Ex Vermibus," "Crowdieknowe," "O Jesu Parvule," and a host of others, all published later in his early collections, *Sangschaw* (1925) and *Penny Wheep* (1926).

It was the energy and originality of this work which seemed to confirm MacDiarmid's view that a Scottish renaissance was a distinct possibility and which drew many supporters to the cause. And the achievement in Scots was further enhanced by the critical commentary which MacDiarmid (as editor Grieve) published on his own work, for he praised the writer for the way in which he had adapted an "essentially rustic tongue to the very much more complex requirements of our urban civilisation" (1, no. 3:62).

The *Chapbook* continued only for fifteen numbers, until November/December 1923. Perhaps by that time MacDiarmid had decided that he needed to spend more time working on his poetry and could not keep pace with the demands of publishing a periodical. Or perhaps he was already planning more ambitious publications. Whatever the reason, the spirit of the *Chapbook* survived, for despite its short life it provided the stimulus for a new literary movement in Scotland, a movement which had MacDiarmid as its undisputed leader.

Information Sources

BIBLIOGRAPHY
Buthlay, Kenneth. *Hugh MacDiarmid (Christopher Murray Grieve)*. Writers and Critics Series. Edinburgh, 1964.

Glen, Duncan. *Hugh MacDiarmid and the Scottish Renaissance*. Edinburgh, 1964.
Kerrigan, Catherine. *"Whaur Extremes Meet": The Poetry of Hugh MacDiarmid, 1920–1934*. Edinburgh, 1983.
Watson, R. B. *Hugh MacDiarmid*. Milton Keynes, 1976.
INDEXES
> None.
REPRINT EDITIONS
> None.
LOCATION SOURCES
> *American*
>> Complete runs: Newberry Library, Chicago; New York Public Library; North-western University Library.
>
> *British*
>> Complete runs: Aberdeen University Library; British Museum; Edinburgh Public Library; Edinburgh University Library; Glasgow University Library; National Library of Scotland, Edinburgh.

Publication History

MAGAZINE TITLE AND TITLE CHANGES
> *The Scottish Chapbook: A Monthly Magazine of Scottish Arts and Letters*
VOLUME AND ISSUE DATA
> Volume 1, numbers 1–12, August 1922–July 1923. Volume 2, numbers 1–3, August 1923–November/December 1923.
FREQUENCY OF PUBLICATION
> Monthly, except for the last two issues, which were bimonthly.
PUBLISHERS
> Hugh MacDiarmid (Christopher Murray Grieve).
EDITOR
> Hugh MacDiarmid (Christopher Murray Grieve).

Catherine Kerrigan

SCRUTINY

For most of its two decades, 1932–1953, the print run of *Scrutiny* was only 750 copies; the modest zenith of 1,500 was only reached three years before its demise. Despite these small numbers, *Scrutiny* was one of the best known, and certainly the most influential and controversial, of the British literary periodicals of the first three-quarters of the twentieth century. It was edited and produced at Cambridge by a small nucleus, the composition of which changed over the years but always included F. R. Leavis and his wife Q. D. Leavis. Although during its existence *Scrutiny* had more than 150 contributors, the Leavises between them wrote 168 of the journal's 850 articles and many of its reviews. L. C. Knights, Denys Thompson, and D. W. Harding made major contributions over a long period, but from first to last it was F. R. Leavis who was the journal's chief "editorial protagonist."[1] Leavis was also one of the greatest, and certainly the most controversial, British literary critic of his age. It would be both artificial and virtually impossible to draw a clear distinction between him and *Scrutiny*, though one must use with caution his 1963 essay, "*Scrutiny*: A Retrospect," in which Leavis inscribed the authorized version of the history of the journal.

It was of essential importance to the character and personality of *Scrutiny* that its nucleus was situated at an ancient university. Cambridge provided "a base, [with] accompanying opportunities for recruitment, and for enlisting collaboration and support in other universities and in the academic world generally." Many of the early contributors, like M. C. Bradbrook, were young graduates, products of Cambridge English who were at the research stage. But the relationship of the university to *Scrutiny* was not simply a matter of personnel. As the editors wrote in a 1942 editorial, the university asserts "a view of cultural tradition as representing the active function of human intelligence, choice, and will; that is, as a spiritual force that can direct and determine . . . the *raison d'être* of a university [was] to be, amid the material pressures and dehumanizing complications of the modern world, a focus of humane consciousness, a centre . . . bringing to bear a mature sense of values [on] the problems of civilization" (10, no. 4:327). So defined, the function of the university and of *Scrutiny* was identical. Indeed, the same Arnoldian concern with cultural crisis and the need for standards was forcefully expressed in two books by members of the nucleus that were published around the time of the journal's founding: Q. D. Leavis's *Fiction and the Reading Public* (1932) and F. R. Leavis and Denys Thompson's *Culture and Environment: The Training of Critical Awareness* (1933), the latter of which included *Scrutiny* in its bibliography: "a quarterly review, 2s. 6d. a copy, 10s. a year, intended to keep those concerned about the drift of civilization (and especially those in schools) in touch with literature and the movement of ideas."[2]

The editors regarded English studies as a central discipline within the university and within the pages of *Scrutiny*. Literature mattered greatly; indeed, the main thrust of *Scrutiny* may be described as the attempt to locate in English literature an autonomous culture independent of any economic or social system. Critical judgment, evaluation, and discrimination were vital activities intimately connected with cultural and moral health, for there was "a necessary relationship between the quality of an individual's response to art and his general fitness for a humane existence" (1, no. 1:5). This being so, *Scrutiny*, though based at a university, was anti-academic in its dislike of linguistic-philological studies as an end in themselves and of the nonevaluative, annalistic treatment of English literature as found, for example, in *The Cambridge History of English Literature*. As Leavis succinctly put it in his *Education and the University: A Sketch for an English School* (1948), most of which first appeared in *Scrutiny*, the concern was with "the problem of making the study of literature a discipline—not a discipline of scholarly industry and academic method, but a discipline of intelligence and sensibility."[3] On the other hand, the Scrutineers, as they came to be called, were equally antagonistic to literary criticism that smacked of the belletristic, the purely aesthetic, or the middlebrow, be it found in the Sitwells, in those aspects of Cambridge that exfoliated into Bloomsbury, or in the London literary establishment whose organs included the *Times Literary Supplement*, the *New Statesman** (see VEA), the Sunday newspapers, and the literature of the British Council.

In the editorial at the beginning of its first issue, the editors of *Scrutiny* could find little to admire in the world of British literary magazines. They did applaud three American reviews: *Hound and Horn*, *Symposium*, and the *New Republic*, particularly praising the last-named journal's combination of "literary criticism with sensitive attention to modern affairs." But these publications had "no English counterparts." There was T. S. Eliot's *Criterion*,* "the most serious as it is the most intelligent of our journals. But its high price, a certain tendency to substitute solemnity for seriousness, and . . . a narrowing of its interests, prevent it from influencing more than a small proportion of the reading public" (1, no.1:2–4). And there had been *Calendar of Modern Letters** (1925–1927), the closest recent journal in principle, intelligence, and liveliness to what *Scrutiny* aimed at. (Indeed, the new journal's title was taken from the "Scrutinies" section of its predecessor.) But *Calendar of Modern Letters* had sunk after less than three years, its editors observing in a closing "Valediction Forbidding Mourning" that in "the present literary situation" an organization different from theirs was required to keep afloat a literary review of uncompromisingly high standards."[4]

The organization that kept *Scrutiny* afloat for two decades is best described as shoestring. There were no subsidies; contributors were not paid; stamps and envelopes were licked by the editors; a note at the end of an early issue thanked an anonymous admirer for the gift of two pounds. For its entire lifespan the journal was run "without secretary, without business-manager, without publicity manager, and without publicity" (19, no. 4:257). In 1941, in a brilliant issue that contains the first of Mrs. Leavis's articles on Jane Austen and her husband's on Joseph Conrad, the editors announced that they thought they could keep going through another year if only another hundred subscribers could be found (10, no. 1:87).[5] Difficulties mounted during the war because of paper restrictions, the bombing of Cambridge, and, most importantly, the dispersal of collaborators and contributors. Demobilization did not solve this last difficulty; as Leavis explained in his "Valedictory" in *Scrutiny*'s final issue, the postwar period proved "preoccupying and distracting . . . for those who came back to civilian life. . . . never again was it possible to form anything like an adequate nucleus of steady collaborators" (19, no. 4:254).

"*Scrutiny*: A Manifesto, " the lead editorial in the journal's first issue, spoke of "the general dissolution of standards," the need to "cultivate awareness" and to keep "informed of 'the best that is known and thought in the world.' " Literature and education would be the subjects of most articles, but the journal would also feature "disinterested surveys" of other departments of modern life, and there would be reviews of carefully selected books on a wide range of subjects (1, no. 1:3, 5, 6). Early numbers of *Scrutiny* answered to this description;

articles and reviews were as varied as they were sparkling. In addition to the pieces on literature and education, G. Lowes Dickinson contributed "The Political Background," I.A. Richards "The Chinese Renaissance," Herbert Butterfield "History and the Marxian Method." James Smith wrote on Alfred North Whitehead, and H. E. Batson contributed "Amateurism and Professionalism in Economics." The young W. H. Auden reviewed Winston Churchill's *Thoughts and Adventures*; J. L. Russell reviewed a philosopher's book about science; books on music, art, architecture, and eugenics were reviewed, as well as the first volume of Leon Trotsky's *History of the Russian Revolution*. As early as the last number of the second volume, however, the editors recognized that "we have not made such a direct approach to the problems of economics, social order and international relations as their terrible urgency might seem to demand of us" (2, no. 4:331). Since the decade was the "decidedly . . . Marxist" 1930s, *Scrutiny* was criticized for not being more politically engagé; but in a retrospective editorial in 1940 the editors went out of their way to applaud their "anti-Marxism," which was an essential correlative to "the fostering of a free play of critical intelligence"(9, no. 1:71, 70).

As the years passed, it was mainly through its literary criticism that *Scrutiny* fostered this free play (though the first of W. H. Mellers's contributions on musical subjects did not appear until the fifth volume). Periodic attention was given to foreign literatures: in the early years Henri Fluchère wrote on French literature, and Martin Turnell later contributed over twenty articles on French writers; in addition to their contributions on English literature, James Smith wrote on Stéphane Mallarmé and D. A. Traversi on *I Promessi Sposi*; and D. J. Enright contributed a number of articles on German writers, as did Marcus Bewley on American literature.

But it is unquestionably in its criticism of the literature of England that the principal achievement of *Scrutiny* is found. The journal accomplished nothing less than "a comprehensive revaluation of English literature, shaping and reordering."[6] In an article published shortly after *Scrutiny*'s demise L. D. Lerner rightly observed:

> The achievement of *Scrutiny* is, in a way, peculiar to the twentieth century: it is the building up of a body of practical criticisms, of substantiated literary judgements, that has surely no equal in extent and quality. The conception of practical criticism, explicitly formulated, is certainly modern. In Dr Leavis's essay on him, Coleridge is suggested as the first practical critic of importance, and even he is said to show more promise than achievement. Its real founders are of this century: Eliot, Graves, Richards, Middleton Murry, and the American New Critics. *Scrutiny* set out from the beginning to apply their methods not sporadically but systematically, over the whole field of English Literature.[7]

On medieval literature there were John Speirs's provocative contributions. Through the work of several critics, particularly L. C. Knights and D. A. Traversi,

Scrutiny effected a major reorientation in Shakespeare criticism, demonstrating (as Leavis was to put it) that "it would not do to discuss a Shakespeare play as if it were a character-novel answering to the established Victorian (and post-Victorian) convention.[8] Following the lead of T. S. Eliot, but with far greater specificity, *Scrutiny* "reconsidered the main streams of English poetry, tracing out the dominant traditions and vital inter-relationships of the major and minor poets, ignoring reputation and returning again and again to the text for new judgment, carefully but passionately eliciting a new view of the poetry of the past" that was immensely stimulating even when one disagreed with such new valuations, as, for example, the notorious lowerings of Milton and Shelley.[9]

On the English novel *Scrutiny*'s valuations and revaluations were perhaps even more pioneering and influential. The journal developed a new way to read a novel (as a "dramatic poem") and identified "the great tradition" of English novelists. Q. D. Leavis's articles on Jane Austen (uncollected until her husband's two-volume *Selections from Scrutiny* came out in 1968) effected a decisive change in that novelist's reputation; Leavis rediscovered George Eliot for his generation; important work was done on Conrad, and *Nostromo* placed at the center of his achievement; sophisticated appreciation of Henry James was furthered; and it was in *Scrutiny* that D. H. Lawrence (the fifth and last of the journal's great tradition) was unequivocally shown to be a great novelist and critic.

Scrutiny's judgments on the writers of the 1930s and 1940s were usually sharply critical; this "offending 'negative' criticism" and "consistent severity of standard," which Leavis regarded as essential aspects of the proper performance of the critical function, were major factors in the often antagonistic controversy between what he perceived as the key elite of *Scrutiny* and "dominant coterie[s]" outside its walls.[10] The later T. S. Eliot more than once had his knuckles rapped; *Finnegans Wake* was deflated; Hemingway's emotional formulae were "cheap," his attitudes "second-rate," and his structural patterns "limited and monotonous" (5, no. 3:297); Auden was periodically censured for not having developed; Dylan Thomas was eviscerated; and Graham Greene savaged. Many of the gratuitously severe judgments meted out in *Scrutiny* come from its last years; a large number of them were written by students of Leavis who took from him "an attitude and a tone that only he had earned."[11] But a similar hardening can also be found in some of Leavis's own postwar essays, and it was perhaps for the best that *Scrutiny* ceased publication in 1953. It was not a torch that could be passed easily (if at all), and by that time its major task—the revaluation of English literature—had been accomplished.

The great influence of *Scrutiny* can be documented in numerous ways. One would be to list the substantive number of important critical books— by Leavis, Knights, Harding, Speirs, Traversi, Mellers, Bewley, and Turnell—that were largely based on material first published in the journal. Another would be to point up its influence in schools and universities and to mention the once widely used seven-volume *Pelican Guide to English Literature*, whose editor and many of whose contributors were ex-Scrutineers. A third way would be to note the unprecedentedly handsome act of Cambridge University Press, which in 1968 reissued all nineteen volumes of *Scrutiny* and in a twentieth included Leavis's retrospect as well as Maurice Hussey's eight-part index of almost 200 pages.

Still another way to indicate the magnitude of influence would be to list the articles, books, and other publications (C. S. Lewis's *An Experiment in Criticism*, and C. B. Cox and A. E. Dyson's *Critical Quarterly** are two examples) which were tacitly or explicitly brought into being as a reaction either to *Scrutiny*'s critical stance or to some of its specific discriminations. Such a compilation would be long, and according to the chief Scrutineer it would be germane: "hostility," Leavis insisted in 1963, "belongs to the central significance" of *Scrutiny*.[12] One cannot help reflecting, however, that the list need not have been so long if in the judgments on contemporary writers the *Scrutiny* contributors had looked down rather than up for their standards of comparison. It has also been suggested that the *Scrutiny* nucleus might have more often ignored than done battle with negative criticism if they had better grasped the simple fact that they were more intelligent and more gifted critics than most of their detractors, and that in the end their work would permanently affect the history of education and of literary criticism.[13]

Notes

1. F. R. Leavis, *"Scrutiny*: A Retrospect," in *Scrutiny: A Retrospect, Indexes, Errata* (Cambridge, Eng., 1963), p. 22.

2. F. R. Leavis and Denys Thompson, *Culture and Environment: The Training of Critical Awareness* (London, 1933), p. 150.

3. F. R. Leavis, *Education and the University: A Sketch for an English School* (New York, 1948), p. 7.

4. *Calendar of Modern Letters* 4 (1927):175–76.

5. Robert Gottlieb, in "Scrutiny Bound," *New Republic*, 7 December 1963, p. 28, calls this *Scrutiny*'s "most touching moment."

6. Leavis, *"Scrutiny*: A Retrospect," p. 16.

7. L. D. Lerner, "The Life and Death of *Scrutiny*," *London Magazine* 2, no. 1 (1955):69.

8. Leavis, *"Scrutiny*: A Retrospect," p. 12.

9. Gottlieb, "Scrutiny Bound," p. 21.

10. Leavis, *"Scrutiny*: A Retrospect," pp. 16, 24.

11. Richard Poirier, "The Great Tradition," *New York Review of Books*, 12 December 1963, p. 20.

12. Leavis, *"Scrutiny*: A Retrospect," p. 19.

13. Review of *A Selection from Scrutiny, Times Literary Supplement*, 25 April 1968, p. 424.

Information Sources

BIBLIOGRAPHY

Bateson, F. W. "The Alternative to Scrutiny." *Essays in Criticism* 14 (1964):10–20.
Bentley, Eric. *The Importance of "Scrutiny": Selections from "Scrutiny: A Quarterly Review" 1932–1948*. New York, 1948.

Brower, Reuben A. "*Scrutiny*: Revolution from Within." *Partisan Review* 31 (1964):297–314.

Gottlieb, Robert. "*Scrutiny* Bound." *New Republic*, 7 December 1963, pp. 21–29.

Knight, G. Wilson. "*Scrutiny* and Criticism." *Essays in Criticism* 14 (1964):32–36.

Leavis, F. R., ed. *A Selection from "Scrutiny."* 2 vols. Cambridge, Eng. 1968.

Lerner, L. D. "The Life and Death of *Scrutiny*." *London Magazine* 2, no. 1 (1955):68–77.

Poirier, Richard. "The Great Tradition." *New York Review of Books*, 12 December 1963, pp. 20–21.

Rosenberg, Harold. "Insurrection." *New Yorker*, 14 March 1964, pp. 169–84.

INDEXES

Maurice Hussey, comp., in *Scrutiny* (Cambridge, 1963), volume 20.

REPRINT EDITIONS

Cambridge University Press, 1963.

Microform: Kraus Microform, Millwood, N.Y.

LOCATION SOURCES

American

Complete runs: Amherst College Library; Columbia University Library; Dartmouth College Library; Enoch Pratt Library; New York Public Library; Princeton University Library; University of Cincinnati Library; University of North Carolina Library; University of Wisconsin Library.

Partial runs: Widely available.

British

Complete runs: Birmingham University Library; British Museum; Edinburgh University Library; National Library of Scotland, Edinburgh; Reading University Library; Roborough Library, University College, Exeter; University of Bristol Library.

Partial runs: Widely available.

Publication History

MAGAZINE TITLE AND TITLE CHANGES

Scrutiny: A Quarterly Review.

VOLUME AND ISSUE DATA

Volume 1, number 1–volume 19, number 4, May 1932–October 1953.

FREQUENCY OF PUBLICATION

Quarterly.

PUBLISHER

The Editors, 13 Leys Road, Cambridge (later 6 Chesterton Hall Crescent, Cambridge, and Downing College, Cambridge).

EDITORS

L. C. Knights and Donald Culver, volume 1, numbers 1–2. L. C. Knights, Donald Culver, F. R. Leavis, and Denys Thompson, volume 1, number 3–volume 2, number 1. D. W. Harding, L. C. Knights, F. R. Leavis, and Denys Thompson, volume 2, number 2–volume 8, number 1. D. W. Harding, L. C. Knights, and F. R. Leavis, volume 8, number 2–volume 10, number 2. D. W. Harding, L. C. Knights, F. R. Leavis, and W. H. Mellers, volume 10, number 3–volume 14, number 3. L. C. Knights, F. R. Leavis, H. A. Mason, and W. H. Mellers, volume

14, number 4–volume 15, number 3. L. C. Knights, F. R. Leavis, and H. A. Mason, volume 15, number 4–volume 19, number 4.

Kerry McSweeney

SCYTHE, THE. See TOWNSMAN, THE

SEVEN

In its brief run of eight numbers, from the summer of 1938 to the spring of 1940, *Seven: The New Magazine* printed fiction, verse, and criticism by writers as diverse as Kay Boyle, Hugh MacDiarmid, Frederick Prokosch, Herbert Read, George Seferis, Wallace Stevens, and Dylan Thomas. Although the editors, John Goodland and Nicholas Moore, made no statement of policy until Moore's editorial comment in the final issue, the magazine published many of the so-called Apocalyptic poets (among them Dorian Cooke, G. S. Fraser, J. F. Hendry, Norman MacCaig, Tom Scott, Henry Treece, Parker Tyler, and editor Moore himself) and experimenters in surrealist poetry and quasi-autobiographical prose fantasies (Lawrence Durrell, David Gascoyne, Henry Miller, Anaïs Nin, and William Saroyan). *Seven* may be linked in philosophy and personnel with the *Booster/Delta* sequence of magazines edited in Paris from 1937 to 1939 by Alfred Perlès. Many of the writers who were published in *Seven* had already appeared in *Booster* or *Delta* (for instance Boyle, Durrell, Gascoyne, Miller, Nin, Saroyan) and, moving in the other direction, Moore was to contribute to all three issues of *Delta*. Goodland, coeditor of the first three numbers of *Seven*, distributor of the fourth, and publisher of the fifth, is also listed as the publisher of the final number of *Delta* (Easter 1939). Finally, the summer 1939 *Seven* was distributed by Cooke, contributor to five numbers of *Seven* and to the last *Delta*. The writers published most frequently in *Seven* are Cooke (nos. 2, 3, 5, 6, 8), Durrell (nos. 1, 3, 4, 6, 8), and Fraser (nos. 1, 2, 5, 6, 7, 8); many other significant authors, including George Barker, Richard Eberhart, Roy Fuller, William Plomer, Keidrych Rhys, and Anne Ridler, also appeared in the magazine. The editors consistently divided the pages among fiction (45 percent), verse (35 percent), and criticism (20 percent).

Viewed as a retrospective, Moore's statement in the final issue of *Seven* defines both the literary freedom and the sociopolitical bias of the magazine. Moore rejected the apolitical stance of a magazine like Cyril Connolly's *Horizon*,* and quoted Dylan Thomas, from *New Verse*,* that the writer should work for " 'the right of all men to share, equally and impartially, every production of man from man and from the sources of production at man's disposal.' *Seven* will therefore continue to publish the best writing it can get hold of, until such time as the desired society becomes possible" (no. 8:32). *Seven* did not, in fact, print much, if anything, to support the establishment of a socialist Utopia, but its editors did show preference for both surrealist and Apocalyptic writing.

The surrealists arrived in a group from *Booster*: the first number of *Seven* contains passages of highly evocative and poetic prose by Durrell, Miller, and Nin. Sometimes referred to as "psychic fiction," these selections are grounded in literal autobiography but merge with fantastic and seemingly disconnected events and emotions which suggest more the workings of the subconscious than of the unconscious mind.[1] Durrell's "Ego," a passage from *The Black Book*, just published in Paris and barred from England, implies the breakdown of the discrete ego into connected yet separate fragments; this concept Durrell would continue to explore in his fiction into the 1980s. Writing of "the air-conditioned quality of the American nightmare" (no. 1:7) in "The Brooklyn Bridge," Miller prefigures in language and messianic tone much of his later writing about the United States. Nin's "Fragment from a Diary" marked the first appearance in England of an excerpt from her extraordinary diaries. The second number of *Seven* contains further surrealist writing by Nin, Perlès, Saroyan, and Laurence Vail; and in number 3, with Montagu O'Reilly's "The Influence of Harps and Laundry on Railway Commitments," another surrealist joined the lists. In the same issue, Treece's critical essay, "Dylan Thomas and the Surrealists," distinguishes between the "self-imposed form" of the Welsh poet and the "succession of bewildering images" of the surrealists.

It is no accident that the quadrumvirate of W. H. Auden, C. Day Lewis, Louis MacNeice, and Stephen Spender is absent from the pages of *Seven*, virtual house organ to the "New Apocalypse" group, which "claim[ed] as ancestors the Book of Revelation, Shakespeare, [John] Webster, [William] Blake, [Franz] Kafka, and D. H. Lawrence."[2] As Fraser makes clear in his discussion of Hendry, Moore, and Treece in his "Introduction" to *The White Horseman* anthology, the Apocalyptics regarded Auden and his compeers as a different poetic generation from their own, as having less "social value" in their writing, of being overly bound by form in verse, of writing poetry demanding more intellection than was proper on the part of the reader; of being, in short, classical, whereas the Apocalyptics saw in themselves a basic Romantic affinity.[3] Indeed, several of them later acquiesced to the "neo-Romantic" label. The Apocalyptics were criticized for their extravagant juxtaposition of images, for their fascination with horror and death. A superficial but significant distinction is that whereas the Auden circle members were nearly all public school followed by Oxford or Cambridge, the New Apocalypse was a "provincial, non-London-Oxford-Cambridge movement (although G. S. Fraser had gone from St. Andrews to Cambridge, and represented *Seven* there). It was also a Celtic movement. Hendry, Scott, Fraser and MacCaig were Scots; Treece was half-Welsh."[4]

In opening *Seven* to considerable surrealist writing, the Apocalyptic poet-editor Moore seemed to be recognizing kinship and even debt. Fraser saw this relationship clearly:

The discoveries of Freud, and the work of the Surrealists . . . have convinced the Apocalyptics that every poet has enough to write about in the contents of his own mind, and that the struggle to be classic, social, relevant, and so on, is unnecessary; because if a poet describes honestly his private perspective on the world, his private universe, human minds are sufficiently analogous to each other for that private universe to become (ultimately though certainly not immediately) a generally accessible human property.[5]

Most of the contributors to *Seven* show a tendency to turn to the subjective inner world, the realm of the subconscious and of the unconscious, for an angle of repose to the chaotic foreground of a Europe plunging into war.

Seven provided an alternative to such established forums for surrealist writing as Eugene Jolas's *transition*, and it helped focus and encourage the Apocalyptics. Although most of the best of the writers who contributed surrealist work to the magazine—Durrell, Gascoyne, Miller, Nin—later abandoned or modified the surrealist mode, *Seven* gave them important early exposure to the public. While the Apocalyptic poets may not have deserved entirely the harshness of John Lehmann's condemnation, "a cliché-ridden, sentimental style 'like a sickly fungoid growth in decaying jam,' "[6] the archetypal Apocalyptics have largely vanished from the anthologies of modern poetry, and only those whose kinship to them was superficial at best, such as Dylan Thomas, have held high reputations in later years. Considering its very short life span, however, *Seven* did extremely well, publishing some very good poetry and prose and representing at least two significant literary movements within its twenty-nine to fifty-seven pages. It printed the first writing by Gerald Durrell and Nin to appear in England, as well as early work by Audrey Beecham, Lawrence Durrell, and Henry Miller. The poets Cooke and J. C. Hall had been published before only in school literary magazines.

Seven ceased publication with the Spring 1940 number, but not because of any failings of the editor, a lack of suitable material, or a dropping readership. It fell victim to what Robert Hewison termed the "grand slaughter of magazines" after the declaration of war: faced with the uncertainty of the situation, publishers turned away from magazines, and among those which also vanished during 1939 and 1940 were the *Cornhill Magazine** (see *VEA, MA*), *The Criterion,** *Fact, The London Mercury,** *New Stories,** *New Verse, Purpose,** *Twentieth Century Verse,** *Voice of Scotland, Wales,** and the *Welsh Review.*[7]

Notes

1. Frederick J. Hoffman, Charles Allen, Carolyn F. Ulrich, *The Little Magazine: A History and a Bibliography* (Princeton, 1946), p. 343.
2. Paul Ray, *The Surrealist Movement in England* (Ithaca, N.Y., 1971), p. 290.

3. George Sutherland Fraser, "Apocalypse in Poetry," in *The White Horseman: Prose and Verse of the New Apocalypse*, ed. J. F. Hendry and Henry Treece (London, 1941), pp.25–29.

4. A. Trevor Tolley, *The Poetry of the Thirties* (London, 1975), pp. 366–67.

5. Fraser, "Apocalypse in Poetry," p. 29.

6. John Lehmann, *I Am My Brother* (London, 1960), p. 230.

7. Robert Hewison, *Under Siege* (London, 1977), p. 11.

Information Sources

BIBLIOGRAPHY

Baker, Denys Val. *Little Reviews, 1914–1943*. London, 1943.

Fraser, George Sutherland. "Apocalypse in Poetry." In *The White Horseman: Prose and Verse of the New Apocalypse*. Edited by J. F. Hendry and Henry Treece. London, 1941.

————. *The Modern Writer and His World*. Rev. ed. London, 1964.

Hoffman, Frederick J., Charles Allen, and Carolyn F. Ulrich. *The Little Magazine: A History and a Bibliography*. Princeton, 1946.

Ray, Paul. *The Surrealist Movement in England*. Ithaca, N.Y., 1971.

Stanford, Derek. "Nicholas Moore." In *The Freedom of Poetry: Studies in Contemporary Verse*. London, 1947.

Tolley, A. Trevor. *The Poetry of the Thirties*. London, 1975.

INDEXES

An Author Index to Selected British Little Magazines, 1930–1939, ed. B. C. Bloomfield (London, 1976).

Comprehensive Index to English-Language Little Magazines, 1890–1970, series 1, ed. Marion Sader (Millwood, N.Y., 1976).

REPRINT EDITIONS

Kraus-Thomson Organization Ltd., Millwood, N.Y.

Microform: Marvin Sukov Collection, University of Wisconsin, BHP/9. Brookhaven Press, La Crosse, Wis.

LOCATION SOURCES

American

Partial runs: Columbia University Library; Harvard University Library; New York Public Library; Pennsylvania State University Library; University of California Library, Los Angeles; University of Virginia Library; Yale University Library.

British

Complete run: British Museum.

Publication History

MAGAZINE TITLE AND TITLE CHANGES

Seven: The New Magazine.

VOLUME AND ISSUE DATA

Number 1, Summer 1938. Number 2, Autumn 1938. Number 3, Winter 1938. Number 4, Spring 1939. Number 4 [i.e., 5], Summer 1939. Number 6, Autumn 1939. Number 7, Christmas 1939. Number 8, Spring 1940.

FREQUENCY OF PUBLICATION

Quarterly.

PUBLISHERS
  Summer-Winter 1938: John Goodland and Nicholas Moore, The Poplars, Taunton, Somerset. Spring-Summer 1939: John Goodland, 8 Englebert Street, London E.C. 1. Autumn 1939–Spring 1940: A. D. Nightall (Production), [n.p.].
EDITORS
  John Goodland, Summer-Winter 1938. Nicholas Moore, Summer 1938–Spring 1940.

Ian S. MacNiven

SOLSTICE

The first issue of *Solstice*, a Cambridge students' magazine, appeared in 1966. Originally conceived as a place to publish poetry of quality by Cambridge students, it had been expanded by the time of its first issue to include translations of young writers in Europe and the Soviet Union. This change in scope and purpose is typical of *Solstice*, which can claim a dazzling array of exciting, fresh contributors and an admirable eye for talent, but cannot claim consistency. After the first year, *Solstice* changed editors with almost every issue, which, even considering that the editors were presumably undergraduates, is a remarkable turnover rate. Thus, nearly every issue carries an editorial which redefines policy, realigns commitments, and outlines the new direction of its publishing future.

Editorial permutations aside, *Solstice* managed to attract some of the most interesting writers of the 1960s. In its first year, under the editorship of Phil Short, the magazine focused mainly on the poetry of young but not unknown writers. In the first issue, poets of such substantial reputation as Anselm Hollo, Jim Burns, Harry Guest, Gael Turnbull, John James, Tom Raworth, Spike Hawkins, and Henry Graham appeared in what was clearly an auspicious start. Anselm Hollo, who by 1966 had had close to a dozen volumes of poetry published, in addition to major editing and translation work, appeared again in *Solstice* number 2 with "Fennica," a long, comic poem with accompanying graphics by John Furnival. Also in this issue were poems by twenty-year-old Brian Patten; these include "Little Johnny's Confession," which became the title poem of his first published volume two years later and which helped establish his reputation. *Solstice* number 3, the September issue, featured new translations of ten poems by Pablo Neruda, selections from Tom Raworth's *A Serial Biography*, and two poems by Gordon Printz-Pahlson, described in the notes as "Sweden's leading poet and critic," who was in residence as lecturer in Swedish that year at Cambridge. The spectacular fourth issue added an American section, featuring works by Daniel Hoffman, Robert Bly, Edward Dorn, and Galway Kinnell. Although Phil Short had announced plans for this impressive number, Sue Limb, one of the coeditors, actually prepared the American section. She and her two coeditors replaced Short, whose name disappeared from the masthead.

Solstice number 5, the first of only two issues in 1967, dropped Limb's name to adviser. An editorial explained that the magazine would include prose as well as poetry, and work "both by new writers and by those already established," and would appear three times a year. The editorial policy did not constitute a new approach, for the mixture of new and known writers characterized *Solstice* from the start, but the inclination was clearly toward the radically new, the shocking, the experimental. But it is to *Solstice*'s credit that, while remaining in the avant garde, it did not compromise the caliber of the work for the merely sensationally current.

The editors of number 6 declared themselves opposed to "self-consciously introspective poetry" and pressed for more contributions in concrete poetry, artwork, and prose. The next issue accordingly contained some very impressive poetry: D. M. Thomas's "Gully" and "It Is a Strange Demesne," followed by a number of translations, including Derek Wavell's from the third century B.C. *Tao Te Ching*, and Daniel Weissbrot's translation of several Russian poets, including Bella Akhmadulina, Viktor Sosnora, and Alexander Kushner. There were three translations from contemporary German poetry, all very political, by Michael Hamburger. To this had been added a section for fiction (which contained a fairly amateurish antiwar story) and more concrete poetry, including extracts from Furnival's six-foot-high screens. Not surprisingly, number 7 also carried an editorial which began, "SOLSTICE is now under new editorship. Our policy . . . " Brian Morse and Steve Bradshaw went on to inveigh against the "paucity" of much university-produced poetry, the university representing all forces which subordinate creativity and social awareness to formal competence.

Solstice number 8 brought back John Cotton and Daniel Hoffman, and added photography by Rick Czartoryski as well as a section devoted to three Cuban poets translated by Nathanial Tarn, a prolific poet in his own right and a noted translator of Neruda.

In contrast to the power that preceded it, number 9, the magazine's last issue, seems much more the undergraduate magazine it was originally conceived to be. It is both interesting and sad to note that the contributors to this issue, most of whom were undergraduates, are unknown and, it seems, have remained so. The editorial in this last issue bravely began with the reassurance that *Solstice*'s difficulties—financial and otherwise—had been solved. The editors went on to survey the poetry scene and intelligently rejected both the "wildly 'uneducated'" ersatz-Blakean variety and the "correct and academic poem," which is "formally perfected but ultimately dead and trite." In its short but splendid existence, *Solstice* seems to have done a very difficult thing: without succumbing to either extreme, it managed to stay on the cutting edge of poetry. Very much a reflection of the 1960s, in its youth, its leftist political inclinations, and its urgent struggle to do something fine, perhaps it is appropriate that *Solstice* should have ceased publication in 1969.

Information Sources

INDEXES
> None.

REPRINT EDITIONS
> None.

LOCATION SOURCES
> *American*
>> Complete runs: University of Chicago Library; University of Iowa Library; University of Kentucky Library, Lexington; University of Pennsylvania Library.
>> Partial runs: Cornell University Library; Northwestern University Library; University of California Libraries, at Berkeley, Santa Barbara, and San Diego.
>
> *British*
>> Complete runs: Glasgow University Library; National Library of Scotland, Edinburgh.

Publication History

MAGAZINE TITLE AND TITLE CHANGES
> *Solstice*.

VOLUME AND ISSUE DATA
> Numbers 1–4, 1966; numbers 5, 6, 1967; numbers 7, 8, 1968; number 9, 1969. No months or seasons are listed.

FREQUENCY OF PUBLICATION
> Irregular.

PUBLISHERS
> Numbers 1–4: W. Heffer and Sons, Ltd., Cambridge. Numbers 5–8: Stanhope Press. Number 9: Pigotts, Cambridge.

EDITORS
> Phil Short, numbers 1–3, 1966. Susan Limb, number 4, 1966. Philip Prowse and Robin Ritzema, number 5, 1967. Jim Manley and Dave Miller, number 6, 1967. Brian Morse and Steve Bradshaw, numbers 7–8, 1968. John Cook and Graham Swift, number 9, 1969.

Toby Silverman Zinman

STAND

Stand was begun in 1952 by poet Jon Silkin, who reputedly sold the first mimeographed issue for eight pence by going from table to table in Soho restaurants. Certainly an activist, embattled position for poetry emerges from re-reading Silkin's editorials in the earliest issues. The first describes a situation that should be favorable to new poetry—improved education, a weakening of the class system, a constant flux of new ideas—but "the appalling gap between what is written and what is actually read" made it necessary for poets to put aside "private intellectualisms, brilliant techniques. . . . [for] the only self-respect an artist can have is to be paid by the society he works in as a labourer is paid for his effort" (1, no. 1:2). What evolves through *Stand*'s early polemics is a real development and sophistication of the early hope to rehabilitate the modern writer's relation to an audience that will not read him or her, into an attempt to demonstrate, literally, how reading is to be performed.

From the early pronouncements, the editorials moved from soliciting subscriptions, the perennial issue of survival, to engaging public policy for the arts. Through 1970–1971, the problems of poetry translation were aired through reviews, editorials, and readers' comments. Can poetry be translated? What kind of poems translate willingly? Should one be suspicious of the success of a translation? What happens to our sensitivity to native English? The first debate over translation began with Gordon Brotherton's "Vallejo in English" (11, no. 1) and ended with his "Some Remarks on Literary Translation" (12, no. 2:53), while regretting their limits. In the next issue the "Forum" section printed the unsolicited responses of readers who questioned the whole project, and invited more comment.

A second polemic took place over the reception of *Poetry of the Committed Individual*, an anthology of verse from *Stand* prefaced by a restatement of editorial position.[1] Silkin argued that a *New Statesman** (see *VEA*) reviewer favored personal, directly observed, "de-sloganised" poetry over committed (political) poetry. Such a position was "prohibitive and circular in that it implies the impossibility of feeling personally bound up with social expression.... The argument does not allow for any shift in attitudes such as would make possible the penetration of public concerns with the writer's personal feelings." Silkin argued for the responsibility of committed poets in democracies: a commitment to theme, but also to the language. However, commitment "for its own sake" was ultimately "a barbarous investment. It reduces still further the area occupied by the poet, and, at the same time, attempts to demarcate territory that should never be at the sole dictation of any group of people" (14, no. 4:7). In the following editorial Terry Eagleton argued that a nonrevolutionary epoch which might not produce the committed poet in the manner of Milton or Blake could at least, through magazines like *Stand*, support the poetry of the committed individual (15, no. 2:3–5). Jon Glover worried that, if Eagleton were right, and effective and beneficial change to society were a liberal pipe-dream, then the limited goal of communication, collaboration between author and reader of the "essentially human" as the only politics possible, was vulnerable to "crisis hysteria and political oppression" (15, no. 3:6).

The introduction of "The Reader's *Stand*" (20, no. 1), which invited an oppositional voice into the magazine, a stand against *Stand*, was inaugurated by the intense objections of one editor, Lorna Tracy, to a story accepted by the other, male editors. She set off a chain of readers' speculations whether the story's phallic bravado was innocent, culpable, or a send-up.

Stand's most controversial polemic, the 1979 "Common Values?" issues (20, nos. 2–3), featured attacks between *Stand* and the *PN Review** (see *Poetry Nation*). Silkin, Eagleton, Raymond Williams, E. P. Thompson, and Craig

Cairns took on *PN Review* editors Michael Schmidt, C. H. Sisson, and Donald Davie as to whether the writer is a reflection or the agent of a new consciousness of his society. The argument, beginning with Cairns's assessment of "Two Conservatisms of English Poetry," identified Davie and Sisson as advocates of that favoring of local poetry of English histories which somehow achieves universality. For Cairns, such parochialism could only see itself as universal in the British Empire which, in fact, instituted global culture (20, no. 2:12–19). In "Poetry and Politics" Sisson allowed *Stand*'s call for commitment, for the writer's values to come up in the poem, but objected to the notion that "the poet must *make his poems come right*, in the sense of making them fit in with his political pre-conceptions" (20, no. 2:23–26). Silkin's "The Rights of England" attacked *PN Review*'s "royalist" version of English history, and was answered separately by Davie and Schmidt. Raymond Williams, while acknowledging the social determining of writing ("the inherited forms write it; the dominant institutions commission it"), reserves the possibility that "a commitment to examining our most settled commitments might be the most literate thing we could attempt" (20, no. 2:8–11).

While the most interesting features of *Stand* have been the critical debates the editors fomented, the range of poetry it has published is no less remarkable. *Stand* had foresight in publishing major figures early, especially Geoffrey Hill, Tony Harrison, and Eagleton, who has reviewed recent poetry since 1967. It enjoys an excellent record for securing a poet's best work: in successive issues, Hill's "Funeral Music" and "September Song" (8, nos. 3, 4), Robert Bly's "Johnson's Cabinet Watched by Ants" (9, no. 1) and "The Teeth Mother Naked at Last" (11, no. 2), Tony Harrison's "National Trust" (12, no. 2), and his sonnets from "The School of Eloquence" (19, no. 2).

Since 1952 *Stand* has maintained an exemplary balance of both fiction and poetry, national and foreign literature. Issues have featured Eastern European literature (7, no. 2), new German poetry (7, no. 3), Arabic folk poems (9, no. 1), Peruvian poetry (10, no. 1), Czechoslovakian works (10, no. 2), Quebec poetry (13, no. 1), Turkish poetry (14, no. 4), Dutch poetry (18, no. 1), Polish poetry (20, no. 1), Australian literature (16, no. 2; 20, no. 4), contemporary East German poetry (21, no. 1), new Arabic writing (22, no. 1), and modern Norwegian writing (23, no. 3). Most recently, *Stand* has committed scarce resources of editors' time and publishers' money (2,000 pounds) to sponsor an international fiction contest.

Note

1. *Poetry of the Committed Individual: A "Stand" Anthology*, ed. Jon Silkin (London, 1973).

Information Sources

INDEXES
   None.

REPRINT EDITIONS

Numbers 1–12: Johnson Reprint (New York).

LOCATION SOURCES

American

Complete runs: Louisiana State University Library; Mississippi State University, State College Library; New York Public Library; Oberlin College Library; Ohio State University Library; St. Louis Public Library; U.S. Library of Congress; University of California Library, Riverside; University of California Library, Santa Barbara; University of Illinois Library; University of Michigan Library; Washington State University Library; Yale University Library.

Partial runs: Widely available.

British

Complete run: University College Library, London.

Partial runs: Widely available.

Publication History

MAGAZINE TITLE AND TITLE CHANGES

Stand.

VOLUME AND ISSUE DATA

Numbers 1–12, 1952–Winter 1956/1957. Volume 2, number 1, 1957–.

FREQUENCY OF PUBLICATION

Irregular until volume 3, then quarterly.

PUBLISHERS

Jon Silkin. Numbers 1–10, 1952–1955: 40 Lee Park, Blackheath, London. Numbers 11–12–volume 3, 1956–1959: 63 St. George's Drive, Victoria, London. Volume 3– volume 7, number 3, 1959–1965: 144 Otley Road, Leeds 16. Volume 7, number 4–volume 23, number 3, 1966–1982: 58 Queens Road, Jesmond, Newcastle-on-Tyne, 2. Volume 23, number 4–, 1983–: 179 Wingrove Road, Newcastle-on-Tyne.

EDITORS

Jon Silkin. Coeditors named are: Gordon Wharton, volume 1, number 5 (1952). Ken Smith, volume 7, number 1–volume 13, number 3 (1965–1971). Catherine Lamb, volume 10, number 1–volume 15, number 2 (1968–1973). Edward Brunner, volume 10, number 4–volume 19, number 4 (overseas editor) (1969–1978). Lorna Tracy, volume 11, number 2 (1970). Howard Fink, volume 12, number 3 (overseas editor) (1971). Robert Ober, volume 13, number 4–volume 20, number 1 (1972–1978). David Heal, volume 15, number 4 (1974). Michael Wilding, volume 15, number 4 (overseas editor) (1974). Victor Kureczko, volume 18, numbers 1–2 (1977). Rodney Pybus, volume 18, number 1–volume 20, number 3 (overseas editor) (1977–1979). Ian Wedde, volume 18, number 1–volume 20, number 3 (1977–1979). A. G. Jones, volume 18, number 1– volume 20, number 3 (1977–1979). Neil Astley, volume 19, number 3–volume 20, number 1 (1978–1979). David Bradshaw, volume 19, numbers 3–4 (1977–1978). David Wise, volume 20, numbers 1–3 (1978–1979). Michael Blackburn, volume 23, number 2 (1982). Brendan Cleary, volume 23, number 3–volume 24, number 3 (1982–

1983). Richard Morgan, volume 24, number 4–volume 25, number 4 (1983–1984). Lawrence Jones, volume 25, number 1– (overseas editor) (1984–).

W. A. Johnsen

STRAND MAGAZINE, THE. SEE VEA

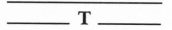

T

TEAPOTH 23. See *POOR. OLD. TIRED. HORSE.*

TIME AND TIDE

The story of *Time and Tide* (1920–1979) is largely the story of Margaret Haig, Viscountess Rhondda, who founded the magazine and who, for many years, edited it, influenced its policy, and controlled its management. Under her leadership it became one of the most outstanding and influential journals of the twentieth century. After her death in 1958 some effort was made to retain the tone and quality which she had so persistently maintained, but the attempt eventually failed. The magazine passed into other hands, assumed a new form, and rapidly declined from its former brilliance before it ceased publication in 1979.

Lady Rhondda's intentions in the review are to some extent explained by the events of her early life. Born in 1883, she was the daughter of Viscount Rhondda, a coal magnate and politician. As a young woman she supported the militant suffragette movement and, after an attempt to plant a bomb in a pillar box, was sent to prison, where she remained for five days before she forced her release by going on a hunger strike. Shortly after her marriage in 1908 her businessman father appointed her his personal assistant. A shrewd and forceful personality, Lady Rhondda rapidly demonstrated her ability in this position. When her father died in 1918, his title passing to his daughter, she continued to manage his business interests and became one of the first women to gain success as a director of a large corporation. But she had other aims and ambitions. Turning away from a business career, she determined in 1919 to take up a long-considered plan and found a weekly review. She was fortunate, as she freely admitted, in having the means to fulfill her ambition. She had money, she had freedom, and she had the ability and determination to proceed. The project was no mean challenge: the public for the kind of review she had in mind was small, and no woman had yet achieved success as a review editor. Yet it was a challenge which Lady Rhondda accepted vigorously. Assisted by a group of like-minded women, she want ahead with her plans, and the first issue of *Time and Tide* appeared on 14 May 1920.

From its inception, *Time and Tide* combined a witty and entertaining style with the promulgation of serious ideas about politics, literature, and the arts. In her autobiography, *This Was My World*, Lady Rhondda explained that she designed the review in order to propagate the new ideas which she saw as the only salvation for society in the postwar world. "I wanted," she remarked of that time, "to find, to test, and to spread the customs and ideas that could be health-giving and life-saving."[1] By presenting new views she hoped to "find the people who were worth hearing, and see that they were heard—heard, if not by the big multitude, at least by the inner group, the keystone people who ultimately directed that multitude. I could put before the public that mattered the things that I wanted them to hear." In her early days as a suffragette she had aimed at changing laws; with *Time and Tide* she wanted to change a "nation's habit of mind" and to establish a fresher, more liberal climate of opinion.[2]

Time and Tide was immediately recognized as something new and valuable in the newspaper world. Its first issue contained messages of good wishes from dignitaries in politics, the church, and education, and statements from many women of achievement. In the first two numbers figures as diverse as the Prime Minister, Lloyd George; the Right Honorable H. H. Asquith; the Archbishop of York; Margaret Tuke, Principal of Bedford College; Lady Baden-Powell; Lilian Faithful, Principal of Cheltenham Ladies' College; Dame Sidney Browne, former Matron-in-Chief of the Territorial Force Nursing Service; Ethel Smyth; and John Galsworthy, all voiced their support. The quality of the magazine was at once apparent, and it received favorable comment from the most distinguished sources. The *Times*, for example, found it to be "well and wittily written," and the *Manchester Guardian* considered it a "worthy piece of journalism that deserves success" (1:116).

The first stage of *Time and Tide* spans the period from 1920 to 1928. In these early years it remained a relatively small magazine, containing fewer articles and reviews than in its later years. In 1921 about 200 books were reviewed. By the end of the decade the number had risen to 700 annually, still far short of the number it was later to cover. The basic format and style, however, were already well established, although inevitably they received some modification over the next forty years. The items in each issue included a review of the week's events, leading articles, original stories and poems, reviews of books, theater, art, and music, a miscellany section, and a section on foreign travel. Urbane, witty, and sophisticated, the review had a style which Malcolm Muggeridge had in mind when he wrote of the "slightly haphazard, out-of-the-way, non-professional quality which is part of the charm, and distinction, of *Time and Tide*"

(37:1390). When Muggeridge used the term "non-professional," he was apparently referring to the personal, iconoclastic tone which typically pervaded the review and set it apart from conventional journalism of the time.

Above all, during those first years *Time and Tide* established its most fundamental and consistent quality: its independence. For many years it carried beneath its title the words "Independent—Non-Party." Tied to no single viewpoint, it was receptive to articles of a wide range of opinion in both literature and politics. Indeed, it encouraged controversy, believing that it could best serve society by stimulating the free play of the mind on the object, a characteristic of the liberal ideal. *Time and Tide* was directed at the informed, liberal, intellectual thinker, at those persons who, in Lady Rhondda's words, were "capable of hearing a man put the opposite point of view to their own without supposing him to be a scoundrel and a liar."[3] This was the point she chose to emphasize in a speech on 30 November 1927, reported in *Time and Tide* on 9 December 1927. She distinguished the weekly review from the daily newspaper: the review tried not merely to talk but to think and thereby gained the highest function of journalism (8:1114). Lady Rhondda recognized the need for a "delicate balance" between maintaining a consistent editorial position and presenting as many sides of an issue as possible. "One must," she wrote, "allow the views one believes the right ones to be shot at and be able to show that they can survive bombardment."[4]

The feminist approach of *Time and Tide* was strong in the first stage, particularly under Helen Archdale, the first editor, who was succeeded in 1926 by Lady Rhondda. At this period *Time and Tide* was closely connected with the Six Point Group, the feminist organization which took its name from its six goals: pensions for widows, equal rights of guardianship for parents, improvement of the laws dealing with child assault and with unmarried mothers, equal pay for teachers, and equal opportunities in the civil service. In addition to many articles dealing with these topics, the periodical provided thorough coverage of the position of women in society. Women in business, women in industry and in factories, women and the trade unions, the education of women, women and the priesthood, women musicians, women and the creative power, and leisured women were just a few of the topics considered. A long-running series entitled "The World Over" was mainly devoted to a depiction of women abroad, and another extended series, "Personalities and Powers," while not restricted to women, most often took as its subject the careers and achievements of distinguished women. In all these articles *Time and Tide* held fast to the principle that the basic goal of feminism should be equality with men. In the 1920s this position came to be known as the "old feminism" to distinguish it from the "new feminism," which asserted that women should now work not so much for equality with men as for those things which they needed to fulfill their own natures. The resulting conflict occasioned an ongoing debate in *Time and Tide* in 1926 and 1927 and engendered a voluminous correspondence.

But even in these early years the concern of *Time and Tide* was just as much with literature as with feminism. Included in the contents were not merely book reviews but short stories, poems, and features on many different writers and aspects of literature. Short stories by writers as diverse as Stella Benson (6:109), Edith Nesbit (1:267), Viola Meynell (5:477), Katherine Mansfield (8:473), Katherine Anne Porter (6:1269), Sylvia Townsend Warner (8:79), Alec Waugh (1:610), and Rabindranath Tagore (2:645) appeared in this period, as well as poems by— among others—V.Sackville-West (8:1007), W. H. Davies (9:964), and D. L. Sayers (1:492). Articles on literary figures were regularly included, especially in the "Personalities and Powers" series, which provided portraits of almost every writer of significance of the day—Arnold Bennett, Joseph Conrad, Thomas Hardy, W. B. Yeats, John M. Synge, H. G. Wells, Robert Bridges, Eugene O'Neill, and May Sinclair, to name only a few. Reviews dealt with books of solid quality, and the reviewers included some important names. Rose Macaulay was the first regular book reviewer; others were Theodora Bosanquet, Winifred Holtby, Vera Brittain, and Stephen King-Hall. D. H. Lawrence reviewed Nathaniel Hawthorne's *Blithedale Romance* in the issue of 5 August 1921 (2:744). The reviews already were of a quality to take them out of the field of ephemeral notices and into the area of genuine criticism. Sylvia Lynd, for example, on 20 June 1924 described *A Passage to India* as "a book of large plan and sustained achievement, a book of new knowledge as well as wisdom and imagination, a book that illumines a social and political problem and leaves it so revealed that the old revelations of it fade into trumpery insignificance" (5:592). This awareness of the Indian question—so much a part of the liberal consciousness in England in the 1920s and 1930s—was combined with perceptive literary evaluation as Lynd wrote on the simultaneously comic and agonizing quality of the novel.

In its articles *Time and Tide* was already attracting writers of outstanding talent or genius, some who were already famous, and some who would shortly become so. Politicians, academics, and professional writers all contributed to its pages. G. K. Chesterton, whose views seldom corresponded with the editorial policy, on 3 December 1926 contributed by invitation an article entitled "Candida and a Candid Friend" (7:1098), a response to a series of articles by "Candida" on "Women of Leisured Classes." Aldous Huxley's satirical "Socratic Dialogues of the Moment," a dialogue between a newspaper editor and a man in the street, appeared on 12 January 1923 (4:39). Bertrand Russell discussed "The Chinese Intelligentsia" on 13 January 1922 (3:29), and G. B. Shaw, "Women since 1860" on 8 October 1920 (1:443). Other important writers were St. John Ervine and Stephen Gwynn, both of whom wrote extensively on Irish affairs; Ethel Smyth, who contributed articles on music; Rebecca West, who wrote book reviews, theater reviews, and general articles; and Winifred Holtby, who reviewed books and contributed many feminist and pacifist articles. West was connected with the review from its inception; she wrote theater reviews in the first year and became a director in 1923. Holtby's first article appeared in 1924

(5:173); she became a director two years later and wrote regularly for nine years. On her death in 1935 Lady Rhondda declared that "she had as large a share in building [*Time and Tide*] as it is today as any one in the world."[5]

The theater criticism of this period was distinguished by the same perception and breadth of knowledge as the literary articles. Reviews of Shakespeare, for example, often included illuminating comments on the plays themselves as well as on the immediate performances. Anne Doubleday, in a review of *Macbeth* on 21 January 1927, saw the play as the tragedy of a man who acts out of character, who is fundamentally introspective but who resorts to violence (8:63). Christopher St. John used a modern-dress performance of the same play as the opportunity for a discussion, on 24 February 1928, of the nature of illusion in the theater (9:181). The judgments of contemporary plays, even those that have not always withstood the test of time, also contained provocative comments. Thus Christopher St. John on 14 March 1924 saw *Back to Methuselah* as Shaw's masterpiece, embodying the intellectual experiences and visionary speculations of a lifetime (5:249). Anne Doubleday was on more secure ground when on 4 April 1924 she described *St. Joan* as Shaw's best play and a great poetic drama which brings history alive (5:330). The play reviews at this time were the more notable because theater criticism was not one of the major concentrations of *Time and Tide*. Theater reviews formed part of a general section on the arts; the notices were usually fairly short and, especially in the late 1930s and the war years, irregular.

The middle years from 1929 to 1945 saw *Time and Tide* rise to the peak of success. Lady Rhondda herself felt that it entered this second stage when she persuaded Shaw to contribute a major article. In "Reminiscences of an Editor," which was printed on 17 May 1941, she recounts how early in 1929 she and Winifred Holtby wanted to broaden the slant of the paper and increase the circulation. Accordingly they planned for 22 February 1929 a bumper number to which Shaw contributed the main feature, a sketch entitled "The King and the Doctors." Later she wrote, "That issue, with that grand G.B.S. in it put *Time and Tide* on the map" (22:398). From then on the review rapidly increased in size, in the number of contributors, and above all in prestige.

The form remained essentially the same, but the number of articles rose steadily until 1939, when the war forced some curtailments. An important new column of personal comment and speculation, "Notes on the Way," was conceived in 1929 by St. John Ervine, who wrote it himself for two years. Thereafter the column was continued by many contributors, who were invited to express their ideas on contemporary issues or indeed on any matter they wished to take up. "Notes on the Way" rapidly became a vehicle for short personal or provocative essays by major authors. Another significant column, "Men and Books," formed the lead article in the book review section. From the start *Time and Tide* sought to provide a forum for the exchange of ideas, and its correspondence page always attracted important contributors; by the 1930s the correspondence was almost as notable as the articles. Lady Rhondda spoke with pride rather than irritation of the violent controversy which often occurred as the contributors spilled over to the letter page. "I must say," she once wrote, "I had some sympathy with the gentlemen who recently, after a week or so of particularly impassioned correspondence, wrote to inquire whether we had ever thought of changing our title to *Tooth and Claw*."[6]

The enlargement of *Time and Tide* in its middle years was to a great extent the result of its use of supplements and special numbers. In 1930 the first Christmas number was issued; by 1933 the Christmas number had become a major anthology of special contributions, the collection being further increased by a children's supplement. Another type of supplement emerged in 1931. In the spring of that year *Foreign Affairs* ceased publication, and Lady Rhondda agreed to take it over in the form of a monthly commentary on international affairs. This commentary, written by Sir Norman Angell, editor of *Foreign Affairs* and the 1933 Nobel Peace Prize winner, was published along with *Time and Tide* under the title *Foreign Affairs Supplement*. The arrangement continued for nine years until Sir Norman left to take up work in New York. Other special supplements included regular travel supplements and book supplements or sections for spring, summer, and autumn. Starting in October 1934 the review also began to publish a large monthly double issue so as to increase both its general and political articles and its book and theater reviews. In 1935 a series of eight University Supplements appeared. The articles in these supplements, each one the work of a major authority, provided a thorough and comprehensive investigation of British universities. Representative entries were essays by Arthur Quiller-Couch on "The Scholarly Don" (16, no. 8 supp.:3–5), G. G. Coulton on "The Medieval Scholar" (16, no. 8 supp.:10–12), C. M. Bowra on "Science and the Humanities" (16, no. 21 supp.:35–36), and Aldous Huxley on "Literature and Examinations" (16, no. 21 supp.:775–76). One last noteworthy supplement was that entitled *Supplement on Persecution of the Jews*, published on 26 November 1938, with articles by Shaw, Sigmund Freud, Harold Nicolson, Norman Angell, Baron Rothschild, and Herbert Morrison (19:1647–62).

In this second stage *Time and Tide* gradually shifted its viewpoints and political stance. The feminist interest which had been the mainspring of the early years continued in the early 1930s with such items as extracts (on 22 and 29 November 1929) from Virginia Woolf's *A Room of One's Own*, the 1930 serialization of E. M. Delafield's *Diary of a Provincial Lady*, Lady Rhondda's article on 18 August 1934 on debutantes, whom she termed a "parrot-educated group" (15:1026), and the many essays by Winifred Holtby.

As events in Europe took on an ever more ominous tone, the emphasis inevitably shifted to the pressing political issues—disarmament, isolationism, pacifism, the rise of the Nazi Party, the war in Spain. Lady Rhondda was throughout her life the champion of personal freedom and the opponent of tyranny either from the right or from the left. In the darkening thirties she took an early stand against Nazism, totalitarianism, and racial prejudice, and under her leadership *Time and Tide* presented the case for reason, compassion, and integrity in a world that was rapidly undermining all such values. More than one commentator remarked that the period constituted "her really great days" (39:935). Yet throughout these troubled times *Time and Tide* still welcomed the interchange of opposing ideas. In his review of the *Time and Tide Anthology* on 17 November 1956, Malcolm Muggeridge remembered with gratitude how in the Munich days he and writers of his ilk, attached to no party or ideology, could find in *Time and Tide* alone an outlet for their unorthodox opinions (37:1390).

While affairs in Europe dominated the political section, *Time and Tide* managed to keep its readers informed both about domestic policy and about American affairs. The paper retained its left-wing orientation, with articles by such figures as Ellen Wilkinson, Labour M.P. for Jarrow, who contributed regularly until she joined the coalition government in 1940. American affairs were mainly covered by Walter Lippmann, who in 1932 began a series entitled "The American View." Other writers on America were Gertrude Stein, who on 9 March 1935 wrote on American newspapers (16:335); and Theodore Dreiser, who on 31 October 1931 contributed "America and Her Communists" and attacked the barring of communism in America and the work of the Fish Committee (12:1247). The sensitivity to American attitudes was a mark of *Time and Tide*'s liberal slant and sometimes produced unexpected bonuses. In 1939, for instance, Herbert Morrison, soon to be Home Secretary, submitted an unsolicited profile on President Roosevelt which became the lead article for the issue of 22 April (20:493).

The political emphases of the 1930s by no means prevented the growth of the literary side of the review. With frequent supplements and double numbers, the literary section expanded rapidly. To take care of this growth it became necessary to appoint a full-scale literary editor, and in 1933 Ellis Roberts became the first to hold this position. A year later Theodora Bosanquet took over the office, to be succeeded by C. V. Wedgwood and John Betjeman. The largest part of the literary section was devoted to book reviews, which by 1937 had increased to more than 1,300, with ninety-seven reviewers. From then on the number dropped slightly, but in most years during Lady Rhondda's editorship about 1,000 books were reviewed. Practically every book of significance on any topic received some notice, and practically every writer of note at one time or another served as a book reviewer: poets Ezra Pound (15:1009), C. Day Lewis (24:663), and Stephen Spender (24:686); academics Gilbert Murray (15:859), Edmund Blunden (14:502), and Harold Laski (10:88); and novelists ranging from Rose Macaulay (13:122) to Storm Jameson (11:1047) to George Orwell (21:927).

The general literary articles in the thirties and the war years form a varied collection, ranging in subject from the predictable to the highly unusual. Notices of the deaths of major authors, an expected feature in a literary review, often provided the occasion for discerning appraisals and comments on their literary principles. Thus the article of 12 April 1941 on Virginia Woolf celebrated her as a "highly individual artist" and a "unique personality," and added the further comment: "Far as her experiments led her, she never lost sight of her human responsibility as an artist to communicate with her fellow creatures, never allowed herself to stray off arrogantly into a private world, never willingly left her meaning obscure'' (22:306). Some of the literary essays reflected the continued feminism of the review. Such were E. M. Delafield's series issued in the spring of 1931, ''Women in Fiction'' (12:158), followed in the same year by ''Children in Fiction'' (12:672) and ''Men in Fiction'' (12:742), and by Lady Rhondda's two series, ''Shaw's Women'' (11:300) and ''Wells on Women'' (11:1327). A more purely academic approach is exemplified by a series of articles which appeared in January, February, and March 1930, ''The Function of Literary Criticism.'' In this series four writers—John Galsworthy, Sylvia Lynd, Laurie Magnus, and Winifred Cullis—examined the function of criticism from the perspective of the writer, the reviewer, the publisher, and the reader. A less conventional analysis of the reading public appeared in August 1932 when the trade union official Jack Jones contributed a series of three articles entitled ''Miners' Welfare and Books—The Literary Renaissance of Britain's Black Lands,'' in which he identified the miners as serious readers whose interests, ranging from Shaw, Huxley, and Lawrence to Joyce and Woolf, made them a public deserving of recognition.

As the articles and reviews increased in number, the amount of creative work slightly diminished. Fewer short stories and sketches appeared in the middle years, though a variety of works was still published by such authors as Pamela Hansford Johnson (16:8), Phyllis Bentley (12:938), Graham Greene (16:1522), and Richard Hughes (21, no. 49 supp.:1). The decline in fiction was, moreover, counterbalanced by the number of short poems. Poetry was a regular feature of each issue, and the Christmas numbers always contained a two- or three-page spread of new poems. The poets ranged from the obscure to the most distinguished, with a fair number of poems by writers who were better known for other forms of literature. Among the poets of this period were Richard Aldington (11:925), W. H. Auden (17:754), Roy Campbell (16:268), W. H. Davies (14:756), Walter De la Mare (11:336), Stella Gibbons (11:1460), F. L. Lucas (16:680), Herbert Read (16:123), L. A. G. Strong (12:248), Edith Sitwell (10:7), C. S. Lewis (23:460), and Edward Thompson (21:365). Special mention may be made of D. H. Lawrence; his poems appeared frequently in 1929, and in the spring of 1933, three years after his death, his poems were published weekly for a period of three months. Contributions were not restricted to English writers. Sketches by Ernst Toller appeared in 1934 (15:342) and poems by Rainer Maria Rilke (15:8) in the same year. American writers also added to the variety: several stories by William Saroyan appeared in the late thirties (e.g., 18:1614), and poems by Vachel Lindsay (12:1183), Countee Cullen (10:685), and Langston Hughes (12:1062) in 1929 and 1931. *Time and Tide* thus was one of the first periodicals in England to publish works by black authors.

Perhaps the most notable feature of *Time and Tide*, however, was its general essays. In its pages novelists, poets, dramatists, and professional journalists were all able to express themselves with a directness and openness often found nowhere else in their works. Writing on 5 January 1935 in ''Notes on the Way,'' T. S.

Eliot made a lively defense of Christianity against the skeptical, scientific spirit of which he took Huxley to be representative (16:6). The following week in the same series of articles he opposed the confused thinking on war underlying A. A. Milne's *Peace with Honour* (16:33). The pacifist viewpoint was presented by George Lansbury, who set out his proposals for world peace in an article on 9 January 1937 (18:33). In the issue for 2 March 1940, on the other hand, A. A. Milne discussed the Peace Pledge Union and the necessity of war. Two articles represent a positive approach to Russian affairs and to communism in the thirties. On 29 July 1933 Sidney Webb, in an essay entitled "Family Life in Soviet Russia," defended Russian social morality (14:909); and on 1 July 1939 Pamela Hansford Johnson, while admitting the tragedy of the tsars, pointed out that the fall of the monarchy was caused by the countless tragedies of the poor and the oppressed (20:885). E. M. Forster contributed a number of personal essays for "Notes on the Way" as well as an article on 27 October 1934 on the Sedition Bill, in which he spoke out for civil liberties as opposed to violence and prejudice (15:1340). Lord David Cecil wrote in the issue for 8 March 1941 on the public school system and the overemphasis in the modern world on the need for equality (22:187). At the other end of the political spectrum, Shaw remained the unorthodox spokesman for socialism, writing frequently for the paper until 1940. After that time he contributed very little since his views on the war differed so widely from the editorial policy. It was, however, characteristic of Lady Rhondda that she did print on 13 January 1940 an article entitled "Danakil Women," which dealt with the Abyssinian war, appending a note to explain that the opinions presented were not those of the paper (21:34).

During the war years *Time and Tide* continued without missing an issue. Although somewhat reduced in size, it retained much the same format and appearance. As the war continued, staff and contributors left—most going into the army, some into government work—but the gaps were somehow filled. Old friends rallied round—stalwarts like Rebecca West, E. M. Delafield, Cicely Hamilton, and Rose Macaulay. Lady Rhondda recalled in "Reminiscences of an Editor" that "distinguished people with a thousand other calls on their time and energy found time to write for us—for no better reason than that we were a weekly review trying to carry on in war time" (22:402).

After the war *Time and Tide* entered a third stage, which extended through the next thirteen years until the death of Lady Rhondda. In this last stage a notable development in editorial policy took place. While the periodical still retained its independence and encouraged in its columns an ongoing dialogue and exchange of ideas, the original feminist slant was now replaced by a firm orientation to the political right. This shift reflected a change not so much in Lady Rhondda's own basic principles as in the world of events to which she applied those principles. Where in the 1920s she had seen personal freedoms as restricted by a male-oriented and class-conscious society, in the late 1940s and 1950s she felt that individualism was threatened on the one hand by totalitarianism and on the other by the bureaucracy of the welfare state. This was the view which she expressed in a series of articles in 1947 and 1948. She wrote on the importance of respect for the law and attacked Marxism and the planned state, which reduced the individual to a cog in a machine. As she saw it, the Labour government, by putting through its program of nationalization, was rushing the country toward the condition of the collective state. Lady Rhondda was in fact in accord with a widespread sentiment. Many of the radicals of the thirties were now disillusioned by the intensifying Cold War, and similar views were expressed by a number of writers. Stephen Spender, in "Open Letter to Pravda," published on 3 April 1948, defended the change in his own attitude to communism, asserting that true democracy must protect the rights of minorities. It was the duty of intellectuals and writers, he declared, to speak for victims and not to withdraw either into the realms of mysticism or into the world of power politics (29:345). Likewise, on 26 February 1949 Rose Macaulay, in "Tyranny and Liberalism," attacked "the vile tyranny of Communism," seeing true liberalism as the only weapon against it (30:197). The same year C. V. Wedgwood, in her review of George Orwell's *1984* on 11 June, found the world of the novel to be already "uncomfortably close" (30:594).

While the political emphases shifted, the literary section of the paper remained as impressive as ever. If anything, the galaxy of writers became even more brilliant. This was in large part due to the efforts of C. V. Wedgwood. Herself a historian of distinction, Wedgwood served as literary editor from 1944 to 1952, and in those years she consolidated the reputation of *Time and Tide* for literature and literary criticism. Although stories and sketches were sparse, short poems continued to appear regularly in every issue and in the Christmas numbers. W. H. Auden (37:1460), John Betjeman (31:1198), Dietrich Bonhoeffer (27:32), Rumer Godden (27:824), Robert Graves (31:36), Kathleen Raine (28:512), Stevie Smith (37:1460), Walter De la Mare (30:1222), John Heath-Stubbs (27:487), and Siegfried Sassoon (33:1429) are among the poets whose works were published in these years.

Even more impressive than the poetry section was the number of writers who contributed book reviews, essays, or feature articles. A long line of new authors at this time made their first appearance. Books were often reviewed by academics of distinction, among them C. S. Lewis (35:1082), H. J.C. Grierson (31:475), Muriel Bradbrook (31:680), Helen Darbishire (35:215), A. J. Ayers (35:967), C. M. Joad (32:114), A. L. Rowse (27:679), G. M. Trevelyan (29:1221), Martin Turnell (37:336), and Jacquetta Hawkes (29:740). Evelyn Waugh wrote several reviews on matters of literature and art, starting with a review of Rex Whistler's *The Konigsmart Drawings*, which appeared in the Christmas number for 1952 (33:1456).

At this time, too, the general essays became more literary and less political. On 10 and 17 June 1950 *Time and Tide* published essays by T. S. Eliot entitled "The Aims of Poetic Drama"; these two essays were extracts from a lecture given in Germany in which he had analyzed the purposes and achievements of the new drama. Stephen Spender's essay of 23 March 1946, "Good Taste and the Critic,'' was a consideration of the opposition between highbrows and low-brows among the reading public (27:271). Louis MacNeice discussed a related problem in his "Notes on the Way" for July 1952 when he reflected on the predicament of the artist in the modern world and the need to be both artist and craftsman, and to deal with both the universal and the temporal (33:779). T. H. White surveyed the development of the horror story or thriller in an article that appeared on 8 September 1951 (32:843), and Lord Tweedsmuir (John Buchan) wrote an essay on the adventure story for the 7 May 1955 issue (36:594). Informal personal essays were also frequent in these years. Typical are Graham Greene's account of a sudden meeting with an old school acquaintance (35:1602), V. Sackville-West's reflections on language (30:1212), and Denton Welch's story of a morning with Lord Berners (33:747).

Despite the stature of the writers and the dedication of the editorial staff, *Time and Tide* was always beset with financial difficulties. The paper had never really paid its way, and by 1958 Lady Rhondda had almost come to the end of the large personal fortune with which she had supported it. After her death it was revealed that she had spent a quarter of a million pounds on the review. In the spring of 1958 she tried to obtain new financial backing or to find a suitable buyer, and ultimately she raised enough money from friends and subscribers to keep the paper going. But the victory was short-lived. It seems probable that the worries of these months were a factor in her death in July of the same year.

Without her leadership the journal as she had established it could not long continue. Although *Time and Tide* lasted for another twenty-one years, it became in fact a totally different publication from the one which she had started in 1920. The decline was rapid. For two years the new owner, Leonard Skevington, a paint manufacturer, attempted to retain as much of the old form and spirit as possible. In 1960, however, he transferred the paper to the Reverend Timothy Beaumont, later Lord Beaumont, president of the Liberal Party. Eventually he too, like Skevington, found the cost of maintaining the journal too great, and in 1962 he sold it to newspaper magnate William J. Brittain.

Under Brittain's editorship the paper was rapidly transformed. In January 1963 it merged with the literary magazine *John O'London's*; the two magazines were issued together as one publication, but each retained its separate identity under separate editors and with separate tables of contents. Under the new arrangement *Time and Tide* continued in its usual form, while *John O'London's* provided additional coverage of books, authors, television, theater, cinema, and people at home and abroad. The merger did not last long. In May 1964 the two magazines separated again. *John O'London's* joined with *Books of the Month* as a monthly magazine, and *Time and Tide* was redesigned as a complete news magazine on the model of the American *Time* and *U.S. News and World Report*. From then on books and literature had little part in it. Attempts to lure new types of readers resulted in totally new emphases: in 1966 the journal became *Time and Tide and Business World*; in 1967, *Time and Tide, the British News Magazine*; and in 1976, *Time and Tide, Business World*. It is a final irony that in February 1977 this once ardently feminist publication now began to carry the subtitle "The Business Man's Weekly Newspaper." The intent of all these changes was to popularize the paper among the mass reading public; and the scholarly articles, learned reviews, and thoughtful commentaries on social and political problems were replaced by popular journalism. From 1966 onwards the frequency of publication varied, ranging from weekly to biweekly to monthly.

In 1965, in a BBC talk on weekly magazines, Anthony Lejeune, personal friend of Lady Rhondda and editor for a short time after her death, remarked that the periodical was "weirdly changed" since her day. The changes became only sharper in the next fourteen years. It was left to Anthony Lejeune to give the final epitaph on the closure of the paper: "I'm not sure that the proprietors for the past 20 years, since Lady Rhondda died, have known what they were doing with it. It's been dying for a long time."[7] The last issue of *Time and Tide* appeared in July 1979. In effect, however, it is the year 1958 that marked the end of *Time and Tide* as one of the great literary and political reviews in the history of British periodical literature.

Notes

1. Margaret Haig, Viscountess Rhondda, *This Was My World* (London, 1933), p. 301.
2. Ibid., pp. 304, 300.
3. Margaret Haig, Viscountess Rhondda, *Notes on the Way* (London, 1937), p. 50.
4. Ibid., pp. 55–56.
5. Ibid., p. 207.
6. Ibid., p. 54.
7. Quoted in the *Daily Telegraph*, 18 May 1979, p. 18.

Information Sources

BIBLIOGRAPHY

Brittain, Vera. *Testament of Experience*. London, 1957.
———. *Testament of Friendship*. London, 1940.
Delafield, E. M., ed. *Time and Tide Album*. London, 1932.
Lejeune, Anthony, ed. *Time and Tide Anthology*. London, 1957.
Rhondda, Viscountess, Margaret Haig. *Notes on the Way*. London, 1937.
———. *This Was My World*. London, 1933.

INDEXES

Indexes were compiled in the *Time and Tide* office, but they are not always included in bound library copies. Even the British Library does not have an index for every volume of the periodical.

REPRINT EDITIONS

Microform: British Library, London.

LOCATION SOURCES

American

Complete run: New York Public Library.
Partial runs: Duke University Library; U.S. Library of Congress.

British

Complete run: British Library.

Partial runs: Bodleian Library; Cambridge University Library; Manchester Public Library.

Publication History

MAGAZINE TITLE AND TITLE CHANGES

Time and Tide, 1920–1963. *Time and Tide, John O'London's*, 1963–1964. *Time and Tide*, 1964–1966. *Time and Tide and Business World*, 1966–1967. *Time and Tide, the British News Magazine*, 1967–1976. *Time and Tide, Business World*, 1976–1977. *Time and Tide, Business Guide*, 1977–1978. *Time and Tide*, 1979.

VOLUME AND ISSUE DATA

Volumes 1–59, May 1920–July 1979. Each volume numbered separately; some irregularities in numbering after 1970.

FREQUENCY OF PUBLICATION

Weekly, 1920–1970. Monthly, 1970–1973. Weekly, 1973–1977. Biweekly, 1977–1978. Monthly, 1978–1979.

PUBLISHERS

1920–1979: Viscountess Rhondda; Leonard Skevington; Rev. Timothy Beaumont; William J. Brittain; Sir Charles Forte. 88 Fleet Street, London E.C.4 (1920–1929)/32 Bloomsbury Street, London W.C.1 (1929–1961)/177 Regent Street, London W.1 (1961–1962)/40–43 Chancery Lane, London W.C.2 (1962–1969)/Classified House, New Bridge Street, London E.C.4 (1969–1977)/58 Russell Square, London W.C.1 (1977)/14 Bolton Street, London W.1 (1977–1979).

EDITORS

Helen Archdale, 1920–1926. Margaret Haig, Viscountess Rhondda, 1926–1958. Anthony Lejeune, 1958–1959. R. Sinclair, 1959–1960. Rev. Timothy Beaumont, 1960–1962. William J. Brittain, 1962–1972. Juliet Brittain, 1972–1977. Ian Lyon, 1977–1979.

Muriel J. Mellown

TO-DAY. See VEA

TOWNSMAN

When Ronald Duncan began his outspoken journal, *Townsman*, in January 1938, he devoted it to literature and other fine arts. It ended in June 1945 as an agricultural journal. Duncan admitted, "We have changed our format five times, our printer six times, our price four times, and even our title has had its vicissitudes" (no. 21:1). For most of its history it appeared as *Townsman*. The last few issues were called the *Scythe*. The May 1942 issue (no. 16) was unusual in that some of the copies had *Townsman* on the cover and others had *Scythe*.

Duncan's interest in agriculture was apparent early in *Townsman* and gradually assumed importance until the last few issues emphasized the subject. Duncan, who became a farmer the year after he began the journal, wrote that he could not tell the difference between farming and literary works, for "what else is literature but the proper husbanding of words?" (no. 21:2).[1] Duncan's editorials and essays showed that three of his concerns—the loss of vitality in the English language, the importance of finding meaning in life, and the need for Great Britain to be self-sufficient—all led to his love of agriculture.

From the first issue, he asserted that "VALID WORK evolves out of an individual's direct impact with reality" (no. 1:1), and later he defined reality as agriculture: "The reality behind words is things. The reality behind things is soil" (no. 16:1). Hitler's and Mussolini's speeches (no. 7:10–12) had vitality, but the British, having lost contact with reality, spoke imprecisely and in clichés. The artist, Duncan believed, must know how to plant onions (no. 5:4). Stressing the need for Britain to be self-sufficient, Duncan advocated regionalism rather than centralization. And the country must stop depending on Canada, India, and particularly the United States (no. 15:1–2). It must look to its own land for food: "food to be eaten where grown" (no. 12:3).

Duncan also wrote that people must have a myth or religion to sustain them. It could not be democracy, communism, or any belief which implied a foolish belief in human perfectibility. It also could not be an Allied victory because there would always be another war (no. 14:1). The answer—echoing the first line of Pound's poem "The Inedible," which appeared earlier in *Townsman*: "Only a WHEAT GOD can save Europe" (no. 10:2)—was a belief in "an Earth God, a Wheat God" (no. 16:2).

Known primarily as a verse dramatist, Duncan published three of his early plays in his journal—*The Unburied Dead* (nos. 1–6), *Pimp, Skunk and Profiteer* (no. 8), and *Ora Pro Nobis* (nos. 8, 10). His shorter poetry included "Post Card" (no. 11:5), a highly visual, compressed poem in celebration of the outdoors; "Practical Ballad No. 5" (no. 13:24); and "Practical Ballad No. 1" (no. 13:24), which detailed how to build a pig sty and forced the similarities between that activity and making poetry.

"The Rexist Party Manifesto" (no. 4:19–23) was an economic satire. To prevent Britain from "sliding into a *War*, a *Slump* or a *Second Industrial Revolution*" (4:20), the fictitious authors of the manifesto proposed that the working class be prevented from breeding and be killed if they could provide no useful services. Once the English working class died out, workers would be provided from British colonies. "Our Strategy in War," the entire contents of number 9, minimized the seriousness of Germany's threat to England. In this satire, a fictitious major general proposed to defeat Germany by, among other things, poisoning its water supply, bombing the sewer system, and letting diseased rats loose behind enemy lines. Duncan's refusal to take Germany's threat to England seriously was echoed elsewhere in the journal when he wrote that Britain had more to fear from Wall Street than Germany (no. 15:1–2).

Reviews in the *Townsman* are less startling. Those by Duncan showed that he admired George Crabbe's poetry (no. 2:22–24) and liked many of W. B.

Yeats's poems, although he himself was not interested in Gaelic mythology (no. 7:19–21). In "Epitaph on the Illiterate Left," he damned W. H. Auden with the epitaph "always a virgin" (no. 10:10). He also wrote (no. 4:24) an obscene poem of condemnation on *Phoenix*, an American quarterly dedicated to the ideas of D. H. Lawrence.[2] Reviews by others tended to support the editor's viewpoint. John Drummond also damned Auden's work (no. 3:23–26), and T. R. Barnes gave high marks to Yeats's poetry while, like Duncan, he was bothered somewhat by the Gaelic mythology (no. 5:25–26). Ezra Pound, Duncan's friend,[3] expectedly received high praise from K. Noel Weston for Cantos 52–61 (no. 12:27–29), but Duncan also published Denys Thompson's criticism of Ezra Pound's *Guide to Culture* (no. 5:30–31). Thompson also criticized reviewers who compared minor authors to Milton or Homer, and he singled out as good critics only Edwin Muir and Herbert Read (no. 1:28–30). Thompson's review of *Poetry and Anarchism* was ambivalent. The subject was timely, but Thompson felt that Read's book "generally raises more questions than it answers" (no. 4:25). In another review, Richard March condemned the poems of William Carlos Williams as "mere nervous twitches, gasps and stutters" (no. 6:19). T. S. Eliot's works were usually favorably reviewed in *Townsman*, and E. W. F. Tomlin wrote about the important contribution the *Criterion** had made (no. 6:13–15).

Ezra Pound was a frequent contributor to *Townsman*, writing on music, religion, and economy. He provided an introduction to music by Francesco da Milano (no. 1:18), and the journal included the musical score "Heaulmiere" from the opera *Villon* by Pound with his own commentary (no. 2:12–18). In his essays on religion Pound objected to Calvinism, calling Calvin's god "a maniac sadist" (no. 11:13). In "Religio" and "Ecclesia" he wrote that, while he did not object to European influences in Christianity, he would not admit to any Semitic influence (no. 8:3–4). He blamed Jews for usury, the major problem confronting the world, especially in his poem "Slice of Life" (no. 5:5). While his essay "The Central Problem" did not specifically target Jews for blame, it also asserted the importance of money in the world and the horror of usury (no. 13:13–16).

Besides Pound and Duncan, the only other important poet to publish in the journal was E. E. Cummings. Three of his poems, including the condemnation "american critic ad 1935" (no. 1:2), appeared in the first issue. The Duke of Bedford (no. 12:12–13; no. 15:20–22) and William Saroyan (nos. 2–4) wrote essays for the journal. T. S. Eliot's "Five Points on Dramatic Writing," originally from a letter to Pound, also appeared.

Besides Pound's music, Duncan's journal included part of Mozart's *The Magic Flute* with commentary by Soulima Strawinksy (no. 6:8–10) and Spanish and Portuguese songs translated by Duncan (no. 18:23–26). There were reproductions of paintings by William Johnstone (no. 1:following 24) and Hilaire Hiler (no. 2:following 18), and drawings by Gaudier-Breszka (no. 6:4–7; no. 11:22).

Short stories were "Death by Misadventure" by Jean Canayenne (no. 1:23–24) and "Idyl on Soutra," written in Scottish dialect by Robert Garioch (no.

2:19–21). For those interested in *Townsman* as a literary magazine, the first ten or eleven issues—with Duncan's plays and satires, the bulk of Pound's contributions, and the works of Cummings, Eliot, Saroyan, and Garioch—are the essential issues to read. All of the organ is valuable, even the later issues, for those who wish to study the early years of Duncan's literary career.

Notes

1. E. W. F. Tomlin, "Ronald Duncan," in *Great Writers of the English Language: Dramatists*, ed. James Vinson (New York, 1979), p. 179.
2. Frederick J. Hoffman, Charles Allen, and Carolyn F. Ulrich, *The Little Magazine: A History and a Bibliography* (Princeton, 1946), pp. 184–86.
3. Tomlin, "Ronald Duncan," p. 182.

Information Sources

BIBLIOGRAPHY

Davis, Earle. *Vision Fugitive: Ezra Pound and Economics*. Lawrence, Kans., 1968.
Duncan, Ronald. *All Men Are Islands*. London, 1964.
———. *How to Make Enemies*. London, 1968.
Haueter, Max Walter. *Ronald Duncan: The Metaphysical Content of His Plays*. London, 1969.
Wahl, William B. *Ronald Duncan: Verse Dramatist and Poet Interviewed*. Vienna, 1973.
INDEXES
> Volume 1, number 1–volume 2, number 8 in *An Author Index to Selected British Little Magazines*, ed. B. C. Bloomfield (London, 1976).

REPRINT EDITIONS
> Kraus Reprint, Nendeln, Liechtenstein, 1972. Scholars' Facsimiles and Reprints, Delmar, N.Y.

LOCATION SOURCES
American
> Complete runs: Hamilton College Library; Harvard University Library; New York Public Library; Princeton University Library; University of Chicago Library; Yale University Library.
> Partial runs: University of Alabama Library; University of Buffalo Library; University of Virginia Library.

British
> Complete run: British Museum.
> Partial run: National Library of Scotland, Edinburgh.

Publication History

MAGAZINE TITLE AND TITLE CHANGES
> *Townsman*, numbers 1–15, 17–18 January 1938–January 1943; number 20, Spring 1944. *The Scythe*, number 16, May 1942; number 19, Summer 1943; numbers 21–24, July 1944–June 1945.

VOLUME AND ISSUE DATA
> Volumes 1–5, numbers 1–24, January 1938–June 1945.

FREQUENCY OF PUBLICATION
   Quarterly, January 1938–November 1940; then two or three times a year, 1941–
   1945.
PUBLISHER
   Ronald Duncan, West Mill, Morwenstow, North Cornwall, England.
EDITOR
   Ronald Duncan.

Margaret Ann Baker Graham

TRACE

The history of *Trace* is a success story. The little magazine began in 1952 as a thin pamphlet, and by 1970 its last issue was a double number 300 pages long. *Trace*'s one editor in all those years, James Bolton May, devoted himself and his finances to what he called in a retrospective editorial "the most fruitful experience of a lifetime" (no. 72/73:417). Edited in the United States but published in London, the magazine was never distinctly British or American. Initially, the function of *Trace* was bibliographical; it provided information about the existence of little magazines to the editors and readers of little magazines. This function began with May's regular contribution to another journal, *Matrix*, called "Towards Print"—a name he retained for his editorials in *Trace*. Some of the contents of early issues seem to be preaching to the converted, with compilations of quoted comments from letters written by editors of other little magazines, all about the necessity of little magazines. This self-serving quality endured in *Trace*, as well as a tone reminiscent of a nineteenth-century belle. The contents were still glaringly unprofessional and quirky. In "A Personal Interview with W. H. Auden," for example, George Stillman writes that the steps to Auden's apartment were "quickly conquered" and then relates, "It happened! The door opened, and there stood Mr. Auden in person. . . . The time flew quickly."

In 1961 a new column, the "Creative Window," was allotted to literature and graphic art. Although no major authors or artists were among the contributors, the feature nonetheless gave the magazine a substance and interest beyond the bibliographical clearinghouse function. *Trace* began to specialize in new writers and in aiding "a few older writers of rather fading reputation" (no. 67:196).

Most of the time editorial decisions were May's alone. An editorial board existed for three years, but May felt that the magazine was losing direction, and he resumed sole power. As editor, he declared his preference for works which treat positive rather than negative themes, as well as his resistance to literary trends. He renounced the Beats in the 1950s and misjudged the importance and permanence of the radical experimentation of the 1960s. He maintained that he was neither pro- nor anti-academy, and that he chose work solely on the basis of its quality, regardless of the author's affiliations or lack thereof. These personal preferences shaped and governed *Trace* for all of its eighteen years.

In 1960–1961, the original impetus for *Trace*, the directories of little magazines, became a separate publication, *The International Guide*, which operated under separate financial supervision. When the *Guide* collapsed a year later, *Trace* again published the directory. The 1962 *Trace* contained the first comprehensive directory, which it continued to publish in subsequent issues. As little magazines proliferated, the directory became primarily a listing reference rather than a reviewing tool.

By 1964 *Trace*, nearly 100 pages long, had become a glossy magazine as well, printing photography and graphic art as well as poetry and short stories. Its fat, sleek appearance masked deeper financial pressures. In 1968 an editorial note informed readers that, contrary to publicity, *Trace* received no grant money; publication by a commercial British firm precluded such financial assistance. May himself had underwritten even the payments to contributing authors and artists. Late in its career several special issues appeared, including number 67 in 1968, which focused on the "Prose/Art/Poems of India," and number 70 in 1969, which focused on humor. When *Trace* succumbed it was not because of financial hard times. May's failing health in 1970 was the determining factor in the decision to stop publishing; without its one editor, there could be no magazine. The flashy final issue in the magazine's eighteenth year of publication was visually impressive and remarkably various in its content, providing an attractive farewell.

Information Sources

INDEXES
>   Each volume indexed.

REPRINT SOURCES
>   None.

LOCATION SOURCES
>   *American*
>>   Widely available.
>
>   *British*
>>   Complete runs: Birmingham Public Library; Bodleian Library; British Museum; Cambridge University Library; London University Library; National Library of Scotland, Edinburgh.

Publication History

MAGAZINE TITLE AND TITLE CHANGES
>   *Trace, A Chronicle of Living Literature*.

VOLUME AND ISSUE DATA
>   Numbers 1–72, February 1952–Autumn 1970.

FREQUENCY OF PUBLICATION
>   Three times a year.

PUBLISHER
>   Villiers Publications, Ltd., Ingestre Road, Tufnell Park, London, N.W. 5.

EDITOR
    James Bolton May.

Toby Silverman Zinman

TRANSATLANTIC REVIEW, THE

Ford Madox Ford, novelist, essayist, and editor, was fifty years old in the fall of 1923, when his brother Oliver, chancing to meet him on a boulevard in Paris, offered him the editorship of the new *Transatlantic Review*. Ford saw the *Transatlantic* as an opportunity for the rebirth of his prewar *English Review** (see *VEA*). Ford was able to find John Quinn, James Joyce, Ezra Pound, and, later, Ernest Hemingway to serve as advisers to the new magazine and as contributors of money, editorial expertise, fiction, nonfiction, or poetry. An organizational meeting with Quinn, Joyce, and Pound took place on 12 October 1923.[1] A manifesto/prospectus was circulated in November, and by December the first issue had been published in Paris in blue and white covers (soon changed to blue and buff). The British and American issues were published in January 1924, in London by Duckworth and Company and in New York by Thomas Seltzer. By January Ford had also relocated his magazine at its permanent address of 29 quai d'Anjou, Ile Saint-Louis.

Ford's express aims were to found a magazine that would create anew an international Republic of Letters for Anglo-Saxondom—one which would benefit from a civilizing French influence. The magazine would unite seemingly incongruous periods and offer a medley of unknowns and knowns. English artists, Ford felt, had been left in a waste land by the war, and were out of touch "with racial life" (1:62). Deadening political and social interests oppressed their spirits, as they had for the past hundred years. In effect, people who might have been creative were merely bored (1:103). "Racial assertiveness" was needed (1:55). The artist should shed edifying bilge and not bother with any system of morals (1:171). Sex in literature would be difficult for Ford to deal with, yet he had faith that in the realm of thought and the arts all conflicts would be resolved (1:197).

Ford was certain of the value and importance of art for its own sake. He thought that the artist, young or old, past or present, must be concerned with "methods" (1:198) and must approach the arts with indirection. Except for informing the reader that the artist must be familiar with the psychology of his own day, Ford did not specify precisely what he meant by methods of style. He offered some ancestral figures as models, elevating Edgar Allan Poe to a primary position, and recommending, in varying degrees, Henry James, O. Henry, Walt Whitman, Rudyard Kipling, and Stephen Crane. These artists would assist and inspire modern artists in their escape from the stultifying moral hypocrisy and commercial oppression of a perpetual Victorianism, and would also help bring into being a great literature, which, Ford believed, could only arise from the masses. He especially looked to America for the emergence of great modern literature. The Young Americans showed the paradoxical—perhaps simply contradictory—character of Ford's literary standards, at least as far as style is concerned. Beginning with the first issue, Ford published his and Joseph Conrad's *Nature of a Crime* (first published about fifteen years earlier), featuring an amoral, agnostic narrator, who declared to his beloved at one point, "Ah my dear one— that is why I have so loved you" (1:18). In contrast, E. E. Cummings wrote on page 4, "It is ourselves against the worms."

It was left to the Young Americans to enter the lists against Ford in their attempt to define the "modern." In the issue edited by Hemingway, for August 1924, the American writer printed brisk items about artists—but also about fighters and bullfighters. He was not attracted to Jean Cocteau's linguistic elitism (1:102–3) and believed Dada had expired (1:356). In backhanded compliments that escape notice, largely due to the famous depiction of Conrad as worth more than the dust of T. S. Eliot made particulate matter in a sausage-grinder, Hemingway mourned Conrad's death. Conrad was also superior to "some great, acknowledged technician of a literary figure" (Ford?) (2:342). Ford, unruffled and unflappable, apologized to Eliot in the same issue.

The first issue of the *Transatlantic Review* might appear from today's vantage point to signal the arrival of a distinguished journal of modern and transitional literature and culture. The title was printed with avant-garde lowercase letters— an accident of space requirements, as Ford later explained.[2] Poetry was contributed by Ezra Pound, E. E. Cummings, and A. E. Coppard (then a well-known writer); stories by Jean Cassou and Robert McAlmon. Ford's essay on literature (printed serially under the pseudonym "Daniel Chaucer"), the serialized *The Nature of a Crime*, the memoirs of a Greek octogenarian, Luke Ionides (related by marriage to the Pre-Raphaelite circle), and references to the 1890s and the art for art's sake movement exemplified both a certain tradition and the idea of internationalism in the arts. But the first issue contained little that was new. Pound and Cummings were already established figures; Coppard was a prominent, commercially successful writer. The French stories integrated cubism in literature at a time when cubism was already secure in the history of art and had become somewhat passé in advanced artistic circles. Ford's authorship of *The Nature of a Crime* was prewar, and the tone, if not the content, was, for the writers of the twenties—for the iconoclastic, antibourgeois, and anti-Victorian—as bourgeois as anything composed by those whom Lytton Strachey had ridiculed in *Eminent Victorians*. A new style and attitude had come into being with the postwar period. The advertisements Ford solicited for his magazine from such figures as Thomas Hardy, H. G. Wells, and T. S. Eliot were of doubtful value. Hardy did not contribute any poetry, and both he and Conrad indicated that they thought the magazine should be for the young. Moreover, Ford's old Tory expostulations against the political left troubled the literary and cultural context of the magazine.

The second issue seemed, to the untutored eye, to include much that was modern: poetry by H. D. (Hilda Doolittle) and F. S. Flint; an impressionistic story by Ethel Colburn Mayne; a brief note by Lincoln Steffens; an article by George Antheil and Ezra Pound on music; and Pound's "Treatise on Harmony." The Steffens article raised eyebrows, with Ford's assistance. Perhaps, Ford mocked, the editor was a Bolshevik, despite his antileftist harangues and philippics (1:62). The serials continued from the first issue, and various letters from capital cities or cultural centers of other countries (mostly written in Paris, however, by exiles or quasi-exiles) concluded the issue.

The third issue attempted to outline an "internationally revelatory purpose" (1:62) and included a tale by the conservative, Carlylean epic writer Selma Lagerlöf, a poem by William Carlos Williams, impressionistic stories by B. M. W. Adams and Mary Butts, and Gertrude Stein's *Making of Americans*. (The first installment was hand-copied by Hemingway from Stein's original manuscript.) An art supplement contains reproductions of Georges Braque, Man Ray, and Gwen John, and Braque contributes some *Notes sur l'Art*.

The April issue contained more pages than its predecessors, but, typically, very little poetry: two poems by Coppard; five, in French, by Jacques Baron; one by J. J. Adams. There was another installment of Stein's *Americans*, Djuna Barnes's story, "Aller et Retour," a Dada test, a Hemingway story, and Joyce's *Work in Progress*, the first publication of any item from *Finnegans Wake*. Ford's "Chroniques" and "Communications" conclude the issue.

The presence of such figures as Stein and Hemingway foreshadowed a development in the magazine toward the new and modern, capping as they did the contributions of early modernists such as Joyce and Pound. New voices were to be heard. The young modernists were clear about what they liked and did not like from the past. The struggle for dominance of the *Transatlantic Review* developed between Ford and Hemingway, between distinctive views of at least two prior generations and a future not clear and definite as of 1924. Ford's position became increasingly defensive on the magazine, and, at least from the vantage point of today, it seems all but inevitable that the *Transatlantic* would eventually have to be born again with new aims or cease publication.

For the next three issues, Ford retained control. The May issue continued to publish Coppard, Ethel Colburn Mayne, and B. M. W. Adams. H. G. Wells's wife Catherine contributed "The Afternoon." Only the end section of the magazine exposes the magazine's conflicts, with Ford and Hemingway disputing about Dada and McAlmon. The June issue brought more of Luke Ionides and some modernist contributions: a story by D. M. Garman, a friend of Hemingway; five surrealistic poems, in French, by Georges Designes; and additional installments by Stein and Ford. Kennon Jewett's letter from the United States, but dated Paris, also illustrated one of the magazine's problems: it was in reality more Paris-based than international, more an exiles' production than a magazine to which internationally minded writers and artists sent contributions from their own countries.

At the midpoint of the publication year, Ford seems to have concluded that the magazine was not moving in the direction he wished. In pursuit of funding and support, he visited the United States. Before leaving, he set up a traditional, conservative July issue with contributions by such established figures as Paul Valéry and William Carlos Williams; a second installment of a lecture on art by Juan Gris; new installments of Stein's *Making of Americans*, Ionides' *Memories*, his own *Some Do Not*, and Conrad and Ford's *Prefaces* to *The Nature of a Crime*; a reproduction of Jacob Epstein's Conrad; and Basil Bunting's review of Conrad's late novel, *The Rover*. Younger writers were represented only by Ivan Beede's violent "A Prairie Summer Morning" and Carlos Drake's melodramatic story, "The Last Dive." Hemingway commented unflatteringly on Cocteau's lack of knowledge of English and deprecated Tristan Tzara and Gilbert Seldes.[3]

The eighth issue, under Hemingway's editorship, brought young American writers to the fore—at least while Ford was in America. There were poems by expatriates, by Bryher (McAlmon's wife), by the Greenwich Village eccentric Baroness Elsa Freytag-Loringhofen. John Dos Passos's "July" was also published, along with another installment of Stein, and contributions by Dorothy Richardson, Nathan Asch, and Guy Hickok. Ford's contributors were generally excluded: Mary Butts, Luke Ionides, Daniel Chaucer, Ford himself. A communication from William Carlos Williams favoring McAlmon affirmed the subeditor Hemingway's independence; the *Chicago Tribune* termed the issue "one of the most virile and important documents of present-day art." Since the American edition of the magazine was printed later than the Paris edition, Ford had an opportunity to respond. He indicated that the magazine would return in its next issue to its usual conservative style.

The September 1924 issue did indeed reassert conservative and international values; Daniel Chaucer reappeared, as did Luke Ionides, along with Ford and his friend Mary Butts. Three poems by George O'Neill, a friend of Hemingway, Hannah Berman's meditative monologue "The Beggar," and D. M. Garman's "Visiting Day" were also published, along with Jean Cassou in a new stylistic experiment (in French), another installment of Stein, and a letter from London by T. S. Eliot's friend, J. Isaacs. The "letter" from the United States was signed Krebs Friend, a friend of Hemingway and a Paris resident. Mina Loy contributed an article on Stein's style, and letter from Tzara answered Hemingway's charges. Hemingway's letter, with its mocking address, "The Republic of Letters," continued the quarrel with Ford. By the end of August, Ford had been relieved of financial responsibilities in the management of the magazine. Krebs Friend became president and Ezra Pound became music editor.

The October issue was unexceptional. Ford's *Some Do Not*, which had been serialized, was not included; his contribution was thus reduced to his "Stocktaking" column (by Daniel Chaucer) and the serialized *Portrait of Conrad*. There were poems by Benjamin Gilbert Brookes and H. Stuart, and serials such as Ionides' *Memories* and Stein's *Americans*. Two war stories, by Geoffrey Coulter and Ivan Beede, captured modern American themes. An article on Czechoslovakia was perhaps designed to highlight the magazine's internationalist theme. There were also poems by Angus McPhail, Natalie Barney, Eyre de Lanux (an American), and Nancy Cunard, who also had by this time acquired a financial interest in the magazine.

Compared to the emotional, aesthetic coherence of the American issue and the more conservative issues controlled by Ford, the October issue seems highly unfocused. The disarray continued in the last two issues, which contained fragments from a diary by Havelock Ellis; twelve poems by Richard Cheever During; and stories by Djuna Barnes ("The Passion") and Hemingway ("The Doctor and the Doctor's Wife"). Kate Buss, stationed in Paris, and an admirer of Pound and Stein, contributed a letter from the United States.

The final issue, the twelfth, for December 1924, concluded the magazine's life. Stein's *Americans* and Ford's *Portrait of Conrad* were serialized, and there were poems by Havelock Ellis, J. J. Adams, Evan Shipman, and Tzara (in French). Donald Stewart, Nathan Asch, Hemingway, Ivan Beede, A. William-Ellis, McAlmon, Jean Rhys, and Elma Taylor all contributed stories. A letter from America signed Elizabeth Krebs may actually have been written by Ford. A violent attack on Antheil (by Arthur Moss) is followed by Ford's *Portrait of Conrad* in an eerie stylistic contrast.

At the end of the twelve-month life of the *Transatlantic*, Ford had succeeded in publishing some of the major established figures of the early and later modern period. And he had published one young writer, Hemingway, destined to be a world literary celebrity for the next thirty-seven years of his life. It would be remarkable in any period for a little magazine to publish writers in a single year who were the equal of Pound, Joyce, Stein, Hemingway, E. E. Cummings, Conrad, and Ford himself, as well as Valéry, Barnes, Cocteau, Tzara, H. D., F. S. Flint, William Carlos Williams, and A. E. Coppard. But the magazine has a further importance: it dramatized the generational struggle between the older group Ford had been part of and the newer one he attempted to join. It is the story in miniature of the aggressive American victory on the literary and cultural battlefield of postwar Europe. This was an important feature of internationalism which Ford did not, however, include in his own definition of "international." Although its life was brief, the *Transatlantic* is a fine example of the little magazine that, fragile as the boat in its logo, manages to master the tides well enough to remain afloat in our imagination. Its motto was well chosen, "Fluctuat nec mergitur."

Notes

1. Bernard J. Poli, *Ford Madox Ford and "The Transatlantic Review"* (Syracuse, N.Y., 1967), p. 20.

2. Ford Madox Ford, *It Was the Nightingale* (London, 1936), p. 284.

3. Poli, *Ford Madox Ford*, p. 108.

Information Sources

BIBLIOGRAPHY

Anderson, Elliott, and Mary Kinzie, eds. *The Little Magazine in America: A Modern Documentary History*. Stamford, Conn., 1978.

Ford, Ford Madox. *It Was the Nightingale*. London, 1936.

Mizener, Arthur. *The Saddest Story: A Biography of Ford Madox Ford*. New York and Cleveland, 1971.

O'Brien, Edward. *Best Short Stories of 1924*. Boston, 1924.

Poli, Bernard J. *Ford Madox Ford and "The Transatlantic Review."* Syracuse, N.Y., 1967.

INDEXES

Each volume indexed. *Comprehensive Index to English Language Little Magazines 1890–1970*, series 1, ed. Marion Sader (Millwood, N.Y., 1976).

REPRINT EDITIONS

Kraus Reprint, New York, 1967.

Microform: New York Public Library.

LOCATION SOURCES

American

Complete runs: Widely available.

British

Complete runs: Bodleian Library; British Museum; Cambridge University Library; Trinity College Library.

Publication History

MAGAZINE TITLE AND TITLE CHANGES

Transatlantic Review.

VOLUME AND ISSUE DATA

Volume 1, numbers 1–6, January-June 1924 (Paris and London editions. Paris edition of issue number 1 printed in December 1923). Volume 1, numbers 1–4, January-April 1924; number 5, May-June 1924; number 6, July 1924. Volume 2, numbers 1–6, July-December 1924 (Paris and London editions). Volume 2, numbers 1–5, August-December 1924 (American edition). Some additions to American issues not included in Paris and London issues.

FREQUENCY OF PUBLICATION

Monthly.

PUBLISHER

Transatlantic Review Company, Paris; Duckworth and Co., London; Thomas Seltzer, New York.

EDITOR

Ford Madox Ford.

Warren Herendeen

TRIPOD, THE. See VEA

TRUTH. See VEA

TWENTIETH CENTURY

In 1877, James Knowles, former editor of the *Contemporary Review** (see *VEA, MA*), established the *Nineteenth Century** (see *VEA*), a journal devoted to publishing "signed writing" by prominent figures and to encouraging debate between public figures on important issues. Around 1895, Knowles discovered that the title *Twentieth Century* was already being used, and began to think of other titles which might be used after 1900: *Nineteen Hundred*; *Nineteenth Century: A Sequel*; and *Nineteenth Century: A Survival.*[1] When January 1901 arrived, however, he had decided upon *Nineteenth Century and After*; this title continued until 1951, when the title changed to *Twentieth Century*.

The first edition of *Nineteenth Century and After* in January 1901 carried a symbol which it was to continue through 1950: a two-faced head, one face that of a bearded old man looking down, and presumably, back, the other of a young woman gazing up and forward. The male figure was labeled XIX, the female XX. Knowles's comment on the addition to the cover is as follows: "This Janiform head, adapted from a Greek coin of Tenedos at the request of the Editor, by Sir Edward J. Poynter, P.R.A., tells, in a figure, all that need be said of the alteration made to-day in the title of the Review." Knowles continued as editor until his death in 1908. His successor was William Wray Skilbeck, his son-in-law, who continued the monthly with few changes. From Knowles's death until 1948, the editors were not identified in the pages of the journal.

National and international affairs were the topics of many of the articles. For much of the life of the periodical, considerable space and attention were devoted to questions regarding the colonies and British imperial policy. This was especially true in the years following the Boer War. Pieces on religion, theology, and dogma were regularly printed as well, often written by prominent churchmen. Historical articles appeared, as did biographical pieces on literary and political figures. Articles on scientific subjects were published, but technical language was avoided. Astronomy, especially, seemed to be a popular topic. During both world wars, of course, much was written about the war effort, the home front, causes of the conflicts, and suggestions and predictions for postwar activities and policies.

One of the reasons for the *Nineteenth Century*'s success was the fact that many prominent writers contributed signed articles to its pages. Alfred Lord Tennyson, Matthew Arnold, William Gladstone (who contributed sixty-five articles), T. H. Huxley, Herbert Spencer, and Algernon Charles Swinburne, to name just a few, were regular contributors. Both *Nineteenth Century and After* and *Twentieth Century* continued in this tradition. Some writers who contributed to the later periodicals were Stephen Spender, Robert Bridges, Hilaire Belloc, Neville Chamberlain, Havelock Ellis, Ramsay Muir, Ford Madox Ford, Virginia Woolf, E. M. Forster, André Maurois, and Sean O'Casey. Later writers included Bonamy Dobrée, Asa Briggs, George Barker, Malcolm Muggeridge, Elizabeth Jennings, Colin Wilson, Norman Mailer, V. S. Naipaul, Thom Gunn, Arnold Toynbee, Christopher Isherwood, and Julian Huxley.

From 1901 until after World War II, the publication varied little in emphasis or physical appearance. In announcing the title change to *Twentieth Century*, an editorial asserted that the world was entering a "new intellectual period" in which nineteenth-century skepticism must be thrown off if totalitarianism was to be avoided. Skepticism must be replaced by "positive beliefs," the editor went on to say, and *Twentieth Century* would foster these ideas (146:887). Physical changes in the periodical occurred at this time as well. The page size was reduced and the type changed from Monotype Garamond to Monotype Baskerville. The 1950s saw the introduction of published correspondence as well as book reviews.

In July 1961 *Twentieth Century* became a quarterly. From this time on, editorial policy was to publish each edition on one major topic or subject, such as the economics of the arts or anthropology. Illustrations were introduced at this time as well. In an editorial in the Autumn 1962 number, it was announced that this policy had proved successful and that it would continue. The editor went on to say that the publication's approach wold be henceforth "more dominantly sociological" and that a new advisory board, consisting of persons working in that area, had been appointed.

In 1965 the periodical was restyled physically. In addition, the editor announced that *Twentieth Century* was widening its interests and "providing a forum for opinions which might otherwise not be expressed." To reflect the "permissive" age, the magazine would henceforth be less restrictive in its language and subject matter. There was no reason, new publishers John Goldsmith and Dennis Hackett asserted, to "avoid things with which everyone is familiar" (no. 1026:3). Over the next seven years the magazine, in its large three-column format, focussed on such topics as "God, Where Art Thou?" (no. 1027), "Aggression" (no. 1031), and "The World of the British Newspaper Cartoon" (no. 1041). The last issue took as its special focus "The Exotic" (no. 1049). There was no indication anywhere in that issue, for the third quarter of 1972, that it was the last of the *Twentieth Century*, as it silently ceased publication.

Note

1. Priscilla Metcalf, *James Knowles: Victorian Editor and Architect* (Oxford, 1980), p. 343.

Information Sources

BIBLIOGRAPHY
"James Knowles." (London) *Times*, 14 February 1908, 12e.
Metcalf, Priscilla. *James Knowles: Victorian Editor and Architect*. Oxford, 1980.
Ward, Wilfred P. *Ten Personal Studies*. London, 1908.
INDEXES
Each volume indexed.
REPRINT EDITIONS
Microform: UMI; Princeton Microfilm Corporation, Princeton, N.J.
LOCATION SOURCES
American
Widely available.
British
Widely available.

Publication History

MAGAZINE TITLE AND TITLE CHANGES
> *Nineteenth Century and After*, 1901–1950. *Twentieth Century*, 1951–1974.

VOLUME AND ISSUE DATA
> Volumes 49–179, numbers 287–1049, January 1901–3d Quarter, 1972. (Continues numbering of *Nineteenth Century*.)

FREQUENCY OF PUBLICATION
> Monthly, 1901–1961; quarterly, July 1961–3d quarter 1972.

PUBLISHERS
> 1901–1904: Sampson Low, Marston, & Co., London. 1904–1920: Spottiswoode (Ballantyne) & Co., London. 1921–1950: Constable & Co., London. 1950–1954: The Nineteenth Century and After, Ltd., London. 1954–1965: The Twentieth Century, Ltd., London. 1966–1968: The Twentieth Century Magazine, Ltd., London (John Goldsmith and Dennis Hackett). 1968–1972: The Twentieth Century Magazine, Ltd., London (Dennis Hackett). 1972 (nos. 1048, 1049): Omnific Advertising, Ltd., London.

EDITORS
> James Thomas Knowles, Jr., 1901–1908. William Wray Skilbeck, 1908–1919. Carrol Romer, 1929. Arnold Wilson, 1934–1938. F. A. Voigt, 1938–1946. Michael Goodwin, 1948–1952. Bernard Wall, 1959–1960. Richard Findlater, 1962–1965. Robert Ottaway, 1965. Michael Wynn Jones, 1966–1968. Michael Wynn Jones and Michael Ivens, 1968–1972.

James W. Parins
Marilyn Parins

TWENTIETH CENTURY VERSE

Twentieth Century Verse had its beginnings in January 1937 in a house in Croydon which was shared by three young aspiring poets, Julian Symons, H. B. Mallalieu, and Derek Savage. Symons, as editor, also provided the requisite financial backing for the magazine with savings accrued from his less-than-elevated position with the Victoria Lighting and Dynamo Company. As Symons later recalled, *Twentieth Century Verse* was "pretty well a single-handed enterprise," although Mallalieu and his wife helped with the "donkey work of the first few issues and with the last one or two."[1] Appearing as it did during the Spanish Civil War, the time of the Popular Front and the Left Book Club—when the imagination of many writers was shaped and even dominated by political turbulence at home and abroad—one might assume that *Twentieth Century Verse* could not escape at least some political motivation and orientation. But its interests were literary rather than ideological. Symons admits that he, Mallalieu, and Savage were motivated by the desire to see in print their work and that of poets from their background:

There was a real difference of attitude then between poets who had been
to a university like Auden, Spender, Day-Lewis, Empson, Lehmann, and
those who hadn't like Thomas, Barker, Ruthven [Todd], Roy Fuller, and
the three of us. There was a whole range of subjects from which we were
cut off and about which most of them wrote, but also they seemed to have
a common tone as of friends talking to each other in a way that excluded
strangers.[2]

The public school and university ethos—if not red in political dye, then
certainly pink—was to be avoided. In his opening editorial Symons denied that
he wished "to cultivate poetry in an atmosphere as rarefied as possible," reiterated that his magazine was not being run as "an advertising campaign for any
literary clique or party," and asserted that poetry "need not be concerned with
politics. . . . to discuss in detail poetry and politics is to tread worn and we believe
barren ground" (no. 2:22).

Plainly, Symons was attempting to carve out his own territory between the
various poetic schools of the 1930s. Not only did he wish to distinguish his
endeavors from those of *New Verse*,* but also from the overtly propagandist
poetry contained within the pages of *Left Review** and from the surrealists, who
were then enjoying something of a vogue. Despite the apparent clarity of Symons's theoretical position, the practical application of his principles (as manifest
in the poetry he published) is less easily categorized. It was perhaps inevitable,
given the editor's anxious seeking of middle ground, that the worst poetry in
Twentieth Century Verse consisted of oblique arguments developed through the
juxtaposition of bizarre imagery with the flattest, most prosaic of statements.
Poets like Ruthven Todd, H. B. Mallalieu, D. S. Savage, and Symons himself,
however, who were regular contributors to the magazine, managed in their better
work to rise slightly above this miasma. Although none of them created a
distinctive voice, together they achieved something of a house style which owed
little to either Auden or Dylan Thomas, having neither the ironic wit and moral
intentions of the former nor the bardic verbal exuberance of the latter. Avoiding
Georgian flourishes, Symons and his friends produced a poetry often dour and
costive, which valued the cerebral development of images in an attempt to express
a fundamanetally private vision. Roy Fuller, a frequent contributor to the magazine, addressed a verse-letter to Symons in the early 1940s, remarking upon
the "crabbed, uncompromising verses" they "used to write" and wondering
"what they mean."[3]

Fuller's own early work is among the most distinguished that Symons published. Unlike Todd, Savage, and Mallalieu, he has become a poet of sustained
and considerable achievement. Although Fuller shared Symons's taste for poems
with tight structures, intellectual arguments, and earnest tones, his Marxist orientation led him to recognise in his work the objective world beyond the self.
He gave voice to personal intellectual conflicts which arose from a central problem he shared with many others: how to reconcile his position as a bourgeois

and an artist with his political belief in Marxism. His language was plainer than that of most contributors to *Twentieth Century Verse*, and his imagery more familiar and more concretely realized.

Symons was something of an ambassador between English and American letters, contributing columns to several American magazines.[4] He was thus well placed to bring out a double issue of *Twentieth Century Verse* (no. 12/13 [September/October, 1938]) dedicated to the work of young American poets: Delmore Schwartz, Wallace Stevens, Theodore Roethke, Yvor Winters, Conrad Aiken, R. P. Blackmur, and John Berryman. The issue also contained an "Enquiry" in the form of a questionnaire to the poets concerned. The American responses to the English questions are quirky and impatient, but Symons was rewarded well for his enterprise; the double number sold the entire 1,000 copy print run as opposed to the usual circulation of 700 copies.[5]

The only other issue of the magazine to sell as well constituted another bold venture on Symons's part: a double number for November-December 1937 dedicated to that self-styled "great professional outcast of the pen," Wyndham Lewis. In 1931 the editor of *Blast** published a book entitled *Hitler*, which approved with some reservations the program of National Socialism. Lewis was inevitably alienated from the dominant liberal writers and the hard-line Marxist propagandists. Despite the fact that in 1937 Lewis published a recantation of his earlier position in *The Hitler Cult*, Symons's symposium may still be regarded as an act of some courage, integrity, and insight. His editorial argued that Lewis's "width of vision" outstripped all "other respected literary figures" of the day and concluded that Lewis was "the most valuable and interesting writer of our time" (no. 6/7:105). There followed a typically combative "Letter to the Editor" by Lewis himself, who, anticipating his critics, denied that he was a "counter-revolutionary" and asserted on the contrary that he was "the pure revolutionary." He also argued that art was "of no use to politics" since it "functioned in the abstract" and spoke "only with God" (no. 6/7:106), a point of view to which Symons was entirely sympathetic. The subsequent seventeen essays written by people of such diverse literary and political affiliations as T. S. Eliot, Hugh Gordon Porteus, Rex Warner, Gavin Ewart, Glyn Jones, and H. B. Mallalieu, provided a fitting testament to Lewis's importance. There were those, however, for whom Lewis could not be redeemed, and in subsequent issues Symons was obliged to defend his championship of Lewis. In number 9, clearly undaunted by his critics, Symons printed Ruthven Todd's checklist of Lewis's works, the first Lewis bibliography.

In view of Symons's consistent promotion of aesthetic values independent of politics, it is ironic that his magazine was a casualty of developments in world events. Moreover, the last issue of the magazine, for July 1939, was a symposium on a topic Symons had disdained; entitled "The Poet and the Public," the subject inevitably evoked political response. Roy Fuller, in "The Audience and Politics," detailed some of Christopher Caudwell's Marxist notions. Desmond Hawkins took a vaguely left-wing position in "Poetry and Braodcasting." George

Barker, though a supporter of the Republicans in Spain, took the view in his "Note on Narrative Poetry" that "poetry is poison to the people" and apparently saw no reason why it should be otherwise. But the most interesting contribution was the editor's dialogue with H. B. Mallalieu, who was to have become an associate editor of *Twentieth Century Verse* following that issue. Their "Conversation after Dinner" constituted Mallalieu's criticism of the magazine and Symons's responses. Mallalieu, who became a Labour politician after the war, argued that Symons had laid undue emphasis on individuality and privacy; too many poems had been printed which were willfully obscure and placed unnecessary barriers between the poet and his audience. Symons reiterated his position of concentration on individuality and aesthetic standards. The dialogue demonstrates that Symons was prepared to tacitly admit some of the charges laid against him and to allow changes by giving Mallalieu the associate editorship.

But change was not to be; the outbreak of the war brought the magazine to a close. Symons has since written fairly accurately about the achievements of *Twentieth Century Verse*, noting a number of "embarrassing pages" and the fact that he "nursed his own ugly ducklings many of whom turned out to be geese." On the positive side, he is "pleased to have printed so many of Roy Fuller's early poems, the first poem of Robert Conquest and some poems by Kenneth Allott."[6] While *New Verse* may have printed a higher proportion of good poetry in the 1930s than *Twentieth Century Verse*, Symons's magazine reflects the variety of styles and the richness of the literary output of that decade. The magazine tempers the argument that the Audenesque was entirely representative of the 1930s. By encouraging the writings of those outside the public school and Oxbridge circle, Symons shows another dimension of twentieth-century letters in Britain.

Notes

1. Julian Symons, "Twentieth Century Verse," *The Review*, no. 11/12 (1964):22–24.
2. Julian Symons, *Notes from Another Country* (London, 1972), p. 59.
3. Julian Symons, *The Thirties: A Dream Revolved* (London, 1960), pp. 152–53.
4. See Symons, "Twentieth Century Verse," pp. 22–24.
5. Ibid.
6. Symons, *Notes from Another Country*, p. 63; "Twentieth Century Verse," pp. 22–24.

Information Sources

BIBLIOGRAPHY
Skelton, Robin, ed. *Poetry of the Thirties.* Harmondsworth, Eng., 1964.
Symons, Julian. *The Thirties: A Dream Revolved.* London, 1960.
———. "Twentieth Century Verse." *The Review*, no. 11/12 (1964):22–24.
———. *Notes from Another Country.* London, 1972.
Tolley, A. T. *The Poetry of the Thirties.* London, 1975.

INDEXES

Numbers 1–18 in *Comprehensive Index to English Language Little Magazines 1890–1970*, series 1, ed. Marion Sader (Millwood, N.Y., 1976). Numbers 9–16 indexed in number 15/16. *An Author Index to Selected British Little Magazines*, ed. B. C. Bloomfield (London, 1976).

REPRINT EDITIONS

Kraus Reprint, New York, 1966.

LOCATION SOURCES

American

Complete runs: Dartmouth College Library; New York Public Library; Pennsylvania State University Library; University of Buffalo Library.

Partial runs: Princeton University Library; University of Chicago Library; Yale University Library.

British

Complete run: British Library.

Partial runs: Cambridge University Library; National Library of Scotland, Edinburgh.

Publication History

MAGAZINE TITLE AND TITLE CHANGES

Twentieth Century Verse.

VOLUME AND ISSUE DATA

Numbers 1–18, January 1937–June/July 1939. Numbers 6/7, 12/13, and 15/16 are double issues. (Although no volume numbers are given, issues 1–9, 9–16, and 17–18 are paginated consecutively.)

FREQUENCY OF PUBLICATION

Twice quarterly.

PUBLISHERS

January–September 1937: The Noble Fortune Press, 1191, Finchley Road, London. November/December 1937–July 1938: Julian Symons, 17, The Waldrons, Croydon. September/October 1938–June/July 1939: Julian Symons, 9, Cedars Road, London.

EDITOR

Julian Symons.

A. D. Caesar

U

UNIVERSITIES' POETRY

In a burst of undergraduate enthusiasm *Universities' Poetry* published its first issue at University College of North Staffordshire, Keele, in March 1958, promising to offer "enlightenment" and the opportunity for "comparative criticism" by bringing together in one volume a selection of poetry written by students in British universities. The anthology received support from the Keele Students' Union and a group of patrons, including G. Wilson Knight.

In his "Foreword" advisory editor John Harvey described the ambitions of the student editors, Bryan Reed and R. Bryan Tyson, who hoped to publish a total of 120 poems a year in biannual volumes, and characterized the poems to follow. Although he did not want to overemphasize either the poems or the role of the university, Harvey believed that creativity was increasingly centered in universities and that a growing audience had its taste shaped in the undergraduate experience. The poems produced by undergraduates provided an index to the culture and a guide to future talent. Expecting to find contrived poems, Harvey was pleased to discover little of the "University Wit" tradition. He was not troubled by the derivative nature of most of the work, so long as the writer's literary debts were owed to the best of the poets.

The anthology quickly gained the financial support of the Arts Council and several other universities. To provide continuity and stability to a national undergraduate publication, a managing committee was formed in 1959 under the chairmanship of Bonamy Dobrée, who became the committee president in 1963, succeeded by V. de Sola Pinto as chairman. It instituted a policy of changing undergraduate editors each year, with a member of the committee advising them.

Twenty-two institutions of higher learning from Aberystwyth to Sheffield were represented in the first issue. The poems were clever, often technically skillful, and clearly influenced by literature, imitating or referring to Wallace Stevens,

Dylan Thomas, and W. H. Auden. Some of the works read like literary poses on nature, such as "Songs from a Southern Shire" by William A. S. Serjeant or "Illuminatio Mea" by Patricia Miles, but others begin to capture and convey experience. Gerald Morgan's "The Terrorists" concretely details the violent acts of a shy man who would betray the government for a blue-eyed girl's kiss. In "No Angel" Marney Matchett explores the paradoxical attraction of Jesus and Mary Magdalene. Zulfikar Ghose of Keele would remain associated from the first issue on in one capacity or another.

Ghose coedited volume 2, which did not appear until October 1959, with three other students: Anthony Smith (of Cambridge), John Fuller (Oxford) and Bryan Johnson (London). A letter from Smith to Ghose served as the "Introduction." Pleased with the quality of the selections and with the length of the pieces, believing that a poem must be long enough to be "testable," he believed that the poems, which could not have been written even five years before, cohered around a common notion of the poet as detached observer. Although the work was good, he predicted that in three to four years it would "look as dead as the Georgians" (2:6) and anticipated a new Romanticism influenced by symbolism and by new language from the "attitude" of the American tradition.

The cover price of *Universities' Poetry* for volume 2 dropped from three shillings, six pence, to two shillings. Advertising appeared, and the binding and paper became more durable. Copy became less academic and moved closer to experience, a shift seen in Ghose's poem recalling his home, "Prologue: Sialkot." The reader encountered a direct memory of childhood—guava and pomegranate trees, a cow and its dung, and grandpa's threat that the barber waits with his razor to remove hair or foreskin. The most amusing, and one of the most insightful poems, was Francis Hope's "Deluded Bears Are Wrecking Telephone Poles." He begins with a newspaper clipping about New England bears that, believing the humming in the wires to be caused by bees, destroy telephone poles in a misguided search for honey. So, his poem develops in a thoughtful parallel, we project our assumptions on to others and "wreck our methods of communication . . . Thinking that humming always leads to honey" (2:52).

Universities' Poetry 3 appeared in March 1961 under the editorship of Edward Lambton (Keele), Andrew Roberts (Cambridge), and Christopher Williams (Oxford), with Ghose as advisory editor in charge of production. Originally promised for October 1960, the magazine, in a preface, explained the delay. The editors wanted to represent all of Great Britain, but in October there was not one poem from anywhere but Oxford and Cambridge worth publishing. The provincial universities were poetically barren ground. Ghose consoled himself that thirty good poems a year from anywhere is an achievement, and noted especially those by Janet Burroway, William Dunlop, John Fuller, and Jon Silkin. Silkin had already established himself as a poet, founding the quarterly *Stand** in 1952 and publishing three volumes of poetry since them, including in 1961 *The Re-ordering of the Stones*, but he had never taken a degree and, so, was a thirty-one-year-old undergraduate at Leeds. John Fuller's *Fairground Music* was published the same year as his appearance in *Universities' Poetry*.

In 1962 and 1963 the managing committee worked to put *Universities' Poetry* on a firmer financial and aesthetic basis. It found additional funding and began to sponsor student poetry conferences that included lectures, readings, and group critiques. More ambitiously, it published the first in a series of collections of poems by promising undergraduates: Janet Burroway's *But to the Season*. The series was designed to create an audience and to find publishers for emerging poets.

In April 1962, *Universities' Poetry* 4, the last issue published at Keele, was edited by Anthony Tillinghast (Nottingham) and Clive Jordan (Oxford), with Dax MacColl of Keele as managing editor. From more than a thousand entries, the editors selected thirty-five poems. The magazine contined the move away from literary allusion toward personal experience, as in Angus Calder's "The Red Birds" and Michael Fried's "Miscarriage" (4:30).

Tom Lowenstein (Cambridge) and Ken Smith (Leeds), the editors for *Universities' Poetry* 5 in May 1963, wrote what was to become the standard introduction: a complaint that most of the entries were poor and that the provincial universities were not producing the quality necessary for them to be represented. As a result, the publication had lost its national balance. They "opened" the magazine by choosing works that focused outside the private world of academia: Seamus Heaney's "Turkeys Observe," which describes the fowls in a butcher shop window; Norman Talbot's "Beet-Pullers," describing their labors; Michael Longley's "Odysseus to the Sirens," an intense reinterpretation of the siren's song, which fills the listener with despair at the memory of the mean ordinariness of the land he longs for.

Universities' Poetry seemed to be on strong footing. It offered cash prizes from the *Transatlantic Review*, sponsored poetry conferences, received secretarial assistance from the *Critical Quarterly*,* and promised a 1964 anthology. But it did not publish again. As the acknowledgments regularly revealed, although *Universities' Poetry* was a showcase for undergraduate poetry, it was not always the writers' first time in print. The anthology used material from college literary magazines, but some work had been published in more widely circulating periodicals, such as the *New Yorker*, *Stand*, and *Critical Quarterly*. More and more its poets continued to encounter a widening audience, thus fulfilling the first editors' intentions and, ironically, ending the mission of the magazine.

Information Sources

BIBLIOGRAPHY
Ghose, Zulfikar. *Confessions of a Native-Alien*. London, 1965.
Schmidt, Michael. *A Reader's Guide to Fifty Modern British Poets*. London, 1979.
INDEXES
    None.

REPRINT EDITIONS
    None.
LOCATION SOURCES
    American
        Complete runs: Northwestern University Library; University of Kansas Library;
        University of Washington Library.
        Partial runs: Harvard Univeristy Library; U.S. Library of Congress; University of
        California Library, Los Angeles; University of Chicago Library.
    British
        Complete runs: Birmingham University Library; Bodleian Library; British Mu-
        seum; University of London Library.

Publication History

MAGAZINE TITLE AND TITLE CHANGES
    Universities' Poetry.
VOLUME AND ISSUE DATA
    Number 1, March 1958. Number 2, October 1959. Number 3, March 1961.
    Number 4, April 1962. Number 5, May 1963.
FREQUENCY OF PUBLICATION
    Irregular (annual).
PUBLISHERS
    University College of North Staffordshire, Keele (1958–1962). Managing Com-
    mittee of *Universities' Poetry*, 34, Claremont Square, London (1963).
EDITORS
    Bryan A. Reed [Keele] and R. Bryan Tyson [Keele]; John Harvey, M.A. (Oxon),
    advisory editor, 1958. Zulfikar A. Ghose (Keele), Anthony Smith (Cambridge),
    John Fuller (Oxford), and Bryan Johnson (London), 1959. Edward Lambton
    (Keele), Andrew Roberts (Cambridge), and Christopher Williams (Oxford); Zul-
    fikar A. Ghose, advisory editor and production, 1961. Anthony Tillinghast (Not-
    tingham) and Clive Jordan (Oxford); Dax MacColl (Keele), managing editor,
    1962. Tom Lowenstein (Cambridge) and Ken Smith (Leeds); Anthony C. Smith,
    advisory and managing editor, 1963.

                                                                    Frank Edmund Smith

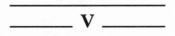

V

VANITY FAIR. See VEA

VE-TIME DRAMA. See DRAMA

VJ-TIME DRAMA. See DRAMA

VOICES

When *Voices* appeared in January 1919, two months following the Armistice, an early admirer, Arthur Quiller-Couch, found it

> strangely fresh and full of faith. . . . I could not decide whether it resembled dreaming amid hideous realities or waking from a hideous nightmare. But the stabbing poignancy of some of the lyrics settled that question. These young men had suffered, and were awake and abundantly hopeful. [3, no. 1:1]

The young men Quiller-Couch so powerfully responded to were four writers who were responsible for much of the work that appeared in the monthly during its lifetime of a little less than three years. A hundred or more writers contributed to this small shilling magazine, but four—Thomas Moult, Louis Golding, F. V. Branford, and Neville Cardus—provided the publication with its identifying "voices." During its first eight months of publication, 80 percent of its contributions were signed by these four writers. After that time, other contributors assumed greater importance in the magazine until, with its last issues, these four writers are infrequently represented except for brief review articles and notes on artistic matters provided mostly by only one of them, *Voices'* editor, Thomas Moult. All four of them were young: at the time *Voices* first appeared, none was yet thirty years old. All of them drew on World War I as subject matter for some of their writing, and at least two were veterans of that war. All four writers either spent their formative years in Manchester or wrote for the *Manchester Guardian*. An editorial note acknowledges the support of that newspaper and actual contributions from two of its staff members of reviews in the first number of *Voices* which appeared over the initials "M.G." ("Chimney Corner," 5, no. 3:105).

Moult was only twenty-four years old when he took on the editorship of *Voices*; as was the case for the other three young men, a career as a man of letters lay before him. During the next twenty years he was to distinguish himself as a journalist and anthologist, as well as achieving some success as a critic, novelist, and poet. For nearly twenty years he edited the annual *Best Poems*. He served as art and sports writer for several publications, including the *Manchester Guardian*, the *Athenaeum** (see *RA*) and the *English Review** (see *VEA*). He served as chair of the editorial board of *Poetry Review** for ten years. Besides serving as editor of *Voices*, Moult contributed something—whether poems, fiction, or criticism—to every issue of his magazine. His first contribution to *Voices* memorializes the dead of World War I in "How Beautiful They Are . . . " (1, no. 1:7–8), and one of his later contributions, a review of Thomas Hardy's "And There Was a Great Calm," claims epochal authority for that poem of the kind *Voices* aspired to. The poem is, he says, "a magnificent piece of work, expressing the attitude of every human soul that was not made hopelessly askew by the events of 1914–18, when as Mr. Hardy puts it with characteristic bluntness, 'old hopes that earth was bettering slowly were dead and damned' " ("Poetry," 4, no. 6:248–49). As editor and contributor, Moult devoted himself to "the spiritual healing of men and women" ("Declaration," 4, no. 3:79). This devotion found expression in lyrics pertaining to the Great War (1, no. 2:93–95) and in the examination of difficult relationships in a love lyric, "Before the Nightfall" (2, no. 6:2–3), and in prose fiction, "Stucco" (2, no. 3:98–101).

Louis Golding, also twenty-four years old in 1919, was Moult's most frequent contributor, having provided nearly every issue of *Voices* with several items which, in all, total about sixty pieces. A native of Manchester and a war veteran, Golding provided the magazine with several prose pieces, including the prefatory piece, "Voices," and essays on the London theater. He also contributed fiction to *Voices*, such as "Forward from Babylon: The Opening of a Novel" (2, no. 1:5–17). Most often, however, Golding's contributions were poems, for which he received critical praise: "Lyric in Gloom" (2, no. 2:67–68) and "Numbers" (1, no. 2:68–70). The poem that was to provide the title of a volume of Golding's poetry also appeared in *Voices*, "Shepherd Singing Ragtime" (1, no. 5:229–32).

F. V. Branford, who published under his military designation as "Flight-Lt.," contributed nearly as many pieces to *Voices* as did Golding, nearly all of them war lyrics. One prose contribution of his, "The Kingdom of Confusion: A Romance" (1, no. 2:80–92; 1, no. 3:144–54), is an autobiographical fragment which stands as lighthearted relief to his more grim poetical endeavors, such as "The Secret Treaties" (1, no. 1:14), "Any Daisy" (1, no. 3:130–31), and "Return" (1, no. 1:18–19).

Neville Cardus, who had been rejected as an army recruit, served part of the war period as a contributor to the *Manchester Guardian*. He was responsible for filling much of the relatively small amount of space in *Voices* devoted to serious art criticism: "Sir Thomas Beecham and Conducting," (1, no. 3:157–64; "Form in Opera," 3, no. 4:155–58). Cardus was eventually to establish himself as a journalistic authority on music and cricket, and many of his essays on those subjects were published in book form following their appearance in periodicals. One of his most significant contributions to *Voices* appeared in the first issue, a rebuke pointed specifically at Arthur Symons. Beauty for beauty's sake, Cardus asserts, is the "root evil of modern art": "The artist must stand face to face with life, and enter into its ways and days of average humanity" ("Beauty for Beauty's Sake," 1, no. 1:47–58). The spirit of that remark pervades *Voices*.

The first issues of *Voices* assume the appearance of small anthologies rather than magazine issues. The second number, for example, consists of twenty-three contributions, of which nineteen are by the magazine's four principal writers. Of the remaining four pieces, one is on the work of Golding. Typically in the early issues of the magazine, each contributor of poetry is represented by three, four, or even five lyrics and—in addition—a selection of prose. After six months or so, the format changed to accommodate a greater number of contributors as well as the regular inclusion of review columns on art, theater, music, and literature. From October 1919 on, there appears "A Survey of Periodicals," consisting of comments by Moult and others on specific contributions—often of poetry—to be found in other periodicals of the day.

Beginning in July 1919, each issue contains reproductions of drawings and woodcuts, including works by artists known for their treatment of war subjects: Paul Nash's "Tree Garden" (2, no. 3:frontispiece); C. Lovat Fraser, a woodcut of engraver Robert Gibbings (3, no. 5/6:190); and Robert Gibbings's "Dublin under Snow" (2, no. 2:frontispiece). Other artists represented in *Voices* include the French sculptor killed in the war, Gaudier-Brzeska ("Drawing," 3, no. 3:facing 87); Lucien Pissarro ("Portrait of the Artist," 3, no. 4:facing 128; "Queen of the Fishes," 4, no. 6:facing 211); war veteran and sculptor Frank Dobson (drawings of a young girl, 5, no. 3:frontispiece; and of a young man, 5, no. 3:facing 68); painter Laura Knight who, following the next war, was to do scores of sketches of the Nuremberg trials ("Portrait of William H. Davies," 3, no. 5/6:facing 171); Jacob Kramer ("Jews Praying on the Day of Atonement," 3, no. 5/6:facing 228; "Suggested Design for Mr. Louis Golding's 'Forward from Babylon,' " 4, no. 2:facing 164); the founder of vorticism, Wyndham Lewis (drawings of a man's head, 5, no. 1:frontispiece; and of a woman in a chair, 5, no. 1:23); Elizabeth Sadler ("London Houses: Westbourne Park," 2, no. 1:frontispiece; and "Willows," 2, no. 5:frontispiece), Anne Estelle Rice ("Harbour," 2, no. 4:frontispiece; "Palms," 2, no. 6:facing 231; and "At the Theatre," 5, no. 2:facing 40); and Edward X. Kapp, successor to Max Beerbohm for personality drawings ("George Graves," 4, no. 2:facing 43; "Doctor Clifford—Preacher," 4, no.3:facing 4).

A number of well-known writers contributed to *Voices*, including Richard Aldington (3, no. 5/6:239–40); Sherwood Anderson (5, no. 4:107–9); D. H. Lawrence (2, no. 1:1–4; 2, no. 4:129–34); May Sinclair (4, no. 3:118; 4, no. 3:80–84; 3, no. 3:87–88; 3, no. 5/6:173–86); John Galsworthy (4, no. 1:1); Amy Lowell (3, no. 3:100–101); Robert Graves (3, no. 1:16; 5, no. 4:110). Vivienne Dayrell, the teenage poet whose first volume of poems, *The Little Wings*, appeared in 1921, was reviewed in *Voices* (5, no. 3:97) and contributed two poems (3, no. 4:159–60). Other well-known writers to appear include Edward Gordon Craig (2, no. 4:154–61), St. John Ervine (2, no. 3:110–17), Storm Jameson (5, no. 1:10–12), H. L. Mencken (5, no. 2:46–47; 5, no. 4:115–21), and W. H. Davies (4, no. 4:119–22).

The magazine appeared monthly through February 1921, except for one double number issued for two summer months of 1920. After February 1921, two issues appeared, one dated Summer and the other Autumn of that year. The first of these seasonal issues acknowledged the difficult times that had fallen on journalistic enterprises generally and promised, if circulation increased, to return to its most frequent publication schedule. Apparently circulation did not increase, at least not sufficiently, and the next issue marked the end of a magazine remarkable most of all for its youthful, hopeful attempt to move forward from the war without either forgetting it or ignoring its significance.

Information Sources

BIBLIOGRAPHY
Bergonzi, Bernard. *Heroes' Twilight: A Study of the Literature of the Great War*. New York, 1965.
Fussell, Paul. *The Great War and Modern Memory*. New York, 1975.
INDEXES
None.
REPRINT EDITIONS
Kraus Reprint, Nendeln, Liechtenstein, 1975. Scholars' Facsimiles and Reprints, Delmar, N.Y.
LOCATION SOURCES
American
Partial runs: Harvard University Library; New York Public Library; University of Michigan Library.

British

Complete run: British Museum.

Partial runs: Bedford College Library; Manchester Public Library; National Library of Scotland, Edinburgh.

Publication History

MAGAZINE TITLE AND TITLE CHANGES

Voices.

VOLUME AND ISSUE DATA

Volumes 1–4, January 1919-December 1920 (six numbers each with volume 3 concluding with one double number 5/6). Volume 5, numbers 1–4, January, February, Summer, and Autumn 1921.

FREQUENCY OF PUBLICATION

Monthly until last two numbers; then quarterly.

PUBLISHER

Hendersons, 66, Charing Cross Rd., London.

EDITOR

Thomas Moult.

Carol de Saint Victor

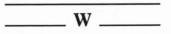

W

WALES (1911). SEE VEA

WALES (1937)

The first series of *Wales* appeared from the summer of 1937 to the winter of 1939–1940 with eleven numbers. The first two numbers featured contributions almost exclusively from Welsh writers, if names are any guide; but later numbers included other writers, as its editor, Keidrych Rhys, developed a more eclectic editorial policy. The writers whose work had been selected for the first number became a group of regular contributors, among them Dylan Thomas, Glyn Jones, John Prichard, Nigel Heseltine, Ken Etheridge, Idris Davies, Ll. Wyn Griffith, Vernon Watkins, Charles Fisher, Aneirin ap Gwynn, and, of course, Rhys himself. This issue included twenty-one poems, a story by Thomas that began on the front cover, and a couple of reviews. Although Rhys wrote no editorial, he added to the last page an advertisement for the magazine, asserting that the English have no culture, that the greatest of present-day writers are Celts, that the Welsh know the beauty of the English language better than the English, that the title is *Wales* to deter the English from claiming the magazine as their own, and that Welsh writers are ordinary people, not a literary clique. Despite this pro-Welsh manifesto, however, by number 5 for summer 1938 Rhys was including more non-Welsh writers than Welsh.

In number 2 for August 1937 Rhys wrote an editorial in which he set forth some of his goals and pleaded for support. He said that *Wales* "ought to be a sort of forum where the 'Anglo-Welsh' have their say as poets, story writers and critics chiefly." This issue, he claimed, "shows the new interest of the Celt in the social scene." He wanted to print "our younger writers" because the English reviews refused to publish them. He also included some of the criticism of the first number, mostly accusations of nationalism and racism. These last became almost a regular feature, as Rhys continued to print excerpts of public comments about his first number. On the title page of number 3, for example, the *Times Literary Supplement* is quoted as describing Thomas as "a young poet of undoubted but wilful talent [who] wastes his strength to achieve obscurity."

Presumably, the coming war had its effect on literary journals very early; and *Wales* was more or less forced to combine numbers 6 and 7 in March 1939. Even at that, the double number had only sixteen pages of actual text; and what is still more baffling, it listed Dylan Thomas as coeditor. One wonders why the smallest number of the series needed two editors. A clue might be found in the next number, also a double one, number 8/9 (August 1939); it listed Nigel Heseltine as editor. Perhaps Rhys had already been looking for a successor in early 1939 and had considered Thomas a likely candidate; but Thomas even more likely needed something less time-consuming and more remunerative than the editorship. Rhys also left some "Notes for a New Editor" in this double issue and took parting shots at the Welsh for their mistreatment and neglect of writers, at Welsh youths for their exodus to England ("There must be some attraction beyond the economic one"), at *John O'London's*, at Aberystwyth University College, at English publishers, and at T. S. Eliot.

The next number, the tenth (October 1939) continued with Heseltine as editor, but he was in the Royal Air Force without a fixed address. Consequently, Rhys was named acting editor. Heseltine continued to contribute an editorial on the continuing fight against fascism "now and after the last Nazi 'Plane is shot down." An interesting feature begun in number 8/9, "Answer to a Question-naire" (answered in that issue by George Ewart Evans), was retained in number 10 and answered by John Cowper Powys. It asked such questions as "Do you consider yourself an Anglo-Welsh writer? For whom do you write? What is your opinion of the relationship between Literature and Society? and Should 'Anglo-Welsh Literature' express a Welsh attitude to life and affairs, or should it be merely a literature 'about' Welsh things?"

Apparently the editors had no inkling that number 11 (Winter 1939–1940) would be the last in this series because they announced the next number for 25 March 1940, with Keidrych Rhys as editor. Heseltine remained as editor of number 11. This issue contained only eighteen pages of contributions by Rhys, James Findlay Hendry, Hugh MacDiarmid, Celia Buckmaster, Philip O'Connor, Davies Aberpennar, Glyn Jones, Lynette Roberts, Oswell Blakeston, Nigel Heseltine, and Julian Symons, nearly half of them non-Welsh. One of the three reviews in the issue was Heseltine's of Flann O'Brien's *At Swim-Two-Birds*, the title a literal translation of the Irish *Snamh-Da-Ean*. The inclusion of non-Welsh writers attested not only to Rhys's attempt to reach a wider audience, but too of his (and probably Heseltine's) taste in modern literature.

Whether because of the war, and a consequent distraction from literary con-cerns, or merely because of dwindling funds, *Wales* ceased publication with number 11 and did not resume until July 1943. This second series ran until

October 1949, during which time the editor was at Ty Gwyn, Llanybri, until 1946, and afterwards at Carmarthen. It was followed by a third series from September 1958 to December 1959. At first the new series numbered each issue as if it were a new journal, but in December 1945, with a double number (8/9), the editors noted that it was number 21, from the beginning series, and soon shifted to the higher numbers. The issue for Autumn 1946, for example, is number 23. Among the contributions to the new series are those attesting to the magazine's principal interest and concern for things Welsh: W. Moelwyn Merchant's "The Relevance of the Anglo-Welsh" (July 1943), George Ewart Evans's "An Emergent National Literature" (October 1943), Dylan Thomas's "Our Country," a Ministry of Information filmscript (also October 1943), Dilys Rowe's "The Significance of Welsh Short Story Writing" (December 1945), Dylan Thomas's "Quite Early One Morning" (Autumn 1946), his "Memories of Christmas" (Winter 1946), and Dilys Rowe's "Thoughts on the Tenth Anniversary of 'Wales' " (February-March 1948).

Meanwhile, *Wales* had gathered some competition for subscribers as well as for writers. The *Welsh Review* had begun in 1939 and appeared regularly until its last issue in the winter of 1948, a fact which suggests that more than the war brought about the demise of the first series of *Wales*. Besides, the magazine had begun its second series in 1943 when the war was far from over, and the editor had managed to keep it alive for several years after the war ended. More than likely Rhys's berating of the Welsh public for its lack of support of the arts in number 8/9 had a stronger cause than mere cantankerousness. Yet *Dock Leaves*, edited by Raymond Garlick and Roland Mathias, was suffering its birth pangs as Rhys's second series was ending. Rhys tried once more, in a third series in 1958, just before the strengthening *Dock Leaves* transformed itself into the *Anglo-Welsh Review.** This new series ran for about eight months, publishing such articles as the anonymous "How I Nearly Met Dylan Thomas: or Another Story of an Artist as a Young Dog" (April 1959).

In his article on Welsh writing in the 1930s, Peter Elfed Lewis observes that "the thirties saw a beginning of a surge of new writing in Wales, which was given encouragement by the advent of *Wales* and *The Welsh Review*."[1] Probably, however, the "surge of new writing" encouraged Keidrych Rhys to launch his journal in the first place, and then later a kind of mutual encouragement must have developed. Certainly an editor of a new journal or magazine needs to assess possible sources of material as well as possible markets for a finished product. Rhys, it is clear from his list of contributors, encouraged young and unknown writers; and *Wales* emphasized work by poets who, as Lewis says, "have absorbed the lessons of modernism and have discarded the old fashioned techniques and literary trappings of older generations."[2] In his concluding remarks comparing the two Anglo-Welsh literary magazines of the thirties, Lewis notes, "*Wales* certainly gives a much fuller picture of the way poetry was developing at the time than *The Welsh Review*."[3] Indeed, from Lewis's survey of the contents, a third of the pages in the entire first series of *Wales* were given to poetry, though both magazines gave more space to prose, particularly the short story. *Wales* was the first English-language magazine to serve literature in Wales and felicitously appeared as a receptive vehicle at a time when there occurred a welcome revival of Anglo-Welsh writing.

Notes

1. Peter Elfed Lewis, "Poetry in the Thirties: A View of the 'First Flowering,' " *Anglo Welsh Review*, no. 71 (1982):53.
2. Ibid., p. 58.
3. Ibid., p. 73.

Information Sources

BIBLIOGRAPHY

Lewis, Peter Elfed. "Poetry in the Thirties: A View of the 'First Flowering.' " *Anglo-Welsh Review*, no. 71 (1982):50–74.

Maud, Ralph. *Dylan Thomas in Print*. Pittsburgh, 1970.

Thomas, Dylan. *Letters to Vernon Watkins*. London, 1957.

Watkins, Gwen. *Portrait of a Friend*. Llandysul, Wales, 1983.

INDEXES

None.

REPRINT EDITIONS

Numbers 1–11: Frank Cass, London.

LOCATION SOURCES

American

Complete runs: Columbia University Library; New York Public Library; University of Buffalo Library; University of Illinois Library.

Partial run: University of Alabama Library.

British

Complete runs: British Museum; University College of North Wales Library.

Partial runs: Bodleian Library; Cambridge University Library; London University Library; Swansea Public Library; University College of South Wales Library; University College of Swansea Library; University College of Wales Library.

Publication History

MAGAZINE TITLE AND TITLE CHANGES

Wales.

VOLUME AND ISSUE DATA

Number 1, Summer 1937-number 11, Winter 1939/1940. New series, number 1, July 1943-number 8/9, December 1945. This series constitutes whole numbers 12–20/21. Issues for August 1944–October 1949 were also called volumes 4–9. Issues for September 1958–April 1959 omitted numbering but constitute numbers 32–35. New series, numbers 36–47, September 1958–December 1959.

FREQUENCY OF PUBLICATION

Quarterly, with fewer issues in a year occasionally.

PUBLISHER

Wales Publications Ltd., 40 Heath St., London N.W.3.

EDITORS
    Keidrych Rhys, 1937–1939, 1943–1959 (with Dylan Thomas, March 1939). Nigel
    Heseltine, 1939–1940.

Martin E. Gingerich

WARTIME DRAMA. See DRAMA

WAVE

Wave, published in eight issues from the autumn of 1970 until the spring of 1974, was the sole effort of its editor, Edwin (Ted) Tarling. Unassuming, nearly slight in its appearance, *Wave* went into production because Tarling found himself dissatisfied with the spate of poetry magazines available at the time. He solicited contributions for his first issue before considering printing costs. With poems waiting to be printed, Tarling found his project redeemed by a family endowment: his sister purchased for him a small hand printing press and a how-to book on printing. One month later—"misprints and all"—the Sonus Press was in operation and Tarling's arduous entry into the field of poetry magazines was under way.[1]

The first volume includes many of the most distinguished names in British poetry and criticism: Alan Brownjohn, Michael Hamburger, Elizabeth Jennings, Philip Larkin, Peter Porter, Peter Redgrove, Vernon Scannell, R. S. Thomas, and Anthony Thwaite. The entries in the first issue range over the respective styles and themes of the "Movement" and the "Group" as well as allowing for an experiment with form by Bob Cobbing in "Fragment" and a wry techno-vernacular poem by Edwin Morgan, "The Computer's First Dialect Poems." But as a whole, the issue reflects Tarling's preference for "conventional poetry which rhymes and scans" and avoids, for the most part, "poetry which appears to be nonsense until, after reading some academic on the subject, one begins to imagine one ought to see something in it."

Subsequent volumes included further entries by some of the first contributors; they were joined by Dannie Abse, Stewart Conn, D. J. Enright, Philip Hobsbaum, Edward Lucie-Smith, and John Wain. Robert Conquest, in two of his *Wave* entries, captures the general humanity, variety, and delight that intermingled and marked *Wave*'s tenure. In "Technique," Conquest queries the challenge of the poetic process that informed his own poetry and hallmarked his tribute Movement anthology, *New Lines* (no. 2:27). Just after "Technique," he reinvokes the quandary of the Movement with a self-deprecating limerick.

Tarling published as many poems as time, energy, and funds permitted, emphasizing those he liked while at times feeling obliged to include poems he was less enthusiastic about, but which were considered interesting to some of the magazine's "clever subscribers." Word-of-mouth assessment of *Wave* generally judged it a success. Tarling reports that it was noted for its clarity and recalls special, enthusiastic praise for it from Sir John Betjeman. But costs and the toll of sheer labor prohibited Tarling from including reviews, and as a result *Wave* failed to receive any critical attention in print. But prizes for many of its contributors in the ensuing years and a staggering list of renowned poets more than confirm the success of Tarling's modest ambition: "I suppose this is what I was after—providing, of course, something interesting or moving [that] was being said in a competent manner. I had no broader policy."

In most ways *Wave* is a celebration of the conventional, urbane, and stylish. It is guilty at times of what Ian Hamilton diagnoses as the sameness that generally marked the Movement's poetry.[2] *Wave* preserves the obligatory poems on Italy, art and artists, animals, cathedrals, holidays, lost loves, and travels through the countryside. Laurence Lerner and others provide Tarling with a balance of whimsy through poems about sneezes and chromosomes (no. 7:24–25), while others like Molly Holden record the ache of the everyday while acknowledging that "Such bastard odds-and-ends are often best" (no. 5:38). More often than not, the magazine presents the British caught in their most essential postures and delightedly, if sometimes poignantly, aware of it.

Although *Wave* succumbed to the temptation of many presses during the period to favor the "established talents," Tarling himself was quite central in fostering, even sponsoring, some new talent.[3] Joan Barton, for example, had been publishing poetry since the late 1920s, but she had been largely isolated except for encouragement from Walter De la Mare and John Betjeman. She credits Tarling with contacting her in the late sixties; he praised her poems, and asked for some. She obliged by contributing to five issues of *Wave*.[4] One of her submissions, "A House under Old Sarum," would ultimately become the title poem for her third volume of poetry published in 1981, eight years after its appearance in *Wave* (no. 6:38). Tarling's faith in Barton led him to interrupt his quarterly publication of *Wave* and put the Sonus Press to work in order to publish her first volume of poetry, *The Mistress and Other Poems* (1972). And the poem "The Mistress" was later chosen by Philip Larkin for *The Oxford Book of Twentieth-Century English Verse* (1973).[5]

The last volume of *Wave* appeared in the spring of 1974. Despite help with the business affairs by Jean Hartley, formerly of *Listen*, and Brenda Evans, Tarling had "had enough of the life literary." Sonus Press and Tarling continue, and their most recent enterprise is Tarling's own collection, *The Wild Whistle: Ballad Airs for Whistle and Other Melodic Instruments* (1983).

Notes

1. All quotations referring to *Wave* are taken from the author's correspondence with Ted Tarling, dated 15 June 1985.
2. Ian Hamilton, "The Making of the Movement," in *British Poetry since 1960: A Critical Survey*, ed. Michael Schmidt and Grevel Lindop (Oxford, 1972), p. 72.
3. Michael Schmidt and Grevel Lindop, "Introduction," in ibid., p. 5.

4. "Joan Barton," interview in Janet Todd, ed., *Women Writers Talking* (New York, 1983), p. 200.

5. "The Mistress" first appeared in *Listen* in 1960.

Information Sources

BIBLIOGRAPHY

Conquest, Robert, ed. *New Lines: An Anthology*. London, 1957.

Lasdun, James. "In the Swendon Tradition." Rev. of *A House under Old Sarum*, by Joan Barton. *Times Literary Supplement*, 17 July 1981, p. 816c.

Lucie-Smith, Edward, and Philip Hobsbaum, eds. *A Group Anthology*. London, 1963.

Schmidt, Michael, and Grevel Lindop, eds. *British Poetry since 1960: A Critical Survey*. Oxford, 1972.

Todd, Janet, ed. *Women Writers Talking*. New York, 1983.

INDEXES
None.

REPRINT EDITIONS
None.

LOCATION SOURCES
American
Partial runs: Harvard University Library (nos. 1–5); University of Michigan Library (nos. 1–6); University of Virginia Library (nos. 1–5, 7–8).

British
Complete runs: Bodleian Library (unverified); British Museum; Hull University, Brynmore Jones Library (unverified).

Publication History

MAGAZINE TITLE AND TITLE CHANGES
Wave: A Magazine of New Poetry, 1970–1974.

VOLUME AND ISSUE DATA
Number 1, Autumn 1970; number 2, Winter 1970; number 3, Spring 1971; number 4, Summer 1971; number 5, Autumn 1971; number 6, Spring 1973; number 7, Summer 1973; number 8, Spring 1974.

FREQUENCY OF PUBLICATION
Quarterly through number 5.

PUBLISHER
Edwin [Ted] Tarling, Sonus Press; formerly 3 Bewick Grove, Preston Road, Hull, England HU93QY; currently 17 Pearson Avenue, Hull, England HU52SX.

EDITOR
Edwin [Ted] Tarling.

Dawn Trouard

WHEELS

Although the idea of beginning *Wheels* was undoubtedly a group decision, Edith Sitwell is the most important figure in its life (1916–1921); and although twenty-one poets contributed to *Wheels*, the three Sitwells—Edith and her brothers Osbert and Sacheverell—contributed to the six issues over two-fifths of all the poems published. Moreover, nearly all of the other contributors were part of the small social circle that the Sitwells occupied in London during and just after World War I. Most of the anthologies and little magazines sprouting up in London to celebrate the new poetry had narrow lists of contributors, but the smallness and perhaps above all the privileged, upper-class quality of the *Wheels* group led to the accusation that it was less a serious literary magazine than a vanity organ, an accusation reflected in F. R. Leavis's well-known statement many years later that "the Sitwells belong to the history of publicity rather than of poetry."[1]

The Sitwells were certainly eager for publicity, but in this they were hardly different from any other group of young poets at this time, be they imagists, vorticists, or Georgians. Like those groups, the *Wheels* poets were quite serious about separating themselves from the literary establishment of their childhood, and such revolt can have very little effect unless it is recognized. Unlike the Georgians, the *Wheels* poets were also out to attack the social establishment, and the fact that they knew it from the inside gave a special bitterness to their anger. These young people, writes David Daiches, "sublimated their own sense of decay into verses sometimes bizarre, sometimes satirical, sometimes artificial. Beneath it all lay a subdued hysteria."[2] The major source of the sense of decay lay near at hand: by 1916 World War I had settled into the seemingly endless horror of trench warfare, with seemingly endless lists of dead and wounded. Confidence in the established order was gone. A large proportion of the poems in *Wheels* mock or rage at the generals and the society around them, but even the slightest and most seemingly trivial poem, so long as it did not praise the accepted virtues or cheer on the war, could take its stand for "civilization."

By 1916 the two older Sitwells had long been taking a stand against the established order, at least as that order was represented by their father, Sir George Sitwell of Renishaw Hall, Derbyshire. As Edith and Osbert tell the story of their family life in their autobiographies, life with Sir George was a constant confrontation with irrationality and bullying.[3] Edith, the eldest, felt herself rejected by both mother and father for being a girl, and a tall, homely, dreamy, and impractical girl at that. Unhappy at home, poetry was from childhood her chief interest and consolation. In 1913, encouraged by the publication of her first poem in the London *Daily Mirror* and emotionally supported by her governess and friend Helen Rootham, she left Renishaw Hall with nothing except her own small income, and set up housekeeping with Helen in a dreary part of London. Osbert, the first son and conventionally good looking, was always popular with his mother; but his conflict with his father was constant through adolescence and reached a climax when his father sent him not to Oxford but to a military life in the local yeomanry. Miserable, Osbert soon used a nervous breakdown to convince his father to let him transfer to the Grenadier Guards, another military life, but one with more compatible associates and, above all, stationed in London.

The months between his arrival in Wellington Barracks at the end of 1912 and the outbreak of World War I in August 1914 were filled with formal dinners and club life, but also with introductions to literary figures, and the discovery of modern art and the Diaghilev ballet.

In London, Osbert spent much of his time with a group of lively and artistic young socialites who frequented the Eiffel Tower restaurant. The idea of a new poetry anthology, one daring enough to contrast with the enormously popular *Georgian Poetry* anthologies, probably arose spontaneously within this group. Who did the actual editorial work for the first issue has been disputed: Nina Hamnett, years later, gave credit to Nancy Cunard; Edith Sitwell said that she herself was its first editor.[4] At any rate, the new magazine was accepted for publication by B. H. Blackwood, and 500 copies appeared on 13 December 1916. On the frontispiece was its symbol, a wheel with the names of the authors forming eight spokes.

Except for the Sitwells themselves and Helen Rootham, the contributors to the first issue were recruited by Osbert: Victor Perowne, Arnold James, Wyndham Tennant, Iris Tree, and Nancy Cunard. Osbert had known Victor Perowne at Eton. Edward Wyndham Tennant, known as "Bimbo," was a close friend from the Grenadiers. Just nineteen years old, he was killed in action in September 1916. Iris Tree and Nancy Cunard had met each other as children; they were both living socially and artistically exciting lives in London. Iris, daughter of the actor Sir Beerbohm Tree, was a student at Slade. Nancy Cunard, daughter of the heir to the steamship line and his American wife, was just beginning a career of artistic production and patronage that would span decades.

Compared to *Blast** or the American *Others*, the first issue of *Wheels* does not display radically new techniques or themes. It does suggest a new mood of overpowering gloominess. As the London *Times* put it, the poets are "dour and morose; they see nothing bright in the present, and no bright hopes in the future."[5] Nancy Cunard's title poem sets the tone with images of wheels rolling through a "painted world" and moved by "a thousand clowns" (1:vii). Osbert Sitwell's "things of slime" (1:11), Iris Tree's waiting worm, "flabby, boneless, brainless, senseless, soulless" (1:61), Edith Sitwell's murderous drunkard and murdered mother (1:43–48), are all images of emptiness or decay. The war intrudes not just in the work of soldiers Tennant and Osbert Sitwell, but in poems by Nancy Cunard (1:30), Iris Tree (1:60), and Helen Rootham (1:77–78). *Wheels* seems tamer today than in its time because the poetry almost entirely lacks a form as revolutionary as its attitudes. The poems echo the 1890s in their language as well as in their melancholy, a language without the specificity and the daring imagery that were to become characteristically modern. Osbert's poem on the bombed town ends with the generalities of "tragic star" and "world disease"; Helen Rootham's elegy on Tennant relies for its effect on capitalized abstractions.

Critical response was mixed, as might be expected, but there was enough of it to encourage that rarity among poetry magazines, a second printing. In the 500 copies of the second edition, in a sober black cover as contrasted with the bright yellow of the first edition, there were two important additions. One was Osbert's first satirical poetry, a violently antiwar poem titled "In Bad Taste." The second addition was a generous selection from those mixed reviews, favorable and unfavorable. These quotes, and Edith's responses to some of them, became a tradition in *Wheels*.

With such success for the first *Wheels*, a second was all but demanded; it was issued in time for the Christmas trade, on 4 December 1917. *Wheels: A Second Cycle* was larger than the first—nearly 100 pages of poetry plus 11 pages of reviews of the first number—and had a larger initial printing, 750 copies. Its cover, a design of green and red whorls, was by C. W. Beaumont; its endpapers by a young Chilean artist who was part of the Eiffel Tower circle, Alvaro Velez Ladron de Guevara.

Of the eight poets in the first number, all but Nancy Cunard and Victor Perowne are in the second. New to the anthology are Sherard Vines, fresh from editing the *Oxford Poetry Review*, and Aldous Huxley; both would publish in all subsequent issues. Huxley's initial attitude to the Sitwells, at least in the letters he wrote to Ottoline Morrell and to his brother Julian, gives no hint that his appearance in *Wheels* was to be the beginning of a long and close association. In a letter to Julian he calls the Sitwells "Shufflebottoms," "each of them larger and whiter than the others. . . . Their great object is to REBEL, which sounds quite charming; only one finds that the steps they are prepared to take, the lengths they will go are so small as to be hardly perceptible to the naked eye." (It should be noted that in the same letter Huxley refers to the *Egoist** as a "horrid little paper.")[6]

The second issue is just as gloomy and much angrier than the first. After two years of trench warfare, even *Georgian Poetry 1916–1917* published one poet, Siegfried Sassoon, who bitterly attacked the war, but in *Wheels* anger is expressed throughout. The volume opens with another of Osbert's "In Bad Taste" poems, this time an attack on all men past fighting age who do their part by sending sons or grandsons to die, by planting potatoes on the lawn (like Sir George Sitwell), by governing with "toothless jaws, / Chattering constantly," and by bullying the poor (2:v-vi). The late Wyndham Tennant is not represented by the nostalgia of "Lavertine," but by "The Mad Soldier," spoken by a soldier who feels himself in a pile of corpses being eaten by rats (2:91–92). Death is no longer a Great Adventure for Helen Rootham; in "Aetat 19," the dead are underground, listening to the tramp of their comrades' marching (2:96). Vines contributes a poem mocking civilians who quickly are bored with "a Stupid sensual soldier" (2:66).

With a good eye for publicity, the editor chose to quote from a variety of press notices at the back of the volume. The most favorable was from the *Morning Post*: "much achievement and more promise . . . the publication of 'Wheels' will be remembered as a notable event in the inner history of English literature" (2:106). Several other encouraging reviews are included, as well as the mockery of the *Weekly Dispatch*, which reduces Nancy Cunard's poetry to "Cunard lines"

(2:112), and the disgust of the *Pall Mall Gazette*—"the foetidness of the whole clings to the nostrils" (2:114). Only one American review is included, an admonitory passage by Ezra Pound, published in Chicago's *Poetry* (2:110–11). Showing the growing success of the young authors is *Wheels*'s first bibliography section, listing seven books by six of the authors.

Wheels: A Third Cycle was late, not appearing until January 1919. The symbol was changed: the wheel was surrounded with flying leaves as if to indicate speed, and Edith's name finally took its proper place in the hub. This is the first issue in which she is identified as editor. The cover is a jagged black-and-white semi-abstraction, "The Sky Pilot," by Laurence Atkinson; for endpapers de Guevara provided line drawings of bicylists. The volume held almost as much poetry as the second cycle, and the run was even larger—1,000 copies. Still, Edith felt that it was weak and blamed the authors' success: the volume was "very bad" because "most of us have had books, all our better work was exhausted."[7] It is true that much of the book seems familiar. Helen Rootham is not included, but Huxley's prose poems echo the translations she contributed. The only new poet is the artist de Guevara, with two very slight translations from the Spanish. Osbert Sitwell, James, Tree, and Vines contribute the now familiar mixture of cynicism, melancholy, and bitterness. However, for Sacheverell and especially for Edith, this volume marks a real step forward. Both had found distinctive voices. Edith set aside her attempts at late Victorian narratives and verse plays, and nearly all of her contributions confidently exploited her own world of images drawn from fairy tale and commedia dell'arte, of startling rhythms and serious play with language.

Wheels' most distinguished volume is its fourth, because of the contributions of one poet, Wilfred Owen, killed in action almost exactly one year before its publication. Owen was originally recruited for *Wheels* by Osbert, during that very brief period when Owen, through introductions provided by Siegfried Sassoon, met the London literary world. He met Osbert in May 1918, and in June 1918 wrote to his mother that the Sitwells had requested poetry for *Wheels*. In July he wrote to Osbert that he was still trying to find the time to "copy out and generally denebulize a few poems acceptable to you either as Editor or— may I not say—friend."[8] He never finished preparing the poems before he was killed in action November 4. The next year, Edith, who had never met Owen, began negotiations for the poetry with his mother. Her letters grew more and more effusive as the weeks went on. In March she spoke of "your son's very beautiful poems; in June the poems were "so magnificent that it has been almost impossible to chose"; in September Owen's had become "the greatest poetry of our time. Though shorter than Dante's *Inferno*, they rank with that poem."[9] She spent hours editing the manuscripts, which often were covered with mud and filled with revisions. The seven she choose for *Wheels: Fourth Cycle* serve as an excellent introduction: "The Show," "A Terre," "The Sentry," "Disabled," "The Dead Beat," "The Changes," and Owen's unfinished work, "Strange Meeting" (4:52–64).

The grimness, if not the quality, of Owen's poems is matched by Osbert Sitwell's "Corpse-Day" (4:9–11). It is echoed by Williams Roberts's cover, with a red tower of jagged figures at gun drill, and his endpapers, where helmeted soldiers with half-human faces play at darts. Even the wheel on the frontispiece is grimmer, with lines around and through it expressing frantic speed. (Owen's name on a spoke is unfortunately misspelled "Wilfid.") The other material in the volume strikes no new note, but Edith's "Nine Bucolic Poems," especially "Clown's Houses," include some of her best early work (5:79–92).

After the introduction of a major new poet in the 1919 volume, it might have been expected that the fifth cycle, 1920, would break new ground also. It did have a new publisher, Leonard Parsons, and a new look, slightly slimmer and more elegant. Instead of designs reflecting the war, the Gino Severini cover showed a stylized, elegant lute player. Arnold James and Iris Tree, who for the first four issues had contributed more quantity than quality to the publication, were gone, and five new poets were added: Alan Porter, Leah McTavish Cohen, Geoffrey Cookson, William Kean Seymour, and John J. Adams. Both Porter and Seymour became well-known, conservative poets. Porter was anthologized by the Sitwells' arch enemy, the champion of the Georgians, J. C. Squire. McTavish Cohen's one poem could have been written by Sherard Vines; Cookson and Seymour strike the faintly sadistic tone of the 1890s. What is most interesting in the issue is Edith's poetry—more "Bucolic Poems" including "King Cophetua and the Beggar Maid"—and the variety of images three poets find for a favorite *Wheels* theme, the wasteland of the modern city. In Huxley's "Theatre of Varieties," the vaudeville stage provides cheap thrills to substitute for lost beauty and truth (5:33–39). Adams's poems mock the social-climbing profiteer and the artistic young woman (5:85); Osbert Sitwell brutally satirizes the society hostess in the poem "Mrs. Kinfoot," whose gospel is, "The world was made for the British bourgeoisie" (5:23), and who cannot endure heaven because all the exciting dinner guests are in hell (5:26).

All contributions by the Sitwells are interesting, but one sign of the weakness of *Wheels* is that in this issue and the next, the Sitwells provided a higher proportion of the poems—half of the total. *Wheels* was not publishing a wide range of poets, and not collecting poets with reputations that would endure. Other publications, *Art and Letters** and *Coterie**, at the same period published Ford Madox Ford, Siegfried Sassoon, Herbert Read, Richard Aldington, and T. S. Eliot. *Wheels* was not competing, either in range or in quality.

The sixth issue announced in many ways that it was to be the last. It had yet another publisher (C. W. Daniel), fewer pages than any previous issue (sixty-two), and an uncompromising cover—the head of a mechanical monster of a soldier by William Roberts. Of the new poets in the fifth cycle, only Alan Porter reappeared in the sixth. Of the four new poets, three contributed only light parodies satirizing the London literary world. The fourth, "Charles Orange," took himself quite seriously as a poet; he was Brian Howard, a schoolboy at Eton but already famous as an aesthete—some years later he would serve as model for Anthony Blanche in Evelyn Waugh's *Brideshead Revisited*. Edith admired his poetry, which was, like much of the material in *Wheels*, derived from the French decadents.

According to Howard, a few months later Edith asked him to help with another *Wheels*, but he was busy with his own magazine, *The Eton Candle* (1922), and refused. *Wheels* died with its 1921 issue, and few felt great regret at its passing. It had grown too repetitive. Its lack of range is often blamed on its editor's lack of taste, but it is known that she was an admirer, and often a friend, of the very poets she was not publishing. *Wheels* was always primarily a family operation, and by 1921 the family no longer needed it. The Sitwells, all but unknown to the literary public in 1916, in six years had become well established. They were publishing in many magazines, they had many friendships and feuds in the London literary world, and among the three of them they had published eleven books. Their careers, which would span another half century, were well launched. *Wheels* was not a sign of their failure but a casualty of their success.

Notes

1. F. R. Leavis, *New Bearings in English Poetry* (London, 1942), p. 73.
2. David Daiches, *Poetry and the Modern World* (Chicago, 1940), p. 86.
3. Edith Sitwell, *Taken Care Of* (New York, 1965); Osbert Sitwell, *Left Hand, Right Hand!* (Boston, 1944) and *Laughter in the Next Room* (Boston, 1948).
4. Hamnett wrote in her autobiography, "Nancy Cunard, who was often at the Eiffel Tower, started a magazine of poetry called *Wheels*. Three young poets called Sitwell, wrote for it, and there was a great deal of discussion as to their merits." *Laughing Torso* (London, 1932), p. 98. All other evidence points to Edith.
5. London *Times*, 4 January 1917, p. 11b.
6. *The Letters of Aldous Huxley*, ed. Grover Smith (London, 1969), p. 132.
7. *Edith Sitwell: Selected Letters*, ed. John Lehmann and Derek Parker (London, 1970), p. 15.
8. *Wilfred Owen: Collected Letters*, ed. Harold Owen and John Bell (London, 1967), p. 562. Owen was not familiar with the magazine and described a fruitless search for a copy in Scarborough—in one shop he was accused of being Osbert.
9. Sitwell, *Selected Letters*, pp. 13–19.

Information Sources

BIBLIOGRAPHY

Owen, Wilfred. *Collected Letters*. Edited by William Harold Owen and John Bell. London, 1967.
Pearson, John. *The Sitwells: A Family's Biography*. New York, 1978.
Sitwell, Edith. *Fire of the Mind*. Edited by Elizabeth Salter and Allanah Harper. London, 1976.
———. *Selected Letters*. Edited by John Lehmann and Derek Parker. London, 1970.
———. *Taken Care Of*. New York, 1965.
Sitwell, Osbert. *Laughter in the Next Room*. Boston, 1948.
———. *Left Hand, Right Hand!* Boston, 1944.

INDEXES
>   None.
REPRINT EDITIONS
>   Kraus Reprint.
LOCATION SOURCES
>   *American*
>   Widely available. (Many libraries catalogue *Wheels* as an anthology rather than a periodical.)
>   *British*
>   Widely available.

Publication History

MAGAZINE TITLE AND TITLE CHANGES
>   *Wheels, An Anthology of Verse*, 1916. *Wheels: A Second Cycle*, 1917. *Wheels: A Third Cycle*, 1918. *Wheels 1919 Fourth Cycle*, 1919. *Wheels 1920 Fifth Cycle*, 1920. *"Wheels" 1921 (Sixth Cycle)*, 1921.
VOLUME AND ISSUE DATA
>   Volumes 1–6, 1916–1921.
FREQUENCY OF PUBLICATION
>   Annually.
PUBLISHERS
>   1916–1919: B. H. Blackwood, Broad St., Oxford. 1920: Leonard Parsons, London. 1921: C. W. Daniel, Ltd., Tudor St., London.
EDITOR
>   Edith Sitwell.

Susan J. Hanna

WIND AND THE RAIN, THE

In 1941, when they founded the *Wind and the Rain*, Michael Allmand and Neville Braybrooke were schoolboys at Ampleforth, one of Britain's great Catholic public schools. One formative influence on the magazine was the environs of a monastery school with its staff monks. Another was World War II. The first issue of the journal was printed by the Benedictine nuns of Stanbrook Abbey, and expressed "a genuine desire to help the Red Cross" (1, no. 1:4). The editorial in the second issue, for Summer 1941, strikes a representative note of religious commitment and independence. "This magazine," the opening sentence asserted, "contains a sample of the temper of the nation." It continued, "The editors are all young, as yet unbiased in any direction save in one—the Christian tradition." It informed its readers that the *Wind and the Rain* was not "financed by a rich individual nor managed by a capitalist board of directors; when something is decided upon, it is done in unison for their unity in purpose and inspiration is their delight" (1, no. 2:50). These are youthful, idealistic words, quickly destroyed by the realities of warfare.

In an editorial for the Spring 1946 number (3, no. 2), the editor, Neville Braybrooke, used the quarter-century anniversary of the publication of Oswald Spengler's *Decline of the West* as the springboard for an analysis of the state of a world in which "a major disaster" has been followed by a "lack of faith," mankind has taken "refuse in a form of mental defeatism." The war, Hiroshima, and Nagasaki—the specter of which haunted many of the postwar contributions— had resulted in a desire in the West "to sacrifice any ideal—be it moral or spiritual—provided it can substitute in its place success with the world." A decline in spirituality was a factor in the decline of the West; it is hardly surprising, then, that the *Wind and the Rain* is less than sympathetic to Marxism or to developments in Eastern Europe. Its emphasis upon "the spiritual side of Christianity: on the need for prayer, example and charity" (3, no. 2:50, 52) inevitably placed it ideologically with the antileft forces of the Cold War ideology prevalent in intellectual circles of the late 1940s. There are, however, no attacks upon Stalinism in its pages.

In a 1951 editorial, the journal's last, Braybrooke revealed that over a decade the *Wind and the Rain* received annually between twenty to thirty manuscripts. Of these potential contributions, 70 percent were poems, 10 percent short stories, and 20 percent articles. The magazine's contents regularly included a two- to three-page editorial; several poems; memoirs, diaries, or other autobiography; a critical essay, usually on a literary topic; extracts from a work in progress— short stories or novel; and selected notices or book reviews. Advertising rarely went beyond the inside front cover and the end back papers. Exhortations to buy National Savings Certificates are found alongside advertisements for the *Catholic Herald* and notices of other small magazines such as the *Poetry Quarterly*,* *Outposts*,* and Braybrooke's own publishing venture, the Phoenix Press. In addition to the *Wind and the Rain*, Braybrooke published *Translation*, a biannual volume of English translations from various European languages. And beginning with the post–1945 issues, Braybrooke included translations in each number of the *Wind and the Rain*.

The unsigned reviews at the end of each issue of the *Wind and the Rain* imitate the mode of the great early nineteenth-century *Quarterly Review** (see *RA, MA*). A review of George Orwell's critical essays, for example, in the Autumn 1946 issue, is detailed, analytical, perceptive, and wide-ranging, placing Orwell in a broad context, and unfavorably contrasting him with Arthur Koestler. "Orwell does not touch upon a possible means of synthesis, as Koestler has done, he simply records, as it is the business of the listening artist to do." Orwell's weakness is "that he has the urge of the creative artist to tilt his lance at the opinions of others, in favour of his own." Orwell's essay on Koestler is limited, for he has not "really assimilated Koestler's message for his age." But the review concludes with the fine distinction that Orwell's "is a free intelligence in an unfree age! a lonely figure with much talent and more kindliness than he will be given credit for. In thinking of him it should always be remembered that he is a creative artist by inheritance—a critic by necessity" (3, no. 3:159).

Perceptive words, written (we now know) during a period in which Orwell was writing *1984*, his last great masterpiece, amid the barren wilderness of Jura in the far north of Scotland.

The same issue reviewed Robert Graves's *Poems 1938–1945* and Dylan Thomas's *Death and Entrances*. Graves and Thomas were both found to be obscure and difficult. The latter's poetry is favorably compared with that of Thomas Traherne, S. T. Coleridge, George Herbert, and Gerard Manley Hopkins. Thomas's output "is a poetry of vision, of interior states akin to, but not to be identified with, the mystics, because it is not necessarily of the same spiritual order." Lines from "Poem in October," "A Winter's Tale," and "Vision and Prayer" are analyzed and discussed. The review concludes that Thomas's "increasing pre-occupation with ends and origins, with an intensely personal reaction to ultimate values, shows evidence of his becoming one of the most significant religious poets of our time." There is none of the dismissive high-mindedness prevalent in, for instance, *Scrutiny*'s* reaction to Dylan Thomas. Graves's verse is characterized by a "concise logic"; the poet is "perhaps primarily a satirist" (3, no. 3:160–61).

Contributions by important postwar British thinkers included Christopher Dawson's "Tradition and Inheritance" (4, no. 4; 6, no. 1), the only autobiographical statement Dawson ever published, and John Heath-Stubbs's remarkable reassessment of Charles Williams, which opens: "In my opinion Charles Williams is one of the most important as well as one of the most neglected thinkers and poets of our present century" (3, no. 2:86)—an opinion still far ahead of critical consensus. A glance through the contents shows a lengthy poem by Charles Williams in the Spring 1942 issue (2, no. 2), François Mauriac's "Fragments from an Occupation Journal" (6, no. 3), W. H. Auden on Graham Greene (6, no. 1), Malcolm Cowley on William Faulkner (5, no. 4), and some of the first translations of August Strindberg into English (5, no. 4). An Anglo-Indian issue for the summer of 1948, published to coincide with the declaration of Indian independence, includes a letter from Gandhi to Chiang Kai-Shek (5, no. 1). Wilson Knight wrote on fascism (2, no. 3:133–44). Other contributors included Arthur Machen, Sean Jennett, T. A. Birrell, Andrew Young, Walter De la Mare, and John Betjeman.

A representative issue, for Spring 1947 (3, no. 4:178), included Francis Berry's poem "Soviet Town Statue," Andrew Young's "The Salmon Leap," reviews of W. Mellers's *Music and Society*, Geoffrey Grigson on Samuel Palmer, Wilson Knight on the consequences of Hiroshima, and one of Betjeman's major poems, "To My Son Aged Eight."

Clearly, the importance of the *Wind and the Rain* lies in the ability of its editor to attract major contributors and major contributions. The summer issue of 1949 (6, no. 1) contains a short, ten-paragraph notice by W. H. Auden, "A Note on Graham Greene." Auden uses Greene's *The Ministry of Fear* as the foundation for general comments on Greene's art. His thrillers are allegories, projections into "melodramatic action of the struggles which go on unendingly in every mind and heart.'' Maybe, Auden adds, ''this is why we like reading thrillers because each of us is a creature at war with himself.'' He continues, ''There is, therefore, not a good side and a bad.'' It does ''matter who wins'' although ''victory does not finally solve anything.'' Auden's words reflect the Cold War situation of post–World War II Europe as much as his own predicament, and his comments on *The Ministry of Fear* were broadcast on American television in the spring of 1949.

The *Wind and the Rain* was a creature of its time. It tried to hold on to spiritual values, especially those with a Catholic orientation, in a world of chaos, turmoil, and change. Its longevity in the world of little magazines, ten years, is a tribute to the quality of its contributions and to the perspicacity and dedication of its editor. The tastes of the magazine were completely those of its editor, Neville Braybrooke, who recalls:

> I was running a ''little review'' with some school friends, and whenever I saw a poem which pleased me, I would write to the poet and suggest that he should contribute to *The Wind and the Rain*. I remember receiving one such poem, accompanied by a note signed ''Starving and Forgotten John Betjeman.'' Others came from Frances Bellerby, Richard Church, Clifford Dyment, James Kirkup, Lilian Bowes Lyon, Hal Summers and Vernon Watkins.[1]

Almost all of them found, early on, a place in Braybrooke's schoolboy review.

Notes

I thank Neville Braybrooke and Brother Terence Richardson (Librarian, Ampleforth Abbey, York), who kindly sent me very early issues of the *Wind and the Rain*, and Professor T. A. Birrell, for their help in preparing this essay.

1. Neville Braybrooke, ed., *The Letters of J. R. Ackerley* (London, 1968), p. xv.

Information Sources

INDEXES

Comprehensive Index to English Language Little Magazines, series 1, ed. Marion Sader (Millwood, N. Y., 1976).

REPRINT EDITIONS

Kraus Reprint, New York. Scholars' Facsimiles and Reprints, Delmar, New York.

LOCATION SOURCES

American

Complete run: St. Louis, Mo., University Library.

Partial runs: Widely available.

British

Partial runs: Bodleian Library, British Museum; Cambridge University Library; Institute of Education Library; Leeds University Library; National Library of Scotland, Edinburgh.

Publication History

MAGAZINE TITLE AND TITLE CHANGES
  The Wind and the Rain.
VOLUME AND ISSUE DATA
  Volume 1, number 1–volume 7, number 3, January 1941–Autumn 1951.
FREQUENCY OF PUBLICATION
  Announced as quarterly, but irregular.
PUBLISHER
  No publisher listed. Editorial and publishing offices; 15 Newton Court Kensington,
  London W.8.
EDITORS
  Michael Allmand, Neville Braybrooke (1, nos. 1, 2); Neville Braybrooke, Terence
  Mark (1, no. 3); Neville Braybrooke, Roland Brown, and Terence Mark (1, no.
  4). Neville Braybrooke's name remains throughout, as does that of Michael All-
  mand as founding editor.

William Baker

WINDMILL, THE

The firm of William Heinemann Limited first brought out a miscellany called
the *Windmill*, a single volume edited by L. Callender, in 1923, then waited
twenty years to resume publication. Reginald Moore and Edward Lane (a pseudonym) were the editors of the first issue of the new series, which appeared in
1944. In an introductory note it promised to supply "a selection of essays,
papers, stories and verses which, by reason of their varied opinions and styles,
make especial claim to the attention of the thoughtful reader in search of entertainment and the stimulation of original ideas" (no. 1:n.p.). Readers apparently
wanted a clearer statement of editorial policy, and Moore and Lane dutifully
supplied an "Argument" to lead off the second issue (1945); but they committed
themselves only to catholicity—the encouragement of diverse points of view and
interests, as expressed by known and unknown contemporary writers. Later the
editors would speak of the "dandyism of personal taste" guiding their selections
(no. 4:1). From the start, then, the *Windmill* sought to avoid the tendentiousness,
aesthetic theorizing, and political factionalism characteristic of so many little
magazines of the forties. It was deliberately bookish and somewhat old-
fashioned, in the tone of the best-known essay to appear in its pages, George
Orwell's "In Defence of P. G. Wodehouse" (1945).

In its four-year existence the *Windmill* anthologized a good deal of poetry—
by Wrey Gardiner (no. 1:28), Kenneth Patchen (no. 1:89), James Courage (no.
2:47), Stevie Smith (no. 2:69), Julian Symons (no. 6:21), Kathleen Raine (no.
6:24), F. T. Prince (no. 3:104), James Reeves (no. 6:27), and many others—
but its poetry is less interesting than its criticism and fiction. In addition to Orwell
on Wodehouse, it printed Graham Greene on François Mauriac (no. 3:80), John

Heath-Stubbs' "The City of Dreadful Night" (no. 4:22), Malcolm Muggeridge on the beginning of the forties (no. 4:138), Roy Fuller on George Meredith (no. 7:12), Julian Symons on George Eliot (no. 8:9), and Douglas Goldring on Violet Hunt (no. 7:4); the young P. H. Newby supplied excellent book reviews. Fiction writers to appear in its pages included Elizabeth Bowen (no. 1:39), Henry Miller (no. 1:72), Frank O'Connor (no. 2:71), C. P. Snow (no. 2:95), Joyce Cary (no. 2:120), Robert Graves (no. 3:143), A. E. Coppard (no. 4:53) and Somerset Maugham—whose novel *Catalina*, in a throwback to nineteenth-century publishing practice, was serialized over four numbers. It is conceivable that lack of interest in *Catalina* hastened the end of the *Windmill* itself. The last installment of the Maugham novel appeared together with a publisher's note suspending publication and (in a pleasant historical juxtaposition) an editorial note praising the young Truman Capote's *Other Voices, Other Rooms*.

To the contemporary reader the most engaging feature of the *Windmill* is the opening essay of each issue, which is always a survey of likes and dislikes by some well-known man or woman of letters. This essay quickly assumed the form of "An Alphabet of Literary Prejudice"—a letter-by-letter excursion into the dandyism of personal taste. William Plomer (no. 5), Rose Macaulay (no. 4), Daniel George (no. 3), G. W. Stonier (no. 2), James Agate (no. 6), Geoffrey Grigson (no. 6), Edward Sackville-West (no. 7), Nigel Balchin (no. 8), Louis MacNeice, (no. 9), V. S. Pritchett (no. 10), and L. P. Hartley (no. 12) all supplied alphabets, and in the competition to see who could deal most wittily with the most intractable letters, Pritchett won handily. For W he wrote "Worry— George Eliot's great subject," and for X "Xanadu—this has never happened to me. I never had a printable dream. I have always had to work" (no. 10:42).

Information Sources

BIBLIOGRAPHY
Hoffman, Frederick J., Charles Allen, and Carolyn F. Ulrich. *The Little Magazine: A History and a Bibliography*. 2nd ed. Princeton, 1947.
INDEXES
None.
REPRINT EDITIONS
Kraus Reprint, Millwood, N.Y., 1967.
LOCATION SOURCES
American
Complete runs: Columbia University Library; Harvard University Library; New York Public Library; University of Buffalo Library; University of California Library, Los Angeles; University of Chicago Library; Yale University Library.
Partial runs: Ohio State University Library; U.S. Library of Congress.
British
Complete runs: British Museum; Cambridge University Library; Liverpool Public Library.
Partial runs: Birmingham Public Library; Bodleian Library; Gloucester Public Library; Manchester Public Library.

Publication History
MAGAZINE TITLE AND TITLE CHANGES
  The Windmill.
VOLUME AND ISSUE DATA
  Volume 1, 1944. Volume 2, 1945. Volumes 3–5, 1946. Volumes 6–8, 1947. Volumes 9–12, 1948.
FREQUENCY OF PUBLICATION
  Irregular.
PUBLISHER
  William Heinemann Ltd., London.
EDITORS
  Reginald Moore and Edward Lane, 1944–1946. Edward Lane, 1947–1948.

Jefferson Hunter

WINDSOR MAGAZINE. See VEA

WORKSHOP

Despite changes in format over the run of *Workshop/New Poetry* from 1967 to 1981, its central aims remained fixed: to give talented unknown poets the opportunity to get their work into print and to foster an enjoyment of poetry among the reading public. An editorial in the second number asserted that *Workshop* "may best be thought of as a gallery in which the works of new writers are displayed side by side with those of their elders." Developing as it did as an offshoot of the cooperative Writers' Workshop, the magazine, initially at least, was seen by its editors as one of a number of efforts, including public readings, to bring together new poets and a new audience for their work. Like most projects of this sort, its staff apparently never saw *Workshop* as a commercial venture. They initially declined to accept advertising, relenting only after the seventh number, and the magazine never directly accepted grants from the Arts Council. Such idealism, however, did not inhibit its growth or its popularity, and when it ceased publication in 1981 it had the largest circulation of any poetry magazine then publishing in Great Britain.

Workshop's publication history can be divided into experimental, developmental, and mature stages. The first thirteen numbers, under the joint editorship of Michael Johnson and Norman Hidden, reflected their efforts to settle on a character and structure for the magazine. (John Pudney also shared editorial duties for the first two numbers.) The first five issues drew on a coterie of poets. Early numbers included the work of Pudney, Alan Brownjohn, Bob Cobbing, Jeni Couzyn, and George MacBeth, but most of the contributors were relatively unknown poets associated with the Writers' Workshop. By the sixth issue the journal had broadened its group of contributors considerably. Impetus for the shift may have come about in part from the practice, begun in *Workshop* number 3 and continued with some regularity until number 15, of inviting guest editors such as Jon Stallworthy, Philip Toynbee, Edward Lucie-Smith, G. S. Fraser, John Horder, William Plomer, and Brian Patten to form particular issues. Guest editors drew contributions from Adrian Henri, Louis Zukofsky, George Barker, Ted Hughes, Roger McGough, Seamus Heaney, W. H. Auden, Michael Hamburger, and Thom Gunn, and included as well the work of a number of little-known writers. The appearance of so many established poets may have raised policy questions within the magazine and among its readership, for in the eleventh number the editors felt the need to reaffirm their intention to give as many new poets as possible a chance to publish, while acknowledging the appearance of "a limited number of established poets to contribute alongside these, so as to enable a critical comparison to be made." Whatever the perception may have been, from a quantitative measurement one can clearly see that the journal's commitment to new poets never wavered. During this period editorials and announcements continued to call attention to the efforts made by the Writers' Workshop to stimulate a general interest in poetry, and they also urged readers to aid in promoting the magazine.

With the fourteenth number, the journal changed its name to *Workshop/New Poetry*, and it began a period of stable and consistent development. (Shortly after the appearance of the fourteenth issue, Michael Johnson, one of the editors, died unexpectedly, and Norman Hidden assumed sole editorship, a position he retained until the journal ceased publication.) A series of features added to the format of the magazine accompanied the change in title. Writing under the pseudonym "Kryptos," Hidden began a column of opinion reflecting his ironic, mildly iconoclastic, idiosyncratic views of the state of contemporary poetry. Hidden also used the column to announce poetry readings and to acknowledge the efforts of readers to enhance circulation. The magazine also began to feature regularly a "Schools Page" given over to contributions from students in the primary and secondary grades and a poetry contest, initially reserved for subscribers, but ultimately expanded to include anyone willing to pay the entry fee of twenty-five pence for each poem or page of poetry. Hidden also experimented with devoting various individual numbers to a single long poem by a new author. (After a few such numbers, Hidden chose to publish such works exclusively through the Workshop Press, another endeavor of the cooperative.) D. M. Thomas, Jeni Couzyn, Ian Hamilton Finlay, and Sister Mary Agnes were some of the most frequent contributors during this period, and articles of various poetic forms appeared with some regularity.

With the twenty-eighth number, the magazine changed its name to *New Poetry* and entered into its final, mature phase. The format and editorial policy that had evolved through numbers 14–27 remained stable. Contributions generally came from relatively unknown British writers, although Hidden did give attention to poets in Scotland, Ireland, and Wales. Poems from other countries, in many cases translations, regularly appeared, including works by Lawrence Ferlinghetti and the Jamaican poet A. L. Hendricks. Hidden also encouraged an interest in contemporary poetry through a variety of means: "Kryptos" continually took up various developments and issues facing contemporary poetry, and he provided a series of useful articles directed at practical concerns facing new poets, such as copyright laws, poetry competitions, and vanity presses. *New Poetry* conducted an extensive reader survey and then published the results, detailing readers' tastes and opinions. The magazine printed interviews with established poets—John Wain, Kathleen Raine, Peter Redgrove, and Brian Patten—on the craft of poetry, and in a series of numbers it featured original work by established figures—R. S. Thomas, D. J. Enright, Charles Causley, and Donald Davie—followed by critiques of their careers. Margaret Diggle frequently contributed essays on contemporary poetry.

Despite the widespread acceptance of the magazine, finances remained a nagging problem. In his "Kryptos" columns Hidden repeatedly took up the topic of raising funds for the journal's production, broadening circulation, and stimulating the general public's interest in poetry. Although the Arts Council had agreed to distribute copies of *New Poetry*, free of charge, to any library that requested them, money still seemed a prominent issue to the end. In his announcement in number 49 of the imminent cessation of publication, however, Hidden did not cite money as a reason for the magazine's demise. Rather, he mentioned a lack of support from established poets and a desire to devote more time to the Workshop Press. Publication ceased with the double issue 51/52.

Information Sources

INDEXES
　　Each number indexed.
REPRINT EDITIONS
　　None.
LOCATION SOURCES
　　American
　　　　Widely available.
　　British
　　　　Complete run: University College, London.
　　　　Partial runs: Bodleian Library; National Library of Scotland; University of Hull.

Publication History

MAGAZINE TITLE AND TITLE CHANGES
　　Writers' Workshop, 1967. *Workshop*, 1968–1971. *Workshop/New Poetry*, 1972–1975. *New Poetry*, 1975–1981.
VOLUME AND ISSUE DATA
　　Numbers 1–52, September 1967–January 1981.
FREQUENCY OF PUBLICATION
　　Numbers 1–13, three times per year; numbers 14–52, quarterly.

PUBLISHERS
   Writers' Workshop/Workshop Two/Workshop Press Ltd./Workshop Press. 2 Cul-
   ham Court, Granville Road, London, N4 4JB (1967–1981).
EDITORS
   Norman Hidden, Michael Johnson, and John Pudney, 1967–1968. Norman Hidden
   and Michael Johnson, 1968–1972. Norman Hidden, 1972–1981.

                                                    Michael Patrick Gillespie

WRITER'S WORKSHOP. See WORKSHOP

WRITING TODAY

The July 1957 premier issue of *Writing Today* announced a modest statement
of principles: a hope of providing "some indication of what is being written at
the moment . . . as a stimulus to our readers to read and judge for themselves"
(no. 1:1). Uniform in format and size (7 1/2 by 9 3/4″) during its five-year life,
it remained, as it began, an inexpensive (nine pence) twelve-page assortment of
short reviews and brief features devoted to contemporary literature, designed to
assist the potential book buyer in his or her purchases. It was intentionally cozy,
emulating conversation in which an informed reader shared general impressions
after having recently sat down with the book concerned. Its taste was catholic
and conventional, assuming an audience of amateurs seeking guidance for their
reading regimes—students studying for "A" level examinations or busy people
seeking a worthy weekend read.

Emphasis usually fell on poetry and fiction recently published in Britain or
America, but discussions of writers from other countries, of the theater, cinema,
television, the visual arts, literary criticism, and miscellaneous cultural subjects
appeared on occasion as well. Most volumes under review had appeared in
England in the year previous; some, however, went back as far as a decade.
Generally, reviews did not exceed 300 words in length. Their function consistently was to popularize rather than cause controversy. Less a champion of the
avantgarde than of writers recognizably worth their purchase price, the magazine
chose to keep its comments brief. Writers chosen for review were usually those
already safely on the rise to reasonable prominence, and sometimes excerpts
from their works were printed. Loosely pedagogical, *Writing Today* aimed at
advising its readership on its contemporary version of Matthew Arnold's "best
that has been thought and said."

The writers from the 1950s and early 1960s whose volumes were reviewed
in various issues of *Writing Today* include Kingsley Amis, Philip Larkin, Iris
Murdoch, John Braine, Saul Bellow, Theodore Roethke, Patrick White, Richard
Wilbur, Jack Kerouac, Brendan Behan, John Berryman, Alain Robbe-Grillet,
Bertolt Brecht, Lawrence Durrell, Carson McCullers, Lionel Trilling, Edmund

Wilson, William Empson, Charles Tomlinson, Ted Hughes, Alan Sillitoe, Muriel Spark, and Albert Camus. Among its better-known contributors, *Writing Today*'s list included Peter Digby Smith on N. F. Simpson's farce *One Way Pendulum* (no. 10) and on British political support for the arts (no. 12:12); John Wain on a reissue of Stendhal's letters (no. 4); and Bernard Bergonzi reviewing Sir Herbert Read's *The Tenth Muse*, D. J. Enright's *The Apothecary's Shop* (no. 3:4), and Edmund Wilson's *The American Earthquake* (no. 4). Although no official designation of editor ever occurred; K. S. Toulson had at least one piece in each of the twelve issues and was the most frequent contributor. Most reviewers offered their work regularly; Marie Peel, E.S.D. Barton, G. Bott, and Alan Brownjohn were among the most frequent. Brownjohn's assignments serve as a sufficiently typical illustration of *Writing Today*'s critical choices: Aldous Huxley's *Collected Stories* (no. 1:8) and *Brave New World Revisited* (no. 6:4–5), Vladimir Dudintsev's *Not by Bread Alone* (no. 2:6), *The Plays of John Whiting* (no. 3:3), Samuel Beckett's *Malone Dies* and *Endgame* (no. 4:7), Boris Pasternak's *Doctor Zhivago* (no. 5:3), John Berryman's *Homage to Mistress Bradstreet* (no. 7:2), recent plays by Harold Pinter, John Osborne, and Arthur Adamov (no. 8:6–7), and Michel Butor's *Passing Time* (no. 11:3).

For each of the first seven numbers, an interview with a noted author also was a regular feature: sequentially, Sir John Betjeman, Jacquetta Hawkins, Roy Fuller, Sir Herbert Read, Marghanita Laski, Anthony Powell, and William Carlos Williams. The initial interview with Betjeman set the tone of those to follow, focusing as it did alternately on collecting second-hand Victorian books and the ranking of English poets: Tennyson first, then Browning, Hardy, and Yeats.

Other features made the magazine much more than a digest of reviews. Occasional articles on the changing face of the British countryside—the spread of prefabricated housing or the motorway network—while not fitting strictly within the magazine's avowed subject, nonetheless helped to establish a distinctive flavor. Features on European and American films were reliable early perceptions in a medium often regarded at the time—especially in Great Britain—as inadequate for the category of art. (Most film reviewers followed recent screenings of the subjects at the National Film Theatre in London.) A. P. Wells, for example, praised the Polish feature *Last Day of Summer* (no. 5:10), Paddy Whannel analyzed the screen version of *Room at the Top* (no. 6:10) and reviewed Jay Leyda's book *Kino*, a history of Soviet cinema (no. 10:11).

Bernard Bergonzi, in a *Writing Today* article entitled "The Need for Criticism," argued that the critic "should help us enlarge our own response to a work . . . and perhaps enable us to see more than we might otherwise have noticed" (no. 9:4). During its five-year, twelve-issue run, *Writing Today* asked the critics it printed to seek an audience somewhere between the amateur reader and the professional, yet closer to the former. Caught between the more timely releases of the daily (or even monthly) press and more detailed scholarly approaches to literary criticism, *Writing Today*—perhaps not so surprisingly—simply had too optimistic a view of its potential clientele. As its original statement of principles and the function for the critic stated above both attest, *Writing Today* was neither radical nor highbrow. While it did not alter fundamental views of writing in this century, it is a refreshingly honest example in its admission of its intended educational role as an arbiter of taste.

Information Sources

INDEXES
 None.
REPRINT EDITIONS
 None.
LOCATION SOURCES
 American
 Complete runs: New York Public Library; University of California Library, Los Angeles.
 British
 Complete run: British Museum.

Publication History

MAGAZINE TITLE AND TITLE CHANGES
 Writing Today.
VOLUME AND ISSUE DATA
 No volume numbers assigned; twelve issues. Number 1, July 1957. Number 2, November 1957. Number 3, March 1958. Number 4, July 1958. Number 5, December 1958. Number 6, May 1959. Number 7, October 1959. Number 8, April 1960. Number 9, July 1960. Number 10, December 1960. Number 11, March 1961. Number 12, March 1962.
FREQUENCY OF PUBLICATION
 Generally, three times a year (numbers 1–11). There were only two issues for 1959, a single issue in 1961 and 1962.
PUBLISHER
 None named or listed. The magazine's address was listed as 10 Parkfields, Putney, London S.W. 15. Printer: Villiers Publications. July 1957–March 1958: 47 Landseer Road, London N19. July 1958–March 1962: Ingestre Road, London, NW5.
EDITOR
 None named or listed.

Ronald L. Dotterer

X. A QUARTERLY REVIEW

The editors of *X. A Quarterly Review*, poet David Wright and painter Patrick Swift, launched their magazine in November 1959, well aware of the expectations established by scores of "little magazines" over the preceding half century. Noting in their fourth number that they may have "mystified" some readers by appearing without a manifesto, they argued that their policy ought to be clear in what they selected for publication. The first indication of their intent in bringing out yet another little magazine is their title, which they justify on the masthead by quoting *The Concise Oxford Dictionary*: "x = algebraic symbol 'the unknown quality.' 'Incalculable or mysterious factor in influence.' " Prepared to risk being called "mystical, religious, or too *serious*," the editors further justified that "incalculable or mysterious factor" in their "Preface to Volume Two": "Any attitude based upon the notion that there exists a total and rational explanation for the artistic impulse and activity is for us the enemy of real poetry." At another point they expressed support for the "gay untrammelled spirit of a man operating freely on the material of life." Praising one such man, George Barker, Swift rejects that which would "make a science of art or of a man" and applauds Barker's view of the poet as "mantic, Sybilline, Dionysian, in fact, mad." They print Brian Higgins's poetry because it is written from the "standpoint of the individual man opting out of the bureaucratised mass." Elsewhere they condemn the "business of art consumerism" from which poets and painters happily may escape, since theirs are "solitary activities."

One impulse to launch *X* may have been the editors' awareness that as the fifties drew to a close there would be inevitable attempts to label the decade. In this regard they supported a neutral "postwar" designation. Clearly *X* sought to minimize the stature of the Beats in America; the first contribution to the first number is George Barker's long satirical poem, lampooning Jack Kerouac, Kenneth Rexroth, and Gregory Corso for mindlessness and lack of original ideas. (American writers are notably absent in the seven numbers of *X*.) Elsewhere the editors condemned the Beats as a travesty of artistic independence, for "asking credit from society for being bohemian—thereby denying . . . the whole essence of real freedom of spirit." On their own side of the Atlantic, they were suspicious of "anger-mongers" and other "official oppositions" to the literary establishment, concerned that the "Emperor and his exposeurs engage in a tolerant and profitable appraisal of their mutual nakedness." These comments were supported by an essay on John Osborne, Arnold Wesker, and others tellingly entitled "New Wave in a Dead Sea."

In opposition to such fashionable writing, the editors preferred "first rate work by poets now in their prime (and some of them, perhaps for that reason, very much out of fashion)." These included Ezra Pound, Hugh MacDiarmid, Stevie Smith, George Barker, Patrick Kavanagh, Vernon Watkins, Malcolm Lowry, David Gascoyne, and C. H. Sisson, among the older poets, as well as young poets such as Geoffrey Hill, Dannie Abse, and Dom Moraes. One editorial comment found some hope in the refusal of an "Oxbridge 'little review' " to publish new poets lacking the "desire to experiment." In addition, *X* was willing to print longer poems and identified itself as "almost the only periodical in these islands prepared to find space for poems of more than snippet area."

In their selection of original fiction (comparatively little) and their comments on contemporary fiction, the editors supported the unfashionable "experimental writing" of Samuel Beckett and Alain Robbe-Grillet, arguing that *Molloy* is "not an experiment but a rip-roaring success." Critic Martin Gerard called Beckett's trilogy, beginning with *Molloy*, the "most important prose event for thirty-seven years." *X* printed a piece by Beckett, lamenting that his work was "virtually neglected, certainly misunderstood," and decried the lack of influence by Beckett's fiction in their country, pointing to French writers like Robert Pinget (of whose work they print excerpts) and Robbe-Grillet. Other fiction writers supported by *X* ranged from Boris Pasternak to Aidan Higgins, and both contributed excerpts from their forthcoming novels. *X* also was responsible for publication of the opening chapters of Irish novelist John McGahern's book *The Dark* (1966), which cost him his teaching post.

In their commentaries on writing and art, the editors emphasized respect for the vulnerability of the creative imagination. Eschewing "those stone mausoleums wherein the dissected corpses of poems and other works of art are permitted to accumulate dust," the editors opted for the "living idea." Thus, Swift, in "Prolegomenon to George Barker," focused on Barker's notion of himself as Romantic poet rather than on Barker's poems. Elsewhere, in "Poets on Poetry," Hugh MacDiarmid, Watkins, Kavanagh, and Stevie Smith discuss their work. In a similar vein Alberto Giacometti explored how an image emerged from a dream. *X* also featured accounts by painters of their creative experiences and reproduced their work: Frank Auerbach, Michael Andrews, David Bomberg, André Masson, Craigie Aitchison, Francis Bacon, and Swift himself. As practicing artists, both editors opposed the "dense triviality characteristic of analytic discussion."

Later numbers of *X* offered excerpts from reviews of the magazine to indicate that it was not being ignored. These remarks range from John Wain's "misgivings" in the *Observer*, through the *New Statesman and Nation*'s* (see *VEA*) declaration, "It's the Counter-Revolution," to the unrestrained praise of Cyril Connolly in the Sunday *Times*: "*X* is performing a real service." Probably the most important was a review in the *Times Literary Supplement*, which applauded *X*'s "articulate expression" of dissatisfaction with fifties "commitment."[1]

Despite this generally positive reception, the editors announced their decision to suspend regular publication. Well before this announcement, they had acknowledged the limited influence of any little magazine upon general attitudes; expecting such influence, they say, is like "holding back the sea with a pitch fork." The magazine, however, was not entirely without influence. One notes, for example, its support for writers like Patrick Kavanagh and Stevie Smith, who had experienced difficulty getting their work published, as well as their boosting of John McGahern's career. Others continue to acknowledge the patronage of *X* for new writers. Michael Schmidt, for example, in his edition of C. H. Sisson's essays, notes that only *X* published Sisson's poems "substantially," and provides a comment that proves the function and worth of literary magazines like *X*: "David Wright, who has been a key figure in Sisson's development as a poet (as in the development of many other poets), promoted his work assiduously, and it was entirely due to Wright's intervention that Sisson's first commercially marketed book of poems . . . appeared."[2]

Notes

1. "After Commitment," *Times Literary Supplement*, 27 November 1959, p. 693.
2. C. H. Sisson, *The Avoidance of Literature: Collected Essays*, ed. Michael Schmidt (Manchester, Eng., 1978), p. 11.

Information Sources

BIBLIOGRAPHY

"After Commitment." *Times Literary Supplement*, 27 November 1959, p. 693.
Kavanagh, Patrick. "A Letter and an Environment from Dublin." *Nimbus* 3, no. 3 (1956):12–15.
Sisson, C. H. *The Avoidance of Literature: Collected Essays*. Edited by Michael Schmidt. Manchester, Eng., 1978.
World Authors 1950–70. Edited by John Wakeman. New York, 1975.
INDEXES
Volume 1 indexed.
REPRINT EDITIONS
Kraus Reprint, Nendeln, Liechtenstein. Scholars' Facsimiles and Reprints, Delmar, N.Y.

LOCATION SOURCES
> *American*
>> Widely available.
>
> *British*
>> Complete run: National Library of Scotland, Edinburgh.

Publication History

MAGAZINE TITLE AND TITLE CHANGES
> *X. A Quarterly Review.*

VOLUME AND ISSUE DATA
> Volume 1, numbers 1–4, November 1959–October 1960. Volume 2, numbers 1–3, March 1961–July 1962.

FREQUENCY OF PUBLICATION
> Quarterly.

PUBLISHER
> Barrie and Rockliff, 2 Clement's Inn, Strand, London, W.C.2.

EDITORS
> David Wright and Patrick Swift.

Earl G. Ingersoll

Titles Included in
The Augustan Age and the
Age of Johnson,
1698–1788

Aberdeen Magazine, Literary Chronicle and Review, The, 1788–91
Adventurer, The, 1752–54
Analytical Review, The, 1788–99
Babler, The, 1763–67
Bee, The, 1759
Bristol and Bath Magazine, The, 1782–83
British Champion, The, 1742–43. See *Champion, The*
British Magazine, The, 1746–51
British Magazine, The, 1760–67
Busy Body, The, 1759
Censor, The, 1715–17
Champion (or Evening Advertiser), The, 1739–43
Common Sense: or, the Englishman's Journal, 1737–43
Connoisseur, The, 1754–56
Country Journal; or the Craftsman, The, 1727–50. See *Craftsman, The*
Court and City Magazine, The, 1763. See *Court Magazine, The*
Court, City, and Country Magazine, The, 1764–65. See *Court Magazine, The*
Court Magazine, The, 1761–65
Court Miscellany, The, 1765–71
Covent Garden Journal, The, 1752
Craftsman, The, 1726–50
Critical Review (or Annals of Literature), The, 1756–1817
Critick, The, 1718
Delights for the Ingenious, 1711
Drury Lane Journal, The, 1752. See *Have At You All*
Edinburgh Magazine, or Literary Amusement, The, 1779–82. See *Weekly Magazine, The*
Edinburgh Magazine, or Literary Miscellany, The, 1785–1803
Edinburgh Magazine and Review, The, 1773–76

Parentheses indicate that the additional title appeared only during part of the run of the magazine.

Edinburgh Weekly Magazine, The, 1783–84, See *Weekly Magazine, The*

Englishman, The, 1713–15

English Review (or An Abstract etc.) *(of Literature, Science,* etc.), *The*, 1784–96

European Magazine, The, 1782–1826

Examiner (or Remarks upon Papers etc.), *The*, 1710–14

Female Spectator, The, 1744–46

Free-Holder, The, 1715–16

Freethinker, The, 1718–21

General Magazine and Impartial Review, The, 1787–92

Gentleman's Magazine (or Monthly Intelligencer) (and Historical Chronicle) (and Historical Review), The, 1731–1907

Gray's Inn Journal, The, 1752–54

Grub-Street Journal, The, 1730–37

Guardian, The, 1713

Have At You All, 1752

Hibernian Magazine, The, 1771–1811

History of the Works of the Learned, The, 1737–43

Idler, The, 1758–60

Imperial Magazine, The, 1760–62

Intelligencer, The, 1728–29

Jacobite's Journal, The, 1747–48

Ladies Magazine, or, the Universal Entertainer, The, 1749–53

Lady's Magazine, The, 1770–1819

Literary and Antigallican Magazine, The, 1756–58. See *Literary Magazine, The*

Literary Journal, A, 1744-49

Literary Journal or a continuation of the Memoirs of Literature, A, 1730–31

Literary Magazine; or the History of the Works of the Learned, The, 1736–37. See *History of the Works of the Learned, The*

Literary Magazine; or, Universal Review, The, 1756–58

London Magazine, The, 1732–85

London Magazine, The, 1791. See *New London Magazine, The*

London Review of English and Foreign Literature, The, 1775–80

London Spy, The, 1698–1700

Lounger, The, 1785–87

Lounger's Miscellany, The, 1788–89

Memoirs for the Curious, 1709. See *Monthly Miscellany, The*

Memoirs of Literature, 1710–17

Midwife, The, 1750–52/53

Monthly Miscellany: or, Memoirs for the Curious, The, 1707–9

Monthly Review (or Literary Journal) (or New Literary Journal), The, 1749–1844

Muses Mercury, The, 1707–8

Museum, The, 1746–47

New Lady's Magazine, The, 1786–97

New London Magazine, The, 1785–97

New Novelist's Magazine, The, 1786–88

New Review, A, 1783–86

Northern Gazette, Literary Chronicle, and Review, The, 1707. See *Aberdeen Magazine, The*

Novelist's Magazine, The, 1780–89

Olla Podrida, The, 1787–88

Oxford Magazine, 1768–76

Payne's Universal Chronicle, or Weekly Gazette, 1758. See *Idler, The*

Plain Dealer, The, 1724–25

Present State of the Republick of Letters, The, 1728–36

Prompter, The, 1734–36

Rambler, The, 1750–52

Reformer, The, 1748

Review (of the Affairs of France) (of the State of the English Nation), 1704–13

St. James's Magazine (or Literary Chronicle) (or the Literary Transactions of Europe), The, 1762–64

Scots Magazine (Containing a General View etc.) *(or General Repository* etc.) *(and Edinburgh Literary Miscellany), The*, 1739–1817

Sentimental Magazine, The, 1773–77

Spectator, The, 1711–15

Student, The, 1750–51

Tatler, The, 1709–11

Templar, and Literary Gazette, The, 1773

Town and Country Magazine, The, 1769–95

True Patriot, The, 1745–46

Universal Chronical, 1758–60. See *Idler, The*

Universal Magazine (of Knowledge and Pleasure) (or Miscellany of Historical etc.), *The*, 1747–1815

Universal Museum (or Gentlemen's and Ladies' Polite Magazine) (and Complete Magazine of Knowledge and Pleasure), The, 1762–72

Universal Spectator and Weekly Journal, The, 1728–46

Universal Visiter, and Memorialist, The, 1756

Walker's Hibernian Magazine, 1786–1811. See *Hibernian Magazine, The*

Weekly Magazine, or Edinburgh Amusement, The, 1768–84

Weekly Review of the Affairs of France, A, 1704. See *Review*

Westminster Magazine, The, 1773–85

Wit's Magazine, The, 1784–85

World, The, 1753–56

Titles Included in
The Romantic Age,
1789–1836

Album, The, 1822–25
Annals of the Fine Arts, 1816–20
Anti-Jacobin Review (and True Churchmen's Magazine) (and Protestant Advocate), The, 1797–1821
Athenaeum and (London) Literary Chronicle, The, 1828–1921
Augustan Review, The, 1815–16
Beau Monde, Le, 1806–10
Bee, The, 1790–94
Belle Assemblée, La, 1806–37
Blackwood's Edinburgh Magazine, 1817–1980. See also *MA*
British and Foreign Review, The, 1835–44
British Critic, The, 1793–1843
British Lady's Magazine, The, 1815–19
British Magazine, The, 1830
British Review and London Critical Journal, The, 1811–25
Cabinet, The, 1807–9
Cabinet Magazine, or Literary Olio, The, 1796–97
Cambrian (and Caledonian) Quarterly Magazine (and Celtic Repertory), The, 1829–33
Chambers's Edinburgh Journal, 1832–53. See *Chambers's Journal*
Chambers's Journal, 1832–1956
Champion (and Sunday Review etc.), The, 1813–22
Companion, The, 1828
Country Literary Chronicle, 1820–24. See *Literary Chronicle and Weekly Review, The*
Court Magazine and Belle Assemblée, The, 1832–37. See *Belle Assemblée, La*
Director, The, 1807
Drakard's Paper, 1813. See *Champion, The*
Dublin Literary Gazette, The, 1830–31
Dublin Review, The, 1836–1969

Parentheses indicate that the additional title appeared only during part of the run of the magazine.

Dublin University Magazine, The, 1833–77
Eclectic Review, The, 1805–68
Edinburgh Magazine and Literary Miscellany, The, 1817–26
Edinburgh Monthly Magazine, The, 1817. See *Blackwood's Edinburgh Magazine*
Edinburgh Monthly Review, The, 1819–23
Edinburgh Review, The, 1802–1929
Englishman's Magazine, The, 1831
Examiner (and London Review), The, 1808–81
Foreign Quarterly Review, The, 1827–46
Fraser's Literary Chronicle, 1835–36
Fraser's Magazine for Town and Country, 1830–82
Gossip, The, 1821
Honeycomb, 1820
Imperial Magazine, The, 1819–34
Imperial Review, The, 1804–5
Indicator, The, 1819–21
Inquirer, or Literary Miscellany, The, 1814–15
Investigator (or Quarterly Magazine), The, 1820-24
Investigator, The, 1822. See *Champion, The*
John Bull, 1820–92
Journal of the Royal Institution of Great Britain, The, 1830–31. See *Quarterly Journal of Science, Literature, and the Arts, The*
Knight's Quarterly Magazine, 1823–25
Leigh Hunt's (London) Journal 1834–51
Liberal, The, 1822–23
Literary and Statistical Magazine for Scotland, The, 1817–22
Literary Chronicle and Weekly Review, The, 1819–28
Literary Examiner, The, 1823
Literary Gazette, The, 1817–63
Literary Gossip, The, 1821–22. See *Gossip, The*
Literary Guardian, The, 1831–32
Literary Journal, The, 1803–6
Literary Journal and General Miscellany, The, 1818–19
Literary Magnet, The, 1824–28
Literary Museum, The, 1822–24
Literary Panorama, The, 1806–19
Literary Sketch-Book, The, 1823–24
Literary Speculum, The, 1821–23
Loiterer, The, 1789–90
London and Westminster Review, The, 1836–40. See *Westminster Review, The*
London Magazine, The, 1791. See *New London Magazine, The (AAAJ)*
London Magazine, The, 1820–29
London Museum, The, 1822–23. See *Literary Museum, The*
London Quarterly Review, The, 1834–83. See *Quarterly Review, The*
London Review, The, 1809
London Review, The, 1835–36. See *Westminster Review, The*
McKay's New British Lady's Magazine, 1817–19. See *British Lady's Magazine, The*
Metropolitan Magazine, The, 1831–50

Mirror Monthly Magazine, The, 1847–49. See *Mirror of Literature, Amusement, and Instruction, The*

Mirror of Literature, Amusement, and Instruction, The, 1822–49

Monthly-Censor, The, 1822–23

Monthly Magazine (and British Register) (of Literature, Science, and Belles Lettres), 1796–1843

Monthly Mirror, The, 1795–1811

National Magazine, The, 1830–31. See *Dublin Literary Gazette, The*

New Bon Ton Magazine, The, 1818–21

New British Lady's Magazine, The, 1817–19. See *British Lady's Magazine, The*

New Edinburgh Review, The, 1821–23. See *Edinburgh Monthly Review, The*

New European Magazine, The, 1822–24

New Monthly Magazine (and Universal Register) (and Literary Journal) (and Humorist), The, 1814–84

New Review, or Monthly Analysis, of General Literature, The, 1813–14

New Universal Magazine, The, 1814–15. See *Universal Magazine, The (AAAJ)*

Nic Nac (or, Oracle of Knowledge) (or Literary Cabinet), The, 1822–28

Poetical Magazine, 1809–11

Printing Machine, The, 1835. See *Leigh Hunt's (London) Journal*

Quarterly Journal of Science, Literature, and the Arts (of Literature, Science, and the Arts), The, 1816–31

Quarterly Magazine, The, 1825. See *Knight's Quarterly Magazine*

Quarterly Review, The, 1809–1962. See also *MA*

Reflector, The, 1810–11

Repository of Arts, The, 1809. See *Poetical Magazine*

Retrospective Review, The, 1820–54

Satirist, The, 1807–14

Scottish Episcopal Review and Magazine, The, 1820–22. See *Literary and Statistical Magazine for Scotland, The*

Scourge (and Satirist), The, 1811–16

Spectator, The, 1828–1925

Sylph, The, 1795–96

Tait's Edinburgh Magazine, 1832–61

Tatler, The, 1830–32

Theatrical Inquisitor (and Monthly Mirror), The, 1812–20

Tripod, or New Satirist, The, 1814. See *Satirist, The*

Watchman, The, 1796

Westminster Review, The, 1824–1914

Wright's London Magnet, 1828. See *Literary Magnet, The*

Yellow Dwarf, The, 1818

Titles Included in
The Victorian and
Edwardian Age,
1837–1913

Academy, The, 1869–1916
Academy and Literature, The, 1902, 1910, 1914. See *Academy, The*
Ainsworth's Magazine, 1842–54
All the Year Round, 1859–95
Anglo Saxon Review, 1899–1901
Arrow, The, 1906–9
Art and Poetry, 1850. See *Germ, The*
Author, The, 1890–
Belgravia, 1866–99
Bentley's Miscellany, 1837–68
Blue Review, The, 1913
Bookman, The, 1891–1934
Bookseller, The, 1858–
British Review and National Observer, The, 1897. See *Scots Observer, The*
Cambridge Review, The, 1879–
Cambridge University Magazine, The, 1839–43
Century Guild Hobby Horse, The, 1884–92. See *Hobby Horse, The*
Chambers's Journal, 1832–1956. See *Chambers's Journal (RA)*
Chambers's Journal of Popular Literature, Science and the Arts, 1854–57. See *Chambers's Journal (RA)*
Chambers's London Journal, 1841–43
Chapbook, The, 1913–14; 1919–25
Christian Teacher, The, 1835–44. See *Prospective Review, The*
Contemporary Review, The, 1866–. See also *MA*
Cornhill Magazine, The, 1860–1975. See also *MA*
Cosmopolis, 1896–98
Court Magazine and Monthly Critic, 1838–47
Critic, The, 1843–63

Parentheses indicate that the additional title appeared only during part of the run of the magazine.

Critic: (The London Literary Journal), The, 1850–58. See *Critic, The*

Critic; (A) Weekly Journal of Literature, Art, Science, and the Drama, The, 1858–59. See *Critic, The*

Critic of Books [etc.], *The*, 1848–50. See *Critic, The*

Critic of Literature, Art, Science, and the Drama, The, 1843–44. See *Critic, The*

Dana, 1904–5

Dickensian, The, 1905–

Dome, The, 1897–1900

Douglas Jerrold's Shilling Magazine, 1845–48

English Association Bulletin, 1907–35. See *English (MA)*

English Review, The, 1908–37

Examiner and London Review, The, 1869–70. See *Examiner, The* (1808) (RA)

Fortnightly (Review), The, 1865–1954. See also *MA*

Fun, 1861–1901

Germ, The, 1850

Golden Hynde, The, 1913–14

Good Words, 1860–1911

Granta, The, 1889–

Green Sheaf, The, 1903–4

Hobby Horse, The, 1884–94

Hood's Magazine, 1884–49

Household Words, 1850–59

Idler, The, 1892–1911

Lady's World, The, 1886–87. See *Woman's World, The*

Leader, The, 1850–60

Leader and Saturday Analyst, The, 1860. See *Leader, The*

Leigh Hunt's Journal, 1850–51. See *Leigh Hunt's (London) Journal (RA)*

Library, The, 1889–

Literary Guide (and Rationalist Review), 1885–

Literature, 1897–1902

London and Edinburgh Weekly Review, 1865–66. See *Weekly Review*

London Quarterly and Holborn Review, The, 1853–1968

London Review, The, 1850. See *Mirror of Literature . . . , The (RA)*

Longman's Magazine, 1882–1905

Macmillan's Magazine, 1859–1907

Mirror Monthly Magazine, The, 1847–49. See *Mirror of Literature . . . , The (RA)*

Month, The, 1864–

Monthly Chapbook, The, 1919. See *Chapbook, The*

Monthly Chronicle, The, 1838–41

Monthly Review, The, 1900–1907

National Observer, 1890–97. See *Scots Observer, The*

National Review, 1855–64

National Review, 1883–1960

New Age, The, 1894–1938

New Freewoman, 1913. See *Egoist, The (MA)*

New Quarterly Review, 1852–62

New Review, The, 1889–97

New Statesman (and Nation), 1913–

Nineteenth Century, The, 1877–1900

North British Review, The, 1844–71
Notes and Queries, 1849–1981
Novel Review, The, 1892. See *Tinsley's Magazine*
Once a Week, 1859–80
Open Window, 1910–11
Oxford and Cambridge Magazine, The, 1856
Pageant, The, 1896–97
Pall Mall Magazine, 1893–1914
Pearson's Magazine, 1896–1939
Poetical Gazette, 1909–12. See *Poetry Review, The*
Poetry and Drama, 1913-14. See *Chapbook, The*
Poetry Review, The, 1909–
Prospective Review, The, 1845–55
Punch, 1841–
Quiver, The, 1861–1926
Rambler, The, 1848–62
Reader, The, 1863–67
Review of Reviews, The, 1890–1953
Rhythm, 1911–13
St. Martin's Review (in-the-Field Monthly) (Messenger), 1890–
Saint Paul's (Magazine), 1867–74
Samhain, 1901–8
Saturday Analyst and Leader, The, 1860. See *Leader, The*
Saturday Review, The, 1855–1938
Savoy, The, 1896
Scots Observer, The, 1888–97
Sharpe's London Magazine, 1845–70
Shilling Magazine, 1845–48. See *Douglas Jerrold's Shilling Magazine*
Strand Magazine, The, 1891–1950
Symposium, The, 1839–41. See *Cambridge University Magazine, The*
Temple Bar, 1860–1906
Thrush, 1901–2; 1909–10
Tinsley's Magazine, 1867–92
To-Day, 1893–1905; 1916–23
T.P.'s Weekly, 1902–16. See *To-Day*
Tripod, The, 1912–13
Truth, 1877–1957
Universal Review, The, 1888–90
Vanity Fair, 1868–1928
Victoria Magazine, The, 1863–80
Wales, 1911–14
Watt's Literary Guide, 1887–94. See *Literary Guide*
Westminster and Foreign Quarterly Review, The, 1846–51. See *Westminster Review, The*
  (RA)
Windsor Magazine, 1895–1939
Woman's World, The, 1886–90
Yellow Book, The, 1894–97

Titles Included in
The Modern Age,
1914–1984

Abinger Chronicle, 1939–44

Adam. International Review, 1929–

Adelphi, The, 1923–55

Agenda, 1959–

Akros, 1965–83

Anglo-Welsh Review, The, 1949–

Arena: A Literary Magazine, 1949–52

Art and Letters: An Illustrated Quarterly, 1917–20

Athenaeum, 1921–31. See *Nation and Athenaeum, The*

Aylesford Review, The, 1955–68

Bell, (A Survey of Irish Life) (A Magazine of Creative Fiction) (A Magazine of Ireland Today), The, 1940–50

Bermondsey Book, The: Quarterly Review of Life and Literature, 1923–30

Black Art, The, 1960–65

Blackfriars: A Monthly Review (Edited by the English Dominicans) (New Blackfriars), 1920–

Blackwood's Edinburgh Magazine, 1817–1980. See also *RA*

Blast: The Review of the Great English Vortex, 1914–15

British Museum Quarterly, 1926–73

British Museum Yearbook, 1976–. See *British Museum Quarterly*

Calendar (of Modern Letters), The, 1925–27

Cambridge Journal, The, 1947–54

Catholic Review, The, 1913–18. See *Blackfriars*

Contemporary Poetry and Prose, 1936–37

Contemporary Review, 1866–. See also *VEA*

Cornhill Magazine, The, 1860–1975. See also *VEA*

Coterie / A Quarterly / Art, Prose, and Literature, 1919–21, 1925–27

Criterion: A Quarterly Review (A Literary Review) (Monthly Criterion) (New Criterion), The, 1922–39

Parentheses around part of a title indicate that the wording appeared only during part of the run of the magazine.

Critical Quarterly, The, 1959–

Decachord, The: A Magazine (for Poets and Students of Poetry) (for Students and Lovers of Poetry) (of New Verse, Critical Essays, Reviews, etc.) (of Verse) (for Poetry-Lovers), 1924–46

Dock Leaves, 1949–57. See *Anglo-Welsh Review, The*

Drama, 1919–

Dublin Magazine, The (A quarterly review of literature, science and art), 1923–58

Egoist, An Individualist Review, The, 1914–19

Encore: (The Magazine) (of the Students' Association) (of the Central School) (of Speech Training and Dramatic Art) (A Quarterly Review for Students of the Theatre) (The Quarterly Review of World Theatre) (The Voice of Vital Theatre), 1954–65

Encounter, 1953–

Enemy, A Review of Art and Literature, The, 1927–29

English, 1936–

English Association Bulletin, 1907–35. See *English*

Enquiry: A Journal of Modern Thought, 1948–50

European Quarterly, The, 1934–35

Experiment, 1928–31

Folios of New Writing, 1940–41. See *New Writing*

Fortnightly (Review), The, 1865–1954. See also *VEA*

Gambit (An International Drama Quarterly) (Bi-Monthly) (International) (International Theatre Review), 1963–

Gangrel, 1945–46

Golden Hind, A Quarterly Magazine of Art and Literature, The, 1922–24

Horizon: A Review of Literature and Art, 1940–50

Humanist, 1956–71. See *Literary Guide (VEA)*

Interim Drama, 1945–46. See *Drama*

Kingdom Come (The Magazine of War-Time Oxford) (Founded in War-Time Oxford) (The First Literary Magazine to Appear in War-Time), 1939–43

Left Review, 1934–38

Life and Letters (Today) (continuing) (and) (The London Mercury) (and Bookman), 1928–50

Life of the Spirit, The, 1944–64. See *Blackfriars*

Lilliput: The Pocket Magazine for Everyone, 1937–60

Lines: New Poetry, Scotland, 1953. See *Lines (Review)*

Lines (Review), 1952–

London Aphrodite, The, 1928–29

London (Gallery) Bulletin, 1938–40

London Magazine, 1954–

London Mercury, The, 1919–39

London Mercury and Bookman, The, 1935–39. See *Life and Letters*

London Quarterly and Holborn Review, The, 1932–68. See *VEA*

Lovat Dickson's Magazine (Devoted Solely to the Short Story) (A Magazine for Thoughtful People), 1933–35

Mandrake, 1945–56

Mint, The, 1946, 1948

Monthly Criterion, The, 1927–28. See *Criterion, A Quarterly Review, The*

Nation and (The) Athenaeum, The, 1921–31

New Adelphi, The, 1930–41. See *Adelphi, The*
New Blackfriars, 1964–. See *Blackfriars*
New Coterie, 1925–27. See *Coterie*
New Criterion, The, 1928–39. See *Criterion, The*
New Departures, 1959–84 (?)
New English Weekly (And the New Age) (A Review of Public Affairs, Literature, and the Arts), (The), 1932–49
New Humanities, 1972–. See *Literary Guide (VEA)*
New Measure, 1965–69
New Poetry, 1945, 1946
New Poetry, 1967. See *Workshop*
New Review, The, 1974–78. See *Review, The*
New Road (New) (Directions in European Art and Letters), 1943–46, 1949
New Saltire, 1961–64. See *Saltire Review of Arts, Letters, & Life, The*
New Stories, 1934–36
New Verse, 1933–39
New Writers, 1961–70
New Writing (and Daylight), 1936–46
Nimbus (A Magazine of Literature, the Arts and New Ideas) (New English Review), 1951–58
Nine: A Magazine (of Poetry and Criticism) (of Literature and the Arts) (of Literature and Criticism), 1949–56
Nineteenth Century and After, 1901–50. See *Twentieth Century*
Northern Review: A Progressive Monthly of Life and Letters, The, 1924
Now (A Journal of Good Writing), 1940–47
Orion (A Miscellany), 1945–47
Our Time: Incorporating Poetry and the People (and New Theatre), 1941–49
Outposts (Poetry Quarterly), 1943–
Owl (Winter Owl), The, 1919–23
Penguin New Writing, 1940–50
Penguin Parade, 1937–45, 1947–48
Plays and Players (Incorporating Theatre World and Encore), 1953–
PN Review, 1973–76. See *Poetry Nation*
Poetry Commonwealth, 1948–51
Poetry (London), 1939–51
Poetry Nation (PN Review), 1973–
Poetry Quarterly, 1939–53
Poetry Studies, 1933–39. See *Poetry Quarterly*
Poetry Wales, 1965–
Poor. Old. Tired. Horse (P. O. T. H.), 1961–67
P. O. T. H. (undated). See *Poor. Old. Tired. Horse.*
Priapus, 1962–71
Purpose: A Quarterly Magazine, 1929–40
Quarterly Review, The, 1809–1967. See also *RA*
Review, The (New), 1962–78
Review of English Literature, A, 1960–67
Right Review, 1936–47
Saltire Review, of Arts, Letters, and Life (New . . .), 1954–64

Samphire (New Poetry) (East Anglia), 1968–81
Scottish Chapbook: A Monthly Magazine of Scottish Arts & Letters, The, 1922–23
Scrutiny: A Quarterly Review, 1932–53
Scythe, The, 1942–45. See *Townsman*
Seven: The New Magazine, 1938–40
Solstice, 1966–69
Stand, 1952–
Teapoth 23 (undated). See *Poor. Old. Tired. Horse.*
Time and Tide (and Business World) (Business Guide) (the British News Magazine) (John O'London's), 1920–79
Townsman (The Scythe), 1938–45
Trace, A Chronicle of Living Literature, 1952–70
Transatlantic Review, 1924
Twentieth Century (Nineteenth Century and After), 1901–72
Twentieth Century Verse, 1937–39
Universities' Poetry, 1958–63
VE-time Drama, 1945. See *Drama*
VJ-time Drama, 1945. See *Drama*
Voices, 1919–21
Wales, 1937–40
War-time Drama, 1939–45. See *Drama*
Wave: A Magazine of New Poetry, 1970–74
Wheels (An Anthology of Verse) (A Second . . . Sixth Cycle), 1916–21
Wind and the Rain, The, 1941–51
Windmill, The, 1944–48
Winter Owl, The, 1923. See *Owl, The*
Workshop (New Poetry) (Writers' Workshop), 1967–81
Writers' Workshop. See *Workshop*
Writing Today, 1957–62
X. A Quarterly Review, 1959–62

A Chronology of Social and Literary Events and British Literary Magazines, 1914–1984

BRITISH LITERARY PERIODICALS	YEAR	SOCIAL & LITERARY EVENTS
	1914	
John Gould Fletcher and Ezra Pound persuade Dora Marsden to broaden her feminist *Freewoman* into the literary *Egoist*. Joyce's *Portrait of the Artist* is serialized.		World War I erupts. John Tenniel, *Punch* cartoonist, dies. Joyce publishes *Dubliners*, Conrad "Chance," George Moore "Hail and Farewell."
Wyndham Lewis begins *Blast* to promote Pound's vorticism and attack futurism.		
	1915	
T.S. Eliot's first publications in England—"Preludes" and "Rhapsody on a Windy Night"—appear in *Blast*.		German blockades of British ports. British merchant ships lose more than a million tons. Einstein advances the theory of relativity. D. H. Lawrence publishes *The Rainbow* (subsequently banned), Conrad *Victory*. Rupert Brooke dies in battle, Alun Lewis is born.

BRITISH LITERARY PERIODICALS	*YEAR*	*SOCIAL & LITERARY EVENTS*

1916

Edith Sitwell publishes the first of six annual anthologies, *Wheels*; the contents are given over to work by her brothers, herself, and their friends.

Lloyd George becomes Prime Minister. Beatty commands British Navy. Shipping losses mount.

Henry James, Jack London die; David Gascoyne, Philip O'Connor are born.

Tristan Tzara and Hans Arp promote Dadism in Zurich.

1917

When Richard Aldington leaves for war service, T. S. Eliot edits the *Egoist*.

War poets—Wilfred Owen, Siegfried Sassoon, Isaac Rosenberg—are featured in the new *Arts and Letters*.

German aircraft attack London. Shipping losses mount to 4 million tons. Food is rationed in Britain.

United States enters war.

T. S. Eliot publishes *Prufrock and Other Observations*, Freud *Introduction to Psychoanalysis*.

First jazz records are pressed.

Anthony Burgess is born.

1918

Seven poems by Wilfred Owen appear in *Wheels* 4, making it the most prestigious issue.

Armistice is signed. British shipping losses total 9 million tons. War casualties total 8.5 million.

Food shortage in Britain; soup kitchens open.

Hopkins's *Poems* are published posthumously.

Wilfred Owen and Isaac Rosenberg die in battle; Muriel Spark is born.

United States Post Office confiscates *Little Review* for publishing Joyce's *Ulysses*.

BRITISH LITERARY PERIODICALS	YEAR	SOCIAL & LITERARY EVENTS
	1919	

The *London Mercury* and *Coterie* begin publication. In spite of the occasional appearance of modernists D. H. Lawrence, E. M. Forster, Virginia Woolf, and T. S. Eliot, both magazines come to represent Edwardian or late Victorian sensibility.

Thomas Moult begins *Voices*, attracts such figures as Aldington, D. H. Lawrence, Galsworthy, Crane, H. L. Mencken, and W. H. Davies.

Newly established British Drama League begins *Drama* to promote its interests—such as the establishment of a national theater—and publish criticism and reviews.

Robert Graves publishes the Oxford circle in the *Owl*.

Joyce's *Ulysses* is serialized in the *Egoist*.

George Curzon succeeds A. J. Balfour as Foreign Secretary.

British forces battle Indian and Afghan troops.

Eamon De Valera controls Sinn Fein; Edward Carson calls for the repeal of Irish Home Rule.

Doris Lessing, Iris Murdoch are born.

| | 1922 | |

Eliot's *Criterion* begins, featuring *The Waste Land*, criticism by Pound, stories by D. H. Lawrence.

In his *Scottish Chapbook* Hugh MacDiarmid publishes a series on the "Theory of Scots Letters" to promote a Scottish renaissance.

The *Golden Hind* combines elaborate artwork with contributions by the imagists, notably F. S. Flint, Aldous Huxley, and Ford Madox Ford.

A. Bonar Law replaces Lloyd George as Prime Minister; Conservatives win 344 of 599 seats.

Unemployed Scots begin a march to London.

Irish Free State is proclaimed.

Kingsley Amis, Philip Larkin, Donald Davie are born.

Ulysses is published in Paris, confiscated in the United States.

BRITISH LITERARY PERIODICALS	*YEAR*	*SOCIAL & LITERARY EVENTS*

1923

John Middleton Murry begins the *Adelphi*, publishing T. S. Eliot (35 works), D. H. Lawrence (19), Arnold Bennett, H. G. Wells, Dorothy Richardson, Aldous Huxley, Edwin Muir, George Santayana.

John Maynard Keynes forms a board to purchase the *Nation and Athenaeum* (merged in 1921); Leonard Woolf becomes literary editor.

Ethel Gutman's *Bermondsey Book* publishes work by articulate laborers alongside that by such contributors as Shaw, Woolf, Walpole, Hardy, Huxley, and De la Mare.

A. Bonar Law resigns, dies later in year; Stanley Baldwin becomes Prime Minister; Neville Chamberlain, Chancellor of the Exchequer. Conservatives hold 258 seats, Labour 191, Liberals 158.

Dock workers strike in London as trade union movement grows.

Yeats wins Nobel Prize for Literature.

Nadine Gordimer and Denise Levertov are born; Katherine Mansfield dies.

1924

Ford Madox Ford publishes the *Transatlantic Review* from Paris, with the assistance of Hemingway, Robert McAlmon, and Pound. Stein's *Making of Americans* and Joyce's *Finnegans Wake* appear.

Charles John Arnell begins the *Decachord*; protests against modern poetry; publishes Day Lewis, Graves, Sassoon, and MacDiarmid.

Hugh MacDiarmid begins the *Northern Review* to promote literary works in the Scots vernacular.

Baldwin is reelected. Winston Churchill joins Conservative Party and becomes Chancellor of the Exchequer. Baldwin resigns; Ramsay MacDonald forms Britain's first Labour government.

Strikes spread throughout Britain.

Anti-British politician J.B.M. Hertzog becomes Prime Minister of the Union of South Africa.

Michael Hamburger is born; Conrad, Marie Corelli, Kafka, Anatole France die.

Forster publishes *A Passage to India*, Shaw *Back to Methuselah* and *Saint Joan*, O'Casey *Juno and the Paycock*.

BRITISH LITERARY PERIODICALS	*YEAR*	*SOCIAL & LITERARY EVENTS*

1925

Calendar of Modern Letters begins publication; attracts contributors from Russia, the United States, and virtually every European country; publishes Englishmen D. H. Lawrence, Edwin Muir, Desmond MacCarthy; supports rational criticism of I. A. Richards.

Britain passes an unemployment insurance act.

Hitler reorganizes the Nazi Party, publishes first part of *Mein Kampf.*

First image is transmitted by television invented by Scotsman John Logie Baird.

Hemingway publishes *In Our Time*, Huxley *Those Barren Leaves.*

Noel Coward's *Hay Fever* opens in London.

Ian Hamilton Finlay, John Wain are born.

1926

General strike cripples Britain.

D. H. Lawrence publishes *The Plumed Serpent*, Hemingway *The Sun Also Rises*, Faulkner *Soldier's Pay.*

J. P. Donleavy, John Fowles are born; Ronald Firbank, Israel Zangwill die.

1927

Pound publishes the *Exile* from Dijon, France; for three issues, the only significant work to appear is Yeats's *Sailing to Byzantium.*

Wyndham Lewis begins his one-man campaign, the *Enemy*; attacks the "time-mind" of Joyce and Stein.

Allied military control of Germany ends, economic system collapses.

First talking film, *The Jazz Singer*, is released.

Lindbergh flies from New York to Paris.

BRITISH LITERARY PERIODICALS	YEAR	SOCIAL & LITERARY EVENTS
	(1927)	
		Proust's *A la recherche du temps perdu* is published, Woolf's *To the Lighthouse*, Yeats's *The Tower*.
		Charles Tomlinson is born.
	1928	
Desmond MacCarthy's new *Life and Letters* attracts work by D. H. Lawrence, Sherwood Anderson, E. M. Forster, George Santayana, Kenneth Clark, and Evelyn Waugh.		H. H. Asquith becomes Prime Minister.
		Age for women's suffrage in Britain is lowered from 30 to 21.
Jack Lindsay and P. R. Stephenson begin their *London Aphrodite*, publishing only six numbers, as intended, as a "joke."		Thomas Kinsella, Alan Sillitoe are born; Thomas Hardy, George Trevelyan die.
William Empson begins the modernist *Experiment* at Cambridge; contributes chapters of *Seven Types of Ambiguity*.		D. H. Lawrence publishes *Lady Chatterley's Lover*, Shaw *The Intelligent Woman's Guide to Socialism and Capitalism*, Aldous Huxley *Point Counter Point*, Evelyn Waugh *Decline and Fall*.
	1929	
Established to promote the Social Credit scheme of C. H. Douglas and the individual psychology of Alfred Adler, *Purpose* attracts Pound, Eliot, and Herbert Read—who declare their faith in Social Credit—as well as Dylan Thomas, Lawrence Durrell, Auden, and Spender.		Labour Party edges the Conservative, 287 seats to 261. Ramsay MacDonald forms a new government.
		United States stock market collapses.
Evelyn Waugh publishes a seminal essay on Firbank in *Life and Letters*.		Second Surrealist Manifesto is published. Faulkner's *The Sound and the Fury*, Hemingway's *A Farewell to Arms*, Hughes's *A High Wind in Jamaica* appear.
		Thom Gunn and John Osborne are born; dramatist Henry Arthur Jones dies.

BRITISH LITERARY PERIODICALS	*YEAR*	*SOCIAL & LITERARY EVENTS*
	1930	

Time and Tide publishes its first Christmas number, a major anthology.

Last Allied troops leave Germany, as Nazi Party gains 107 seats.

T. S. Eliot publishes *Ash Wednesday*, Hart Crane *The Bridge*, Somerset Maugham *Cakes and Ale*, Evelyn Waugh *Vile Bodies*.

John Arden, Ted Hughes, Harold Pinter are born; D. H. Lawrence dies.

1931

When *Foreign Affairs* ends, *Time and Tide* takes it over as a monthly commentary.

In *Experiment*, William Empson assesses Auden's *Paid on Both Sides* and provides an accurate document of the 1930s sensibility.

The *Nation and Athenaeum* merges with the *New Statesman* to become *New Statesman and Nation*. Kingsley Martin is editor.

Ramsay MacDonald forms a second National Government after a vote of 558–556.

Oswell Mosley leaves the Labour Party to form new fascist party.

Colin Wilson is born; Arnold Bennett, Frank Harris, Hall Caine die.

1932

Alfred Orage begins the *New English Weekly* primarily to advance the idea of Social Credit. Amid essays on economics appear Eliot's *Four Quartets*, Pound's Canto 38, and Dylan Thomas's first London publication.

From Cambridge, *Scrutiny* begins its role as academic arbiter of British literary taste for the next two decades.

Unemployment climbs to 30 million worldwide: 2.8 in Britain, 13.7 in the United States. Roosevelt wins American presidential election by a landslide vote.

The Nazi Party gains 230 seats in Germany.

John Galsworthy receives Nobel Prize for Literature.

BRITISH LITERARY PERIODICALS	YEAR	SOCIAL & LITERARY EVENTS

(1932)

The *Oxford Outlook*, with Richard Goodman as editor, publishes one Marxist issue, then expires for a year before reissue as the leftist *New Oxford Outlook*.

Richard Rees becomes editor of the *Adelphi* (until 1937). A friend of George Orwell, he secures much of his work for the magazine.

Huxley publishes *Brave New World*, Auden *The Orators*, Greene *Stamboul Train*.

Michael Roberts's Oxford anthology *New Signatures* introduces Auden, Spender, and Day Lewis, solidifies their identification as a group.

Malcolm Bradbury, Geoffrey Hill, Adrian Mitchell, Peter Redgrove, Arnold Wesker are born; Lady Gregory, Lytton Strachey, G. Lowes Dickinson, Harold Monro die.

1933

Geoffrey Grigson's *New Verse*, the best poetry magazine of the decade, is established to promote the work of Auden, MacNeice, and to a lesser degree, Spender and Day Lewis. Special issues focus on Hopkins, the nature of poetry, Freud, and Marx.

Lovat Dickson's Magazine promotes the short story, offers a history of the genre. Stories by Hemingway, D. H. Lawrence, and Kay Boyle appear.

Edwin Muir, after seeing the effects of the new Nazi regime in Germany, plans the *European Quarterly* to make England aware of the Continental situation.

Contemporary Review supports Jewish and political refugees from the Continent and welcomes essays by and about exiles.

The Enabling Law makes Hitler dictator; Goering is Prime Minister, Goebbels Minister of Propaganda. Boycott of Jews begins; first concentration camps open.

United States court allows *Ulysses* to be sold.

Orwell publishes *Down and Out in Paris and London*, Stein *The Autobiography of Alice B. Toklas*, Wells *The Shape of Things to Come*.

Joe Orton and David Storey are born; John Galsworthy, George Moore, George Saintsbury die.

BRITISH LITERARY PERIODICALS	YEAR	SOCIAL & LITERARY EVENTS
	(1933)	
F. R. Leavis, admirer of the *Calendar of Modern Letters*, publishes an anthology of critical essays from the magazine.		
	1934	
The *Adelphi* reports on the Independent Socialist Party; publishes Dylan Thomas, W. H. Auden, Orwell, Spender, Day Lewis, and George Barker.		Oswald Mosley holds Fascist meetings in Britain; Churchill warns Parliament of Germany's air force.
		Greene publishes *It's a Battlefield*, Graves *I, Claudius*, Fitzgerald *Tender Is the Night*, Pound *An ABC of Reading*.
Left Review succeeds *Viewpoint* as the organ of the British complement of the pro-Soviet Writers' International; advocates social realism; publishes Auden, Spender, Day Lewis.		Gorki leads first Soviet Writers' Conference in Moscow.
	1935	
		Stanley Baldwin forms a National Government.
		George V's Silver Jubilee is celebrated.
		Victor Gollancz begins the Left Book Club.
		T. S. Eliot publishes *Murder in the Cathedral*, Auden and Isherwood *The Dog beneath the Skin*.
		Edward Bond and Michael Horovitz are born.
	1936	
Count Potocki begins his *Right Review*, promotes the divine right of kings as the ''sanest'' form of government.		Spanish Civil War begins.
		Edward VIII succeeds George V, abdicates to his brother, George VI.

BRITISH LITERARY PERIODICALS	*YEAR*	*SOCIAL & LITERARY EVENTS*

(1936)

Previously apolitical, *Life and Letters Today* announces support for Republicans in the Spanish Civil War, joining *Left Review, New Verse*, and other, more political magazines.

Oswald Mosley is driven out of Whitechapel for his anti-Jewish demonstration.

German troops move into the Rhineland, build the Siegfried Line.

English includes in its first issue works by Sean O'Casey, Laurence Binyon, and T. Sturge Moore.

International Surrealist Exhibition opens in London.

Nineteen-year-old Roger Roughton begins *Contemporary Poetry and Prose*, remembered primarily as a surrealist journal. Contributors include Picasso, Lorca, Lautreamont, Dylan Thomas.

Dylan Thomas publishes *Twenty-five Poems*, Huxley *Eyeless in Gaza*, John Strachey *The Theory and Practice of Socialism*.

A. E. Housman, G. K. Chesterton, Rudyard Kipling die.

1937

Julian Symons begins *Twentieth Century Verse* as an outlet for poets not included in the Oxbridge circle of *New Verse* or the radical *Left Review*.

Baldwin retires, replaced by Neville Chamberlain as Prime Minister; British begin policy of appeasement when Lord Halifax visits Hitler.

Left Review comes under the control of the Communist Party and focuses on Soviet culture.

Spanish rebels destroy Guernica; Picasso begins *Guernica* mural for Paris exhibition.

Time and Tide becomes one of the first publishers of Alun Lewis.

Orwell publishes *The Road to Wigan Pier*, Auden and Isherwood *The Ascent of F. 6*.

Tom Stoppard is born; J. M. Barrie dies.

1938

Founded to notice all avant-garde art shows and movements, E.L.T. Mesens's *London Bulletin* focuses on surrealism. The December issue explores the therapeutic value of surrealist art. Later issues focus on constructivists, expressionists.

Churchill leads opposition to Chamberlain's policy of appeasement; Anthony Eden resigns. Citizens are given gasmasks.

Germany and America withdraw ambassadors.

BRITISH LITERARY PERIODICALS	*YEAR*	*SOCIAL & LITERARY EVENTS*

(1938)

Seven succeeds *Booster* and *Delta* (Paris), publishing many of the same writers—Boyle, Durrell, Gascoyne, Miller, Nin—as well as the Apocalyptics.

Townsman begins as a literary magazine, regularly publishing Pound, before its interests shift almost completely to agriculture.

Pogroms begin in Germany. Mussolini gets anti-Jewish legislation in Italy.

Greene publishes *Brighton Rock*, Isherwood *Goodbye to Berlin*.

1939

War brings an end or preparations to close *Cornhill, Criterion, London Mercury, New Stories, New Verse, Purpose, Twentieth Century Verse, Wales*, the *Welsh Review*.

Tambimuttu begins *Poetry (London)*, one of two poetry magazines in wartime London. Despite its catholic tastes, the magazine is identified with the Apocalyptics.

Kingdom Come early on supports John M. Murry's call in the *Adelphi* for peace negotiations instead of aggression, later publishes essays on the social and aesthetic problems posed by the war.

Britain declares war on Germany, begins conscription, sends expeditionary forces into France, uses radar stations to detect enemy aircraft.

Joyce publishes *Finnegans Wake*, Eliot *The Family Reunion*.

Margaret Drabble is born; Yeats, Freud, Ford Madox Ford, Llewelyn Powys die.

1940

The two most important magazines of the decade begin publication: Cyril Connolly's *Horizon*, and John Lehmann's *Penguin New Writing*, a serial anthology.

Sean O'Faolain begins the *Bell* to present "the best Irish writers." O'Faolain himself, Patrick Kavanagh, Elizabeth Bowen, Louis MacNeice, and Flann O'Brien contribute frequently.

Chamberlain resigns, dies later in year. Churchill becomes Prime Minister, Eden Foreign Secretary.

Germany begins heavy air raids over London, RAF night raids over Germany. Britain joins Free French under De Gaulle.

Oswald Mosley imprisoned under war acts.

BRITISH LITERARY PERIODICALS	YEAR	SOCIAL & LITERARY EVENTS
	(1940)	
George Woodcock begins *Now*, to be edited from an anarchist point of view. D. S. Savage and Julian Symons contribute frequently.		Greene publishes *The Power and the Glory*, Koestler *Darkness at Noon*. Tom McGrath is born.
	1941	
The pamphlet *Poetry and the People* becomes the glossy *Our Time*, which Beatrix Lehmann, Alan Bush, and Sylvia Townsend Warner cooperatively produce.		United States enters war; Britain joins United States in declaring war on Japan; establishes the Air Training Corps; rations clothing.
Henry Treece, Stefan Schimanski, and Alan Rook take over *Kingdom Come* and try to make the undergraduate Oxford magazine a vehicle for the Apocalyptics.		Noel Coward produces *Blithe Spirit*, Brecht *Mother Courage and Her Children*. J. F. Hendry and Henry Treece publish a key anthology of *New Apocalypse* poets.
Lilliput enjoys phenomenal success, with a circulation of a quarter of a million; publishes V. S. Pritchett, Wyndham Lewis, Evelyn Waugh.		Dave Cunliffe is born; James Joyce and Virginia Woolf die.
	1942	
John Lehmann merges *Folios of New Writing* with Czech author Jiří Mucha's *Daylight* to form *New Writing and Daylight*; publishes European writers exiled in London.		Americans bomb Tokyo, win at Midway.
Orwell publishes in *New Road* his long essay, "Looking Back on the Spanish War," which prefigures the totalitarianism of *1984*.		Germans sink the *Eagle* and the *Manchester*. Britain rations food. Gandhi demands India's independence, is arrested.
Wrey Gardiner, editor of *Poetry Quarterly*, notes the complete triumph of the neoromantic Apocalyptics over the 1930s "objective" poets.		

BRITISH LITERARY PERIODICALS	YEAR	SOCIAL & LITERARY EVENTS
	(1942)	
Wartime shortages force the *Adelphi* to publish quarterly instead of monthly.		
	1943	
Alex Comfort and John Bayliss's *New Road* attracts the most important young British poets, recognizes and encourages the Apocalyptics and surrealists.		Italy surrenders. Churchill, Stalin, and Roosevelt meet at Teheran. RAF raids Berlin. Eighth Army advances in Tripoli.
		Sidney Keyes dies in battle; his *Collected Poems* appears posthumously two years later.
	1944	
Horizon gives increasing space to American writers, culminates in a special issue in 1947.		Allies invade Normandy, Eighth Army takes Florence. Battle of the Bulge begins.
William Heinemann brings back the *Windmill* (1923).		Joyce Cary publishes *The Horse's Mouth*, Maugham *The Razor's Edge*, Huxley *Time Must Have a Stop*.
		Keith Douglas, L. H. Myers, Arthur Quiller-Couch die.
	1945	
The *Contemporary Review* lends its support to Attlee's Labour government and advocates the welfare state.		War ends. Black markets proliferate.
		United Nations is established.
John Wain begins *Mandrake* while an undergraduate at Oxford, publishing J. B. Leishman, Kingsley Amis, and Michael Hamburger.		Labour Party wins; Clement Attlee becomes Prime Minister.
J. B. Pick establishes *Gangrel* in the belief that literary reviews can counter ''the world-wide advance towards totalitarianism'' with ''moral'' criticism.		Evelyn Waugh publishes *Brideshead Revisited*, Orwell *Animal Farm*.

BRITISH LITERARY PERIODICALS	*YEAR*	*SOCIAL & LITERARY EVENTS*
	(1945)	

Horizon awards its annual prize to Dylan Thomas; publishes "Fern Hill," "Refusal to Mourn," "Poem in October."

George Orwell includes the best of his *Horizon* essays—on Kipling, Koestler, Wells, Yeats—in *Critical Essays*.

Windmill publishes Orwell's "In Defense of P. G. Wodehouse."

1946

Simon Watson Taylor's anthology of surrealist art, *Free Unions Libres*, is seized by police. Unable to understand it, they believe the journal is in code.

The British Arts Council is formed to provide financial support for the arts.

Dylan Thomas publishes *Deaths and Entrances*, Rattigan *The Winslow Boy*.

John Maynard Keynes, Gertrude Stein die.

1947

Edgell Rickword is removed by the Communist Party from the editorship of *Our Time*. Circulation had drastically declined as Communist sympathies became more suspect.

Angus Wilson's first publication, a short story, appears in *Horizon*.

Cambridge Journal is established to support traditional humanistic education against the encroachment of scientific and technical disciplines.

Princess Elizabeth marries Philip Mountbatten, Duke of Edinburgh.

India gains independence, is divided into India and Pakistan.

Camus publishes *The Plague*, Mann *Doktor Faustus*, H. E. Bates *The Purple Plain*.

BRITISH LITERARY PERIODICALS	*YEAR*	*SOCIAL & LITERARY EVENTS*

1948

Under Lionel Monteith, *Poetry Commonwealth* favors Apocalyptic poetry, publishes Henry Treece and G. S. Fraser.

British Rail is nationalized.

Auden receives Pulitzer Prize for *The Age of Anxiety*, Eliot the Nobel Prize.

Alan Paton publishes *Cry, the Beloved Country*, Waugh *The Loved One*, Rattigan *The Browning Version*.

1949

Enquiry combines an interest in parapsychology and literature, publishes Graves's "The White Goddess."

Pound admirer, bookseller Peter Russell begins *Nine*, calls for new "objective" poetry that does not merely imitate modernist techniques.

Pembroke Dock Grammar School faculty begin a house organ, *Dock Leaves*; by its fifth issue it dubs itself "A National Review . . . of Welsh Arts and Letters."

Time and Tide systematically attacks Marxism, the socialist collective state, and the Labour Party.

Communist Jack Lindsay, assisted by Randall Swingler, transforms *Our Time* into *Arena* to promote Continental literature, rejects Marxist aesthetics, and promotes Romantic principles.

Britain recognizes the independence of the Republic of Eire.

T. S. Eliot publishes *The Cocktail Party*, Orwell *1984*, Nancy Mitford *Love in a Cold Climate*.

Faulkner receives the Nobel Prize.

1950

Horizon, Life and Letters Today, Penguin New Writing cease publication.

Bertrand Russell receives the Nobel Prize for Literature.

George Bernard Shaw dies.

BRITISH LITERARY PERIODICALS	YEAR	SOCIAL & LITERARY EVENTS
	1951	
British Museum Quarterly, which suspended publication in 1940, begins again with a special retrospective on the years 1941–1950 (vol. 15).		Churchill forms government after Conservatives win. Korean War begins.
	1953	
The Congress for Cultural Freedom founds *Encounter* to break down the "departmentalization" of arts and politics; Spender and Irving Kristol (U.S.) are editors.		Elizabeth II is crowned Queen. Korean War ends. Churchill receives the Nobel Prize for Literature. G. S. Fraser and Iain Fletcher publish the anthology *Springtime*, harbinger of a new literary movement in poetry. Dylan Thomas dies. John Wain publishes his first novel, *Hurry On Down*.
	1954	
John Lehmann begins the *London Magazine*; recalling the venerable tradition of that title, he secures *au courant* contributors, the Movement poets. When J. B. Priestley attacks Waugh in the *New Statesman*, Waugh annihilates Priestley in a reply to the *Spectator*. The intellectual review, *Cambridge Journal*, succumbs to the competition of specialized academic journals. The *Fortnightly* is absorbed by the *Contemporary Review*.		Iris Murdoch publishes her first novel, *Under the Net*, Amis *Lucky Jim*, Golding *Lord of the Flies*, C. P. Snow *The New Men*, Rattigan *Separate Tables*, Huxley *The Doors of Perception*. Thom Gunn, still an undergraduate, debuts with *Fighting Terms*. Hemingway receives the Nobel Prize.

BRITISH LITERARY PERIODICALS	YEAR	*SOCIAL & LITERARY EVENTS*

1955

George Hartley publishes *Listen* to promote Movement poets.

Nimbus opposes Movement fiction and poetry in its reviews.

Churchill resigns; Anthony Eden becomes Prime Minister. Hugh Gaitskell leads Labour Party.

British rail and dock workers strike.

Commercial television is first broadcast in Britain.

Philip Larkin's first collection, *The Less Deceived*, establishes him as an important postwar poet.

1956

Encore encourages new audiences for plays, publishes, for the first time, plays by Pinter, and continues the fight for a national theater.

Robert Conquest introduces the Movement poets in the anthology *New Lines*.

Angus Wilson publishes *Anglo-Saxon Attitudes*.

Brecht's Berliner Ensemble visits London.

The English Stage Company is established at the Royal Court Theatre. Osborne's *Look Back in Anger* lends its title to a new school of "angry young men."

Bertolt Brecht, Max Beerbohm, Walter De la Mare die.

1957

Harold Macmillan succeeds Anthony Eden as Prime Minister.

European Common Market is established.

BRITISH LITERARY PERIODICALS	YEAR	SOCIAL & LITERARY EVENTS
	(1957)	
		Ted Hughes publishes his first collection of poems, *Hawk in the Rain*, Charles Tomlinson his first work, *Solo for a Glass Harmonica*.
		Durrell begins to publish his Alexandria Quartet.
		Samuel Beckett's *Endgame*, Osborne's *The Entertainer* are staged.
		Wyndham Lewis, Dorothy Sayers, Joyce Cary, Roy Campbell die.
	1959	
Influenced by Ezra Pound, William Cookson begins *Agenda* to introduce Continental and American authors to Britain.		Muriel Spark publishes her first novel, *Memento Mori*, Brendan Behan *The Hostage*.
Michael Horovitz begins the avant-garde *New Departures* as one of his efforts for literature to reach the masses. Samuel Beckett, Alan Brownjohn, Stevie Smith contribute.		John Arden's *Sergeant Musgrave's Dance* opens in London.
		D. H. Lawrence's *Lady Chatterley's Lover* is declared obscene and banned from the U.S. mails.
		Edwin Muir dies.
	1960	
The *Stage Yearbook* contrasts Pinter's *Homecoming* with older ones by Bagnold and Coward, and applauds the public's developing taste.		Prince Andrew is born.
		Arnold Wesker's *Trilogy* is staged at the Royal Court Theatre; Pinter's *The Caretaker* opens in London.
C. P. Snow publishes "Two Cultures" in *Encounter*.		Philip Larkin publishes his seminal poetry collection, *The Less Deceived*, Sillitoe *The Loneliness of the Long Distance Runner*, John Betjeman *Summoned by Bells*.

BRITISH LITERARY PERIODICALS	YEAR	SOCIAL & LITERARY EVENTS
	1961	

In a *Time and Tide* interview John Whiting discusses the staging and impact of *The Devils*, and the recent transformations in British theater.

Alan Ross takes over *London Magazine*, mixing popular discussions (Beatles' music) with literary contributions by Roy Fuller, Gavin Ewart, Philip Larkin, and Jean Rhys.

Encounter celebrates its 100th issue.

British begin negotiations to enter the Common Market.

Spy trials open in London for George Lonsdale, George Blake, the Krogers.

John Osborne's *Luther*, Christopher Fry's *Curtmantle*, Shelagh Delaney's *A Taste of Honey* are performed.

Irish Murdoch publishes *A Severed Head*.

Hilda Doolittle (H.D.), Hemingway die.

1962

Priapus begins as an outlet for new poets.

Alfred Alvarez publishes the definitive anthology, *The New Poetry*.

1963

Ian Hamilton Finlay's *Poor. Old. Tired. Horse.* gains a reputation as international journal of concrete poetry, is virtually ignored in its native Scotland.

Gambit introduces non-British works and furnishes line-copies to groups staging or reading the plays it prints.

New Writers' editor John Calder commissions ''happenings'' at the Edinburgh Festival for the fourth issue; the theme is decline in the theater.

Sir Alec Douglas-Hume becomes Prime Minister when Macmillan resigns.

Harold Wilson succeeds Hugh Gaitskell as leader of the Labour Party.

Britain gets permanent homes for two theater groups: the Royal Shakespeare Company and the National Theatre.

Edward Lucie-Smith publishes *A Group Anthology* to promote poets published by his Turret Press and to challenge Movement principles of verse.

BRITISH LITERARY PERIODICALS	YEAR	SOCIAL & LITERARY EVENTS
	(1963)	
		John Arden's *The Workhouse Donkey*, Joe Orton's *Entertaining Mr. Sloan* are staged.
		Louis MacNeice, Tristan Tzara, John Cowper Powys die.
	1965	
Plays and Players absorbs *Encore* (along with *Shows Illustrated, Play Pictorial, Theatre World*) and becomes the most important journal for British theater.		Edward Heath heads the Labour Party.
Agenda publishes Ted Hughes's "Cadenza" from *Lupercal*.		Bombing in American war in Vietnam escalates on both sides. New universities open in Kent and Warwick.
Image publishes an important special issue, "Kinetic Art: Concrete Poetry."		T. S. Eliot, Winston Churchill, Somerset Maugham die.
Duncan Glen attracts work from the best-known Scots poets for his new *Akros*.		
	1966	
Cambridge students begin *Solstice*; the first issue includes Anselm Hollo, Harry Guest, Gael Turnbull.		Edward Bond's controversial *Saved* is staged in London. Keith Douglas's *Collected Poems* appears, raises his importance as a war poet.
	1967	
Theatre at Work publishes series of interviews with new playwrights, assesses new plays.		Tom Stoppard's *Rosencrantz and Guildenstern Are Dead*, Pinter's *The Homecoming* debut in London.
Ramparts produces evidence for the funding by the American Central Intelligence Agency of *Encounter*.		Golding publishes *The Pyramid*, Isherwood *A Meeting by the River*, Auden *Collected Shorter Poems*.

BRITISH LITERARY PERIODICALS	YEAR	SOCIAL & LITERARY EVENTS
	(1967)	
English publishes a special issue including most of the major Scots poets.		Clement Attlee, John Masefield, Siegfried Sassoon die.
	1968	
Poets Michael Butler and Kemble Williams promote experiments in contemporary poetry in the East Anglian *Samphire*.		C. Day Lewis becomes poet laureate. Frederick Rolfe's *Hadrian VII*, Kingsley Amis's *I Want It Now* appear.
	1969	
Michael Horovitz publishes an anthology of underground poetry, *Children of Albion*, featuring many *New Departures* poets.		Prince Charles's investiture takes place at Caernarvon Castle. British army sends troops to quell rioting in Belfast. Samuel Beckett receives the Nobel Prize. Walter De la Mare's *Complete Poems* are published. Joe Orton's *What the Butler Saw* debuts in London. Osbert Sitwell, Ivy Compton-Burnett die.
	1970	
Contemporary Review begins a variety of articles regularly on British theater.		Prime Minister Edward Heath succeeds Harold Wilson in Conservative victory. C. P. Snow concludes the *Strangers and Brothers* novels. Muriel Spark publishes *The Driver's Seat*, Iris Murdoch *A Fairly Honorable Defeat*.

BRITISH LITERARY PERIODICALS	*YEAR*	*SOCIAL & LITERARY EVENTS*
	(1970)	
		The Royal Court Theatre stages David Storey's *Home* and *The Contractor*.
		E. M. Forster dies.
	1972	
		Britain imposes direct rule on Northern Ireland, enters the Common Market.
		Alan Ayckbourne's *Absurd Person Singular* opens in London.
		Ezra Pound, C. Day Lewis die.
	1973	
		Patrick White receives the Nobel Prize.
		David Storey's *The Changing Room* is named best play of the season by New York Drama Critics.
		Philip Larkin edits *The Oxford Book of Modern Verse*.
		Noel Coward, Elizabeth Bowen, W. H. Auden, J.R.R. Tolkien die.
	1975	
Workshop changes its name to *New Poetry*, continues to discover minor poets in Britain and publish them alongside better known poets D. M. Thomas, Ferlinghetti.		Margaret Thatcher leads the British Conservative Party.
		Inflation rate is 25 percent in Britain.
Martin Dodsworth becomes editor of *English*.		Peter Shaffer's *Equus* wins New York Drama Critics' and Tony awards in New York.

BRITISH LITERARY PERIODICALS	*YEAR*	*SOCIAL & LITERARY EVENTS*

	(1975)	
		Anthony Powell completes his twelve-volume *roman fleuve, A Dance to the Music of Time*.
		P. G. Wodehouse, Lionel Trilling die.
	1976	
Lines Review devotes the June issue to an appraisal of Robert Lowell by Philip Hobsbaum.		James Callaghan succeeds Harold Wilson as Prime Minister.
		Alan Ayckbourne's *Norman Conquests*, Stoppard's *Travesties* are performed in London and New York, respectively.
		Isaac Rosenberg's *Collected Poems* affirms his importance.
	1977	
Harold Hobson and John Russell Taylor join *Drama* and make it the most prestigious theater review in Britain.		Queen Elizabeth celebrates her Silver Jubilee.
		Simon Gray's *Otherwise Engaged* wins the New York Drama Critics' Award.
		John Fowles publishes *Daniel Martin*.
		Anthony Eden, Terence Rattigan, Anaïs Nin, Robert Lowell die.
	1978	
Lines Review reasserts its Scottish character, focusing on Aberdeen poets.		Margaret Thatcher moves to control immigration from the Caribbean and India.
Rising costs force the closing of London Magazine Editions.		First test-tube baby is born in Lancashire.

BRITISH LITERARY PERIODICALS	YEAR	SOCIAL & LITERARY EVENTS

(1978)

Spectator celebrates its 150th anniversary, *Encounter* its 25th.

The Arts Council contribution to *London Magazine* rises to 24,000 pounds.

G. Wilson Knight contributes a series of essays to the *Contemporary* on John Cowper Powys.

Iris Murdoch's *The Sea The Sea* wins the Booker Prize. Greene publishes *The Human Factor*.

F. R. Leavis, Hugh Ross Williamson, Hugh MacDiarmid die.

1979

Time and Tide, in decline since the death of founder and editor Margaret Haig, Viscountess Rhondda, in 1958, ends.

The *Contemporary* begins a series of essays on modern British theater. Charles Morovitz of the Open Space Theatre contributes several essays, one on "Ibsen, Strindberg, and the Sex War."

PN Review petitions to retain the older version of the *Book of Common Prayer*.

The *Times Literary Supplement* is closed over labor disputes.

Tambimuttu, at 65, publishes *Poetry London/Apple Magazine*, features rock lyricists.

Margaret Thatcher replaces Callaghan as Prime Minister.

Soviet Union invades Afghanistan; Khomeini deposes the Shah of Iran, takes American hostages.

Sir Anthony Blunt is revealed as a Soviet spy in World War II.

Kingsley Amis publishes *Collected Poems*, Ted Hughes *Remains of Elmet* and *Moortown*, Nadine Gordimer *Burger's Daughter*.

1980

New poets featured in *Lines Review* include Ian Abbot, Christopher Rush, Robert Preston Wales, and Iain Banforth.

Thatcher successfully protests the British share of payments to the European Economic Community.

BRITISH LITERARY PERIODICALS	YEAR	SOCIAL & LITERARY EVENTS

(1980)

In an essay in *London Magazine* Philip Larkin reaffirms Movement attitudes about poetry.

Gambit devotes issues to Steven Berkoff's London Theatre Group, Tom Stoppard, Polish and German theater.

In the *London Review of Books* Michael Sisson protests that too many books (45,000) are published in the U.K.

100,000 steelworkers strike the British Steel Corporation for thirteen weeks.

Olympic Games are held in Moscow.

Soviet dissident Sakharov stirs world attention when he is exiled to Gorky.

William Golding publishes *Rites of Passage* (which wins the Booker Prize), Burgess *Earthly Powers*, Margaret Drabble *The Middle Ground*.

C. P. Snow, Olivia Manning, Kenneth Tynan die.

1981

Samphire becomes a victim of its success; editors Michael Butler and Kemble Williams decide to end the magazine rather than rely on an editorial staff.

Thatcher applauds U.S. President Reagan's economic policies on a visit to the U.S.

The British Social Democratic Party gains official recognition as the third largest party.

Minorities in Brixton (Lambeth) riot for two days against British police harrassment.

Bobby Sands of the I.R.A. dies in a hunger strike, seeking to be classed as a political prisoner.

Prince Charles, Lady Diana marry.

D. M. Thomas publishes *The White Hotel*, Salman Rushdil *Midnight's Children*, Christopher Hope *A Separate Development*.

BRITISH LITERARY PERIODICALS	YEAR	SOCIAL & LITERARY EVENTS
	1982	
		Britain fights Argentina, reclaims the Falkland Islands.
		Queen Elizabeth signs agreement for Canada's statutory independence.
		John Paul II makes the first trip by a pope to Britain, meets Archbishop Runcle at Canterbury.
		Doris Lessing publishes her fourth novel in the *Canopus in Argos* series, Durrell *Constance*, Greene *Monsignor Quixote*.
		Archibald MacLeish, Kenneth Rexroth die.
	1983	
Plays and Players no longer publishes complete playscripts, citing the new Methuen "Theaterscripts."		Thatcher receives 397 of 650 votes to remain Prime Minister.
The thirtieth anniversary issue of *Encounter* includes a "conversation" by U.N. Ambassador Jeane Kirkpatrick on "American Foreign Policy in a Cold Climate."		Amid protests against U.S. missiles in Europe, the Anglican Church speaks out against unilateral disarmament.
		William Golding wins Nobel Prize.
		John Berger gives his earnings from the Booker Prize to a black liberation movement in protest of the Booker McConnel Company (West Indies).
		Donald Davie's *Collected Poems*, Ted Hughes's *The River*, Geoffrey Hill's *The Mystery of . . . Charles Péguy* are published.
		Beverly Nichols, Christina Stead, Rebecca West, Tambimuttu die.
	1984	
Agenda protests the parochialism of poets Ted Hughes and Philip Larkin.		

Scottish Literary Periodicals: A Selected List

Books in Scotland. Quarterly. Edinburgh. Published by the Ramsey Head Press. 1978–continuing. "A quarterly review of new books by Scottish writers, books about Scotland and books in general" which features articles on "contemporary writing, Authors Who's Who, Reading Lists, News and comments." Contributors: Allan Massie, Edwin Morgan, Iain Crichton Smith, Douglas Gifford, Ian Campbell, Marinell Ash, Naomi Mitchison. Editor—Norman Wilson.

Broadsheet. Irregular. Dublin, then Edinburgh. February 1967–June 1978. Format was a broadsheet with poems on either side and, occasionally, graphics. Almost all the work was previously unpublished and included Welsh, Russian, Gaelic, and "concrete" poetry, as well as work and commentary on the Irish situation. Contributors: Thomas Kinsella, Edwin Morgan, George MacBeth, Patrick Kavanagh, Seamus Heaney, John Montague, Yevgeny Yevtushenko, Earle Birney, Tom McGrath, Donald Campbell, Iain Crichton Smith, Norman MacCaig, Tom Leonard, Hamish Henderson. Editor—Hayden Murphy.

Cencrastus. Quarterly. Edinburgh. Autumn 1977– continuing. Designed to cover "Scottish and International Literature, Arts and Affairs." Emphasis is primarily literary, but also includes items on art, film, and contemporary politics. Contributors: David Daiches, Angus Calder, George Bruce, Michael Keating, Christopher Harvey, Edwin Morgan, Colin McCabe, Cairns Craig. Editors—initially a committee, but by summer 1981, Editor/Manager—Glen Murray; Autumn 1982—Sheila G. Hearn.

The Free Man. Weekly. Edinburgh. 6 February 1932–5 May 1934. "A Journal of Independent Thought" which combined literary and political content. Hugh MacDiarmid ran a regular column ("At the Sign of the Thistle") under his own name, Christopher Murray Grieve. Contributors: Robert Garioch, Neil Gunn, William Soutar, Lewis Grassic Gibbon (James Leslie Mitchell). Editor—Robin Black with the assistance of Dr. Stanley Robinson. Continued as *New Scotland* (1935–1936) and again as *The Free Man* until 1947.

Gairm. Quarterly. Glasgow. 1952–continuing. The leading Scottish Gaelic periodical for the last thirty years, it spearheaded the modern Gaelic literary renaissance. Content includes fiction, poetry, current affairs, criticism, and reviews. Contributors: George Campbell Hay, Feargus MacFhionnlaigh, Sorley MacLean, and Gaelic writers worldwide. Present editor—Derick S. Thomson.

Lallans. Biannually, May and November. Edinburgh. November 1973–continuing. "The Magazine for writing in Lowland Scots," carrying on the tradition set by Hugh Mac-Diarmid, who published his first poems in Lallans in the 1920s. Content includes poems, stories, articles, reviews, and editorials—all in Scots. Contributors: James King Annand, Robert Garioch, Ian Bowman, William Graham, A. D. Mackie, Alastair Mackie, Donald Campbell, Robert McLellan, George Campbell Hay, David Murison. Editors—1973–1983, James Annand King; 1983–present, Donald Campbell. There is an index to numbers 1–20.

The Literary Review. Fortnightly, then monthly. Edinburgh, then London. October 1979–continuing. Content includes poetry, short stories, reviews, articles, television and theater, notices, interviews, and essays on feminism. Contributors: Doris Lessing, Asa Briggs, Frank Johnson, Marina Warner, A. L. Rowse, Lisa St. Aubin de Teran, James Baldwin, Nadine Gordimer, Edwin Morgan, David Lodge, George MacBeth, Geoffrey Grigson. Editors—1979–1981, Anne Smith; 1982–present, Gillian Greenwood. In September 1982 became *"The Literary Review* incorporating *Quarto"* and was thereafter published in London.

The Modern Scot. Quarterly. Dundee (later St. Andrews). Spring 1930–January 1936. "Organ of the Scottish Renaissance," it continued the work begun by Hugh MacDiarmid's periodicals of the 1920s. Content mainly literary and political. Contributors: Sean O'Faolain, Hugh MacDiarmid, A. R. Orage, W. H. Auden, Major C. H. Douglas, Edwin Muir, Catherine Carswell, Herbert Read. Editor—J. H. Whyte. In April 1936 amalgamated with the *Scottish Standard* to form the *Outlook.* Selections from the periodical were published as *Towards a New Scotland: Being a Selection from 'The Modern Scot,'* ed. James H. Whyte (London, 1935).

*The New Edinburgh Review.*Triannually. Edinburgh (published by Edinburgh University Student Publications Board). February 1969–continuing. Content: not primarily literary but contains a considerable amount of articles, interviews, reviews, poems, short stories, etc., by Scottish writers. Contributors: Iain Crichton Smith, Alan Spence, Ron Butlin, Douglas Dunn, Edwin Morgan, Marcella Evaristi, Tom Nairn, Robert Garioch, Robin Fulton, Walter Perrie. Editors—1969, David Cubbitt; 1970, Julian Pollock and Brian Torode; 1971, Paul Atkinson; 1976, Murray Grigor; 1977, Tom Nairn; 1978, Owen Dudley Edwards; 1978, Bill Campbell; 1979, James Campbell; 1983, Allan Massie.

Poetry Scotland. Irregular. Glasgow, then Edinburgh. 1943–1946. Content: contemporary Scottish poetry. Contributors: Hugh MacDiarmid, Edwin Muir, Maurice Lindsay, William Jeffrey. Editor—Maurice Lindsay.

Scottish Arts and Letters. Intermittently. Glasgow. 1944–1950. Content: articles, reviews, literary criticism, poems, short stories, articles on fine art, and reproductions of work by Scottish artists (mainly J. D. Fergusson and William MacTaggart). Contributors: W. S.

Graham, Norman MacCaig, G. S. Fraser, William Soutar, Sorley MacLean, A. S. Neill, James Bridie, Sydney Goodsir Smith, Hugh MacDiarmid, Edwin Muir, William Jeffrey, Douglas Young, Robert Garioch, George Campbell Hay. Editors—R. Crombie Saunders and J. D. Fergusson (art editor).

Scottish International. "A Quarterly Review incorporating *Feedback*." Edinburgh. January 1968–1974 (published monthly in 1972). Content: poetry, short stories, reviews, and articles of international interest. Contributors: Edwin Morgan, Hamish Henderson, Christopher Harvey, Stanley Eveling, Anthony Ross, Iain Crichton Smith, Archie Hind, Alisdair Grau, Alan Spence, Tom McGrath. Editors—Robert Garioch, Edwin Morgan, Robert Tait (managing); 1974, Tom Buchan.

Scottish Literary Journal. Biannually. Aberdeen. July 1974–continuing. Published by the Association for Scottish Literary Studies as "A Review of Studies in Scottish Language and Literature." Content: emphasis is on scholarly articles on Scottish subjects, but also contains poems, reviews, etc. Publishes an annual supplement containing "The Year's Work in Scottish Literary and Linguistic Studies." Contributors: Kenneth Buthlay, Douglas S. Mack, Elizabeth Waterston, Alan Bell, Edwin Morgan, Ian Campbell, and Christopher Rush. Editor—Thomas Crawford.

Scottish Literary News. Biannually. Aberdeen. October 1970–December 1974. "Newsletter of the Association for Scottish Literary Studies," it grew out of the University Committee for Scottish Literature, founded in August 1970. Content: "The Year's Work in Scottish Literary Studies," scholarly articles, Gaelic studies, and folk literature. Contributors: Matthew P. MacDiarmid, Hamish Henderson, Edwin Morgan. Editors—1970, Thomas Crawford; December 1974, Alexander Scott. In 1974 many of its functions were taken over by the *Scottish Literary Journal*.

The Scottish Review: Arts and Environment. Quarterly. Glasgow (published by the Scottish Civic Trust and the Saltire Society in association with the Scottish Arts Council). Winter 1975–continuing. Content: social and literary. Contributors: Iain Crichton Smith, Derick Thomson, Edwin Morgan, Alan Spence, George Bruce, David Daiches, Maurice Lindsay, Naomi Mitchison, Alastair Fowler, Anthony Burgess, Liz Lochhead, Norman MacCaig, Robert Garioch. Editors—Lindsey MacLeod (Managing Editor), George Bruce, A. C. Davis, Gordon Huntly, Maurice Lindsay, Lorn M. Macintyre, Tom Markus, Alexander Scott.

Scottish Studies. Biannually from 1953–1973, then annually. Edinburgh. 1957–continuing. The journal of the School of Scottish Studies, Edinburgh University. Content is a "wide range of research into Scottish traditional life" contributed mainly by the staff of the school and other scholars in the field. Includes work in English, Scots, and Gaelic on folklore, songs, place names, riddles, the oral tradition, and transcripts from manuscripts and the tape-recorded archives of the school. Contributors: Hamish Henderson, I. A. Crawford, G.W.S. Barrow, A. J. Aitken, T. C. Smout, Alan Bruford, John MacQueen, David Craig, Anne Ross, Peter Cooke. Editors—1957–1964, J. Wreford Watson; 1964–1969, B.R.S. Megaw; 1969–present, John MacQueen.

Tocher. Triannually. Edinburgh. 1971–continuing. The sister journal to *Scottish Studies*, its content is based on "a selection of traditional material and memories from the archives of the School of Scottish Studies, Edinburgh University—directly transcribed with a minimum of editing, close attention given to dialect features from field recordings of informants, singers, storytellers and their families." Includes translations from Gaelic, music transcriptions and scores, poetry, place names, etc. Editor—Alan Bruford; Assistant Editor—Mary MacDonald.

The Voice of Scotland. Quarterly (irregular). Dunfermline, 1938–1939; Glasgow, 1945–1949; Edinburgh, 1955–1958. June 1938–1958. Content: "Scottish art and affairs" which included poetry, short stories, articles, book reviews, etc. Contributors: Norman MacCaig, Sydney Goodsir Smith, Edwin Morgan, Thurso Berwick, David Craig, Robert Garioch, Jessie Kocmanova. Editor—Hugh MacDiarmid. The numbers for 1938–1939 are indexed in *An Author Index to Selected British "Little Magazines," 1930–1939*, ed. Barry C. Bloomfield (London, 1976).

Catherine Kerrigan

Magazines with Short Runs

This appendix includes magazines with short runs, either in number of issues or length of time. The list of libraries includes only those with complete runs, unless complete runs are not available. The two indexes noted are: B. C. Bloomfield, ed., *An Author Index to Selected British Little Magazines, 1930–1939* (London, 1976); Marion Sader, ed., *Comprehensive Index to English-Language Little Magazines, 1890–1970*, series 1 (Millwood, N.Y., 1976).

Adelphi Magazine. One issue, June 1922. London. Edited by Henry Danielson. Decorations by C. Lovat Fraser. Not connected with the *Adelphi*,* 1923–1955.

Aengus. An All Poetry Journal. Midsummer, 1919. Dublin.

Air Force Poetry. 1944. Edited by John Pudney and Henry Treece.

Alba. A Scottish Miscellany in Gaelic and English. 1948. Glasgow.

Albananch. One issue, 1938. Edited by C. J. Russell and J. F. Hendry.

Albion. 1944–1947. Oswestry. Title changes: numbers 1–3: *New Saxon Pamphlets*; numbers 4–5: *New Saxon Review*.

The Antidote. Irregular. Numbers 1–4, 21 December 1912–12 June 1915. London. Edited by T.W.H. Crosland (numbers 1–3) and Lord Alfred Bruce Douglas (numbers 1–4). Number 4 includes Lord Alfred Douglas's attack on Robert Ross, in the aftermath of Wilde's "De Profundis."

Anvil: Life and the Arts. A Miscellany. Book 1, 1947.

The Apple (of Beauty and Discord). 1920–1922. Volume 1, numbers 1–4 in 1920; one number each in 1921 and 1922. London. Edited by Herbert Furst. Published by Colour Publishing Company. An elaborate and eclectic magazine, with many excellent reproductions. Among the contributors were John Rodker, Robert Graves, and Osbert Sitwell.

Arena. A Quarterly Review. Numbers 1–4, April 1937–January/March 1938. London. Edited by Martin Turnell. Not connected with the journal of the same title edited by Randall Swingler, 1912–1913. British Library, National Library of Scotland. Index: Bloomfield.

Argus: Political, Financial, Satirical and Theatrical. Numbers 1–15, October 1925– December 1926.

Arson. An Ardent Review. Part One of a Surrealist Manifestation. One issue, March 1942. London. Edited by Toni del Renzio, with associates John and Robert Melville and Conroy Maddox. Articles include a long essay by André Breton and one on surrealist poetry by Nicholas Calas.

The Arts. Numbers 1–2, 1946–1947. London. Edited by Desmond Shaw-Taylor.

The Arts and Philosophy. Numbers 1–2, Spring 1950–Autumn 1951. New series, numbers 1–?, Spring, 1962–? Edited by Sidney Arnold.

The Arts in War Time: A Report on the Work of C.E.M.A. (Council for the Encouragement of Music and the Arts) 1942/1943.

Axis. A Quarterly Review of Contemporary "Abstract" Painting and Sculpture. Numbers 1–8, 1935–Winter 1937. London. Edited by Myfanwy Evans. Index: Bloomfield.

Banba. Volumes 1–3, 1921–1922. Dublin. Printed in Gaelic and English.

Bill-o' Jack's Summer Annual. 1913, 1914. Rochdale. Edited by William Baron.

The Black Hat: An Unusual Review. Numbers 1–8, September 1930–October 1932. Edited by D. Thompson and H. Kelly.

The Blue Book. Conducted by Oxford Undergraduates. 1 May 1912–June 1913. London.

The Bond of Peace. Pamphlets 1–4, 1940. London. Published by the Peace Pledge Union. Contributors include Eric Gill and J. Middleton Murry.

The Book for the Train. One issue, 1946. Hunstanton.

A Book (Second Book, Third Book) of Poems by the Poet's Fellowship. 1920–1922. Bristol.

The Bookworm. Numbers 1–5, September/October 1929–May/June 1930. Incorporates *Onward*.

The Booster. A Monthly Magazine in French and English. Founded by the American Country Club of France. 1937–1938. Title, April–December 1938: *Delta*. Paris. Managing editor: Alfred Perles. In September 1937 *Booster* became a leading avant-garde magazine, with a staff of editors/contributors including Henry Miller, William Saroyan, Lawrence

Durrell, and Anaïs Nin. Three issues appeared as *The Booster*, three as *Delta*. Reprint: Johnson. Index: Sader.

Bristol Poets Fellowship Quarterly. Numbers 1–4, 1925–1926.

Broadsheet. 1942–1943.

The Burning Bush. Numbers 1–6, 4 June 1928–1930. Eton.

Cambridge Left. Volumes 1–2, Summer 1933–Autumn 1934.

Cambridge Writing. Numbers 1–8, 1948–1952. Cambridge University Young Writers Group.

The Candle. Numbers 1–4, January 1938–June 1940. Edited by Oliver W.F. Lodge. Numbers 1–3 published by Holmburg St. Mary; number 4 by College of William and Mary, Virginia.

Carmina. A Review Devoted to Poetry. Numbers 1–12, August 1930–1932. London. Westcliff-on-Sea. Edited by Maurice Leahy.

Carnaval. Numbers 1–6, June 1946–July 1947. London.

The Cartoon. Numbers 1–14, 4 February–6 May 1915.

The Catacomb. Numbers 1–14, April 1949–May 1950. Monthly. New series, number 4, Summer 1950–Winter 1951/1952. Quarterly. Edited by Robert Lyle and Roy Campbell.

Causerie: The Intimate Magazine. Numbers 1–4, November 1939–February 1940. Edited by Horace Shipp.

Cerebrilist. One issue, December 1913. Edited by E. H. Preston; founded by E. C. Grey.

Change: The Beginning of a Chapter in Twelve Volumes. Volumes 1–2, January–February 1919. Edited by John Hilton and Joseph Thorpe.

The Chapbook. The Magazine of the Glasgow Literary Club. Numbers 1–4, 1934–1935. No connection with London *Chapbook*.

Cheerio! A Magazine Produced and Published by the Unemployed Clerical Workers in the Occupational Centres of Birkenhead. Volume 1, number 1–volume 2, number 5, December 1932–March 1934. Birkenhead. Reproduced from typewriting.

The Chelsea Review. Numbers 1–2, March–April 1928.

Circus: The Pocket Review of Our Times. Numbers 1–3, April–June 1950. Edited by Randall Swingler, with John Davenport and Paul Hogarth.

Civvy Street: The Magazine for All Ex-service Men and Women. June 1946–1947. Absorbed *Khaki and Blue.*

The Colosseum: The Quarterly of Action, Not a Polite Review. Volumes 1–5, numbers 1–22, March 1934–July/September 1939. Subtitle varies.

Contemporaries and Makers. 1933. Continued as *Contemporaries.* Summer 1933–1935. Quarterly. Cambridge. Edited by John Kaestlin.

Contemporary Issues. Summer 1948. London.

Contemporary Poetry and Prose.* Numbers 1–10, May 1936–Autumn 1937. London.

Convoy. Numbers 1–6, February 1944–1947. Number 2 as *Convoy File*, number 6 as *Christmas Convoy.* London.

The Country Heart. A Quarterly Magazine. Numbers 1–8, January/March 1921–October/December 1922. Supersedes *Vineyard Magazine.*

The Critic. 1 January 1914.

The Critic. A Quarterly Review of Criticism. Volume 1, numbers 1–2, Spring, Autumn, 1947. London. Published by the Critic Press, Mistley. Incorporated in *Politics and Letters.* Edited by Wolf Mankowitz, Clifford Collins, and Raymond Williams.

Critic. Literature, Art, Music, Drama. Numbers 1–2, March 1928, April 1929. London. Titled also *Free Critic.* New York Public Library.

Crux: Controversial—Constructive—Critical. 1940. Glasgow. British Library.

David. An International Review of Politics and Literature. Numbers 1–3, March–May 1932. Edited by A. J. Henderson, Allan N. Taylor, and Erik Warman.

Delphic Review. An Anarchistic Quarterly. Volume 1, numbers 1–2, Winter 1949–Spring 1950. Fordingbridge. Edited by Albert J. McCarthy.

Delta. See *The Booster.*

Dial Monthly. A Magazine for Church Women and Others. Volume 1, number 1–volume 2, number 19, January 1913–July 1914. Contributors include Katherine Tynan and Thomas Moult.

Dope. Numbers 1–2, 1932. Edited by Bernard Causton. Index: Bloomfield.

Down West. Being the Year Book of the West Country Essay Club. 1923–1924.

Emotionism. One issue, February 1928. Contributors include Peggy Ashcroft.

English Life and Language. Volume 1, number 1–volume 2, number 24, January 1946–December 1947.

Envoy. A Review of Literature and Art. Volumes 1–5, numbers 1–20, December 1949–July 1951. Dublin.

Epilogue. A Critical Summary. Volumes 1–4, 1935–1938. Annual. Deya, Majorca; London. Edited by Laura Riding and Robert Graves. Number 4 is a monograph, *The World and Ourselves*, by Laura Riding.

Equator. Numbers 1–2? December 1945–? Mombassa Arts Club. Edited by Edward Lowbury. Contributors include Roy Campbell, Roy Fuller, and John Press.

The Eton Candle. Volume 1, March 1922. Eton. Edited by Brian Howard. This school magazine includes a supplement with material from Old Etonians, including Osbert and Sacheverell Sitwell and Aldous Huxley.

Exile. Numbers 1–4, Spring 1927–Autumn 1928. Dijon, France; Chicago. Edited by Ezra Pound. Index: Sader.

Farrago. Numbers 1–6, February 1930–June 1931. Quarterly. Oxford. Edited by Peter Burra. Index: Bloomfield.

The Fight Against Superstition, Clericalism and Cultural Revolution. Numbers 1–4, January ?–December 1934. Published by the League of Socialist Freethinkers.

The Fig Tree. A Douglas Social Credit Quarterly Review. Numbers 1–12, 1936–1939. Belfast; London. Published by the Social Credit Secretariat, Ltd. Contributors include Ezra Pound and Eric Gill.

Focus. Numbers 1–4, Summer 1938–Summer 1939. London.

Focus One (-Five). 1945–1950. Edited by B. Rajan and Andrew Pearse.

Form. A Monthly Magazine Containing Poetry, Sketches, Essays of Literary and Critical Interest. Volume 1, numbers 1–2, April 1916–April 1917. Edited by Austin O. Spare. Published by John Lane.

Form. A Monthly Magazine: New Series. Volume 1, numbers 1–3, October 1921–January 1922. Edited by Austin O. Spare, W.H. Davies. Published by Morland Press Ltd. Subtitle varies. Reprint: Kraus. Index: Sader.

The Forum. Numbers 1–9/10, November 1921–August 1922. Edited by C. F. Holland and W. R. Marshall.

Forum. Stories and Poems. Numbers 1–2, Summer 1949–1950. Edited by Muriel Spark. Derek Stanton was coeditor for the second number.

Free Expression. Numbers 1–9(?), December 1939–August 1941(?) Contributors include Ethel Mannin.

Free Unions. One issue, July 1946. Edited by Simon Watson Taylor. Associated with Surrealist Group in England.

Frontline. Bulletin of Front Line Generation. One issue, 1946.

Gemini. A Pamphlet Magazine of New Poetry. Numbers 1–5, May 1949–September 1950. Edited by Frederick Vanson. Derby.

Germinal. Illustrated Monthly. Numbers 1–2, July 1923, July 1924.

The Glass. A Literary Magazine Devoted to Imaginative and Introspective Writing. Numbers 1–8, 1948–1953. Lowestoft. Edited by Antony Borrow.

Golden Star. Numbers 1–76, 4 March 1939–17 August 1940.

Good Luck. The New Paper for Men and Women. Numbers 1–28, May–November 1919. Merged into *Home Companion*.

Grangewood Magazine. March 1933.

Gypsy. Volume 1, numbers 1–2, May 1915, May 1916. London. Pomegranate Press.

The Hamyarde. Volume 1, number 1, October 1922; volume 2, number 1, November 1922. Edited by Anthony Praga with Charles Beard and George Hill.

Harlequin. Numbers 1–2, 1949–1950. Oxford. Edited by Oliver Carson and Anthony Blond. Merged with *Panorama*.

Here and Now. A Group Production. Poetry—Prose—Drawing. Subtitle varies. Numbers 1–5, 1941–1949. Edited by Peter Albery and Sylvia Read.

Here Today. Numbers 1–4, 1944–1945. Reading. Edited by Pierre Edmunds and Roland Mathias. Emphasis on local drama and local writing.

Hillmn. Numbers 1–5, July 1920–July 1921. Edited by Ernest Collings and Vera Millar.

Indian Writing. A Quarterly. Numbers 1–4, 1940–1941, number 5, ?

Irish Review. A Monthly Magazine of Irish Literature, Art & Science. Volumes 1–4, numbers 1–42, March 1911–November 1914.

The Island. A Quarterly. Numbers 1, 2/3, 4, June, September, December 1931. London. Edited by Josef Bard. Index: Bloomfield.

I Spy. Spring 1939. Saint Leonards. Edited by Donald B. Cameron.

Jazz Forum. Quarterly Review of Jazz and Literature. Numbers 1–5, 1946–Autumn 1947. Fordingbridge. Edited by Albert J. McCarthy.

Khaki and Blue. Numbers 1–5, Summer 1944–1945. London. Edited by Peter Ratazzi. Merged with *Civvy Street.*

Leaven. One issue, Easter 1946. Croydon. Edited by John Bate. Supersedes *Oasis.*

Letters. A Journal of Correspondence and Debate. One issue, 10 September 1922. Conducted by J. L. Hornibrook.

The "Lisp of Leaves." A Magazine for Discerning People. Volume 1, numbers 1–9, April–December 1949. Lancaster. Continued as *The North-west Monthly Incorporating The "Lisp of Leaves."*

Literary Review. Numbers 1–11, 1936–1937. Index: Bloomfield (except issues 6, 7, 9).

The Little Revue. Numbers 1–3, February–April 1939. Edinburgh.

The Liverpool Chapbook. One issue, 1920. Liverpool.

Lloyd's Saturday Stories. Numbers 1–44, 1921–1922.

London Forum. One issue, July 1931. Edited by Harold Kelly and Bonar Thompson.

London Forum. A Quarterly Review of Literature, Art and Current Affairs. Numbers 1–4, 1946–1947. London. Edited by Peter Baker and Roland Gant (number 1), Warwick Charlton (numbers 3–4).

Loqueia Mirabilis. Volume 1, number 1–volume 2, number 1, November 1936–May 1937. Langford (Bristol). University of Kansas, New York Public Library; British Library.

The Magazine of Today. An Illustrated Review of Modern Life and Literature. Numbers 1–5, May–September 1930. Succeeded by *Today and Tomorrow. A Review of Modern Life.*

Man. One issue, March 1915. Continued as *Superman*, 1915–1916.

Manuscript: A Bimonthly. Numbers 1–3, June, August/September, November/December 1941. Southampton.

Melody. Volume 1, number 1–volume 2, number 2, 1931–1933. Cambridge. National Poetry Circle. Merged with *Rejection.*

Mid-day. 1946–1947. Oxford. Quarterly. Edited by Antoinette Pratt Barlow.

Million. New Left Writing. The People's Review. Numbers 1–3, 1943. Glasgow. Occasional. Early issues undated. Edited by John Singer.

The Modern Scot. Volumes 1–6, Spring 1930–January 1936. Dundee. Merged with *Scottish Standard* to form *Outlook.* Index: Bloomfield.

The Monologue. Numbers 1–24, 1 February 1934–5 February 1935. Edited by Lyn Irvine. Reproduced from typewriting.

Motley. One issue, 1 November 1930. Oxford.

My Queen Magazine. Numbers 1–12, 21 July–17 November 1914.

New Britain. A Weekly Organ of National Renaissance. Volume 1, number 1–volume 3, number 64, 24 May 1933–8 August 1934. New series, volume 1, number 1, Autumn 1934. London. Edited by C. B. Purdom. Merged into *Eleventh Hour for New Order in Great Britain.*

New Days. Volume 1, number 1–volume 2, number 3, 18 September 1915–1 April 1916. London. Edited by Louis Vincent. Subtitle varies.

New Era. 1946.

New Generation. Numbers 1–2, Spring/Summer 1946, Winter 1947. Edited by Peter Ratazzi. Affiliated with the "Front Line Generation."

The New Keepsake. One issue, 1931. Decorations by Rex Whistler.

The New Keepsake for the Year 1921. Le Nouveau Keepsake pour l'année 1921. London; Paris. Edited by X. M. Boulestin. Plates selected by J. E. Laboureur. Published by Chelsea Book Club. Includes work by Harold Monro, Richard Aldington, Aldous Huxley, D. H. Lawrence.

New Numbers. Numbers 1–4, February–December 1914. Ryton. Works solely of Rupert Brooke, Lascelles Abercrombie, John Drinkwater, and W. W. Gibson; includes Brooke's war sonnets.

The New Oxford Outlook. Volume 1, number 1–volume 2, number 3, May 1933–November 1935. Supersedes *Oxford Outlook.* Index: Bloomfield.

New Poetry. One issue, 1945. Edited by Nicholas Moore.

The New Review. An International Notebook for the Arts. Volume 1, numbers 1–5, January/February 1931–April 1932. Paris.

The New Saxon Pamphlets. Numbers 1–5, March 1944–1947. Numbers 4–5 as *New Saxon Review.* Irregular. Oswestry. Edited by John Atkins.

The New Saxon Review. See *The New Saxon Pamphlets.*

New Scotland (Alba Nuadh). Numbers 1–9, 12 October–7 December 1935. Glasgow.

The New Weekly. 1914. London.

Night and Day. Numbers 1–26, July–December 1937. Index: Bloomfield.

Northern Lights. Numbers 1–2, 1939. Harrogate. Edited by Alan Hadfield.

Now-a-days. Book Reviews, Theatre, Music, Poetry, Art. Volume 1, numbers 1–5, 1947–1948. Brighton. Edited by Cyril Stone.

Oasis. 1951. Cambridge.

Oasis. An Anthology to Divert an Idle Hour. 1943–1944. Croydon. Edited by John Bate and Conan Nicholas. Superseded Easter 1946 by *Leaven*.

Onward. Numbers 1–2, 1928. Became *Bookworm*.

Opus. Numbers 1–14, 1940–1943. Tring. Edited by Denys Val Baker.

Orpheus. A Symposium of the Arts. Volumes 1–2, 1948–1949. London. Edited by John Lehmann. Supersedes *New Writing and Daylight*.

Outlook. Incorporating The Modern Scot and The Scottish Standard. Numbers 1–10, April 1936–January 1937. Glasgow.

Out of Bounds. Against Reaction in the Public Schools. Numbers 1–4, March/April 1934–June 1935. Subtitle varies. Edited by Esmond Romilly.

The Outpost. A Monthly Magazine of Literature, Art & National Life. Numbers 1–5, June–December 1925.

The Palatine Review. Numbers 1–5, January/February 1916–March 1917. Oxford. Edited by T. W. Earp (?).

The Panton Magazine. Literature, Art, Music, Drama. Numbers 1–4, January/March–October/December 1927. London. Organ of the Panton Arts Club.

The Patch-box. One issue, 1914.

Personal Landscape. Volume 1, parts 1–4, 1942(?)–1945. Cairo. Edited by Lawrence Durrell, Bernard Spencer, and Robin Felden.

Phoenix. Numbers 1–2, December 1938–July 1939. Eastbourne. Edited at Eastbourne College in aid of distressed areas.

Phoenix: A Literary Journal. 1942–1946? Manchester; Lewes. Edited by Norman Swallow and Nigel Storm.

Phoenix: A Magazine for Young Writers. 1939–1942. Ayton. Edited by Cynthia Crashaw, Norman Hampson, Norman Swallow, and Basil Widger.

Phoenix Quarterly: A Journal Devoted towards the Recovery of Unity in Religion, Politics and Art. Numbers 1–3, Autumn 1946–April 1948. London. Edited by Maurice Cranston.

Ploy. 1945. Glasgow. Edited by R. Crombie Saunders.

Poesy. Volume 1, number 1–volume 2, number 15, July 1915–November 1917. Bishop Auckland. Edited by E. Herdman. Volume 1 bound as *Gathered Leaves*.

The Poet. Volume 1, number 1–volume 4, number 3, 1936–1939. Bolerno (Midlothian).

Poetry and the People. Numbers 1–20, July 1938–September 1940. London. Poetry Group of the Left Book Club. Merged with *Our Time*. Index: Bloomfield.

Poetry Folios. Numbers 1–10, 1942–1946. London; Barnet. Edited by Alex Comfort and Peter Wells.

Poetry Ireland. Numbers 1–19, number 20 supplement to *Irish Writing*, April 1948–October 1952. Cork.

Poetry Manchester. June 1951. Manchester Public Library.

Poetry of To-Day. Numbers 1–2, January/February 1919–November/December 1920. New series, volumes 1–10, June 1924–1938. London. Subtitle varies. Two series of supplements to the *Poetry Review*.

Poetry Quarterly. Volume 1, numbers 1–6, 1933–1934. Spring 1934 issue entitled *Poetry Quarterly and Dramatic Review*. London. Edited by William Kingston Fudge, George Whybrow. Not connected with *Poetry Quarterly*,* 1939, which succeeded *Poetry Studies*. Index: Bloomfield.

Poetry—Scotland. Numbers 1–3, 1943–1946; number 4, 1949. Glasgow. Edited by Maurice Lindsay. Hugh McDiarmid guest editor for number 4.

Poets Now in the Services. Numbers 1–?, 1942–? London. Edited by A. E. Lowry. A small collection of war verse.

Poets of Tomorrow: First (-Third) Selection. 1939–1942. Number 2 also entitled *Cambridge Poetry, 1940*. London.

Polemic. A Magazine of Philosophy, Psychology and Aesthetics. Numbers 1–8, September 1945–1947. Edited by Humphrey Slater.

Politics and Letters. Numbers 1–7, Summer 1947–Summer 1948. London. Edited by Raymond Williams, C. S. Collins, Wolf Mankowitz. Incorporated *Critic*.

Prose. Numbers 1–4, August–November 1936. Index: Bloomfield.

Prospect. See *Resistance*.

The Quiet Hour. Numbers 1–12, November 1937–October 1938. Birmingham. Edited by James Bailey.

Quill Magazine. A Quarterly of Letters and Poems. 1963.

The Quorum. A Magazine of Friendship. One issue, 1920.

Rann. A Quarterly of Ulster Poetry. Numbers 1–17, 1948–1953. Belfast. Subtitle varies slightly.

The Reading Lamp. Numbers 1–9, August 1946–August 1947.

The Realist. A Journal of Scientific Humanism. Volumes 1–3, April 1929–January 1930. Edited by Archibald Church, Gerald Heard. Contributors include Arnold Bennett, Rebecca West, John Galsworthy.

Rejected Mss. Number 1, January 1934. Oxford. Continued as *Rejected Mss. and Other*, number 2, December 1934. Edited by N. F. Hidden, H. D. Wilcock, N. R. Cohn. Index: Bloomfield.

Rejection. A Magazine of Literary and General Interest. Volume 1, number 1–volume 2, number 11, 1932–1934. Absorbed *Melody*.

Resistance. A Social-Literary Magazine. One issue, October 1946. London. Edited by Derek Stanford and David West. Merged with *Prospect*.

"Resurgam" Younger Poets. Broadsheets Written under the Impact of War. Numbers 1–8(?), 1940–(?) London. Contents in anthology, *Today's New Poets*, 1944.

Reveille. Devoted to the Disabled Sailor and Soldier. Numbers 1–3, August 1918–February 1919. Edited by John Galsworthy; assistant editor C. S. Evans. Continuation of nonliterary journal, *Recalled to Life*.

Review–43 (–46). Winter 1943/Summer 1946.

Root and Branch. A Seasonal of the Arts. Bognor, Flansham. Volumes 1–3, Spring 1912–1926? Edited by James Guthrie. Includes work by W. H. Davies and Edward Thomas.

Salamander. Egypt; Southsea 1941–? Edited by John Cromer and John Gawsworth.

Satire and Burlesque. Volume 1, number 1–volume 2, number 5, October 1934–July/August 1935.

Scots Writing. Glasgow. 1943(?)–? Occasional. Edited by P. McCrory and Alec Donaldson. British Library, National Library of Scotland.

Scottish Art and Letters. Numbers 1–5, 1944–1950. Edited by R. Crombie Saunders; art editor J. D. Ferguson. Annual. Hugh MacDiarmid was literary editor for number 5.

The Scottish Bookman. Numbers 1–6, September 1935–February 1936. Edinburgh. Edited by David Cleghorn Thomson. Young Scottish writers contributed.

Scottish Periodical. Numbers 1–2, Summer 1947, Summer 1948. Edinburgh. Edited by Ronald Gregor Smith.

The Scottish Standard. Volume 1, numbers 1–13, February 1935–February 1936. Glasgow. Merged with the *Modern Scot* to form *Outlook*.

Seascape. The Coast Quarterly. Summer 1946–Autumn 1948(?) Edited by A. William Ellis.

Seed. A Quarterly Journal. January–April/July 1933. London. Edited by Herbert Jones, Oswell Blakeston.

Selected Writing. Numbers 1–5, 1941–1946. Occasional. Edited by Reginald Moore.

Short Stories. Volume 1, numbers 1–19, 30 May–3 October 1914.

Signature. Numbers 1–3, 4 October–1 November 1915. Edited by John Middleton Murry, D. H. Lawrence, Katherine Mansfield. Made up of contributions by the editors; Mansfield's are signed "Matilda Berry."

Soma. Numbers 1–5, June 1931–1934. Published by K. S. Bhat. Index: Bloomfield.

Songs for Sixpence. A Series of Single New Poems by Young Cambridge Poets. Numbers 1–6, 1929.

Static. Numbers 1–3?, 1931? Edited by Richard Kersey, T.J.B. Spencer.

Stories. A Magazine Devoted to Fiction. Numbers 1–2, July, August 1923.

Storm. Stories of the Struggle. A Magazine of Socialist Fiction. Numbers 1–3, 1933. Index: Bloomfield.

Superman. Continuation of *Man*.

The Survey. Numbers 1–3, November 1933–January 1934.

Tattoo. A Pegasus Publication. Numbers 1–4, 1946–1947. Glasgow. Edited by Patrick McCrory.

Tempest. A Collection of Prose Writings. October 1943–? London. Edited by John Leatham, Neville Braybrooke. Emphasized works of fantasy, allegory.

This Week. Numbers 1–6, 1939.

Today. New series, numbers 1–2, 6 May 1916–6 January 1917. London. Supersedes *T. P.'s Weekly* (1902–1916) and superseded by *To-Day** (see *VEA*).

Today and Tomorrow. A Review of Modern Life. Volume 1, number 1–volume 4, number 2, October 1930–New Year 1934. London. Incorporates *The Magazine of Today*.

Tomorrow. Numbers 1–2, August–September 1924. Dublin.

Translation. Two issues, 1945, 1947. Edited by Neville Braybrooke, Elizabeth King.

Triad. Volumes 1–2, 1946–1947. Edited by Jack Alstrop. A miscellany.

The Trifle. A Monthly Magazine. Numbers 1–2, July–August 1915.

The Tyro. A Review of the Arts of Painting, Sculpture and Design. Numbers 1–2, 1921–1922. Edited by P. Wyndham Lewis. Published by Egoist Press. Lewis's second magazine, after *Blast** (1914–1915). Partly supported by Sydney Schiff and Edward Wadsworth. Work by Lewis, T. S. Eliot (in part under the pseudonym "Gus Krutzsch"), Herbert Read, Jacques Lipschitz, and former vorticists. Reprint: Frank Gass & Co., 1970.

Ulster Parade. Numbers 1–12, 1941–1947. Belfast. Some numbers lack date.

Ulster Voices. 1943. Belfast. Edited by Ed Roy McFadden, Robert Creacen.

The Venture. Numbers 1–6, October 1928–June 1930. Cambridge. Edited by Anthony Blunt, H. Romily Fedden, Michael Redgrave. Index: Bloomfield (numbers 5, 6).

Viewpoint. A Critical Review. Numbers 1–2, April–September 1934. Croydon. Edited by D. A. Willis. Absorbed by *Left Review*.* Index: Bloomfield.

The Vine. A Volume from the Symbolists' Press. 1917. Birmingham.

Vision. A Magazine and Review of Mysticism. Volume 1, number 1–volume 2, number 7, 1920. Edited by Dorothy Grenside, Galloway Kyle.

Voice of Scotland. A Quarterly Magazine of Scottish Arts and Affairs. June 1928–August 1939. Dumfermline. Reappeared 1945–1949, 1955–1958. Index: Bloomfield.

Voices. An Anthology of Individualist Writings. Numbers 1–6, 1943–1946; new series, 1946. Wigginton and Port Isaac. Edited by Denys Val Baker. Supersedes *Opus*.

The Voyager. Numbers 1–4, March–June 1924. Bristol. Edited by S. W. Smith.

Wanderer. Numbers 1–11/12, December 1933–November 1934. Larling. Edited by John Middleton Murry. Index: Bloomfield.

West Country Magazine. Volume 1, number 1–volume 7, number 3, Summer 1946–Autumn 1952. Denham.

The Window. Numbers 1–8, 1951–1955. Edited by John Stankey, Philip Inman.

The Window. A Quarterly Magazine. Numbers 1–4, January–October 1930. London. Edited by Eric Partridge, Bertram Ratcliffe. Index: Bloomfield.

Writers of the Midlands. Numbers 1–2, 1946–1947. Birmingham. Edited by Stanley Derricourt.

Writing Today. Numbers 1–4, October 1943–December 1946. Tring. Edited by Denys Val Baker.

Yellowjacket. Numbers 1–2, March–May 1939. London. Index: Bloomfield.

Youth. The Authors' Magazine. Numbers 1–3, 15 February–June 1922. Not connected with *Youth*, 1920–1934.

Susan J. Hanna

Index

Abbot, Ian, 235
Abel, Deryck, 96, 98
Abercrombie, Lascelles, 238
Abinger Chronicle, 1–4
Abse, Dannie, 26, 331–32, 372, 487, 510; *Poems, Golders Green*, 394
Abyssinian War, 449
Academic magazines: *Cambridge Journal*, 80–82; *Critical Quarterly*, 121–24; *English*, 164–68; *Experiment*, 177–79; *Kingdom Come*, 211–15; *Mandrake*, 261; *New Measure*, 282–83; *Poetry Nation*, 364–65; *Solstice*, 434–36; *Scrutiny*, 423–28; *Review of English Literature*, 406–8; *Universities' Poetry*, 473
Achebe, Chinus: *Things Fall Apart*, 406
Action, 277
Action Française, 115, 409
Actors' Studio, 147
Aczel, John, 282
Adagio Press, 52
Adam International Review, 4–7, 151, 153
Adamov, Arthur, 506
Adams, B. M. W., 461
Adams, John J., 461, 463, 494
Adams, Sam, 370, 372
Addison, Joseph, 107, 391
Adeane, Louis: "A Visit to Madame Zena," 319

Adelphi, 8–18, 279, 360
Adler, Alfred, 380–85
Adler, Henry, 278
A. E. *See* Russell, George
Aeschylus, 197; *Prometheus Bound*, 407
Afrikaans poetry, 22. *See also* South African literature
Agar, Eileen, 242
Agate, James, 501
Agenda, 18–21, 365
Agnes, Mary, 503
Agriculture, 453–54
Aiken, Conrad: American editor for *Coterie*, 110–13; "Blind Date," 285; contributes to *Bermondsey*, 46; to *Criterion*, 118; to *Experiment*, 178; to *Horizon*, 205; to *London Mercury*, 251; to *New Poetry*, 284; to *Twentieth Century Verse*, 469; *Ushant*, 111
Aitchison, Craigie, 510
Aitchison, James, 416
Aitchison, John, 104
Akhmadulina, Bella, 435
Akhmatova, Anna, 129
Akros, 21–24
Alcock, R. A., 178
Alden Press, 216
Aldington, Richard: "Concert," 33; contributes to *Adelphi*, 16; to *Arts and Letters*, 33; to *Coterie*, 112; to *Crite-*

rion, 116; to *Encounter*, 157; to *Ex-periment*, 178; to *Time and Tide*, 448; to *Voices*, 480; defends D. H. Lawrence, 157; edits *Egoist*, 144; futurist manifesto in *Blast*, 63, 65; on *Nine*, 312; "Postlude," 33

Algren, Nelson, 340

Allen, Carleton Kemp, 96, 391

Allen, M. E., 131

Allen, Percy, 136

Allen, W. Gore, 36

Allen, Walter, 156–57, 167, 303, 312, 324, 338–39

Allied Artists Association, 61

Allmand, Michael, 496–97

Allott, Kenneth, 284, 293, 361, 470

Almansi, Guido, 401

Alvarez, Alfred: contributes to *Encounter*, 159; to *London Magazine*, 246; to *Mandrake*, 262–63; to *Review*, 393–95, 397–98; in *Review* anthology, 395; *The New Poetry*, 394; *The Shaping Spirit*, 98; *Twelve Poems*, 398

Alvinsleben, Werner, 243

Amata, Mara, 274

American Scholar, 85

American writers: in *Agenda*, 19; *Calendar of Modern Letters*, 77; *Contemporary Poetry and Prose*, 87; *Coterie*, 110–12; *Critical Quarterly*, 122; *Encounter*, 154–58; *Horizon*, 203, 206; *Kingdom Come*, 212–14; *Lilliput*, 229; *London Magazine*, 246, 247, 249; *New Measure*, 283; *New Road*, 287; *Penguin New Writing*, 340; *Penguin Parade*, 346; *Review*, 396–97; *Solstice*, 434; *Time and Tide*, 448; *Transatlantic Review*, 459–63. *See also* specific authors

Amis, Kingsley: *Alterations*, 400; contributes to *Encounter*,156; to *London Magazine*, 245–46; to *Mandrake*, 263; to *Outposts*, 331; to *Priapus*, 379; *I Want It Now*, 400; in *Priapus* anthology, 378; *Lucky Jim*, 307; reviewed in *Mandrake*, 262; in *Nimbus*, 307; in *Review*, 401; in *Writing Today*, 505

Amis, Martin, 400–402; *It's Disgusting at Your Age*, 401

Anand, Mulk Rah, 338

Anderson, Lindsay, 148, 149

Anderson, Sherwood, 14, 223, 480; "The Corn Planting," 346

Andrews, Michael, 510

Angell, Norman, 446

Anglo-Welsh Review, 24–27, 485

Angold, J. P., 277

Annand, J. K., 22, 23, 233, 234

Anouilh, Jean, 98, 137

Anson, Peter, 56

Ansorge, Peter, 350, 354

Antheil, George, 461, 463

Antisemitism, 390, 410, 455

Antonucci, Emil, 375

Anvil Press Poetry, 282

ap Dafydd, Gwilym, 372

ap Gwynn, Aneirin, 483

Apocalyptic poets: featured in *Kingdom Come*, 212–14; in *Life and Letters*, 226; in *New Road*, 287; in *Poetry Commonwealth*, 357; in *Poetry Quarterly*, 367–68; in *Seven*, 430–32; identified with *Poetry (London)*, 359–60; reviewed in *Our Time*, 328

Apollinaire, Guillaume, 374; *Bestiary*, 374

Appel, Benjamin, 290

Aquinas, Thomas, 56

Arabic folk poems, 438

Aragon, Louis, 28, 325, 367

Arbuthnot, Malcolm, 65

Arbuzov, Aleksey: *Fiddler on the Roof*, *The Promise*, 187

Archard, Cary, 372

Archdale, Helen, 443

Archer, E., 112

Archer, William, 46, 136, 182

Arden, John, 146, 149, 189

Arden, Mary. *See* Le Maistre, Violet

Ardizzone, Edward, 6

Arena, 28–31

Arena Publications, 28, 31

ARIEL: A Review of International English Literature, 408

Armitage, John, 184

Armstrong, William, 166
Arnell, Charles John, 127–29
Arnold, Audrey M., 261
Arnold, G. L., 83
Arnold, Matthew, 78, 106, 465
Aron, Raymond, 156
Arp, Hans, 294
Arrabal, Fernando: *The Solemn Communion*, 187
Arson, an Ardent Review, 88
Art and Artists, 350
Art and Letters, 31–34, 111
Art and Science, 220
Art criticism: in *Blast*, 65; *Enquiry*, 171; *Golden Hind*, 196; *Horizon*, 203–4; *New English Weekly*, 278; *Penguin New Writing*, 339; *Poor. Old. Tired. Horse.*, 374-75; *Scrutiny*, 426; *Transatlantic Review*, 461; *Writing Today*, 505; *X: Quarterly Review*, 510. *See also* Surrealism; Vorticism
Art reproductions: in *Adam*, 5, 7; *Blast*, 68; *Coterie*, 110; *Golden Hind*, 194–95; *Horizon*, 206; *Kingdom Come*, 219; *Lilliput*, 229; *London Bulletin*, 241–42; *London Magazine*, 247; *London Mercury*, 251, 254; *New Departures*, 273–74; *New English Weekly*, 278; *Orion*, 324, 325; *Owl*, 334; *Penguin New Writing*, 340; *Penguin Parade*, 348; *Poor. Old. Tired. Horse.*, 374-75; *Priapus*, 378; *Solstice*, 434, 435; *Time and Tide*, 450; *Townsman*, 455; *Transatlantic Review*, 461; *Voices*, 479; *Wheels*, 491–94
Arthur Press, 164
Arts Council: aids *Anglo–Welsh Review*, 26–27; *Lines Review*, 234; *London Magazine*, 248; *New Departures*, 275; *New Measure*, 282; *Nimbus*, 306; *Poetry Wales*, 370; *Review*, 399; *Saltire Review*, 415; *Universities' Poetry*, 473; effect on *Our Time*, 329; urged to support theater, 100
Arundel, Honor, 331
Asch, Nathan, 462, 463
Ascham, Roger: *The Scholemaster*, 52
Ashbery, John, 366

Asquith, H. H., 442
Astley, Neil, 439
Aston, George, 181
Athenaeum, 8–9; *See also Nation and Athenaeum*
Atkins, John, 192
Atkinson, Lawrence, 65, 69, 493
Atthill, Robin, 168
Attlee, Clement, 81, 97
Attwater, Rachel, 36
Auden, W[ystan] H[ugh]: contributes to *Adam*, 5; to *Adelphi*, 15; to *Agenda*, 20; to *Contemporary Poetry and Prose*, 87; to *Criterion*, 118; to *Encounter*, 157; to *Horizon*, 205; to *Left Review*, 219; to *Life and Letters*, 224; to *London Mercury*, 254; to *Mint*, 264; to *New Departures*, 274; to *New Measure*, 283; to *New Verse*, 292–94; to *New Writing*, 300–302; to *Nimbus*, 306; to *Penguin New Writing*, 339, 342; to *Purpose*, 387; to *Scrutiny*, 426; to *Time and Tide*, 448, 450; to *Wind and the Rain*, 498; to *Workshop*, 503; criticized in *Scrutiny*, 427; influences *Universities' Poetry*, 474; leaves *Encounter* because of CIA backing, 159; on Graham Greene, 498–99; on mystery novels, 498–99; on Shakespeare's Falstaff, 157; on surrealism, 294; parodied in *Review*, 400; recollections in *Trace*, 457; reviewed in *Encounter*, 158; in *Experiment*, 178; in *London Mercury*, 252; in *New Verse*, 292–94; in *Poetry (London)*, 362; in *Samphire*, 418; in *Townsman*, 455. Works: *The Age of Anxiety*, 356; "Allendale," 293; "At the Grave of Henry James," 205; "The Carter's Funeral," 293; "Criticism in a Mass Society," 264–65, 268; *An Epistle to a Godson*, 418; "The Fall of Rome," 205; "In Praise of Limestone," 205; *In Time of War*, 293; "Lay Your Sleeping Head," 301; "A Literary Transference," 387; "Meiosis," 293; "Memorial for the City," 205; *Paid on Both Sides*, 178; "Palais des Beaux Arts," 301; "Sep-

tember 1, 1939," 318; *Thank You, Fog*, 400
Auerbach, Frank, 510
Austen, Jane: letter in *Cornhill*, 107; reviewed in *Cornhill*, 106; in *Northern Review*, 316; in *Now*, 318; in *Scrutiny*, 425, 427
Australian literature, 347, 356
Ayer, A. J., 206, 450
Aylesford Review, 35–40
Ayrton, Michael, 325, 340

Babel, Isaac, 77, 90
Bacon, Francis, 510
Baden-Powell, Lady, 442
Bagehot, Walter, 83
Bagnold, Enid, 223
Baker, Ernest A., 95
Balchin, Nigel, 501
Baldwin, Faith, 346
Balzac, Honoré de, 116
Bamforth, Iain, 235
Banks, J. R., 125
Banks, Paul, 278
Banting, John, 331
Bantock, Gavin, 283
Barclay, Thomas, 181
Bard, Joseph, 278
Barea, Arturo, 203
Barfield, Owen, 252, 264
Barilsford, H. N., 95
Barker, Clive, 136
Barker, George: contributes to *Adelphi*, 15; to *European Quarterly*, 174; to *Horizon*, 205; to *London Mercury*, 254; to *Nimbus*, 306; to *Orion*, 326; to *Penguin New Writing*, 339, 342; to *Poetry (London)*, 360; to *Twentieth Century*, 465; to *Twentieth Century Verse*, 469-70; to *Workshop*, 503; to *X: Quarterly Review*, 509; "Note on Narrative Poetry," 470; reviewed in *Nimbus*, 307; in *X: A Quarterly Review*, 510; "Six Poems from America," 361
Barker, J. Ellis, 181
Barker, Ronald, 354
Barlas, Chris, 189

Barlow, George, 93
Barlow, K.D., 385
Barnes, Clive, 352
Barnes, Djuna, 241; "Aller et Retour," 461; "The Passion," 463
Barnes, J. S., 117
Barnes, Peter, 189
Barnes, T. R., 455
Barnes, William, 264
Barney, Natalie, 462
Baron, Jacques, 461
Barrie and Rockliff, 512
Barrie, James M., 6, 78, 92, 134, 138, 384
Barry, Iris, 77
Barry, Philip, 137
Barton, E. S. D., 506
Barton, Joan: "A House under Old Sarum," *The Mistress and Other Poems*, 488
Bartsch, Kurt, 398
Bates, H. E.: contributes to *Adelphi*, 12; to *Cornhill*, 108; to *Horizon*, 205; to *Kingdom Come*, 214; to *Lovat Dickson's Magazine*, 257, 259; to *Penguin Parade*, 346; "Mademoiselle," 214; "A Note on the English Short Story," 257; on editorial board of *New Stories*, 289
Bateson, F. W., 398
Batson, H. E., 426
Baudelaire, Charles, 5, 77
Baughan, E. A., 136
Baultier, Jules de, 12
Baumann, Arthur, 181
Bax, Arnold, 42
Bax, Clifford, 136, 137, 193–95
Baxter, James K., 356
Bayley, John, 365, 398
Bayliss, Ben, 75
Bayliss, John, 285–88
Beachcroft, T. O., 15
Bean, Robin, 354
Beardsley, Aubrey, 37
Beat poetry, 457, 509
Beattie, George, 99
Beaumont, C. W., 492
Beaumont, Timothy, Lord, 451

Beck, Julian, 150
Beckett, John, 45
Beckett, Samuel: *Breath*, 187; contributes to *Encounter*, 156; to *Gambit*, 187; to *London Bulletin*, 241–42; to *New Departures*, 273, 274; to *New Writers*, 298; to *X: Quarterly Review*, 510; *Endgame*, 150; *Happy Days*, 150, 186; *Malone Dies*, 100, 506; *Molloy*, 510; "PSS," 274; reminiscence in *Contemporary Review*, 100; reviewed in *Encore*, 149, 150; in *Gambit*, 186; in *Writing Today*, 506; in *X: Quarterly Review*, 510; *Waiting for Godot*, 150
Beecham, Audrey, 360, 361, 432
Beeching, Jack, 331
Beede, Ivan, 462, 463
Beerbohm, Max, 1–2, 105, 107, 223, 252, 334
Behan, Brendan, 42, 505
Bell, 41–45, 139, 140
Bell, Clive, 107, 108, 223, 224
Bell, Daniel, 156
Bell, John, 181
Bell, Quentin, 224, 407
Bellamy, Frank, 47
Bellerby, Frances, 325, 499
Belloc, Bessie Raynor, 92
Belloc, Hilaire, 55, 60, 182, 251, 465
Bellow, Saul, 156, 157, 340, 400, 505
Beloff, Max, 156
Benda, Julien, 115
Benét, Stephen Vincent, 346
Bennett, Arnold: centenary tribute in *Gambit*, 187; contributes to *Adelphi*, 10; memoirs in *London Mercury*, 202; quarrel in *Blackfriars*, 55; reprinted in *Review*, 400; reviewed in *Calendar of Modern Letters*, 78; in *Contemporary Review*, 97; in *Drama*, 134; in *Time and Tide*, 444
Bennett, Richard, 230
Bennett, Roy: "Xanthippe," 379
Benson, Arthur C., 105
Benson, Stella, 444
Bentley, Eric, 151
Bentley, Nicholas, 5, 6
Bentley, Phyllis, 448

Beresford, J. D., 11
Bergé, Carol, 39
Bergonzi, Bernard, 37, 122, 310, 362, 400, 506
Berkeley, George: *Siris*, 84
Berkoff, Steven, 189
Berlin, Isaiah, 108
Berliner Ensemble, 148, 150
Berlioz, Hector, 5
Berman, Hannah: "The Beggar," 462
Bermondsey Book, 45–51
Bermondsey Bookshop, 45–46, 49
Berners, Gerald Tyrwhitt–Wilson, Lord, 451
Bernhardt, Sarah, 105
Bernstein, Carl: *The Final Days*, 401
Berridge, Elizabeth, 108
Berry, Francis, 166; "Soviet Town Statue," 498
Berryman, John: contributes to *New Departures*, 274; to *Twentieth Century Verse*, 469; *Homage to Mistress Bradstreet*, 506; in *Review anthology*, 395; promoted by *Review*, 397; reviewed in *London Magazine*, 246; in *Review*, 399; in *Writing Today*, 505, 506
Best Poems, 478
Beste, R. Vernon, 331
Betjeman, John: contributes to *Cornhill*, 107; to *Criterion*, 118; to *Horizon*, 204; to *London Magazine*, 245; to *London Mercury*, 252; to *Time and Tide*, 450; to *Wind and the Rain*, 498; interview in *Writing Today*, 506; leaves *Encounter* because of CIA backing, 159; literary editor for *Time and Tide*, 447; reviewed in *Blackwood's Edinburgh Magazine*, 60; "To My Son Aged Eight," 498
Bewley, Marius, 263, 426
Bianchi, Tony, 27
Bianco, Pamela, 334
Biederman, Charles, 375
Bielski, Alison J., 370
Bien, P., 6
Biermann, Wolf, 398
Biggs, J. R., 346
Billington, Michael, 350

Billington-Grieg, Teresa, 92

Binyon, Laurence, 46, 167

Birney, Earle, 355, 356, 406

Birnstingl, H. J., 196

Birrell, Augustine, 94, 96

Birrell, Francis, 118

Birrell, T. A., 498

Bishop, Elizabeth, 284, 287, 397; "The Gentleman of Shallot," 285

Bishop, G. W., 136

Bishop, John Peale, 285

Bjorkman, Edwin, 93

Black Art, 51–53

Black, Victor, 195, 197

Blackburn, Michael, 439

Blackburn, Thomas, 167

Blackfriars, 53–58

Blackfriars Publications, 57

Blackmur, R. P., 394, 469

Blackwell, Basil, 57, 289

Blackwood, B. H., 491

Blackwood, George Douglas, 61

Blackwood, George William, 61

Blackwood, James H., 61

Blackwood, Michael, 60

Blackwood, William, and Sons, 61

Blackwood's Edinburgh Magazine, 58–61

Blair, Hamish, 59

Blake, William: featured in *New Departures*, 273; reviewed in *Adelphi*, 12; in *Arena*, 30; in *British Museum Quarterly*, 74; in *Cambridge Journal*, 85; in *Kingdom Come*, 219; in *Northern Review*, 316; in *Now*, 318; in *Our Time*, 328

Blakeston, Oswell, 278, 484

Blakestone, Bernard, 85

Blast, 61–70, 146

Bliss, Percy, 346

Blok, Alexander: "The Downfall of Humanism," 175

Bloomfield, Paul, 215

Blumenfeld, Simon, 220

Blunden, Edmund C.: contributes to *Adelphi*, 11; to *Calendar of Modern Letters*, 77; to *Coterie*, 212; to *English*, 167–68; to *Kingdom Come*, 212; to *London Mercury*, 251; to *Orion*,

324; to *Owl*, 334; to *Review of English Literature*, 407; reviewed in *Quarterly Review*, 390; reviewer for *Time and Tide*, 447

Bly, Robert, 434; "Johnson's Cabinet Watched by Ants," "The Teeth Mother Naked at Last," 438

Boakes, R. A., 166

Boas, Frederick S., 96, 136–37, 182

Boas, Guy, 165–66

Bobowski, Prince, 409

Bobrowski, Johannes, 398

Bockris, Victor, 401

Bode, Carl, 98

Bodkin, Maud, 15

Bodley Head, 69, 301, 302

Boldero, Martin. *See* Grigson, Geoffrey

Bolgar, R. R., 83, 84

Böll, Heinrich, 156, 159

Bolt, Robert, 149

Bomberg, David, 69, 510

Bond, Edward, 137, 188, 351–52; *Black Mass*, 188; *Saved*, 351

Bone, Stephen, 326

Bonhoeffer, Dietrich, 450

Book Design and Production, 51

Bookman, 254

Books and Bookmen, 350

Books of the Month, 451

Booster, 430

Booth, Martin, 419

Borges, Jorge Luis, 156, 157; "Death and the Compass," "The Library of Babel," 310

Borrow, Antony, 310

Borroway, Janet, 474

Bosanquet, Theodora, 444, 447

Bosman, H. C.: "Makapan's Caves," "The Rooinek," 307

Boswell, James, 59, 107

Bott, G., 506

Bottomley, Gordon, 118, 134

Bottrall, Ronald, 192, 361

Bowen, Elizabeth: contributes to *Bell*, 42; to *Cornhill*, 107; to *Horizon*, 205; to *London Mercury*, 252; to *New Writing*, 300, 301; to *Orion*, 324–25; to *Penguin New Writing*, 340; to *Purpose*,

385, 387; to *Windmill*, 501; reviewed in *Orion*, 325
Bowes & Bowes, 86
Bowes-Lyon, Lilian, 324
Bowles, Patrick, 273
Bowles, Paul, 156, 245, 340
Bowra, Maurice, 107, 324, 446
Boyajian, Zabelle C., 94
Boyars, Arthur, 261–62, 309
Boyars, Marion, 187
Boyle, Kay, 118, 254, 287, 430
Boyle, Patrick, 341
Boyser, Yves de, 7
Bozhovitch, G., 175
Bracco, Roberto: *The Little Saint*, 186
Bradbrook, Frank, 84
Bradbrook, M. C., 424, 450
Bradbury, Malcolm, 122, 400, 402, 407
Bradley, A. C., 100
Bradshaw, David, 439
Bradshaw, Steve, 435
Braga, Edgard, 374, 375
Bragg, Melvyn, 400, 401, 403
Brahms, Caryl, 230
Braine, John, 192, 505; *Last Day of Summer*, *Room at the Top*, 506
Branford, F. V., 477–80
Braque, Georges, 278, 461
Braun, Volker, 398
Braybrooke, Neville, 17, 25, 496–97
Brazilian poetry, 375
Brecht, Bertolt: contributes to *Encore*, 151; to *Encounter*, 156; to *Life and Letters*, 225; to *New Review*, 403; to *Nimbus*, 306; to *Penguin New Writing*, 340; to *Review*, 398; excerpted in *Left Review*, 219; model for *Encore*, 148–51; *Mother Courage and Her Children*, 150; on Chinese theater, 225; "The Private Life of Mister Julius Caesar," 307; reviewed in *Contemporary Review*, 96; in *Drama*, 137; in *Review*, 398; in *Writing Today*, 505
Bredin Publishing Co., 224, 228
Brenton, Howard, 189
Breton, André, 86, 213, 241–42, 287; *Second Manifesto*, 242; "Towards an Independent Revolutionary Art," 242

Brevet Publishing Ltd., 354
Brew, Kwesi, 356
Breytenbach, Breyten, 403
Brezina, Otokar, 174
Bridges, Robert, 105, 252–53, 465
Bridges-Adams, W., 136
Bridgwater, Patrick, 397
Bridie, James, 137
Briggs, Asa, 83, 465
Bright, Lawrence, 58
British Drama League. *See* British Theatre Association
British Library. *See British Museum Quarterly*
British Museum Quarterly, 71–76
British Museum Yearbook, 74–78
British Periodicals, Ltd., 18, 272
British Poetry Association, 357
British Theatre Association, 133–34, 327
British Weekly, 25
Brittain, Juliet, 453
Brittain, Vera, 259, 441
Brittain, William J., 451
Britting, Georg, 175
Broad, C. D., 169
Brogan, Denis, 81, 98
Brokenau, Franz, 156
Bromberger, Norman: "South Africa Journal," 403
Bronowski, Jacob, 177
Brontë, Charlotte, 104, 106
Brook, Peter, 150
Brooke, Rupert, 68, 94, 251
Brookes, Benjamin Gilbert, 462
Brooks, Cleanth: *Modern Poetry and the Tradition*, 262
Brooks, F. Vincent, 334
Brooks, Gwendolyn, 98
Brooks, Harold, 168
Brophy, Brigid, 248
Brotherton, Gordon, 437
Brown, George Mackay, 168, 374, 375, 414, 415
Brown, Ivor, 135–36, 137, 182
Brown, John Russell, 136
Brown, Roland, 500
Browne, Dame Sidney, 442
Browne, E. Martin, 100, 138

Browne, Wynyard, 253, 278, 385
Browning, Elizabeth Barrett, 106
Browning, Robert, 2, 94
Brownjohn, Alan: contributes to *New Departures*, 273; to *New Measure*, 283; to *Review*, 396, 403; to *Wave*, 487; to *Workshop*, 502; on American poets, 396; reviews for *Writing Today*, 506
Bruce, George, 415, 416
Bruce, Lenny, 149
Brun, Padraic de, 139
Brunner, Edward, 439
Brustein, Robert, 350
Bryher. *See* Ellerman, Winifred
Buchan, Alastair, 156
Buchan, John, 59, 315
Buchner, Georg: *Lenz*, 262
Buck, Pearl, 259
Buckley, Peter, 353
Buckmaster, Celia, 484
Bukowski, Charles, 249
Bull, A. J., 192
Bullen, Frank, 105
Bulletin (English Association). *See English*
Bullock, Michael, 332
Bunin, Ivan, 117
Bunting, Basil, 19, 462
Bunting, Percy, 91–92, 94–96
Buñuel, Luis, 86
Bunyan, John, 85, 328
Burke, Kenneth, 77
Burne-Jones, Edward, 334
Burnett, Frances Hodgson, 105
Burnham, James, 156
Burns, Alan, 298
Burns, Carol, 298
Burns, Emile, 329–30
Burns, Jim, 434
Burns, Robert, 23, 421
Burroughs, William, 401
Burroway, Janet: *But to the Season*, 474
Bury, J. B., 391
Bush, Douglas, 264
Buss, Kate, 463
Butler, A. Maynard, 93
Butler, Josephine, 92
Butler, Michael, 418–19

Butor, Michel, 247; *Passing Time*, 506
Butt, John, 406
Butter, Peter, 176
Butterfield, Herbert, 83, 98, 426
Butts, Mary, 461, 462
Buxton, Noel, 95
Buzzati, Dino, 298
Byrne, Donn, 139
Byron, George Gordon, Lord, 106, 137, 391, 409

Cable, Boyd, 105
Cage, John, 274
Cahill and Company, Ltd., 45
Cairns, Craig, 437–38
Calas, Nicolas, 287
Calder and Boyars, 186, 300
Calder, Angus: "The Red Birds," 475
Calder, John, 187, 188, 297–99
Calder, Robert, 233
Calder-Marshall, Arthur, 7, 257, 289, 290
Caldwell, Erskine, 259
Calendar of Modern Letters, 33, 77–80, 219, 425
Callender, L., 500
Calvino, Italo, 247, 401, 403
Cambridge Apostles, 223
Cambridge Journal, 80–86
Cambridge University Press, 428
Camden Town Group, 61
Cameron, Norman, 205, 293, 398
Cammaerts, Emile, 46
Campbell, Donald, 22, 23
Campbell, Patrick, 230, 231
Campbell, Roy: attacked in *New Verse*, 295; contributes to *Calendar of Modern Letters*, to *Mandrake*, 262; to *Nimbus*, 306; to *Nine*, 310; to *Right Review*, 409; *Light on a Dark Horse*, 311; model for *Nine*, 311–12; reviewer for *Enquiry*, 171
Campos, Augusto de, 374, 375
Camus, Albert, 28, 155–57, 307, 506
Canadian literature, 348, 356, 438
Canayenne, Jean, 455
Candlin, Clara, 129
Capek, Karel, 238

Capetanakis, Demetrios, 340
Capote, Truman, 107, 206; *Other Voices, Other Rooms*, 501
Carcanet Press, 366
Cardrew, Cornelius: "Piano Piece February 1959," 273
Cardus, Neville, 479
Carlyle, Jane Welsh, 106
Carlyle, Thomas, 93–94, 182, 414
Carmelite Institute (Rome), 39
Carmelus, 39
Carne-Ross, D. S., 309–11
Carpenter, Edward, 14
Carroll, Lewis, 106
Carruthers, James, 385
Carson, Robert, 74
Carswell, Catherine, 10, 14
Carter, Angela, 39
Carter, Frederick, 11
Cartier-Bresson, Henri, 178
Carver, Raymond, 249
Cary, Joyce, 5, 108, 306, 501
Casson, Lewis, 137
Cassou, Jean, 460, 462
Castro, Fidel, 157
Catholic Herald, 497
Catholic magazines, 35–40, 53–58
Catholic Review, 53. See also *Blackfriars*
Catlin, George, 98
Cattaui, Georges, 5
Caudwell, Christopher, 469
Causley, Charles, 16, 504
Causton, Bernard, 95
Cavafy, C. P., 116, 398
Cavalcanti, Alberto, 44
Caxton, John, 362
Caxton, William, 51–52
CCF [Congress for Cultural Freedom], 153–54, 158–59
Cecchi, Emilio, 262
Cecil, David, 326, 449
Celan, Paul, 274
Céline, Louis-Ferdinand, 192, 403
CEMA [Council for the Encouragement of Music and the Arts], 327. See also Arts Council
Cendrars, Blaise, 156

Central Intelligence Agency (U. S.), 158–59
Central Register of Charities, 26
Central School of Speech Training and Dramatic Art, 147
Cervantes, Miguel de, 94
Chabrol, Claude, 403
Chagall, Marc, 5
Chamberlain, Neville, 465
Chambers, Jessie: *D. H. Laurence: A Personal Record*, 174-75
Chambers's Journal, 60
Champion, H. H., 84
Chamson, André, 301, 338–39
Chandos Group, 381
Channing Press, 369
Chaplin, Charles, 11
Chaplin, Sid, 339, 341
Chapman, 23
Chapman and Hall, 184, 199
Chapman, R. W., 252
Chatto and Windus, 133, 250, 400
Chaucer, Daniel. *See* Ford, Ford Madox
Chaucer, Geoffrey, 107, 130
Cheever, John: "The Falconer," 400
Chekhov, Anton, 77, 137, 197, 257, 339
Chesser, Elizabeth Sloan, 92
Chesterton, G. K., 39, 93, 119, 224, 252; "Candida and a Candid Friend," 444
Chiang Kai-shek, 498
Chiari, Joseph, 326
Childe, William Rowland, 129
Childers, Erskine, 42
Children of Albion, 273, 274
Chilman, Eric, 129
Chinese literature, 19, 129, 227
Chirico, Giorgio de, 157, 213, 241–42; "Mystery and Creation," 242
Chopin, Frédéric, 6
Christo, Javachoff, 401
Church, Richard, 77, 194, 197, 499; "The Last Summer," 195; "The Past," 195; *Philip*, 197; "Workshop," 195
Churchill, Charles, 78
Churchill, Winston, 107; *Thoughts and Adventures*, 426

CIA (U.S.), 158–59
Circulation: *Adam International Review*,
    6; *Anglo–Welsh Review*, 24, 25; *Ayles-
    ford Review*, 39; *Bell*, 42; *Bermondsey
    Book*, 49; *Blackwoods*, 60; *Cornhill*,
    108; *Coterie*, 112; *Critical Quarterly*,
    122–23; *Drama*, 138; *Encore*, 147;
    Encounter, 157, 159; *European Quar-
    terly*, 176; *Horizon*, 6, 207; *Left Re-
    view*, 218; *Lilliput*, 229, 230; *London
    Aphrodite*, 238; *London Mercury*, 251;
    Our Time, 329; *Penguin New Writing*,
    303, 342; *Poetry Wales*, 370; *Review*,
    399; *Samphire*, 419; *Scrutiny*, 423;
    Twentieth Century Verse, 469; *Wheels*,
    491
Clapham, Walter, 231
Clare, Anthony, 402
Clare, John, 182
Clark, Colin, 156
Clark, Kenneth, 107, 108, 223
Clark, Laurence, 360
Clark, Le Gros, 385
Clark, Stephen, 298–99
Clarke, Austin, 42, 274
Clarke, Gillian, 27
Clarke, I. F., 391
Claudel, Paul, 5
Clayton, Bertram, 391
Cleary, Bredan, 439
Clemo, Jack, 283, 325
Clinkard, Mildred, 216
Cluer, Elizabeth, 325
Cobban, Alfred, 83
Cobbing, Bob, 487, 502
Cobden-Sanderson, Richard, 114
Cocteau, Jean, 4, 5, 117, 460–63
Coe, Katherine Hunter, 367
Coghill, Neville, 137, 262, 310
Coghill, Rhoda, 141
Cohen, Leah McTavish, 494
Cole, G. D. H., 14
Coleman, Emily Holmes, 175
Coleridge, Samuel Taylor, 29, 33, 72,
    78, 85, 88, 406
College Press, 358
Collet's Bookshop, 222
Collins, Churlton, 105

Collins, H. P., 13
Colquhoun, Archibald, 38
Colquhoun, Ithell, 241, 242
Colum, Padraic, 41, 139
Colvin, Clare, 100
Comedie Française, 150
Comfort, Alex, 286–88; "Art and Social
    Responsibility," 318
Commentary, 153
Common, Jack, 15
Commonwealth writers: in *English*, 167;
    Gambit, 187, 189; *London Magazine*,
    249; *New Measure*, 283; *Penguin New
    Writing*, 341; *Penguin Parade*, 346;
    Poetry Commonwealth, 354, 355–57;
    Review of English Literature, 406
Communist magazines. *See* Socialist
    magazines
Communist Party, 29, 211, 218–19, 329,
    449–50. *See also* Political issues; So-
    cialist magazines
Compton-Burnett, Ivy, 324
Compton-Rickett, Leonard A., 146
Concrete poetry, 64, 123, 249, 374–75,
    418, 435
Condé, David, 247
Congress for Cultural Freedom, 153,
    154, 158–59
Conn, Stewart, 487
Connolly, Cyril, 7, 201-7, 223, 511
Connors, Bruton, 370
Conquest, Robert, 246, 394, 470, 487
Conrad, Joseph: *The Arrow of Gold*, 384;
    contributes to *Blackwood's Edinburgh
    Magazine*, 58; to *Transatlantic Review*,
    460; *Lord Jim*, 58, 96; *The Nature of a
    Crime*, 460, 462; *Nostromo*, 427; re-
    viewed in *Contemporary Review*, 96,
    98; in *Purpose*, 384; in *Scrutiny*, 425,
    427; in *Time and Tide*, 444; in *Trans-
    atlantic Review*, 460; *The Rover*, 462
Conran, Anthony, 25, 370
Constable and Co., 224, 467
Contemporary Poetry and Prose, 86–91,
    241, 294
Contemporary Review, 91–102, 183
Continental writers: in *Adelphi*, 13–14;
    Arena, 28; *Calendar of Modern Let-*

ters, 77; *Contemporary Poetry and Prose*, 86–90; *Contemporary Review*, 95–96; *Criterion*, 115, 117, 118; *Critical Quarterly*, 122; *Decachord*, 129; *Egoist*, 144; *Encounter*, 158; *European Quarterly*, 173–76; *Gambit*, 185–89; *Golden Hind*, 196–97; *Horizon*, 203; *Kingdom Come*, 213–14; *Life and Letters*, 225–27; *Lilliput*, 229–30; *Lines Review*, 234–35; *London Magazine*, 247, 249; *Mandrake*, 262; *New Measure*, 283; *New Review*, 403; *New Road*, 287; *New Writers*, 298; *New Writing*, 300–301; *Nimbus*, 307; *Nine*, 310; *Orion*, 324–26; *Penguin New Writing*, 338–41; *Solstice*, 434–35; *Time and Tide*, 448; *Transatlantic Review*, 461–63. See also specific authors, countries
Cook, John, 436
Cooke, Dorian, 361, 430, 432
Cooke, William, 168
Cookson, Geoffrey, 494
Cookson, George, 165
Cookson, William, 19, 21, 365
Coombes, B. L., 220, 301, 303, 339, 341
Cope, R. K., 356
Coppard, A. E., 77, 290, 460–61, 501; "Fine Feather," 47
Corbett, James, 181
Corbière, Tristan, 307
Corday, Charlotte, 65
Cordell, Alexander, 26
Corke, Hilary, 156
Cornford, Frances, 12, 325
Cornhill Magazine, 60, 103–10
Corso, Gregory, 274, 510
Corvo, Baron. See Rolfe, Frederick
Cosmoi, M. M. See Mitrinovic, Dmitri
Coterie, 110–13
Cotton, John, 365, 376, 377-79, 435
Coulter, Geoffrey, 462
Coulthard, G. R., 310
Coulton, G. G., 446
Council for the Encouragement of Music and the Arts, 327. See also Arts Council

Courage, James, 500
Courbet, Gustave, 324
Cournos, John, 62, 118
Courtney, Janet, 181
Courtney, William Leonard, 181–82
Cousin, Victor, 84
Couzyn, Jeni, 502, 503
Coveney, Michael, 354
Coward, Noel, 137
Cowley, Malcolm, 284, 498
Cowper, William, 84, 96
Cox, C. B., 121, 364
Cox, Horace, Ltd., 173
Cox, Nigel, 169
Cozzens, James Gould, 346
Crabbe, George, 454
Craig, David, 403, 416
Craig, Edward Gordon, 134, 138, 197, 480
Craig, Randall, 136
Crane, Hart, 77
Crane, Stephen, 459
Cranston, Maurice, 247
Craxton, John, 340
Creeley, Robert, 159, 274
Cregan, David, 100
Crick, Bernard, 401
Crimean War, 95
Criterion, 11–12, 33, 111, 113–21, 410–11, 425, 455
Critical Quarterly, 85, 121–23, 365, 407, 428, 475
Croce, Benedetto, 1, 116, 197, 203
Crockenedge, Edmund, 298
Cronin, Anthony, 45, 307
Crookshank, F. G., 383
Crosland, C. A. R., 156
Crosland, Margaret, 368
Crowley, Aleister, 172
Cuban poets, 435
Cullen, Countee, 448
Cullis, Winifred, 448
Culver, Donald, 429
Cummings, E. E.: "American Critic Ad 1935," 455; contributes to *Contemporary Poetry and Prose*, 87; to *New English Weekly*, 279; to *Now*, 319; to *Transatlantic Review*, 460; reviewed in

Aphrodite, 279; in *Review*, 397; "What If a Much of a Which of a Wind," 319

Cunard, Nancy, 328, 463, 491, 492

Cundall, Peter: "Ballsgame," 379

Cunninghame, A. T., 174

Cuppy, Will, 14

Czartoryski, Rick, 435

Czechoslovakian literature, 438

D'Annunzio, Gabriele, 77

D'Wit, Vivan, 367

Dada, 460, 461

Daiches, David, 156, 159, 490; "The Writing of Scottish Literary History," 415

Daily Herald, 111

Daily Mirror, 244, 247

Daily News, 47

Daily Worker, 29

Dale, Peter, 21

Dali, Salvador, 86, 241

Danby, John F., 84

Dance and Dancers, 350

Daniel, C. W., 388, 494

Dante Alighieri, 95, 130

Darbishire, Helen, 450

Darwin, Charles, 95, 106

Dataller, Roger, 15

Davenport, Diana, 402

Davenport, John, 28, 178, 284, 402

Davey, Norman, 197

Davie, Alan, 274

Davie, Donald: contributes to *Adelphi*, 16; to *Cambridge Journal*, 84; to *Critical Quarterly*, 122; to *New Departures*, 274; to *Poetry (London)*, 362; to *Review*, 393–95, 397; to *Samphire*, 419; to *Workshop*, 504; edits *Review*, 365–66; *Essex Poems*, 395; influence on *Critical Quarterly*, 122; "January," 419; letter in *London Magazine*, 245; *Purity of Diction in English Verse*, 245; quarrel with *Stand*, 438; reviewed in *Poetry Nation*, 365; "The Varsity Match," 365

Davies, Aberpennar, 484

Davies, Aneirin Talfan, 25, 370, 371

Davies, Christopher, Ltd., 373

Davies, Emily, 92

Davies, Hugh Sykes, 87, 242, 294

Davies, Idris, 220, 372, 483

Davies, James Kitchener, 373

Davies, John, 27

Davies, Nora E., 25

Davies, Pennar, 26, 373

Davies, Rhys, 15, 264

Davies, Russell, 400, 402

Davies, William H.: contributes to *Golden Hind*, 194–95; to *London Mercury*, 251; to *Time and Tide*, 444, 445; to *Voices*, 480; portrait in *Voices*, 479; special issue of *Poor. Old. Tired. Horse.*, 373

Dawson, Christopher, 498

Day, Bertram, 367

Day, John, 52

Day–Lewis, Sean, 323, 325

Daylight, 303, 340

Dayrell, Vivienne, 480

De la Mare, Walter: contributes to *Adam*, 5; to *Adelphi*, 11; to *Bermondsey Book*, 46; to *English*, 168; to *Enquiry*, 170; to *Horizon*, 204; to *London Mercury*, 251, 252; to *Northern Review*, 315; to *Orion*, 324; to *Owl*, 334; to *Poetry (London)*, 360; to *Time and Tide*, 448, 450; to *Wind and the Rain*, 498; reviewed in *Bermondsey Book*, 49; in *Calendar of Modern Letters*, 79; *Stories from the Bible*, 49

Deakin, Tom, 378

Dean, Mabel, 47

Decachord, 127–33

Defoe, Daniel: "A Tour through England and Wales," 96

Delafield, E. M., 448, 449; *Diary of a Provincial Lady*, 446

Delaney, Bernard, 57

Delaval, Seaton, 324

Delta, 430

Delteil, Joseph, 37

Delvaux, Paul, 242

Demant, V. A., 383

Demuth, Norman, 215

Denis, Terence, 278

Denning Report, 38
Dennis, Nigel, 155
Der Monat, 153, 156
Derleth, August W., 290
Des Imagistes, 62
Design: *Blast*, 64; *British Museum Quarterly*, 73; *Gambit*, 188; *Golden Hind*, 194; *Kingdom Come*, 211; *Lilliput*, 229, 230; *London Aphrodite*, 237; *London Magazine*, 247–48; *New Departures*, 273-74; *New Review*, 403; *Penguin Parade*, 344–45, 347–48; *Right Review*, 408–9; *Twentieth Century*, 465, 466; *Wheels*, 491–94
Designes, Georges, 461
Dial, 114, 297
Dickens, Anthony, 364
Dickens, Charles: evaluated as dramatist in *Drama*, letters in *Adam*, 5; *Public Dinners*, 52; reprinted in *Cornhill*, 104; reviewed in *Arena*, 30; in *Cornhill*, 106; in *Fortnightly Review*, 182; in *Kingdom Come*, 219; in *Our Time*, 328; in *Review of English Literature*, 406
Dickens, Monica, 229
Dickinson, G. Lowes, 426
Dickinson, Patric, 168, 324
Dickson, Lovat, 255–59
Didion, Joan, 400
Diggle, Margaret, 504
Dillon, E. J., 95, 181
Dismorr, Jessica, 65, 67, 68
Disraeli, Benjamin, 107
Distributism, 55–56
Dixon, Jeannette, 406
Dobrée, Bonamy, 465, 473
Dobson, Austin, 105, 391
Dobson, Frank, 479
Dobson, Rosemary, 356
Dock Leaves. *See Anglo–Welsh Review*
Dodsworth, Martin, 166–67, 388, 395, 398
Dolgoronsky, Sophy, 129
Dominicans, 53–58
Donleavy, J. P., 306
Donne, John, 144

Donoghue, Denis, 394, 399; *Connoisseurs of Chaos*, 394
D[oolittle], H[ilda]: contributes to *Coterie*, 112; to *Egoist*, 144; to *Life and Letters*, 225, 227; to *Transatlantic Review*, 460; supported by Pound in *Egoist*, 144; *Tribute to Freud*, 227
Dorn, Edward, 434
Dos Passos, John, 316, 319, 389; "July," 462
Dostoevsky, Fyodor, 77, 115, 384, 422; "Baal: Impressions of London," 175
Doubleday, Anne, 445
Douglas, C. H., 173, 276-78, 380–85
Douglas, Gavin, 421
Douglas, James, 238
Douglas, Keith, 213, 295, 361, 362; "Haydn Clock Symphony," "Russians," "Search for a God," 213; translation of *Aeneid*, 421
Dowden, Edward, 93
Doyle, A. Conan, 105
Drabble, Margaret, 400
Drake, Carlos, 462
Drama, 133–39, 353
Draper, Theodore, 157
Dreiser, Theodore, 49, 252; "America and Her Communists," 447
Driberg, Tom, 206
Drinkwater, John, 46, 94, 167, 182
Dru, A., 175
Drummond, John, 455
Dryden, John, 84
Dublin Magazine, 41, 139–42
Duchamp, Marcel, 241–42
Duckworth and Co., 459
Dudintsev, Vladimir: *Not by Bread Alone*, 506
Dugdale, T. C., 171
Duhamel, Georges, 5
Dumesnil, René, 325
Dunbar, William, 421
Duncan, Isadora, 238
Duncan, Kunigunde, 129
Duncan, Ronald, 138, 277, 453–56
Dunlop, William, 474
Dunn, Douglas, 235, 248, 365, 396–99, 402

Dunn, Fergus, 376

Dunsany, Edward J. M. D. Plunkett, Lord, 42, 223, 229

Duran, Father Leopoldo, 6

Durey, René, 110

During, Richard Cheever, 463

Durrell, Gerald, 432

Durrell, Lawrence: *The Black Book*, 431; contributes to *Blackwood's Edinburgh Magazine*, 60; to *Encounter*, 156; to *Gangrel*, 191, 192; to *Kingdom Come*, 213; to *New English Weekly*, 279; to *New Poetry*, 284; to *New Writing*, 300; to *Penguin New Writing*, 340; to *Poetry (London)*, 361; to *Purpose*, 386; to *Seven*, 430, 431, 432; "Egyptian Pastiche," 386; "In Crisis," 386; letter in *Right Review*, 409; "The Prince and Hamlet," 279; reviewed in *Purpose*, 387; in *Writing Today*, 505; translation of Sikelianos, 340

Durrenmatt, Friedrich, 137, 247

Dutch poetry, 438

Dvořák, Anton, 44

Dyment, Clifford, 278, 499

Dyson, A. E., 121

Dyson, Betty, 278

Dyson, Will, 277, 278

Eagleton, Terry, 365, 437–38

Earley, Tom, 370

Earp, Thomas, 110, 238

East German poetry, 438

Eberhart, Richard, 20, 159, 178, 285, 310, 319; "At the End of the War," 319

Economic issues, 380–86. *See also* political issues

Edgett, E. F., 197

Edinburgh Festival, 298, 347, 414

Education reform, 81–82, 85, 347, 424–26

Edwards, Christopher, 139

Egoist, 62, 143–46

Ehrenpreis, Irvin, 400, 401

Einstein, Albert, 162

Eisentein, Sergei, 225

Elder, Smith Co., 103–4, 106

Eliot, George, 83, 167, 427, 501

Eliot, T. S.: contributes to *Adelphi*, 16; to *Arts and Letters*, 33; to *Blast*, 61, 67; to *Coterie*, 112; to *Drama*, 134, 138; to *Egoist*, 144; to *Enemy*, 162; to *Horizon*, 206; to *London Mercury*, 252; to *New English Weekly*, 277, 279; to *Nine*, 309; to *Purpose*, 386; to *Time and Tide*, 449, 450–51; to *Twentieth Century Verse*, 469; criticized in *Wales*, 484; in *Transatlantic Review*, 460; edits *Criterion*, 113; featured in *Agenda*, 19; in *Review*, 398; influence on *Adam*, 5; on *Scrutiny*, 427; literary editor of *Egoist*, 144; offered editorship of *Nation and Athenaeum*, 270; on editorial board of *Coterie*, 110; of *New English Weekly*, 280; opinion of Charles Whibley, 58–59; of Gordon Craig, 138; *Poems 1909–1925*, 252; promotes *Transatlantic Review*, 460; relationship with J. M. Murray, 11; reviewed in *Adelphi*, 15; in *Anglo–Welsh Review*, 25; in *Aphrodite*, 237, 238; in *Arena*, 28; in *Aylesford Review*, 38; in *Contemporary Review*, 98; in *English*, 167; in *Experiment*, 178; in *London Mercury*, 252, 253; in *Poetry (London)*, 362; in *Quarterly Review*, 389–90; in *Scrutiny*, 427; in *Townsman*, 455; reviews Harold Monro, 144; satirized in *Contemporary Poetry*, 87; supported by Pound in *Egoist*, 144; supports Social Credit, 386. Works: *After Strange Gods*, 279; "The Aims of Poetic Drama," 4, 450; "The Ballad for Big Louise," 68; "Bullshit," 68; "Burbank with a Baedeker," 33, 398; "Commentaries," 116–18; *Complete Plays*, 398; "Culture and Politics," 16; *The Elder Statesman*, 98; "Euripides and Gilbert Murray," 33; *The Family Reunion*, 15; "Five Finger Exercises," 398; "Five Points on Dramatic Writing," 455; *Four Quartets*, 279, 362; "Fragment of an Agon," 117; "The Future of Poetic Drama," 134; "Gerontion," 398; "The Hollow

Men," 5; "The Idea of a Christian Society," 386; "The Idea of a Literary Review," 116; "Last Words," 119; *Little Gidding*, 277; "The Love Song of J. Alfred Prufrock," 68, 389; "Marina," 5; *Murder in the Cathedral*, 167; "Note on Poetry and Belief," 162; "Notes on the Blank Verse of Christopher Marlowe," 33; *Notes Towards a Definition of Culture*, 279, 398; "On a Recent Piece of Criticism," 386; *On Poetry and Poets*, 398; *Poems 1920*, 33; *Poems 1909–1925*, 252; *Poetry and Drama*, 5; "The Poetry of W.B. Yeats," 386; "Preludes," 68; "Reflections on the Unity of European Culture," 4; "Rhapsody on a Windy Night," 5, 362; *The Sacred Wood*, 252; "Salutation," 117; "The Social Function of Poetry," 16; "A Song for Simeon," 5; "Sweeney Erect," 33; "Tradition and the Individual Talent," 145; "The Unity of European Culture," 119; *The Use of Poetry and the Use of Criticism*, 279; *The Waste Land*, 30, 252. *See also Criterion*

Eliot, Vivienne, 114–15
Ellerman, Winifred, 225, 462
Elliot, Ebenezer, 83
Ellis, A. E., 249
Ellis, Havelock: "The Celtic Spirit in Literature," 93; contributes to *Contemporary Review*, 93; to *Enquiry*, 171; to *Golden Hind*, 194, 196; to *Life and Letters*, 225; to *Transatlantic Review*, 463; to *Twentieth Century*, 465
Ellis, Lionel, 237
Ellis–Roberts, R., 10
Ellis, S. M., 182
Ellmann, Richard, 159, 399
Elsom, John, 99; *Postwar British Theatre*, 100
Elton, Oliver, 241
Eluard, Paul, 28, 86–88, 213, 241, 288, 294, 367
Elwell-Sutton, A. S., 278
Elwin, Malcolm, 36, 391

Elyot, Kevin, 352
Elytis, Odysseus, 301, 340
Emmet, Alfred, 148
Empson, William: contributes to *Contemporary Poetry and Prose*, 87; to *Horizon*, 205, 206; to *Nimbus*, 306, 307; to *Review of English Literature*, 407; edits *Experiment*, 177-78; featured in *Review*, 398; "Just a Smack at Auden," 87; reviewed in *London Mercury*, 253; in *Mandrake*, 262; in *Penguin New Writing*, 339; in *Poetry (London)*, 362; in *Review*, 395; in *Writing Today*, 506; *Seven Types of Ambiguity*, 178; *The Structure of Complex Words*, 262
Encore, 146–53, 350, 353
Encounter, 153–61
Enemy, 161–64
English, 164–69
English Association, 164–68
English Carmelite Fathers, 35
English Review, 66, 459
English Stage Society, 246
Enigma, 378
Enquiry, 169-73
Enright, D. J.: *The Apothecary's Shop*, 506; contributes to *Cambridge Journal*, 85; to *Critical Quarterly*, 122; to *Encounter*, 155; to *English*, 167; to *London Magazine*, 245; to *Nimbus*, 306; to *Scrutiny*, 426; to *Wave*, 487; to *Workshop*, 504; on German literature, 426
Enslin, Ted, 375
Epstein, Jacob, 63, 69
Erculisse, Emile, 47
Ernst, Max, 88, 241, 242, 287
Ervine, St. John, 224, 444, 480
Esher, Oliver Brett, Viscount, 222
Essays in Criticism, 85
Essenin, Sergei, 174
Essex, Edwyn, 57
Esslin, Martin, 136, 156, 167, 350, 351
Etchells, Frederick, 62, 68, 69
Etheridge, Ken, 483
Eton Candle, 495
Euclid: *Elements of Geometrie*, 52
European Common Market, 156
European Quarterly, 173-77

Evans, B. Ifor, 16, 96, 168, 182
Evans, Brenda, 488
Evans, George Ewart, 484, 485
Evans, Illtud, 57
Evans, Margiad, 324
Evans, Maurice, 84
Evans, Richard, 370
Evans–Pritchard, E. E., 56
Evergreen Review, 297
Every, George, 278
Ewart, Gavin: "Audenesque for an Initia-
    tion," 293; contributes to *London
    Magazine*, 249; to *New Verse*, 293; to
    Poetry (London), 360; to *Review*, 400;
    to *Samphire*, 419; to *Twentieth Century
    Verse*, 469; influence of folk forms,
    88; "Inner Circle," 290; "Journey,"
    293; "Phallus in Wonderland," 293
Experiment, 177-79
Express Printers, 321
Ezekiel, Nissim, 406; "Marriage," 332

Faber and Faber, 114, 272
Fagan, Stephen, 352
Fainlight, Ruth, 331
Faithful, Lilian, 442
Falck, Colin, 394–99, 402
Fanfarlo. *See* Stonier, George
Fanfrolico Press, 236
Fantasy Press, 378
Farrar, James, 16
Farrell, James T., 156, 264
Farrell, Michael, 43
Fascism, 117, 154–58, 409–10, 498. *See
    also* Antisemitism; Political issues; So-
    cialist magazines, World War II
Fassbinder, Rainer Werner: *Pre-Paradise
    Sorry Now*, 188
Faulkner, Edwin, 129
Faulkner, William, 156, 316–19, 498;
    *Light in August, The Sound and the
    Fury*, 224
Fausset, Hugh l'Anson, 12, 14
Favil Press, 333
Fawcett, Millicent Garrett, 92
Feminist literature, 92–94, 105–6, 129,
    443–45
Fenollosa, Ernest, 62

Fenton, James: *Terminal Moraine*, 395
Ferguson, John, 98
Ferguson, Peter, 273
Ferlinghetti, Lawrence, 503
Fermor, Patrick Leigh, 107
Ferris, Paul, 25
Ferry, Antony, 147, 153
Ferry, Jean, 247
Ffrench, Yvonne, 252
Fiedler, Leslie, 155, 156
Field Press, 251, 255
Fielding, Henry, 84
Fielding, K. J., 168
Film criticism: in *Bermondsey Book*, 49;
    Contemporary Review, 99; *Drama*,
    134; *Encounter*, 155; *Experiment*, 178;
    Life and Letters, 224–27; *New English
    Weekly*, 278; *Review*, 403; *Quarterly
    Review*, 391; *Writing Today*, 506
Films and Filming, 350
Findlater, Richard, 136, 149, 350, 467
Fingleton, David, 99
Finlay, Ian Hamilton, 39, 374-76, 503
Finlayson, Henry G., 278
Firth, C. H., 105
Firth, J. B., 181
Fish Committee, 447
Fish, Winifred E., 383
Fisher, Charles, 483
Fisher, H. A. L., 95
Fisher, Roy, 372, 419
Fitchett, W. H., 105
Fitt, Mary. *See* Freeman, Kathleen
Fitzgerald, Percy, 94
Fitzgerald, Robert D., 356
Fitzmaurice, George, 141
Five Arches Press, 24
Flaubert, Gustave, 391; *Three Tales*, 197
Fleischmann, Julius, 158
Fleming Report on Education in Post-War
    Britain, 347
Fletcher, David, 60
Fletcher, Iain, 37, 309, 361
Fletcher, John Gould, 112, 117, 143–44
Flight, Claude, 385
Flint, F. S., 117, 460
Fluchère, Henri, 426
Foakes, R. A., 168

Focus, 381

Fogazzaro, Antonio, 175

Folios of New Writing, 300. *See also New Writing*

Forbes, Duncan, 83

Ford, Ford Madox: contributes to *Blast*, 65; to *Cornhill*, 105; to *Criterion*, 116; to *Golden Hind*, 196, 197; to *Twentieth Century*, 465; edits *Transatlantic Review*, 459–63; featured in *Agenda*, 19; *The Good Soldier*, 65; *Mister Bosphorus and the Muses*, 197; *The Nature of a Crime*, 462; *Portrait of Conrad*, 462–63; *Some Do Not*, 197, 462

Fore Publications, 28, 328

Foreign Affairs, 446

Form, 194

Forsdyke, Edgar J., 76

Forsdyke, John, 73

Forster, E. M.: *Abinger Harvest*, 1; contributes to *Abinger Chronicle*, 1–3; to *Adam*, 5; to *Calendar of Modern Letters*, 77–78; to *Criterion*, 116; to *Encounter*, 158; to *Life and Letters*, 223; to *New Writing*, 301; to *Time and Tide*, 449; to *Twentieth Century*, 465; *A Passage to India*, 444; reviewed in *Adelphi*, 17; in *Contemporary Review*, 98; in *Time and Tide*, 444; "The Torque," 158

Forster, Peter, 136

Forte, Charles, 453

Fortnightly Review, 62, 85, 97, 181–84

Fortune Press, 284

Forzano, Giovacchino: *A Gust of Wind*, *To Live in Peace*, 186

Four Pages, 18–19

Fowles, John, 108, 401

Foxall, Edgar, 88

Frame, Robert, 374

France, 4

France, Anatole, 290

Francis, Frank C., 76

Frank, Waldo, 12, 14

Frankel, Ben, 331

Franklin, Roger, 276

Fraser, C. Lovat, 479

Fraser, G[eorge] S[utherland]: at Cambridge, 431; coedits *Nine*, 309; contributes to *Adam*, 5; to *Kingdom Come*, 212; to *Lines Review*, 235; to *New Road*, 387; to *Nine*, 310; to *Poetry Commonwealth*, 357; to *Poetry (London)*, 361, 362; to *Seven*, 430; "Elegy for Certain Resolutions," 367; guest editor for *Workshop*, 503; reviewed in *Review*, 398; satirized in *Review*, 394

Fraser, Norrie, 385

Frazer, James G., 391

Freedgood, Morton, 338

Freedom Press, 321

Freeman, John, 32

Freeman, Kathleen, 196

Freewoman. *See Egoist*

French literature, 19, 95, 189, 203–4, 426

French, Cecil, 194, 195, 197

Freud, Sigmund, 116, 225–27, 382–83, 446

Freytag-Loringhofen, Elsa von, 462

Fried, Michael, 393, 395, 396; *Appetites*, 398; "Miscarriage," 475

Friedman, Milton, 156

Friend, Krebs, 462

Frisch, Max: *Philipp Hotz's Fury*, 186

Frost, Robert, 77, 251, 397

Fry, Christopher, 137, 138, 254

Fry, Geoffrey, 247

Fry, Maxwell, 174

Fry, Roger, 61, 115

Fuller, John: *The Art of Love*, 398; *Cannibals and Missionaries*, 395; contributes to *Review*, 395, 398–99; to *Universities' Poetry*, 475; edits *Universities' Poetry*, 474; *Fairground Music*, 474; *The Tree That Walked*, 379, 395

Fuller, Roy: "The Audience and Politics," 469; *A Reader's Guide to W. H. Auden*, 395; *Collected Poems*, 395; contributes to *Kingdom Come*, 212; to *London Magazine*, 245; to *New Verse*, 293; to *Orion*, 324; to *Penguin New Writing*, 339; to *Review*, 393; to *Twentieth Century Verse*, 468–69; to *Windmill*, 501; in *Review* anthology, 395;

interview in *Writing Today*, 506; *New Poems*, 395; "October 1940," 319; on Laura Riding, 397; reviewed in *Northern Review*, 316; in *Now*, 318
Fulton, Robin, 233, 234, 416
Furnival, John, 374, 375
Furnival Press, 53
Futurism, 58, 63

Gabain, Marjorie, 385
Gabo, Naum, 242
Gairm, 21
Gait, John W., and Sons, 321
Galbraith, John Kenneth, 155
Galil Publishing Company, 216
Galletley, Leonard, 129
Galloway, David, 298
Galsworthy, John: centenary tribute in *Gambit*, 187; contributes to *Bermondsey*, 46; to *Owl*, 334; to *Time and Tide*, 442; to *Voices*, 480; praised in *Decachord* for Nobel Prize, 130; reviewed in *Drama*, 134–38; in *New Stories*, 290
Gambit, 185–90, 350
Gandhi, Mahatma, 498
Gangrel, 190–93
Gappmayr, Heinz, 374
Garcia Lorca, Federico, 89, 175, 219, 301, 310, 339, 398
Gardiner, C. Wrey, 287, 288, 367, 500
Gardiner, Leslie, 59
Gardiner, Rolf, 16
Gardner, Diana, 368
Gardner, Helen, 303
Garioch, Robert, 23, 168, 234, 235, 455
Garlick, Raymond, 24–26, 370, 371
Garman, Douglas M., 77–79, 329, 461, 462; "Visiting Day," 462
Garnett, David, 407
Garrett, George, 338
Garrick, David, 2
Gascoyne, David: contributes to *Adam International Review*, 7; to *Contemporary Poetry and Prose*, 86, 88–89; to *European Quarterly*, 175; to *Kingdom Come*, 213; to *New Verse*, 293; to *New Writing*, 302; to *Poetry (London)*, 361,

362; to *Purpose*, 385; to *Seven*, 430, 432; featured in *X: Quarterly Review*, 510; "The Light of the Lion's Mane," 89; reviewed in *New Verse*, 293; *A Short Survey of Surrealism*, 87, 241; "The Very Image, to Rene Magritte," 88
Gaskell, Elizabeth, 104
Gaskill, William, 149, 188
Gates, Barrington, 290
Gaudier-Brezska, Henri, 62–65, 67–68, 455, 479
Gawsworth, John, 39, 170, 171, 361; *Collected Poems*, 171
Gellner, Ernest, 83
Genet, Jean, 149, 306, 403
Geoffrey, Gordon: "It's Good To Be Young," 213
George, Daniel, 501
George, Lloyd, 442
George, W. L., 181
Georgian Poetry, 131, 491
Georgian poets: attacked by moderns, 127, 292; published in *Decachord*, 131; in *English*, 167; in *Horizon*, 204; in *London Mercury*, 32, 251–54; tolerated by T. S. Eliot, 144
Gerard, Martin, 510
Gerhardi, William, 77
German literature, 84, 95, 189, 426, 435–38
Gershenzon, M. O., 174
Gertler, Mark, 10
Ghika, 204
Ghose, Zulfikar A., 332, 474
Giacometti, Alberto, 510
Gibbings, Robert, 479
Gibbon, Monk, 141
Gibbons, Stella, 12, 448
Gibson, Douglas, 2
Gibson, W. W., 168
Gibson, Wilfred, 46
Gide, André, 5, 107, 213, 301, 340
Giedion, Siegfried, 242
Gifford, William, 391
Gilbert, William S., 106
Gilby, Thomas, 56
Gill, Eric, 37, 54

Gill, Richard, 174, 175
Gill, Sarah Shore, 2
Gillatt, Penelope, 149
Gilleat-Smith, Baptista, 211
Gillett, Eric, 197
Gillis, Astrid, 375
Gillman, James, 72
Gilloux, Louis, 338
Gilman, H., 31
Ginner, Charles, 31
Ginsberg, Allen, 274
Ginzberg, Natalia, 249
Giono, Jean, 340
Girsavicius, J. O., 178
Gissing, George, 92
Gittings, Robert, 99
Gladstone, William, 465
Glasgow, George, 96
Glazer, Nathan, 156
Glebe, 62
Glen, Duncan, 21–24, 375
Glenday, Michael K., 22
Glover, Jon, 437
Godden, Rumer, 450
Godfrey, Gordon, 98, 99
Godwin, George, 16
Goethe, Johann Wolfgang, 14, 85, 89;
    Faust, 170
Gogarty, Oliver St. John, 42
Gold, Eric, 23
Golden Hind, 193–99
Golding, Louis, 477–80
Golding, William, 122
Goldsmith, John, 466
Golightly, Alan, 379
Gollomb, Joseph, 181
Gomringer, Eugen, 374, 375
Goncharov, Ivan, 159
Gooch, George Peabody, 91–98, 101
Good, Thomas, 192
Goodland, John, 430
Goodman, Paul, 284, 287
Goodwin, Clive, 147, 153
Goodwin, Michael, 467
Gordimer, Nadine, 108, 156, 249, 400;
    "The Dogs," 400
Gordon, Caroline, 118
Gordon, Giles, 136, 415, 416

Gorell, John G. Barnes, Lord, 97, 107
Gorky, Maxim, 219, 270
Gosse, Edmund, 6, 92, 105, 182, 256,
    391
Gourmont, Rémy de, 182
Gower Street Lecture Club of Individual
    Psychology, 381, 382
Gowing, Laurence, 325
Graham, A[ngus] C[harles], 398
Graham, Cunningham, 315
Graham, Henry, 434
Graham, Rigby, 378
Graham, W. H., 97
Graham, W. S., 361
Grahame, Kenneth, 100
Granger, Frank, 175
Granger, Muriel, 192
Gransden, K. W., 156
Granville-Barker, Frank, 354
Granville-Barker, Harley, 107, 134, 138,
    182
Grass, Gunter, 156, 158
Graves, Robert: attacked in *New Verse*,
    295; contributes to *Adelphi*, 11, 14; to
    Calendar of Modern Letters, 77; to
    Cornhill, 108; to *Decachord*, 129; to
    Enquiry, 170; to *Fortnightly Review*,
    182; to *London Magazine*, 245; to *New
    Writing*, 303; to *Poetry Wales*, 372; to
    Time and Tide, 450; to *Voices*, 480; to
    Windmill, 501; edits *Owl*, 333–35; "A
    Frosty Night," 334; "Ghost-Raddled,"
    334; *Poems 1938–1945*, 498; reviewed
    in *Quarterly Review*, 390; in *Wind and
    the Rain*, 498; "The White Goddess,"
    170. *See also Owl*; Seizin Press
Gray, John, 37
Gray, Ruth: "Chagrin," 213
Gray, Simon, 352, 401; *Dog Days, Two
    Sundays*, 401
Gray, Thomas, 59
Greacen, Robert, 287, 361
Greek literature, 19, 181, 340
Green, Carolyn, 147
Green, Henry, 301, 340, 387
Green, Hugh, 6
Green, Lawrence G., 59
Green, Roger Lancelyn, 261

Green, Russell, 110–11
Greenberg, Clement, 203
Greene, Graham: "The Coming," 197; contributes to *Decachord*, 129; to *Golden Hind*, 197; to *Horizon*, 205, 206; to *Life and Letters*, 224; to *London Magazine*, 245, 248; to *London Mercury*, 252; to *Mint*, 264, 265; to *Orion*, 326; to *Penguin New Writing*, 340; to *Time and Tide*, 448, 451; to *Windmill*, 500; "Convoy to West Africa," 265; featured in *Adam International Review*, 6; *The Ministry of Fear*, 498; on François Mauriac, 500; "The Potting Shed," 97; reviewed in *Adelphi*, 17; in *Contemporary Review*, 97; in *Northern Review*, 316; in *Now*, 318; in *Wind and the Rain*, 498–99
Greenwood, Arthur, 95
Gregg, Frances, 12
Gregory, Horace, 90, 284
Greig, Andrew, 23
Grein, J. T., 136
Grey Owl, 259. *See also Owl*
Grey Walls Press, 216, 288, 367
Gribble, Vivien, 197
Grierson, Francis, 98
Grierson, H. J. C., 450
Grieve, Christopher Murray. *See* MacDiarmid, Hugh
Griffith, Hubert, 136
Griffith, Ll. Wyn, 483
Griffiths, Bryn, 370
Grigg, Malcolm: "Sonata for a Young Man," 178
Grigson, Frances Franklin, 297
Grigson, Geoffrey: attacked in *Kingdom Come*, 214; contributes to *Encounter*, 156; to *Review*, 398; to *Wind and the Rain*, 498; to *Windmill*, 501; edits *Mint*, 264–65; *New Verse*, 291–96; on Norman Cameron, 398; on Dylan Thomas, 205, 360
Grillo, John, 187
Grimond, Joseph, 97
Grindea, Carol, 4
Grindea, Miron, 4–7
Gris, Juan, 462

Grodeck, Georg, 383
Gross, Fritz, 96
Group poets, 487
Gruffydd, Peter, 370, 371
Guest, Harry, 434
Guevara, Alvaro Velez Ladron de, 492
Guilbert, Yvette, 277
Guild socialism, 173. *See also* Social credit
Guinness, Alec, 341
Guinness, Bryan, 15
Gumilev, Nicolai, 3
Gundolf, Friedrich, 118
Gunn, Neil, 192, 315, 414–16, 421
Gunn, Thom: contributes to *Agenda*, 20; to *Critical Quarterly*, 122; to *London Magazine*, 245; to *Twentieth Century*, 465; to *Workshop*, 503; in *Priapus* anthology, 378; in *Review* anthology, 395; reviewed in *Critical Quarterly*, 122; in *Priapus*, 379; in *Review*, 395, 396; in *Review* anthology, 395; *Touch*, 379
Gurnard, Joseph. *See* Stonier, George
Guthrie, Tyrone, 147
Gutkind, Erich, 385
Gutman, Ethel, 45–46
Gwynn, Stephen, 444

H. D. *See* Doolittle, Hilda
Hackett, Dennis, 466
Haggard, H. Rider, 37, 93
Hair, 188
Haldane, J. B. S., 47
Hale, Owen, 147
Hall, Bill, 232
Hall, Donald, 397
Hall, J. C., 368, 394, 432
Hall, Peter, 147, 149
Hall, Radclyffe: *The Well of Loneliness*, 238
Halward, Leslie, 338
Hamburger, Michael: "Brecht and His Successors," 398; contributes to *Agenda*, 20; to *Mandrake*, 263; to *Nine*, 310; to *Poetry (London)*, 361; to *Wave*, 487; to *Workshop*, 503; reviewed in *Review*, 398; translation of

Lorca, 310; "The Unity of Eliot's Poetry," 398
Hamilton, Cicely, 449
Hamilton, Cuthbert, 62, 65, 69
Hamilton, George Rostrevor, 12, 325
Hamilton, Ian, 393–404, 488; *Pretending Not To Sleep*, 398
Hamilton, Robin, 235
Hamnett, Nina, 110, 491
Hampton, Christopher, 137
Handke, Peter, 352
Hanley, James, 99
Hansom Books, Ltd., 354
Hapgood, Norman, 93
Harding, D. W., 423, 429
Harding, Harold, 196
Harding, Joan, 97
Hardy, Barbara, 167, 168
Hardy, Thomas: "And There Was a Great Calm," 478; contributes to *Bermondsey Book*, 46; to *Cornhill*, 104–5; to *Fortnightly Review*, 182; to *Life and Letters*, 223; to *London Mercury*, 251; to *Owl*, 334; eulogized in *Cornhill*, 106; *Far from the Madding Crowd*, 106; featured in *Agenda*, 19; "The Master and the Leaves," 334; "The Missed Train," 334; promotes *Transatlantic Review*, 460; reviewed in *Adelphi*, 12; in *English*, 167; in *Northern Review*, 316; in *Now*, 318; in *Time and Tide*, 444; in *Voices*, 478
Hare, David, 137, 352; *How Brophy Made Good*, 188
Harker, Diana, 147, 153
Harris, Frank, 112
Harris, John H., 181
Harris, Kenneth, 211
Harris, Mary, 319
Harrison, Frederic, 182
Harrison, Tony, 249; "National Trust," "The School of Eloquence," 436
Harrisson, Tom, 206, 293
Harrold, R. F., 82
Harsent, David, 395–99, 401–3; *Tonight's Lover*, 398
Hartley, Jean, 488
Hartley, L. P., 6, 78, 99, 245, 248, 501

Harvey, John, 476
Harwood, H. C., 77, 78
Harwood, Lee, 396
Haskell, Arnold C., 16, 278
Hassall, Christopher, 213
Hauptmann, Gerhardt, 116, 137
Hawkes, Jacquetta, 450
Hawkes, John, 401
Hawkesyard Review, 53
Hawkins, A. Desmond, 278, 385–87, 469
Hawkins, Jacquetta, 506
Hawkins, Spike, 375, 434
Hawthorne, Nathaniel: *Blithedale Romance*, 444
Hayman, Ronald, 136, 138, 307, 400
Hayter, William, 158
Haywood, John, 223
Hazlitt, William, 182, 328–30
Heal, David, 439
Heaney, Seamus, 249, 274, 372, 394, 503; "The Play Way," 332; "Turkeys Observe," 475
Heard, Gerald, 170, 172
Hearsey, Richard, 378
Heartfield, John, 242
Heath, Frederick, 49
Heath-Stubbs, John: contributes to *Kingdom Come*, 214; to *New Road*, 287; to *Penguin New Writing*, 339; to *Poetry (London)*, 361–62; to *Time and Tide*, 450; to *Wind and the Rain*, 498; to *Windmill*, 500–501; on Charles Williams, 362, 498
Hebblethwaite, Eleanor, 128
Heffer, W., and Sons, Ltd., 436
Heinemann, William, 247, 500
Heller, Erich, 84
Heller, Joseph, 401
Hemingway, Ernest, 38, 259, 316, 319, 427; "The Doctor and the Doctor's Wife," 463; edits *Transatlantic Review*, 461–62; quarrel with Ford Madox Ford, 461–62
Henderson, Alexander, 324
Henderson, Hamish, 232, 341
Henderson, Hubert Douglas, 270
Hendersons, 110, 481

Hendricks, A. L., 504
Hendry, J[ames] F[indlay], 214, 285, 374, 375, 430–31, 484
Henri, Adrian, 503
Henry, O. *See* Porter, William Sydney
Henryson, Robert, 421
Heppenstall, Rayner, 14, 15, 192, 278, 324
Herbert, Zbigniew, 393, 398
Herdman, John, 22, 23
Herford, C. H., 96
Heron, T. M., 277
Herring, Robert, 224–25
Herrmann-Neise, Max, 96
Hertz, Frederick, 83
Heseltine, Nigel, 411, 483, 484
Hesketh, Phoebe, 97, 168
Hesse, Hermann, 115
Hewitt, R. M., 174
Hickok, Guy, 462
Hidden, Norman, 502, 503
Higgins, Aidan, 510
Higgins, Bertram, 77–79
Higgins, F. R., 141
Hiler, Hilarie, 455
Hill, Edmund, 57–58
Hill, Geoffrey, 19, 306, 365, 397, 438, 510; "Our Word Is Our Bond," 20
Hill, George F., 76
Hill, Greg, 27
Hill, Holly, 100
Hillyer, Robert, 12
Hilton, R. W. K., 82
Hind, C. Lewis, 197
Hinde, Thomas: *Agent*, 400
Hindu literature, 227
Hirst, Francis, 95
Hoare, Samuel, 77, 197
Hobday, C. H., 331
Hobman, D. L., 96
Hobsbaum, Philip, 235, 332, 379, 487; "The Rock Pool," 332
Hobsbawm, E. J., 83, 84
Hobson, Harold, 188
Hockney, David, 273, 274, 402
Hodges, Cyril, 370
Hoffman, Daniel, 434, 435
Hoffman, Frederick J., 238

Hoffmannstahl, Hugo von, 116
Hogarth Press, 302, 337
Holbrook, David, 329, 330
Holdane, Elizabeth, 181
Hölderlin, Friedrich, 11, 398; *Patmos*, 175
Hole, Phillipa, 129–30
Hollo, Anselm, 39, 283, 375; "Fennica," 434
Holloway, Geoffrey: *Rhine Jump*, 418
Holloway, John, 84–85, 167, 245, 414, 415
Holms, J. F., 78
Holtby, Winifred, 444–45
Holub, Miroslav, 403
Homer, 294; *Iliad*, 264; *Odyssey*, 279
Hone, William, 328
Hook, Sidney, 156
Hope, Anthony, 105
Hope, Francis, 395; "Deluded Bears Are Wrecking Telephone Poles," 474
Hopkins, Gerard Manley, 84, 219
Hopkins, Kenneth, 37
Hopkinson, Tom, 230, 231
Horder, John, 503
Horizon, 6, 42, 153, 201–8, 226, 342, 360
Horovitz, Adam, 275
Horovitz, Frances, 39, 275; *The High Tower*, 274
Horovitz, Michael, 39, 272-75, 419; *Children of Albion*, 273, 274; *19 Poems of Love, Lust, and Spirit*, 274
Hort, G. M., 195
Hough, Graham, 17, 84, 407
Hound and Horn, 425
House, Jack, 414
Housman, A. E., 316, 318
Housman, Laurence, 170, 194
Houston, Libby, 375
Howard, Albert, 277, 278
Howard, Birkin, 331
Howard, Brian, 494–95
Howard, Charles, 242
Howell, Jane, 188
Howells, William Dean, 17, 105
Hronstein, Yakov, 3
Huchel, Peter, 398

Huddleston, Sisley, 181
Hueffer, Ford Madox. *See* Ford, Ford
Madox
Hueffer, Oliver, 459
Hughes, Langston, 274, 448
Hughes, Richard: *A High Wind in Ja-maica*, 223
Hughes, Ted: contributes to *Critical Quarterly*, 122; to *London Magazine*, 249; to *New Departures*, 274; to *Work-shop*, 503; *Crow*, 379; *Hawk in the Rain*, 246; leaves *Encounter* because of CIA backing, 159; reviewed in *Agenda*, 20; in *Critical Quarterly*, 122; in *London Magazine*, 246; in *Priapus*, 378-79; in *Writing Today*, 506; *Wodwo*, 379
Hughes, Thomas, 95
Huizinga, J. H., 401
Hull, R. F. C., 324
Hull, Tristram, 305
Hull University, 124
Hulme, T. E., 63, 116
Hulton, Edward, 229
Hume, David, 416
Humphreys, Emyr, 26
Hungarian poetry, 234
Hunley, T. H., 465
Hunt, Hugh, 136
Hunter, G. K., 122
Huntley, Francis E. *See* Mayne, Ethel
Colburn
Hunyedi, Sandor, 229
Hurd, Archibald, 181
Hurry, Leslie, 340
Husain, Adrian, 283
Hutchings, W., 125
Hutchinson, Horace G., 391
Huxley, Aldous: contributes to *Bermond-sey Book*, 46; to *Calendar of Modern Letters*, 78; to *Coterie*, 112; to *Crite-rion*, 117; to *Golden Hind*, 194, 197; to *London Aphrodite*, 238; to *Now*, 318; to *Time and Tide*, 444, 446; to *Wheels*, 492, 494; defended in *London Aphrodite*, 238; letter in *Enquiry*, 171; letter in *Right Review*, 409; on editorial board of *Coterie*, 110; opinion of Sit-

wells, 492; reviewed in *Adelphi*, 12; in *Aylesford Review*, 38; in *Life and Let-ters*, 223; in *Writing Today*, 506.
Works: "Albert: Prince Consort," 197; "The Ambassador of Capripedia," 197; *Antic Hay*, 238; "Art as a Social Function," 318; *Brave New World Re-visited*, 506; *Collected Stories*, 506; "Literature and Examinations," 446; *Point Counter Point*, 9; "Socratic Dia-logues of the Moment," 444; "Theatre of Varieties," 497
Huxley, Julian, 46, 95, 105–7, 316, 465, 492; "Art as a Social Function," 316; "The Courtship of Animals," 48
Huxley, Leonard, 105-7
Hyde, Lawrence, 12

Ibsen, Henrik: contributes to *Contempo-rary Review*, 93; reviewed in *Adelphi*, 12; in *Contemporary Review*, 93, 100; in *Drama*, 134, 137; in *Kingdom Come*, 219; in *Life and Letters*, 223; "The Saga and the Ballad," 93
Illustrations. *See* Art reproductions
Imagist poetry, 9, 31, 62, 110, 144, 177, 292
Indian literature, 458
Interim Drama. See Drama, 135, 139
International Arts Guild, 4
International Bulletin of Surrealism, 241
International Guide, 458
International Surrealist Exhibition (June 1936), 88
Ionesco, Eugene, 4, 156–57, 247, 274; "Have I Written Anti-Theatre?" 186
Ionides, Luke, 460, 462; *Memoirs*, 462
Irish Academy of Letters, 140
Irish literature, 41–44, 93, 139–41, 167, 234, 503
Irish Statesman, 41
Isaacs, J., 462
Isherwood, Christopher: contributes to *Encounter*, 155; to *New Verse*, 301; to *New Writing*, 301; to *Penguin New Writing*, 338; to *Twentieth Century*, 465; *Goodbye to Berlin*, 301; reviewed in *Review*, 401

Italian literature, 22, 95–96, 197, 262, 414

Ivens, Michael, 467

Ivor, B. F., 394

Jackson, Alan, 234

Jackson, Barry, 137

Jackson, Norman, 378, 379

Jackson, T. A., 328

Jacobson, Dan, 396, 401; *The Maturity of Josef Baise*, 400

Jacobson, H. M., 403

Jacobson, Sydney, 231

Jaffin, David: *The Half of a Circle*, 418

James, Arnold, 491–94

James, C. L. R., 153

James, Clive, 395, 397; *The Metropolitan Critic*, 395; "Peregrine Prykke's Pilgrimage," 402

James, Henry: contributes to *Cornhill*, 105; "The Golden Bowl," 84; reviewed in *Blackwood's Edinburgh Magazine*, 58; in *Cambridge Journal*, 84; in *Cornhill*, 108; in *Enquiry*, 170; in *Horizon*, 205; in *Northern Review*, 316; in *Now*, 318; in *Orion*, 325, 326; in *Scrutiny*, 427; in *Transatlantic Review*, 459; letters in *Adam*, 6; *The Wings of the Dove*, 84, 325; "Within the Rim," 182

James, John, 434

Jameson, Storm, 5, 278, 447, 480

Jandl, Ernst, 374, 375

Jarosy, Ivo, 306, 307

Jarrell, Randall, 203, 285, 395; "The Death of the Ball-Turret Gunner," 203

Jarrett, Bede, 54, 57

Jarry, Alfred, 86

Jay, Peter, 282

Jean-Jouve, Pierre, 362

Jeffares, A. Norman, 168, 406–8

Jeffrey, Francis, 252

Jeffrey, William, 12

Jellicoe, Ann: *The Knack*, 149

Jellinek, Frank, 331

Jenkins, Heinke, 378

Jenkins, Robin, 415

Jennett, Sean, 498

Jennings, Elizabeth: contributes to *Aylesford Review*, 39; to *London Magazine*, 245; to *Outposts*, 331; to *Twentieth Century*, 465, to *Wave*, 487; reviewed in *Contemporary Review*, 98; in *Review*, 394

Jennings, Humphrey, 86, 178, 242, 244; "The Boyhood of Byron," 89

Jentzsch, Bernd, 398

Jerome, Helen, 197

Jewett, Kennon, 461

Jhabvala, Ruth Prawer, 249

Jiminez, Juan, 398

Joad, C. E. M., 170, 450

John O'London's, 451, 484

John, Augustus, 5, 112

John, Gwen, 197, 461

Johnson, B. S., 332; "The Son of Jesus," 379

Johnson, Bryan, 474

Johnson, Geoffrey, 168

Johnson, Louis, 355–57

Johnson, Michael, 502, 503

Johnson, Pamela Hansford, 448, 449

Johnson, Patricia: "The Choice," 319

Johnson, Ronald, 374, 375

Johnson, Samuel, 59, 106, 326, 334

Johnson, Terry, 352

Johnston, Denis, 42

Johnstone, William, 455

Jones, A. G., 439

Jones, Bobi, 370

Jones, Brian, 249

Jones, D. A. N., 403

Jones, David, 19, 26, 371, 372, 373

Jones, Gerallt, 371

Jones, Glyn, 25, 26, 469, 483, 484

Jones, Jack, 26, 448

Jones, John Idris, 370

Jones, Lawrence, 440

Jones, Lewis, 220

Jones, Michael Wynn, 467

Jones, Peter, 365; *British Poetry Since 1970*, 365–66

Jones, Simon, 354

Jong, Erica, 307, 418

Jonson, Ben, 188; *Volpone*, 187

Jopson, N. B., 175

Jordan, Clive, 475
Josephs, Bertram, 262
Journal of the Printing Historical Society, 51–52
Jouvenal, Bertrand de: *Sovereignty*, 38
Joyce, James: censored by *Calendar* printers, 77; contributes to *Arts and Letters*, 33–34; to *Criterion*, 116; to *Egoist*, 144; to *Experiment*, 178; to *Transatlantic Review*, 461–63; editorial advisor to *Transatlantic Review*, 459–61; *Finnegans Wake*, 226, 427; model for *Scottish Chapbook*, 422; *A Portrait of the Artist as a Young Man*, 33, 144; reviewed in *Aphrodite*, 237; in *Criterion*, 116; in *Enemy*, 162, 163; in *Life and Letters*, 223, 226; in *Nimbus*, 307; in *Orion*, 326; in *Purpose*, 387; in *Quarterly Review*, 390; in *Scrutiny*, 427; supported by Pound in *Egoist*, 144; *Ulysses*, 11, 144, 307, 390; *Work in Progress* (*Finnegans Wake*), 461
Juenger, Ernst, 288
Jung, Carl G., 12, 170, 306, 307, 384

Kafka, Franz, 118, 174, 387; *Diaries*, 324; "Him," 279
Kahlau, Heinz, 398
Kaiser, Ernst, 306; "The City," *The Murder Story*, 307
Kandinsky, Vasily, 69
Kantorowicz, Alfred, 338
Kapp, Edward, 480
Kavanagh, Patrick, 42, 205, 306, 361, 510
Kay, George, 232
Kazin, Alfred, 108
Keats, John, 12, 85, 99, 107, 197
Keith, Arthur, 170
Kelleher, John, 43
Keller, Hans, 402, 403
Kelly, Bernard, 56
Kelmscott Press, 52
Kendrick, Thomas, 75–76
Kennan, George F., 156
Kennaway, James, 248
Kennedy, Stetson, 308
Kennedy, X. J., 108

Kenner, Hugh, 310
Kenny, Rowland, 280
Kent, Rockwell, 334
Kenyon, Frederick, 71–74
Kermode, Frank, 84, 155, 156, 158, 400, 407
Kerouac, Jack, 274, 505, 509
Kerr, Fergus, 58
Kershaw, John R. C., 181
Kettle, Arnold, 28
Keyes, Sidney, 214, 215, 287, 361–62; "Rome Remember," "Seascape," 362
Keynes, John Maynard, 269-70
Khlebnikov, Velimir: "From a Zoological Garden," 374
Kiely, Benedict, 42
Kierkegaard, Søren: "A Personal Confession," 175
King, Cecil, 244, 247
King, Francis, 249
Kingdom Come, 211–16, 360
King-Hall, Stephen, 444
Kingsland, William G., 94
Kingsley, Charles, 95
Kinnell, Galway, 434
Kinsella, Thomas, 42
Kipling, Rudyard, 32, 258, 459
Kirk, G. S., 83
Kirkpatrick, Jean, 157
Kirkup, James, 15, 192, 287, 325, 362, 499
Klee, Paul, 88, 242
Klein, John, 137
Klingender, F. D., 328, 329
Knight, G. Wilson, 99, 168, 182, 473, 498
Knight, Holford, 181
Knight, Laura, 194, 479
Knights, L. C., 423, 426, 429
Knowles, James, 464–66
Koestler, Arthur: compared to Orwell, 497; contributes to *Encounter*, 156; to *Horizon*, 203, 206; to *Lilliput*, 229; to *New Writing*, 303; "The Foulest Christmas I Ever Had," 229–30; "The Intelligentsia," 206; "The Mixed Transport," 203; *The Sleepwalkers*,

157; *Suicide of a Nation*, 156; "The Yogi and the Commissar," 206
Kokoschka, Oskar, 242, 287
Komroff, Manuel, 229
Kops, Bernard, 6, 273
Koteliansky, S. S., 9–10, 77
Kott, Jan, 28
Kramer, Jacob, 67, 479
Kristol, Irving, 153–56
Krook, Dorothea, 84
Kropotkin, Peter, 317
Kunert, Gunter, 398
Kureczko, Victor, 439
Kushner, Alexander, 435
Kustow, Michael, 153

Labour Party, 13, 328–29, 450. *See also* Political issues; Socialist magazines
Lagerlöf, Selma, 461
Lahr, John, 136
Laing, Ronald, 402
Lall, Chaman, 110
Lamb, Charles, 72, 107
Lamb, Mary, 72
Lambert, J. W., 136, 137
Lambeth Conference, 55
Lamblett, Charles, 273
Lambton, Edward, 474
Lane, Allen, 220, 337, 344–45, 348
Lane, Edward, 500
Lane, John, 64, 69, 305
Lane, Margaret, 107, 108, 325, 326
Lang, Andrew, 93, 105
Lange, Monique, 298
Langland, William, 36, 130
Lannon, Tom, 99
Lansburgy, George, 449
Lanux, Eyre de, 462
Larbaud, Valéry, 11
Larkin, Philip: contributes to *Cornhill*, 108; to *Critical Quarterly*, 122; to *London Magazine*, 245–46, 249; to *Wave*, 487; *A Girl in Winter*, 262; in *Priapus* anthology, 378; in *Review* anthology, 395; influence on *Critical Quarterly*, 122; reviewed in *Critical Quarterly*, 122; in *Mandrake*, 262; in

Poetry Nation, 365; in *Writing Today*, 505
Larminie, William, 93
Laski, Harold, 10, 46, 117, 447
Laski, Marghanita, 506
Lasky, Melvin J., 155–56
Lasserson, Michael, 6
Latin (classical) literature, 22, 181
Lattimore, Richmond, 254
Laughlin, James, 279
Laval, Pierre, 84
Lavin, Mary, 42
Lavrin, Janko, 173-76
Lawrence and Wishart, 302
Lawrence, C. E., 392
Lawrence, D. H.: attacked by Wyndham Lewis, 163; biography in *European Quarterly*, 174-75; contributes to *Adelphi*, 8–13; to *Calendar of Modern Letters*, 77; to *Egoist*, 144; to *Fortnightly Review*, 182; to *Life and Letters*, 223; to *London Mercury*, 252; to *Lovat Dickson's Magazine*, 259; to *New Coterie*, 112; to *Time and Tide*, 444; to *Voices*, 480; "Creative Evolution," 10; essay on Hawthorne, 444; eulogy in *Adelphi*, 13; in *London Mercury*, 253; *Fantasia of the Unconscious*, 9–10; "Hopi: Snake Dance," 10; "Indians and an Englishman," 10; letters in *Encounter*, 158; in *Samphire*, 419; letters to Katherine Mansfield, 13; "Nottingham and the Mining Countryside," 13; on *Adelphi*, 10; relationship with J. M. Murray, 9–13; reviewed in *Adelphi*, 17; in *European Quarterly*, 175; in *Life and Letters*, 223; in *London Aphrodite*, 238; in *Lovat Dickson's Magazine*, 258; in *Purpose*, 386; in *Quarterly Review*, 389; in *Review*, 397; in *Scrutiny*, 427; reviews Frederick Rolfe, 10; "Snake, The," 252; supported by Pound in *Egoist*, 144; translations of Giovanni Verga, 10
Lawrence, T. E., 6, 334
Lawrence, W. J., 181
Lax, Robert, 374-75
Lea, F. A., 14

Leakey, L. S. B., 170

Leautreamont, Comte de: *Les Chants de Maldoror*, 88

Leavis, F. R., 78, 121–23, 423–28, 490; *Culture and Environment*, 424; *Education and the University*, 424; *Re–Reading English*, 366; *Towards Standards of Criticism*, 78–79

Leavis, Q. D., 423–28; *Fiction and the Reading Public*, 424

LeBreton, Louis, 178

Lechmere, Kate, 62, 65

Lee, Laurie, 108, 205, 324, 325, 341

Lee, Vernon. *See* Paget, Violet

Leeper, Janet, 136

Leeston, Osyth, 108–9

Lefebvre, Marcus, 58

LeFoe, Dominic, 98

Left Review, 217–22, 293, 300, 409, 468

Legge, Sheila, 241

Lehmann, Beatrix, 331

Lehmann, John: assists with *Encounter*, 153; attacked in *Kingdom Come*, 214; contributes to *Adam*, 5; to *Experiment*, 177; to *New Writing*, 303; to *Orion*, 324; edits *London Magazine*, 244–47; *New Writing*, 300–304; *Penguin New Writing*, 337–42; letter in *Horizon*, 204; on *Experiment*, 177; on proletarian literature, 301; opposes Marxist criticism, 300; satirized in *Penguin New Writing*, 342

Lehmann, Rosamond, 244, 300, 323, 339

Leishman, James Blair, 261

Leith, Mrs. Disney, 94

Lejeune, Anthony, 452

Le Maistre, Violet, 12

Lemasson, Sophie: *1789*, 188

Le Mesurier, Lilian, 49

Lenin, Vladimir I. U., 14

Leonardo da Vinci, 223

Leonov, Leonid, 28, 77

Lerner, L. D., 85, 488

Leslie, Shane, 390

Lesser, J., 96

Lessing, Doris, 149, 156, 230, 401; "A Home for the Highland Cattle," 230

Le surrealisme au service de la revolution, 241

Le Theatre du Soleil, 188

Letwin, Shirley, 83, 84

Leverson, Ada, 117

Levertov, Denise, 192, 319; "Folding a Shirt," 319

Levi, Peter, 274

Levidov, M., 175

Levine, Ellen, 372

Lewes, George Henry, 97

Lewis, Alun: contributes to *Kingdom Come*, 214; "In Hospital Poona," 361; in *Review* anthology, 395; reviewed in *Northern Review*, 316; in *Now*, 318; in *Review*, 399; "Postscript for Gweno," 361; "The Public Gardens," 361; special issue of *Poetry Wales*, 372; "To Edward Thomas," 361

Lewis, C. Day: castigated in *Review*, 394; co-editor for *Orion*, 323, 325; contributes to *Adam*, 5; to *Adelphi*, 15; to *Bell*, 42; to *Contemporary Poetry and Prose*, 87; to *Cornhill*, 108; to *Encounter*, 155, 156; to *English*, 167, 168; to *Horizon*, 205; to *Kingdom Come*, 213; to *Left Review*, 219; to *Life and Letters*, 224; to *London Mercury*, 254; to *New Verse*, 292–93; to *New Writing*, 300–302; to *Orion*, 324; to *Penguin New Writing*, 339, 342; "An Experiment in Criticism," 428; "Georgics" (translation), 213; leaves *Encounter* because of CIA backing, 159; portrait in *Orion*, 325; reviewed in *New Verse*, 292–93; reviewer for *Time and Tide*, 447; "The Sitting," 325

Lewis, Monk, 243

Lewis, Peter Elfed, 485

Lewis, Saunders, 25

Lewis, Wyndham: art in *Voices*, 480; attacked in *Aphrodite*, 237; contributes to *Arts and Letters*, 33; to *Calendar of Modern Letters*, 78; to *Criterion*, 116; to *Life and Letters*, 224; to *Lilliput*, 230; defended by Pound, 144; edits *Blast*, 61–68; *Enemy*, 161–63; effects

of fascism, 117; featured in *Agenda*, 19; model for *New Verse*; 292; reviewed in *Experiment*, 178; special issue of *Twentieth Century Verse*, 469. Works: *The Art of Being Ruled*, 162–63; *Before Antwerp*, 68; "The Crown Master," 68; *The Diabolical Principle*, 163; "Enemy of the Stars," 66; *Hitler*, 469; *The Hitler Cult*, 469; *Paleface*, 163; *The Revolutionary Simpleton*, 162; *Time and Western Man*, 162; "Timon," 144
Leyda, Jay: *Kino*, 506
Liberalism. *See* Political issues
Liddell, Robert, 340
Lidgett, J. Scott, 94
Life and Letters, 153, 222–38, 254, 360
Life and Letters To–Day. See Life and Letters
Life of the Spirit. See Blackfriars
Lilliput, 229–31
Limb, Sue, 434–35
Lindsay, Cressida, 39
Lindsay, David, 234
Lindsay, Jack, 28, 220, 236–39, 254, 327–30
Lindsay, Maurice, 235, 415
Lindsay, Norman, 238
Lindsay, Philip, 238
Lindsay, Vachel, 251, 334, 448
Lines. See Lines Review
Lines Review, 23, 231–36, 414
Linklater, Eric, 414
Lippmann, Walter, 447
Lissitsky, El, 374
Literaturnaya Gazeta, 342
Little, Lawrence, 295
Littlewood, Joan, 149
Littlewood, S. R., 136
Livesay, Dorothy, 356
Living Theatre, 150
Lloyd, A. L., 175
Lock, Ursula, 129
Locke–Ellis, Vivian, 9
Locker-Lampson, Frederick, 107
Lockhart, John Gibson, 391
Locre, Elza de, 238
Lodge, David, 400

Lodge, Oliver W. F., 2
Loewe, Roland, 278
Logue, Christopher, 306
Lohr, Frederick, 192
London Aphrodite, 29, 236–40
London Bulletin, 88, 241–44
London Gallery, 241–42
London Gallery Bulletin. See London Bulletin
London Library, 6
London Magazine (1820), 244
London Magazine (1954), 244–50
London Magazine Editions, 249
London Mercury, 32, 111, 177, 225, 236–38, 250–55
London Mercury and Bookman. See London Mercury
London Theatre Group, 189
London, Jack: "The House of Mapuhi," 257
Long, Robert Crozier, 181
Longley, Michael: "Odysseus to the Sirens," 475
Longmans, Green and Co., 406, 408
Looney, J. Thomas, 196
Lorant, Stefan, 229–31
Lorca, Federico Garcia, 89, 175, 219, 301, 310, 339, 398
Lovat Dickson's Magazine, 255–60
Low, Sidney, 181
Lowbridge, Peter, 398
Lowell, Amy, 112, 144, 397–99, 480
Lowell, Robert, 19, 20, 159, 235, 246, 395–97
Lowenstein, Tom, 475
Lowry, Malcolm, 284, 400, 510
Loy, Mina, 462
Lubbock, Percy, 389
Lucas, E. V., 105
Lucas, F. L., 252, 448
Lucas, Walter, 135–36, 138
Lucie-Smith, Edward, 379, 394, 487, 503
Ludovici, Anthony M., 181, 384
Luethy, Herbert, 156
Lund, Sylvia, 444, 448
Lurie, Alison, 400, 401
Luxemburg, Rosa, 14

Lymington, Gerard V., Lord, 117
Lyon, Ian, 453
Lyon, Lilian Bowes, 499
Lyttelton, E., 95

Mabille, Pierre, 243
Macaulay, Rose, 107, 324, 444, 447,
  449–50, 501
Macbeth, George, 20, 378, 379, 394,
  406, 502
MacCaig, Norman: contributes to *Eng-
  lish*, 168; to *Kingdom Come*, 213; to
  Lines Review, 232, 235; to *Saltire Re-
  view*, 415; to *Seven*, 430; on concrete
  poetry, 431; on editorial board of *Lines
  Review*, 232
MacCarthy, Desmond, 2, 78, 222–24,
  227
MacColl, Dax, 475
MacDiarmid, Hugh: contributes to *Adam*,
  5; to *Arena*, 28; to *Criterion*, 118; to
  English, 168; to *Enquiry*, 171; to *European Quarterly*, 174; to *Kingdom
  Come*, 212; to *Lines Review*, 234, 235;
  to *New English Weekly*, 278; to *New
  Road*, 288; to *Nimbus*, 306; to *Saltire
  Review*, 415; to *Seven*, 430; to *Wales*,
  484; to *X: Quarterly Review*, 510; edits
  Northern Review, 314–16; edits *Scot-
  tish Chapbook*, 420; featured in
  Agenda, 19; in *X: Quarterly Review*,
  510; honored by *Lines Review*, 232;
  influence on *Akros*, 21–22; on editorial
  board of *Lines Review*, 232; on *Nine*,
  313; *Penny Wheep*, 422; *The Purple
  Patch*, 316; *Sangschaw*, 422; "A The-
  ory of Scots Letters," 422
Macdonald, Dwight, 156
Macdonald, M., 232, 236
MacDonald, Ramsay, 46
MacGowran, Jack; *Beckett at Sixty*, 186
Machado, Antonio, 398; *The Garden in
  the Evening*, 398
Machen, Arthur, 36, 498
Machiavelli, Nicolo: *Il Cucchiaio Lungo*,
  186
Machray, Robert, 181
Mackay, George, 235

Mackenzie, Compton, 59, 414
Mackenzie, Faith Compton, 112
Mackesy, Marjorie, 129
Mackie, Alastair, 23, 415
Mackie, Albert, 233
Mackworth, Cecily, 325
Maclaren, Hamish, 374
Maclaren-Ross, J., 204–5, 230, 339
MacLean, Alastair, 372
MacLean, Sorley, 232, 234, 235
MacLeish, Archibald, 117
MacLennan, Hugh, 406
MacLiammoir, Michael, 42
Macnab, Roy, 355, 356
MacNeice, Louis: contributes to *Bell*, 42;
  to *Criterion*, 118; to *Encounter*, 156;
  to *Horizon*, 205–6; to *Life and Letters*,
  224; to *London Magazine*, 245; to
  London Mercury, 254; to *New Verse*,
  292–93; to *New Writing*, 303; to *Or-
  ion*, 325; to *Penguin New Writing*,
  339; to *Poetry (London)*, 360; to *Time
  and Tide*, 451; to *Windmill*, 501; edits
  Bell, 45; poetry judge for *Anglo–Welsh
  Review*, 25; reviewed in *New Verse*,
  292–93; satirized in *Penguin New
  Writing*, 339, 342
MacPherson, C. B., 83
MacRae, Mary, 324
Madariaga, Salvador de, 96
Maddox, Conroy, 241
Madge, Charles, 206, 293–94, 361
Magarshack, David, 339
Magnus, Laurie, 448
Magnusson, Magnus, 416
Magritte, René, 88, 219, 241–42
Mahon, Derek, 400
Mailer, Norman, 465
Mair, Mary, 131
Mairet, Philip, 276–80, 381–85
Makins, Williams, 201
Malahat Review, 400
Malina, Judith, 150
Malines Conversations, 55
Mallalieu, H. B., 467-70
Mallarmé, Stephane, 116, 426
Malloch, George Reston, 315
Malraux, André, 118, 158, 204, 290

Mamet, Louis: "Episode from Life,"
   290
Manchester University Press, 124
Mandelstam, Osip, 403
Mander, John, 7
Mandeville Publications, 364
Mandrake, 261–64
Manhood, H. S., 290
Mankowitz, Wolf, 262
Manley, Jim, 436
Mann, Golo, 158
Mann, Heinrich, 96
Mann, Thomas, 5, 96, 158, 225, 403
Mansfield, Katherine, 8–13, 33, 252,
   258, 444
Mansour, Joyce, 298
Mao Tse-Tung, 310
Marceau, Marcel, 401
March, Richard, 359, 361, 455
Marchant, Tony, 352
Marcoussis, Louis, 242
Mariani, Yoi, 47
Marinetti, E. F. T., 58, 63, 129
Marius, 84
Mark, Terence, 500
Markham, E. A., 100
Marlow, Jack. *See* Lehmann, John
Marlow, John, 383, 388
Marlowe, Christopher, 137
Marnau, Fred, 287
Marowitz, Charles, 100, 147, 149
Marriott, Charles, 197
Marriott, J. A. R., 181
Marsden, Dora, 143
Marsden, Francis, 194
Marsh, Peter. *See* Hamilton, Ian
Marshall, Horace, 184
Marshall, Norman, 135
Martin, George, 331
Martin, Graham, 395
Martin, Kingsley, 215
Martin Secker and Warburg Ltd., 161
Marx, Karl, 14, 56, 107, 385
Martin, Mary, 352
Marxism. *See* Communist Party, Socialist
   magazines
Marxist aesthetics and criticism: in
   Arena, 29; *Blackfriars*, 56; *Contempo-*

rary Poetry and Prose, 89; *Criterion*,
   115, 117; *Left Review*, 218–19; *Pur-*
   pose, 385–86; *Scrutiny*, 426; *Stand*,
   437–38; *Twentieth Century Verse*, 469
Masefield, John, 79, 94, 182, 334
Masingham, H. J., 172
Mason, A. E. W., 105
Mason, H. A.. 429
Mason, Michael, 403
Mass Observation, 206, 293–94
Masse, René, 47
Massingham, H. J., 112
Massingham, Henry William, 269-70
Masson, Andre, 241, 510
Matchett, Marney: "No Angel," 474
Mathers, Powys, 238
Mathew, David, 56
Mathews, Ray, 299
Mathias, Roland, 24–27, 370
Matisse, Henri, 44
Matrix, 457
Matthewman, S., 129
Matthews, Herbert L., 157
Maugham, Somerset, 98, 107, 501
Maupassant, Guy de, 257
Mauriac, François, 5, 500; "Fragments
   from an Occupation Journal," 498
Maurois, André [Emile–S.–W. Herzog],
   46, 47, 259, 465
Maurras, Charles, 409
Maxwell, Annette, 356
Maxwell, H. H., 181
May, Derwent, 378, 379
May, James Bolton, 457–58
Mayakovski, Vladimir, 219, 374–75,
   393, 397
Mayne, Ethel Colburn, 196–97, 461
McAlmon, Robert, 460, 463
McCabe, Herbert, 58
McCarthy, Mary, 156–57, 203
McCullers, Carson, 235, 505
McEwan, Ian, 401
McGahern, John: *The Dark*, 510
McGough, Roger, 503
McGrath, John, 273, 274
McGuffie, J., 374, 377
McKane, Richard, 274
McLaverty, Michael, 141

McLeod, Fiona. *See* Sharp, William
McNabb, Vincent, 54–56
McNeill, J. G. Swift, 181
McPhail, Angus, 462
McQuillan, Ruth, 23
McWilliams, F. E., 242
Mead, Matthew, 283
Megroz, R. L., 141
Meli, Giovanni: *La Bucolica*, 310
Meller, W. H., 426, 429; *Music and Society*, 498
Mellor, Oscar, 378
Melville, Lewis, 181
Melville, Robert, 216, 242
Men Only, 230
Menai, Huw, 252
Mencken, H. L., 480; *In Defense of Women*, 197
Mendes, Alfred H.: "Lulu Gets Married," 290
Mennon, Krishna, 349
Merchant, W. Moelwyn, 136, 485
Mercier, Vivian, 42
Mercury. See London Mercury.
Meredith, George, 30, 93, 105–6, 384, 501
Merrill, James, 397
Merriman, Henry Seton, 105
Merrythought Press, 52
Merton, Thomas, 39, 52, 56
Merwin, W. S., 159
Mesens, E. L. T., 241–42
Mew, Charlotte, 17
Meyerstein, Edward H. W., 129, 261
Meynell, Gerard T., 336
Meynell, Viola, 444
Micinski, Tadeusz, 175
Mickel, Karl, 398
Middleton, Christopher, 159, 283, 398
Milano, Francesco de, 455
Miles, Hamish, 224, 289, 291
Miles, Patricia: "Illuminatio Mea," 474
Milicic, Sibe, 129
Mill, James Stuart, 83
Millar, John, 83
Millay, Edna St. Vincent, 46
Miller, Betty, 108
Miller, Christopher, 20

Miller, Dave, 436
Miller, Henry: "The Brooklyn Bridge" 431; contributes to *Aylesford Review*, 37; to *Criterion*, 118; to *Encounter*, 156; to *Gangrel*, 191; to *Horizon*, 206; to *New Road*, 287; to *Now*, 319; to *Purpose*, 386; to *Seven*, 430–32; to *Windmill*, 501; on D. H. Lawrence, 386
Miller, Karl, 405
Millin, Sarah Gertrude, 11
Millner-Cullard, R., 274
Mills, John Orme, 58
Milne, A. A., 46, 134, 449
Milne, Ewart, 394
Milne, Tom, 153
Milton, John, 2, 130, 181–82, 252, 325
Miner, Edmund, 100
Mint, 264–67, 285
Minton, John, 340
Miró, Joan, 5, 219, 242
Mitchell, Adrian, 402
Mitchison, Naomi, 235, 414; *The Conquered*, 196; "The Wine Merchant," 196
Mitford, Nancy, 157, 205–6
Mitrinovic, Dmitri, 381–82
Modern Review, 62
Modigliani, Amedeo, 110
Mole, John, 419; "Lay–By," 379
Molnar, Ferenc, 229
Moncheur, Charles, 5
Moncrieff, C. K. Scott, 252–53
Mondrian, Piet, 242
Monro, Alida, 17
Monro, Harold, 112, 117, 144
Monroe, Harriet, 62
Montague, John, 42
Montale, Eugenio, 28, 249, 262
Monteith, Lionel, 354–57, 368
Montgomerie, William, 233, 235
Montgomery, Neil, 384–85
Montgomery, Stuart, 283
Montmorency, Arnold De, 98
Montmorency, J. E. G., 94, 96
Moore, Brian, 400
Moore, George, 182, 253

Moore, Henry, 4, 206, 242; "Lyre–Bird," 362

Moore, Marianne, 87, 118, 144, 225, 312, 395; "Smooth Gnarled Crape Myrtle," 279

Moore, Nicholas, 284, 359, 361, 368, 430,

Moore, Reginald, 500

Moore, T. Inglis, 355

Moore, T. Sturge, 129, 167, 196, 391

Moorehead, Alan, 204

Moorman, Mary, 99

Moraes, Dom, 510

Moran, Helen, 252

Moran, James Charles, 51

Moravia, Alberto, 203

More, Julian, 147

Morgan, David, 100

Morgan, Edwin, 23, 235, 374–75, 414–16; "The Computer's First Dialect Poems," 487

Morgan, Gerald, 370–71; "The Terrorists," 474

Morgan, Richard, 440

Morgan, Robert, 370

Morley, Frank, 114

Morpurgo, J. E., 347–48

Morrell, Ottoline, 492

Morris, Elita, 290

Morris, William, 30, 51, 52

Morrison, Herbert, 446–47

Morrison, Stanley, 54

Morrison, Theodore, 12

Morse, Brian, 435

Mortimer, Raymond, 5

Morton, A. L., 175

Morton, James, 99

Mosley, James, 52

Mosley, Oswald, 36, 38, 410

Moss, Arthur, 463

Mottram, R. H.: "The Churchyard Path," 171

Moult, Thomas, 477–80; "How Beautiful They Are," 478

Mountford, John, 52

Movement poets: in Critical Quarterly, 122; London Magazine, 245–46; Poetry (London), 362; Poetry Quarterly,

368; Priapus anthology, 378; Waves, 487–85; opposed by Nimbus, 306–7; by Poetry Nation, 365

Mozart, Wolfgang, 455

Mrozek, Slawomir, 403

Mucha, Jiri, 303, 340

Muggeridge, Malcolm, 134, 156, 442–43, 465, 501

Muir, Edwin: attacked in New Verse, 295; co-editor for Orion, 323, 325; contributes to Adelphi, 11–12; to Calendar of Modern Letters, 77; to Horizon, 206; to London Magazine, 245; to London Mercury, 253, 254; to Lovat Dickson's Magazine, 258; to New Writing, 303; to Northern Review, 315; to Orion, 324; to Saltire Review, 414; to Scottish Chapbook, 421; edits European Quarterly, 173-76; in Review anthology, 395; "The Natural Man and the Political Man," 303; reviewed in Akros, 22; in Calendar of Modern Letters, 78; in Contemporary Review, 95; in Townsman, 455; "The Voyage," 324

Muir, Kenneth, 406

Muir, Ramsay, 269, 465

Muir, Willa, 173–74, 176, 324

Mulkerns, Val, 45

Münchner Illustrierte Presse, 229

Munro, Neil, 59

Munson, Gorhan, 77

Murdoch, Iris, 122, 246, 505

Mure, G. R. G., 83

Murphy, J. T., 14

Murras, Charles, 117

Murray, Andrew: "Arthur's Evening Out," "Don Juan," 213

Murray, Gilbert, 95, 137, 270, 447

Murray, John II, 106-7, 391

Murray, John V, 392

Murray, John VI, 106–9

Murry, John Middleton: attracts Dylan Thomas to Adelphi, 279; contributes to Aylesford Review, 36; to Enquiry, 172; to Kingdom Come, 211; to Quarterly Review, 389; edits Adelphi, 8–18; The Free Society, 172; influenced by D. H.

Lawrence, 9–12; *The Life of Jesus*, 11; on Henry Williamson, 36; *Things to Come*, 11; *To The Unknown God*, 11; *Son of Woman*, 11, 13

Murry, Richard, 13

Murry, Robert, 96

Music and Musicians, 350

Music criticism: in *Adam*, 5; *New Departures*, 273; *New English Weekly*, 278; *Right Review*, 409; *Scrutiny*, 426; *Time and Tide*, 444; *Townsman*, 455; *Voices*, 479

Mussolini, Benito, 129, 386

Myers, Elizabeth, 36

Nabokov, Vladimir, 156, 259

Naipaul, Shiva, 400

Naipaul, V. S., 159, 465

Nalkowska, Zofja, 174

Napoleon I [Buonaparte], 170

Narayan, R. K., 406

Nash, Ogden, 229

Nash, Paul, 479

Nathan, David, 352

Nation. See Nation and Athenaeum

Nation and Athenaeum, 269–72

Nation, Ltd., 272

National Festival of Community Drama, 133

National Film Theatre, 506

National Theater (Britain), 147, 150, 189, 350

National Theatre Bill (1951), 134

Nazism. *See* Political issues

Neame, Alan, 39

Nehru, Jawaharlal, 219

Neill, Charles, 190–91, 192

Nemerov, Howard, 284

Nersh, Alex, 298

Neruda, Pablo, 28, 156, 219, 274, 306, 434; *The Earth is Called John*, 307

Nerval, Gerard de, 139

Nesbit, Evelyn, 444

Nevinson, C. R. W., 62, 63, 69

New Adelphi. See Adelphi

New Age, 62, 111, 114, 173, 381

New Biology, 344

New Blackfriars. See Blackfriars

New Coterie. See Coterie

New Country, 174, 300

New Criticism, 285

New Departures, 272–76

New English Weekly, 276–82, 385

New Freewoman, 62. *See also Egoist*

New Lines, 487

New Measure, 282–84

New Poetry (1945), 284–86

New Poetry (1975–81). *See Workshop*

New Quarterly, 222

New Republic, 42, 425

New Review. See Review

New Review, Ltd., 405

New Road, 286–89

New Saltire. See Saltire Review

New Signatures, 87, 174, 292, 300

New Soundings, 245

New Square Publications, Ltd., 142

New Statesman (and Nation), 42, 170, 222, 270

New Stories, 257, 289–91

New Verse, 88, 264–65, 291–97, 300, 360, 468

New Writers, 297–300

New Writing, 202, 300–305, 323, 337, 360

New Writing and Daylight. See New Writing

New Writing in Europe, 337

New Yorker, 14, 112, 400

New Zealand literature, 348

Newbolt, Henry, 32

Newby, P. H., 501

Newman, John Henry, 46, 106

Newport Publications, 331

Newton, Eric, 215

Nexus Publications, 405

Niccodemi, Dario: *Dawn, Day, Night*, 186

Nichols, Rayner, 278

Nichols, Robert, 77, 238

Nichols, Ross, 192

Nicholson and Watson, 327, 364

Nicholson, Ben, 242

Nicholson, Jim, 375

Nicholson, Irene, 324

Nicholson, Nancy, 334

Nicholson, Norman, 167, 287, 361; "Carol for Holy Innocents," 213; "Songs of the Island," 367
Nicholson, William, 334
Nicoll, Allardyce, 134, 136
Nicolson, Harold, 107, 446
Niedecker, Lorine, 374
Nietzsche, Friedrich, 237, 384–85, 422
Nievierov, Alexander, 77
Nimbus, 305–9
Nin, Anaïs, 387, 430–32; "Fragment from a Diary," 431
Nine, 262, 309–14
Nineteenth Century and After. See Twentieth Century
Nixon, Richard M., 401
Noble Fortune Press, 471
Norris, Leslie, 370, 378, 379
Northern Review, 314–17
Norwegian writing, 438
Nott, Kathleen, 159
Nott, Stanley, 173–76
Nougé, Paul, 241, 242
Now, 207, 317–21, 360
Noxon, Gerald F., 178, 284
Noyes, Alfred, 59, 97, 105, 168
Nutall, Jeff: *Sixties Christmas*, 418
Nye, Robert, 39, 234, 235, 370

Oakeshott, Michael, 80, 82–83
Oasis, 361
Oates, Joyce Carol, 400, 401
Obaldia, René de: *Edward and Agrippina*, 186
Ober, Robert, 439
O'Brien, Edward J., 257, 289, 291
O'Brien, Flann, 42; *At Swim-Two-Birds*, 484
O'Brien, Ruth: "An Accident," 290
O'Casey, Sean: contributes to *Bell*, 42; to *Encore*, 147; to *English*, 167; to *Life and Letters*, 223; to *Mint*, 264; to *Twentieth Century*, 465; excluded from *Dublin Magazine*, 140; reviewed in *Drama*, 137; reviews Beckett in *Encore*, 147–50
O'Connor, Frank: contributes to *Bell*, 41, 42; to *Cornhill*, 108; to *Dublin Maga-*

zine, 141; to *Horizon*, 205; to *Life and Letters*, 224; to *London Mercury*, 254; to *Orion*, 324; to *Penguin New Writing*, 340; to *Review of English Literature*, 407; to *Windmill*, 501; poetry editor in *Bell*, 13; reviewed in *New Stories*, 290
O'Connor, John, 39
O'Connor, Philip, 273, 294, 326, 484
O'Donnell, Martin, 45
O'Donnell, Peadar, 43–44, 140
O'Dwyer, M. F., 181
O'Faolain, Julia, 249
O'Faolain, Sean, 41–45, 108, 140, 205, 259, 346
O'Flaherty, Liam: contributes to *Aphrodite*, 238; to *Bell*, 42; to *Bermondsey Book*, 47; to *Calendar of Modern Letters*, 77; to *Coterie*, 112; to *Dublin Magazine*, 140; to *Lilliput*, 229; "Going into Exile," 140; "The Strange Disease," 47
Ogilvie, Elizabeth, 405
Ognev, Nikolai, 338
Okara, Gabriel, 357
O'Kelly, Seumas, 139
Oliver, George, 232
Olivier, Laurence, 150, 351
Olson, Charles, 274
Omega Workshop, 61–62
Omnific Advertising, Ltd., 467
O'Neill, Eugene, 134, 137, 444
O'Neill, George, 462
O'Neill, Moira, 59
Onslow-Ford, Gordon, 241, 244
Open Space Theatre, 100
Oppenheimer, Joel, 283
Orage, Alfred Richard, 114, 276–80; *Apologia*, 385
Orage, Jesse R., 280
Orage, Richard, 280, 381
Order of Preachers. *See* Dominicans
O'Reilly, Montagu, 431
Origo, Iris, 108
Orion, 323–27
Ormond, John, 370, 371, 372
Orpheus, 304

Ortega y Gasset, José: *The Task of Our Times*, 383

Orton, Joe, 149, 352

Orwell, George: contributes to *Adelphi*, 14; to *Gangrel*, 191, 192; to *Horizon*, 203, 206; to *New English Weekly*, 278; to *New Road*, 287; to *New Writing*, 301; to *Now*, 319; to *Penguin New Writing*, 338; to *Windmill*, 500; influence on Cyril Connolly, 202; letters in *Encounter*, 158; on Movement poets, 287; quarrel with Comfort, 288; reviewed in *Contemporary Review*, 98; in *Time and Tide*, 450; in *Wind and the Rain*, 497–98; reviewer for *Time and Tide*, 447. Works: *Animal Farm*, 206; "Boys' Weeklies," 206; "A Hanging," 14; "How the Poor Die," 319; "In Defence of P. G. Wodehouse," 500; "Looking Back on the Spanish War," 287; *1984*, 30, 206, 450; "Raffles and Miss Blandish," 206; "Rudyard Kipling," 206; "Shooting an Elephant," 301, 338; "Why I Write," 192

Osamu, Dazai, 155

Osborne, Dorothy, 326

Osborne, John, 122, 149, 506, 510; *Look Back in Anger*, 246, 352, 401

Osborne, W. H., 326

O'Sullivan, Seamus, 41

Ottaway, Robert, 467

Our Time, 28, 220, 327–31

Outposts, 331–33, 497

Outposts: Modern Poets Series, 331

Ou-Yang-Hsiu, 196

Owen, Alun: *The Rough and Ready Lot*, 149

Owen, Wilfred, 32, 112; "Anthem for Doomed Youth," 402; "Arms and the Boy," 32; "The Charges," 493; "The Dead Beat," 493; "Disabled," 493; "Greater Love," 32; "The Next War," 32; "The Sentry," 493; "The Show," 493; "Strange Meetings," 493; "A Terre," 493

Owl, 333–36

Oxford Poetry Review, 492

Oxford University Press, 124, 169

P.E.N., 4, 129, 173; *New Poems, 1965*, 379

Paalen, Wolfgang, 242

Pacifism, 13–14, 211

Pagan, Robert. *See* Plomer, William

Page, Alun, 25

Page, Louise, 352

Page, P. K., 356

Paget, A., 48

Paget, Violet, 93

Pailthorpe, Grace, 242

Painter, George Duncan, 325

Palmer, Cecil, 336

Palmer, D. J., 124

Palmer, John, 182

Palmer, Samuel, 498

Pankratov, Iuri Ivanovich: "Slow Song," 374

Panzini, Alberto, 46

Parapsychology, 169–71

Parker, Alexander, 56

Parker, Gilbert, 37

Parker, Louis N., 196

Parker, W. M., 391

Parson, Donald, and Co., 284

Parsons, Geoffrey, 326

Parsons, Leonard, 494

Parthasarathy, R., 406

Partisan Review, 7, 42, 156, 203, 207, 365

Partledge, William, 104

Partridge, Eric, 238

Pasternak, Boris: *Doctor Zhivago*, 506; reviewed in *Writing Today*, 506; works in *Adelphi*, 15; *Encounter*, 156; *Experiment*, 178; *New Measure*, 283; *New Writing*, 301; *Orion*, 324; *Penguin New Writing*, 340; *X: Quarterly Review*, 510

Patchen, Kenneth, 192, 274, 500

Pater, Walter, 92, 100

Patten, Brian, 434, 503, 504

Paulin, Tom, 365

Pavey, L. A., 289, 291

Payment to contributors, 289

Payn, James, 106
Payne, Robert, 310
Paz, Octavio, 156
Peace News, 14
Peace Pledge Union, 14–15, 449
Peake, Mervyn, 254, 362
Pears, Edwin, 95
Pearsall, Logan, 324
Pearson, Gabriel, 395, 397, 405
Peel, Marie, 506
Peguy, Charles, 58
Pelican Guide to English Literature,
    427–28
Pelling, H. M., 83
Pemberton, Max, 37
Penchenat, Jean-Claude: *1789*, 188
Penguin Books Ltd., 344
Penguin Modern Poets, 379
Penguin New Writing, 153, 220, 244,
    337–46
Penguin Parade, 323, 344–49
Penrose, Roland, 241, 242, 244
Penrose, Valentine, 87
Pepler, Hilary, 37, 56
Peploe, Denis, 232
Péret, Benjamin, 241; *Remove Your Hat*,
    90
Perles, Alfred, 192
Perloff, Marjorie, 365
Perowne, Victor, 491
Persian literature, 227
Personal Landscape, 361
Peruvian poetry, 438
Peter, John, 136
Pethick-Lawrence, Frederick, 97
Petrarch, 77
Pettet, E. C., 325
Pevsner, Nikolaus, 264
Phare, Elsie, 178
Phelan, Jim, 339
Philips, Peter, 331
Phillips, Douglas, 370
Phillpotts, Eden, 129, 171
Phoenix, 455
Phoenix Press, 497
Photography. *See* Art reproductions
Picasso, Pablo, 5, 241–242, 274, 328,
    362; *Guernica*, 242

Pick, J. B., 190–92
Picture Post, 229
Pilikian, Hovhanness, 137
Pinder–Wilson, Ralph, 74
Pinero, Arthur Wing, 100
Pinget, Robert, 298, 510
Pinker, Robert, 147
Pinter, Harold 146, 149, 156, 506; *The
    Birthday Party*, 149; *The Caretaker*,
    149; "A Letter to Peter Wood," 138;
    No Man's Land, 401
Pinto, Vivian de Sola, 168, 473
Piper, John, 242, 324
Pirandello, Luigi: contributes to *Ber-
    mondsey Book*, 46; to *Calendar of
    Modern Letters*, 77; to *Criterion*, 115;
    to *Lovat Dickson's Magazine*, 259; re-
    viewed in *Contemporary Review*, 95;
    in *Drama*, 134, 137; in *Gambit*, 187
Pissarro, Lucien, 33, 479
Pitter, Ruth, 213
Pitts, Denis, 231
Pitts, M. C., 320
Plaid Cymru, 370
Plath, Sylvia, 56, 122–23, 395, 397
Play Pictorial, 353
Play texts, 350–52
Plays and Players, 138, 151, 185, 350–
    54
Plomer, William: consulted for *New
    Writing*, 300; contributes to *Adelphi*,
    12, 15; to *Calendar of Modern Letters*,
    77; to *Encounter*, 156; to *New Verse*,
    301; to *New Writing*, 301; to *Orion*,
    324; to *Windmill*, 501; guest editor for
    Workshop, 503; satires in *Penguin New
    Writing*, 339
Plotinus, 391
Plowman, Max, 12–14
Plunkett, James, 42
Plutarch: *Moralia*, 161
PN Review. See Poetry Nation
Pocket Publications, 231
Poe, Edgar Allen, 33, 459
Poetry (Chicago), 62, 90, 295
*Poetry: A Magazine of Verse, Comment,
    and Criticism*, 127
Poetry (London), 287, 358–64, 367–68

Poetry 1960, 123
Poetry and Audience, 379
Poetry and Drama, 62
Poetry and the People, 327
Poetry and the Play, 127
Poetry Commonwealth, 354–58
Poetry League, 127
Poetry Nation, 364–67
Poetry of the Committed Individual, 437
Poetry Olympics, 273–274
Poetry Publishing Company, 132
Poetry Quarterly, 367–69, 497
Poetry Studies, 367. *See also Poetry Quarterly*
Poetry Wales, 369–73
Poetry Wales Press, 373
Polanyi, Michael, 83, 156, 157
Polish poetry, 438
Polish theater, 189
Political issues: in *Adelphi*, 13–15; *Arena*, 29–30; *Aylesford Review*, 38; *Blackfriars*, 54; *Blackwood's Edinburgh Magazine*, 58–59; *Blast*, 67; *Cambridge Journal*, 80–83; *Contemporary Poetry and Prose*, 89; *Contemporary Review*, 92, 95–97; *Criterion*, 115, 117–18; *Encounter*, 153–59; *Enemy*, 162–63; *European Quarterly*, 173–76; *Experiment*, 178; *Fortnightly Review*, 182; *Gangrel*, 191–92; *Horizon*, 202–3; *Kingdom Come*, 211–13, 215; *Left Review*, 217–19; *Life and Letters*, 225; *New English Weekly*, 277–78; *New Road*, 287; *New Writing*, 300, 302–3; *Purpose*, 381; *Quarterly Review*, 390–91; *Right Review*, 409–10; *Saltire Review*, 414; *Time and Tide*, 446–47, 449; *Townsman*, 454–55; *Twentieth Century*, 465. *See also* Antisemitism; Fascism; Marxist aesthetics and criticism; Socialist magazines; Spanish Civil War; World War I; World War II
Pomerance, Bernard: *High in Vietnam, Hot Damn, Hospital,Thanksgiving Before Detroit*, 189
Pond, P., 374, 377
Ponge, François, 204

Poor. Old. Tired. Horse., 373–77
Pope, Alexander, 78
Pope-Hennessy, James, 108
Por, Odon, 277
Porter, Alan, 381, 382, 494
Porter, Katherine Anne, 157, 444; "Pale Horse, Pale Rider," 346
Porter, Peter, 235, 248, 396, 487; *Last of England*, 395
Porter, William Sydney, 459
Porteus, Hugh Gordon, 278, 361–62, 469
Posegate, Mabel, 367
Potocki, Count, of Montalk, 408
Potter, Dennis: *Brimstone and Treacle*, 401
Pound, Ezra: association with *Egoist*, 143–44; banned from *Quarterly Review*, 67; contributes to *Blast*, 61–68; to *Criterion*, 115; to *Fortnightly Review*, 182; to *New Departures*, 274; to *New English Weekly*, 277–79; to *Purpose*, 386; to *Townsman*, 454–55; correspondence in *Agenda*, 19; editorial advisor to *Transatlantic Review*, 459–61; effects of fascism, 117; featured in *Adam*, 7; in *Agenda*, 19; in *X: Quarterly Review*, 510; influenced by C. H. Douglas, 381–85; influence on *Nine*, 309, 311; letters in *Encounter*, 158; music criticism in *Townsman*, 455; in *Transatlantic Review*, 462; opinions on religion, 455; on surrealism in *Contemporary Poetry and Prose*, 88; on *Wheels*, 493; reviewed in *Aphrodite*, 237; in *London Magazine*, 246; in *Nine*, 311; in *Purpose*, 386; in *Quarterly Review*, 389; in *Townsman*, 455; reviews Eliot in *New English Weekly*, 279–80; reviews for *Time and Tide*, 447; satirizes Rupert Brooke, 68; supports Social Credit, 381, 385–86. Works: "Ancient Music," 67; "As Sextant," 309; Canto 38, 279; "Consegna," 386; "Dogmatic Statement on the Game and Play of Chess," 67; *Ezra Pound Talking*, 20; "Fratres Minores," 64; *Guide to Culture*, 455; *Hugh Selwyn Mauberley*, 33; *The In-*

edible, 454; "Treatise on Harmony," 461; *Villon*, 455

Powell, Anthony, 401, 506

Powys, John Cowper, 36, 99–100, 406, 484

Powys, Llewelyn, 36, 77, 278

Powys, Theodore F., 36, 118, 290

Poynter, Edward J., 465

Praz, Mario, 253, 262

Preece, Peter, 370

Press run. *See* Circulation

Preuves, 153

Priapus, 377–80

Priapus Press, 365

Price, Habberley, 170

Price, Jessup, 74

Price, Julius, 181

Price, K. Arnold, 196

Price, Mona, 140

Prices: *Black Art*, 52; *Contemporary Poetry and Prose*, 90; *Contemporary Review*, 91; *Cornhill*, 105–7; *Coterie*, 112; *English*, 165–66; *Gangrel*, 191; *Lilliput*, 229; *Lines Review*, 231–32; *New Departures*, 274; *New Review*, 403; *New Writing*, 337; *Orion*, 324; *Our Time*, 329; *Penguin New Writing*, 337; *Penguin Parade*, 344; *Review*, 399; *Right Review*, 408; *Scrutiny*, 424; *Stand*, 436; *Universities' Poetry*, 474; *Writing Today*, 505

Prichard, Hesketh, 105

Prichard, John, 483

Priestley, J. B., 5, 46, 137, 182, 206

Prince, F. T., 500; "Soldiers Bathing," 361

Print Design and Production, 51

Printz–Pahlson, Gordon, 434

Pritchett, V. S.: acknowledges importance of *Penguin New Writing*, 341; contributes to *Horizon*, 205; to *Lilliput*, 230; to *London Magazine*, 245, 249; to *Lovat Dickson's Magazine*, 259; to *New Writing*, 301–2; to *Orion*, 324; to *Penguin New Writing*, 338–39; to *Windmill*, 501

Profumo affair, 38

Prokosch, Frederick, 430

Proletarian literature: in *Bermondsey Book*, 45–51; *Gangrel*, 191–92; *Left Review*, 219–20; *New Writing*, 301–3; *Stand*, 436–37; *Time and Tide*, 448, 450

Prothero, George W., 67, 391

Prothero, Rowland, 391

Proust, Marcel, 5–6, 38, 77, 84, 116, 384; *A la recherche du temps perdu*, 389

Prowse, Philip, 436

Prys–Jones, A. G., 25

Psychology, theories of, 382–87

Publicist, 239

Pudney, John, 225, 230, 502

Punch, 230

Purcell, Henry, 273

Purdom, C. B., 136

Purpose, 380–88

Putt, S. Gorley, 325, 326

Pybus, Rodney, 439

Pygge, Edward. *See* Hamilton, Ian

Quarterly Review, 58, 62, 67, 389–92

Quasimode, Salvatore, 262

Quennell, Peter, 77, 107–8, 118, 223

Quiller-Couch, Arthur, 105, 129, 182, 446, 477

Quilter, Harry, 93

Quinn, John, 68, 459

Rabagliati, A.: "Has Nature a Purpose?" 382

Radice, Amanda, 406

Raine, Kathleen: contributes to *Experiment*, 178; to *New Verse*, 294; to *Now*, 319; to *Poetry (London)*, 361–62; to *Time and Tide*, 450; to *Windmill*, 500; interviewed in *Workshop*, 504; satires in *Penguin New Writing*, 342

Ramanujan, A. K., 357

Ramparts, 158

Ramsey, T. W., 192

Rank, Otto, 387

Rankin, James, 416

Ransom, John Crowe, 77, 399; "Philomela," 334; "Winter Remembered," 334

Ratcliffe, Dorothy Una, 196, 197
Rattenbury, Arnold, 331
Rattigan, Terence, 100, 137
Raverat, Gwen, 346
Raworth, Tom, 283, 396, 434
Ray, Man, 241, 242, 461
Read, Herbert: contributes to *Adam*, 5; to *Adelphi*, 13, 16; to *Arts and Letters*, 33; to *Bermondsey Book*, 46; to *Coterie*, 112; to *Criterion*, 115; to *Encounter*, 156; to *Kingdom Come*, 214–15; to *Life and Letters*, 224; to *London Bulletin*, 242; to *New English Weekly*, 278; to *Northern Review*, 316; to *Now*, 318; to *Penguin Parade*, 346; to *Poetry (London)*, 361, 362; to *Purpose*, 386; to *Seven*, 430; to *Time and Tide*, 448; to *Writing Today*, 506; interview in *Writing Today*, 506; on Picasso's *Guernica*, 242; on surrealism, 87, 241; organizes London Exhibition (1936), 241; reviewed in *Left Review*, 218; in *Townsman*, 455; supports Social Credit, 386. Works: "A Community of Individuals," 386; "The Cult of Leadership," 316, 318; "Definition Toward a Modern Theory of Poetry," 33; "Ode without Rhetoric," 213; "The Paradox of Anarchism," 316, 318; *Poetry and Anarchism*, 214, 455; "Promenade Solennelle," 33; *The Tenth Muse*, 506; "Winter Grief," 33
Reavey, George, 178; translations of Pasternak, 244
Rebel Art Centre, 62–63
Rechy, John, 249
Reckitt, Maurice B., 277–78, 280, 381–85
Redgrave, Vanessa, 147
Redgrove, Michael, 355
Redgrove, Peter, 39, 331, 393, 419, 487, 504
Reed, Bryan, 473
Reed, C. C., 25
Reed, Henry, 324, 326
Rees, Alun, 370
Rees, Goronwy, 157, 202–3
Rees, Morwyth, 25

Rees, Olwyn, 25
Rees, Richard, 13
Reeves, James M., 178, 398, 500
Reger, Mark, 101
Reid, Alexander, 415
Reid, Alistair, 235
Reid, James M., 414
Reinhardt, Ad, 375
Religious issues, 12, 115, 170, 455, 465
Remarque, Erich Maria, 49
Remizov, Aleksey, 77
Renan, Ernest, 84
Renny, Peter, 195
Renzio, Toni del, 287
Resurgence, 272, 274
Review, 393–406
Review of English Literature, 406–8
Review of English Studies, 85
Review of Reviews, 256
Revolution surréaliste, 241
Rexroth, Kenneth, 319, 367, 509–10
Reynolds, O. W.: "The Dansant: Moment," 178
Rhine, J. B., 170
Rhondda, Margaret Haig, Lady, 441–53; *This Was My World*, 442
Rhys, Ernest, 129, 130–31
Rhys, Jean, 248, 463; "Sleep It Off Lady," 400
Rhys, Keidrych, 361, 483–85
Rhythm, 8
Rice, Anne Estelle, 480
Richards, Ceri, 362
Richards, Glasbrook, 278
Richards, I. A., 33, 78, 117, 292, 366, 426
Richardson, Dorothy, 11, 13, 97, 224–25; "Helen," 197; "Law," 383; "Resolution," 382
Richardson, Edward, 174, 175
Richardson, Henry Handel, 259
Richardson, Maurice, 230, 231
Richardson, Samuel, 84
Richardson, William, 231
Richmond, Bruce, 114
Ricks, Christopher, 398, 400
Rickword, Edgell, 28, 77–79, 217–19, 238, 328–30

Riddell, Alan, 232, 233
Ridgway, Alfred, 169
Riding, Laura, 52–53, 77, 172, 237, 290, 295, 397
Ridler, Anne, 136, 205, 287, 310, 361;"Geordie," 213
Rietty, Robert, 185–87
Right Review, 408–11
Riley, Bridget, 375
Rilke, Rainer Maria, 279, 310, 448; *Duino Elegies*, 361; *Sonnets to Orpheus*, 324
Rimbaud, Arthur, 77, 175, 325; "Drunken Ship," 325
Ritchie, Anne Thackeray, 106; *The Blackstick Papers*, 104
Ritzema, Robin, 436
Rivera, Diego: "Towards an Independent Revolutionary Art," 242
Robbe-Grillet, Alain, 247, 505, 510
Roberts, Andrew, 474
Roberts, C. E. Bechhofer, 278
Roberts, Denys Kilham, 323, 325–26, 345
Roberts, Ellis, 447
Roberts, Lynette, 484
Roberts, Michael, 12, 15, 253; "The Critic and the Public," 386
Roberts, Philip, 351, 353
Roberts, R. Ellis, 224, 258
Roberts, Sally, 370
Roberts, William, 65, 68–69, 494
Robins, Elizabeth, 92
Robinson, E. A., 197
Robinson, Lennox, 42, 140
Robinson, M., 13
Robson, Vivian, 197
Robson, W. W., 263, 398
Rochester, University of, 8
Rodgers, W. R., 42
Roditi, Edouard, 15
Roethke, Theodore, 15, 19, 295, 469, 505
Rogers, Pat, 168
Rogers, Timothy, 168
Rogoff, Gordon, 153
Rolfe, Frederick, Baron Corvo: *Hadrian the Seventh*, 38

Rolls House Publishing Company, 57
Romains, Jules, 259; *Quinette's Crime*, 256
Romanoff, P. A., 47
Romer, Carroll, 467
Rook, Alan, 211, 213, 214; "Dunkirk Pier," "Lager," "The Retreat," 361
Roose-Evans, James, 136
Roosevelt, Franklin, 107
Roosevelt, Theodore, 447
Root, Howard, 56
Rootham, Helen, 490–94
Roper, David, 190, 353
Rosanov, Vasili, 77
Roscoe, Theodora, 96
Rose, Henry, 93
Rosenberg, Anne, 32
Rosenberg, Harold, 156
Rosenberg, Isaac: "Heart's First Word," "If You Are Fire," "In Piccadilly," 32
Rosenthal, M. L., 376, 400
Rosoman, Leonard, 340
Ross, Alan, 157, 247–49, 339, 361
Ross, Leonard Q., 229
Rossetti, Christina, 107
Roth, Philip, 401
Rothenberg, Jerome, 375
Rothenstein, William, 112
Rothermere, Lady, 114
Rothschild, Lionel Walter, Baron, 446
Rougemont, Denis de, 155
Roughton, Roger, 86–90, 294
Round, Dora, 174
Rouse, W. H. D., 279
Routledge and Kegan Paul, 267
Rowe, Dilys, 485
Rowse, A. L., 60, 99, 100, 117, 213, 450
Royal Court Theatre, 148, 186, 188, 350
Royle, Trevor, 23, 233, 236
Rozanov, Vasily Vasilyevich, 175
Rozewicz, Tadeusz, 403; *An Interrupted Act*, 187
Rubens, Robert, 100
Rudd, Maxwell Billens, 409
Ruddock, Gilbert, 372
Rudkin, David, 149

Rumanian poetry, 19
Runciman, Steven, 156
Rural Life Movement, 55
Rush, Christopher, 235
Ruskin, John, 30, 52, 106
Russell, Bertrand A. W., Lord: contributes to *Bermondsey Book*, 46–48; to *Calendar of Modern Letters*, 78; to *Contemporary Review*, 92; to *Encounter*, 156–57; to *Horizon*, 206; to *Life and Letters*, 444; to *Time and Tide*, 444; to *Townsman*, 455; "Liberalism and Women's Suffrage," 92; on Chinese intelligentsia, 444; reviewed in *Blackwoods's Edinburgh Magazine*, 58; in *Kingdom Come*, 213
Russell, George, 41, 139
Russell, J. L., 426
Russell, John, 204, 324
Russell, Peter, 262, 309–13
Russian literature, 22, 95, 157
Rutter, Frank, 31, 33
Ryder, Charis, 405
Ryder, David Warren, 277
Rye, Anthony, 324, 326
Rypins, Stanley I., 110

Sackville, Margaret, 38
Sackville-West, Edward, 77, 302, 325, 501
Sackville-West, Vita, 46, 223, 252, 444, 451
Sadler, Elizabeth, 480
Sainsbury, Geoffrey, 12
Saint–Exupéry, Antoine de, 301
Saintsbury, George, 119, 253, 256
Saints Press, 52
Salamander, 361
Salle, Marguerite, 409
Salmon, Christopher, 265
Salter, Ada, 46
Salter, Alfred, 46
Saltire Review, 413–17
Saltire Society, 413–16
Saltmarshe, Christopher, 178
Samphire, 417–20
Sampson, Ashley, 385
Sampson, Low, Marston, 467

Samsom, William, 107, 204, 245, 249, 325, 339
Samuel, Edwin, 99
Sandeman, Margot, 374
Sanders, John, 312
Santayana, George, 157, 223–24, 252
Sargeant, Howard, 368
Sargeson, Frank, 341
Saroyan, Aram, 375
Saroyan, William, 42, 229, 290, 430–31, 445, 448; "Seventy Thousand Assyrians," 259
Sarton, May, 108, 254
Sartre, Jean-Paul: antinuclear speech, 44; contributes to *Adam*, 5; to *Bell*, 44; to *Encounter*, 156; to *Gambit*, 186; to *Horizon*, 204; to *New Writing*, 301; to *Penguin New Writing*, 340; interview in *Encounter*, 158; leaves *Encounter* because of CIA backing, 159; "Myth and Reality in the Theater," 186; quarrel in *Nimbus*, 307; reviewed in *Encore*, 149; in *Horizon*, 204; "The Room," 301
Sassoon, Siegfried: contributes to *Bermondsey Book*, 46; to *Calendar of Modern Letters*, 77; to *Decachord*, 129; to *Enquiry*, 171; to *Life and Letters*, 224; to *Owl*, 334; to *Time and Tide*, 450; meeting with Wilfred Own, 402; reviewed in *Contemporary Review*, 98; "Ultimate Values," 171; "Wraith," 32
Saunders, Helen, 65, 67
Saurat, Denis, 315; *L'Actuel*, 384
Savage, D[erek] S., 295, 316, 318–19, 467–68
Sayers, Dorothy L., 167, 252
Sayers, Michael, 278
Scannell, Vernon, 16, 167, 394, 419, 487
Scarfe, Francis, 87, 90, 205, 362
Schehade, Georges: *Vasco*, 186
Schiff, Sydney, 1
Schiff, Violet, 1
Schimanski, Stefan, 211, 214–15
Schlesinger, Arthur, Jr., 156, 158

Schmidt, Michael, 365, 438, 511; *British Poetry since 1970*, 365–55
Schoenberg, Friedrich, 273
Schonfield, Andrew, 156, 158
Schwartz, Delmore, 203, 287, 469
Science News, 344
Scot, Michael, 141
Scott, Alexander, 23, 235, 375, 414
Scott, Francis George, 315
Scott, Michael, 308
Scott, Tom, 233–34, 430–31
Scott, Walter, 83, 106
Scott-James, R. A., 16, 251, 253–54
Scott-Kilvert, Ian, 310
Scott-Moncrieff, Michael, 415
Scottish Arts Council, 22. *See also* Arts Council
Scottish Chapbook, 420–23
Scottish Home Rule, 421
Scottish Literary Journal, 23
Scottish literature: featured in *Akros*, 21; *English*, 167; *Life and Letters*, 227; *Lines Review*, 231; *Saltire Review*, 413; *Scottish Chapbook*, 420; *Workshop*, 503
Scottish Review, 416
Scrutiny, 121–23, 246–47, 253, 295, 423–30
Searle, Ronald, 5
Secker, Martin, 161
Sedition Bill, 449
Seferis, George, 156, 430
Seizin Press, 52
Seldes, Gilbert, 116, 462
Selincourt, Hugh de, 14
Seltzer, Thomas, 459
Selver, Paul, 112, 175
Selvon, Samuel, 247
Sen, Nikhil N.: "L'Etoile de Mer," "Scenario," 178
Sergeant, Howard, 98, 331–32, 355
Serjeant, William A. S., 474; "Songs from a Southern Shire," 474
Seton-Watson, Hugh, 156
Seven, 430–34
Severini, Gino, 494
Sewell, Brocard, 35–40

Sexton, Anne, 246, 274; *45 Mercy Street*, 418
Seymour, William Kean, 98, 99, 494
Shakespeare, Dorothy, 67
Shakespeare Memorial Theatre, 347
Shakespeare, William: Falstaff, 157; first folio, 51; *Hamlet*, 137, 150, 385; *Lear* quotation for *Samphire* title, 417–18; letters to de Vere in *Golden Hind*, 196; *Macbeth*, 445; radio productions reviewed in *Drama*, 134; reviews in *Adelphi*, 12; in *Aylesford Review*, 38; in *Contemporary Review*, 94; in *Drama*, 137; in *Encore*, 150; in *English*, 167; in *European Quarterly*, 175; in *Fortnightly Review*, 181, 182; in *Kingdom Come*, 219; in *Life and Letters*, 223; in *New Review*, 401; in *Purpose*, 385; in *Review of English Literature*, 406; in *Time and Tide*, 445
Shand, A. I., 105
Shand, John, 12
Shanks, Edward, 32, 238, 251
Shapiro, Karl, 156, 203, 285
Sharma, Partap: *A Touch of Brightness*, 187
Sharp, Alfred, 330
Sharp, William, 93
Sharpley, C. Elissa, 129
Shaw, D. A., 325
Shaw, George Bernard: *Back to Methuselah*, 445; contributes to *Bell*, 42; to *Bermondsey Book*, 46; to *Drama*, 134, 138; to *Lilliput*, 230; to *Time and Tide*, 444, 446, 449; correspondence in *Cornhill*, 108; featured in *Drama*, 137; *The Intelligent Woman's Guide to Socialism and Capitalism*, 49; "The King and the Doctors," 445; on dramatists' fees, 134; on Granville Barker, 138; reviewed in *Bell*, 42; in *Calendar of Modern Letters*, 79; in *Cornhill*, 106; in *Drama*, 134, 138; in *London Aphrodite*, 238; in *Time and Tide*, 445; *St. Joan*, 445; "Women since 1860," 444
Shaw, Helen: "Bonestone and Spirit," 332

Shaw, Irwin, 346, 401; "Main Currents of American Thought," "Weep in Years to Come," 346
Shawcross, John, 96
Sheeler, Dick, 375
Shelley, Percy Bysshe, 93, 130, 196, 253
Shenstone, W. A., 105
Sheppard, Canon Dick, 15
Sherrock, Roger, 166
Shiel, M. P., 37–38
Shils, Edward, 156, 158
Shipman, Evan, 463
Sholokhov, Mikhail, 301, 340
Short, Dudley, 278
Short, John, 213
Short, Phil, 434
Short story magazines, 255–60, 289–91
Shorter, Eric, 136
Shows Illustrated, 353
Shuttle, Penelope, 39, 379
Sicilian literature, 22–23
Sickert, Walter, 325
Sidgwich, M. C., 131
Siegel, Eli, 374–75
Signet Press, 52
Sikelianos, Angelos, 340
Silkin, Jon, 235, 274, 436–38, 474
Sillitoe, Alan, 156, 331, 400, 506
Silone, Ignazio, 156, 287, 301, 340
Simenon, Georges, 5, 230
Simon, S. J., 230
Simpson, Louis, 122, 397
Simpson, Lucie, 182
Simpson, N. F.: *One Way Pendulum*, 506
Sinclair, May, 116, 444, 480
Sinclair, R., 453
Sinclair, Upton, 278
Singer, Burns, 235, 415
Sisson, C. H., 310, 365, 372, 438, 510, 511
Sitwell, Edith: attacked in *New Verse*, 295; contributes to *Adam*, 5; to *Arena*, 28; to *Arts and Letters*, 32; to *Coterie*, 112; to *Encounter*, 155, 156; to *Golden Hind*, 194, 196; to *Life and Letters*, 225; to *London Magazine*, 245; to *Orion*, 324, 325; to *Penguin*

New Writing, 339; to *Time and Tide*, 448; edits *Wheels*, 489–94; "The Lady with the Sewing Machine," 32; "Nine Bucolic Poems," 494; praises *Nine*, 312; reviewed in *Contemporary Review*, 98; "Undergrowth," 196
Sitwell, George, 490
Sitwell, Osbert: contributes to *Bell*, 42; to *Criterion*, 116; to *Life and Letters*, 224, 225; to *Orion*, 325; to *Penguin New Writing*, 340; to *Wheels*, 490–94; "Corpse-Day," 494; *Great Morning*, 326; "In Bad Taste," 492; "Mrs. Kinfoot," 494
Sitwell, Sacheverell, 32, 116, 238, 490–94; "Bird–Actors," 32
Six Point Group, 443
Size (format). *See* Design
Skeat, T. C., 72
Skelsey, Geoffrey, 187
Skelton, John, 14, 78
Skelton, Robin, 400
Skene, Brenda, 129
Skevington, Leonard, 451
Skilbeck, William Wray, 465
Skilton, Charles, Ltd., 286
Sladen-Smith, F., 135
Slater, Montagu, 218, 331
Slayden, David, 273
Slessor, Kenneth, 238
Smart Set, 62
Smiles, Samuel, 83
Smith, Adam, 83
Smith, Anthony, 474
Smith, Ashley, 47
Smith, Elder, Co., 103–4, 106
Smith, F. Newland, 139
Smith, George Murray, 104
Smith, Iain Crichton, 168, 234, 235, 415
Smith, James, 426
Smith, Ken, 439, 475
Smith, Peter Digby, 506
Smith, R. D., 324
Smith, Reginald John, 103–6
Smith, Stevie: contributes to *Aylesford Review*, 39; to *Lilliput*, 229; to *London Mercury*, 254; to *New Departures*, 273–74; to *Nimbus*, 306; to *Orion*,

324, 325; to *Poetry (London)*, 361; to *Time and Tide*, 450; to *Windmill*, 500; to *X: Quarterly Review*, 510

Smith, Sydney Goodsir, 168, 232–35, 415, 416

Smyth, Ethel, 442, 444

Smythyman, Kendrick, 356

Snaith, Stanley, 238

Snell, Reginald, 280

Snow, C. P., 407, 501; "Two Cultures," 157

Snyder, Gary, 283; *The Back Country, Six Sections from Mountains and Rivers*, 378

Social Credit, 173, 276, 381

Social issues. *See* Political issues

Socialist magazines, 13–14, 28–29, 217, 329–30, 450. *See also* Political issues

Soissons, Count de, 390

Soldati, Mario, 247

Solomon, J. D., 178

Solstice, 434–36

Solt, Mary Ellen: "E PLURIBUS UNUM," 374

Solzhenitsyn, Aleksandr, 158

Somerville, H., 56

Sommerfield, John, 339

Sonus Press, 488

Sorabji, Haikhoisru Shapurji, 278

Sosnora, Viktor, 435

Soutar, William, 415, 421

South Africa, 56, 158, 308, 403

South African literature, 348, 356

Southey, Robert, 391

Soyinka, Wole, 156, 357; *The Lion and the Jewel*, 186

Spalding, Helen 325

Spanish Civil War: discussed in *Blackfriars*, 56; in *Horizon*, 202; in *Left Review*, 219; in *New Road*, 287; in *Review*, 398; effects on *Adelphi*, 13–14; on *Contemporary Poetry and Prose*, 87; on *Encounter*, 154; on *Kingdom Come*, 212; on *Life and Letters*, 225

Spanish literature, 116, 414

Spare, Austin O., 194–97

Spark, Muriel, 331; *Speaker*, 269

Speirs, John, 426

Speirs, Ruth, 361

Spencer, Bernard, 248, 293, 361, 395, 398; "Allotments: April," 293

Spencer, Herbert, 465

Spender, Harold, 181

Spender, Hugh F., 181

Spender, Stephen: coedits *Horizon*, 201; contributes to *Adam*, 5; to *Adelphi*, 15; to *Contemporary Poetry and Prose*, 87; to *Criterion*, 118; to *Left Review*, 219; to *Life and Letters*, 224; to *London Mercury*, 253–54; to *New Departures*, 274; to *New Stories*, 290; to *New Verse*, 292–93, 301; to *New Writing*, 300–302; to *Penguin New Writing*, 338, 342; to *Poetry (London)*, 360, 362; to *Purpose*, 387; to *Time and Tide*, 450–51; to *Twentieth Century*, 465; edits *Encounter*, 153–55; founds International Arts Guild, 4; on wartime publishing, 341; reviewed in *New Verse*, 292–93; in *Nine*, 311–12; in *Northern Review*, 316; in *Now*, 318; in *Review*, 394; reviewer for *Time and Tide*, 447; satirized in *New Review*, 402; in *Penguin New Writing*, 341. Works: "By the Lake," 290; *European Witness*, 204; *The Generous Days*, 395; "Good Taste and the Critic," 450–51; "Notes from a Diary," 155; "Open Letter to Pravda," 450; "Some Notes on Being a Poet Today," 387; *The Struggle of the Modern*, 395; *World Within Worlds*, 311

Spengler, Oswald, 175, 422; *The Decline of the West*, 497

Spenser, Edmund, 130, 219

Spiritualism, 169–71

Sprigge, Cecil Jackson Squire, 1

Sprigge, Elizabeth, 138

Sprigge, Sylvia, 1–4

Squire, J. C., 32, 238–39, 250–53, 334, 494

St. Albert's Press, 36–38

St. Clements Press, 8

St. Dominic's Press, 37

St. John, Christopher, 445
St. John, Henry, 57
St. Martin's Press, 297
Stafford, William, 20, 400
Stallworthy, Jon, 402, 503
Stanbrook Abbey, 496
Stand, 436–40
Stanford, Derek, 68, 97, 287
Stanford, J. K., 59
Stanhope Press, 436
Stanislavsky, Constantin, 147
Staples, Ronald, 16
Stark, Freya, 107
Starkey, James Sullivan, 139–41
Statesman Publishing Co., 228
Steele, Jeffrey, 374
Steffens, Lincoln, 461
Stein, Gertrude: attacked in *Enemy*, 162–63; contributes to *Criterion*, 117; to *Life and Letters*, 225; to *London Bulletin*, 242; to *Time and Tide*, 447; edits *Wheels*, 489–96; *The Making of Americans*, 461–63; reviewed in *Aphrodite*, 237
Steinbeck, John, 259, 387
Steiner, George, 168; *Language and Silence*, 123
Stendhal [Marie–Henri Beyle], 506
Stephen, Leslie, 103; "Mausoleum Book," 407
Stephens, James, 41, 139
Stephens, Meic, 369–71
Stephensen, Percy Reginald, 236–39
Stern, James, 252, 339
Stevens, Wallace: "The Bed of Old John Zeller," 285; contributes to *Contemporary Poetry and Prose*, 87; to *Life and Letters*, 225; to *New Poetry*, 284; to *Poetry Quarterly*, 367; to *Seven*, 430; "Less and Less Human, O Savage Spirit," 285; on Marianne Moore, 225; reviewed in *London Mercury*, 252; special issue of *Twentieth Century Verse*, 469
Stevenson, Anne, 235
Stevenson, Robert Louis, 37, 92, 104, 106
Stewart, Donald, 463

Stewart, Gervase, 213
Stillman, George, 457
Stokes, Adrian, 366
Stokes, Stanley, 129
Stone, Helen, 129
Stonier, George W., 339, 387, 501
Stopes, Marie C., 211
Stoppard, Tom, 189, 352, 401; *Travesties*, 7
Storey, David, 138, 352
Story, 257, 289
Strachey, John, 103, 218, 324
Strachey, Lytton, 72, 223, 253, 270
Strand Magazine, 60
Strawinsky, Soulima, 455
Strindberg, August, 100, 137, 498
Strong, L. A. G., 141, 230, 257, 259; "Talk at the Inn," "Storm," 195–96
Stuart, H., 462
Stuart, Jesse, 15
Sudermann, Hermann, 134–35
Sullivan, Arthur Seymour, 106
Sullivan, J. W. N., 9
Summerfield, John, 331
Summers, Hal, 499
Summers, Montague, 134
Sundar, Kaval, 298
Supervielle, Jules, 340
Surrealism: criticized in *Kingdom Come*, 214; discussed in *New Verse*, 294; excluded from *Twentieth Century Verse*, 468; featured in *Contemporary Poetry and Prose*, 86–90; in *Experiment*, 177; in *Left Review*, 219; in *Lilliput*, 230; in *London Bulletin*, 241–43; in *Seven*, 431–32. *See also* Art criticism; Art reproductions; specific artists
Surrealisme au service de la revolution, 241
Surrealist Group in England, 243
Svevo, Italo, 306; *Confessions of Zeno*, 307
Swallow Press, 52
Swedish literature, 227, 234
Swift, Graham, 436
Swift, Jonathan, 78, 107, 219, 406
Swift, Patrick, 509–11

Swinburne, Algernon Charles, 93–94, 465
Swingler, Randall, 28, 219–20, 302, 329
Swinnerton, Frank, 10, 171
Sykes, Hugh, 177–78
Sykes, Norman, 83
Sylvanus, V., 196
Symonds, John Addington, 93, 171–72
Symons, Arthur, 93, 197, 223, 479
Symons, Julian: contributes to *New English Weekly*, 278; to *Northern Review*, 316; to *Now*, 318; to *Review*, 398; to *Wales*, 484; to *Windmill*, 500, 501; edits *Twentieth Century Verse*, 467; influences Conrad Aiken, 284; on *Horizon*, 207; on *Kingdom Come*, 211; on *Left Review*, 217; on *Poetry (London)*, 363; on the Spanish Civil War, 225; reviewer for *New Review*, 403
Symons, Travers, 381–85
Symons, W. T., 280
Symposium, 425
Synge, John Middleton, 97, 137, 444
Szasz, Thomas, 402

T. P.'s Weekly, 62
Tagore, Rabindranath, 182, 444; "The Foundling Hero," 196
Takl, George, 287
Talbot, Norman: "Beet-Pullers," 475
Tambimuttu, J. M., 5, 358–63
Tanguy, Yves, 242
Tanner, Tony, 407
Tansley, Ronald, 290
Tao Te Ching, 435
Tarling, Edwin, 487–88
Tarn, Nathaniel, 435
Tarr, John C., 52
Tate, Allan, 15, 77, 203, 284, 310
Taurus Press, Ltd., 53
Taylor, A. J. P., 206
Taylor, Elizabeth, 108
Taylor, Elma, 463
Taylor, Geoffrey, 45
Taylor, John Russell, 136–37, 149, 350–51
Taylor, Peter, 264, 400
Tchang T'ien-Yih, 301, 338

Television, 134, 505
Television plays, 401
Tempo Presente, 153
Tennant, Wyndham, 493
Tennyson, Alfred, Lord, 94–95, 107, 465
Tertz, Abram, 155
Tessimond, A. S. J., 15, 325
Thackeray, William Makepeace, 104, 106
Thayer, Scofield, 114
Theater criticism: in *Contemporary Review*, 100, 101; *Critical Quarterly*, 122; *Drama*, 133–38; *Encore*, 146–52; *Encounter*, 155; *English*, 167; *Experiment*, 178; *Gambit*, 185–90; *Life and Letters*, 224, 226–27; *New English Weekly*, 278; *Plays and Players*, 350–53; *Review*, 403; *Time and Tide*, 444–45; *Voices*, 478; *Writing Today*, 505
Theater guides (London), 352–53
Theater scripts, 351, 353
Theatre du Soleil, 188
Theatre Quarterly, 138
Theatre Workshop, 149
Theatre World, 353
Theroux, Paul, 159, 400
Thibaudet, Alfred, 253
This Quarter, 241
Thomas, D. M.: contributes to *New Review*, 400; to *Outposts*, 331; to *Priapus*, 379; to *Samphire*, 419; to *Solstice*, 435; to *Workshop*, 503; "Gully," 435
Thomas, Dylan: contributes to *Adelphi*, 15; to *Contemporary Poetry and Prose*, 87; to *Criterion*, 118; to *Horizon*, 205; to *Life and Letters*, 225; to *New English Weekly*, 278; to *New Stories*, 290; to *New Verse*, 293; to *New Writing*, 300; to *Penguin New Writing*, 341; to *Poetry (London)*, 360; to *Purpose*, 386; to *Seven*, 430; to *Wales*, 483–85; criticized in *Scrutiny*, 427; defended by Tambimuttu, 360; eulogized in *Adelphi*, 17; in *Poetry Wales*, 372; influence on *Universities Poetry*, 474; listed as coeditor of *Wales*, 484; obituary in *Lines Review*, 233; reviewed in

Anglo–Welsh Review, 26; in *Contemporary Review*, 97, 98; in *London Magazine*, 245; in *New Verse*, 293; in *Poetry Quarterly*, 368; in *Saltire Review*, 414; in *Wind and the Rain*, 498; special issue of *Adam*, 6; of *Anglo–Welsh Review*, 25. Works: *Adventures in the Skin Trade*, 341; "Altarwise by Owl Light," 225; "And Death Shall Have No Dominion," 279; *Collected Poems*, 245; *Death and Entrances*, 498; *The Death of the King's Canary*, 402; "Deaths and Entrances," 205; "The Enemies," 290; "Fern Hill," 205; "Fine Meats on Bones That Soon Have None," 386; "Memories of Christmas," 485; "Our Country," 485; "Poem in October," 205; "Quite Early One Morning," 485; "Refusal to Mourn the Death by Fire," 205; "Then Was My Neophyte," 386; "Today, This Insect, and the World I Breathe," 386

Thomas, Edward, 372
Thomas, Gilbert, 96
Thomas, R. George, 26
Thomas, R. S.: contributes to *Anglo–Welsh Review*, 25; to *Critical Quarterly*, 122; to *English*, 167; to *Poetry (London)*, 361; to *Poetry Wales*, 370–72; to *Wave*, 407; to *Workshop*, 504; reviewed in *Anglo–Welsh Review*, 26; in *Poetry Wales*, 371
Thompson, David, 136
Thompson, Denys, 423, 429; *Culture and Environment*, 424
Thompson, E. P., 28, 328–29, 437
Thompson, Edward, 448
Thompson, Francis, 39
Thompson, P. Gilchrist, 256–58
Thomson, David Cleghorn, 98, 415
Thomson, Derick, 232–35, 415
Thornely, Thomas, 129
Three Candles Press, 52
Thurber, James, 206; "The Night the Bed Fell," 14
Thwaite, Anthony, 155, 158–61, 331, 402, 487

Tibbs, Molly, 98
Tikhonov, Nikolai, 301, 342
Tiller, Terence, 361, 362
Tillinghast, Anthony, 474
Tillotson, Geoffrey, 168, 252
Tillotson, Kathleen, 168
Tillyard, E. M. W., 407
Time and Tide, 441–53
Todd, Ruthven, 205, 225, 241, 294, 468–69
Toller, Ernst, 46, 230, 448; "As Others See Us," 135
Tolley, A. T., 88
Tolstoy, Leo, 93, 134, 219
Tomlin, E. W. F., 278, 386, 455
Tomlinson, Charles, 20, 122, 310, 365, 506; "The Way In," 365
Tomlinson, H. M., 9, 270
Tonybee, Francis, 95
Torbet, Ronald, 57
Toulmin, Stephen, 83
Toulson, K. S., 506
Townshend, Margaret, 410
Townshend, Petrie, 224–25
Townsman, 277, 453–57
Toynbee, Arnold, 108, 157, 465
Toynbee, Philip, 156, 203–5, 213, 303, 503; "The Decline and Future of the English Novel," 339
Trace, 457–59
Tracy, Lorna, 437, 439
Trafford, John, 309
Transatlantic Review, 459–64, 475
Transition, 90, 163, 432
Translation, 497
Travers, Pamela, 278, 280
Traversi, D. A., 426
Tredell, Nicolas, 366
Tree, Iris, 491–94
Treece, Henry: contributes to *Anglo–Welsh Review*, 25; to *Poetry (London)*, 360–61; to *Seven*, 430–31; "Dylan Thomas and the Surrealists," 431; edits *Kingdom Come*, 211; *How I See Apocalypse*, 357; on Dylan Thomas, 26; on *Nine*, 312; "Ophelia," 367; *The White Horseman*, 357, 431
Tremaine, Herbert, 129

Tremayne, Sydney, 415
Trevelyan, Elizabeth, 1
Trevelyan, George M., 105, 197, 450
Trevelyan, R. C., 1–3
Trevelyan, Robert, 1
Treves, Paolo, 96
Trevor, William, 249
Trevor-Roper, Hugh, 107, 156–57,
    206
Trewin, J. C., 136, 137, 352
Trilling, Lionel, 17, 156–59, 206, 366,
    505
Tripp, John, 370
Triskell Press, 373
Trocchi, Alexander, 298, 307, 416,
    298
Trollope, Anthony, 83, 104, 107, 316,
    318
Tronson, R. F., 356
Trotsky, Leon: *History of the Russian
    Revolution*, 426
Tuke, Margaret, 442
Tunnard, John, 242
Tuophy, Frank, 249
Turkish poetry, 438
Turnbull, Gael, 375, 434; *Scantlings*,
    418
Turnbull, Ivor, 232
Turnbull, John, 68
Turnell, Martin, 426, 450
Turner, W. J., 334
Turner, W. Price, 415
Tvardovsky, Aleksandr, 374
Tweedsmuir, John Buchan, Lord, 451
Twentieth Century, 294, 363, 464–67
Twentieth Century Verse, 201, 292, 398,
    467–71
Tyler, Parker, 243, 430
Tynan, Katherine, 105
Tynan, Kenneth, 97, 146, 148–49,
    262
Tyrrell, G. N. M., 169–70
Tyson, R. Bryan, 473
Tyutchev, Fyodor, 374
Tzara, Tristan, 5, 28, 462–63

Uglow, Jack, 46
Ullman, Liv, 401

Underhill, Evelyn, 391
Ungaretti, Giuseppi, 19
United Nations, 43
United States, attitude toward, 30
Unity Theatre, 327
Universities' Poetry, 473–76
"University Question," 81–83
Unwin, J. D., 385
Upward, Edward, 219, 301, 303, 398
Urban, George, 157

V-E Time Drama. See Drama
V-J Time Drama. See Drama
Vail, Laurence, 431
Valentine, E. S., 164
Valéry, Paul, 77, 115, 324, 462–63
Valle Inclán, R. M. del, 174
Van der Post, Laurens, 108
Van Orden, Bianca, 247
Van Velde, Bram, 242
Vaughan, Henry, 95
Vaughan, Keith, 339, 340
Vazov, Ivan, 175
Venison, Alfie. *See* Pound, Ezra
Venture, 177
Venturi, Lionello, 262
Vere, Edward de, 196
Verne, Jules, 37
Vestdijk, Simon, 298
Vettese, Raymond, 23
Vickridge, Alberta, 129
Victoria and Albert Museum, 347
Viewpoint, 217
Villiers Publications, Ltd., 458
Vines, Sherard, 492–93
Viogt, F. A., 467
Visiak, E. H., 5, 37
Vivian, Arthur, 192
Vivis, Tony, 187
Vogelweide, Walther von de, 310
Voices, 111, 477–81
Von Stern Press of Luneberg, 52
Vorticism, 61–68, 182
Voznesensky, Andrei, 274, 375; "Para-
    bolic Ballad," 374

Wade, Rosalind, 99
Wadsworth, Edward, 62, 63, 69

Wagner, Geoffrey, 368

Wagner, Richard, 196

Wain, John: "Ambiguous Gift" 339; contributes to *Critical Quarterly*, 122; to *London Magazine*, 245; to *Penguin New Writing*, 339; to *Review of English Literature*, 407; to *Wave*, 487; edits *Mandrake*, 261–63; interviewed in *Workshop*, 504; on Stendhal's letters, 506; "Poem Without a Main Verb," 245; reviewed in *Nimbus*, 307; satirized in *Review*, 394

Walcott, Derek, 249, 357, 394, 406

Wales, 26, 483–87

Wales Publications, Ltd., 486

Walker, Ted, 377–79; *Fox on a Barn Door*, 378

Wall, Bernard, 467

Wall, Max, 100

Wall, Stephen, 405

Wallach, Eli, 147

Waller, Elizabeth, 216

Waller, John, 211–13, 361, 362

Walpole, Hugh Seymour, 46, 116

Walters, H. G., Ltd., 28

Ward, A. W., 105

Ward, J. P., 372

Ward, Mrs. Humphry, 104–8

Ward, Stephen, 38

Wardle, Irving, 187–88

Warner, Rex, 219, 302, 469

Warner, Sylvia Townsend, 46, 108, 230, 366, 444

Warnke, Janice, 247

Warren, Robert Penn, 156

War-Time Drama. See Drama

Warwick, Dulcie, 367

Watkins, Vernon: castigated in *Review*, 394; contributes to *Life and Letters*, 225; to *Nimbus*, 306–7; to *Poetry (London)*, 361; to *Poetry Wales*, 370–72; to *Wales*, 483; to *Wind and the Rain*, 499; to *X: Quarterly Review*, 510; reviewed in *Anglo–Welsh Review*, 25–26

Watling, E. F., 136

Watson, E. L. Grant, 195–96

Watson, Janet, 327

Watson, Peter, 201, 207

Watson, William, 32

Watt, David, 147

Watts, Doreen C., 367

Watts, S. G., 213

Waugh, Alec, 193, 197, 444; *Myself When Young*, 197

Waugh, Arthur, 181; "The New Poetry," 389–90

Waugh, Evelyn: *Black Mischief*, 223; *Brideshead Revisited*, 42, 495; contributes to *Bell*, 42; to *Cornhill*, 107; to *Encounter*, 157; to *Horizon*, 206; to *Life and Letters*, 223; to *Lilliput*, 230; to *Time and Tide*, 450; reviewed in *Northern Review*, 316; in *Now*, 318

Wave, 487–89

Wavell, Derek, 435

Weaver, Harriet Shaw, 146

Webb, Harri, 370

Webb, Kaye, 230

Webb, Paddy, 379

Webb, Sidney, 105, 449

Weber, Eugen, 83

Wedde, Ian, 439

Wedgwood, C. V., 447, 450

Wedgwood, Julia, 92

Weidenfeld and Nicolson, 274

Weil, Simone, 264

Weiss, Peter, 137, 149, 352

Weissbrot, Daniel, 435

Welch, Denton, 15, 325, 451

Weld, Agnes Grace, 94

Wellard, James H., 47, 49

Wells, A. P., 506

Wells, Catherine, 461

Wells, Geoffrey, 11

Wells, H. G.: *The Common Sense of World Peace*, 49; contributes to *Adam*, 5; to *Adelphi*, 10; to *Contemporary Review*, 92; to *Cornhill*, 107; to *Fortnightly Review*, 182; to *Horizon*, 206; featured in *Adam International Review*, 6; promotes *Transatlantic Review*, 460; reviewed in *Bermondsey Book*, 49; in *Calendar of Modern Letters*, 79; in *Lovat Dickson's Magazine*, 258; in *Time and Tide*, 444, 448

Wells, Robert Preston, 235
Welsh Church Funds Committees, 26
Welsh literature, 227, 369–73, 483–86,
    503
Welsh Outlook, 370
Welsh Review, 25, 485
Welty, Eudora, 206, 340; "Hello and
    Good-bye," 348
Wenzelides, Arsen, 175
Wesker, Arnold, 146, 149, 156, 401,
    510
West, Alick, 218–19
West, Geoffrey, 13, 289, 291
West, Rebecca, 13, 62, 66, 156, 444–45,
    449
Westminster Press, 336
Weston, Alban, 58
Weston, K. Noel, 455
Weyman, Stanley John, 37, 105, 106
Whannel, Paddy, 506
Wharton, Edith, 389
Wharton, Gordon, 439
Wheels, 32, 111, 489–96
Whelan, John Francis. *See* O'Faolain,
    Sean
Whelpley, James D., 181
Wheway, John, 283
Whibley, Charles, 58–59
Whistler, Laurence, 360–61
Whistler, Rex, 450
Whitaker, Malachi, 12, 15
White, Beatrice, 168
White, E. B., 14
White, Patrick, 406, 505
White, R. J., 83
White, T. H., 178, 451
Whitehead, Alfred North, 162, 426
Whitehead, Philip, 401
Whiting, John, 149; *Marching Song*, 307;
    Plays, 506
Whitman, Walt, 130, 459
Whittington-Egan, Richard, 98
Whitworth, Geoffrey, 133–35, 137
Wickham, Glynne, 100
Wilbur, Richard, 306, 505
Wild Hawthorne Press, 377
Wilde, Gerald, 362
Wilde, Oscar, 106

Wilding, Michael, 439
Wilenski, R. H., 242
Wilkinson, Anne, 356
Wilkinson, Ellen, 447
Willet, F. W., 298
William-Ellis, A., 463
Williams, Charles, 100, 310, 361–62,
    498
Williams, Christopher, 474
Williams, Heathcote, 274; *AC/DC*,
    188
Williams, Herbert, 370
Williams, Hugo, 396, 399
Williams, John Stuart, 370, 371
Williams, Kemble, 418–19
Williams, Melvin G., 52
Williams, Miles Vaughan, 216
Williams, Orlo, 12
Williams, Ralph Vaughn, 1–3
Williams, Raymond, 122, 303, 437,
    438
Williams, Stephen, 136
Williams, T. F. D., 80–81
Williams, T. H. Parry, 372
Williams, Tennessee, 340
Williams, William Carlos: contributes to
    Egoist, 144; to *Transatlantic Review*,
    461–62; interview in *Writing Today*,
    506; reviewed in *Review*, 395, 397; in
    Townsman, 455; solicited by Pound for
    Blast, 62; special issue of *Agenda*,
    19
Williams-Ellis, Amabel, 218
Williamson, Alan, 400
Williamson, Henry, 16, 36
Williamson, Hugh Ross, 316, 318
Willy, Margaret, 165–66
Wilmers, Mary Kay, 402
Wilson, A. E., 136
Wilson, Angus, 122, 134, 204–5, 401,
    407; "Mother's Sense of Fun," *The
    Wrong Set*, 205
Wilson, Arnold, 467
Wilson, Colin, 36–38, 465
Wilson, Edmund, 158, 206, 505; *The
    American Earthquake*, 506; "Art, the
    Proletariat, and Marx," 14
Wilson, Effingham, 150

Wilson, Ethel, 326
Wilson, Romer, 12, 290
Wilton, Andrew, 74
Winchilsea, Anne, Countess of, 12, 178
Wind and the Rain, 496–500
Windmill, 500–502
Windmill Press, 250
Wine and Food Quarterly, 7
Wing, Giles, 259
Winter's Tales, 297
Winters, Yvor, 366, 395, 397, 469
Wintringham, T. H., 218, 301
Wise, David, 439
Wishart Co., 80
Witheford, Hubert, 356
Wodehouse, P. G., 290
Wolfe, Humbert, 46, 259
Wolfendon, John F., 76
Wollheim, Richard, 83
Women's literature. *See* Feminist literature
Women's Printing Society, Ltd., 133
Wood, DerWent, 334
Woodcock, George, 191–92, 213, 317–20, 407
Woodcock, Ingeborg, 321
Woods, Charles H., 181
Woodward, Bob: *The Final Days*, 401
Woolf, Leonard, 95, 215, 324
Woolf, Virginia: contributes to *Bermondsey Book*, 46; to *Cornhill*, 105; to *Criterion*, 115; to *Encounter*, 155; to *Life and Letters*, 223; to *London Mercury*, 252; to *Nation and Athenaeum*, 270; to *New Writing*, 300, 301; to *Time and Tide*, 446; to *Twentieth Century*, 465; early manuscripts, 6; featured in *Time and Tide*, 447; "The Leaning Tree," 301, 303; letters in *Life and Letters*, 224; in *Orion*, 325; literary editor of *Nation and Athenaeum*, 270; meets with Potocki, 410; *A Room of One's Own*, 446; reviewed in *Abinger Chronicle*, 2; in *London Mercury*, 252
Word in the Desert, 123
Worde, Wynkyn de, 52
Wordsworth, Dorothy, 99

Wordsworth, William, 130, 167
Working class literature. *See* Proletarian literature
Workshop, 502–5
Workshop Press, 503
World Peace Council (1954), 44
World War I: and *Blackfriars*, 54–56; *Contemporary Review*, 94; *Fortnightly Review*, 181–83; *Penguin Parade*, 346–47; *Voices*, 478; *Wheels*, 490, 492
World War II: and *Abinger Chronicle*, 1–3; *Adam*, 4; *British Museum Quarterly*, 73–74; *Criterion*, 118; *Decachord*, 130; *Drama*, 135; *European Quarterly*, 173; *Horizon*, 201–4, 206; *Kingdom Come*, 212–13; *Life and Letters*, 226; *New English Weekly*, 280; *New Writing*, 302–3; *Now*, 318–19; *Penguin New Writing*, 337–47; *Seven*, 432; *Time and Tide*, 445–47; *Wales*, 484; *Wind and the Rain*, 496–97; list of magazines closed by, 432; paper shortages, 323
Wright, Basil, 178
Wright, David, 509–11
Wright, Judith, 356
Wright, Richard, 191
Writers' Workshop, 502
Writing Today, 505–7
Wyatt, Woodrow, 213

X: A Quarterly Review, 509–12
Xiste, Pedro, 374, 375

Yates, Peter, 301
Yeats, Jack, 42
Yeats, W[illiam] B[utler]: contributes to *Adelphi*, 11; to *Bell*, 42; to *Contemporary Review*, 92–93; to *Cornhill*, 105; to *Criterion*, 115; to *Life and Letters*, 224; to *London Mercury*, 251; featured in *Agenda*, 19; "Ireland Bewitched," 92; "Literature and the Living Voice," 93; memoirs in *London Mercury*, 252; *The Resurrection*, 11; reviewed in *Cambridge Journal*, 84; in *English*, 167; in *Purpose*, 386; *Review of Eng-*

lish Literature, 406; in *Townsman*,
454–55; *The Speckled Bird*, 42; "What
Is 'Popular Poetry'?" 105
Yellow Book, 244
Yevtushenko, Yevgeny, 403
York Mystery Plays, 100
Young, Andrew, 378, 498; "The Salmon
Leap," 498; *The New Poly Olbion*,
378
Young, Edward: "Night Thoughts,"
294

Young, James, 13
Young, James Carruthers, 384–85

Zadkine, Ossip, 110
Zaehner, Robert Charles, 56
Zaina, Alexandra, 38
Zangwill, Israel, 46
Zukofsky, Louis, 19, 118, 374, 503
Zweig, Stefan, 5
Zwemmer Gallery, 243

Contributors

R. VICTORIA ARANA teaches twentieth-century British literature at Howard University.

WILLIAM BAKER, who also contributed to *British Literary Magazines: The Victorian and Edwardian Age*, resides in the West Midlands.

HALLMAN BELL BRYANT, professor at Clemson University, has just completed a critical bibliography of Robert Graves for Garland Press.

JOHNNIE WADE BURNS is assistant professor of English at Tennessee Technological University.

A. D. CAESAR, who formerly taught at the Flinders University of South Australia, has written on the poetry of Sidney Keyes.

WILLIAM CLARKIN is emeritus professor of the School of Library and Information Science at S.U.N.Y. at Albany.

LAURENCE COUPE completed a thesis on Rickword's *Calendar of Modern Letters* and has published on Rickword in *Stand*.

FRANK DAY teaches English literature at Clemson University.

RONALD L. DOTTERER is associate professor of English at Susquehanna University and author of *Clad in Shining Armor: The Novels of Flann O'Brien*.

BARBARA J. DUNLAP is on the staff of City College of New York.

TED R. ELLIS III, professor of English at East Carolina University, also contributed to *British Literary Magazines: The Romantic Age*.

STEVEN GALE, who teaches at Missouri Southern State College, is the author of a critical analysis of Harold Pinter's works and editor of a Pinter bibliography.

PAUL L. GASTON is associate vice-president at Southern Illinois University at Edwardsville.

MICHAEL PATRICK GILLESPIE is assistant professor of English at Marquette University.

MARTIN E. GINGERICH teaches at Western Michigan University and is the author of *Contemporary Poetry in America and England, 1950–1975: A Guide to Information Sources*.

MARGARET ANN BAKER GRAHAM teaches at Iowa State University.

TERENCE L. GRIMES is professor at Atlantic Christian College.

SUSAN J. HANNA teaches English at Mary Washington College.

WARREN HERENDEEN is a member of the Department of Speech, Hearing, and Drama at Mercy College.

JEFFERSON HUNTER teaches English literature at Smith College.

WILLIAM HUTCHINGS, assistant professor of English at the University of Alabama at Birmingham, is working on a book about the plays of David Storey.

EARL G. INGERSOLL is on the English faculty of S.U.N.Y. at Brockport.

W. A. JOHNSEN teaches English at Michigan State University.

THOMAS J. KENNY has published on James Joyce in the *Journal of Modern Literature* and *James Joyce Quarterly*.

CATHERINE KERRIGAN teaches English at the University of Western Ontario.

ADRIENNE E. KERTZER is on the English faculty at the University of Calgary and is associate editor of *Ariel*.

RAYMOND N. MACKENZIE teaches at Mankato State University.

IAN S. MACNIVEN teaches in the Humanities Department at S.U.N.Y. Maritime College in the Bronx. He is coeditor of *Literary Lifelines: The Richard Aldington—Lawrence Durrell Correspondence* and *The Richard Aldington—Ezra Pound Correspondence*.

KERRY McSWEENEY, Molson Professor of English at McGill University, is author of *Tennyson and Swinburne as Romantic Naturalists*. He also contributed to *British Literary Magazines: The Victorian and Edwardian Age*.

LAWRENCE H. MADDOCK is associate professor of English at the University of West Florida.

ELGIN W. MELLOWN is associate professor of English at Duke University and author of numerous essays on modern British literature.

MURIEL J. MELLOWN is professor of English at North Carolina Central University.

PETER MORGAN, professor at the University of Toronto, is author of *Literary Critics and Reviewers in Early Nineteenth Century Britain*.

MARGARET ANNE O'CONNOR teaches English at the University of North Carolina at Chapel Hill.

HANS OSTROM is coauthor of *Leigh Hunt: A Reference Guide*. He also contributed to *British Literary Magazines: The Augustan Age and the Age of Johnson* and *Victorian and Edwardian Age*.

JAMES W. PARINS teaches at the University of Arkansas. He also contributed to *British Literary Magazines: The Victorian and Edwardian Age*.

MARILYN PARINS teaches English at the University of Arkansas.

MARK REGER, a lecturer at the University of Missouri at Columbia, also contributed to *Black Journals of the United States*, another volume in the Greenwood reference series, Historical Guides to the World's Periodicals and Newspapers.

DAVID S. ROBB is secretary of the Association for Scottish Literary Studies and contributor of biographies of Scots writers to *The Dictionary of Literary Biography*.

CAROL DE SAINT VICTOR, professor of English at the University of Iowa, is the only contributor with profiles in all four parts of *British Literary Magazines*.

THOMAS M. SAWYER, who was on the faculty of Clarkson College, died in 1984.

MARGARET SCANLAN teaches at Indiana University at South Bend and contributes frequently on modern British subjects to academic journals.

BARBARA QUINN SCHMIDT, associate professor of English at Southern Illinois University at Edwardsville, edits the *Victorian Periodicals Review*.

CHARLES L. P. SILET, associate professor of English at Iowa State University, also contributed to *British Literary Magazines: The Victorian and Edwardian Age*.

FRANK EDMUND SMITH teaches English at William Rainey Harper College.

HILDA D. SPEAR teaches at Dundee University. Her book on the literature of World War I, *Remembering, We Forget*, appeared in 1979.

DICKIE A. SPURGEON, professor of English at Southern Illinois University at Edwardsville, also contributed to *British Literary Magazines: The Romantic Age* and *The Victorian and Edwardian Age*.

CHRISTIAN C. STOUGH recently taught at the Center for the Humanities at the University of Southern California.

ALAN C. THOMAS teaches English at Scarborough College at the University of Toronto.

VINCENT L. TOLLERS is on the faculty of S.U.N.Y. College at Brockport and editor of *Literary Research Newsletter*.

DAWN TROUARD teaches English at the University of Akron.

CRAIG WERNER teaches Afro-American studies at the University of Wisconsin and has recently published *Paradoxical Resolutions: American Fiction since James Joyce*.

TOBY SILVERMAN ZINMAN, associate professor of English at the Philadelphia College of Art, is working on a book about the plays of Sam Shepard.

About the Editor

ALVIN SULLIVAN is Professor of English at Southern Illinois University/ Edwardsville, and Editor of *Papers on Language and Literature*. A specialist in modern British literature and literary criticism, he has written *D. H. Lawrence and The Dial, The Dial—Two Author Indexes*, and articles for *Journal of Modern Literature, Explicator, D. H. Lawrence Review, Modern Fiction Studies*, and *Studies in English Literature*.